HUMAN
BEHAVIOR
AND
INTERNATIONAL
POLITICS

HUMAN
BEHAVIOR
AND
INTERNATIONAL
POLITICS

*Contributions from the
Social-Psychological Sciences*

Edited by

J. DAVID SINGER

Mental Health Research Institute
and
Department of Political Science
University of Michigan

RAND McNALLY & COMPANY • CHICAGO, ILLINOIS

RAND McNALLY POLITICAL SCIENCE SERIES

MORTON GRODZINS, Advisory Editor

BAYLEY, *Public Liberties in the New States*

BECKER, *Political Behavioralism and Modern Jurisprudence*

BOBROW, ed., *Components of Defense Policy*

ELDERSVELD, *Political Parties: A Behavioral Analysis*

FROMAN, *Congressmen and Their Constituencies*

GOLDWIN, ed., Rand McNally Public Affairs Series
   America Armed: Essays on United States Military Policy
   A Nation of States: Essays on the American Federal System
   Why Foreign Aid?
   Political Parties, U.S.A.
   100 Years of Emancipation

GOLEMBIEWSKI, *Behavior and Organization: O & M and the Small Group*

HAIGHT and JOHNSTON, eds., *The President: Roles and Powers*

HANNA, ed., *Independent Black Africa: The Politics of Freedom*

MILBRATH, *Political Participation*

MILBRATH, *The Washington Lobbyists*

PEABODY and POLSBY, eds., *New Perspectives on the House of Representatives*

PRESS, ed., *The Polity: Selected Essays by Norton E. Long*

SCHMIDHAUSER, ed., *Constitutional Law in the Political Process*

SCHUBERT, ed., *Judicial Behavior: A Reader on Theory and Research*

SINGER, ed., *Human Behavior and International Politics*

STRAUSS, *The City and Man*

STRAUSS and CROPSEY, eds., *History of Political Philosophy*

ULMER, ed., *Introductory Readings in Political Behavior*

WILLIAMS and PRESS, eds., *Democracy in Urban America: Readings on Government and Politics*

Dedicated to QUINCY WRIGHT, who showed us the way.

ACKNOWLEDGMENTS

In presenting this volume, three distinct types of acknowledgment are appropriate. First, there is my intellectual debt to the Ford Foundation which provided me, on two separate occasions, with the opportunity to "tool up" in the behavioral sciences. One such occasion was the Seminar on the Teaching of International Politics, held during the summer of 1956 at the State University of Iowa, under the direction of Vernon Van Dyke.[1] Here I had a chance to read, hear, and talk with some of the nation's most rigorous and creative social scientists, only a few of whom were themselves international relations specialists. Out of that experience came my appreciation of sociology, psychology, anthropology, and economics as sources of data, ideas, and methods. As a consequence, I applied for one of the Ford Foundation's post-doctoral training grants, and spent 1957-58 at Harvard's Department of Social Relations, studying the social-psychological sciences. For both of these opportunities my gratitude goes not only to the Foundation, but to the people from whom I learned so much: Professors Van Dyke and Lerche, the eleven other fellows, and the visiting consultants at the Iowa Seminar; and Gordon Allport, Herbert Kelman and many others who welcomed and assisted me in so many ways at Harvard.

My second debt is to those students and colleagues who helped me to comb the endless journals with a degree of thoroughness that could not have been achieved single-handedly: Lloyd Jensen, Ellen Samuels, Marc and Phyllis Pilsuk, and George Levinger.

Finally, one cannot put together a collection of articles until they have

---

[1]Three successive seminars were held, with Professor Van Dyke directing the first two, and Charles O. Lerche (who assisted in 1956) directing the third at Emory University in 1957; about a dozen young scholars attended each year. See Vernon Van Dyke, "The Improvement of Teaching in International Relations: The Iowa Seminars," *American Political Science Review*, LI (1957), 579-81; and Ronald J. Yalem, "The Ford Foundation Seminars on International Politics," *Background*, VII (1963), 65-75.

been written and published elsewhere. Thus, my third debt is to those social scientists who, unwittingly, wrote up their work not only for their disciplinary colleagues but for what will be, I hope, a goodly number of political-science eavesdroppers as well. I am also grateful to those hard-working social scientists who provide both the academic and administrative leadership required for the publication of the journals from which I borrowed. Publishing these is a time-consuming job essential to the growth of science, and one which is taken on in addition to normal teaching and research activities. I would therefore like to thank, as warmly as possible, the editors of all the journals from which I have drawn material, and the publishers of the four books from which I have taken excerpts, as well as the authors, for making their work available to me in this somewhat unorthodox enterprise.

CONTENTS

INTRODUCTION

Among students of international politics today, there seems to be a growing dissatisfaction with the "state of the art." In one way or another, many of us feel that we have progressed but a short distance since Thucydides. Some of us, of course, are *not* disturbed by that realization, and are quite persuaded not only that the ancient Greek scholar knew all there was to know about inter-nation relations then, but that there is nothing new to be added even now, more than 2300 years later. Such antiquarianism may be vanishing, but it has left its scars on a field of study too important to be dealt with in the same artistic and intuitive fashion as literature, religion, or art.

The purpose of this volume is to help, however modestly, to carry the discipline of international politics from the prescientific to the scientific stage in its development. As such, it is intended for teachers, researchers, advanced students, and practitioners, especially those who view the current ferment in the field with some ambivalence — and curiosity. It will interest those whose approach is prescientific or nonscientific, but will largely bore or even antagonize those of the antiscientific predisposition.[1] Among the latter will be those who are convinced that a field of study so complex *cannot,* and so socially important *should not,* be subjected to scientific treatment. For their pedagogical purposes, however, it might make a useful devil's advocate. The practitioner, however sophisticated, will also tend to take a dim view of the enterprise; for him it will seem too abstract and unreal, and thus irrelevant for his purposes. Unfortunately, he will not be far from the truth, since this book appears toward the close of what seems to be only the first phase in the transition to which I hopefully referred, and it will probably be a good many years before we

---

[1]It may also have one or both of these effects on those who are already committed to, and knowledgeable regarding, the enterprise which this volume represents.

have a body of empirical generalization solid enough to be of any value to those who must act and decide, day in and day out, on behalf of their nations.

The State of the Art

Be that as it may, I address the book primarily to my academic colleagues and to their more mature students, graduate and undergraduate, with the hope that they will find it usefully provocative in a variety of settings. Thus, before going any further, let me dispel any impression that I would deride or belittle all that has gone before in diplomatic history or international relations. Over the past decades and centuries political scientists have built up an impressive body of information concerning relations among nations, and to ignore or reject this store of knowledge and ideas would indeed be frivolous. It is just that each discipline seems destined to pass through a number of stages from the normative and the intuitively descriptive to the operational and the scientific. For a number of reasons, political science and history have tended not to move along at the same rate as sociology or psychology, though it is perfectly evident that these, too, have a long way to go. But they have, at least, crossed the first important threshold and need no longer expend precious intellectual (and emotional) energy on those issues which currently engage political scientists.

Let me try to suggest, albeit briefly, why international political relations as a branch of political science has tended to lag in its evolution toward a scientific discipline. First, there is the subject matter itself: nations cannot be placed in a purely experimental situation, whereas the psychologist's object of study—the individual or the small group—can. The major activity of nations—diplomacy—is most difficult to observe, classify, and measure since it goes on in a realm too large or too invisible to be watched by the scholar, whereas the phenomena of interest to the sociologist—employment, social mobility, demographic trends—are considerably more observable, with the added advantage that they are often recorded for him by governmental statisticians. The economist, of course, is in the best position of all. Most of his data—income, trade balances, sales, jobs—are already in quantified form, and there is no lack of incentive for nonacademics to gather these data for him.

Then there is the recruitment process itself; scientifically oriented people tend to gravitate toward those fields which are already more or less scientific and in which the norms encourage the scientific spirit. Conversely, those who prefer less rigorous, more speculative activity gravitate in another direction, ending up in subcultures compatible with their own intellectual styles.[2] Thus, we have a vicious circle, in which the fields more susceptible to scientific inquiry attract those who advance the field further, while the more elusive fields recruit scholars who are most likely to leave them pretty much as they found them.

Finally, there is the matter of the roles which scholars in various disciplines are called upon to fill. Government, as the major large-scale decision-maker of modern times, is more likely to call upon political scientists for help in making political decisions than upon psychologists or sociologists. Moreover, political scientists themselves have tended to admire and honor those of their colleagues with "practical" experience in government, however worm's eye the view may have been, while they feel slightly embarrassed to lecture or write about phenomena which they have never experienced directly. For other social scientists this is hardly a problem. Psychologists have unlimited opportunity to experience their own and others' attitudes, beliefs, and behavior, nor do sociologists lack the opportunity to participate in the activities of families, ethnic groups, professions, or even social strata; *all* of us do all of these things almost every day. Furthermore, as a consultant to, or a practitioner in, government, the political scientist comes to identify with the one he knows and works for, while his colleagues in the behavioral sciences, studying as they do *many* individuals, professions, or classes, while working for none of them, are hardly likely to identify so completely with any of their objects of study. This identification, of course, strongly inhibits both the incentive and the ability to examine with great precision and objectivity.

For these, and perhaps other reasons, political science finds itself entering the crucial and exciting transition stage somewhat later than economics, sociology, and psychology, and at more or less the same time as, perhaps, anthropology or clinical psychology; history, I fear, is still so steeped in the tradition of the humanities that political science is likely to

---

[2]This is as good a place as any to emphasize as firmly as possible that I am not advocating the exclusion of imagination, creativity, and speculation from our discipline or any other. These activities are absolutely essential to the development of a science, but they are also far from sufficient.

be well along in its development before that discipline is even stirred by the sort of controversy which political science has experienced in the past decade or so.[3]

In any event, the political scientist's objective is to make international politics a discipline capable of accurate description, comprehensible explanation, and statistically reliable prediction. This requires, of course, a body of theory, but theory in turn requires a broad base of empirical data, intellectual constructs which can give meaning and coherence to the data, and rigorous, replicable procedures by which the data may be gathered, classified, and analyzed. In short, the aim is to develop a science, and the assumption is that the more advanced social sciences can make a major contribution toward the realization of that aim.

The Relevance of the Behavioral Sciences

Let me now try to be more specific and indicate, in somewhat greater detail, the nature of the possible contribution of the behavioral sciences to international politics as a systematic, scientific field of investigation. As I see it, that contribution might take three distinct forms.

First, there are *the findings* of these disciplines—the empirical data and the generalizations which summarize those data. Many of these findings may be directly, as well as indirectly, applicable to international relations. For example, social psychology has accumulated an impressive body of data concerning (a) the attitudes which people in general (especially American college students!) hold regarding foreign nations, their elites, and their publics; and (b) the sorts of events, experiences, and conditions which go to shape those attitudes. The social psychologist can tell his colleagues in international relations, for instance, which personality types will tend to be more hostile toward foreigners, which will prefer aggressive behavior and which lean toward withdrawal and isolation,

---

[3]Among the general treatments of this controversy are: David Easton, *The Political System* (New York: Knopf, 1953); Heinz Eulau, *The Behavioral Persuasion in Politics* (New York: Random House, 1963); Charles Hyneman, *The Study of Politics* (Urbana: University of Illinois Press, 1959); Vernon Van Dyke, *Political Science: A Philosophical Analysis* (Stanford, Calif.: Stanford University Press, 1960); James C. Charlesworth (ed.), *The Limits of Behavioralism in Political Science* (Philadelphia: American Academy of Political and Social Science, 1962); and Austin Ranney (ed.), *Essays on the Behavioral Study of Politics* (Urbana: University of Illinois Press, 1962).

Two polemics against the trend are: Bernard Crick, *The American Science of Politics* (Berkeley: University of California Press, 1959); and Herbert James Storing (ed.), *Essays on the Scientific Study of Politics* (New York: Holt, Rinehart & Winston, 1962).

which economic brackets or social status will have more internationalists, or how the educational level of an individual can predict to his attitudes on international organization. Somewhat less directly applicable, but equally germane, are the findings of the small-group researchers (in both sociology and social psychology) regarding the speed and accuracy of problem-solving when the group's size, leadership, organization, or communication net is varied. These groups are by no means *exact replicas* of national decision-making ones (and this matter of analogy will be discussed below), but they are, in certain respects, *similar enough* to provide useful insights into the decision process.

Second, there are *the concepts and models* which these disciplines have developed by both the inductive and deductive methods. I am referring here to the ideas which have been found useful for organizing and grouping specific findings in a coherent and parsimonious fashion. To illustrate again, there are the concepts of mobility in sociology, of diffusion in anthropology, and of response-set in psychology. Further, there are some powerful and useful concepts coming to the behavioral sciences from mathematical economics via game theory: zero-sum game, mixed strategy, or expected utility. These and many other concepts, by which vague and elusive notions become clear-cut and coherent ideas, could be of inestimable assistance in the development of the field of international relations, and they will be introduced during the unfolding of this volume.

Third, and in the long run most important, there are *the methods* of the behavioral sciences, quite similar to those of the physical sciences, but different enough to preclude any slavish imitation. Without methodological self-consciousness, at least until rigorousness becomes habitual, a science just cannot be developed. By combining ingenuity with discipline, social and experimental psychology and sociology have devised techniques by which many of their slippery and qualitative phenomena may be observed, recorded, and measured. Thus, each researcher normally has a clear idea of the procedures used by his predecessors in classifying and quantifying these ambiguous events and conditions, and, as a consequence, the results are generally comparable and cumulative. The key notion here is "operationalism," a term used to convey visible, articulated, and replicable procedures, as distinct from procedures that are invisible, implicit and utterly *un*reproducible.

To summarize, I would contend that we in political science have not only failed to utilize much of the ready-at-hand data from the behavioral sciences, but, more seriously, have limped along with vague and open-ended concepts such as collective security, functionalism, balance of power, or alliance, which we define in a multitude of private ways, and with modes of data-gathering and data-interpretion that are no more operational and replicable than those of literature, art, theology, or journalism. If this criticism seems unduly harsh, let me ask the reader how many well-established propositions about the behavior of nations or the operation of the international system he can state,[4] and even more compellingly, what procedures might be used to put such propositions to the empirical test. I venture to say that I would be far from inundated!

Is Social Science Possible?

There are, of course, some serious epistemological criticisms that can be levelled at all of the social sciences, and it would be cavalier of me to bypass them in my enthusiasm for this particular enterprise. Some of these criticisms apply to research *within* any one discipline and others apply to the problem of *transferring* findings and concepts from one discipline to another. The latter class, which will be discussed in the next section, is my primary concern, but let me refer briefly to the others first.

One of the promptest criticisms to come from the superskeptic (moderate skepticism is essential to science, but the extreme form may lead to an intellectual nihilism and a denial of all knowledge or knowledgeability) is that concerning the differences between physical and social science. Prominent among these differences is the fact that, as social scientists, *our* objects of analysis are ourselves: living, thinking, perceiving, and goal-seeking entities; whereas the physical scientist's object of analysis is the cell, the atom, a molecule, a tissue, a nerve fiber—all allegedly inanimate or at least nonthinking. The argument that flows from this distinction is that we are actually interacting with our objects of analysis and they with us, whereas no such interaction plagues the chemist, biologist, astronomer or physicist.

The observation is unexceptional, yet it hardly invalidates social science; it merely imposes an additional need for care and control. In order to assure that the social scientist, in his role as observer, inter-

---

[4]To qualify, such propositions must not be at so high a level of abstraction as to be tautological, or at so low a level as to apply only to a single, discrete case.

viewer, or experimenter, does not influence his objects and hence contaminate the results, he must be somewhat more ingenious and rigorous in his research design than, perhaps, some physical scientists need to be. All sorts of things can contaminate the data emerging from a scientific investigation, and just as the social scientist must avoid investigator influence, for example, the physical scientist needs to worry about controlling for such sensitive factors as absence of bacteria, atmospheric pressure, sound waves or other vibration, temperature fluctuation, and so on. He might argue that it is the social scientist who has it easy, not having to control for such difficult variables!

A second, and less serious argument is that social phenomena are inherently more complex than physical ones. If this were not so widespread a notion, it would be unnecessary to point out that human physiology, still only partially understood, was perhaps a greater mystery half a century ago than a complex social organization is today. The less scientific scrutiny invested in a subject, the more complex it seems—at least to intelligent and perceptive observers. Furthermore, it should be emphasized that apparent complexity is a function of the models and theories in use, and the nature of the variables employed in such models. If, for example, one's model of international politics were based upon the child-rearing techniques or the high school curriculum to which every citizen of each nation has been exposed, or upon all the interpersonal relations of all legislators and foreign ministry personnel, the resultant theory would be most cumbersome and the foreign policy process would appear even more complex and conceptually unmanageable than it already is. However, as solid, operational data are collected and as efficient, parsimonious models at the appropriate level of abstraction are constructed, order and comprehensibility begin to emerge.

Another distinction which is used to emphasize the difficulty, if not impossibility, of applying scientific procedures to social and psychological affairs is the relative insusceptibility of these phenomena to measurement and quantification—a *sine qua non* of science. This, like other contrasts, reflects a rather naive understanding of physical phenomena. Imagine putting a molecule on a scale, or laying a cell alongside a ruler, or putting calipers around a planet! In other words, these elusive, microscopic, or distant moving objects (or mental constructs, to be more accurate) became measurable only when extremely ingenious techniques of classification, separation, and observation had been developed, and there is no reason to assume that opinions or social distances or inter-group interactions should prove any more difficult to measure than their chemical, biological, and physical counterparts.[5] As a matter of fact, many of the selections in this book will illustrate the considerable progress that has already been made. Also, it should be emphasized that measurement can take a variety of forms, from such primitive ones as greater-lesser, through simple rank-ordering, on down to metric or cardinal measurement; and quite often there is not even a legitimate need for great precision.

Finally, perhaps the most serious criticism concerns experimental control and the manipulation of variables. It is argued that the physical scientist, working as he does with objects that are devoid of any will of their own, may hold certain of his variables constant while systematically modifying those which interest him in any particular investigation; thus he is able to *repeat* his experiments over and over. This, we are told, can only be done in the laboratory, where the presence, absence, quantity, strength, position, or rate of change of all variables remains under the researcher's control. First of all, this is by no means always true of physical science, even within the laboratory. Can we possibly assert that the astronomer, for example, is able to hold some of his objects of inquiry steady in one place while moving others about to satisfy his experimental requirements? Obviously not; yet his is certainly a well-advanced science, already enjoying excellent measurement and description, and impressive prediction, even though it may still be weak on the explanatory side.

In order to cope with the nonlaboratory situation, social scientists have developed three additional types of strategy: the field experiment, the natural experiment, and the *ex post facto* experiment. The *field experiment* is closest in design to the laboratory one, but its setting makes control and manipulation somewhat trickier; that is, an event, condition, or person is deliberately injected into what is in all other respects a normal field setting, and then the effects of that artificial stimulus are observed. The *natural experiment* also occurs in the normal field setting and in the

---

[5]The skepticism which meets most efforts to measure and operationalize in international relations is by no means a phenomenon peculiar to that discipline. As recently as 1928, L. L. Thurstone, a leader in psychological measurement, felt compelled to publish "Attitudes Can Be Measured" in the *American Journal of Sociology*, XXXIII (1928), 529-54. And the problem in biology is nicely summarized in Ralph W. Gerard, "Quantification in Biology," *Isis*, LII (1961), 334-52.

presence of the investigator, but no artifical stimulus or condition is injected; rather, the researcher merely waits for the desired stimulus to occur naturally and then records the effects. Both types of experiment are widely used in sociology and social psychology as well as in some of the physical sciences, with astronomy and meteorology as typical examples of the latter. The most difficult research strategy, but the one most germane to international politics, is the *ex post facto* experiment. Here, the investigator neither observes the events as they unfold nor injects artificial stimuli into the field setting. Rather, he goes back to the records, observations, or other traces left by past events and tries to select — by visible and explicitly articulated criteria — a number of comparable historical cases for which "adequate" descriptions are available or reconstructable, and assumes, for convenience, that they have not yet taken place. Then the variables are identified, observation and measurement procedures specified, and hypotheses spelled out. Finally the case is examined *as if* it were unfolding before his very eyes in order to ascertain the extent to which his hypotheses were borne out. As for holding some variables constant while manipulating others, it is merely (!) a matter of finding those cases in which the desired control conditions existed.

Let me suggest a simple example, based on a project of mine now under way. Suppose one wanted to test the following hypothesis, not always made explicit, but central to what we call the balance-of-power theory: The *closer* the international system is to bipolarity, the greater the frequency and magnitude of war, and the *further* it is from bipolarity, the less the frequency and magnitude. First the investigator selects that historical period which holds most theoretical interest for him; it can be several decades, a century, or many centuries, but his generalization, whether confirmed or disconfirmed, normally holds only for that period.[6] Next, he develops quantitative measures of his *independent* variable (polarity of the system) and his *dependent* variables (magnitude of war, frequency of war), and then he goes on to code and score the independent variable and the two dependent variables for each year. Finally, he runs simple statistical correlations between the two sets of variables,

[6]Literally speaking, there is no such outcome as confirmation of an hypothesis; one states the hypothesis in the negative form and then seeks *disconfirmation* over a series of experiments. The more often this "null hypothesis" is disconfirmed, the greater statistical confidence one can have in the original hypothesis. In contrast to law, the defendant is assumed to be guilty until proven innocent, compellingly and often!

and concludes that, for the period under study, the hypothesis is (or is not) strongly (or weakly) disconfirmed. The major problem is that of devising reliable measures and classification procedures, but, as I suggested earlier, this is difficult, but not impossible. As to the complaint that many factors in the international system *other than* polarity may have accounted for the results, all the investigator can do is go on to study, in a similar fashion, the correlation between *those* factors and his outcome, noting which were present in what strength and combinations for each year or other time period selected. This is, of course, a grossly simplified summary of what can be done but it should suggest the possibilities of the *ex post facto* experiment for political science and history; in a more sophisticated form, sociology has been employing it for years.[7]

In returning to the admittedly rhetorical question which titles this section, the answer would seem to be an unequivocal "yes," although we in *social* science do have somewhat greater difficulties to overcome than do most *physical* scientists. But the problems are not impossible to surmount, and we might well devote as much effort to attacking them as we do to asserting and demonstrating that they are insurmountable.

Analogy and Reality

Having addressed myself to some of the more telling issues of social science in general, I must now turn to a matter peculiar to this specific book, and examine one of the key epistemological problems involved in any effort to transfer knowledge from one field to another. I am referring, of course, to the procedure known as analogizing. Thus, even if the skeptic is persuaded that psychology and sociology do qualify as sciences, he may still boggle at any effort to utilize *their* models and *their* data in the study of international politics. In other words, what of the argument that the findings in one empirical world — and the ideas used to organize those findings — cannot legitimately be transferred to another, and distinctly different, empirical world?

First of all, it depends upon the literalness of the transfer under

---

[7]For a discussion and rather primitive illustration of this approach in anthropology, see Morris Freilich, "The Natural Experiment, Ecology, and Culture," *Southwestern Journal of Anthropology*, XIX (1963), 21-39. Also relevant here is Ernest Nagel, *The Structure of Science* (New York: Harcourt, Brace & World, 1961), especially Ch. 13, "Forms of Controlled Inquiry."

consideration. No one would argue, for instance, that since most individuals tend to respond to frustration with aggressive behavior against the source of the frustration, most nations can be expected to do likewise; or that if a "wheel" communication-net produces optimum problem-solving performance in ten-person groups, the same pattern would follow in a ministry of defense or a legislative or interdepartmental committee.

While recognizing how absurd it would be to make any one-to-one extrapolation from the psychological or sociological experiment to the "real" world because of the important discrepancies between the two, it is worth noting that there are other discrepancies of a less obvious, but equally germane, nature. After all, *no* two social—or physical— phenomena are exactly identical; they must always differ, if only in time and place.[8] If every event or condition is, in fact, unique and not quite like any other, the question becomes one of whether it is possible to generalize at all, since generalization requires a large number of comparable cases. Therein, of course, lies the point: there is a world of difference between *identical* and *comparable,* and if we could only generalize on the basis of *identical* cases, conditions, or experiments, all science would be impossible. Thus, we must settle for that degree of identity which is sufficient for our theoretical needs; in other words, all we ask is that the cases be similar enough to be comparable in terms of the specific variables that concern us in any particular inquiry.

Another point worth noting in this regard concerns the problem of distortion from reality. Traditional political scientists and historians are fond of pointing out that, whatever they may lack in scientific method or theory-building, they are able to provide extremely accurate descriptions of political reality. Well, it depends on the meaning assigned to "accurate"; if it means a perfect replication of the actual events, social conditions, thoughts, and words that occurred, the claim has no legitimacy. First of all, only a portion of these phenomena have been recorded, or even *could* have been recorded, merely because diplomatic and political activity has a large private sector; and even if all such activity *were* in the public domain, it would require a massive battery of highly trained observers to record everything that transpired. Secondly, even with such an observation and data-recording team, any classificatory

---

[8]An article which raises this and related issues in a sophisticated and clear fashion is Carey B. Joynt and Nicholas Rescher, "The Problem of Uniqueness in History," *History and Theory,* I (1961), 150-62.

scheme conceivable by the mind of man would require considerable screening of the events and conditions, with some retained by the screening criteria and many others necessarily filtered out. Moreover, if an encyclopedic and nondiscriminating scheme were possible, it would be almost useless. In other words, data become valuable only when the trivial and the substantive have been separated from one another, with the distinction between them largely a function of the theoretical interests and needs of the scholarly observer.

Leaving the issue of *quantitative* accuracy, or completeness, now let us examine the matter of *qualitative* accuracy: that is, for those events and conditions which *are* observed and recorded, how far does reality remain undistorted—what is the relationship between an event and the verbal record of it? Clearly, words are *symbols* of social reality, as are graphs, charts, or mathematical equations, and as such they must necessarily be some distance from the phenomena they represent. The point is, of course, that there is no possible way, even using a sound-track, techni-color, motion-picture camera, or a battery of them, of reproducing social phenomena in a quantitatively or qualitatively accurate fashion; selection and interpretation are unavoidable, so that the recorded result cannot be anything but a *simulation* or *representation* of reality.

Given these conclusions, we can now return to our problem of analo-gizing from the literature of the behavioral sciences to international politics and comparative foreign policy. Perhaps the most useful way of tackling this question is to ask: To what extent do such analogies "simulate" the world of diplomacy, which is what primarily interests us? Is the simulation close enough to be useful, or is it likely to be so far-fetched that it is either misleading or irrelevant? The answer, of course, depends upon whether the variables we are using are comparable when taken from the one setting to another. If intergroup conflict in the social psychology laboratory is best described, predicted, or explained in terms of the same variables necessary to understand such conflict within the foreign policy decision-making group of a nation, then the comparabil-ity is sufficient. Using the same illustration, would the comparabil (or isomorphism) become inadequate if the same model were applied to inter-*nation* conflict? Intuitively, we would tend to think that it would, given the evident discrepancies between the motives, decision processes, capabilities, and social environments of men and of nations. The varia-bles seem just too incomparable to be useful in this latter case, whereas they *might* be comparable enough for drawing an analogy between the small laboratory group and the national decision-making group.[9]

However, no matter how comparable the variables may be, or how compelling the analogy, an important distinction remains to be made. Is the analogy drawn for descriptive and predictive purposes, or merely for heuristic purposes? If "heuristic" means here "suggestive" (or "productive of tentative ideas and hypotheses") it is easy to see how crucial this distinction can be. To put it another way, in the absence of better data and better models from the "real" world, the analogy may well *have to* serve as evidence, albeit evidence of a clearly interim nature. Its main value, then, is to generate reasonable hypotheses, whose confirmation ultimately requires testing in the empirical world about which we want to generalize. Until such testing, by operational, and therefore replicable, procedures occurs, we are a goodly distance from our objective of data-based theory. But given the tremendous gap which now separates us from that aspiration, it will be no great crime to treat our more sophisticated and careful analogies as a tentative variety of empirical evidence. In examining the many analogies suggested in this volume, it will be up to the reader to decide how close each of them comes to the standards described.

Selection Criteria

What are the criteria by which the excerpts in this volume have been selected? As suggested above, the disciplines from which I have borrowed are assumed to have a potential applicability in terms of their findings, concepts, and methods. Therefore, selections were chosen because they seemed to do one or more of the following:

(a) provide *data* or information which may fill a relevant empirical gap in our present descriptions and explanations of national behavior and international relationships;

(b) offer a more useful (i.e., insightful or understandable, systematic or coherent, parsimonious or efficient) *way of looking* at our subject than has hitherto been employed; and

(c) suggest a *technique* by which we might make our data-making, data-

---

[9]For an excellent discussion of the problems involved in extrapolating from experimental findings in the laboratory to the "real" world, see Sidney Verba, *Small Groups and Political Behavior* (Princeton, N.J.: Princeton University Press, 1961), especially Ch. IV.

gathering, or data-interpretation more accurate, reliable, replicable, complete, or economical; this includes techniques which might permit the quantification or operationalization of variables which we have tended to regard as highly elusive and not susceptible to such clarification.

Some of the excerpts will do only one of these things, and some will be useful for two or all three of these purposes; generally, my reason for selecting the material will be indicated. Moreover, almost all of the selections are intended to convey that intangible element of intellectual "style" which distinguishes the intuitionist and the social "poet" from the scientist.

Given these particular requirements, it must be immediately recognized that no one (especially a disciplinary outsider) could possibly claim to have read—or even glanced through—all of the English-language journals in sociology, social anthropology, and the relevant psychologies (clinical, experimental, and social) since their appearance. I have, however, over the past six years made a serious attempt to keep up with a large segment of this literature and to read back to the late 1940's when the recent upsurge in social science research first became manifest. Moreover, a number of my students and colleagues have made themselves self-appointed (not without encouragement!) surveyors, constantly on the lookout for relevant papers which I might have missed; a fair proportion of those presented here were discovered in just such a fashion.

To be somewhat more specific now, let me indicate which fields have been included or ignored in this search. First, economics has been completely ignored, but not because it is irrelevant. On the contrary, the models and schemes used by economists could, and to some extent already do, largely enrich our conceptual storehouse, and a study of the evolution of their methods would be invaluable to the international relations specialist.[10] Even though some of the economists' basic variables are, in a sense, ready-made in quantitative form, they have had to overcome a number of equally difficult problems in devising their measures, indices, and other classification criteria. Perhaps one of us will

---

[10]As a matter of fact, two contemporary economists have already made major contributions to our discipline, particularly in the study of international military relations. See Kenneth Boulding, *Conflict and Defense* (New York: Harper & Row, 1962); and Thomas Schelling, *The Strategy of Conflict* (Cambridge, Mass.: Harvard University Press, 1961).

one day prepare a volume similar to this in which the impressive relevance of economics might be fully illustrated; it could be a most valuable contribution.

Second, when this book began to take shape in my mind, I had every intention of including quite a few articles and studies from cultural and social anthropology. But as my search progressed, I was reminded that, while the field is rich in *concepts,* it is almost *methodless,* so that these insightful ideas are so far from operational that they are often useless for the purposes of this volume. And as for the voluminous body of *information* gathered by that discipline, two difficulties were present. First, the great bulk of it is based upon the study of pre-industrial societies and would, thus, not be susceptible to direct application. Second, what relevant data they could provide suffer largely from the same liability as their models: so unoperational and intuitive in the gathering as to be of relatively low reliability. After all, one of my purposes here is to accelerate the development of scientific method in international politics, and it would serve little purpose to introduce data gathered by methods which are no more rigorous and replicable than those already used in international relations.[11]

Having circumscribed the disciplinary areas from which the readings here have been drawn, let me now indicate another range of selection criteria that needed consideration. Under the general rubric of international relations and the social-psychological sciences, we might distinguish three classes of research: first, that conducted by international relations specialists who are using the techniques, ideas, and data of the behavioral sciences; second, that done by sociologists and psychologists in which they explicitly apply their skills to substantive matters in the international relations field; and, third, work done by the latter group, but with no intentional application to our field. It is material from this third class, of course, which comprises the present volume. The other two classes are represented in the bibliography at the end of the book.

However, the length of those two listings should not be misinter-

---

[11] One contribution from anthropology which now seems to be getting some attention is the parallelism between the forms of political organization found in some primitive groups and those found in today's international system; the term "stateless society" may well be applicable to both settings. See for example, Roger Masters, "World Politics as a Primitive Political System," *World Politics,* XVI (1964), 595-619; and Chadwick Alger, "Comparison of Intranational and International Politics," *American Political Science Review,* LVII (1963), 406-19.

preted,[12] since, in order to illustrate the general nature of what has already been done in those first two classes, my selection criteria have not been particularly stringent. Thus, little of the work listed in either of them can honestly be identified as scientific; as long as the sociologist or psychologist was addressing himself to matters of our concern, and as long as the international relations scholar utilized *some* of the formers' skills or styles, they were included. On the other hand, there are a few items in each class which clearly demonstrate that scientific work in the field can, indeed, be done, and that rigorous research need not be limited to trivial aspects of international relations.[13]

Why much of the material in these two classes should be somewhat below par is not difficult to explain. As to the first class, international relations scholars have only recently begun to borrow from the behavioral sciences and few of us are yet well trained in their methods and concepts.[14] While most of us have been largely self-trained in this regard, our recent and future students will be considerably better prepared, and the next few years should, therefore, see a sharp increase in both the quantity and quality of operational and imaginative work.

Turning now to the opposite side of the interdisciplinary coin, there is also an increasing amount of research relevant to international relations being undertaken by psychologists and sociologists, some of which is of extremely high quality. However, much of it suffers from three faults. First, very few of these behavioral scientists have any detailed or thorough familiarity — however anecdotal and intuitive — with the empirical world which concerns us here: that of past and present international politics. Thus, they have considerable difficulty fitting their own kinds of

[12]Other useful bibliographies are in Jessie Bernard, T. H. Pear, Raymond Aron, and Robert C. Angell, *The Nature of Conflict* (Paris: UNESCO, 1957); and Seymour Beardsley and Alvin Egdell, *Human Relations in International Affairs* (Washington: Public Affairs Press, 1956). See also Leon Bramson and George Goethals (eds.), *War: Studies from Psychology, Sociology, and Anthropology* (New York: Basic Books, 1964).

[13]Several of the political scientists and historians whose work is listed, plus a few others, have joined with me in an effort to conduct and publish a volume of individual studies, each of which attempts to "test" an interesting theoretical question by means of operational procedures and quantitative data. Tentatively entitled *Quantitative Research in International Politics*, it will appear in early 1966 as Volume VI of the International Yearbook of Political Behavior Research.

[14]Though it is accurate to describe the development as recent — i.e., the 1950's and 1960's — one scholar and his students really began the trend in the late 1930's. This was, of course, Quincy Wright whose two-volume *Study of War* (Chicago: University of Chicago Press, 1942), includes an impressive number of operational measures and testable propositions. A one-volume edition, abridged by Louise L. Wright (Chicago: University of Chicago Press, 1964), is now available. In light of that project, plus his multi-disciplined *Study of International Relations* (New York: Appleton-Century-Crofts, 1955), dedication of this collection to him seems to be a most appropriate, if insufficient, recognition.

research into the larger picture. Second, they tend to work with a limited number of variables, only some of which have any meaningful "fit" in the world of foreign policy and international politics. Third, many of those who have tried their hand in our field have done so out of a sense of deep personal commitment to the problem of peace in the nuclear-missile area, and with a feeling of utmost urgency. I certainly share these feelings, as do many of us, but these scholars often permit that sense of urgency to overcome their excellent training and genuine capabilities, with the result that they seem to be working by a double standard. That is, little of their work in the realm of international politics reflects the same care and rigor which marks their more traditional research and teaching activities. Again, the bibliography reveals numerous exceptions, and we can certainly hope that this hurdle will be cleared before too long.[15]

A final consideration regarding the selection of the readings is one concerning which the serious scholar is always ambivalent: the need to communicate effectively with readers who, for the most part, will be unfamiliar with the lexicon and literature of the behavioral sciences. I have sought to meet this problem in two ways. First, I have often passed up what might be thought of as the best work on a given problem, selecting instead a paper which some of the *cognoscenti* might consider mediocre. All I can do is ask the latter's indulgence and reiterate that my primary purpose has not been to present the most sophisticated, but rather the most relevant and understandable, work of which I was aware.[16]

Second, I have – from the point of view of the original authors – committed an unpardonable sin: tampering with their labors of love. As to deletions, I have screened out a great deal of the material dealing with essentially mechanical problems of methodology, and presented passages of a procedural or statistical nature only on occasion. Likewise,

---

[15]One way of overcoming a portion of these problems is to provide graduate students in these disciplines with some formal training in our field, even if that training be quite traditional. Under a program recently introduced at the University of Michigan, doctoral candidates in economics, sociology, and psychology may offer international relations as a graduate field by taking several courses in the political science department plus an interdisciplinary seminar. In other words, a student need no longer take his Ph.D. in political science in order to become an international relations specialist.

[16]It might not be amiss at this point to urge our colleagues in psychology and sociology to give greater attention to literary grace and semantic craftsmanship; sophisticated models and operational data are valuable, but even more so when presented in the context of coherent verbalization, especially if they are to be useful to those of us outside their disciplinary subculture.

many charts and tables, as well as footnotes, have been omitted.[17] On the other hand, I have rather often italicized words and phrases that may not have required such emphasis for communication within the discipline concerned, and I have less often inserted in brackets a clarifying word or two. The authors have been most gracious in permitting this sort of alteration. Finally, on occasion, my introductory comments include a passage intended to clarify an idea or technique which seemed likely to confuse or escape the uninitiated reader.

Organization of the Volume

A glance at the table of contents will indicate the degree to which the arrangement implies and reflects a particular model of the international system. Part One deals with that system as *the environment* within which nations interact with one another. For the nation, as for any other social actor, the system which serves as its environment has three specific aspects: the physical-technological, the institutional-structural, and the attitudinal-cultural. Though the lines between them are far from neat and unambiguous, some sort of classification is essential, and I have found that this is still a useful distinction. These selections have been presented at the beginning in order to emphasize the degree to which the international system and *its* environment (both of which constitute the environment of the nations) are relatively stable factors which markedly limit and restrict the freedom and independence of the nations.

In Part Two we look in considerable detail at *the actors* themselves — the nations and their component parts. Here our concern is with the specific characteristics of a nation which affect its mode of behavior in the international system: its history, cultural values, formal ideology, social institutions, decision-making procedures, and capabilities. The purpose of dealing with the nation in this temporarily isolated context is to permit a degree of analysis which would be far more difficult if it were conducted in the complicating context of ongoing interactions. We temporarily suspend this dynamic in order to look inside the "black box" for relevant similarities and differences between and among our national actors.

But in Part Three we return to the ongoing interactions between nations, and shift our focus from their internal characteristics to their

---

[17]Brief omissions are indicated by ellipsis marks (...) within the text, and larger omissions by a line of asterisks or an editorial note.

external behavior. Here are the real dynamics of inter-nation politics — the interaction between and among those complex social organizations known as national states. I should warn the reader, however, that this part will be considerably shorter than Part Two, primarily because the behavioral sciences seem to have much more that is directly applicable to say about *organizational behavior* (i.e., behavior which occurs *within* organizations) than about *interorganizational phenomena.* As I suggested earlier, one is much less nervous about "plugging in" well-established data or analogizing between an experimental group and a foreign ministry, than analogizing from the interpersonal level to the international level.

In sum, the volume is organized very much as if it *were* a text or theory book on international politics, with Part Two quite clearly thought of as the section on comparative foreign policy and Parts One and Three conceived of as the static and dynamic treatments, respectively, of international politics. In Part Four, there are no selections, partially because I could not find anything really compelling and partially because it is the place where the material of the three preceding parts comes together; since I could not be especially creative here, there was no point in being repetitive. Therefore, in the conclusion I have tried only to tie together some of the generalizations that seemed to emerge throughout and to reiterate the central purpose of the volume.

Integrating the Diverse Disciplines

Assuming, then, the reader's willingness to consider the possible value to international relations of these other disciplines, a serious problem still remains. The data and concepts which emerge do so from a welter of diverse milieus and they are staggeringly noncomparable. How, if at all, can they be combined and collated into anything approximating a coherent whole? One intellectual preoccupation that reappears from time to time in man's search for knowledge is that of the "unity of the sciences." Periodically, over the centuries, philosophers — amateur as well as professional — seek to discover, or impose, order and coherence on the then-existing body of knowledge and/or belief. During the past decade of the current "information explosion," another resurgence of such interest has developed, and prominent among the contending unifiers is the general systems approach.

This period has seen, on both the basic research and the applied research fronts, and even in the formulation of public policy, an impressive degree of interdisciplinary activity. In the universities, psychiatrists have collaborated with anthropologists, economists with sociologists, and statisticians with philosophers; and in the counsels of government, mathematicians, law professors, engineers, physicists, and political scientists have had to work together on complex problems whose parameters clearly fall beyond the boundaries of any one academic discipline.

Now in order for any effective communication to take place among specialists of such diverse intellectual backgrounds and vocabularies, some sort of common language and associated taxonomy becomes nearly indispensable. Naturally that language must be at a level of abstraction high enough to embrace the multiplicity of objects and relationships used in these disparate fields of inquiry. Thus, despite the misgivings which inevitably accompany any effort to move toward a unification of the sciences, the general systems, and other related approaches, seem to be "catching on" among many physical and social scientists in North America and elsewhere.

In order to indicate the flavor and orientation of these efforts, it seems appropriate to open the book with excerpts from one of the classic statements on this approach. The author of this selection—a mathematical biologist—is generally recognized as the intellectual father of this orientation in integrated science, and his allusions will indicate his non-social-science background. The reader should not, however, be put off by his reliance on physical and biological examples; those which I have retained are both understandable and relevant to the student of international politics. The two final sections have also been retained, in an effort to meet those critics who contend that those of us who favor a scientific approach to the study of human affairs are out to dehumanize man.

GENERAL SYSTEM THEORY

Ludwig von Bertalanffy

The Quest for a General System Theory

Modern science is characterized by its ever-increasing specialization, necessitated by the enormous amount of data, the complexity of techniques and of theoretical

From Ludwig von Bertalanffy, "General System Theory," *General Systems,* I (1965), 1-10 (the footnotes have been omitted). Reprinted by permission of the author and the Society for General Systems Research.

structures within every field. This, however, has led to a breakdown of science as an integrated realm: The physicist, the biologist, the psychologist and the social scientist are, so to speak, encapsulated in a private universe, and it is difficult to get word from one cocoon to the other.

There is, however, another remarkable aspect. If we survey the evolution of modern science, as compared to science a few decades ago, we are impressed by the fact that similar general viewpoints and conceptions have appeared in very diverse fields. Problems of organization, of wholeness, of dynamic interaction, are urgent in modern physics, chemistry, physical chemistry, and technology. In biology, problems of an organismic sort are everywhere encountered: it is necessary to study not only isolated parts and processes, but the essential problems are the organizing relations that result from dynamic interaction and make the behavior of parts different when studied in isolation or within the whole. The same trend is manifest in *gestalt* theory and other movements as opposed to classical psychology, as well as in modern conceptions of the social sciences. These parallel developments in the various fields are even more dramatic if we consider the fact that they are mutually independent and largely unaware of each other.

Up to recent times, the corpus of laws of nature was almost identical with theoretical physics. Few attempts to state exact laws in non-physical fields have gained universal recognition. However, the impact and the development of the biological, behavioral, and social sciences seem to make necessary an expansion of our conceptual schemes in order to allow for systems of laws in fields where application of physics is not sufficient or possible.

Such [a] trend towards generalized theories is taking place in many fields and in a variety of ways. For example, an elaborate theory of the dynamics of bio logical populations, the struggle for existence and biological equilibria has devel oped, starting with the pioneering work by Lotka and Volterra. The theory operates with biological notions such as individuals, species, coefficients of competition, and the like. A similar procedure is applied in quantitative economics and econometrics. The models of families of equations here applied happen to be similar to those of Lotka or, for that matter, of chemical kinetics, but the model of interacting entities and forces is at a different level. To take another example: living organisms are essentially open systems, that is, systems exchanging matter with their environment. Conventional physics and physical chemistry deal with closed systems, and only in recent years has theory been expanded to include irreversible processes, open systems, and states of non-equilibrium. If, however, we want to apply the model of open systems to, say, the phenomena of animal growth, we automatically come to a generalization of theory referring not to physical but to biological units. In other words, we are dealing with generalized systems. The same is true of the fields of cybernetics and theory of information which have gained so much interest in the past few years.

Thus, there exist models, principles, and laws that apply to generalized systems or their subclasses, irrespective of their particular kind, the nature of their component elements, and the relations of "forces" between them. It seems legitimate to ask for a theory, not of systems of a more or less special kind, but of universal principles applying to systems in general.

In this way we come to postulate a new discipline, called General System Theory. Its subject matter is the formulation and derivation of those principles which are valid for "systems" in general.

(1) A first consequence of the existence of general system properties is the appearance of structural similarities or isomorphies in different fields. There are correspondences in the principles which govern the behavior of entities that are, intrinsically, widely different. This correspondence is due to the fact that they all can be considered, in certain respects, as "systems," that is, complexes of elements standing in interaction. The fact that the fields mentioned, and many others as well, are concerned with "systems," leads to a correspondence in general principles and even in special laws when the conditions correspond to the phenomena under consideration.

In fact, similar concepts, models and laws have often appeared in widely different fields, independently and based upon totally different facts. There are many instances where identical principles were discovered several times because the workers in one field were unaware that the theoretical structure required was already well developed in some other field. General System Theory will go a long way towards avoiding such unnecessary duplication of labor.

System isomorphies also appear in problems which are recalcitrant to quantitative analysis but nevertheless of great intrinsic interest. There are, for example, isomorphies between biological systems and "epiorganisms" (Gerard) like animal communities and human societies. Which principles are common to the several levels of organization and so may legitimately be transferred from one level to another, and which are so specific that transfer leads to dangerous fallacies? Can civilizations and cultures be considered as systems?

It seems, therefore, that a general theory of systems would be a useful tool *providing, on the one hand, models that can be used in, and transferred to, different fields, and safeguarding, on the other hand, from vague analogies* which often have marred the progress in these fields [emphasis added].

(2) There is, however, another and possibly more important aspect of General System Theory. To use an expression of W. Weaver, classical science was highly successful in developing the theory of unorganized or disorganized complexity which stems from statistics, the laws of chance, and, in the last resort, the second law of thermodynamics. Today our main problem is that of *organized* complexity [emphasis added]. Concepts like those of organization, wholeness, directiveness, teleology, control, self-regulation, differentiation and the like are alien to conventional physics. However, they pop up everywhere in the biological, behavioral, and social sciences, and are, in fact, indispensable for dealing with living organisms or social groups. Thus, a basic problem posed to modern science is a general theory of organization. General System Theory is in principle capable of giving exact definitions for such concepts and, in suitable cases, of putting them to quantitative analysis.

(3) If we have briefly indicated what General System Theory means, it will avoid misunderstanding also to state what it is not. It is not pure mathematics or identical with the triviality that mathematics of some sort can be applied to any sort of problem; instead it poses specific problems which are far from being trivial. Further, General System Theory is not a search for vague and superficial analogies between physical, biological, and social systems. Analogies as such are of little value, since beside similarities between phenomena, dissimilarities always can be found as well. The isomorphy we have mentioned is a consequence of the fact that, *in certain aspects, corresponding abstractions and conceptual models can be applied to different phenomena* [emphasis added]. It is only in view of these aspects that system laws will apply. This does not mean that physical systems, organisms and societies are all the same. In principle, it is the same situation as when the law of gravitation applies to Newton's apple, the planetary system, and the phenomenon of tide. This means that, in terms of some rather limited aspects, a certain theoretical system (that of mechanics) holds true; it does not mean that there is a particular resemblance between apples, planets, and oceans in a great number of other aspects.

AIMS OF GENERAL SYSTEM THEORY

Summarizing, the aims of General System Theory can be indicated as follows:

(a) There is a general tendency towards integration in the various sciences, natural and social.

(b) Such integration seems to be centered in a general theory of systems.

(c) Such theory may be an important means for aiming at exact theory in the non-physical fields of science.

(d) Developing unifying principles running "vertically" through the universes of the individual sciences, this theory brings us nearer to the goal of the unity of science.

(e) This can lead to a much-needed integration in scientific education.

A remark as to the delimitation of the theory here discussed seems to be appropriate. The term and program of a General System Theory was introduced by the present author a number of years ago. It has turned out, however, that quite a large number of workers in various fields have been led to similar conclusions and ways of approach. It is suggested, therefore, to maintain this name which is now coming into general use, be it only as a convenient label.

It looks, at first, as if the definition of systems as "sets of elements standing in interaction" is so general and vague that not much can be learned from it. This, however, is not true. Systems can, for example, be defined by certain families of differential equations and if, in the usual way of mathematical reasoning, more specified conditions are introduced, many important properties can be found of systems in general and more special cases.

This mathematical approach followed in General System Theory is not the only possible or most general one. There are a number of related modern approaches, such as information theory, cybernetics, game, decision, and net theories, stochastic models, operations research, to mention only the most important ones. However, the fact that differential equations cover extensive fields in the physical, biological, economical, and probably also the behavioral sciences, makes them a suitable access to the study of generalized systems.

I am now going to illustrate General System Theory by way of some examples.

CLOSED AND OPEN SYSTEMS: LIMITATIONS OF CONVENTIONAL PHYSICS

My first example is that of closed and open systems. Conventional physics deals only with closed systems, that is, systems which are considered to be isolated from their environment. Thus, physical chemistry tells us about the reactions, their rates, and the chemical equilibria eventually established in a closed vessel where a number of reactants is brought together. Thermodynamics expressly declares that its laws only apply to closed systems. In particular, the second principle of thermodynamics states that, in a closed system, a certain quantity, called entropy, must increase to a maximum, and eventually the process comes to a stop at a state of equilibrium. The second principle can be formulated in different ways, one being that entropy is a measure of probability, and so a closed system tends to a state of most probable distribution. The most probable distribution, however, of a mixture, say, of red and blue glass beads, or of molecules having different velocities, is a state of complete disorder; having separated all red beads on one hand, and all blue ones on the other, or having, in a closed space, all fast molecules, that is, a high temperature on the right side, and all slow ones, a low temperature, at the left, is a highly improbable state of affairs. So the tendency towards maximum entropy or the most probable distribution is the tendency to maximum disorder [or randomness].

However, we find systems which by their very nature and definition are not closed systems. Every living organism is essentially an open system. It maintains itself in a continuous inflow and outflow, building up and breaking down of components, never being, so long as it is alive, in a state of chemical and thermodynamic equilibrium but maintained in a so-called steady state.

*   *   *   *   *

INFORMATION AND ENTROPY

Another development which is closely connected with system theory is that of the modern theory of communication. It has often been said that energy is the currency of physics, just as economic values can be expressed in dollars or pounds. There are, however, certain fields of physics and technology where this currency is not readily acceptable. This is the case in the field of communication which, due to the development of telephones, radio, radar, calculating machines, servomechanisms and other devices, has led to the rise of a new mathematical field.

The general notion in Communication Theory is that of information. Information is measured in terms of decisions. Take the game of Twenty Questions, where we are supposed to find out an object by having answered questions about it by yes or no. The amount of information conveyed in one answer is a decision between two alternatives, such as animal or non-animal. With two questions, it is possible to decide for one out of four possibilities, for example, mammal — nonmammal, or flowering plant — non-flowering plant. With three questions it is a decision out of eight, and so forth. Thus, the logarithm at the basis 2 of the possible answers can be used as a measure of information, the unit being the so-called binary unity or "bit." The information contained in two answered questions is $\log_2 4 = 2$ bits, of three answers, $\log_2 8 = 3$ bits, and so forth. This measure of information happens to be similar to that of entropy or rather negative entropy, since entropy also is defined as a logarithm of probability. But entropy, as we have already heard, is a measure of disorder; hence negative entropy or information is a measure of order or of organization since the latter, compared to distribution at random, is an improbable state. In this way information theory comes close to the theory of open systems, which may increase in order and organization, or show negative entropy. But negative entropy can be considered a measure of decisions, taken out of equally probable ones, a measure of improbability or information.

Another central concept of Communication Theory is that of feedback. A simple scheme for feedback is the following. In the classical case of stimulus-response, a stimulus affects a receptor; the message of the receptor is transmitted to some controlling apparatus, and from this to an effector which gives the response. In feedback, the result of the effector's activity is monitored back to the receptor so that the system is self-regulating.

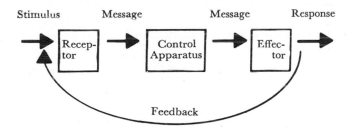

Feedback arrangements are used in modern technology to a wide extent for the stabilization of a certain action, as in thermostats or in radio receivers; or for the direction of actions towards a goal where the aberration from that goal is fed back, as information, till the goal or target is reached. This is the case in self-propelled missiles which seek their target, anti-aircraft fire control systems, ship-steering systems, and other so-called servomechanisms.

There is a large number of biological phenomena which correspond to the feedback scheme. First, there are the phenomena of so-called homeostasis, or maintenance of balance in the living organism, the prototype of which is thermoregulation in warm-blooded animals. Cooling of the blood stimulates certain centers in the brain which "turn on" heat-producing mechanisms of the body, and the body temperature is monitored back to the center so that temperature is maintained at a constant level. Similar homeostatic mechanisms exist in the body for maintaining the constancy of a great number of physico-chemical variables. Furthermore, feedback systems comparable to the servomechanisms of technology exist in the animal and human body for the regulation of actions. If we want to pick up a pencil, report is made to the central nervous system of the amount [by] which we have [missed] the pencil in the first instance; this information then is fed back to the central nervous system so that the motion is controlled till it reaches its aim.

So a great variety of systems in technology and in living nature follow the feedback scheme, and it is well known that a new discipline, called Cybernetics, was introduced by Norbert Wiener to deal with these phenomena. The theory tries to show that mechanisms of a feedback nature are at the basis of teleological or purposeful behavior in man-made machines as well as in living organisms, and in social systems.

*   *   *   *   *

Causality and Teleology

Another point I would like to make is the change the scientific world-picture has undergone in the past few decades. In the world view called mechanistic, born of classical physics of the 19th century, the aimless play of the atoms, governed by the inexorable laws of mechanical causality, produced all phenomena in the world, inanimate, living, and mental. No room was left for any directiveness, order, or telos. The world of the organisms appeared a mere product of chance, accumulated by the senseless play of mutation at random and selection; the mental world as a curious and rather inconsequential epiphenomenon of material events.

The only goal of science appeared to be the analytical, that is, the splitting-up of reality into ever smaller units and the isolation of individual causal trains. Thus, physical reality was split up into mass points or atoms, the living organism into cells, behavior into reflexes, perception into punctual sensations, and so forth. Correspondingly, causality was essentially one-way: one sun attracts just one planet, one gene in the fertilized ovum produces such and such inherited character, one sort of bacterium produces this or that disease, mental elements are lined up, like the beads in a string of pearls, by the law of association. Remember Kant's famous table of the categories, which attempts to systematize the fundamental notions of classical science: it is symptomatic that the notion of interaction and of organization were only space-fillers or did not appear at all.

Now we may state as characteristic of modern science that this scheme of isolable units acting in one-way causality has proved to be insufficient. Hence the appearance, in all fields of science, of notions like wholeness, holistic, organismic, *gestalt* and so forth which all signify that in the last resort, we must think in terms of systems of elements in *mutual interaction* [emphasis added].

Similarly, notions of teleology and directiveness appeared to be outside the scope of science and the playground of mysterious, super-natural or anthropomorphic agencies; or else, a pseudo-problem, intrinsically alien to science, and merely a misplaced projection of the observer's mind into a nature governed by purposeless laws. Nevertheless, these aspects exist, and you cannot conceive of a living organism, not to speak of behavior and human society, without taking into account what variously and rather loosely is called adaptiveness, purposiveness, goal-seeking and the like.

＊　＊　＊　＊　＊

WHAT IS ORGANIZATION?

Similar considerations apply to the concept of organization. Organization also was alien to the mechanistic world. The problem did not appear in classical physics, mechanics, electrodynamics and so forth. Even more, the second principle indicated destruction of order as the general direction of events. It is true that this is different in modern physics. An atom, a crystal, or a molecule are organizations, as Whitehead never failed to emphasize. In biology, organisms, by definition, are organized things. But although we have an enormous amount of data on biological organization, from biochemistry to cytology, to histology and anatomy, we do not have a real theory of biological organizations, that is, a conceptual system which permits explanation of the empirical facts.

＊　＊　＊　＊　＊

As an example of the application of General System Theory to human society, I would like to quote a recent book by Boulding, entitled *The Organizational Revolution*. Boulding starts with a general model of organization and states what he calls Iron Laws holding good for any organization. Such Iron Laws are, for example, the Malthusian law that the increase of a population is greater than that of its resources. Then there is a law of the optimum size of organizations: the larger an organization grows, the longer is the way of communication and this, depending on the particular nature of the organization, acts as a limiting factor and does not allow an organization to grow beyond a certain critical size. According to the law of instability, many organizations are not in a stable equilibrium but show cyclic fluctuations which result from the interaction of subsystems. This, incidentally, could probably be treated in terms of the Volterra theory, Volterra's so-called first law being that of periodic cycles. The important law of oligopoly states that, if there are competing organizations, the instability of their relations and hence the danger of friction and conflicts increase with the decrease of the number of those organizations. Thus, so long as they are relatively small and numerous, they muddle through in some way to coexistence. But if only a few or a competing pair is left, as is the case with the colossal political blocks at the present day, conflicts become devastating to the point of complete mutual destruction. The number of such general theorems for organization can easily be enlarged. They are well capable of being developed in an exact way, as it actually was done for certain aspects.

GENERAL SYSTEM THEORY AND THE UNITY OF SCIENCE

Let me close these remarks with a few words about the general implications of interdisciplinary theory.

The integrative function of General System Theory can perhaps be summarized as follows. So far, the unification of science has been seen in the reduction of all sciences to physics, in the final resolution of all phenomena into physical events. From our point of view, unity of science gains a more realistic aspect. A unitary conception of the world may be based, *not* upon the possibly futile and certainly far-fetched hope finally *to reduce all levels of reality to the level of physics, but rather on the isomorphy of laws in different fields* [emphasis added]. Speaking in what has been called the "formal" mode, that is, looking at the conceptual constructs of science, this means structural uniformities of the schemes we are applying. Speaking in "material" language, it means that the world, that is, the total of observable phenomena, shows structural uniformities, manifesting themselves by isomorphic traces of order in its different levels or realism.

We come, then, to a conception which in contrast to reductionism, we may call perspectivism. We cannot reduce the biological, behavioral, and social levels to the lowest level, that of the constructs and laws of physics. We can, however, find constructs and possibly laws within the individual levels. The world is, as Aldous Huxley once put it, like a Neapolitan ice cake where the levels, the physical, the biological, the social and the moral universe, represent the chocolate, strawberry, and vanilla layers. We cannot reduce strawberry to chocolate—the most we can say is that possibly in the last resort, all is vanilla, all mind or spirit. The unifying principle is that we find organization on all levels. The mechanistic world view, taking the play of physical particles for ultimate reality, found its expression in a civilization glorifying physical technology which eventually has led to the catastrophies of our time. Possibly the model of the world as a great organization can help to reenforce the sense of reverence for the living which we have almost lost in the last sanguinary decades of human history.

GENERAL SYSTEM THEORY IN EDUCATION: THE PRODUCTION OF SCIENTIFIC GENERALISTS

After this necessarily sketchy outline of the meaning and aims of General System Theory, let me try to answer the question what it may contribute to integrative education. In order not to appear partisan, I give a few quotations from authors who were not themselves engaged in the development of General System Theory.

A few years ago, a paper, entitled "The Education of Scientific Generalists," was published by a group of scientists comprising the engineer Bode, the sociologist Mosteller, the mathematician Tukey, and the biologist Winsor. The authors emphasize the "need for a simpler, more unified approach to scientific problems." They write:

> We often hear that "one man can no longer cover a broad enough field" and that "there is too much narrow specialization.". . . We need a simpler, more unified approach to scientific problems, we need men who practice science — not a particular science; in a word, we need scientific generalists.

The authors then make clear how and why generalists are needed in various fields such as physical chemistry, biophysics, the application of chemistry, physics, and mathematics to medicine, and they continue:

> Any research group needs a generalist, whether it is an institutional group in a university, or a foundation, or an industrial group. . . . In an engineering group, the generalist would naturally be concerned with system problems. These problems arise whenever parts are made into a balanced whole.

In a symposium of the Foundation for Integrated Education, Professor Mather discussed "Integrative Studies for General Education." He states:

> One of the criticisms of general education is based upon the fact that it may easily degenerate into the mere presentation of information picked up in as many fields of enquiry as there is time to survey during a semester or a year. . . . If you were to overhear several senior students talking, you might hear one of them say "our professors have stuffed us full, but what does it all mean?". . . More important is the search for basic concepts and underlying principles that may be valid throughout the entire body of knowledge.

In answer to what these basic concepts may be, Mather states:

> Very similar general concepts have been independently developed by investigators who have been working in widely different fields. These correspondences are all the more significant because they are based upon totally different facts. The men who developed them were largely unaware of each other's work. They started with conflicting philosophies and yet have reached remarkably similar conclusions. . . .

"Thus conceived," Mather concludes, "integrative studies would prove to be an essential part of the quest for an understanding of reality."

No comments seem to be necessary. Conventional education in physics, biology, psychology or the social sciences treats them as separate domains, the general trend being that increasingly smaller sub-domains become separate sciences, and this process is repeated to the point where each specialty becomes a triflingly small field, unconnected with the rest. In contrast, the educational demands of training "Scientific Generalists" and of developing interdisciplinary "basic principles" are precisely those General System Theory tries to fill. They are not a mere program or a pious wish since, as we have tried to show, such theoretical structure is already in the process of development. In this sense, General System Theory seems to be an important headway towards interdisciplinary synthesis and integrated education.

SCIENCE AND SOCIETY

However, if we speak of education, we do not solely mean scientific values, that is, communication and integration of facts. We also mean ethical values, contributing to the development of personality. Is there something to be gained from the viewpoints we have discussed? This leads to the fundamental problem of the value of science in general and the behavioral and social sciences in particular.

An argument about the value of science and the impact of its gradual development upon society and the welfare of mankind would run something like this. Our knowledge of the laws of physics is excellent, and consequently our technological control of inanimate nature almost unlimited. Our knowledge of biological laws is not so far advanced, but sufficient to allow for a good amount of biological technology in modern medicine and applied biology. It has extended the span of human life far beyond the limits allotted to a human being in earlier centuries or even decades. The application of the modern methods of scientific agriculture, husbandry, and so forth, would well suffice to sustain a human population far surpassing the present one of our planet. What is lacking, however, is the knowledge of the laws of human society, and consequently a sociological technology. So the achievements of physics are put to use for ever more efficient instruments of destruction; we have famines in vast parts of the world while harvests rot or are destroyed in other parts; war and indiscriminate annihilation of human life, culture, and means of sustenance are the only way out of uncontrolled fertility and consequent overpopulation. *They are the outcome of the fact that we know and control physical forces only too well, biological forces tolerably well, and social forces not at all* [emphasis added]. If, therefore, we could have a well-developed science of the human society and a corresponding technology it would be the way out of the chaos and impending destruction of our present world.

This seems to be plausible enough and is, in fact, but a modern version of Plato's precept that only if the rulers are philosophers, will humanity be saved. There is, however, a catch in the argument. We have quite a fair idea what a scientifically controlled world would look like. In the best case, it would look like Aldous Huxley's *Brave New World,* and in the worst, like Orwell's *1984.* It is an empirical fact that scientific achievements are put just as much, or even more, to destructive as constructive use. The science of human behavior and society is not exempt from this fate. In fact, it is perhaps the greatest danger of the systems of modern totalitarianism that they are so alarmingly up to date not only in physical and biological, but also in psychological technology. The methods of mass suggestion, of the release of the instincts of the human beast, of reflex conditioning and thought control are developed to highest efficiency, and just because modern totalitarianism is so terrifically scientific, it makes the absolutism of former periods appear a dilettantish and comparatively harmless makeshift. Scientific control of society is no highway to Utopia.

The Ultimate Precept: Man as the Individual

We may, however, conceive of a scientific understanding of human society and its laws in a somewhat different and more modest way. Such knowledge can teach us, not only what human behavior and society have in common with other organizations, but also what is their uniqueness. Here the main tenet will be: man is not only a political animal, he is, before and above all, an individual. The real values of humanity are not those which it shares with biological entities, the function of an organism or a community of animals, but those which stem from the individual mind. Human society is not a community of ants or termites, governed by inherited instinct and controlled by the laws of the superordinate whole; it is based upon the achievements of the individual, and is doomed if the individual is made a mere cog in the social machine. This, I believe, is the ultimate precept a theory of organization can give: not a manual for dictators of any denomination more efficiently to subjugate human beings by the scientific application of Iron Laws, but a warning that the Leviathan of organization must not swallow the individual without sealing its own inevitable doom.

PART ONE

THE
INTERNATIONAL
SYSTEM
AS
ENVIRONMENT

It is a truism that every living organism, from the nerve cell to the nation, exists in an environment and interacts with other organisms which exist within the confines of that environment. But the truism fails to answer two more specific questions. First, exactly what constitutes that environment? What are its limits and boundaries, and where is the conceptual line of demarcation between the actors and their environment? Second, what is the nature of the environment's impact on the actors? Or, more specifically, in what directions and to what extent does the environment affect and influence the behavior of these actors?

In answering the first question, the observer always enjoys a considerable amount of latitude. Since the lines between actors and environment are often imaginary rather than tangible, he is generally free to draw them at the place most convenient and useful for his particular intellectual purposes. But draw them he must, if he is to avoid conceptual chaos and imprecision, and it is not always a simple matter to settle on these boundaries. In studying traffic flows, the line between the auto and the highway is relatively clear, and that between the Senator and the Congress is almost equally evident, but, as one moves up the ladder of social complexity, the number of possible alternatives increases and the implications of one's choice of boundary are less obvious.

Thus, in world politics, any one of the following might be selected as the actor: the head of state, the foreign *minister,* the foreign *ministry,* the delegation at the United Nations, the entire government, all or part of the population of a nation, the economic or social elites, or the opinion-makers, to mention a few of the tangible—but by no means easily identifiable—possibilities. Or one may select as his actors the abstraction known as the "state." Or he may decide that one or several international organizations is the most important, and, hence, most theoretically useful, actor.

Traditionally, however, the "nation" has come to be regarded as the key actor in this field, and that choice is reflected in the name normally given to the field: international (or inter-nation) relations. Although a persuasive case can be made for others, I still consider the nation the most important and most useful choice, and will use that level of social organization as my actor in this book.[1]

Having made that choice, however, there still remains the problem of defining and delimiting the nation, so that it may be differentiated from its environment. This brings up the concept of the international system as a large and complex social system and raises the general problem of taxonomy. In this book, the international system will be approached as follows. First of all, there are the many components of the system: not only the nations, but all the other discernible and relevant groups which affect relations among nations but which are outside of any particular nation. Individuals and groups *within* any single nation are conceived of as *components of the nation,* but those groupings that exist across, or *outside of,* several nations are seen as *components of the system.* Regional and global organizations are the most important, and they may be either *inter*governmental, such as the League of Nations or the U.N., their specialized agencies, O.A.S., alliances, lighthouse commissions, and customs unions, or *non*governmental, such as trade union organizations, industrial cartels, Red Cross, Rotary International, World Association of World Federalists, International Political Science Association, and so on.[2]

The international—or any other social—system, however, is more than the sum or aggregate of its subnational, national, cross-national, or supranational components. It has certain distinguishing characteristics of its own, varying over time, and these systemic characteristics are most usefully thought of as falling into three classes. First there is its *technological* character, which refers to the degree to which human ingenuity and resourcefulness permit men and their social organizations to control, adapt to, or overcome the physical characteristics of the earth and its relevant environment. Second, there is the *cultural* (some might call it the attitudinal) dimension. This is the general body of norms, values, and expectations which most of the world's politically relevant people in any

---

[1] I am by no means suggesting that nations are the only actors in world politics, and elsewhere I have discussed this problem of choice of actor and its implications in greater detail. See J. David Singer, "International Conflict: Three Levels of Analysis," *World Politics,* XII (1960), 453-61; and "The Level of Analysis Problem in International Relations," *World Politics,* XIV (1961), 77-92. See also Arnold Wolfers, "The Actors in International Relations," in W. T. R. Fox (ed.), *Theoretical Aspects of International Relations* (Notre Dame, Ind.: University of Notre Dame Press, 1959); and Kenneth N. Waltz, *Man, the State and War* (New York: Columbia University Press, 1959).

[2] There is a detailed description of the latter in Lyman C. White, *International Non-Governmental Organizations* (New Brunswick, N.J.: Rutgers University Press, 1951).

given period believe in—and believe that others believe in. In other words, there is a folklore of widely, but by no means globally, shared preferences and predictions regarding what nations *ought* to do and are *likely* to do in their relations with one another, with their own citizens, and with the cross-national and international organizations.

Finally, the environment has a *structural* or institutional dimension, and among the variables which might be used to describe this systemic characteristic are:

(a) the number of nations and dependencies in the system;

(b) the number of discrete coalitions and alliances;

(c) the number of nonaligned nations;

(d) the ease with which nations may move into or out of alliances;

(e) the number and ratio of super, major, minor, and small powers;

(f) the ease with which nations may move up or down in the power hierarchy; and

(g) the degree of formal and informal organization in the total system, ranging from near-anarchy to world empire, with balance of power, collective security, and federation as three major intermediate degrees of organization.

Admittedly none of these three classes of systemic characteristics is found to be equally distributed among the nations. In the technological realm, for example, not all nations will have the same degree of access to knowledge, an equal number of people to apply it, or similar industrial or natural resources in order to exploit it.[3] But even though the distribution and application of technological knowledge may be radically uneven, and its impact widely different from nation to nation, it cannot be thought of primarily as an *actor* characteristic; it exists in the larger international system and can be expected—no matter how tight the secrecy—to spread in its effects over most of the system. Likewise, the structural or the cultural characteristics of the system, though found and experienced differentially around the globe, are still most usefully conceived of as systemic—rather than actor—characteristics.

Before turning to the readings which are designed to illuminate the reciprocal influence that exists between the actors and the environmental system, however, there is a preliminary problem of some significance.

---

[3]Suggestive in this regard is Harold Sprout, "Geopolitical Hypotheses in Technological Perspective," *World Politics,* XV (1963), 187-212.

Broadly, this is the question of how much importance the scholar attaches to, or attributes to, the environment.[4] Admittedly that decision should not be made until one has examined the data. But every social scientist, no matter how casually he has examined those data, tends to have some sort of predilection on the so-called ecology question. And the fact that I am dealing with the system as environment in Part One indicates a good deal about my own predilections. Note further that I have tended to talk more often about the system's impact on the actors than vice versa. This, of course, is not meant to suggest that the nations are seen to have no impact on the system; that would be a preposterous position, especially in international relations, where the system is relatively "weak" compared to its extraordinarily "autonomous" component parts. But it does reflect a bias which is not too widely shared in our field by either the traditionalists or the more scientifically oriented modernists.

---

[4]The most coherent analysis available is Harold and Margaret Sprout, *Man-Milieu Relationship Hypotheses in the Context of International Politics* (Princeton, N.J.: Princeton University, Center for International Studies, 1956).

A. THE ECOLOGICAL POINT OF VIEW

The purpose of the opening excerpts, then, is to provide an understanding of some of the general issues involved in this question in light of its relevance for sociology. In the opening statement, Amos Hawley seeks — in one of the classical papers on the subject — to describe the content and approach of human ecology. The opening part of his article, which is omitted, is a critique of various interpretations of ecology and is of less interest to us than to the sociologist.

ECOLOGY AND HUMAN ECOLOGY

Amos H. Hawley

Briefly stated, ecology is concerned with the elemental problem of how growing, multiplying beings maintain themselves in a constantly changing but ever restricted environment. It is based on the fundamental assumption that life is a continuous struggle for adjustment of organism to environment. However, the manifest interrelatedness of living forms, which leads students to speak of the "web of life," suggests that adjustment, far from being the action of independent organisms, is a mutual or collective phenomenon. Drawing together the relevant facts, it seems that the inevitable crowding of living forms upon limited resources produces a complex action and reaction of organism with environment and organism with organism in the course of which individuals become related to one another in ways conducive to a more effective utilization of the habitat. As the division of labor which thus develops approaches equilibrium, such that the number of organisms engaged in each of the several activities is sufficient to provide all the needs that are represented, the aggregate of associated individu-

From Amos H. Hawley, "Ecology and Human Ecology," *Social Forces*, XXIII (1944), 398-405 (the footnotes have been omitted). Reprinted by permission of the author and The University of North Carolina Press.

als assumes the aspect of a compact viable entity, a superorganism, in fact. The (biotic) community, as such a functionally or symbiotically integrated population may properly be called, is in effect a collective response to the habitat; it constitutes the adjustment, in the fullest sense of the term, of organism to environment.

The subject of ecological inquiry then is the community, the form and development of which are studied with particular reference to the limiting and supporting factors of the environment. Ecology, in other words, is a study of the morphology of collective life in both its static and its dynamic aspects. It attempts to determine the nature of community structure in general, the types of communities that appear in different habitats, and the specific sequence of change in community development.

Two elements, one implicit and the other explicit, in the conception as outlined here merit special emphasis. Not immediately evident perhaps, though nevertheless of basic importance, is the fact that the units of observation, *i.e.,* the data, are neither physiological processes nor anatomical structures but are rather the activities of organisms. Taxonomic characteristics are relevant only so far as they serve as indexes of behavior traits. "When an ecologist says 'there goes a badger'" writes Elton, "he should include in his thoughts some definite idea of the animal's place in the community to which it belongs, just as if he had said 'there goes the vicar.'" Thus if the term species and species designations recur frequently in ecological discussion, it is simply because that is the most convenient way of referring to the expected or observed occupations of the organisms denoted.

Secondly, as already indicated, life viewed ecologically is an aggregate rather than an individual phenomenon. The individual enters into ecological theory as a postulate and into ecological investigation as a unit of measurement; but as an object of special study he belongs to other disciplines, *e.g.,* physiology, genetics, psychology, etc. The focus of attention in ecology is upon the population which is either organized or in process of becoming organized. This cannot be too strongly emphasized, for it places ecology squarely in the category of social science.

Human ecology, like plant and animal ecology, represents a special application of the general viewpoint to a particular class of living things. It involves both a recognition of the fundamental unity of animate nature and an awareness that there is differentiation within that unity. Man is an organism and as such he is dependent on the same resources, confronted with the same elementary problems, and displays in essential outline the same mode of response to life conditions as is observed in other forms of life. Thus the extension of patterns of thought and techniques of investigation developed in the study of the collective life of lower organisms to the study of man is a logical consummation of the ecological point of view. One important qualification is necessary, however; the extraordinary degree of flexibility of human behavior makes for a complexity and a dynamics in the human community without counterpart elsewhere in the organic world. It is this that sets man apart as an object of special inquiry and gives rise to a human as distinct from a general ecology.

While to reason from "pismires to parliaments" would do violence to the facts, it is nevertheless necessary to keep the phenomenon of culture in proper perspective. When man by virtue of his culture-producing capacity is regarded as an entirely unique type of organism the distortion is no less acute than if this quality were completely ignored. Human behavior, in all its complexity and variability, is but further evidence of the tremendous potential for adjustment inherent in life. Culture is nothing more than a way of referring to the prevailing techniques by which a population maintains itself in its habitat. The component parts of human culture are therefore identical in principle with the appetency of the bee for honey, the nest-building activities of birds, and the hunting habits of carnivora. To argue that the latter are instinctive while the former are not is to beg the question. Ecology is concerned less now with how habits are acquired, than with the functions they serve and the relationships they involve.

Thus despite the great difference between the behavior of men and that of lower forms of life—a difference which appears to be of degree rather of kind, the approach described as general ecology may be applied to the study of man without radical alteration. In simplest terms, human ecology is the descriptive study of the adjustment of human populations to the conditions of their respective physical environments. The necessity that life be lived in a specific place and time, operating upon man as it does upon other organisms, produces an inescapable compulsion to adjustment which increases as population increases or as the opportunities for life decrease. And out of the adaptive strivings of aggregated individuals there develops, consciously or unconsciously, an organization of interdependencies which constitutes the population a coherent functional entity. The human community, in other words, is basically an adaptive mechanism; it is the means whereby a population utilizes and maintains itself in its habitat. Human ecology, then, may be defined more fully as the study of the development and the form of communal structure as it occurs in varying environmental contexts.

The human community, of course, is more than just an organization of symbiotic relationships and to that extent there are limitations to the scope of human ecology. Man's collective life involves, in greater or less degree, a psychological and a moral as well as a symbiotic integration. But these, so far as they are distinguishable, should be regarded as complementing aspects of the same thing rather than as separate phases or segments of the community. Sustenance activities and interrelations are inextricably interwoven with sentiments, value systems, and other ideational constructs. Human ecology is restricted in scope then not by any real or assumed qualitative differences in behavior but simply by the manner in which its problem is stated. The question of how men relate themselves to one another in order to live in their habitat yields a description of communal structure in terms of its overt and visible features. It does not, however, provide explanations of all the many ramifications of human interrelationships. The external and descriptive approach of ecology is ill-suited to the direct study of the psychological counterpart of symbiosis, although it may serve as a fruitful source of hypotheses concerning that aspect of the community.

It may be helpful to call attention to the fact that the problems of human ecology, and ecology in general, are basically population problems. The broad question, as previously indicated, concerns the adjustment of population to the resources and other physical conditions of the habitat. This resolves itself into a number of related problems, such as: (1) the succession of changes by which an aggregate passes from a mere polyp-like formation into a community of interdependencies; (2) the ways in which the developing community is affected by the size, composition, and rate of growth or decline of the population; (3) the significance of migration for both the development of the community and the maintenance of community stability; and (4) the relative numbers in the various functions composing the communal structure, together with the factors which make for change in the existing equilibrium and the ways in which such change occurs.

Clearly, human ecology has much in common with every other social science. The problem with which it deals underlies that of each of the several specialized studies of human social life. Its data are drawn from the same sources and it employs many of the same techniques of investigation. The points of convergence are, in fact, too numerous to detail in this paper. There is no basis therefore to conclude from what has been said that human ecology is an autonomous social science: it is quite unlikely that there is any autonomy in science. The distinctive feature of the study lies in the conception of the adjustment of man to habitat as a process of community development. Whereas this may be an implicit assumption in most social science disciplines, it is for human ecology the principal working hypothesis. Thus human ecology might well be regarded as the basic social science.

In the second selection, the authors (also sociologists) continue the debate over what ecology is and is not, and, in the truncated portion quoted here, attempt to compare it to two other approaches. Note that Duncan and Schnore by no means insist that the social structural environment is necessarily the most important variable in a social system; rather they emphasize more the level-of-analysis problem, and they even suggest that social structure or organization can be viewed as the *dependent* variable, influenced by demographic, physical, or technological dimensions.

CULTURAL, BEHAVIORAL, AND ECOLOGICAL PERSPECTIVES IN THE STUDY OF SOCIAL ORGANIZATION

OTIS DUDLEY DUNCAN AND LEO F. SCHNORE

Although there are various understandings as to the scope and problems of sociology, many would grant that the study of society as a *system or pattern of organization* constitutes the core problem, whatever other preoccupations it may have [emphasis added]. As a result, a rather amorphous area, usually called "social organization," seems to provide sociology's central concern. Admittedly, the boundaries of the area are indistinct, and its conceptual apparatus is notably eclectic.

Tangential to this central area, three distinctive approaches to the study of society have developed within American sociology within the last few decades — the *cultural, behavioral,* and *ecological.* The terms may recall the tripartite scheme of Sorokin and Parsons: society, culture, and personality. The purposes of these authors differ from ours. Focusing on the nature of society as the *explanandum* of sociological theory, we attempt to make clear that the concepts and assumptions in use in sociology today were fashioned largely from these three different ways of regarding society. However, no prospect of integrating them into a "sociocultural" theory or a "general theory of action" is here entertained; the relationships among the three are not taken as evidence that they are special cases of some master scheme.

* * * * *

None of the three perspectives can be regarded as an exclusively sociological specialism. Certainly, each has ramifications carrying it into a whole range of problems lying well beyond the study of society, which is the focus of interest here. Unless sociology is willing to revert to a Comtean encyclopedism, it will hardly wish to claim the entirety of behavioral science, culture theory, and human ecology. In discussing their contributions to the study of society, therefore, one must avoid the appearance of evaluating them as fields or disciplines in their own right — on their "home territory," so to speak. At the same time the character of their extra-sociological preoccupations manifestly directs and limits their mode of attack on the core problems of sociology. This is seen readily in their key problems.

From Otis Dudley Duncan and Leo F. Schnore, "Cultural, Behavioral, and Ecological Perspectives in the Study of Social Organization," *American Journal of Sociology,* LXV (1959), 132-46 (the footnotes have been omitted). Reprinted by permission of the authors and The University of Chicago Press.

The *cultural* approach is derived from classical anthropological theory, which conceives of culture as a more or less integrated totality, comprising cultural patterns or sub-systems of which society is one, along with art, religion, language, technology, and others. A volume such as Kroeber's *Configurations of Culture Growth,* for example, scarcely makes reference to social structure and can hardly be called a contribution to knowledge of *social* change, except indirectly. The original intention of the cultural sociologists was to bring over from culture theory its general concepts and major hypotheses, demonstrating their applicability and fruitfulness in the study of society and of social change in particular. Thus society, like other parts of culture, was described in terms of cultural continuity ("social heritage"), invention, cultural diffusion, and the like.

The enduring contribution of this school, as it turned out, was not the strangely static "cultural determinism" of certain of its epigoni, or the theory which explains social systems in terms of "institutions" derived from "cultural value patterns," or yet the abortive effort to construct a global "sociocultural" theory. It was rather the interpretation of social change as an adjustment to cultural, and particularly technological, accumulation. (As is suggested below, the ecological perspective is perhaps a more congenial milieu for this type of interpretation than culture theory per se.) Hence the theoretical weakness of behavioralism in regard to change is not characteristic of the best cultural sociology. The latter has a well-developed interest—at least on the conceptual level—in innovation and invention and in diffusion and borrowing, all conceived as processes. In practice, except for the global theorists, cultural sociologists seldom concerned themselves with such problems of culture theory as the structure and evolution of linguistic systems, movements in styles of art and philosophy, or diffusion of items of ceremonial culture. But culture theory, insofar as it suggests an effort to treat these matters as aspects of an integrated whole, may distract the student whose business is to deal with social organization.

The *behavioral* approach (we shall refer primarily to the social-psychological version rather than that of "collective behavior") is centrally concerned with how the individual participates in social life: how the person reconciles himself to the necessity of living with others, how he relates to other persons, how he is socialized, how his behavior is controlled or influenced by that of others, and how all these problems are related to the structure of his personality and the content of his attitudes, commitments, orientations, and personal adjustment. The sociological viewpoint appropriate for this range of problems regards society as a pattern of interpersonal relationships or as an arena of social interaction. Here, however, the relevant "structure" is that which is perceived by the individual, just as the relevant "environment" is the social environment, which is again conceived in terms of individual perceptions. One searches this literature in vain for more than superficial reference to the brute facts that men live in a physical environment and that they employ material technology in adapting to it. More important, adaptation itself is conceived in individualistic terms rather than as a collective process.

As a consequence of the behavioralists' focus on the individual, his motivation, and his "tensions . . . as he fits himself into the social system," they find little need for structural or organizational concepts, nor do they like to entertain hypotheses calling for an explanation of social change other than through such intervening variables as dispositional changes or modifications of character structure. Many behavioralists have a thoroughly nominalistic view of societies and groups; as a result, they are methodological reductionists and have a trained incapacity to view social organization as a reality *sui generis* in functional and evolutionary terms. (These remarks do not apply so forcefully to the student of collective behavior, who examines social organization in the process of its emergence from relatively unstructured interaction. But this view, of course, has a built-in bias that precludes its yielding an adequate account of society as a going concern or the underlying factors of social change.)

In fact, the most glaring weakness of the behavioral approach to problems of organization can be seen in the treatment accorded change. One is hard put to find the source of societal dynamics—the causes of the changing objective circumstances perceived by the individual, to which he attends. Thus the overwhelming stress upon the individual's "adjustment" to altered external circumstances and the almost total lack of attention to the mainsprings of change, wherever they may reside. Actually, by adopting a patently static conception of culture as "that which is socially transmitted between generations," the behavioral approach is forced to an impasse: it can "explain" stability over time, but it is unable to cope with change within its own frame of reference without invoking "deviation" from norms. A circular argument often results, for social change is defined as a new pattern of individual behavior, which is brought about by "deviation"—a new pattern of behavior.

The *ecological* viewpoint likewise is easily deflected, in its turn, into studies of the environment in strictly geographic terms or into exercises in formal demography. However, its view of social organization as the collective adaptation of a population to its environment avoids the reductionism of behavioral concepts and the etherealism of the "value-pattern" concepts of some culture theorists. In this sense ecology deals with society in somewhat more concrete terms than either of the other approaches. The concept of a "population" as a system with emergent properties is not found in the behavioral or cultural perspectives, nor is the version of the functions of social organization to which this concept leads.

Judged by their research interests and theoretical concerns, as mirrored in current publications, most sociologists today are inclined to be behavioralists. Some have a familiarity with culture theory, and they eclectically accept elements of the cultural approach; few have an acquaintance with human ecology that goes beyond the chapters on urban ecology in their undergraduate textbooks. A brief exposition of this perspective may be appropriate at this point.

In the most general terms the framework of human ecology embraces four main referential concepts: population, environment, technology, and organization, which define what may be called the "ecological complex." Organization is assumed to be a property of the population that has evolved and is sustained in the process of adaptation of the population to its environment, which may include other populations. Insofar as it is amenable to ecological study, organization tends to be investigated as a ramification of sustenance activities, broadly conceived, which utilize whatever technological apparatus is at the population's disposal or is developed by it.

While in its crudest version this framework suggests that organization is to be viewed as the "dependent variable," influenced by the other three "independent variables," upon a more sophisticated view, organization is seen as reciprocally related to each of the other elements of the ecological complex. In fact, to define any of the elements of this complex adequately, one has to take account of their relationship with organization. The notion of an "ecosystem" may be used as a heuristic designation for the ecological complex in order to bring out this aspect of interrelatedness which some writers have identified as the most fundamental premise in ecological thinking. That to others this notion is one of the central postulates of sociology itself only serves to underscore the sociological character of ecology — whether in its plant, animal, or human version. Darwin's conception of the "web of life" refers to a system of organization first and foremost.

Although ecology is not to be identified with the study of areal distributions, and its subject matter is by no means limited to the "territorial arrangements that social activities assume," the study of spatial relationships continues to play a key role in ecology for several reasons. First, territoriality is a major factor giving unit character to populations. Second, space is simultaneously a requisite for the activities of any organizational unit and an obstacle which must be overcome in establishing interunit relationships. Finally space — like time — furnishes a convenient and invariant set of reference points for observation, and observed spatio-temporal regularities and rhythms furnish convenient indicators of structural relationships.

B. THE ENVIRONMENT AT WORK

The two previous excerpts have given some idea of the ecological approach to social science, and the ways in which it might differ from other approaches. But neither paper emphasized the rather specific causal connection that most ecologists tend to see between the environment and the actions or interactions which occur within that environment. In the following selections, that causal connection will be emphasized, perhaps even overemphasized. The contributions selected will be arranged according to the three-way taxonomy suggested earlier, with one or two papers each dealing with the technological, cultural-attitudinal, and structural dimensions of a social environment. But it should be emphasized that social scientists not only utilize a variety of classifications (many of which differ from mine) but that the distinctions between and among them are not always clear, in reality as well as in conception.

1. The Technological Dimension

As implied above, the impact of any single environmental characteristic upon the events occurring within that environment is seldom easily differentiable from the impact of the other characteristics, and the opening selection brings out this interdependence quite clearly. Here we can see the effect of technological innovation upon the norms and expectations which characterize a particularly primitive social system, and the effect of these changes, in turn, on the social structure itself. As with all of the readings in this book, it is crucial that the reader clarify in his own mind the analogous levels and units of analysis as he moves back and forth between his concern with the world of international political relations and the concern of the various authors with almost all social relations *except* international ones.

STEEL AXES FOR STONE-AGE AUSTRALIANS

LAURISTON SHARP

I

Like other Australian aboriginals, the Yir Yoront group which lives at the mouth of the Coleman River on the west coast of Cape York Peninsula originally had no knowledge of metals. Technologically their culture was of the old stone age or paleolithic type. They supported themselves by hunting and fishing, and obtained vegetables and other materials from the bush by simple gathering techniques. Their only domesticated animal was the dog; they had no cultivated plants of any kind. Unlike some other aboriginal groups, however, the Yir Yoront did have polished stone axes hafted in short handles which were most important in their economy.

Towards the end of the 19th century metal tools and other European artifacts began to filter into the Yir Yoront territory. The flow increased with the gradual expansion of the white frontier outward from southern and eastern Queensland. Of all the items of western technology thus made available, the hatchet, or short handled steel axe, was the most acceptable to and the most highly valued by all aboriginals.

In the mid 1930's an American anthropologist lived alone in the bush among the Yir Yoront for 13 months without seeing another white man. The Yir Yoront were thus still relatively isolated and continued to live an essentially independent economic existence, supporting themselves entirely by means of their old stone age techniques. Yet their polished stone axes were disappearing fast and being replaced by steel axes which came to them in considerable numbers, directly or indirectly, from various European sources to the south.

What changes in the life of the Yir Yoront still living under aboriginal conditions in the Australian bush could be expected as a result of their increasing possession and use of the steel axe?

II. THE COURSE OF EVENTS

*   *   *   *   *

In 1915, an Anglican mission station was established near the mouth of the Mitchell River, about a three-day march from the heart of the Yir Yoront country. Some Yir Yoront refused to have anything to do with the mission, others visited it occasionally, while only a few eventually settled more or less permanently in one of the three "villages" established at the mission.

Thus the majority of the Yir Yoront continued to live their old self-supporting

From Lauriston Sharp, "Steel Axes for Stone-Age Australians," *Human Organization,* XI (1952), 17-22 (the footnotes have been omitted). Reprinted by permission of the author and The Society for Applied Anthropology.

life in the bush, protected until 1942 by the government reserve and the intervening mission from the cruder realities of the encroaching new order from the south. To the east was poor, uninhabited country. To the north were other bush tribes extending on along the coast to the distant Archer River Presbyterian mission with which the Yir Yoront had no contact. Westward was the shallow Gulf of Carpentaria on which the natives saw only a mission lugger making its infrequent dry season trips to the Mitchell River. In this protected environment for over a generation the Yir Yoront were able to recuperate from shocks received at the hands of civilized society. During the 1930's their raiding and fighting, their trading and stealing of women, their evisceration and two- or three-year care of their dead, and their totemic ceremonies continued, apparently uninhibited by western influence. In 1931 they killed a European who wandered into their territory from the east, but the investigating police never approached the group whose members were responsible for the act.

As a direct result of the work of the Mitchell River mission, all Yir Yoront received a great many more western artifacts of all kinds than ever before. As part of their plan for raising native living standards, the missionaries made it possible for aboriginals living at the mission to earn some western goods, many of which were then given or traded to natives still living under bush conditions; they also handed out certain useful articles gratis to both mission and bush aboriginals. They prevented guns, liquor, and damaging narcotics, as well as decimating diseases, from reaching the tribes of this area, while encouraging the introduction of goods they considered "improving." As has been noted, no item of western technology available, with the possible exception of trade tobacco, was in greater demand among all groups of aboriginals than the short handled steel axe. The mission always kept a good supply of these axes in stock; at Christmas parties or other mission festivals they were given away to mission or visiting aboriginals indiscriminately and in considerable numbers. In addition, some steel axes as well as other European goods were still traded in to the Yir Yoront by natives in contact with cattle stations in the south. Indeed, steel axes had probably come to the Yir Yoront through established lines of aboriginal trade long before any regular contact with whites had occurred.

III. Relevant Factors

If we concentrate our attention on Yir Yoront behavior centering about the original stone axe (rather than on the axe—the object—itself) as a cultural trait or item of cultural equipment, we should get some conception of the role this implement played in aboriginal culture. This, in turn, should enable us to foresee with considerable accuracy some of the results stemming from the displacement of the stone axe by the steel axe.

The production of a stone axe required a number of simple technological skills. With the various details of the axe well in mind, adult men could set about producing it (a task not considered appropriate for women or children). First of all a man had to know the location and properties of several natural resources found in his immediate environment: pliable wood for a handle, which could be doubled or bent over the axe head and bound tightly; bark, which could be rolled into cord for the binding; and gum, to fix the stone head in the haft. These materials had to be correctly gathered, stored, prepared, cut to size and applied or manipulated. They were in plentiful supply, and could be taken from anyone's property without special permission. Postponing consideration of the stone head, the axe could be made by any normal man who had a simple knowledge of nature and of the technological skills involved, together with fire (for heating the gum), and a few simple cutting tools — perhaps the sharp shells of plentiful bivalves.

The use of the stone axe as a piece of capital equipment used in producing other goods indicates its very great importance to the subsistence economy of the aboriginal. Anyone — man, woman, or child — could use the axe; indeed, it was used primarily by women, for theirs was the task of obtaining sufficient wood to keep the family campfire burning all day, for cooking or other purposes, and all night against mosquitoes and cold (for in July, winter temperature might drop below 40 degrees). In a normal lifetime a woman would use the axe to cut or knock down literally tons of firewood. The axe was also used to make other tools or weapons, and a variety of material equipment required by the aboriginal in his daily life. The stone axe was essential in the construction of the wet season domed huts which keep out some rain and some insects; of platforms which provide dry storage; of shelters which give shade in the dry summer when days are bright and hot. In hunting and fishing and in gathering vegetable or animal food the axe was also a necessary tool, and in this tropical culture, where preservatives or other means of storage are lacking, the natives spend more time obtaining food than in any other occupation — except sleeping. In only two instances was the use of the stone axe strictly limited to adult men: for gathering wild honey, the most prized food known to the Yir Yoront; and for making the secret paraphernalia for ceremonies. From this brief listing of some of the activities involving the use of the axe, it is easy to understand why there was at least one stone axe in every camp, in every hunting or fighting party, and in every group out on a "walk-about" in the bush.

The stone axe was also prominent in interpersonal relations. Yir Yoront men were dependent upon interpersonal relations for their stone axe heads, since the flat, geologically recent, alluvial country over which they range provides no suitable stone for this purpose. The stone they used came from quarries 400 miles to the south, reaching the Yir Yoront through long lines of male trading partners. Some of these chains terminated with the Yir Yoront men, others extended on farther north to other groups, using Yir Yoront men as links. Almost every older adult man had one or more regular trading partners, some to the north and some to the south. He provided his partner or partners in the south with surplus spears, particularly fighting spears tipped with the barbed spines of sting ray which snap into vicious fragments when they penetrate human flesh. For a dozen such spears, some of which he may have obtained from a partner to the north, he would receive one stone axe head. Studies have shown that the sting ray barb spears increased in value as they move south and farther from the sea. One hundred and fifty miles south of Yir Yoront one such spear may be exchanged for one stone axe head. Although actual investigations could not be made, it was presumed that farther south, nearer the quarries, one sting ray barb spear would bring several stone axe heads. Apparently people who acted as links in the middle of the chain and who made neither spears nor axe heads would receive a certain number of each as a middleman's profit.

Thus trading relations, which may extend the individual's personal relationships beyond that of his own group, were associated with spears and axes, two of the most important items in a man's equipment. Finally, most of the exchanges took place during the dry season, at the time of the great aboriginal celebrations centering about initiation rites or other totemic ceremonials which attracted hundreds and were the occasion for much exciting activity in addition to trading.

Returning to the Yir Yoront, we find that adult men kept their axes in camp with their other equipment, or carried them when travelling. Thus a woman or child who wanted to use an axe—as might frequently happen during the day— had to get one from a man, use it promptly, and return it in good condition. While a man might speak of "my axe," a woman or child could not.

This necessary and constant borrowing of axes from older men by women and children was in accordance with regular patterns of kinship behavior. A woman would expect to use her husband's axe unless he himself was using it; if unmarried, or if her husband was absent, a woman would go first to her older brother or to her father. Only in extraordinary circumstances would she seek a stone axe from other male kin. A girl, a boy, or a young man would look to a father or an older brother to provide an axe for their use. Older men, too, would follow similar rules if they had to borrow an axe.

It will be noted that all of these social relationships in which the stone axe had a place are pair relationships and that the use of the axe helped to define and maintain their character and the roles of the two individual participants. Every active relationship among the Yir Yoront involved a definite and accepted status of superordination or subordination. A person could have no dealings with another on exactly equal terms. The nearest approach to equality was between brothers, although the older was always superordinate to the younger. Since the exchange of goods in a trading relationship involved a mutual reciprocity, trading partners usually stood in a brotherly type of relationship, although one was always classified as older than the other and would have some advantage in case of dispute. It can be seen that repeated and widespread conduct centering around the use of the axe helped to generalize and standardize these sex, age, and kinship roles both in their normal benevolent and exceptional malevolent aspects.

*   *   *   *   *

The stone axe was an important symbol of masculinity among the Yir Yoront (just as pants or pipes are to us). By a complicated set of ideas the axe was defined as "belonging" to males, and everyone in the society (except untrained infants) accepted these ideas. Similarly spears, spear throwers, and fire-making sticks were owned only by men and were also symbols of masculinity. But the masculine values represented by the stone axe were constantly being impressed on all members of society by the fact that females borrowed axes but not other masculine artifacts. Thus the axe stood for an important theme of Yir Yoront culture: the superiority and rightful dominance of the male, and the greater value of his concerns and of all things associated with him. As the axe also had to be borrowed by the younger people it represented the prestige of age, another important theme running through Yir Yoront behavior.

*   *   *   *   *

IV. THE OUTCOME

The introduction of the steel axe indiscriminately and in large numbers into the Yir Yoront technology occurred simultaneously with many other changes. It is therefore impossible to separate all the results of this single innovation. Nevertheless, a number of specific effects of the change from stone to steel axes may be noted, and the steel axe may be used as an epitome of the increasing quantity of European goods and implements received by the aboriginals and of their general influence on the native culture. The use of the steel axe to illustrate such influences would seem to be justified. It was one of the first European artifacts to be adopted for regular use by the Yir Yoront, and whether made of stone or steel, the axe was clearly one of the most important items of cultural equipment they possessed.

The shift from stone to steel axes provided no major technological difficulties. While the aboriginals themselves could not manufacture steel axe heads, a steady supply from outside continued; broken wooden handles could easily be replaced from bush timbers with aboriginal tools. Among the Yir Yoront the new axe was never used to the extent it was on mission or cattle stations (for carpentry work, pounding tent pegs, as a hammer, and so on); indeed, it had so few more uses than the stone axe that its practical effect on the native standard of living was negligible. It did some jobs better, and could be used longer without breakage. These factors were sufficient to make it of value to the native. The white man believed that a shift from steel to stone axe on his part would be a definite regression. He was convinced that his axe was much more efficient, that its use would save time, and that it therefore represented technical "progress" towards goals which he had set up for the native. But this assumption was hardly borne out in aboriginal practice. Any leisure time the Yir Yoront might gain by using steel axes or other western tools was not invested in "improving the conditions of life," nor, certainly, in developing aesthetic activities, but in sleep—an art they had mastered thoroughly.

Previously, a man in need of an axe would acquire a stone axe head through regular trading partners from whom he knew what to expect, and was then dependent solely upon a known and adequate natural environment, and his own skills or easily acquired techniques. A man wanting a steel axe, however, was in no such self-reliant position. If he attended a mission festival when steel axes were handed out as gifts, he might receive one either by chance or by happening to impress upon the mission staff that he was one of the "better" bush aboriginals (the missionaries' definition of "better" being quite different from that of his bush fellows). Or, again almost by pure chance, he might get some brief job in connection with the mission which would enable him to earn a steel axe. In either case, for older men a preference for the steel axe helped change the situation from one of self-reliance to one of dependence, and a shift in behavior from well-structured or defined situations in technology or conduct to ill-defined situations in conduct alone. Among the men, the older ones whose earlier experience or knowledge of the white man's harshness made them suspicious were particularly careful to avoid having relations with the mission, and thus excluded themselves from acquiring steel axes from that source.

In other aspects of conduct or social relations, the steel axe was even more significantly at the root of psychological stress among the Yir Yoront. This was the result of new factors which the missionary considered beneficial: the simple numerical increase in axes per capita as a result of mission distribution, and distribution directly to younger men, women, and even children. By winning the favor of the mission staff, a woman might be given a steel axe which was clearly intended to be hers, thus creating a situation quite different from the previous custom which necessitated her borrowing an axe from a male relative. As a result a woman would refer to the axe as "mine," a possessive form she was never able to use of the stone axe. In the same fashion, young men or even boys also obtained steel axes directly from the mission, with the result that older men no longer had a complete monopoly of all the axes in the bush community. All this led to a revolutionary confusion of sex, age, and kinship roles, with a major gain in independence and loss of subordination on the part of those who now owned steel axes when they had previously been unable to possess stone axes.

The trading partner relationship was also affected by the new situation. A Yir Yoront might have a trading partner in a tribe to the south whom he defined as a younger brother and over whom he would therefore have some authority. But if the partner were in contact with the mission or had other access to steel axes, his subordination obviously decreased. Among other things, this took some of the excitement away from the dry season fiesta-like tribal gatherings centering around initiations. These had traditionally been the climactic annual occasions for exchanges between trading partners, when a man might seek to acquire a whole year's supply of stone axe heads. Now he might find himself prostituting his wife to almost total strangers in return for steel axes or other white man's goods. With trading partnerships weakened, there was less reason to attend the ceremonies, and less fun for those who did.

Not only did an increase in steel axes and their distribution to women change the character of the relations between individuals (the paired relationships that have been noted), but a previously rare type of relationship was created in the Yir Yiront's conduct towards whites. In the aboriginal society there were few occasions outside of the immediate family when an individual would initiate action to several other people at once. In any average group, in accordance with the kinship system, while a person might be superordinate to several people to whom he could suggest or command action, he was also subordinate to several others with whom such behavior would be tabu. There was thus no overall chieftanship or authoritarian leadership of any kind. Such complicated operations as grass-burning animal drives or totemic ceremonies could be carried out smoothly because each person was aware of his role.

On both mission and cattle stations, however, the whites imposed their conception of leadership roles upon the aboriginals, consisting of one person in a controlling relationship with a subordinate group. Aboriginals called together to receive gifts, including axes, at a mission Christmas party found themselves facing one or two whites who sought to control their behavior for the occasion, who disregarded the age, sex, and kinship variables of which the aboriginals were so conscious, and who considered them all at one subordinate level. The white also sought to impose similar patterns on work parties. (However, if he placed an aboriginal in charge of a mixed group of post-hole diggers, for example, half of the group, those subordinate to the "boss," would work while the other half, who were superordinate to him, would sleep.) For the aboriginal, the steel axe and other European goods came to symbolize this new and uncomfortable form of social organization, the leader-group relationship.

The most disturbing effects of the steel axe, operating in conjunction with other elements also being introduced from the white man's several sub-cultures, developed in the realm of traditional ideas, sentiments, and values. These were undermined at a rapidly mounting rate, with no new conceptions being defined to replace them. The result was the erection of a mental and moral void which foreshadowed the collapse and destruction of all Yir Yoront culture, if not, indeed, the extinction of the biological group itself.

From what has been said it should be clear how changes in overt behavior, in technology and conduct, weakened the values inherent in a reliance on nature, in the prestige of masculinity and of age, and in the various kinship relations. A scene was set in which a wife, or a young son whose initiation may not yet have been completed, need no longer defer to the husband or father who, in turn, became confused and insecure as he was forced to borrow a steel axe from them. For the woman and boy the steel axe helped establish a new degree of freedom which they accepted readily as an escape from the unconscious stress of the old patterns—but they, too, were left confused and insecure. Ownership became less well defined with the result that stealing and trespassing were introduced into technology and conduct. Some of the excitement surrounding the great ceremonies evaporated and they lost their previous gaiety and interest. Indeed, life itself became less interesting, although this did not lead the Yir Yoront to discover suicide, a concept foreign to them.

The second selection, also from the anthropological literature, has much in common with the preceding paper. That is, it points up the extent to which the introduction of a new technology will produce profound changes in the structural and organizational characteristics of a social system. But in this case, Julian Steward, summarizing a research conference which he directed, reflects one of the powerful strains in his particular discipline by almost totally ignoring the attitudinal dimension as either an independent or an intervening variable. That is, he and most of his fellow evolutionists think of culture in a manner sharply differentiated from that of most political scientists and sociologists, as well as many anthropologists. For them, culture tends to be nothing more than "the way things are done" or "the way activities are organized," and it is seldom given any psychological connotation. As the Duncan and Schnore paper stated (in an omitted section), "the ecologist is interested in the pattern of observable physical activity itself, rather than the subjective expectations that individuals may entertain of their roles."

IRRIGATION CIVILIZATIONS: A COMPARATIVE STUDY

Julian H. Steward, *et al.*

Irrigation

It is definitely implicit in our approach, even though we may have failed to make it explicit, that we seek causes. Irrigation is not only the principal independent variable from the point of view of correlations but, in terms of functional

From Julian H. Steward, *et al., Irrigation Civilizations: A Comparative Study* (Washington: Pan-American Union, 1955), pp. 71-73. Reprinted by permission of Professor Steward and the Pan-American Union.

hypotheses, an explanation of the necessary and recurrent relationship between irrigation and the various "dependent variables" is in fact a statement of causality. Any such statement must show how use of irrigation brings about great population density and organization of the population in particular ways.

Beals comments that "large-scale irrigation is associated with fairly dense population . . . but which is the antecedent and which the consequent variable cannot possibly be answered at this point." As for sheer numbers of people—but not social patterns—I think the question is answerable if it is somewhat re-phrased. There is obviously a relationship, although not a simple Malthusian one, between food supply and population. An increased food supply permits popula-tion growth, which in turn facilitates the expansion of food production through employing more workers and using more efficient methods. The early stages of irrigation were necessarily small-scale and produced far less food per man hour of labor than the later, larger systems. Through a gradual and continuing process, every improvement in farming permitted further population expansion which led to further improvement. The limitation on such growth apparently was availability of water to a society equipped with pre-industrial techniques. When the limits of water were reached, population probably continued to increase somewhat beyond the food supply, creating an imbalance and social pressures. Meanwhile, a considerable portion of the productive efforts had been released from farming for other cultural activities. This portion could not be returned to food production, however, because water rather than labor supply imposed the limits upon this production.

We have assumed that the construction of dams, canals, and ditches in intercommunity irrigation projects involved a kind and amount of manpower that required a central authority. Beals raises the cogent question of whether the managerial functions in irrigation may not be performed through patterns of community cooperation rather than a central authority, and he rightly observes that this question has been little explored. While more research is of course needed, I think the difficulty also arises from the failure to distinguish different kinds and developmental stages of irrigation societies and from the tendency to think of irrigation in terms of its maximum development in the late Florescent Era and the Militaristic Eras. I suggest the very general and provisional hypothe-sis that informal intercommunity cooperation is feasible in systems having only small dams and a few miles of canals, but that the expansion of these systems increases the need for a labor force and augments the "managerial density" until corvee [forced] labor supplants volunteer workers and a permanent, state-appointed bureaucracy supercedes temporary supervisors. Whether the mana-gerial hierarchy rests upon religious, secular, military or political authority, or various combinations of these, however, depends upon the stage and kind of development.

The Northern Paiute of eastern California irrigated, but theirs was a system of diverting comparatively small mountain streams into ditches two or three miles long that watered only wild seeds. Some of the prehistoric Pueblo of Utah apparently irrigated cultivated plants by this same method, while recent Pueblo impounded rain run-off in dams, much like the modern "tanks" used to water live stock. Any intervillage cooperation needed in Paiute or Pueblo irrigation could readily be arranged on an informal basis. More ambitious systems, how-ever, would require some over-all authority in order to plan canals, impress the necessary labor, and regulate water distribution. Among the Hohokam of southern Arizona, a single irrigation system might comprise several hundred miles of large canals serving many widely separated communities. The precise nature of Hohokam society is not known, since the culture reached its climax in prehistoric times and was not demonstrably perpetuated in any post-Columbian Indian society, but the irrigation surely required a managerial authority far stronger than that of the Paiute or Pueblo. This aspect of Hohokam culture merits far more study than it has yet received.

In the areas under consideration in these papers it might be postulated that, from the point of view of managerial controls, farming developed through the following stages. First, Incipient Farming was based on rainfall and each com-munity or small local settlement was independent. It is conceivable that a supra-community authority might have developed when population density became so great that competition for land led first to mutual or customary understandings regarding rights of cultivation and inheritance and later to state enforcement of laws governing these matters. Control of arable land was possibly a factor in the Mesoamerican development.

Second, irrigation began with small dams and ditches as a supplement to rainfall, probably on the upper tributaries of the main rivers, for small popula-tions could hardly have coped with the main streams. During this initial stage, informal cooperation between neighboring villages probably met the managerial needs.

Third, the more arid, lower areas near the main streams, which ultimately became the key irrigation areas, could not be utilized extensively until it was possible to construct large dams and long canals and to reclaim swampy land. Population growth, however, was probably rapid, owing to natural increase and to the addition of settlers attracted by the greater productivity. When the extent of the irrigation systems required corvee labor and a full-time supervisory class, a centralized authority emerged which, in the absence of other authority patterns, was sanctioned by religion and led to the development of a priesthood. I suggest that a theocratic society developed because shamans had wielded great power over practical affairs in earlier societies lacking a priesthood because rain-making and seasonal changes in temperature, precipitation and the like were interpreted as supernatural phenomena, and because group agricultural ceremonialism is found among most early farmers.

Fourth, when the productive limits of irrigation were approached, the basis of power shifted from the priesthood to a more secular, political, and militaristic

57

bureaucracy. While the state may have wrung slightly more produce from the land by exploiting irrigation to the maximum, it also become interested in canals as means of communications and transportation of goods for administrative purposes. These functions were very highly developed in Mesopotamia and China. In the Central Andes, where the rugged topography prevented this function from assuming importance, it appears that canals were nonetheless constructed for the administrative purpose of relocating populations rather than of increasing production. Thus, the partial amalgamation of the irrigation systems of the Chicama and Moche Valleys and the expansion of Chanchan at the mouth of the latter valley into a huge, planned city were perhaps done primarily to relocate and concentrate the population for state reasons. There is no evidence that greater productiveness or increased overall population followed this change. In China and the Near East, the conversion of the larger settlements from religious centers to more secular, political, administrative and military centers was undoubtedly facilitated by these new uses of canals.

These suggestions, however, are broad and provisional. The Symposium has clearly brought out the need for much more detailed analysis. Local environmental differences, for example, posed dissimilar irrigation problems, the solution of which may well have affected the societies. In the Central Andes the engineering need was to divert streams originating high in the rugged and precipitous mountains and to utilize gravity to bring the flow to a maximum amount of farm land both in the valley bottoms and on the terraced hill sides. Since each river flowed a comparatively short distance from the Highland to the Pacific Ocean, each irrigation system and presumably the state controlling it embraced a single valley. The problem was very different in the case of such Old World rivers as the Hwang-ho, Yang-tsze, Tigris-Euphrates, Indus, and Nile. While these rivers cannot be lumped in a single category, they had in common the need to be diverted well upstream of the lands they watered, a need which may have affected the size if not the nature of the states. Moreover, there were many problems particular to the different areas. In Mesopotamia, as Adams points out, there was the difficulty that the run-off of melting snow in the mountains reached the lowlands during a time disadvantageous for growing crops. The difficulty might have been remedied by impounding water in reservoirs, but it is doubtful that early technology could achieve water storage on an important scale. Another difficulty of these huge systems of canals is that since many of them ran considerable distances with only a slight gradient they were subject to sedimentation.

Among the many technical problems involved in irrigation—and of great importance today in connection with efforts to conserve renewable natural resources—are alkalinization and leaching of farm lands to the point of ruining the soil, formation of such impermeable deposits as caliche, erosion and other topographical changes, alteration of the water table, and possibly changes in rainfall and climate, all produced in part by man's use of the land. It need hardly be added that archaeology, history, irrigation engineering, agronomy, geography, and other disciplines find a common ground in these subjects.

Finally, it is worth considering whether the crops in the irrigation areas were as important in shaping the culture as the method of growing them. In many areas, one or more well adapted crops constitute the principal subsistence — e.g., the potato in the cool climates of Chile and the Andean Highlands, manioc in the Tropical Forests, yams in Oceania, etc. In the irrigation areas, the staples were largely cereal crops — wheat, millet, rice, barley and oats in the Old World and maize in the New World. To a certain extent, the method of cultivation — sowing, propagation by cutting, transplanting, and many others — is dictated by the nature of the plant. There are several compelling reasons, however, for believing that in the case of the key irrigation areas, the use of irrigation was far more important than the plant species.

In the first place, a dense population is a precondition but not a cause of a developed "civilization." The Central Valley of Chile had very productive farming and compared favorably demographically with the Central Andes, but its society consisted only of fairly small, localized lineages. It lacked irrigation or other integrating factors. In the second place, practically all the cereal crops of the irrigation areas were utilized also in a variety of rainfall areas. In the third place, while it is possible that special plant varieties had become adapted to irrigation conditions, the biological ecological adaptability of plants is so great as to be very deceiving. Dr. Inez Adams in a thesis at Columbia University showed that what had been considered for many years to be two quite unlike, genetically-determined kinds of rice (*Oryza*) (namely, "dry rice," which is grown without irrigation in fairly arid areas, and "wet rice," which is always irrigated) were apparently the same plant which flourished under a surprising variety of conditions.

While the extent to which techniques of cultivation are determined by the plant itself is of course an empirical question in each case, there seems little doubt that in the major irrigation areas, technology was the distinctive determinant of increased productivity, of population growth and, according to the different kinds of irrigation, of types of social coordination and managerial authority.

2. The Cultural Dimension

In this section, the emphasis shifts from the technological to the normative and cultural dimension, and seeks to illustrate the extent to which *these* characteristics of a social system impinge upon those individuals and groups for whom the system is environment. The study reported here indicates a relatively high correlation between the norms and values which are dominant in a given neighborhood and the incidence of delinquency; the extent to which the use, or threatened use, of violence, thievery, or blackmail is approved in the international system may likewise exercise an impact on the "delinquency" rate of the nations inhabiting it.

COMMUNITY INTEGRATION AND THE SOCIAL CONTROL OF JUVENILE DELINQUENCY

ELEANOR E. MACCOBY, JOSEPH P. JOHNSON, AND RUSSELL M. CHURCH

The important role that community integration and social control are assumed to play in the prevention of delinquency is highlighted by Shaw, in his discussion of the differences in delinquency rates in various parts of Chicago. In the famous Chicago studies, done more than 25 years ago, it was found that delinquency was highest in the center of the city, areas marked by physical deterioration and declining population. Shaw offered the following hypothesis:

Under the pressure of the disintegrative forces which act when business and industry invade a community, the community thus invaded ceases to function effectively as a means of social control. Traditional norms and standards of the conventional community weaken and disappear. Resistance on the part of the community to delinquent and criminal behavior is low, and such behavior is tolerated and may even become accepted and approved.

Moreover, many of the people who come into the deteriorating section are European immigrants or southern Negroes. All of them come from cultural and social backgrounds which differ widely from the situations in the city. In the conflict of the old with the new the former cultural and social controls in these groups tend to break down. This, together with the fact that there are few constructive community forces at work to re-establish a conventional order, makes for continued social disorganization.

If community disintegration is indeed a factor producing juvenile delinquency, how precisely are the effects produced? In an attempt to devise an empirical study of the effects of community integration, we reasoned that something like the following process might occur: a child who, for a variety of reasons, has an interest in deviating, tries out one or two deviant acts in a tentative way, to see what the reaction of the community will be. If he lives in a disorganized community (where the rate of moving in and out will be high and where neighbors are not closely bound by social, religious, or kinship ties) there

From Eleanor E. Maccoby, Joseph P. Johnson, and Russell M. Church, "Community Integration and the Social Control of Juvenile Delinquency," *Journal of Social Issues*, XIV (1958), 38-51 (the footnotes have been omitted). Reprinted by permission of the authors and the *Journal of Social Issues*.

will be relatively little chance that he will be seen by someone who knows him or knows his parents, so long as the act is committed outside the walls of his own dwelling. The people who do see him may be deviants themselves, and may not consider the behavior especially reprehensible. But even if they do disapprove, they may nevertheless choose not to interfere, being reluctant to mention the incident directly to the child or his parents since they do not know them, and being afraid to attract the attention of the police to themselves by reporting the act to the authorities.

Our basic hypothesis is then, that in disorganized neighborhoods individual adults will feel less responsibility for guiding other people's children into the paths of "good" behavior, and will ignore deviant acts when they see them being committed, unless they themselves are directly involved. Under these circumstances, the children who are making their first tentative explorations into delinquency will find that they have a good chance of escaping any painful consequences of their antisocial activities, and will be emboldened by this knowledge, with the result that delinquency will increase in the disorganized neighborhoods.

To test whether this hypothetical picture represents what actually occurs, we compared two areas of Cambridge, Mass. The areas were chosen to be as similar as possible with respect to socio-economic status of residents, but still highly different in delinquency rates. We set out to test the following specific hypotheses:

1. The high delinquency area will be less "integrated" than the low, in the sense that people living in the "high" area will be less homogeneous with respect to ethnic and religious background, will be more transient, will be less well acquainted with their neighbors, and have fewer perceived common interests with them.

2. In the high delinquency area, values about pre-delinquent acts will be more "permissive" than in the low delinquency area. That is, there will be a tendency for residents to believe that youthful acts such as fighting, drunkenness, minor shoplifting, and minor vandalism are not especially reprehensible, are "natural" and sometimes to be condoned. Attitudes toward such behavior in the low delinquency area, on the other hand, should be relatively severe.

3. In the high delinquency area, private citizens will be less likely to take remedial action when they see other people's children engaging in some kind of delinquent or pre-delinquent activity.

We interviewed a sample of adults in each of our two neighborhoods, and our questions covered (a) the respondent's attitudes toward several categories of juvenile misbehavior, (b) the degree of the respondent's integration in his community, and (c) reports of incidents of juvenile delinquent or pre-delinquent behavior in the neighborhood. We asked each respondent to tell us exactly what action (if any) had been taken by people who observed or knew about the incident.

Before we report our findings, let us describe our criteria for choosing the two neighborhoods, and our methods of obtaining the information we required.

THE TWO NEIGHBORHOODS

It is well known, of course, that delinquency rates are higher in neighborhoods where the residents have low socio-economic status. We were not interested in studying this factor, however, and wanted to hold it constant. We therefore selected two census tracts from the city of Cambridge, one with a high delinquency rate and one with a low rate, with socio-economic factors constant as nearly as possible. We were not able to achieve as close a match on all factors as would have been desirable. Table 1 [not shown] shows how the two areas compared with respect to delinquency and with respect to socio-economic factors. It will be seen that the areas were well matched on education, fairly well matched on occupation, with a difference of over five hundred dollars in median income. The differences in delinquency rates were quite dramatic.

We were unable to find areas which were closer than these two in socio-economic level and which still differed significantly in delinquency rates. It is impossible to tell, of course, whether the differences which exist between the two areas in socio-economic status are sufficient to produce the differences in delinquency rate. All that we can say is that considering the whole socio-economic range in Cambridge, these neighborhoods are fairly similar on such items as rent, occupation, education, and even income, while they differ by a considerably greater part of the range in delinquency rates.

* * * * *

RESULTS

Community Integration

Our high delinquency area was clearly less integrated in terms of the criteria of integration we employed. First of all, the *low* delinquency area was highly homogeneous with respect to religion: 93 per cent were Catholic, as contrasted with 53 per cent in the high delinquency area [emphasis added]. Furthermore, those who were Catholics were more frequent church-goers in the low delinquency area than in the high. Thirty-five per cent of the Catholics in the high delinquency area said they attended church less than once a week, while in area "low" only 15 per cent report this. Area "low" was also more homogeneous ethnically: Here our sample shows a fairly high concentration (32 per cent) of people of Canadian origin, quite a few of these being French Canadian, with virtually no Negroes, or people of Eastern European origin. In contrast, our sample from the high delinquency area had 18 per cent Negroes, and 16 per cent East Europeans, with only 9 per cent Canadians.

We expected that the high delinquency area would contain more people who were "transient" — who had lived in the community only a short time. We found a slight tendency for this to be true, but both areas were highly stable. Sixty per cent of the respondents in the high delinquency area and 71 per cent in the low area had lived in their present neighborhood for ten years or more.

Despite the fact that most of the people in the high delinquency area had lived in their neighborhoods a substantial length of time, they were less integrated in their communities. As Table 2 shows, they knew fewer of their neighbors by name, did not know many people intimately enough to borrow something, less often felt they had common interests with their neighbors, and more often disliked the neighborhood.

These differences between the areas in attitudes toward the neighborhood and relations with neighbors are still found, even if one considers only the people who have lived in the neighborhood ten years or more. Therefore, the differences in "integration" of individual citizens into their communities cannot be attributed primarily to differences in length of residence. We might point out parenthetically that the lower level of integration in our high delinquency area need not reflect a progressively deteriorating situation. This particular low level of social interaction might remain stable for many years.

TABLE 2

Area Differences in Measures of Integration

Per Cent Who:	High Delinquency Area	Low Delinquency Area
Report liking the neighborhood	64%	85%
Know more than ten of their neighbors by name	52	63
Know more than five neighbors well enough to borrow something ("Like a hammer or a cup of sugar")	28	50
Feel they have "pretty much the same interests and ideas" as the other people in the neighborhood	33	59
Number of cases	129	107

We do, then, find evidence for the first of our hypotheses. In the high delinquency area, residents do not know each other as well as in the low delinquency area, and do not feel as much a part of the community. Does this mean that they withdraw from playing any role in the informal control of children's deviant actions in their community? Before we examine the answer to this question, let us take up one other factor that might lead the residents of a high delinquency area to avoid controlling delinquent or pre-delinquent actions;

perhaps they do not take such actions as seriously as do the residents of a low delinquency area. Do the two areas differ in their values about certain actions that the larger society defines as "delinquent"?

Attitudes toward Deviant Behavior

Measuring attitudes toward deviant behavior is a difficult matter. One clearly cannot ask "Do you think excessive drinking is a good or bad thing? How about theft? Assault?" In our first formulations of questions in this area, we found we were getting universally righteous answers, in which everybody reported (at least to our primarily middle-class interviewers!) being "against sin." In pretesting question wording, we found that the only way we could differentiate among respondents in this area was to ask, not whether certain actions were "right" or "wrong," but *how serious* actions were. That is, while all respondents might agree that stealing a candy bar from the dime store was "wrong," some expressed the view that it was not a very serious matter—that it was the sort of thing all children might be expected to do at some time or another, and that they would outgrow it if no issue were made of it; others regarded such actions as the first step toward more serious criminal actions, and felt that drastic disciplinary action was called for. We inquired about seven different kinds of pre-delinquent behavior. Two of our questions are presented below to illustrate the way we approached these issues:

> Every neighborhood has a certain amount of fighting between groups of children. Some people think it's very important to stop these fights, other people think the youngsters are just learning to stand up for themselves and should be left alone. How do you feel?

> Sometimes we hear of children damaging the property of people who live in the neighborhood—for instance, bending over car aerials or letting the air out of tires or ripping up fences. If children do this sort of thing, do you think it's anything to worry about, or are they just letting off steam?

Table 3 shows the proportion of respondents in each area who thought each of the seven kinds of act was "serious," who qualified their answers, or who thought the actions were "not serious." The striking thing about the table is the similarity of the attitudes in the two areas. In both areas, drinking is considered the most serious juvenile offence, fighting the least. People in the low delinquency area took a slightly more serious view of minor thefts from stores, damage to public property, and drinking than did their high-delinquency-area counterparts; but this trend was counterbalanced by a tendency for the high-delinquency-area respondents to take a more serious view of abusive remarks and fighting.

Our findings, then, are not consistent with the point of view that the adults in a high delinquency area take a tolerant or indifferent attitude toward delinquent and pre-delinquent activities on the part of children. We see no evidence that "delinquent values" about the "wrongness" or "seriousness" of these actions prevail in the high delinquency area. This issue will be discussed further below.

TABLE 3
Area Differences in Attitude toward Types of Pre-Delinquent Acts[a]

		Serious	Depends	Not Serious	No Answer	
Abusive remarks	High Delinquency Area	57%	30%	12%	1%	100%
	Low Delinquency Area	47	33	12	8	100
Minor thefts from stores	High Delinquency Area	36	50	12	2	100
	Low Delinquency Area	49	46	5	1	100
Damage to public property	High Delinquency Area	57	26	10	6	100
	Low Delinquency Area	64	22	8	7	100
Damage to private property	High Delinquency Area	40	32	22	7	100
	Low Delinquency Area	41	36	15	8	100
Fighting	High Delinquency Area	28	48	23	2	100
	Low Delinquency Area	22	50	27	2	100
Drinking	High Delinquency Area	79	17	3	1	100
	Low Delinquency Area	87	8	1	4	100
Truancy	High Delinquency Area	42	42	12	4	100
	Low Delinquency Area	41	42	11	6	100

[a]The percentages in this table are based upon 129 cases in the high delinquency area, 107 in the low. In none of the seven instances are the two neighborhoods significantly different in the proportion reporting a "serious" attitude.

Informal Social Control

We have seen that while the two areas did not differ in their views about how serious various kinds of delinquent behavior are (at least if their verbal reports to our interviewers may be trusted), the high delinquency area was less integrated, and we reasoned that this lack of integration might result in individual residents being unwilling to take action if they observed their neighbors' children engaged in some sort of deviant behavior. We asked our respondents hypothetical questions about whether they *would* step in and try to do something about it if they observed abusive language, property damage, fighting, or drunkenness. Table 4 shows that the respondents in the low delinquency area report themselves somewhat more ready to "do something about it," significantly so in the case of fighting and drinking.

The actual controlling behavior in real incidents reported by the respondents showed some area differences in the same direction, although the differences are not large. To study the kinds of action that had been taken in actual incidents of neighborhood delinquency, we first recorded all the incidents from the "incident report sheets" in which action by the respondent was both "possible and necessary," and in which the respondent's own children were not involved. If someone else had already taken remedial action about the incident, we did not regard it as necessary for the respondent to do so, even if the respondent observed the incident. And if the respondent knew about the incident but had not actually seen it and/or did not know the identity of the culprits, we did not regard it as possible for the respondent to act. On the other hand, if the respondent heard about the incident without actually witnessing it, and *did* know the identity of the delinquent children, we included the incident in our list of incidents in which some controlling action by the respondent would have been possible. For example, an incident of vandalism in a parochial school was reported, in which a gang of boys had entered the school by breaking windows, and had thrown ink on the floors and slashed furniture. The police had been unable to learn the identity of the vandals. One of our respondents knew who the boys were, having learned the details through her own sons, who were ostensibly not involved. She could have told either the police or church authorities, but had not done so. This incident would be included in the list of incidents in which action by our respondent was both "necessary and possible."

TABLE 4

Area Differences in Percentages Who "Would Do Something about It" in Hypothetical Instances of Delinquency

Child's Hypothetical Act	High Delinquency Area	Low Delinquency Area
Open rudeness, insulting language	26%	31%
Property damage	32	42
Fighting	12	25
Drinking	8	21
Number of cases	129	107

In all, 206 such incidents were reported by the respondents in our high delinquency area, and 130 were reported by the respondents in our low delinquency area. Of course, some respondents reported no such incidents, while others reported several.

Having listed the incidents in which control by the respondent would have been possible, and in which no one else had already taken remedial action, we wished to determine the number of these incidents in which the respondent actually had taken action. Before doing this, however, we divided the incidents according to whether the respondent had or had not been the *victim* of the delinquent act. Our hypothesis about greater social control in the low delinquency area applies especially to acts of delinquency in which the observer is *not* the victim. That is, in both areas, we might expect that when the respondent himself has been stolen from or had his property damaged, he will be motivated to catch and punish the offenders. But we have hypothesized that in well-integrated neighborhoods, individual citizens will act to stop deviant juvenile behavior even if they themselves are not involved.

Table 5 shows that, as expected, when the respondent is himself the victim of an anti-social act on the part of a juvenile offender, he is very likely indeed to take action, and this is true in both the high and low delinquency areas. The kinds of action taken included calling the police, reproving the child directly, or getting in touch with the child's parents. When the respondent is not the victim,

TABLE 5
Area Differences in the Number of Incidents in Which
the Respondent Took Controlling Action

	Number of Incidents Reported	Respondent Took Action	Respondent Did Not Take Action	% of Incidents in Which Respondent Acted	Number of Respondents Reporting at Least One Incident
Respondent the victim:					
High delinquency area	86	72	14	84%	62
Low delinquency area	78	69	9	88%	47
Respondent not the victim (but control possible):					
High delinquency area	120	48	72	40%	68
Low delinquency area	52	31	21	60%	41

there is a somewhat greater tendency for an observer to take action in the low delinquency area than in the high. In 60 per cent of the non-victim incidents reported from the "low" area in which the respondent was in a position to take action, he did so: in the high delinquency area, the comparable figure is 40 per cent. It is difficult to evaluate the statistical significance of the differences between these last two figures, since they are based upon the number of *incidents* reported, rather than upon the number of respondents reporting them. The fact is that, out of the 68 respondents in the high delinquency area who reported at least one incident in which they could have taken action but were not the victim, 30 took no action and 38 took action in at least one of the incidents he reported. In the low delinquency area, out of the 41 people reporting at least one non-victim incident, 16 took no action and 25 took action in at least one instance. These proportions are quite similar (and not statistically different). The difference between the two areas appears to lie in the fact that in the high delinquency area, each respondent reports more non-victim incidents, and his tendency toward controlling action is not proportional to the number of incidents he reports. That is, the more incidents a respondent reports, the lower the proportion of them he will have attempted to control. And 44 of the respondents in the high delinquency area had *ignored* at least one non-victim incident in which they could have taken action; only 21 respondents in the low delinquency area did this.

One explanation of this fact is that in the high delinquency area, more of the delinquent acts are committed by *gangs* of children (rather than by individual offenders), and the deviant children are older, on the average. Naturally, when an observer sees a delinquent act being committed by a group of five or six boys in their middle or late "teens," the observer will hesitate to interfere because of the physical danger to himself. Several of our respondents told us of people who had been beaten up when they attempted to stop gangs of boys who were engaged in delinquent activity. But the greater frequency of older offenders in the high delinquency area does not fully account for the lower proportion of controlling actions on the part of residents who are not directly involved. Even when the deviant child is young enough so that it would not be dangerous to try to control him, his deviant action is somewhat less likely to meet with a controlling action in the high-delinquency area (see Table 6).

In both areas, many of our respondents expressed reluctance to interfere in the control of other people's children. We asked: "We're interested in how you feel about whether it's all right to correct somebody else's child. When somebody else's child gets into mischief, and you see it, do you think it's up to you to say anything, or do you think it's better to stay out of it?" One third of the respondents in each area said that they thought it was all right for them to do something, but the majority expressed strong doubts about the propriety of interference, and many said categorically that a child's misbehavior is his parents' responsibility and others ought not to interfere. One respondent expressed this reaction as follows:

> We generally keep out of other people's business with their kids. They just don't want us to do anything about them. Definitely — even if I knew them — I'd just go on and not pay any attention. People wouldn't like it — they'd say what does he know about my kids! We get along fine with everybody and I wouldn't want it to change by sticking my nose somewhere where it's not wanted.

TABLE 6

Area Differences in Controlling Action in Relation to the Age of the Deviant Child
(Including Only Incidents in Which the Respondent Was Not the Victim)

	Number of Incidents (Action Necessary and Possible)	Action Taken by Respondent	No Action Taken by Respondent
Child under 13 years old[a]			
High delinquency area	51	29	22
Low delinquency area	29	20	9
Child 13 or over			
High delinquency area	62	16	46
Low delinquency area	23	11	12

[a]When several children were involved in delinquent activity together, the median age of the group was taken as the age for this tabulation. The number of incidents included is less than the number reported in Table 5, since for some incidents the respondent did not report the age of the child or children involved.

It is interesting that while we found no area difference in respondents' *own* opinions about whether it was all right to interfere with other people's children, we did find some differences when we asked whether *other people in the neighborhood* felt it was all right. In the high delinquency area, people more often said that their neighbors believed one ought to mind one's own business (22 per cent said this, as contrasted with 9 per cent in the low delinquency area).

* * * * *

Summary and Discussion

We compared two areas of Cambridge which were similar in socioeconomic status, one having a high rate of juvenile delinquency and the other a low rate. We interviewed a sample of residents in these two communities concerning "community integration," attitudes toward delinquent behavior, and the social control of such behavior. We took 129 interviews in the high delinquency area, 107 in the low, and reached 73 per cent of the people initially designated for interview in a probability sample. Our major findings were:

1. The high delinquency area was less "integrated" than the low. That is, residents of the "high" area, as compared with residents of the low delinquency area, did not like their neighborhood as well, did not know their neighbors as well, and did not so often feel that they shared interests and points of view with their neighbors. This was true despite the fact that both areas had fairly stable residence patterns. The low delinquency area was also somewhat more homogeneous with respect to the religious and ethnic backgrounds of the residents.

2. The areas did not differ in their attitudes toward the "seriousness" of different kinds of deviant juvenile behavior.

3. Residents of the low delinquency area, when they saw a child engaged in deviant behavior in which the observer was not directly involved, were somewhat more likely than residents of the "high" area to take some action — either interfering directly with the child's activities, or informing the police or the child's parents. Area differences in this respect were not great, however, and an attitude of reluctance to interfere prevailed in both areas.

Some of our initial speculations about the processes of social control are supported, and some are not. We found, as expected, that people in the high delinquency area do tend to ignore children's pre-delinquent and delinquent actions somewhat more often, and this provides an atmosphere in which delinquency can grow more easily.

We originally thought that one of the reasons residents in a high delinquency area might be slow to take controlling action when they observed incidents of delinquent behavior was that they hold delinquent values themselves, and feel that actions of delinquent children are actually quite acceptable. We did not find this to be the case; residents of the high delinquent area were just as quick as the residents of the "low" area to tell us that minor vandalism and small thefts from stores, etc. were serious and should be dealt with severely. How shall we interpret this finding? One possibility is that the respondents did not reveal their real conscious attitudes to our interviewers. We do not know; we can only point out that while a number of respondents *did* express indulgent attitudes about juvenile misbehavior, in response to our particular question-wording, these respondents were found equally often in the two areas, so that the attitudes they expressed do not appear to be differentially related to a high delinquency rate.

Assuming for the moment that most of our respondents told us the truth about their conscious attitudes, how are we to explain the fact that the residents of a high-delinquency area appear to share the values of the larger society about the "wrongness" and "seriousness" of such activities as stealing, damaging property, juvenile drunkenness, etc.? We may be dealing here with the ticklish problem of different "levels" of attitudes — perhaps these people are ambivalent, and while they consciously hold pro-social attitudes, they simultaneously have strong anti-social impulses, so that when they see a child deviating they may consciously disapprove but at the same time experience enough vicarious pleasure in the child's anti-social actions that they do not take steps to stop the child. Or perhaps, while sharing the general values about specific criminal activities, they may hold *other* values which interfere. For example, a strong belief in the value of individual autonomy, or the importance of immediate impulse gratification, might run counter to the effective implementation of anti-criminal values.

Another possible explanation is that the "delinquent values" which have been assumed to prevail in high-delinquency areas actually characterize, not the entire delinquent neighborhood, but only the actual families in which the delinquent children are found. We encountered some evidence that when a family of children got the reputation of being "bad," the neighborhood would withdraw from the family and isolate them. Other children would be forbidden to play with the deviant children, and the parents of the neighborhood, who might have made previous efforts to deal with the parents of the delinquent children, would give up such efforts and leave the family alone. Thus the pro-social values of the larger neighborhood might cease to affect delinquent children.

*   *   *   *   *

Our study suggests that a neighborhood pattern of social isolation of families may be an important factor in delinquency. We see no evidence that this social pattern is either the cause or the result of lack of homogeneity of values *about delinquent activities as such*. But the lack of social integration appears to have certain direct effects in a lowered level of social control of delinquent and pre-delinquent activities.

3. *The Structural Dimension*

In addition to the technological and the cultural dimension, the environment always has a structural or institutional dimension. That is, the international system within which nations act and interact may be described in terms of its sociological attributes. As was suggested in the introduction to this part of the book, these attributes may refer to the number and strength of international agencies or organizations, the ratio of dependent to independent political entities, the ratio of major to minor powers, or the alliance patterns of the period in question. The latter is a particularly interesting element because it has a direct impact on the nature and extent of almost all interactions. For example, if it is assumed that when a nation joins a tight military-political alliance it becomes less free to interact with nations outside of that alliance, it can be seen that any trend toward bipolarization in the system will appreciably reduce the total interaction possibilities.[1] In the following selection, Caplow illustrates some of the many consequences of changes in the number of independent actors (individuals, groups, nations, alliances, and so on) in a variety of social systems.

ORGANIZATIONAL SIZE

THEODORE CAPLOW

Not only does the size of an organization affect its character, but changes of size at certain points along a scale of expansion are more important than at other points. A three-person group has certain properties which are lacking in two-person groups and in four-person groups. If a work crew with fifteen members is doubled in size, its structure and its activities are quite certain to change, because the pattern of close interaction possible among fifteen persons is improbable among thirty. On the other hand, a work group of two hundred members might be doubled in size without any striking changes in its structure.

Some organizations, like baseball teams, are of fixed size and cannot function properly except with the exact number of members specified. Others, like

---

[1]For some of the implications of such a diminution, see Karl W. Deutsch and J. David Singer, "Multipolar Power Systems and International Stability," *World Politics,* XVI (1964), 390-406.

From Theodore Caplow, "Organizational Size," *Administrative Science Quarterly,* I (1957), 484-505 (footnotes 1-3, 7-9, and 11-16 have been omitted). Reprinted by permission of the author and *Administrative Science Quarterly.*

legislative committees, are more variable, and can function satisfactorily within a range of sizes. Still other types of organization, like certain voluntary associations, may have any size whatever.

The smallest organizations have two members, this being the least number capable of maintaining an interaction system. It is possible to discover freak organizations with a membership of one, but these are always based upon a fiction that enables a single member to appear as if he were simultaneously in two or more offices and to interact with himself. It sometimes happens that in dying associations, the last survivor inherits the whole organizational system. The last student member of an academic fraternity sometimes holds all of the chapter offices at the same time, and there have been a number of incidents in which the last survivor of a military unit assumed command of himself for the purpose of maintaining a proper record.

The largest organizations are nations and churches, whose membership runs into hundreds of millions. The Roman Catholic church and the Chinese People's Republic both have populations of more than 400 million. The largest membership which an organization theoretically might have would be equal to the population of the earth. At the moment, no examples of a universal or nearly universal organization can be found. The United Nations is explicitly an association of states and not of their respective populations.

The simplest and most adequate way of arranging organizations by size is to count their members and then to array them in the rank order of these counts. This is a measurement rather than a classification, and in scientific work measurements are more accurate and satisfactory than classifications. Nevertheless, classification by size cannot be entirely avoided. It is unrealistic to discuss communities without making a general distinction between villages and great cities. It is almost impossible to draft a workable system of procedures for both the giant factory and the small workshop. Above all, it is impossible in the present state of knowledge to transfer generalizations about the small group to the large group or vice versa. Changes in size are associated with unavoidable changes of structure at some points in the scale of expansion but not at others. Each size category has definite interaction possibilities and limits.

A further complication is introduced by the time element. The significant changes between patterns of interaction do not occur at exactly the same points in organizations of different duration. Thus, for example, the maximum membership of a committee whose members are intended to be a primary group is probably about ten. In a larger committee it would not be possible for all of the theoretical pair relationships to be realized. A more permanent organization, like a Chinese extended family, however, may count a hundred or more members without ceasing to be a primary group.

Any classification of organized groups by size must be somewhat arbitrary in its designation of class limits. The classification we shall use here is based on a criterion of *interaction possibilities*. In other words, the classification reflects the patterning of the interaction network by the sheer size of the group. As the following pages show, this patterning is independent of other classifications. It does not depend upon the nature of the group, nor the cultural setting in which it is found.

The usefulness of such a classification lies precisely in its independence of other organizational characteristics. However, the association of group size and interaction possibilities is not perfect. Hence the class limits proposed in the following scheme should be taken only as approximations. The relative margin of error in the class limits probably increases with increasing size.

CATEGORIES OF SIZE

Small groups are divided into *primary groups,* in which each member interacts individually with every other member, and *nonprimary groups,* in which this condition is not met. Small groups which are primary ordinarily range in size from two to about twenty. Small groups which are not primary may contain from three to about one hundred members.

The *medium group* is too large to permit the development of all possible pair relationships among members or the recognition of all members by all others. But it is small enough so that one or more members may establish pair relationships with all of the others. Under ordinary conditions, the medium group ranges from a lower limit of about fifty to an upper limit of perhaps one thousand members.

The *large group* is too large for any member to know each of the others but not too large for one or more members to be *recognized* by each of the others [emphasis added]. One or more members may interact with all of the other members, but with only one-way recognition, i.e., a key member might be recognized by all others, but not recognize all of them. The large group ranges from a lower limit of about one thousand members to an upper limit in the neighborhood of ten thousand, but this upper limit is especially variable.

The *giant group* is too large to permit direct contact of any individual with *all* of the others [emphasis added]. Certain personalities in the giant group may be recognizable by all other members, however, through the aid of mass communication. For most purposes, a lower limit of ten thousand is approximately accurate for the giant group, and there is no upper limit.

Most of the organized groups in any society are found within the limits of the *small group.* These include practically all households, play groups, cliques, gangs, councils, and conspiracies. Also included are the basic units of larger economic, military, and political organizations: work crews, infantry platoons, and precinct committees.

Most small groups are easily assembled. In fact, it is difficult to find examples of small organized groups which do not assemble a large majority of their members at frequent intervals. Face-to-face interaction is characteristic of most small groups, even those which are nonprimary. Perhaps for these reasons, only a small group can exercise power without delegation. Active directorates, councils-of-war, executive committees, courts of justice, cabinets, and the like seldom have more than fifteen or twenty members. Medium or large power groups, such as legislatures, are always found on close inspection to be controlled by one or more of their component subgroups.

There has been comparatively little discussion of the *medium group,* which has neither the emotional significance of the primary group nor the fascinating complexity of the giant organization. Within its limits, we find a large proportion of the world's enterprises, including most voluntary associations, representative assemblies, religious congregations, schools and academies, factories and mines, prisons and hospitals.

The medium group cannot survive without a formal organizational structure, but its day-to-day activities are largely controlled by the activities of internal cliques. A single member cannot usually exert much influence over a group of this kind even from a position of leadership, but relatively small groups can do so. There is a structural analogy between the triad of three persons, with its inherent instability and its tendency to develop a coalition of two members against the third, and the medium group, with its administrative instability and its tendency to develop coalitions of cliques.

There are two types of *large organized groups,* both very common. On the one hand are the component units of giant organizations: government bureaus, dioceses, regiments, branches, and industrial plants. On the other are overgrown specimens of organizational types which normally fall into the medium category.

The large organization offers especially favorable ground for the development of strong leadership. With so large a membership it is no longer possible for any member to know all of the others. But it is still possible for a number of the members — leaders, specialists, comic or notorious characters — to be known to all of the others on the basis of direct familiarity. The situation of this central group is exceptionally favorable because their unique personal influence may be used to reinforce formal authority and vice versa. A large organization necessarily has a fully developed administrative apparatus, but it does not have the massive inertia which limits any effort to influence a giant organization.

One of the most important characteristics of the large group is the members' illusion of full acquaintance with each other. An employee in a large factory who is familiar with the entire physical plant, the names and personalities of the department heads, the location and purposes of the principal cliques, is often quite unaware that this knowledge fails to circumscribe the entire organization.

Another way of stating the interactional criterion for the large group is that each well-oriented member will have some acquaintances in common with any other member selected at random. In other words, in the ideal case, although no member interacts with all other members, any pair are connected with each other through some third member with whom both of them interact. Some of the most interesting situations of organizational life develop in networks of this kind.

The line between large and *giant groups* is difficult to draw. Some widely dispersed groups with only a few hundred members behave very much like giants. Certain manufacturing companies with thirty or forty thousand employees are very simple in structure. The lower limit of ten thousand members is approximate, and there is no apparent upper limit. There do not seem to be any important structural differences between the lower and upper ranges. The characteristics of the national state are identified as easily in the miniature nations of Switzerland and Denmark as in the United States or India. Armies, enterprises, and churches with fifty thousand members seem to exhibit the same structural elements as those which are ten times as large.

* * * * *

Social interaction takes place at all levels of the giant organization, which can be viewed as a great cluster of suborganizations. These range from dyads and triads to giant organizations in their own right. But the interaction of any single member no longer involves a large proportion of the total membership. In the nature of things it is impossible for anyone to have a detailed familiarity with the entire structure. Familiarity with the structure of suborganizations and personal interaction within one's own sector provide sufficient orientation for ordinary action.

Relational Complexity

The relational complexity of small groups increases rapidly with small increases in size. This phenomenon apparently was first described by V. A. Graicunas in a paper published in 1933.[4] Graicunas was a management consultant who maintained that an executive must be familiar with the relationships among his subordinates in order to direct their activities. Since this requirement includes multiple as well as pair relaionships, it would limit an executive to five or six subordinates. In seminars and informal discussions the application of this idea to other kinds of groups was worked out in some detail by F. Stuart Chapin. The same rather obscure paper by Graicunas also attracted the attention of James H. F. Bossard, who developed a "Law of Family Interaction," as follows: "With the addition of each person to a family or primary group, the number of persons increases in the simplest arithmetical progression in whole numbers, while the number of personal relationships within the group increases in the order of triangular numbers."[5] This analysis eventually led to a more extensive treatment by William H. Kephart, who studied the implications of group size for three types of relationship: between persons, between persons and combina-

---

[4]V. A. Graicunas, "Relationship in Organization," *Bulletin of the International Management Institute,* March, 1933.
[5]J. H. S. Bossard, "The Law of Family Interaction," *American Journal of Sociology,* L (1945), 292.

tions, and between combinations. The following discussion is based upon Kephart's 1950 paper.[6]

Four interactive types are distinguished:

Interactive type Number 1 concerns pair relationships between individual persons in a group. Each member has a potential relationship with every other, excluding himself. The number of possible relationships *for any member* is equal to the size N of the group minus one [emphasis added]. The total number of relationships possible *for the entire group* of N members will be $N \times N-1$ divided by 2, since each possible relationship is counted by two participants [emphasis added].

The number of potential relationships (PR) for any single member increases at the same rate as the size of the group ($PR = N-1$):

$$N = 2 \quad 3 \quad 4 \quad 5 \quad 6 \quad 7 \ldots$$
$$PR = 1 \quad 2 \quad 3 \quad 4 \quad 5 \quad 6 \ldots$$

The number of potential relationships in the whole group increases much faster than group size. It is given by the formula $PR = N(N-1)/2$ which produces the following series:

$$N = 2 \quad 3 \quad 4 \quad 5 \quad 6 \quad 7 \ldots$$
$$PR = 1 \quad 3 \quad 6 \quad 10 \quad 15 \quad 21 \ldots$$

It may be easier to visualize what is involved if we consider an example. In a four-person family, composed of father, mother, son, and daughter, the [six] possible pair relationships will be these:

1. father —mother
2. father —son
3. father —daughter

---

4. mother—son
5. mother—daughter
6. son —daughter

Interactive type Number 2 concerns all of the pair relationships plus all relationships between an individual and a combination. In the small primary group each member has to deal not only with his fellow members individually but on occasion with each possible pair, each possible triad, and so on up to the total of other members. The formula for the total of these relationships is:

$$PR = 2^{N-1} - 1,$$

which produces the following series of potential relationships for each member:

$$N = 2 \quad 3 \quad 4 \quad 5 \quad 6 \quad 7 \ldots$$
$$PR = 1 \quad 3 \quad 7 \quad 15 \quad 31 \quad 63 \ldots$$

---

[6]William M. Kephart, "A Quantitative Analysis of Intragroup Relationships," *American Journal of Sociology*, LV (1950), 544-49.

This is a rapid increase, indeed, but it is almost insignificant compared to the mushrooming total of relationships for the group as a whole. The number of potential relationships for the group as a whole is given by the formula

$$PR = N/2 \times (2^N - N - 1),$$

and this series grows as follows:

$N =$	2	3	4	5	6	7 ...
$PR =$	1	6	22	65	171	420 ...

* * * * *

EMPIRICAL EVIDENCE

There have been a number of observational and experimental studies which deal directly with the subject of group size. The evidence is far from complete, but a number of important statements can be made on the basis of what is now known.

Most unorganized groups are very small. Organized groups are somewhat larger. Thus John James counted informal groups of pedestrians, shoppers, children at play, travelers in a railroad depot, and bathers at public beaches.[10] For purposes of comparison he also studied the groupings which occurred in the fictional situations of two stage plays, four movies, and six hours of radio broadcasting. Finally he recorded the size of clusters of workers in four department stores, a construction project, and a railroad roundhouse. The distributions which occur in these three categories are remarkably similar. There is a variation of less than one-third of 1 per cent in the proportion of two-person groups, for example. The mean group size in each case is somewhat less than three, and it is notable that average group sizes in the neighborhood of three have been reported in a number of educational studies. [See Table 1.]

James concludes that "freely forming and unforming groups undergoing continuous interaction are very small, falling within a size range of about two to seven, having an average size of about three." He supposes that larger groups of whatever complexity must be "molecular" arrangements of small groups and could be analyzed into their component systems.

The same paper presents evidence on the size of organized small groups. Although these have been reduced in some cases to subdivisions of a larger functioning unit, they are strikingly larger, nevertheless, than the free-forming groups. [See Table 2.]

The kind of interaction which takes place is apparently not much affected by small changes in group size. Robert F. Bales and Edward F. Borgatta, using Bales's method [see pp. 349-58] of recording and observing units of interaction

---

[10]John James, "A Preliminary Study of the Size Determinant in Small Group Interaction," *American Sociological Review*, XVI (1951), 474-77; John James, "The Distribution of Free-Forming Small Group Size," *American Sociological Review*, XVIII (1953), 569-70.

TABLE 1
Frequency Distribution of Group Sizes, by Classes of Groups[a]

Group Size	Informal		Stimulated Informal		Work	
	f	%N	f	%N	f	%N
2	5,263	71.07	125	71.02	1,104	71.32
3	1,496	20.20	38	21.59	357	23.06
4	471	6.36	12	6.82	73	4.72
5	133	1.80	1	.57	12	.78
6	41	.56			2	.12
7	1	.01				
	N = 7,405		N = 176		N = 1,548	
Mean group size	2.41		2.37		2.35	

[a]John James, "A Preliminary Study of the Size Determinant in Small Group Interaction," *American Sociological Review,* XVI (1951), 476.

in laboratory discussion groups, experimented with groups ranging in size from two to seven. There were four groups of each size, each meeting for four 40-minute sessions to discuss a human relations case and to reach a solution. Although the authors do see certain trends in the data, the overwhelming impression is one of uniformity from size to size. In no case is there a consistent increase or decrease in the frequency of one kind of behavior as we move across the table.

* * * * *

Indeed, the distribution of participation rates in small groups appears to be governed by a simple mathematical principle. Bales and his associates were

TABLE 2
Some Groupings in the United States, State of Oregon, and
Eugene, Oregon, Governments, and in Four Large Corporations[a]

Organization	Number of Groups	Range of Group Size	Mean Group Size
U.S. Senate subcommittees of 11 committees	46	2-12	5.4
U.S. House of Representatives subcommittees of 14 committees	111	3-26	7.8
State of Oregon executive, legislative, judiciary, boards, departments, commissions	26	2-14	5.7
Eugene, Oregon, executive, council members, committees, boards	19	3-11	4.7
Subgroups in officer and board-of-director organizations of four large corporations	29	3-9	5.3

[a]James, "Preliminary Study of the Size Determinant," p. 474.

apparently the first to notice that the total volumes of participation of individual members of task groups were arrayed in a remarkably regular rank order. In other words, if the volume of activity of each member is carefully measured and the members are ranked with the most active member first, the next most active member second, and so on, the volume of activity will be found to diminish at a predictable rate. Bales and his coworkers supposed that the appropriate model was a harmonic series — one in which the volume of activity of the second most active member would be half that of the first, that of the third most active member would be one-third that of the first, and so on. They found the rank order of individuals to be the same whether they measured the volume of activity directed by them to other individuals, or to all others in the group, or to other individuals or by other individuals to them, or by all others to them. This fairly simple finding has enormous implications for the understanding of interactive networks, and Table 3 is worth close study until the principle is clearly perceived.

TABLE 3

Aggregate Matrix for 18 Sessions of Six-Man Groups[a]

Person Originating Communicative Act	Number of Communicative Acts Received						Total to Indivi duals	To Group as a Whole 0	Total Initiated
	1	2	3	4	5	6			
1	——	1,238	961	545	445	317	3,506	5,661	9,167
2	1,748	——	443	310	175	102	2,778	1,211	3,989
3	1,371	415	——	305	125	69	2,285	742	3,027
4	952	310	282	——	83	49	1,676	676	2,352
5	662	224	144	83	——	28	1,141	443	1,584
6	470	126	114	65	44	——	819	373	1,192
Total received	5,203	2,313	1,944	1,308	872	565	12,205	9,106	21,311

[a]Adapted from Robert F. Bales, Fred L. Strodtbeck, Theodore M. Mills, and Mary E. Roseborough, "Channels of Communication in Small Groups," *American Sociological Review*, XVI (1951), 463 (Table 1).

A year later, Frederick F. Stephan and Elliot G. Mishler replaced the harmonic series by an exponential function, or growth curve, with the formula $P_i = ar^{i-1}$ where P_i is the estimated percentage for participants ranked i, r is the ratio of the percentage for any rank to the percentage of the next higher rank, and a is the estimate for participants ranked 1. They applied this formula to participation data obtained in eighty-one meetings of thirty-six groups of college students, ranging in size from four to twelve members. The formula gives an extraordinarily good fit, as the following extract from their data [Table 4], having to do with fourteen groups of eight persons each, shows:

Stephan and Mishler are careful to stress the limitations on the use of this model. For its successful application, the following three conditions need to be

TABLE 4

Distribution of Participation by and to Members of Small Discussion Groups
(Fourteen Meetings of Eight-Member Groups)[a]

Rank of Member	Participations Originated by the Member				Participations Directed to the Member			
	Partici-pations	Per Cent	Estimated Percentage	Differ-ence	Partici-pations	Per Cent	Estimated Percentage	Differ-ence
	2042		31.9		2042		22.0	
Leader	803	39.2	39.9	+0.7	946	46.3	46.0	−0.3
1	434	21.2	21.3	+0.1	266	12.9	14.1	+1.2
2	294	14.3	14.2	−0.1	218	10.6	9.0	−1.6
3	184	8.9	9.5	+0.6	105	5.1	5.8	+0.7
4	140	6.6	6.3	−0.3	87	4.1	3.7	−0.4
5	98	4.8	4.2	−0.6	49	2.3	2.4	+0.1
6	55	2.6	2.8	+0.2	32	1.5	1.5	0.0
7	34	1.6	1.9	+0.3	17	0.7	1.0	+0.3

[a]Adapted from Frederick F. Stephan and Elliot G. Mishler, "The Distribution of Participation in Small Groups: An Exponential Approximation," *American Sociological Review,* XVII (1952), 603. The original table, from which this is an excerpt, gives data for a total of 18 separate meetings of 36 different groups, varying from four to twelve members each.

fulfilled: a range of potentials for verbal participation, no interference with the subjects' expression of these potentials, and a lack of well-differentiated roles among members. In other words, the model is designed for unorganized groups. In organized groups the influence of size may work in much the same way, but presumably the presence of status factors will affect the volume of activity of members in different positions.

PART TWO

THE
NATION
AS
PRIMARY
ACTOR

Part One has dealt with social systems as the environment within which groups and individuals carry on their activities, and explored some of its characteristics. Analogizing to the international system from a variety of smaller, but not necessarily simpler, social systems, three major dimensions have been differentiated: the technological, the cultural, and the structural. Clearly, no one of these clusters of variables impinges independently upon the component actors, but for the sake of conceptual manageability, the differentiation turns out to be quite useful.

Part Two, however, turns to a study of the actors themselves. That there are a great many more selections here than in Part One is due to two considerations. First, Parts Three and Four will return to the total system, albeit indirectly, where it will be treated in a more dynamic fashion. Second—and this is an important point—the behavioral science literature contains much more material that is directly relevant at the national than at the international level; that is, its relevance to the nation-as-actor is much more *empirical* than *heuristic*. In the Introduction it was argued that the behavioral social sciences have three types of relevance for the field of international relations: the empirical, the heuristic, and the methodological. At the empirical level, there are findings which can be "plugged in" to the political scientist's models of comparative foreign policy or international politics, with little or no extrapolation. The heuristic contribution of the behavioral sciences on the other hand, requires more in the way of imagination; the political scientist finds, not *data,* but *ideas* that he may borrow for application to his own theory-building needs. Thus, much of the material presented in Parts One and Three should not be thought of as *directly* relevant, but only as suggestive in an area where there is a desperate need for ideas by which data may be meaningfully and economically organized. Part Two, however, attempts to sample from a vast mine of data and information whose empirical usefulness to the comparative study of foreign policy (i.e., nations-as-actors) has been only dimly recognized or exploited.

A. TREATING SOCIAL ORGANIZATIONS AS ACTORS

Implicit in everything so far has been the assumption that one may think of anything from the single individual to the large and complex social organization as an "actor." Is it possible, without doing violence to empirical reality and conceptual clarity, to speak of a social organization which is as large and complex as a nation, as if it really were an actor? While I think one can, others would sharply disagree, and perhaps go so far as to insist that all group behavior must be "reduced" to that of its individual members. In any event, it is by no means a closed issue, nor is it an unimportant one.

By way of introduction, it should be noted that until very recently political philosophers and social theorists found themselves embroiled in one version of this debate, as raised by the Nazi and other Fascist movements. Since Nazi ideology borrowed heavily from the writings of Hegel and Nietzsche, both of whom tended to view the state as an organismic entity with a life and purpose of its own, many liberals have thus associated the denial of individual importance and dignity with the many versions of "collectivist" social theory.[1]

The two selections which follow are intended not only to explore the implications of a "group as actor" point of view, but to touch upon the methodological implications involved.[2] That is, unless group characteristics and behavior can be observed, measured, and statistically analyzed — in terms of nonindividual variables — the conceptualization of group as

---

[1]Conservatives, too, have made a somewhat similar leap; see Frederick A. Hayek, *The Counter-Revolution of Science* (Glencoe, Ill.: The Free Press, 1952); and L. von Mises, *Theory and History* (New Haven, Conn.: Yale University Press, 1957).
[2]Two other useful articles, not reproduced here, are Werner S. Landecker, "International Relations as Intergroup Relations," *American Sociological Review,* V (1940), 335-39; and Charles K. Warriner, "Groups Are Real: A Reaffirmation," *American Sociological Review,* XXI (1956), 549-54.

actor is not particularly useful. Finally, it must be emphasized that even while considering a collectivity of individuals as a system or as a coherent social actor, one need not deny the existence and importance of the many components (individuals and subgroups) which go to make up the larger organization.

COMMON FATE, SIMILARITY, AND OTHER INDICES OF THE STATUS OF AGGREGATES OF PERSONS AS SOCIAL ENTITIES

Donald T. Campbell

There is currently considerable interest in efforts to apply concepts about "systems" at the level of social groupings. But for such applications to be meaningful, we should be able to test the hypothesis in specific instances that an aggregate of persons behaves as a system. We should be able to find instances in which the hypothesis of system is confirmed, and instances in which it is not, or in which the systemicity is of lesser degree. Too frequently concepts of "system" or "homeostatis" or "dynamic structure" are made axiomatic and lose their status as testable hypotheses. Too frequently such concepts are used in a way which provides an infinite flexibility in *ad hoc* explanations, and thus lose that essential rigidity which might make them testable. Yet the hypothesis of system is clearly testable in some instances. A pound of hamburger is clearly less of a system than a one-pound living white rat, and there are many measurements possible which would document this difference. If biologists have seldom provided lists of such criteria, it is not because the difference is undemonstrable, but rather because it is so obviously demonstrable as to be a waste of laboratory effort to verify.

Those interested in treating social and political organizations as systems are most frequently offered the biological organism as an example of a system. This is true both of recent conceptualizations in the behavioral science movement and of those available at the founding of modern social science. For those interested in a functional theory of social organization, Herbert Spencer's *Principles of Sociology, Part II, The Inductions of Sociology,* can still be recommended. The behavioral scientist will find it unacceptable in many minor details, but also profoundly modern in spirit and brilliantly suggestive of still untested research leads. Spencer is also free from the unwarranted ethical conclusion which has alienated so many from the organismic analogy, to wit, that not only are societies organism-like, but that it is good for them to become more so. As a militant

From Donald T. Campbell, "Common Fate, Similarity and Other Indices of the Status of Aggregates of Persons as Social Entities," *Behavioral Science,* III (1958), 14-25 (the footnotes and the bibliography and references have been omitted). Reprinted by permission of the author and the Mental Health Research Institute.

antinationalist and pacifist, resisting the temptation to identify with the glories of Queen Victoria's expanding empire, he used the analogy as a source of concepts about process and function, rather than as a pseudoscientific prop for an ethic.

*　　*　　*　　*　　*

Before we can go ahead with testing the hypothesis that political units or social organizations are organism-like systems, there is a prior question which must be answered. Spencer states the problem in his first chapter entitled, "What is a Society?" This chapter is but two pages long. To set the stage more specifically it can be quoted in full:

> This question has to be asked and answered at the outset. Until we have decided whether or not to regard a society as an entity; and until we have decided whether, if regarded as an entity, a society is to be classed as absolutely unlike all other entities or as like some others; our conception of the subject-matter before us remains vague.
>
> It may be said that a society is but a collective name for a number of individuals. Carrying the controversy between nominalism and realism into another sphere, a nominalist might affirm that just as there exist only the members of a species, while the species considered apart from them has no existence; so the units of a society alone exist, while the existence of the society is but verbal. Instancing a lecturer's audience as an aggregate which by disappearing at the close of the lecture, proves itself to be not a thing but only a certain arrangement of persons, he might argue that the like holds of the citizens forming a nation.
>
> But without disputing the other steps of his argument, the last step may be denied. The arrangement, temporary in the one case, is permanent in the other; and it is the permanence of the relations among component parts which constitutes the individuality of a whole as distinguished from the individualities of its parts. A mass broken into fragments ceases to be a thing; while, conversely, the stones, bricks, and wood, previously separate, become the thing called a house if connected in fixed ways.
>
> Thus we consistently regard a society as an entity, because, though formed of discrete units, a certain concreteness in the aggregate of them is implied by the general persistence of the arrangements among them throughout the area occupied. And it is this trait which yields our idea of a society. For, withholding the name from an ever-changing cluster such as primitive men form, we apply it only where some constancy in the distribution of parts has resulted from settled life.
>
> But now, regarding a society as a thing, what kind of thing must we call it? It seems totally unlike every object with which our senses acquaint us. Any likeness it may possibly have to other objects, cannot be manifest to perception, but can be discerned only by reason. If the constant relations among its parts make it an entity; the question arises whether these constant relations among its parts are akin to the constant relations among the parts of other entities. Between a society and anything else, the only conceivable resemblance must be one due to *parallelism of principle in the arrangement of components*.

There are two great classes of aggregates with which the social aggregate may be compared—the inorganic and the organic. Are the attributes of a society in any way like those of a not-living body? or are they in any way like those of a living body? or are they entirely unlike those of both?

The first of these questions needs only to be asked to be answered in the negative. A whole of which the parts are alive, cannot, in its general characters, be like lifeless wholes. The second question, not to be thus promptly answered, is to be answered in the affirmative. The reasons for asserting that the permanent relations among the parts of a society are analogous to the permanent relations among the parts of a living body, we have now to consider.

Forgiving him his haste and superficiality, the non sequitur in the second sentence of the last paragraph, and his mistaken notion about the social life of primitive man, I believe Spencer to be right in his ordering of the problem:

1. Among actual or potential aggregates of persons, there are certain aggregates which meet criteria of being "entities," and other aggregates which do not. The distinction is capable of empirical representation.

2. Among those actual or potential aggregates which meet the criteria of being entities there are some which meet the further and more specific criteria of being organic systems. These criteria are likewise capable of operational specifications.

But I believe his treatment of the first problem is inadequate, and that its specification poses a major obstacle to the development of usable systems theory in the social sciences. For the anthropologist in isolated areas, the specification of the social units of tribe and clan may pose little difficulty. The status of entity and system, the useful boundaries of aggregation, may be as apparent to him as to a vertebrate biologist. But for groups in the modern western world, the problems become difficult. If we are to test whether "it" is a system, we need to know what the "it" we are dealing with is, what its boundaries are, where it begins and leaves off. It may be, for example, that a modern metropolitan area is in certain features a homeostatic system—but how can we test the hypothesis unless we have criteria for defining a metropolitan area? Political units such as wards, cities, townships, and counties, might fail to meet the test merely because they represented arbitrary fragments of social entities.

THE PERCEPTION OF ENTITIES

It is to this first problem of Spencer's that I wish to address myself. I wish to do so by reverting to my role as psychologist and raising the more general problem as to how we "perceive" entities. The paper might well be retitled: "Perceiving invisible entities such as social groups." In this elaboration, I am to some extent following another great sociologist, like Herbert Spencer in receiving less attention today than he might, although otherwise he may seem a strange bedfellow. May I quote from Stuart Rice's *Quantitative Methods in Politics,* in his chapter most appropriately labeled "a statistical view of a perceptual world."

It is true that some of the data reported by human sense organs seem more substantial than others. One sees a saxophone and hears the atmospheric disturbances to which it gives rise, but one cannot see or hear or touch or smell the group relationships which in some perplexing manner bind the members of the jazz orchestra together. The first surmise that each member is wholly independent of the others in thought and action eventually breaks down, and it is perceived that they have organization, but the organization seems less tangible than the saxophone.

In actuality the two types of data are not as dissimilar as they seem. The existence of the saxophone is only inferred from sense impressions of it. If the concert patron should become mentally ill and have an hallucination in which the saxophone played a part, the testimony of his senses would later be rejected, if he were restored to sanity, because of the absence of corroboration for the hallucinatory evidence. Corroboration would be required in the form of other sense impressions received directly by the patient, emanating from or relating to the saxophone, or indirectly from other individuals who in turn received sense impressions relating to the instrument in question. When all possible corroboration is secured, belief in the existence of any material thing remains an inference. Belief in the existence of a group relationship is of the same character. It is an inference, based upon a variety of sense impressions concerning the behavior of individuals who are involved.

All data from the perceptual would turn out to be evidences concerning reality, but not reality itself; or, if preferred, such evidences are reality and the latter is nothing more. Whatever the preferred form of statement, it remains true that what is known of a hypothetical world without one's own individual mind is universally subject to error and inexactitude. Scientific method conceptualizes the perceptual data and treats them *as if* they were real and exact entities. This methodological process, like a great deal more of scientific method, is essentially fictional. Its justification is to be found in the results to which it leads. Hence it is as valid for the scientist to speak of a social group as to speak of an ounce of ether, provided he can do something further with the idea. All he knows of ether is what he infers through the mediumship of his own or (by a secondary process) of another person's sense impressions.

In his subsequent chapters on "Group cohesion and likeness" and "The identification of blocs in small political bodies" he puts into operational terms the question, "when is an aggregate of persons an entity?" While I shall make little use of his specific solutions, the perspective on the problem is the same.

One other source must be acknowledged: Karl Deutsch's chapter on "Mapping and measurement" in his *Political Community at the International Level* represents the sophisticated statement of a behavioral scientist who uses the concepts of system, boundary, and organization in such a way that empirically verifiable exemplifications of his concepts are made explicit. One quotation from this chapter will help further set the stage for the discussions.

The concept of reality will be employed here in its operational meaning. It will be appropriate to speak of reality in those cases where such limited tests, qualitative and quantitative, as are at our disposal indicate some historical or social structure from which we can predict the outcome of other tests, including kinds of tests not yet devised. Tentative descriptions of historical or social processes or structures will of course be in terms of symbols, such as maps or words or numbers, which will describe the inferred structures to which they apply. The more verifiable such descriptions prove to be (that is, the wider the range of mutually independent testing operations by which they are confirmed), the more reality may be ascribed to the tentative models or constructions. In other words, models will be more realistic the larger the number of mutually independent operations, present or future, by which they are confirmed.

You will note a common preoccupation with the "reality" of social units in these three quotations spanning the 80 years since 1876. These represent, however, only mild and methodologically sophisticated statements of the "realist" position. They perhaps should better be called the "as real as" position, recognizing as they do the fallible and mediate nature of our knowledge of common-sense objects as well as of social entities. As such they could also be the expression of a consistent nominalism. More strident denials and affirmations are of course available. The promising aspect of these three statements is that they all propose empirical tests of the "reality" of social units, and it is this feature that I want to elaborate. But there lies behind these chronic protests and denials a stubborn psychological problem which will continue to plague us. The natural knowledge processes with which we are biologically endowed somehow make objects like stones and teacups much more "real" than social groups or neutrinos, so that we are offended by the use of the same term "real" to cover both instances, and are thus tempted to an attitude of conventionalism toward the latter which we would reject if applied to the former. Two sources of the feeling can be suggested. First: according to certain objective criteria to be discussed below, groups are in most instances less "solid," less multiply confirmed, of less sharp boundaries, less "hard." Second, and most important, we have evolved in an environment in which the identification of certain middle-sized entities was both useful and anatomically possible. As a product of this evolutionary process we have the marvelously effective mechanism of vision, which, within a limited range of entities, analyzes entitativity so rapidly and vividly that all other inferential processes seem in contrast indirect, ponderous, and undependable. More important, the visual process is so powerful and seemingly direct that we usually do not stop to notice the inferential steps involved in it and the nature of the clues employed. My proposal is that we look to the empirical clues of entity used in the visual perception of middle-sized physical entities and then employ these clues in the analysis of social aggregates as entities.

Wertheimer has given us a basic list of principles of perceptual organization, demonstrated through research on vision under limiting conditions of low entitativity. His inquiry was as to the factors which lead discrete elements to be perceived as parts of a whole organization, and which determine the organization they will be perceived as parts of. These are his general principles insofar as characteristics of the stimulus elements are concerned:

1. Proximity: elements close together are more likely to be perceived as parts of the same organization.

2. Similarity: similar elements are more likely to be perceived as parts of the same organization.

3. Common fate: elements that move together in the same direction, and otherwise in successive temporal observations share a "common fate" are more likely to be perceived as parts of the same organization.

4. Pregnance, good continuation or good figure: elements forming a part of a spatial organization or pattern, as a line or more complex form, tend to be perceived as a part of the same unit.

These represent by and large objective or operationally specifiable aspects of the stimulus field. In the analysis which follows there will be an effort to state the diagnostic principles which they imply in such fashion as to bypass the direct visual perception of wholes, and in such fashion as to be equally applicable to stones and social groups.

Pregnance or good continuation may be expanded into the notion of closed figure, or completed boundary. How else could the five blind men of the parable have convinced themselves that they dealt with but one entity, with but one and the same elephant, except by extending their surface exploration until they had described a closed surface, at which point they would have joined hands and achieved intersubjective communicability and agreement on the entity and its shape? I will attempt to so state the first three clues so that they generate boundaries which may then be examined for closure or completeness.

COMMON FATE AS A SOURCE OF BOUNDARIES

To start with the stone. Let us at some one moment index the molecules (or some larger, more convenient unit, such as cubic centimeters) of substance in a volume including the stone and adjacent substances. Let us subsequently over a series of occasions record the locus of each unit of substance. From these records let us compute between each pairing of the units a "coefficient of common fate" which will be larger the more frequently the two units have been in the same general region at the same time. If our substance sample is in fact discontinuous, then the coefficients will be very high among those bits of substance which we may subsequently identify as an entity, relatively low between these bits "of it" and other bits which are parts of other "things." The rigidity, solidity, permanence which "real things" are reputed to have are expressions of this "common fate," which, excepting for adamant, is never absolute, is always subject to rupture.

Let us similarly tag a sample of persons, large enough so that all members of one group are included and many more. Let us observe the locations of these persons on a broad sample of occasions, and compute between each person and each other an index of common fate. Such indices could be similarly used to delineate entities. To be sure, the intra-entity coefficients would never run quite as high as those within the stone, and the inter-entity coefficients would run higher, for small groups sampled within a complex western society. The boundaries, in other words, would be empirically less distinct, less sharp. The entities of stone and group are equally "real" insofar as the formal epistemological procedures for knowing them are concerned, but the stone when known turns out to be more solid, harder, and of sharper edges than the group. Similarly, a band of gypsies is empirically harder, more solid, more sharply bound than the ladies aid society, and the high-school basketball team during basketball season falls somewhere in between, as judged by the average level of the intra-entity common fate coefficients and the ratio between these and the intra-to-extra-entity (inter-entity) common fate coefficients. On grounds such as these, the zoologist of social insects has scarcely more trouble identifying colonies of bees, ants, and termits than he does in identifying a single bee as an entity, provided he is privileged to observe the behavior of the colony's members over a period of time. (But then, insect groups have sharper boundaries than do human groups.)

The use of coefficients of common fate, differing from zero to unity, enables us to deal with entitativity as a matter of degree, and even in the physical world intergrades occur. Thus between the teapot and the teapot lid the inter-entity coefficients are high, though not quite as high as the intra-entity coefficients. Lower, but still high, are the inter-entity coefficients between cup and saucer. The intra-entity common fate coefficients are higher for a platoon than for a battalion, and higher for a destroyer crew than for either, etc.

*   *   *   *   *

SIMILARITY AS A SOURCE OF BOUNDARIES

If we were upon a single occasion to describe the attributes of each molecule or person, one could in parallel fashion compute one (or many) coefficients of similarity. These could then be used to draw boundaries. Many of the boundaries would be sharp. But in the gravel pit, among the social insects when several colonies of the same species are pooled, and for human social groupings, the boundaries drawn by similarity seem somewhat secondary to those based upon common fate. Thus "red heads" are less a "real" group than "Negroes," in the sense that the latter boundary is confirmed by some degree of common fate, while the former usually is not (except in the one instance recorded by Watson). But perhaps it is more important to emphasize that usually the boundaries concur, but that one criterion may draw a boundary where another does not. Thus common fate may not separate a stone from the spot of tar adhering to it (unless our sample of occasion includes a solvent bath) while similarity does. Thus the piece of reinforced concrete is less "unified" than a piece of soft limestone by the coefficient of similarity, more unified by the coefficient of common fate, if pulverizing pressures are included in the sample of events.

*   *   *   *   *

PROXIMITY AS A CLUE FOR ENTITY

Contemporaneous spatial contiguity of particles seems still less "essential" than either common fate or similarity as a clue for entity. However, the fact that it is used by the visual perceptual machinery indicates its general usefulness, and certainly the ethnologist finds it highly correlated with social entitativity, although Tyron's data indicate some interesting exceptions for high social level groupings in the San Francisco Bay area.

Perhaps most significant is the employment of proximity to draw group boundaries where the distribution of interparticle spacings becomes large. Certainly boundaries so drawn would confirm most atomic, molecular, indigenous social group, and other entity diagnoses. For human groups, face-to-face communication processes made possible by proximity generate similarity and feelings of belongingness which make coordinated action and hence common fate more likely.

The value of proximity as a predictor of common fate is primarily a function of the kind of adhesives which hold the particles together in common fate. For atoms, molecules, and the run of inanimate physical objects including the solar system, these adhesives require adjacency. For modern social groups, this may not be essential. Thus the FBI may be a group with sharper boundaries, a harder, more solid social entity than is Davenport County, Iowa.

REFLECTION OR RESISTANCE TO INTRUSION OF EXTERNAL ENERGY, MATTER, OR DIAGNOSTIC PROBES

Still more basic to the visual machinery than the Gestalt organizational principles is diagnosis of boundaries through the reflection or alteration of the speed of particles of matter or wave energy. Thus we could locate the boundaries of the stone through the interruption, absorption, or slowing of electromagnetic waves of the light or heat frequencies, of acoustic air compression waves, of tossed ping-pong balls, or of probing fingers. The stone is "opaque" to a wide variety of waves and substances in motion. Its boundaries can thus be plotted, and would be highly coincident or multiply confirmed between the various procedures. It is here that the traditional distinction between primary and secondary qualities has most direct relevance. The primary qualities represent interruptions of the locomotion or manual probes of the diagnosing organisms. The secondary qualities represent probes of lower energy content (as light, sound, or radar waves) when these are employed so as to substitute for the primary ones.

Analogously, group boundaries may occasionally be plotted by the sentry's challenge, by the deceleration locations in the traveler's locomotion, by indoctrination procedures, etc. Hemphill and Westie have suggested permeability as a clue for the rigidity of group formation. It remains to be seen whether practical diagnostic procedures using the reflection of probes will be usable at the group level.

INTERNAL DIFFUSION, TRANSFER, COMMUNICATION

For certain inanimate entities, particularly those of metal, and for animate entities, boundaries can be plotted by diffusion limits and diffusion rate uniformities within the entity, or diffusion rate discontinuities between the entity and adjacent substance, as for heat or electrical potential within metals, and as for blood sugar and oxygen with animals. Thus by use of a radioactive tracer potassium introduced into an animal's food, one could plot the animal's body boundaries with a Geiger counter or photographic paper, plotting essentially the boundaries of internal substance transfer. Plotting the distribution of manufactured products or foodstuffs would similarly diagnose the boundaries of an economic system. Tracings of the boundaries of distribution of a given message have a similar logic. The communication rate between particles, boundaries implied by depressions in the interparticle transaction rate, etc. represent ways of plotting the boundaries of functional social units which Deutsch in particular has emphasized.

*   *   *   *   *

ILLUSIONS AND MULTIPLY CONFIRMED BOUNDARIES

In the diagnosis of middle-sized physical entities, the boundaries of the entity are multiply confirmed, with many if not all of the diagnostic procedures confirming each other. For the more "real" entities, the number of possible ways of confirming the boundaries is probably unlimited, and the more our knowledge expands, the more diagnostic means we have available. "Illusions" occur when confirmation is attempted and found lacking, when boundaries diagnosed by one means fail to show up by other expected checks. Most frequently, these illusions involve "superficial" similarity contours, as in two-dimensional paintings of "real" objects, distracting contours in camouflage, and the wearing of enemy uniforms in espionage.

In the typical arena of the anthropologist, it seems likely that a multiple confirmability of boundaries similar to that for biological and inanimate entities may be found. For the sociologist and political scientist, a preliminary scouting indicates that the redundancy of boundary diagnoses may be so considerably less and the number of empirically justified delineations of units open to him may be so considerably greater, that the common attitude of regarding all such delineations as arbitrary may seem justified. However, even here an emphasis on the potential multiple diagnosability of boundaries seems important, even if the boundaries be more numerous, less sharp, and more overlapping, with multiple group membership being the rule. It might well be alleged that any scientifically useful boundary must be confirmable by at least two independent means. Such an emphasis seems necessary if sociology is to retain those attitudes of discovery, problem solving, independent confirmation and validation of construct which have characterized the successful sciences.

Taking an evolutionary perspective on the visual apparatus, it seems clear that the development was predicated upon an environment populated with stable, solid, clear-cut entities—that it could never have developed in a world of fuzzy-edged amoeboid clouds or in a completely fluid, homogeneous material space. By analogy, one might guess that the development of any science is predicated upon the discovery of such natural nodes of material organization, upon stable discontinuities. If discreteness and multiple-diagnosability of entities at the social level turns out upon examination to be lacking, then the possibility of a social science representing a separate level of analysis from the biological or psychological will be eliminated. Most sociologists and behavioral scientists judge from their preliminary scouting that while confusing or complex, the situation is not that bad, and that there is the possibility of a science of social groups per se. In the end, this is an empirical matter not to be decided on a priori grounds.

It can be noted that the diagnostic procedures here suggested all seem to depend upon the acceptance or achievement of an entity diagnosis at a lower level. Historically this seems not to be so, as we started with diagnosis of middle-sized entities and have worked down to the neutrinos and up to the solar system. In any event, this should provide no qualms for the social scientist who is certainly justified in basing his diagnosis of social entities upon an acceptance of the biologist's diagnosis of organisms. The behavioral scientist should certainly allow himself an applied epistomology which makes use of the achievements of the more advanced and/or more basic sciences, rather than limiting himself to what can be deductively justified on the basis of the contemplations of a mortal philosopher, sitting immobile with both eyes closed, his mind swept clean by intent at least of the biasing effects of all prior learning.

Consistent Nominalism and the Status of Psychology's Individuals as Entities

In the so-called nominalists of Spencer's example and of Warriner's recent discussion there is a basic inconsistency in the application of nominalism. The *sociologist's* entity constructions are treated as fictional while the *psychologist's* entity constructions, such as persons, individuals, or organisms are given a real status, rather than being treated nominalistically [emphasis added]. Needless to say, this inconsistent nominalist is often a psychologist looking over the fence at his neighbor sociologist's area. Given the attunement of the anatomic diagnostic procedures to entities of the size of organisms, this inconsistent position can have great intuitive appeal.

Of course, even as diagnosed by the tedious actuarial procedures suggested by this paper, the biologist's organism of protoplasmic cells would turn out to be a much more discrete, clear-cut, hard, and multiply diagnosed entity than almost any of the sociologist's entities (unless the biologist happened to choose slime mold as an example). But this is the biologist's organism, not the psychologist's. The psychologist's organism would have to be diagnosed or confirmed by common fate and similarity coefficients among responses. Since responses lack reidentifiability, common fate considerations can only be employed to test the hypothesis that biological boundaries are also the boundaries of psychological entities. Analysis of variance procedures with the biological person as a classification criteria are appropriate at this point. Is there variance among a population of responses collected at various times from various persons which is associated with the individual? This turns out to be equivalent empirically to the problem of the reliability coefficient of a psychological measure. These are often high, but occasionally get as low as zero, and uniformly tend to be lower as the persons under study are more homogeneous sociologically. Certainly the boundaries of the psychological person are fuzzy enough to give the psychologist cause for modesty in setting standards for sociological entities. Often enough one can predict responses better from knowing a person's social locus and immediate setting than one can from a knowledge of this biological person's responses in past situations.

CONCEPTS AND METHODS IN THE MEASUREMENT OF GROUP SYNTALITY

Raymond B. Cattell

I. First Things First in Social Psychology

Now that social psychology has recognized its major concern to be the psychology of groups—in relation to one another and to individuals—the time is ripe to discuss research methods and concepts for arriving at *the description of group behavior*.

It is to be hoped that history will not repeat itself by recapitulating in social psychology the unnecessarily wayward and wasteful course of individual psychology. The development of an exact science of prediction in relation to individual personality required, as in other biological sciences, the prior provision of accurate description, measurement and classification of phenomena. Actually amateur speculation and incontinent "explanation," remote from actualities of measurement or observation, ran riot and sadly delayed progress by deflecting the attention of researchers, until recent years, from the basic and unescapable discipline of a true science of personality measurement.

This contribution to social psychology begins, therefore, with the challenge that the solution of the vital practical and theoretical social problems now clamoring for attention requires scientific workers to restrain themselves from superficial "research" until a correct foundation for *the meaningful description and*

From Raymond B. Cattell, "Concepts and Methods in the Measurement of Group Syntality," *Psychological Review*, XLVIII (1955), 48-63 (the footnotes and the bibliography and references have been omitted). Reprinted by permission of the author and the American Psychological Association.

measurement of groups has been achieved [emphasis added]. It then proceeds to propound concepts, methods and experiments for this foundation. It asserts, as a logical premise, that to arrive at laws governing the development and interaction of groups, we must first have some accurate means of defining a group at a given moment.

We have, in short, to establish a branch of psychology concerned with the "personality" of groups. "Establish" is used advisedly; for at present—in spite of much talk about "culture patterns"—methods and concepts simply do not exist. The sociologists, recognizing that a group cannot be defined in merely political or economic terms, have turned to the psychologist for a science of the living group entity, but, for reasons evident in the following section, they have yet done so in vain. Mannheim, typical of sociologists disappointed in constructive synthesis by the psychologists' impotence, well says "The main reason for our failure in this branch of human studies is that up till now we have had no historical or sociological psychology."

II. THE DIMENSIONS OF SYNTALITY

By "personality," *in the individual,* we mean "that which will predict his behavior in any given, defined situation" [emphasis added]. Mathematically we take a pattern of indices which defines the personality and another set defining the situation, arriving therefrom at an estimate of the ensuing behavior. Psychologically we speak of the former—the personality indices—as a structure of traits —a set of more or less permanent "readinesses," which function behaviorally under the impact of a stimulus situation.

For *the corresponding structure in the group* an unambiguous term is needed [emphasis added]. Examination of many possible verbal roots indicates *syntality* as best indicating the "togetherness" of the group, while having sufficient suggestive parallelism to "personality" and "totality." Further, we may perhaps speak appropriately of the syntality of a group as inferred from the "synaction" of its members—the group action as defined below. Syntality covers dynamic, temperamental and ability traits of the group.

* * * * *

Social psychology now stands where the study of individual personality then stood [before the progress of Thurstone and others in developing measures of the unitary trait]. In effect psychologists have accumulated a few fragmentary aspects of group syntality from various isolated studies. They have chanced upon "morale" (although the label probably covers such different variables as group persistence against difficulties and mean level of individual idealism), aggressiveness, authoritarian-democratic structure, isolationism, degree of freedom from internal dissension, etc. Mostly these "dimensions" of group behavior have been seized upon in response to the suggestion of some immediate practical problem, without regard to any over-all theory or to long-term scientific needs in social psychology. The slightest consideration of the whole natural history of groups would probably suggest more important variables than these for describing their total behavior.

An embarrassing harvest of muddle, moreover, is likely to be reaped if the application of large terms for small variables continues very long with respect to the labelling of group traits. Is it fitting, for example, to describe experimental groups as Totalitarian, or Democratic (in science as distinct from journalism) when no proof is offered that these are unitary patterns or when the variables actually measured are perhaps the least important for defining that total pattern, if it exists as a single pattern?

It would seem better to stick to modest, less interpretive, more contingent labels for more completely definable experimental variables, until the true patterns emerge and are confirmed.

Social psychology, therefore, now awaits its foundation of accurately described syntalities, alike at the level of culture patterns, of institutional groups and of small committees. That foundation can be achieved *by factor analysis of a "population" of groups, on a suitably chosen collection of group behavior variables.*

⊥　⊛　⊛　⊻　⁂

III. The Factorizable Characteristics of Groups: Logical Analysis

As we concentrate on the choice of variables we run into certain problems of assortment which can perhaps be solved to a certain degree by armchair reflection. This and the following section constitute attempts thus to achieve the maximum clarity of experimental design and problem formulation, with the adoption of definite hypotheses.

Out of deference to majority opinion we ought perhaps to ask at the outset the supposedly devastating question whether such a thing as a group mentality exists at all. It is of historical if not of scientific importance that McDougall's penetrating pioneer analysis of "the group mind" was badly received by a certain section of American psychologists. In the descendents of this sectional opposition the allergic reaction to his expression is still so strong as to paralyze thought, and writers who pander to irrationality have for years operated with McDougall's concept by circumlocutions. The rejection was not due to opposition to Hegelianism, for McDougall's able philosophical preamble explicitly refuted Hegelian mysticism and accepted Hobhouse's searching anti-idealist criticisms. The probably correct, but more trivial explanation was that this contribution to social psychology was launched at an unfortunate moment. For a large number of callow students in psychology were unable at that time to recognize any manifestation of mind unless formally, or often actually, reduced to the twitching of a dog's hind leg. From the drouth of this sterile atomism they presently rushed, with undiminished lack of judgment, down a steep place into the sea of ineffable, unmeasurable—but far from inaudible—Gestalt.

Fortunately a steady nucleus of naturalistic observation and methodological constructiveness survived and developed, despite those local set-backs, and despite the disturbances from the clamorous medieval tournaments among the pseudo-philosophical "isms" of psychology. Meanwhile the idea was further developed by Gurwitch in sociology, and, in more vague terms, by Whitehead and by Roethlisberger in industrial psychology. Finally, the main line of development in pure psychology has given us better technical methods, notably factor analysis and its variants, for investigating behavioral wholes and dynamic patterns.

It could be argued that any study of total organisms, such as McDougall proposed, should have been postponed until new methods had been invented, but this is quite different from asserting (a) that reflexology is capable of explaining the behavior of organisms as such, or (b) that wholes do not exist. Of the difficulties of the social psychologist at that juncture McDougall wrote, "... to the obscure question of fact with which he deals, it is in the nature of things impossible to return answers supported by indisputable experimental proofs. In this field the evidence of an author's approximation towards truth can consist only in his success in gradually persuading competent opinion of the value of his views." His optimism about the existence of a large reservoir of competent opinion proved unjustified. But the vigor of prejudice has one virtue: that it forces the development of precision methods from the conclusions of which the prejudiced cannot escape.

McDougall himself, unfortunately, failed to develop the method here described, but many of his conclusions about group behavior are likely to prove correct, and his basic contention that *it is rewarding to deal with groups as single entities* remains the springboard whence we take off into new research fields [emphasis added].

$$* \quad * \quad * \quad * \quad *$$

As to the behavior from which the group mentality is to be inferred, however, there runs alike through McDougall's and other psychologists' writings what we consider a rather serious confusion of characteristics. On grounds of logical analysis we suggest that there are *three* aspects or "panels" to be taken into account in defining a group.

(1) Syntality Traits (Behavior of the Group as a Group)

The group behavior recorded here concerns any effect the group has as a totality, upon other groups or its physical environment. Just as the individual may show more willed (conscious), and less organized (neurotic symptom, temperament) behavior, so the group behavior will range from action by (a) whatever organized will and executive agencies the group possesses, to (b) less organized, uncontrolled elements and so to (c) unorganized mass action, expressing largely the average individual as under (3) below. For example, the sheer amount of food the group eats would be largely a function of this last kind.

*   *   *   *   *

Most of these traits will be inferred from external behavior of the group, but the executive will of the group can manifest its properties also in *internal action,* *e.g.,* in deliberately changing internal organization, suppressing internal revolt. Examples of syntality traits are: aggressiveness against groups (*e.g.,* acts of declaration of war), efficiency in exploitation of natural resources, isolationism, energy in trading, reliability in commitments, proneness to trade cycles or to revolutions.

(2) Characteristics of Internal Structure

These concern the *relationships among the members of the group.* The character of unification and of government is primary, and this may vary from a practically unstructured crowd through horde leadership and the incipient democratic leadership in Moreno's vague "tele or the movement of feeling toward leader individuals" to a highly organized legislature and executive. Internal structure characters issue in syntality traits but they are not themselves the behavior of the group.

Examples of structural characters are: all sorts of indices expressing degree of heterogeneity in various characteristics, indices of class structure, pattern of institutions and organs such as church, army, family, modes of government and communication.

(3) Population Traits

These are mere aggregate values — definitions of the personality of the *average* (or typical, modal) member of the group. It is noticeable that in the literature of group characteristics the bulk of observations actually concern the typical member of the population rather than the group syntality.

Examples of population characteristics are: average intelligence, crime incidence, attitudes on moral and religious questions and all that is usually gathered by population polls.

The probable relationship among these three panels is that if we knew all the laws of social psychology we could predict the first from the second and third. Alternatively, if we knew the third and the environment of the group we could predict the second, *i.e.,* the type of group structure which would emerge, and therefore, ultimately, the first, *i.e.,* the group behavior. This is no denial of the principle that the mind of the group is fashioned by individuals and in turn fashions the individual mind. In the extreme instance of the second where we are dealing with a practically unstructured crowd, the first and third become practically identical.

From the interim observations available in our experiments we can already generalize the hypothesis that the changes in syntality traits produced by changes in population traits will be qualitatively as well as quantitatively different from the latter. For example, an increment in average intelligence may change character-like qualities in the group, while a difference between groups in average emotional stability of the population may appear as a difference in the ability of the group *per se* to solve cognitive complexities. This we shall call the *theory of emergents* (or syntal emergents).

IV. SEVEN THEOREMS ON THE DYNAMICS OF SYNTALITY

The implicit conception of group which most people unconsciously adopt in such discussions as the above is of an aggregate composed of a number of individuals whose *whole existence* is bound up with the group. Real groups are rarely of this kind and for the most profitable application of the new method to general group investigation it behooves us first to analyze as far as possible what the situation is with regard to varieties of groups and the modifications of method required to cope with them. This analysis turns principally on the dynamic relations within and between groups, for temperamental and ability characters do not differ in any systematic way, as far as we can see, from those known in individuals.

Sociologists have written a good deal about group classification and, more tangentially, about dynamics, and we must first glance at the evolution of opinion among outstanding representatives. Gumplowicz in his classical treatment out-distanced most of the psychologists of a generation later by conceiving that laws can be formed about the behavior of groups ("The behavior of collective entities is determined by natural laws") but failed to agree with the present integrative psychological position by maintaining somewhat unnecessarily that this behavior had no relation to "the motives and natural qualities of (constituent) individuals." Ross proceeded to carry the study of groups into a classificatory system which included "Fortuitous groups" (crowds), "Natural groups" (families, clans), "Interest groups" (states, confederacies, guilds), and also, but less happily, "Likeness groups" (professions, classes) in which presumably nothing dynamic but only a logical bond might hold the members together. Gillin and Gillin adopt a somewhat similar classification, but descriptively and without implying fundamental psychological differences. To the psychologist a merely logical classification is untenable. *Every* group is an interest group — in the sense that its existence arises from a dynamic need — or else it is not, in any psychological sense, a group. Sorokin and Zimmerman's distinction between "systems" and "congeries" seems to be a statement of this issue in other terms.

Even when sociologists, however, have recognized that a group exists only because and so long as it satifies psychological needs, they have failed to appreciate the nature of the ergic and the metanergic needs that are involved in its support. Hayes, Hart, Von Wiese and others stress or dwell wholly upon security, as if small groups form, and then aggregate into larger groups, only under threat. This may be a common motive—indeed fear and gregariousness may account for practically all association in the lower animals. But in man, with his power of learning ways of long-circuited satisfaction, the whole gamut of primary ergs—hunger, escape, self assertion, curiosity, sex, gregariousness, etc. —may participate in group formation. The sheer fact of groups needing to have adequate dynamic basis, obvious though it may now be, needs emphasis at this juncture in social psychology because the extension of group experiment of the present kind brings the risk that, in the artificial situation of experiments, groups will be employed which are not created by a real purpose of the participants.

Beyond this fundamental character the psychologist has next to recognize the fact of *dynamic specialization,* a phenomenon tied up with the almost universal occurrence of overlapping groups. For the simplification of a first experimental approach we have chosen, as described above, self-contained groups: nations, which have relatively shadowy loyalties beyond themselves, and committee groups in a control "vacuum" situation in which no other loyalties of the members are brought into action or conflict. But the great majority of existing social groups, other than nations, are overlapping, in the sense that individuals belong simultaneously to several groups. This situation exists because, as Cole succinctly puts it, "an association (group) can always be made specific in function, while man can never be made so."

*   *   *   *   *

VI. Summary

1. Social psychological research can advantageously be centered on the behavior of groups as organic, functionally integrated entities. Group syntality has more resemblances than differences with regard to individual personality, suggesting profitable transfer of research methods from one to the other.

2. Effective research on the development, abnormalities and inter-relations of groups can proceed only on a foundation of syntality measurement. The dimensions of syntality can be found by factor analysis.

3. Factor analysis must rest on an even sampling of a wide range of group characteristics. The characteristics of groups have to be sought at three levels: (1) Syntality—the behavior of the group; (2) Structure—the relations of individuals in the group; (3) Population personality traits—the individual characteristics averaged.

4. Groups differ from individuals most radically in their dynamic make-up or synergy, especially because of the structural possibilities of overlapping groups. This does not invalidate the factorization of group characteristics but it intro-

duces complications requiring special attention to the design of investigation.

5. The dynamic relationships which have to be heeded in the design of experiments to investigate group syntalities, and which require investigation in their own right as prime determiners of the behavior of groups, have been expressed in seven theorems. These theorems may be briefly labelled: (1) Dynamic origin of groups; (2) Vectorial measurement of synergy; (3) Subsidiation in the syntal lattice; (4) Subsidiation in the personal lattice; (5) Hierarchies of loyalty from the law of effect; (6) Synergic constancy in a system of overlapping groups; and (7) Isomorphism of syntality change and personality change.

B. NATIONAL GOALS

In Western culture, there is a strong element of the teleological—a belief in the purposiveness of almost all social behavior. Thus, any inquiry into the behavior of individuals and groups generally begins by asking: "What are its goals or objectives?" This is what is usually meant when one asks "why" an actor does this or that. Obviously, there is another meaning to "why;" what are the variables in the environment and the characteristics and capabilities of the actor which impel it in any given direction? That is, one might well argue that there is no such thing as goal-orientation or even goal-awareness in social groups and that they merely move along in time and space, responding to a variety of forces.

In Part One, it should have been apparent that my own view lies somewhere between these two poles of what is essentially the argument over free-will versus determinism. The physical and psychic characteristics of the environment do exercise an important influence on the behavior of a nation; but, however limiting a nation may find its external environment and its own relative capabilities, there nevertheless remains a considerable degree of freedom for it and its decision-makers in the selection of goals and strategies.

In the balance of this part, the nation—and analogues of the nation—will be considered as a goal-pursuing organization, even though that goal may be, on occasion, little more than the search for ways of minimizing losses or minimizing future restraints on its freedom of action. Such activity—or lack thereof—may be seen as flowing from three major sets of variables.

First, there are its preferences: these stem from the cultural values, norms, ideologies, and aspirations of the nation itself, and produce some sort of imaginary, ideal state of affairs. But no social organization makes a heavy investment in the pursuit of utopia; the costs are too great. Rather, some effort is made to reduce aspirations so that environmental resistance may be diminished, or to increase capabilities so that such resistance may be overcome. Thus, the second factor in goal-selection will be those restraints—*and incentives*—created by the international environment: the system and its characteristics as outlined in Part One. The third factor is, of course, national power: the environment imposes restraints, and the power of the actor is intended to match or overcome those restraints.

The next two sections, then, will deal respectively with the two sets of variables which, in interaction with the international environment, determine the goals which nations tend to pursue: preferences and power.

1. National Character as a Source of Preferences

Looking at the matter of preferences in more detail, it is evident that those who act as decision-makers on behalf of social organizations will develop preferences for that organization which are responsive to many factors, some of which are internal and some of which are external or environmental. Among the external ones might be, in addition to those systemic factors discussed in Part One, geographical setting,[1] the history of the region, or the characteristics of a neighboring nation. The internal factors might include the official ideology, the distribution of power among competing subnational groups, the degree of political and social stability, the racial or ethnic composition of the nation, the manner in which decision-makers are selected, and so on. Many of these blend together and find expression in what is known as "national character," but this variable has caused a good deal of controversy in the social sciences. Those who find it a useful construct give it a variety of meanings and a variety of empirical referents, while those who consider it a useless, or dangerous, or misleading notion tend to select the particular version which they find most easy to make into a "straw man."

Basically, there are two dominant meanings of national character. One is essentially a statistical notion which is best expressed by the term

---

[1] A useful summary of the role of geography, an environmental variable which I almost ignore in this volume, is George Kish and J. David Singer (eds.), "The Geography of Conflict, *The Journal of Conflict Resolution,* IV (1960), 1-162.

"modal personality."[2] Simply put, this is the set of values and other personality traits distributed among the *individuals* who make up the society; if one, for example, selected all the crucial dimensions of personality and found where most of a nation's adult population fell on each of them, and then recombined those dominant characteristics into a fictitious "typical ———— man," he would have one description of that nation's national character. The other approach is more anthropomorphic and usually refers to the *nation's* character as if it were a single personality; the incarnation of this approach is John Bull, Uncle Sam, the Hun, and so on. Though I have just finished arguing for the nation-as-actor construct, it does not necessarily follow that I advocate the second of these approaches to national character. On the contrary, it is essentially a poetic and non-operational metaphor which hinders, rather than helps, an understanding of the behavior of a complex society. These and several related issues are systematically explored in the following selection.

AN EVALUATION OF THE NATIONAL CHARACTER CONCEPT IN SOCIOLOGICAL THEORY

EMILY M. NETT

I

The characterization of the social framework known as the nation, and indirectly of the individuals operating within that structure, has occupied social scientists for several decades now. The problem has received varying degrees of interest by the separate disciplines at different times. In American sociology, for example, the tradition dates at least to Sumner who, while trying to establish the structural elements of society, conceptualized the "ethos" of nations. More recently, however, in the midst of a revived interest in so-called national character on the

---

[2] A comprehensive review and analysis of the literature from this point of view is Alex Inkeles and Daniel J. Levinson, "National Character: The Study of Modal Personality and Sociocultural Systems," in Gardner Lindzey (ed.), *Handbook of Social Psychology* (Reading, Mass.: Addison-Wesley, 1954), II, 977-1020.

From Emily M. Nett, "An Evaluation of the National Character Concept in Sociological Theory," *Social Forces,* XXXVI (1958), 297-303 (the footnotes have been omitted). Reprinted by permission of the author and The University of North Carolina Press.

part of anthropologists and psychologists, sociologists appear to be remaining aloof. The writer of the one book on American character by a sociologist denies that the personality types he describes are specific to any nation. Another sociologist severely criticizes the psychoanalytically-oriented anthropological studies and denies the usefulness of the concept of national character. On the other hand, and perhaps not unrelated, present-day sociologists are pursuing avidly the value orientation lead. Several have recognized that certain "dominant" themes can be identified in any social system and have applied the analysis at the national level.

Indeed, the reader of the materials on both value orientations and national character sometimes has difficulty observing the differences between the two; he is frequently confronted with lists of alleged personality traits ascribed to individual persons which coincide with lists of value orientations of nation-societies. The aim of this paper is to examine more closely from the point of view of its usefulness to sociology the concept of national character, by suggesting difficulties which arise in a consideration of the legitimacy of the concept in the sociologist's lexicon. First, however, a brief review of the criticisms leveled against the existing studies of national character will be presented.

If it is at all possible to separate methodological problems from theoretical considerations, it appears safe to say that the majority of the criticisms of national character studies center around weaknesses in methods. Problems of sampling, sufficiently made and recorded observations, quantification, classification, and correlation would appear to fall under the heading of research methods dilemmas. All of these aspects have been thoroughly covered in the critiques by the psychologists, the group of academics most vociferous in this matter.

That many of the statements about national character are hypotheses which require translation from "theoretical" to "empirical" language is one of the main arguments of Leites. Furthermore, he states that those who generalize do not usually make the mistake of failing to indicate they have insufficient evidence upon which to do so; rather they fail to make explicit the difference between required evidence (hypotheses) and available evidence (verification). In other words, they have what Leites calls "a high expectation-of-full-verification feeling" about their hypotheses. Farber goes further to accuse these researchers of abrogating one of the requirements of scientific research; namely, to make visible the procedures employed in the study. Not only do some studies fail to state how the observations were made, but they also make it impossible to determine how the data are ordered and the conclusions drawn. As Klineberg had earlier observed, the psychologists want documentation and verification.

Klineberg also indicated the sampling problem. Although he alluded specifically to analysis of so-called "cultural products" (such as art, literature, folk tales, news items, etc.) when he warned researchers to take necessary precautions to make their sample representative and to apply to the sample careful techniques of content analysis, his dictum might well apply to the interviewing and testing of persons. The question of the applicability of generalizations to the population

106

under study as a whole, he implies, can only be answered if the characteristics of the sample can be assumed to be representative.

Another methodological difficulty is the matter of establishing the causal connection. Klineberg, on Gorer's study of Japanese character structure, raised the inevitable question, "Is the Japanese a rigid, aggressive, formal adult because of his toilet training, or does this rigidity and formality reflect itself in the treatment of the child?" He advances the notion that comparative analysis will help provide the answer. Leites calls the willingness on the part of the observers to posit causes, the "fallacy of translation of correlation to causation." He insists that the kind of relationship which is concluded to exist between two variables is dependent upon other premises in the theory which is being used. Bendix is also concerned with the problem. He demonstrates the circularity of the reasoning in national character studies which imply that specific neurotic symptoms of individuals are widespread and therefore both cause and consequence of certain cultural symbols. His example of such reasoning is the researcher taking a symbol, i.e., Nazi propaganda, from which the character structure of particular groups in German society is inferred, and then using the inference to show why the propaganda had such wide appeal.

That the distinction between methodological and theoretical considerations of national character is in the final analysis an academic one, is clearly illustrated by this last criticism. The technique of making the separation has been employed since it is believed that the question of reliability of findings of the existing studies of national character had to be dealt with, if somewhat summarily, before turning attention to the question of the validity of the construct.

II

American sociologists have for the most part forgone, during more than fifteen years when the most activity occurred in this area, becoming engaged in the questionable pleasure of studying national character. Has such abstinence reflected wisdom? Parenthetically, is the current absorption with value orientations a belated parallel development? What are some of the limitations inherent in the concept of national character other than the lack of a rigorous scientific approach, which the sociologist must consider? These and other questions will be discussed under the headings of *the sociologistic-psychologistic dilemma, the vagueness of the terms relating to socially required behavior, the nation-culture confusion, the problem of the elites,* and *conformity-deviation.*

Because so many of the theoretical problems hinge upon the manner in which the sociologistic-psychologistic dilemma is approached, it will be presented prior to the other discussions. The problem, of course, is an ancient one — that of the relative weight to be assigned, in the explanation of human behavior, to institutions on the one hand and to individual motivation on the other. Earlier theorists had felt that they had to choose between one horn or the other; more recent ones have sought to come to grips with the dilemma by seeking to view behavior as involving elements of both kinds, related in a kind of interdependence. But as Bierstedt points out, they sometimes finish by ". . . constructing instead a superogatory social psychology . . ." rather than sociological theory.

The positions taken with regard to the study of national character can be illustrated as shifting at various periods in time. Ginsberg was the first to point out that there are at least two senses in which the term "national character" could be taken; i.e., as traits common to *individuals in a group* (most frequently distributed), or as behavior patterns of *the group as a whole* [emphasis added]. At that time his opinion was that the bulk of more popular works was concerned with the prevalence of traits in the group, but that, "The indirect method of studying national characteristics by an analysis of the psychological basis of the collective achievements of peoples has undoubtedly proved more fruitful than the direct method based on observation of individual behavior." Klineberg, in a more conciliatory mood, summed up the situation by saying in effect that both approaches are valid — that the group is not merely the sum of its individuals and that much can be learned by studying the individual. Representing a more extreme position than Ginsberg and a reaction to Kardiner's "basic personality type" and to Fromm's "social character" is the point of view of Bendix; that all cultures of Western civilization have essentially the same range of personality types but that they (cultures) all make different demands for social responses upon the individual. His conclusion is:

> When we analyze the "social character" of a society, we are in fact characterizing the emotional problems with which the people are typically faced and which arise out of the institutions and historical traditions of that society. . . . And if we attribute to these people a "social character" or a "national character" or a "basic personality type," we simply confuse the response with the stimulus.

And finally, fifteen years after Ginsberg's statement, Inkeles and Levinson, noting that there are few definitions and no general agreement among what looks to them like at least four different meanings of the term, decided that national character should be equated with "modal personality structure" and that the requirements of society (as in Fromm's "social character") deserve the status of ". . . an independent though significantly related construct . . .". They conclude, "Given this distinction, the degree of congruence between the modal personality structures and the psychological requirements of the social milieu emerges as an important problem for research."

As yet studies of national character in the sense that Inkeles and Levinson suggest, i.e., modal personality structure, are not available. Some monographs describe the modal personality structure of smaller more homogeneous groups as revealed by psychological tests, and raw data for similar populations have been compiled but not analyzed in these terms. The existing studies on the national level appear more correctly to report and analyze certain behavior patterns of the group, or what might better be called the character of nations. Abstractions, on various levels, from these patterns have otherwise been termed dominant orientations, themes, value orientations, master symbols, and ethoses. Inferences about personality structure from these behavior patterns or about their internalization by individuals have most frequently been termed national character, social character, or basic personality structure. This situation induces one to conclude that the studies made to date, despite the application of psychoanalytic theory and the interest in human motivation and personality structure, have had much the same result as if a more sociologistic approach had been taken. That is, the results represent descriptions of *the institutional requirements made upon individuals living in the nation-society and codifications of the manner in which these demands are assumed to be organized* [emphasis added]. This in part explains the overlap in personality traits and value orientations mentioned in the first section of this paper. The concepts do coincide *in so far as national character has been operationally defined.*

Although it is conceded that "ethos," "dominant orientations," or any other term would serve equally well and also that the term "national character" itself might as well be used to mean "modal personality," since empirical data are available under that rubric we shall continue to use it throughout the paper in the sense of abstractions about socially required behavior. One cannot but be curious as to what would have been the results of field study if the data gathered had been done so with the research design of Inkeles and Levinson in mind, on the one hand, and on the other, if sociologists had accepted the challenge to provide some other frame of reference than the psychoanalytic which might in the long run have proven more profitable both for national character studies and for social organization theory itself. Since Inkeles and Levinson have adequately dealt with the problems of personality theory and the delineation of modal personality structures, the remaining discussion will be slanted toward a few of the difficulties which the national character concept demonstrates for sociological theory.

The vagueness of definitions of socially required behaviors, and especially of second-order abstractions such as norms, values, value-orientations, etc., is the first fact imposed upon one by an encounter with the national character concept. Kluckhohn, in his extensive discussion of the term "value," has noted the tendency for anthropologists talking on a high level of abstraction to merge value and culture. This same confusion of terms exists with reference to social norms and values, despite various attempts to classify them. In one classification, systems of value-orientation standards are seen as one element of culture and in turn can be subclassified into further elements, including moral standards. Kluckhohn says that the way in which he defines *value* overlaps with Sumner's concept of the *mores* and he further differentiates norms (rules, in his words) and values on the basis of sanctions which apply to values [emphasis added]. Furthermore, he distinguishes between values and cultural premises, configurations, themes, and focuses. The latter are ". . . structural concepts, primarily intended to map the culture in cognitive terms for the outsider, to help depict the culture as a system. Values always look to action, in particular to the selections made by individual actors between different paths, each 'objectively' open." The findings of existing studies of national character could provide empirical verification to logical frameworks and suggest new formulations which explain more of the facts of socially required behaviors and explain them more simply.

The nation-culture confusion is a problem of a slightly different order than the one discussed above, but equally important and closely connected. The following statement by Farber is about as succinct yet as comprehensive as one might find: "A nation represents one empirically observed type of human grouping and the character of such groupings may be studied as a problem of social organization." He not only locates the object of study, but he also indicates the direction it should take. He foresees, however, one difficulty for which he fails to find a solution; this is that the concept of nation is essentially a political-geographical one, and that any given nation may or may not correspond with a cultural grouping. Examples of cultures spilling over national boundaries or of several cultures contained within one boundary may be found in abundance; in fact, there can hardly be found an example of correspondence in the Western hemisphere. On the other hand, it is in the cultural grouping that orthodox theory locates particular structural characteristics.

The solution to this problem may be found in the same manner as the regionalists found their answer to the quandary of defining their units of study. Political boundaries may be ignored and effort concentrated on locating and studying cultural groups based on some criteria other than political sovereignty and geographical confinement. Riesman has chosen to deal with the problem in somewhat this manner. Although his hypothesis is a unique one and worthy of consideration in its own right [there are correlations between the conformity demands put upon people in a society (social character) and the broadest of social indexes (curve of population growth and distribution used as a key to these indexes)], it does not answer the theoretical question at hand; namely, of what significance to sociological theory is the fact that *nations* have unique ethoses? The term "theoretical" is used not because the statement of differences is hypothesis rather than fact (which it is if one wants to deny common sense observations any validity), but because dominant themes, value orientations, ethoses, national characteristics or whatever appellations one gives them are important to the formulation of theories of social organization. In a sense these themes represent for institutional behavior what motives do for the personality organization of the individual; they are not merely the independent variables in a formula. They are neither cause nor effect, but forces integrating and moving the society; they need to be viewed as dynamic elements in the functioning of large organizations such as nations. Sociologists cannot ignore the fact that national groups differ widely in inner unity and homogeneity and that such factors as these are bound to enter into national character.

Ginsberg has suggested a classification of nationhood to take into account the following: the type of political unity, the degree of social differentiation and type of class structure, the degree of cultural homogeneity with special reference to

110

language and religion, and the age or stage of maturity and growth. Consideration of such specifics as classifications and typologies is not possible in this paper;
it is the purpose at this point only to note the need for more adequate formulation of the kind of groupings which nations represent and the manner in which
this is related to national character.

The problem of the elites, which the national character concept points up, is
also inextricably bound up in the concern of the social theorist with social
organization. Farber raises the following point: "Since policy is made by elites
operating within a special psychological context, a pragmatic objection to the
whole notion of national character arises from the viewpoint of applied psychology: that a description of national character would be of little value in
predicting the international political acts of a nation." Although he insists that
this consideration can be of no primary interest to the pure scientist, this paper
takes the position that it is of the ultimate importance to the theoretically-minded
sociologist although not just from the standpoint of predictability of theory.

The relationship of the power elite or elites, not just to themselves, but to the
system of evaluative symbols operative in the functioning of the society is of the
greatest concern to those interested in the institutional aspects of society. In the
past, both in studies of national character specifically and in sociological theory
generally, "This distinction between peoples and their governments which
Americans seem to feel so intimately . . ." has been somewhat neglected. In recent
years increasing attention has been focused on this area generally, although still
not by those studying national character. Interest in the elites might take a twofold turn: (1) toward the role played by the power elite(s) in determining
national character and reciprocally in the way in which the actions of the power
elite(s) are limited by national character, and (2) toward the degree to which the
discrepancy between the character of the masses and the character of the most
powerful groups acts as a lever in social change; i.e., the part played by
dominant, variant, and deviant orientations, to use F. Kluckhohn's terms.

This brings the discussion to the final problem stressed by the national
character concept to be considered in this paper—the matter of deviation-
conformity, and stemming from it the problem of social change. One of Bendix's
main criticisms of the psychoanalytic approach to national character is: "If the
symbols of a culture are taken as a clue to the characteristic personality types of
its participants, then we underestimate the incongruity between institutions,
culture patterns, and the psychological habitus of a people, and we ignore an
important source of social change." The theorist must not undervalue this
incongruity, and in fact might even seek for the sources of *continuous* social
organization in deviation rather than in conformity. Certainly with regard to the
typology of nationhood discussed above, one important dimension would be the
degree of requiredness which is expected of individuals, or the amount of
conformity to institutionalized patterns which is enforced.

In one study of common values reflected in literature the researcher found that
although short stories strongly upheld moral ideas and values of the American
family at all three cultural levels in which magazines carrying them circulated,

111

the upper level shows a tendency to set itself apart by selecting more *alternatives* to basic themes. As the author suggests, whether the nonconformity at this level is verbal or actual would have to be determined. But it might be presumed that even to support the kind of literary tradition which allows nonconformity a group must be more flexible in its thought-ways than one which does not. Do such differences exist between nations; do they in turn make a difference in the manner in which changes in the social structure (wars, economic recessions, technological changes, power struggles, etc.,) are met? It would be valuable to have a formulation of the way in which conformity demands reduce the effectiveness of the deviation aspect of persons and groups (in this instance nation-societies) in *responding to* and *initiating* social change.

The matter of incongruities is interconnected with the problem of the elites, with regard to which we have already noted the importance of deviant and variant orientations in social change theory. By focusing attention on the disparity resulting from degrees of requiredness of various types of behaviors prescribed by the norms and values of the society as applied to different segments of the society, we should be able to go beyond Riesman's analysis. Because of using the historical approach he has been forced to deal with the problem of change more than some of the others who have studied national character. He notes that the disparity between socially required behavior and characterologically compatible behavior is one of the great levers of change. The discrepancy between different sets of socially required behaviors in the same system has always been considered another source of change, the dynamics of which are little understood.

III

In summary, several statements appear in order. First, the studies of national character made to date consist mainly of a body of hypotheses, not yet adequately verified, about the requirements around which the nation-society is organized. Second, if the term is to be meaningful for sociological theory, it will have to be taken in the above sense rather than in the modal personality structure context, this being a matter of emphasis not to deny the validity of the search for psychological differences between nationals. Third, there is no adequate theory describing the social demands as a configuration and no classification or substantial agreement on terms referring to these requirements. And finally, in the development of social organization theory consideration might be given to two aspects of national character which until this time have received little attention—the interaction between the institutional requirements and the behavior of the elites, and the role that degrees of conformity-deviation in the social structure play as an active ingredient in the dynamics of change.

The next articles represent two somewhat divergent techniques applicable to the search for measures of national character. In the first,

Scott follows the modal personality path, emphasizing a relatively statistical approach which can provide clues as to the sorts of goals social groups might pursue and the kinds of policies they might adopt in that pursuit.

EMPIRICAL ASSESSMENT OF VALUES AND IDEOLOGIES

William A. Scott

Much has been written about the ideology of American culture and of various subcultures within it. In the early days of the nation, Tocqueville saw Americans as preoccupied with freedom, equalitarianism, and physical well-being. The industrial revolution and the rise of capitalism were presumably associated with the Protestant ethic, embodying the ideals of individualism, hard work, and self denial. Recently Fromm, Riesman, and Whyte have noted the emergence of a marketing or other-directed personality orientation, said to be supplanting the ideology of the Protestant ethic. Mead characterizes Americans as at once idealistic and pragmatic; while Gorer stresses their generosity, hatred of authority, and concern with interpersonal relations and the acquisition of money.

Such characterizations of cultural ideology tend to highlight presumed modal patterns while de-emphasizing the diversities which surround them. Certain diversities are treated by Kluckhohn, who points out that heterogeneous cultures are characterized by variant, as well as dominant, value orientations.

But whether cultural ideologies are viewed as unitary or diverse, there is usually considerable ambiguity concerning the empirical bases of such generalizations. Value systems may be read from official documents and pronouncements, such as the Declaration of Independence or the President's State of the Union Message. They may be inferred from content analyses of communications media or from art forms and other cultural artifacts. Or they may be derived by questioning members of the society about the personal values that they hold sacred. Whatever the procedure, the selection of relevant data for value inference involves a sampling problem. What population of documents is to be taken as embodying the overt values of the culture? What population of communication media or art forms is definitive of the group's culture? What population of persons may appropriately be regarded as validators of a society's ideology? Given definitions of these populations, what sorts of sampling procedures should one use to ensure adequate representation of the intended population? Should newspapers be sampled disproportionately according to readership? Should varieties of an art form be differentially weighted depending on the size of their

From William A. Scott, "Empirical Assessment of Values and Ideologies," *American Sociological Review,* XXIV (1959), 299-310 (all footnotes, except note 11, have been omitted). Reprinted by permission of the author and The American Sociological Association.

audience? — or on experts' judgments of their importance to the culture? Should a population of individuals be sampled in random fashion, with equal weight given to all informants? Or should respondents be differentially represented according to their social visibility?

Studies of cultural ideology have given little explicit attention to such problems of research method. Generally the population and sampling procedure are not specified; and the analyst's method of integrating data on which inductions are based is left inexplicit. An astute interpreter may derive insights which are validated by their correspondence either with the reader's common-sense judgments or with another analyst's interpretation. In either case, *the basis of the validation is usually as mysterious as the original interpretation* [emphasis added]. It is not unusual, under such circumstances, for independent investigators to reach quite divergent interpretations of cultural patterns. These divergencies may be attributed to at least two sources: different investigators may collect their data from quite different populations of events; and the inferred cultural patterns are *highly dependent on the interpretive work* of the investigator, which is not duplicated from one researcher to another [emphasis added].

Confusion of interpretations concerning cultural ideologies is also brought about by the theoretical problem of what is meant by "culture." From the standpoint of a culturologist (many students of cultural anthropology appear to share this viewpoint), culture represents *a set of externalized ideas or other products of work and thought* [emphasis added]. Individuals may serve as culture-carriers, but cultural elements themselves are viewed as having a separate existence, functioning within a deterministic system composed only of other cultural elements. From this point of view, the appropriate objects of analysis for cultural investigations are such products as language, art forms, and material artifacts which are not directly dependent for their current existence on the participation of particular individuals (although individual members of society, in a sense, may have been responsible for their origins).

Another definition of culture, widely held among social psychologists, refers to *ideas which are held in common by members of a society or social group* [emphasis added]. Although these cultural elements may display the normative properties characterized by Durkheim as "exteriority" and "constraint," their existence as cultural facts ultimately depends on their being shared by a significant proportion of persons in society. Thus cultural values and ideologies are functions of similarities in the cognitive structures of individuals.

Clarity of discourse, it seems, requires that these two definitions of culture be kept conceptually distinct. And each should be measured by operations appropriate to its definition. Culture as a system of shared meanings should be assessed by questioning individuals and determining the extent of agreement among them. Culture as an external system of ideas and products should be assessed by direct observation and interpretation of these products. But descriptions of cultural ideologies have often confused these two, interpreting data relevant to one definition as if they referred to the other. Thus, members of a particular national group may be assigned traits, such as glorification of feminism, on the basis of content analysis of communication media. It would seem preferable to obtain independent measures from cultural products and from members' cognitive structures, and to treat their degree of correspondence *as a matter for empirical investigation* [emphasis added]. Instances of discrepancy could be every bit as interesting as instances of congruence. In any case, congruence should not be assumed in the absence of evidence from independent sources.

These considerations form the theoretical and methodological context of the research reported below.

Assessing Moral Ideals of Individuals

A *personal value,* or *moral ideal,* has been defined as a particular individual's concept of an ideal state of affairs or relations among people, which he uses to assess the "goodness" or "badness," the "rightness" or "wrongness" of actual relations which he observes. Instruments for assessing "values" have been developed by Allport and Vernon and by Morris, but these were considered inappropriate for the present investigation because they are constructed so as to measure only a limited number of value orientations. Moreover, the Allport-Vernon scale appears more like a test of object-preferences than a test of personal values in the present sense; most of its items do not require moral evaluation of courses of action, but simply selection among them.

In order to avoid artificial restriction of the range of subjects' evaluative responses, an open-question measure of moral ideals was developed for use either in interview surveys or in questionnaires. Although providing, at best, a crude assessment of any particular personal value, it has the advantage of permitting expression of a limitless variety of values, so that the researcher can determine empirically just what standards of "goodness" or "rightness" are expressed voluntarily by members of any given population. For more precise assessment of particular moral ideals, one can develop multiple-item scales by the Guttman, Likert, or Thurstone techniques.

Populations and Samples

Subjects were selected from three different populations: (a) adult residents of "Mountaintown," a predominantly upper-middle class suburban community of approximately 30,000 inhabitants; (b) students at State University in Mountaintown; and (c) students at Fundamentalist College, a minority sect college in the Midwest. Samples from populations (a) and (c) were selected by probability sampling procedures, and 80 per cent or more of the designated respondents were contacted. Their moral ideals were assessed by non-directive interview. Population (b) was not sampled in representative fashion, but students in a large general psychology class (mostly sophomores) were studied. Their moral ideals were assessed by a questionnaire closely similar to the interview questions used on the other two populations.

115

Measures of Moral Ideals

Those parts of the interview schedule dealing with moral ideals were exclusively of the open question type, in which the interviewer attempted to record verbatim the respondent's answers. In accordance with the definition of a moral ideal as an abstract standard for judging concrete actions, the open questions were framed with a view toward eliciting standards of conduct.[11] In the State University sample moral ideals were assessed by mimeographed questionnaires on which subjects answered two questions comparable to those used in the interview.

Responses, as recorded by the interviewer or by the subject, were subsequently coded by the research team. Since the categories of moral ideals were not designated in advance, it was necessary to develop them empirically by perusal of the first fifty interviews returned, with provision for adding categories as necessary. Eventually sixty discriminable categories were established, but only thirteen of these were used with sufficient frequency (thirty or more respondents in the Mountaintown sample) to justify tabular analysis. By combining certain of the low-frequency ideals into more general groupings, it was possible to obtain a set of eighteen categories for correlational analysis of the Mountaintown data. (Three more were subsequently added for the other two populations.) A brief description of each is presented in Table 1. It must be emphasized that these eighteen moral ideals cannot be regarded as a general typology applicable to all populations. They are valid only for Mountaintown at the time of this study (Spring, 1957), and depend on the particular assessment procedures employed here.

Reliability of the Measures

Reliability of the measure of moral ideals was assessed in two ways: first, by the extent to which two different coders agreed in inferring a particular ideal from what the respondent reported; and second, by the degree to which respondents mentioned the same moral ideals in two successive interviews. The figures in the

---

[11]After a brief introductory and not overly informative explanation of the general mission of the interviewer, the respondent was asked: "I wonder if you would think about your various friends and pick out two that you admire most." "Now, what is it about the first person that you particularly admire?" "Anything else?" "Now what is it about the second person that you particularly admire?" "Anything else?" "Now, would you think of a couple of people whom you have very little use for. What about the first person would you say is especially bad?" "Anything else?" "What about the second person would you say is especially bad?" "Anything else?" The purpose of these "warm-up" questions was to encourage the respondent to think about people in an evaluative framework — which many are not accustomed to doing. There followed the questions from which the respondent's moral ideals were assessed: "So far I have asked you about specific people. Now I have a more general question. What is it about any person that makes him good?" "Anything else?" "What kinds of things about a person would make him especially bad?" "Anything else?" And for each item mentioned under "good" and "bad": "Why would you say that is good (or bad)?"

second column of Table 1 report a corrected index of inter-coder agreement, π, which represents the percentage agreement above chance. In general, these figures are reasonably high, indicating, at least for some of the value categories, that trained content analysts can agree on coding of the respondents' answers. The measures of response stability, from the first to the second interview, are

TABLE 1

Coding Reliabilities and Response Stabilities
of Moral Ideals Professed by Mountaintown Residents

	Coefficients of Agreement (π)	
Moral Ideal	*Between Two Coders on Pre-test*	*Between Pre- and Post-test*
1. Self-control; abstinence; cleanliness; orderliness[a]	.90**	.71**
2. Religiousness; belief in God; church-going	.86**	.53**
3. Hard work	.81**	.38*
4. Honesty	.80**	.40**
5. Intelligence; mental development; intellectuality	.79**	.51*
6. Humility; democratic equalitarianism	.77**	.00
7. Genuineness; sincerity	.75**	.16
8. Happiness; optimism; sense of humor; easy-going nature[a]	.71**	.37*
9. Loyalty to family or friends[a]	.70**	.11
10. Fairness; objectivity; universalism[a]	.67**	.00
11. Dependability; responsibility	.60**	.38*
12. Love of people; kindliness toward people	.56**	.10
13. Social interaction skills; ability to get along with people	.56**	.26
14. Friendliness; affability	.43*	.21
15. Integrity; adherence to one's ideals	.30	.39
16. Respect for individual dignity; tolerance for differences	.25*	.19
17. Respect for authority; prestige; power; status[a]	.22	.16
18. Generosity; helpfulness	.17	.16
Mean inter-coder agreement and mean stability	.57	.26

[a]Combined of two or more originally distinct categories with frequencies too small for separate analysis.
**P < .01.
*P < .05.

reported in the third column of the table. It is apparent that reliabilities of respondents' reports are much lower than the reliabilities of judging their values from a single interview. Either there was considerable change in moral ideals in the three-month interval; or the same set of ideals changed in relative saliences, so that some were readily mentioned one time and not the other; or the different approaches of the two interviewers elicited different responses to the same questions. Whatever the sources of instability in responses, clearly this method of assessment may not yield comparable results for some of the moral ideals from one interview to another later one.

Validity of the Measures

Since no independent measures of the moral ideals were available in this study, it was necessary to resort to validation by inference from correlations with other responses. If a person maintains moral ideals in the sense intended here, then he would be expected to use them to evaluate significant others in his environment. Therefore, it is reasonable to expect that criteria used in assessing other people should correlate with the criteria embodied in the moral ideals. At various points in the interview three different kinds of significant others were suggested: the respondent's acquaintances, his children, and the respondent's self. Responses to these questions about specific people were coded according to the same set of categories used to assess the general moral ideals. Hence one can determine the respondents' tendencies to use the same categories to describe admired people and good qualities in general (or, alternatively, their tendencies to use opposites of the favored general qualities to describe bad traits in themselves or others) [Table 2 omitted below].

*   *   *   *   *

CULTURAL VALUES IN THE THREE POPULATIONS

To the extent that many members of a particular social group give responses which can be classified into a single category of moral ideals, one can say that a cultural value exists. It would be unusual, indeed, for an open question technique such as this to yield anywhere near 100 per cent classification within a single category, so one must be careful to interpret the response frequencies in relative terms. If specific questions had been framed for each of the categories, all of them would undoubtedly have elicited much higher rates of assent than were found in this study. But such a procedure would have been unwieldly in the present research context, and would inevitably have focused attention on particular values to the exclusion of others.

Cultural values of the three populations may be inferred from Table 3, which lists the proportions of respondents from each sample who professed each ideal. Although Mountaintown can not be regarded as representative of the entire

United States, it is nevertheless interesting to note the distribution of responses (second column of figures) in the light of interpretations of "American character" based on other kinds of data. Evidently moral ideals associated with "people" and interpersonal relations rank high in popularity, in contrast with moral ideals related to individuality and self sufficiency. Ideals involving self-control are much more popular than those involving expression of impulse. Aside from self-control, the classical values of the Protestant ethic — hard work, stoicism, and achievement — are scarcely mentioned. The ideals of creativity, aesthetic sensitivity, and appreciation of natural beauty were found so rarely that they could not be profitably included in the tabulation. Respect for authority, prestige, and status (combined category) received less frequent mention than their antithesis, democratic equalitarianism (or humility).

Thus the picture of Mountaintown obtained from this interview assessment of moral ideals is suggestive of Riesman's "other directed" type of social character. The popular values in this town tend to be those which concern social relations rather than relations with oneself, values related to the present rather than to the past or future, and values of impulse restraint rather than hedonism or power.

The Mountaintown data may be used as a standard of comparison for the other two populations (first and third columns in Table 3). Significant departures of the student groups from the Mountaintown sample are indicated by asterisks between the appropriate columns of figures. The four values which were relatively more popular in State University include social interaction skills, intelligence, achievement, and individuality. The first three of these correspond to the commonly held picture of the university as encouraging student orientations toward academic and social goals; academic endeavors are presumably stressed largely by the faculty, while concern for social skills is engendered within the fraternity and sorority groups. The relative prevalence of individualism as a value appears inexplicable on an *a priori* basis, unless one attributes it either to the adolescent years or to academically related pressures.

Fundamentalist College presents a picture of striking contrast to that found in Mountaintown. Mentioned relatively more frequently in the former population are a large number of moral ideals: religiousness, self-control, respect for authority, humility (democratic equalitarianism), hard work, individuality, happiness, social interaction skills, friendliness, and being liked by others. Most of these differences can be attributed to three conditions: the strong religious orientation of the college, the need of a deviant group to maintain strong in-group ties, and the correlative need to resist pressures for conformity to out-group demands which are incompatible with its ideology. Such an interpretation leaves unexplained the relatively greater emphasis on happiness as a value, and does not account for the failure of generosity, love of people, integrity, and loyalty to emerge as significantly more popular ideals. (The last three of these values show sample differences in the expected direction, but they are not large enough to warrant conclusions about population differences.)

It is apparent that this method of assessing cultural values indicates some

TABLE 3

Moral Ideals in Mountaintown, State University, and Fundamentalist College

| | Proportion Expressing the Ideal in: | | |
Moral Ideal	State University (N = 295)	Mountaintown (N = 319)	Fundamentalist College (N = 47)
1. Love of people	35% **	50%	55%
2. Honesty	23 **	49 **	28
3. Individual dignity	8 **	32	26
4. Generosity	13 **	31	23
5. Self-control; etc.	24	26 **	55
6. Genuineness	27	26	17
7. Social skills	43 **	19 **	66
8. Friendliness	15	18 **	55
9. Dependability	13	18	17
10. Religiousness	1 **	18 **	49
11. Happiness	20	17 **	43
12. Fairness	7 **	16	15
13. Humility	16	15 **	43
14. Integrity	15	12	21
15. Hard work	13	12 *	28
16. Loyalty	4	12	21
17. Intelligence	31 **	11	9
18. Respect for authority	6	10 **	38
19. Individuality; self-sufficiency; independence	32 **	5 **	32
20. Achievement; striving to do well	24 **	4	6
21. Being liked by others	0	1 **	47

**p < .01 (by t-test) (refers to difference between percentages in adjacent columns).
*p < .05.

substantial differences among the three populations tested. To a considerable degree these differences are consistent with what one might expect on the basis of generally held views of the two academic institutions. Although there are no systematic data to validate these views, casual impressions suggest that if independent measures of the *external* cultures of these institutions could be obtained, they would correspond with the data concerning *internal* cultures reported here.

Valid comparisons between the internal and external cultures would require systematic data from the latter; these might appropriately be obtained from public documents, pronouncements of leaders, and institutional routines. Within a well integrated institution which provides for adequate socialization of its members, one would normally expect to find good correspondence between the two, but cases of perfect congruence are probably rare. Directors of State University would perhaps be disturbed to find that only about a quarter of the students profess the value of academic achievement, while directors of Fundamentalist College might be equally distressed to discover that only half of their students appear to share the value of religiousness. Thus instances of discrepancy between external culture (expected by institutional leaders) and internal culture (actually shared by participants) could provide interesting points of departure for the study of cultural disequilibrium and change.

ASSESSMENT OF CULTURAL IDEOLOGIES

* * * * *

The major differences between the ideologies of Mountaintown and State University may be summarized as follows: Mountaintown emphasizes the combination of religiousness and self-control to a much greater extent than does State University, while the latter places relatively more emphasis on the hard work-achievement combination. Whereas self-control is strongly linked with religiousness in the wider community, it is tied with social skills, happiness, and friendliness at the university. (It is noteworthy that, among these university students, self-control is apparently not seen predominantly as relinquishment of pleasure, but rather as a means toward, or concomitant of, pleasure itself — pleasure being closely linked with social interaction values.) Aside from these three major differences, the intercorrelation matrices from the two populations look about the same. This tempts one to infer that the ideological groupings found at State University parallel those of the wider community represented by Mountaintown. . . . In fact, the university students are probably recruited for the most part from a population whose ideological structure is not greatly different from that of Mountaintown.

Fundamentalist College [Table 6 omitted] displays quite a different ideological structure. Although there are marked associations among many of the ideals, there is little resemblance between these clusters and Mountaintown's. There is an almost recognizable derivative of the "interpersonal opportunism" cluster, but this includes social skills, humility, and self-control, in place of the social skills, humility, respect for authority, and happiness values of the Mountaintown matrix. (It will be recalled that self-control was also a part of this cluster in State University; in this respect the two student populations are alike.) The values of happiness and friendliness are now found as parts of a larger, but somewhat loosely organized, group which forms the dominant ideology of Fundamentalist College. This cluster comprises the seemingly diverse ideals of respect for authority, hard work, being liked by others, friendliness, happiness, and independence. While the value of friendliness forms the most central link in this ideology, the latter is difficult to identify with a single phrase.

Two other major differences between this matrix and those previously observed suggest a marked difference between Fundamentalist College and the other two populations. First, only two value-clusters are found, in contrast with the five in Mountaintown and in State University. Second, there are relatively

121

few negative correlations among the various ideals, compared with their pro-fuseness in the other two matrices. Both of these characteristics suggest an ideologically more homogeneous group, with relatively little conflict among the moral ideals maintained by different members. In view of the population base from which Fundamentalist College students are recruited — nearly all are members of the same religious sect — this homogeneity, as well as the contrast with a community such as Mountaintown, can be readily understood.

Finally, it is noteworthy that the moral ideal of religiousness bears no relation to any of the other ideals, although it is professed by about one half of the students. The independence of this value from the others suggests that it has no unique meaning for all group members. The college is presumably organized around a single, dominant religious theme, but the binding force of this theme is not supplemented — neither is it diluted — by inclusion in an ideology which embodies other popular and dominant moral ideals.

Summary

This paper describes a method for assessing values and ideologies of a culture, when that culture is defined in terms of the shared psychological attributes of its members. The moral ideals professed by the individual participants in a particular social structure are determined by content analysis of their answers to open questions concerning traits which they admire or dislike in other people. A particular moral ideal is judged dominant (and hence a cultural value) to the extent that it is widely shared within the group. Cultural ideologies are inferred from intercorrelations among moral ideals within the group of respondents. Data concerning the values and ideologies of three different populations within the United States are reported, together with interpretations of the differences found among them.

When respondents are selected as a representative sample of the larger population that constitutes a society or sub-society, this procedure would seem to be appropriate for determining the values and ideologies of the entire culture, provided that each individual's moral ideals are given equal weight in the total. However, if the group's culture is defined, not by reference to the shared psychological attributes of its members, but as an external system of ideas and cultural products, then the present assessment procedure is inadequate. Given the latter definition of culture, values and ideologies should be determined from direct assessment of relevant cultural products, such as language, art forms, mass communications, and other patterned behaviors. Unfortunately, studies of such external culture have provided little in the way of explicit guidance for the definition of the relevant population of events or for sampling in such a way as to represent faithfully that which they purport to measure. The provision of such explicit procedures would open the way for investigations concerning the degree of correspondence between culture, as psychologically defined, and culture as an extra-individual system.

In a somewhat different vein, but equally useful, is the content analysis reported below. The authors are looking for the same kinds of variables, but they employ a technique which requires more in the way of inference. In their study they examine those dramatic plays which were most popular in Germany and in America during 1927, and, from the values and attitudes which are expressed therein, they draw inferences about the character of the nations in which the productions were popular.[1]

GERMAN AND AMERICAN TRAITS REFLECTED IN POPULAR DRAMA

Donald V. McGranahan and Ivor Wayne

*   *   *   *   *

Our first assumption in this study is that popular drama can be regarded as a case of "social fantasy" — that the psychological constellations in a dramatic work indicate sensitive areas in the personalities of those for whom the work has appeal; their needs, assumptions and values are expressed ("projected") in the drama. The successful play must be attuned to the audience. There can be no claim that dramatic material reflects the total personality of the individual who enjoys it. Analysis of popular songs, poetry, art, humor, novels and short stories, propaganda, advertising, religious writings, public activities, statistics on crime and mental disease, etc., may well reveal other psychological facets of a historical population that is not accessible to direct study.

Our analysis of the plays is clearly limited by the fact that the play-going audience is not a proper sample of the national population. It represents primarily an educated, urban segment. However, the German and American audiences are roughly comparable. If significant psychological differences can be shown between corresponding segments of two national populations, then this

[1]For an empirical investigation into the usefulness of this technique, see Milton C. Albrecht, "Does Literature Reflect Common Values?" *American Sociological Review*, XXI (1956), 722-29. One other version of the content analysis technique is that used in Juan B. Cortes, "The Achievement Motive in the Spanish Economy between the 13th and 18th Centuries," *Economic Development and Cultural Change*, IX (1961), 144-63. That study is based on the theoretical work of David C. McClelland and John W. Atkinson.

From Donald V. McGranahan and Ivor Wayne, "German and American Traits Reflected in Popular Drama," *Human Relations*, I (1948), 429-55 (the footnotes have been omitted). Reprinted by permission of the authors and *Human Relations*.

indicates a real difference in national character, unless one rejects a statistical definition of that concept and reserves it only for nationally uniform traits. Whether the traits expressed in the plays actually extend to other parts of the population must be determined by study of other sources. The German and American play-going audiences are not, of course, exactly comparable—for example, New York (Broadway) has a greater role in the American theater than does any metropolis in Germany where the theater has been more decentralized. Furthermore, seats in the German theater have tended to be cheaper. This is connected with the important fact that the German theater, unlike the American theater, has been primarily under public ownership, or subsidy from public funds. These considerations must be borne in mind in the evaluation of our results.

METHODS AND PROCEDURE

As a first step in choosing the sample for each country, all reported productions for the calendar year 1927 (including productions first staged in the last weeks of December, 1926) were examined, and musical comedies, operas, revues and follies were eliminated. From the remaining plays, which relied on story content and characters for appeal, were eliminated all revivals and all foreign importations, so far as these could be determined. Austrian, Sudetan and Swiss-German plays were excluded from the German sample. This left about 135 first productions ("try-outs") for each country.

An attempt was then made to select the 45 most popular plays in each country. In the United States, popularity was judged on the basis of: (1) success on Broadway, as measured by the recorded number of performances; (2) success in the rest of the country, as indicated by the frequency and content of reviews in theater journals and local newspapers; (3) over-all success as indicated by various "end-of-the-season" discussions, tabulations, and over-all reviews. In the case of the German plays, popularity was judged on the basis of: (1) the success of the play in spreading through the theaters in the various German towns, as indicated by speed with which reviews of the play followed each other in special theater periodicals, the over-all frequency of such reviews, and the estimate of popular reaction therein contained; and (2) over-all success as indicated by retrospective summaries, etc. No single objective measure being available for national success in the case of either country, it was necessary to combine criteria in estimating the rank order of popularity. The procedure ensured that all recognized successes were included. For the less successful plays, it became increasingly difficult to assess relative order of popularity (the total section was limited to 45 plays in each country rather than an intended sample of 50, because at about this point the plays were becoming uniformly and indistinguishably unsuccessful).

Once the 45 plays for each country were chosen on the basis of popularity estimate, summaries of their contents were written down. The summaries were based upon reading of the play or of an abridged form of the play as given in Burns Mantle, or upon an examination of several independent reviews, since a single reviewer could not be relied upon to give an adequate digest. An element of unconscious bias may have crept into the summarizing of some of the plays, although a careful attempt was made to obtain accurate digests. The summarized contents were then subjected to various types of analysis by three judges. There is no established psychological method of content analysis in handling dramatic material. The three judges independently gravitated toward categories that followed the traditional lines of break-down in drama: the nature of the setting, of the central characters, of the plot, and of the conclusion. An attempt was made by each of the judges to use the categories used in analysis of the Thematic Apperception Test, but the material did not lend itself easily to this type of analysis. A method seemed required by which each plot could be treated as a unit. Furthermore, exploratory attempts at analysis indicated that it would be wiser to let the categories emerge from the material so far as possible, rather than superimpose categories.

It was found that the structure of nearly all the dramas could be described in terms of the pattern of conflict, the interplay of opposing forces, that underlay the plot: conflict between youthful lovers and parents, between honest folk and criminals, between revolutionary and reactionary political forces, between moral and immoral impulses within the individual, etc. Once the patterns of conflict in the different plays were established, it was further found that these conflicts could be classified into six major groups or categories, called the "love theme," the "morality theme," the "idealism theme," the "power theme," the "career theme," and the "outcast theme." These major categories were then defined in some detail according to their typical ingredients (the definitions are given in the following section).

In view of the ease with which prejudice and preconception operate in the field of national psychology, it was felt that the judgments of the two authors should not be the sole basis for determining German-American differences in terms of these categories, since the authors knew which plays were German and which were American. For this reason, seven additional judges were used. The summaries of the plays were arranged in a random order, authors and titles were deleted. A number of the German plays were already set in the United States, England, Russia, or some other non-Germanic country and had non-Germanic characters. These summaries were left in their original form. In the case of the remaining German plays, the settings and the names of the central characters were transformed into American settings and names, with but five exceptions: in one case, a French setting was substituted, and in the remaining four cases the German settings and characters could not be changed without changing the basic content of the play. To off-set the latter situation, four American plays were given German settings and names. The seven independent judges were then provided with the ninety summaries (each summary averaging a third of a single-spaced typewritten page in length), the detailed definitions of the basic themes, and directions to classify a play under a given thematic category "only if the theme is central to the plot; that is, if the theme could not be eliminated without significantly changing the essential nature of the plot and leaving it logically or psychologically incomplete. If a love theme, for example, is merely thrown in for incidental interest, this is not to be counted." Subjects were told a play might contain only one, or it might contain several of the basic themes.

In addition to this thematic analysis, the judges were asked to classify each play "according to whether the ending is (1) happy, (2) unhappy (tragic), or (3) ambiguous (mixed); also according to whether the play is primarily *personal* in content and import (concerned with private affairs of individuals), or primarily *ideological* (concerned with political, social, national or international issues)." The judges were told that the purpose of the experiment was to test the reliability of the categories used.

Each of the authors also classified the plays independently so that there were nine judges all told. In computation of the results, a play was reckoned to fall under a given category if five or more of the nine judges agreed in placing it there. In only seven of the ninety plays did the majority fail to find any one basic theme applying. There is no standard formula for measuring the reliability of categories of content analysis such as used in this study, but inspection of the data indicates that the love theme and the idealism theme were employed with the greatest agreement among judges, the morality and power themes with least agreement. For example, when the majority of the judges agreed on the presence of the love or idealism theme in a given play, this majority was more often a majority of all nine of the judges than a majority of eight, seven, six, or five judges; whereas a majority agreement in the case of the morality and power themes was more frequently a majority of only five or six of the judges. Agreement on the level of action (personal versus ideological) and the nature of the ending of the play (happy, unhappy, ambiguous) was also fairly high, in the sense that when there was majority agreement, it was most frequently universal agreement.

In the statistical results presented, the procedure of defining the presence of a given category by the majority agreement of the nine judges applies only to the data on the basic themes. In the case of the level of action, and the nature of the endings, the results represent majority agreement among only seven judges (because of pressure of time, two of the judges were not asked to use these categories). All other data represent the analysis of the two authors only, and can be distinguished by the fact that they are presented in numerical form, not in percentages).

Definitions of the Basic Themes

The following are the detailed definitions of the basic themes as given to the judges who analyzed the plays.

The Love Theme

This category includes only heterosexual love of the boy-girl, husband-wife, master-mistress variety. It does not include family love — unless incest is clearly indicated — or love of any non-sexual object. However, plays dwelling on the problems married people have in getting along with each other are to be ordinarily included, even if romantic love is not highlighted. In plays falling under the love theme, dramatic interest usually centers about the question whether two lovers, or potential or would-be lovers, will be united in the end. Opposed to the love relationship may be any number of factors: parents, personal misunderstandings and grievances between the lovers, career ambitions, character defects, higher ideals of one form or another. These forces must be overcome or reconciled before the happy union can ensue. Love may, of course, lose to any of the forces conflicting with it.

The Morality Theme

Plays built around a morality theme deal with the problems that arise from the moral standards of society and human weakness or sinfulness in falling below these standards. Morality is used here only in the sense of *conventional personal morals* such as are treated in the Bible and in western criminal law. We are not here concerned with good and bad philosophies of life, political faiths or social systems, but with specific individual behavior. Typical immoralities or sins are: personal crimes of any sort, individual dishonesty, sexual looseness, intentional injury to other persons. Opposed are such virtues as: law-abidingness, honesty, "true love," kindness, and consideration of others. The good and evil forces may be represented externally by good and evil men (e.g., honest folk and criminals) or internally by good and evil impulses. In plays with a basic morality theme (as here defined) the moral is assumed to be the conventional, the expected, the normal behavior of the social majority; the immoral is the deviant, the behavior of the man who falls below the social norm. Indeed, the moral is often treated as having the force of society and perhaps even of "nature" behind it, while the immoral is unsocial, unwholesome, and unnatural. Ordinarily, in plays with a basic morality theme, the guilty person who falls below the social norm *must either reform* (i.e., readjust to society and nature) or *suffer punishment* (or both). The play clearly implies the superiority of virtue, both as desirable and as necessary. Finally, it is assumed in these plays that the choice between good and evil paths of actions is a matter of free choice between possible alternatives, that the individual is therefore responsible for his morality or immorality. Plays of the morality type may be said to provide the spectator with a certain excitement by dramatizing immoral impulses but at the same time they provide him with a moral lesson to the effect that "crime does not pay." Because nearly all plays involve crimes or immoralities of one sort or another, it is desirable to define the morality type negatively and indicate the kinds of play that do not fall under this category: (1) plays that present illicit love-making as charming or amusing, and involve no moral judgment, no character reform or punishment, fall only under the love theme; (2) plays that justify an ordinarily immoral or criminal act in the name of a higher ideal or value (patriotism, "liberalism," art, etc.) or treat ordinary morality as petty and narrow, in comparison with the hero's higher vision, or present a hero who stands far above a corrupt and evil world, fall under the category of "idealism"; (3) plays that present merely a primitive conflict in which moral forces play no role fall only under the power theme; (4) if the central character is a criminal or other deviant type and the play presents him sympathetically, or makes it clear that he is not responsible for his sins, but society or fate is responsible, then the play belongs under the outcast theme.

The Idealism Theme

Plays featuring the idealism theme have a central character who is consciously attempting to pursue a set of high principles. He may be a revolutionary idealist, a humanitarian idealist, or a devoted supporter of the old regime; a nationalistic patriot or an internationalist; a free-thinking liberal, a priest or an art-lover. The important point is that his motives and his character set him apart from, and above, the masses of the people. He is not merely seeking to live an average, conventional private life, and he does not behave in a manner that can be expected of the average citizen. In the pursuit of his principles, he may have to sacrifice some conventional personal value—his reputation, his life, love, social acceptance, personal happiness, normal creature comforts. He may very well commit some act against conventional morals, as in the case of the patriot who kills his friend for the sake of his country. The idealist theme is thus concerned with the conflicts engendered by those who stand above the ordinary; the morality theme with conflicts engendered by those who fall below the ordinary. Unlike the moral individual, the idealist has convention and normality usually arraigned against him. Idealism plays often imply the desirability of reforming society as a whole, of redefining values, or of preventing a social change that is under way. The idealist typically has to fight against materialism, conventional moral scruples, self-interest, prejudice, pettiness, stupidity, weakness of character, personal desires, lesser loyalties, conflicting systems of ideals. These forces may be external or within himself. Included under idealism are plots that stress an extraordinary sense of duty, loyalty or patriotism, or a single-minded devotion to a "cause."

The Power Theme

The power theme deals with the problems that arise from the conflict between two individuals or groups for the same object, territory, position of authority, or controlling influence over a situation. It includes personal conflicts for power, class conflicts, ideological conflicts, revolutions, war, etc. Also included are plays in which a central character seeks power against such obstacles as his own inferiority or his more tender impulses. Frequently the struggle involves the use of violence, ruthlessness, trickery or cold-bloodness on the part of one or both adversaries. In power conflicts, the more powerful side usually comes to dominate the situation; but it is not necessarily the better side that wins—in fact, the reverse is true if the worse side is stronger. Plays that are principally structured and resolved in terms of who is right and who is wrong, or who is good and who is bad, do not, of course, fall under the power category. Power may be represented by a number of different factors: physical material means, strength of character, ruthlessness of purpose in pursuit of a goal, lack of "soft" emotions, courage, cunning, trickery.

The Career Theme

In career themes a central character is attempting to win personal success in his occupation, to make money, create a work of art, or advance his professional status. The goal is personal achievement, not the success of an ideal, system, way of life, nation or other super-individual institutions. Various obstacles block the path to success.

The Outcast Theme

In a number of plays we find as a central character a person who is placed outside normality or normal society by some handicap, abnormality, inferiority or stigma. This may be a physical handicap—deformity or extreme ugliness or illness; a mental handicap—some form of mental disease; a political handicap—the condition of being an exile; or any one of a number of social handicaps, such as being a criminal, prisoner, outlaw, vagabond, pauper, Negro, bastard, prostitute. The play dwells upon the relationship of this person to normal society, his reactions to society or society's reactions to him. It may show, for example, how he seeks normal love and acceptance, how he reacts with cunning or brutality to his outcast status, how he is not himself responsible for his status, how society misunderstands and abuses him. Sometimes the outcast has a superior perspective and is also an idealist. *If a criminal or other outcast is the central character of a play, the play ordinarily falls under the outcast theme.* But if the central character is clearly a normal individual and the criminal is his adversary, representing evil forces, then the play is to be classified under the morality theme, since the interest here is not in portraying the problems of the outcast, but the conflict between good and evil. Not included in this category are plays in which the suspicion or accusation of say, murder, is falsely attributed to innocent persons, and the action of the plot is centered about revelation of the true situation. The outcast status must be real, recognized as such by both society and the individual. Plays are not included in which a person, nominally a deviant, enjoys popularity because of his deviance.

RESULTS

Table 1 indicates the percentage of plays in each national group falling under each of the basic themes, as defined by a majority of the nine judges. American plays, it can be seen, are primarily concerned with love and personal morals. The German plays are considerably more preoccupied with idealism, power, and the problems of the abnormal or outcast. Little difference appears in personal career themes.

TABLE 1
The Basic Themes

| | U.S. | | German | |
	N	%	N	%
Love	27	60%	14	31%
Morality	16	36	4	9
Idealism	2	4	20	44
Power	1	2	15	33
Outcast	0	0	8	18
Career	5	11	4	9
No agreement	6	13	1	2

The love and morality themes often go together — 10 of the 20 plays that contain morality themes (U.S. and German combined) were also scored as having love themes. Similarly, idealism and power tend to go together: 5 of the 16 plays considered to express power conflicts were also considered to contain the idealism theme.

Table 2 indicates that the German plays are strikingly more pre-occupied with social and political problems than are the American plays. Their level of action is primarily ideological; the basic conflict is between forces that represent divergent social, political or economic interests, or divergent philosophies of life. The problems portrayed in the American plays, on the other hand, are overwhelmingly personal — love affairs, family affairs, difficulties and hostilities on a non-ideological level. The German ideological emphasis is obviously tied up closely with the emphasis on the idealism theme.

The German plays also have more unhappy endings than do the American plays (Table 3). Connected with this is the fact that the side of virtue consistently

TABLE 2
The Level of Action

	U.S.	German
Ideological	4%	51%
Personal	96	47
No agreement	0	2

130

wins out in the American plays, but the unsympathetic side often comes out on top in the German. Frequently in the German plays the central character is a ruthless, treacherous, or egotistic individual who wins success because of these very qualities.

TABLE 3
The Endings

	U.S.	German
Happy	67%	40%
Ambiguous	24	29
Tragic or unhappy	9	27
No agreement	0	4

The German central characters tend to be older and more often males than is the case in the American plays (Table 4). More noteworthy than these statistics, however, is the difference in the type of woman who plays a central role. When a female carries the burden of the plot in American drama, she tends to possess in eminent degree qualities that are considered feminine—beauty, emotionality, charm, tenderness, softness, motherliness, etc. But when a female is the central character in a German play, she tends to be strong, and an aggressive type of person who outdoes men in their own territory—she defeats men in economic competition, ruthlessly exploits male weakness, rejects lovers who have too soft a character, refuses to give way to love because this would interfere with her more serious purposes, etc. In short, femininity as such may be as important as masculinity in the American plays, but rarely in the German plays where female equality of importance seems to be possible only by achieving masculine qualities and values.

TABLE 4
The Central Characters

		U.S.	German
Sex	Male	19	33
	Female	15	9
	Couple (male & female)	6	0
	Larger mixed group	5	3
Age	Youthful	23	13
	Middle-aged or elderly	13	19
	Indeterminate or mixed	9	13

In keeping with the fact that more of the German plays are on a social level there is a further distinction at once apparent—the German central characters are more frequently social types; that is, their social status or role plays an important part in the logic of the plot. They behave as they do because they are proponents of a cause, princes, rulers, generals, political functionaries, exiles, typical representatives of a social class, etc. The American central characters, on the other hand, are more "ordinary people" whose role or status has less critical bearing on the plot—their occupation could be changed without basically altering the plot. The social type that seems to be favored as the central character in the American theater of 1927 is the entertainer or artist, although the detective-policeman and the man of great wealth also turn up.

On the basis of what the authors and critics in their respective countries call "light" and "serious" plays, there was no national difference in relative frequency. In both countries the ratio was approximately two light plays to three serious plays. This ratio also holds if we consider not the specific samples chosen but the total number of dramatic productions in each country in 1927. Marked differences appear, however, in the time and place of the action presented in the plays (Table 5).

TABLE 5
Time and Place of Action

	U.S.	German
Contemporary (1920-1927)	42	23
Historical		
1789-1919	1	7
1453-1788	1	9
antiquity	1	1
No specific time: sagas, fairy tales, symbolic fantasies	0	5
Domestic setting	41	26
Foreign or legendary setting	4	19

The figures reflect a German predilection for historical plays. Seventeen plays out of our sample, and thirty-four per cent of the total German drama production in 1927, fall into this category. But the German drama also takes leave of the contemporary domestic scene through legends and fantasies, and through foreign settings. One curious result is the fact that in the year 1927 more plays on a subject of American history were produced in Germany than in the United States. The German departure from the contemporary scene, however, must not be taken as evidence of a flight from current social problems. It indicates rather a German tendency to view these problems *sub specie aeternitatis.* Such plays appear designed to have a deep meaning for the present.

*   *   *   *   *

Summary and Conclusions

1. The 45 most popular new plays in Germany and the United States in 1927 were analysed for psychological content. A smaller sample from 1909-10 were also examined. Independent judges, from whom the difference in national origin was concealed, were used to classify the 1927 plays according to certain major categories of analysis.

2. The German plays are considerably more ideological, philosophical, historical and social-minded than the American plays; the latter dwell on private problems, the difficulties of achieving love and virtue in daily life.

3. The German hero tends to be an individual with a distinct role who stands above or outside of normal society: a visionary pursuing a cause, a prince more far-seeing and liberal than his subjects, a social outcast. The American hero tends to be a more ordinary person from society's midst.

4. The central character is less frequently a woman in the German plays than in the American; and where women do have central roles in the German drama, they tend to take over masculine characteristics and masculine types of action — "femininity" as commonly understood, feminine qualities and feminine emotional reactions, do not get the attention they receive in the American drama.

5. In American love plots, the emphasis is upon the working out of a solution to conflicts and difficulties arising from external obstacles (e.g., parents, criminals) or from the lovers themselves (e.g., misunderstandings, immoral impulses). The path of love is precarious until some final adjustment is made. In the German plays, two individuals may be deeply united in "idyllic" love by virtue of sharing common ideals; or a physical scene or locale, charged with emotion and meaning, may provide a context for idyllic love. The German lovers, however, may be once and for all cut asunder when higher (deeper) values so dictate. The German plays do not feature the love relationship as dependent upon the solution of emotional difficulties in personal relations.

6. The American orientation is essentially moralistic, the German orientation idealistic. The American hero must struggle against immoral or anti-social tendencies in himself or in other specific individuals; such tendencies are portrayed as interfering with the normal realization of personal happiness. The German hero who stands above the masses and is pursuing an ideal goal, a blueprint for society, may have to struggle against the normal practices of society itself. The value pattern expressed in the American plays enjoins the individual to be considerate of the welfare of other specific individuals; at the same time he must watch out for his own welfare. The German idealistic hero, on the other hand, in order to be successful, must consider neither his own welfare nor the welfare of other specific individuals. He must consider only the fulfilment of his high aim.

7. Personal ambitions and satisfactions, which are sanctioned in the American plays, are frequently portrayed as the root obstacle in the German plays, the

133

"materialism" against which the idealist must fight. Similarly, conventional moral standards which in the American plays promote success and happiness, often appear in the German drama to be petty, hypocritical, mean and confining; the German hero must frequently fight against "Philistinism" as well as materialism.

8. Personal crimes and sins, which pose basic problems in the American plays, are frequently excused, or justified in the German plays. Society is pictured as responsible, rather than the individual; or an act judged wrongly by society is interpreted as good because society's judgment is petty and narrow; or a criminal act, though not approved *per se,* is necessitated by Fate and the logic of the German idealism. We find for example, various murders of beloved persons consciously carried out by sympathetically portrayed characters in the German plays. The American hero, placed in the same type of dilemma into which the German hero falls, might well make the same choice of action—but he does not get into the same dilemma.

9. While the American plays carry the lesson that virtue has pragmatic sanction, the lesson to be found in the German plays is that success in worldly conflicts is won through power and ruthlessness. Without power, idealism is doomed to failure. The German drama accordingly places great emphasis upon strength of character, the determined, even ruthless pursuit of long-range goals. The strong and ruthless national idealist was a German favorite of 1909-10, the humanitarian idealist overwhelmed by strong, ruthless enemies a favorite of 1927.

10. The good side usually wins in the resolution of conflicts in the American drama because some individual in a critical position changes his mind. The hero or heroine who has sinned may undergo character reform, an opposing parent, a criminal or an estranged lover may change his attitude, or, in the last analysis, an independent tribunal of law or public opinion may be persuaded to change its opinion and recognize truth and justice. The reform of attitude or character is usually brought about through some persuasive argument or evidence, rational or irrational, such as legalistic evidence, humanitarian reasoning, a dream occasioned by eating a piece of cheese, a slap on the face, a wife's leaving her husband, the presence of a baby, sympathetic love, sickness or injury, strokes of fortune, sudden consequences that teach a lesson. Acts of ingenuity are often the means by which the compelling evidence is marshalled. The assumption that there is a reliable fundament of good will and good sense in society open to persuasion, that human beings can and will change, provided the proper argument is brought to bear upon them, this assumption of educability and reform pervades the American drama, but is relatively lacking in the German drama. There it is assumed, on the contrary, that human beings are inflexible, uncompromising; they are narrow in their vision, petty and rigid in their interpretation of their status and their adherence to the canons of respectability. Even the law does not serve as an ultimate recourse, for it, too, may operate in a petty, narrow manner. It is consistent with this view of human nature and human society that conflicts are not resolved in the German drama so much

through the marshalling of evidence to change attitudes, as through power techniques.

11. Both the German and American plays express rebellion against authority: the American, against parents and others who interfere in the individual's life happiness; the German, against political superiors, classes, or society itself. The American rebels in the name of his personal right to happiness. This right is a positive value, and forces opposed to it are portrayed as immoral, evil, or at least ill-advised. There is no such right to individual happiness clearly presumed to justify rebellion against authority in the German plays. When a German rebels, he must do so, not in self interest, but in the name of an ideal, a set of values that are superior to those of the authority against which he is rebelling. Each individual German rebellion thus tends to be an ideological movement. A solution to the American rebellion is provided — the individual who is wrong, whether the rebel or the authority, can admit his guilt and reform. But the German rebel cannot reform, since his is the superior position; and authority will not reform. Hence there is no solution in the way of reintegration; the losing side must depart or die or drink its bitter cup in silence.

2. *National Power as a Modifier of Preferences*

As was suggested earlier, the goal preferences of a nation, regardless of their extravagance and romanticism, will always be somewhat tempered by the degree of power available for their pursuit. That is, in order to realize certain aspirations within and against a resistant (to put it mildly) environment, the decision-makers must continually develop and appraise their organization's power. The observer's analysis of the power of an actor may follow one of several paths. One way, quite traditional in international relations, is to measure such tangible or intangible bases of power as population size and skill, natural resources, industrial plant, governmental efficiency, weapons technology, men under arms, morale, and so on. These so-called objective indices, separately or in combination, may ultimately pay off as predictors of the outcomes of power-confrontation, but to date progress in this area of research has been slight.[1]

A second approach is to employ a more dynamic measure, based upon an actor's actual *use* of power in attempting to influence another. This latter is, of course, far more difficult to operationalize, but in Part Three

---

[1]One of the more sophisticated efforts to analyze and interpret these objective data is in F. Clifford German, "A Tentative Evaluation of World Power," *The Journal of Conflict Resolution*, IV (1960), 138-44.

(where the focus will be upon the vigorous interaction among actors) two rather successful attempts to use this approach will be presented. The following excerpts, however, are from a paper which uses a method that falls somewhere in between the static and the dynamic. That is, French and Raven seek to identify the bases of power by examining specific types of relationships between influencer (O for Other, in their lexicon) and influencee (P for Person) in given social settings. Although one might argue that few if any of these bases are relevant to inter-nation influence, it is important to bear in mind that all *have been* relevant at one time or another and may well become operative again. Moreover, the type of power base used and emphasized by nations is itself a major factor in determining which ones will be most effective in the future: that is, the more that nations rely upon coercion, the less the likelihood that other forms of power will be developed and exploited.

THE BASES OF SOCIAL POWER

JOHN R. P. FRENCH, JR. AND BERTRAM RAVEN

*　　*　　*　　*　　*

THE BASES OF POWER

By the basis of power we mean the relationship between O and P which is the *source* of that power [emphasis added]. It is rare that we can say with certainty that a given empirical case of power is limited to one source. Normally, the relation between O and P will be characterized by several qualitatively different variables which are bases of power. Although there are undoubtedly many possible bases of power which may be distinguished, we shall here define five which seem especially common and important. These five bases of O's power are: (1) reward power, based on P's perception that O has the ability to mediate rewards for him; (2) coercive power, based on P's perception that O has the ability to mediate punishments for him; (3) legitimate power, based on the perception by P that O has a legitimate right to prescribe behavior for him; (4) referent power, based on P's identification with O; (5) expert power, based on the perception that O has some special knowledge or expertness.

From John R. P. French, Jr., and Bertram Raven, "The Bases of Social Power," in Dorwin Cartwright (ed.), *Studies in Social Power* (Ann Arbor: University of Michigan, Institute for Social Research, 1959), pp. 150-67 (the footnotes and the bibliography and references have been omitted). Reprinted by permission of the authors and the University of Michigan Institute for Social Research.

Our first concern is to define the bases which give rise to a given type of power. Next, we describe each type of power according to its strength, range, and the degree of dependence of the new state of the system which is most likely to occur with each type of power. We shall also examine the other effects which the exercise of a given type of power may have upon P and his relationship to O. Finally, we shall point out the interrelationships between different types of power, and the effects of use of one type of power by O upon other bases of power which he might have over P. Thus we shall both define a set of concepts and propose a series of hypotheses. Most of these hypotheses have not been systematically tested, although there is a good deal of evidence in favor of several. No attempt will be made to summarize that evidence here.

Reward Power

Reward power is defined as power whose basis is the ability to reward. The strength of the reward power of O/P increases with the magnitude of the rewards which P perceives that O can mediate for him. Reward power depends on O's ability to administer positive valences and to remove or decrease negative valences. The strength of reward power also depends upon the probability that O can mediate the reward, as perceived by P. A common example of reward power is the addition of a piece-work rate in the factory as an incentive to increase production.

The new state of the system induced by a promise of reward (for example the factory worker's increased level of production) will be highly dependent on O. Since O mediates the reward, he controls the probability that P will receive it. Thus P's new rate of production will be dependent on his subjective probability that O will reward him for conformity minus his subjective probability that O will reward him even if he returns to his old level. Both probabilities will be greatly affected by the level of observability of P's behavior. Incidentally, a piece rate often seems to have more effect on production than a merit rating system because it yields a higher probability of reward for conformity and a much lower probability of reward for nonconformity.

The utilization of actual rewards (instead of promises) by O will tend over time to increase the attraction of P toward O and therefore the referent power of O over P. As we shall note later, such referent power will permit O to induce changes which are relatively independent. Neither rewards nor promises will arouse resistance in P, provided P considers it legitimate for O to offer rewards.

The range of reward power is specific to those regions within which O can reward P for conforming. The use of rewards to change systems within the range of reward power tends to increase reward power by increasing the probability attached to future promises. However, unsuccessful attempts to exert reward power outside the range of power would tend to decrease the power; for example if O offers to reward P for performing an impossible act, this will reduce for P the probability of receiving future rewards promised by O.

137

Coercive Power

Coercive power is similar to reward power in that it also involves O's ability to manipulate the attainment of valences [positive and negative incentives]. Coercive power of O/P stems from the expectation on the part of P that he will be punished by O if he fails to conform to the influence attempt. Thus negative valences will exist in given regions of P's life space, corresponding to the threatened punishment by O. The strength of coercive power depends on the magnitude of the negative valence of the threatened punishment multiplied by the perceived probability that P can avoid the punishment by conformity, i.e., the probability of punishment for nonconformity minus the probability of punishment for conformity. Just as an offer of a piece-rate bonus in a factory can serve as a basis for reward power, so the ability to fire a worker if he falls below a given level of production will result in coercive power.

Coercive power leads to dependent change also; and the degree of dependence varies with the level of observability of P's conformity. An excellent illustration of coercive power leading to dependent change is provided by a clothes presser in a factory observed by Coch and French. As her efficiency rating climbed above average for the group the other workers began to "scapegoat" her. That the resulting plateau in her production was not independent of the group was evident once she was removed from the presence of the other workers. Her production immediately climbed to new heights.

At times, there is some difficulty in distinguishing between reward power and coercive power. Is the withholding of a reward really equivalent to a punishment? Is the withdrawal of punishment equivalent to a reward? The answer must be a psychological one—it depends upon the situation as it exists for P. But ordinarily we would answer these questions in the affirmative; for P, receiving a reward is a positive valence as is the relief of suffering. There is some evidence that conformity to group norms in order to gain acceptance (reward power) should be distinguished from conformity as a means of forestalling rejection (coercive power).

The distinction between these two types of power is important because the dynamics are different. The concept of "sanctions" sometimes lumps the two together despite their opposite effects. While reward power may eventually result in an independent system, the effects of coercive power will continue to be dependent. Reward power will tend to increase the attraction of P toward O; coercive power will decrease this attraction. The valence of the region of behavior will become more negative, acquiring some negative valence from the threatened punishment. The negative valence of punishment would also spread to other regions of the life space. Lewin has pointed out this distinction between the effects of rewards and punishment. In the case of threatened punishment, there will be a resultant force on P to leave the field entirely. Thus, to achieve conformity, O must not only place a strong negative valence in certain regions through threat of punishment, but O must also introduce restraining

138

forces, or other strong valences, so as to prevent P from withdrawing completely from O's range of coercive power. Otherwise the probability of receiving the punishment, if P does not conform, will be too low to be effective.

Legitimate Power

Legitimate power is probably the most complex of those treated here, embodying notions from the structural sociologist, the group-norm and role oriented social psychologist, and the clinical psychologist.

There has been considerable investigation and speculation about socially prescribed behavior, particularly that which is specific to a given role or position. Linton distinguishes group norms according to whether they are universals for everyone in the culture, alternatives (the individual having a choice as to whether or not to accept them), or specialties (specific to given positions). Whether we speak of internalized norms, role prescriptions and expectations, or internalized pressures, the fact remains that each individual sees certain regions toward which he should locomote, some regions toward which he should not locomote, and some regions toward which he may locomote if they are generally attractive for him. This applies to specific behaviors in which he may, should, or should not engage; it applies to certain attitudes or beliefs which he may, should, or should not hold. The feeling of "oughtness" may be an internalization from his parents, from his teachers, from his religion, or may have been logically developed from some idiosyncratic system of ethics. He will speak of such behaviors with expressions like "should," "ought to," or "has a right to." In many cases, the original source of the requirement is not recalled.

Though we have oversimplified such evaluations of behavior with a positive-neutral-negative trichotomy, the evaluation of behaviors by the person is really more one of degree. This dimension of evaluation, we shall call "legitimacy." Conceptually, we may think of legitimacy as a valence in a region which is induced by some internalized norm or value. This value has the same conceptual property as power, namely an ability to induce force fields. It may or may not be correct that values (or the superego) are internalized parents, but at least they can set up force fields which have a phenomenal "oughtness" similar to a parent's prescription. Like a value, a need can also induce valences (i.e., force fields) in P's psychological environment, but these valences have more the phenomenal character of noxious or attractive properties of the object or activity. When a need induces a valence in P, for example, when a need makes an object attractive to P, this attraction applies to P but not to other persons. When a value induces a valence, on the other hand, it not only sets up forces on P to engage in the activity, but P may feel that all others ought to behave in the same way. Among other things, this evaluation applies to the legitimate right of some other individual or group to prescribe behavior or beliefs for a person even though the other cannot apply sanctions.

Legitimate power of O/P is here defined as that power which stems from internalized values in P which dictate that O has a legitimate right to influence P and that P has an obligation to accept this influence. We note that legitimate power is very similar to the notion of legitimacy of authority which has long been explored by sociologists, particularly by Weber, and more recently by Gold-hamer and Shils. However, legitimate power is not always a role relation: P may accept an induction from O simply because he had previously promised to help O and he values his word too much to break the promise. In all cases, the notion of legitimacy involves some sort of code or standard, accepted by the individual, by virtue of which the external agent can assert his power. We shall attempt to describe a few of these values here.

Bases for Legitimate Power

Cultural values constitute one common basis for the legitimate power of one individual over another. O has characteristics which are specified by the culture as giving him the right to prescribe behavior for P, who may not have these characteristics. These bases, which Weber has called the authority of the "eternal yesterday," include such things as age, intelligence, caste, and physical character-istics. In some cultures, the aged are granted the right to prescribe behavior for others in practically all behavior areas. In most cultures, there are certain areas of behavior in which a person of one sex is granted the right to prescribe behavior for the other sex.

Acceptance of the social structure is another basis for legitimate power. If P accepts as right the social structure of his group, organization, or society, especially the social structure involving a hierarchy of authority, P will accept the legitimate authority of O who occupies a superior office in the hierarchy. Thus legitimate power in a formal organization is largely a relationship between offices rather than between persons. And the acceptance of an office as *right* is a basis for legitimate power — a judge has a right to levy fines, a foreman should assign work, a priest is justified in prescribing religious beliefs, and it is the manage-ment's prerogative to make certain decisions. However, legitimate power also involves the perceived right of the person to hold the office.

Designation by a legitimizing agent is a third basis for legitimate power. An influencer O may be seen as legitimate in prescribing behavior for P because he has been granted such power by a legitimizing agent whom P accepts. Thus a department head may accept the authority of his vice-president in a certain area because that authority has been specifically delegated by the president. An election is perhaps the most common example of a group's serving to legitimize the authority of one individual or office for other individuals in the group. The success of such legitimizing depends upon the acceptance of the legitimizing agent and procedure. In this case it depends ultimately on certain democratic values concerning election procedures. The election process is one of legitimiz-ing a person's right to an office which already has a legitimate range of power associated with it.

Range of Legitimate Power of O/P

The areas in which legitimate power may be exercised are generally specified along with the designation of that power. A job description, for example, usually specifies supervisory activities and also designates the person to whom the job-holder is responsible for the duties described. Some bases for legitimate authority carry with them a very broad range. Culturally derived bases for legitimate power are often especially broad. It is not uncommon to find cultures in which a member of a given caste can legitimately prescribe behavior for all members of lower castes in practically all regions. More common, however, are instances of legitimate power where the range is specifically and narrowly prescribed. A sergeant in the army is given a specific set of regions within which he can legitimately prescribe behavior for his men.

The attempted use of legitimate power which is outside of the range of legitimate power will decrease the legitimate power of the authority figure. Such use of power which is not legitimate will also decrease the attractiveness of O.

Legitimate Power and Influence

The new state of the system which results from legitimate power usually has high dependence on O though it may become independent. Here, however, the degree of dependence is not related to the level of observability. Since legitimate power is based on P's values, the source of the forces induced by O include both these internal values and O. O's induction serves to activate the values and to relate them to the system which is influenced, but thereafter the new state of the system may become directly dependent on the values with no mediation by O. Accordingly this new state will be relatively stable and consistent across varying environmental situations since P's values are more stable than his psychological environment.

We have used the term legitimate not only as a basis for the power of an agent, but also to describe the general behaviors of a person. Thus, the individual P may also consider the legitimacy of the attempts to use other types of power by O. In certain cases, P will consider that O has a legitimate right to threaten punishment for nonconformity; in other cases, such use of coercion would not be seen as legitimate. P might change in response to coercive power of O, but it will make a considerable difference in his attitude and conformity if O is not seen as having a legitimate right to use such coercion. In such cases, the attraction of P for O will be particularly diminished, and the influence attempt will arouse more resistance. Similarly the utilization of reward power may vary in legitimacy; the word "bribe," for example, denotes an illegitimate reward.

Referent Power

The referent power of O/P has its basis in the identification of P with O. By identification, we mean a feeling of oneness of P with O, or a desire for such an identity. If O is a person toward whom P is highly attracted, P will have a desire to become closely associated with O. If O is an attractive group, P will have a feeling of membership or a desire to join. If P is already closely associated with O he will want to maintain this relationship. P's identification with O can be established or maintained if P behaves, believes, and perceives as O does. Accordingly O has the ability to influence P, even though P may be unaware of this referent power. A verbalization of such power by P might be, "I am like O, and therefore I shall behave or believe as O does," or "I want to be like O, and I will be more like O if I behave or believe as O does." The stronger the identification of P with O the greater the referent power of O/P.

Similar types of power have already been investigated under a number of different formulations. Festinger points out that in an ambiguous situation, the individual seeks some sort of "social reality" and may adopt the cognitive structure of the individual or group with which he identifies. In such a case, the lack of clear structure may be threatening to the individual and the agreement of his beliefs with those of a reference group will both satisfy his need for structure and give him added security through increased identification with his group.

We must try to distinguish between referent power and other types of power which might be operative at the same time. If a member is attracted to a group and he conforms to its norms only because he fears ridicule or expulsion from the group for nonconformity, we would call this coercive power. On the other hand if he conforms in order to obtain praise for conformity, it is a case of reward power. The basic criterion for distinguishing referent power from both coercive and reward power is the mediation of the punishment and the reward by O: to the extent that O mediates the sanctions (i.e., has means control over P) we are dealing with coercive and reward power; but to the extent that P avoids discomfort or gains satisfaction by conformity based on identification, regardless of O's responses, we are dealing with referent power. Conformity with majority opinion is sometimes based on a respect for the collective wisdom of the group, in which case it is expert power. It is important to distinguish these phenomena, all grouped together elsewhere as "pressures toward uniformity," since the type of change which occurs will be different for different bases of power.

The concepts of "reference group" and "prestige suggestion" may be treated as instances of referent power. In this case, O, the prestigeful person or group, is valued by P; because P desires to be associated or identified with O, he will assume attitudes or beliefs held by O. Similarly a negative reference group which O dislikes and evaluates negatively may exert negative influence on P as a result of negative referent power.

It has been demonstrated that the power which we designate as referent power is especially great when P is attracted to O. In our terms, this would mean that the greater the attraction, the greater the identification, and consequently the greater the referent power. In some cases, attraction or prestige may have a specific basis, and the range of referent power will be limited accordingly: a group of campers may have great referent power over a member regarding campcraft, but considerably less effect on other regions. However, we hypothesize that the greater the attraction of P toward O, the broader the range of referent power of O/P.

The new state of a system produced by referent power may be dependent on or independent of O; but the degree of dependence is not affected by the level of observability to O. In fact, P is often not consciously aware of the referent power which O exerts over him. There is probably a tendency for some of these dependent changes to become independent of O quite rapidly.

Expert Power

The strength of the expert power of O/P varies with the extent of the knowledge or perception which P attributes to O within a given area. Probably P evaluates O's expertness in relation to his own knowledge as well as against an absolute standard. In any case expert power results in primary social influence on P's cognitive structure and probably not on other types of systems. Of course changes in the cognitive structure can change the direction of forces and hence of locomotion, but such a change of behavior is secondary social influence. Expert power has been demonstrated experimentally. Accepting an attorney's advice in legal matters is a common example of expert influence; but there are many instances based on much less knowledge, such as the acceptance by a stranger of directions given by a native villager.

Expert power, where O need not be a member of P's group, is called "informational power" by Deutsch and Gerard. This type of expert power must be distinguished from influence based on the content of communication as described by Hovland et al. The influence of the content of a communication upon an opinion is presumably a secondary influence produced after the *primary* influence (i.e., the acceptance of the information). Since power is here defined in terms of the primary changes, the influence of the content on a related opinion is not a case of expert power as we have defined it, but the initial acceptance of the validity of the content does seem to be based on expert power or referent power. In other cases, however, so-called facts may be accepted as self-evident because they fit into P's cognitive structure; if this impersonal acceptance of the truth of the fact is independent of the more or less enduring relationship between O and P, then P's acceptance of the fact is not an actualization of expert power. Thus we distinguish between expert power based on the credibility of O and informational influence which is based on characteristics of the stimulus such as the logic of the argument or the "self-evident facts."

Wherever expert influence occurs it seems to be necessary both for P to think that O knows and for P to trust that O is telling the truth (rather than trying to deceive him).

Expert power will produce a new cognitive structure which is initially relatively dependent on O, but informational influence will produce a more independent structure. The former is likely to become more independent with the passage of time. In both cases the degree of dependence on O is not affected by the level of observability.

The "sleeper effect" is an interesting case of a change in the degree of dependence of an opinion on O. An unreliable O (who probably had negative referent power but some positive expert power) presented "facts" which were accepted by the subjects and which would normally produce secondary influence on their opinions and beliefs. However, the negative referent power aroused resistance and resulted in negative social influence on their beliefs (i.e., set up a force in the direction opposite to the influence attempt), so that there was little change in the subjects' opinions. With the passage of time, however, the subjects tended to forget the identity of the negative communicator faster than they forgot the contents of his communication, so there was a weakening of the negative referent influence and a consequent delayed positive change in the subjects' beliefs in the direction of the influence attempt ("sleeper effect"). Later, when the identity of the negative communicator was experimentally reinstated, these resisting forces were reinstated, and there was another negative change in belief in a direction opposite to the influence attempt.

The range of expert power, we assume, is more delimited than that of referent power. Not only is it restricted to cognitive systems but the expert is seen as having superior knowledge or ability in very specific areas, and his power will be limited to these areas, though some "halo effect" might occur. Recently, some of our renowned physical scientists have found quite painfully that their expert power in physical sciences does not extend to regions involving international politics. Indeed, there is some evidence that the attempted exertion of expert power outside of the range of expert power will reduce that expert power. An undermining of confidence seems to take place.

SUMMARY

We have distinguished five types of power: referent power, expert power, reward power, coercive power, and legitimate power. These distinctions led to the following hypotheses.

1. For all five types, the stronger the basis of power the greater the power.

2. For any type of power the size of the range may vary greatly, but in general referent power will have the broadest range.

3. Any attempt to utilize power outside the range of power will tend to reduce the power.

4. A new state of a system produced by reward power or coercive power will be highly dependent on O, and the more observable P's conformity the more dependent the state. For the other three types of power, the new state is usually dependent, at least in the beginning, but in any case the level of observability has no effect on the degree of dependence.

5. Coercion results in decreased attraction of P toward O and high resistance; reward power results in increased attraction and low resistance.

6. The more legitimate the coercion the less it will produce resistance and decreased attraction.

3. Matching Preferences to Power

The preceding selections were meant to indicate the sorts of variables that lead to a fairly *general* formulation of national goals. But no decision-making unit in a nation will be able to function effectively under so vague a rubric; goals must be refined and concretized in order to serve as a useful policy guide. The Thompson and McEwen paper examines the ongoing process of goal-setting and goal-changing in a formal organization which could easily be a Ministry of Defense or Foreign Affairs or an interministry standing committee. The reader should bear in mind the authors' use here of the term "environment" to refer not to the total, larger, environment, but to that segment of it closest at hand to the organization. For the purposes of this selection, the analogy will be to the public at large in a nation or to those other subnational organizations with which a Foreign or Defense Ministry, an Atomic Energy Commission, a legislative committee, or a political faction must interact in the development of over-all national policy.

ORGANIZATIONAL GOALS AND ENVIRONMENT: GOAL SETTING AS AN INTERACTION PROCESS

JAMES D. THOMPSON AND WILLIAM J. McEWEN

In the analysis of complex organizations the definition of organizational goals is commonly utilized as a standard for appraising organizational performance. In many such analyses the goals of the organization are often viewed as a constant. Thus a wide variety of data, such as official documents, work activity records, organizational output, or statements by organizational spokesmen, may provide the basis for the definition of goals. Once this definition has been accomplished, interest in goals as a dynamic aspect of organizational activity frequently ends.

It is possible, however, to view the setting of goals (i.e., major organizational purposes) not as a static element but as a necessary and recurring problem facing any organization, whether it is governmental, military, business, educational, medical, religious, or other type.

This perspective appears appropriate in developing the two major lines of the

From James D. Thompson and William J. McEwen, "Organizational Goals and Environment: Goal Setting as an Interaction Process," *American Sociological Review*, XXIII (1958), 23-31 (the footnotes have been omitted). Reprinted by permission of the authors and The American Sociological Association.

present analysis. The first of these is to emphasize the interdependence of complex organizations within the larger society and the consequences this has for organizational goal-setting. The second is to emphasize the similarities of goal-setting *processes* in organizations with manifestly different goals. The present analysis is offered to supplement recent studies of organizational operations.

It is postulated that goal-setting behavior is *purposive* but not necessarily *rational*; we assume that goals may be determined by accident, i.e., by blundering of members of the organization and, contrariwise, that the most calculated and careful determination of goals may be negated by developments outside the control of organization members. The goal-setting problem as discussed here is essentially determining a relationship of the organization to the larger society, which in turn becomes a question of what the society (or elements within it) wants done or can be persuaded to support.

GOALS AS DYNAMIC VARIABLES

Because the setting of goals is essentially a problem of defining desired relationships between an organization and its environment, change in either requires review and perhaps alteration of goals. Even where the abstract statement of goals remains *constant,* application requires redefinition or interpretation as changes occur in the organization, the environment, or both.

* * * * *

Reappraisal of goals thus appears to be a recurrent problem for large organization, albeit a more constant problem in an unstable environment than in a stable one. Reappraisal of goals likewise appears to be more difficult as the "product" of the enterprise becomes less tangible and more difficult to measure objectively. The manufacturing firm has a relatively ready index of the acceptability of its product in sales figures; while poor sales may indicate inferior quality rather than public distaste for the commodity itself, sales totals frequently are supplemented by trade association statistics indicating the firm's "share of the market." Thus within a matter of weeks, a manufacturing firm may be able to reappraise its decision to enter the "widget" market and may therefore begin deciding how it can get out of that market with the least cost.

The governmental enterprise may have similar indicators of the acceptability of its goals if it is involved in producing an item such as electricity, but where its activity is oriented to a less tangible purpose such as maintaining favorable relations with foreign nations, the indices of effective operation are likely to be less precise and the vargaries more numerous. The degree to which a government satisfies its clientele [citizens] may be reflected periodically in elections, but despite the claims of party officials, it seldom is clear just what the mandate of the people is with reference to any particular governmental enterprise. In addition, the public is not always steadfast in its mandate.

* * * * *

146

ENVIRONMENTAL CONTROLS OVER GOALS

A continuing situation of necessary interaction between an organization and its environment introduces an element of environmental control into the organization. While the motives of personnel, including goal-setting officers, may be profits, prestige, votes, or the salvation of souls, their efforts must produce something useful or acceptable to at least a part of the organizational environment to win continued support.

In the simpler society, social control over productive activities may be exercised rather informally and directly through such means as gossip and ridicule. As a society becomes more complex and its productive activities more deliberately organized, social controls are increasingly exercised through such formal devices as contracts, legal codes, and governmental regulations. The stability of expectations provided by these devices is arrived at through interaction, and often through the exercise of power in interaction.

It is possible to conceive of a continuum of organizational power in environmental relations, ranging from the organization that dominates its environmental relations to one completely dominated by its environment. Few organizations approach either extreme. Certain gigantic industrial enterprises, such as the *Zaibatsu* in Japan or the old Standard Oil Trust in America, have approached the dominance-over-environment position at one time, but this position eventually brought about "countervailing powers." Perhaps the nearest approximation to the completely powerless organization is the commuter transit system, which may be unable to cover its costs but nevertheless is regarded as a necessary utility and cannot get permission to quit business. Most complex organizations, falling somewhere between the extremes of the power continuum, must adopt strategies for coming to terms with their environments. This is not to imply that such strategies are necessarily chosen by rational or deliberate processes. An organization can survive so long as it adjusts to its situation; whether the process of adjustment is awkward or nimble becomes important in determining the organization's degree of prosperity.

However arrived at, strategies for dealing with the organizational environment may be broadly classified as either *competitive* or *co-operative*. Both appear to be important in a complex society—of the "free enterprise" type or other. Both provide a measure of environmental control over organizations by providing for "outsiders" to enter into or limit organizational decision process.

The decision process may be viewed as a series of activities, conscious or not, culminating in a choice among alternatives. For purposes of this paper we view the decision-making process as consisting of the following activities:

1. Recognizing an occasion for decision, i.e., a need or an opportunity.
2. Analysis of the existing situation.
3. Identification of alternative courses of action.
4. Assessment of the probable consequences of each alternative.
5. Choice from among alternatives.

147

The following discussion suggests that the potential power of an outsider increases the earlier he enters into the decision process, and that competition and three sub-types of co-operative strategy—*bargaining, co-optation,* and *coalition*—differ in this respect. It is therefore possible to order these forms of interaction in terms of the degree to which they provide for environmental [or extra-agency] control over organizational goal-setting decisions.

Competition

The term competition implies an element of rivalry. For present purposes competition refers to that form of rivalry between two or more organizations which is mediated by a third party. In the case of the manufacturing firm the third party may be the customer, the supplier, the potential or present member of the labor force, or others. In the case of the governmental bureau, the third party through whom competition takes place may be the legislative committee, the budget bureau, or the chief executive, as well as potential clientele and potential members of the bureau.

The complexity of competition in a heterogeneous society is much greater than customary usage (with economic overtones) often suggests. Society judges the enterprise not only by the finished product but also in terms of the desirability of applying resources to that purpose. Even the organization that enjoys a product monopoly must compete for society's support. From the society it must obtain resources—personnel, finances, and materials—as well as customers or clientele. In the business sphere of a "free enterprise" economy this competition for resources and customers usually takes place in the market, but in times of crisis the society may exercise more direct controls, such as rationing or the establishment of priorities during a war. The monopoly competes with enterprises having different purposes or goals but using similar raw materials; it competes with many other enterprises, for human skills and loyalties, and it competes with many other activities for support in the money markets.

* * * * *

Competition, then, is one process whereby the organization's choice of goals is partially controlled by the environment. It tends to prevent unilateral or arbitrary choice of organizational goals, or to correct such a choice if one is made. Competition for society's support is an important means of eliminating not only efficient organizations but also those that seek to provide goods or services the environment is not willing to accept.

Bargaining

The term bargaining, as used here, refers to the negotiation of an agreement for the exchange of goods or services between two or more organizations. Even where fairly stable and dependable expectations have been built up with impor-

148

tant elements of the organizational environment—with suppliers, distributors, legislators, workers and so on—the organization cannot assume that these relationships will continue. Periodic review of these relationships must be accomplished, and an important means for this is bargaining, whereby each organization, through negotiation, arrives at a decision about future behavior satisfactory to the others involved.

*   *   *   *   *

Unlike competition, however, bargaining involves direct interaction with other organizations in the environment, rather than with a third party. Bargaining appears, therefore, to invade the actual decision process. To the extent that the second party's support is necessary he is in a position to exercise a veto over final choice of alternative goals, and hence takes part in the decision.

Co-Optation

Co-optation has been defined as the process of absorbing new elements into the leadership or policy-determining structure of an organization as a means of averting threats to its stability or existence. Co-optation makes still further inroads on the process of deciding goals; not only must the final choice be acceptable to the co-opted party or organization, but to the extent that co-optation is effective it places the representative of an "outsider" in a position to determine the occasion for a goal decision, to participate in analyzing the existing situation, to suggest alternatives, and to take part in the deliberation of consequences.

The term co-optation has only recently been given currency in this country, but the phenomenon it describes is neither new nor unimportant. The acceptance on a corporation's board of directors of representatives of banks or other financial institutions is a time-honored custom among firms that have large financial obligations or that may in the future want access to financial resources. The state university may find it expedient (if not mandatory) to place legislators on its board of trustees, and the endowed college may find that whereas the honorary degree brings forth a token gift, membership on the board may result in a more substantial bequest. The local medical society often plays a decisive role in hospital goal-setting, since the support of professional medical practitioners is urgently necessary for the hospital.

*   *   *   *   *

Coalition

As used here, the term coalition refers to a combination of two or more organizations for a common purpose. Coalition appears to be the ultimate or extreme form of environmental conditioning of organizational goals. A coalition may be unstable, but to the extent that it is operative, two or more organizations act as one with respect to certain goals. Coalition is a means widely used when two or more enterprises wish to pursue a goal calling for more support, especially for more resources, than any one of them is able to marshall unaided. American business firms frequently resort to coalition for purposes of research or product promotion and for the construction of such gigantic facilities as dams or atomic reactors.

* * * * *

Coalition requires a commitment for joint decision of future activities and thus places limits on unilateral or arbitrary decisions. Furthermore, inability of an organization to find partners in a coalition venture automatically prevents pursuit of that objective, and is therefore also a form of social control. If the collective judgment is that a proposal is unworkable, a possible disaster may be escaped and unproductive allocation of resources avoided.

DEVELOPMENT OF ENVIRONMENTAL SUPPORT

Environmental control is not a one-way process limited to consequences for the organization of action in its environment. Those subject to control are also part of the larger society and hence are also agents of social control. The enterprise that competes is not only influenced in its goal-setting by what the competitor and the third party may do, but also exerts influence over both. Bargaining likewise is a form of mutual, two-way influence; co-optation affects the co-opted as well as the co-opting party; and coalition clearly sets limits on both parties.

Goals appear to grow out of interaction, both within the organization and between the organization and its environment. While every enterprise must find sufficient support for its goals, it may wield initiative in this. The difference between effective and ineffective organizations may well lie in the initiative exercised by those in the organization who are responsible for goal-setting.

* * * * *

The activities involved in winning support for organizational goals thus are not confined to communication within the organization, however important this is. The need to justify organizational goals, to explain the social functions of the organization, is seen daily in all types of "public relations" activities, ranging from luncheon club speeches to house organs. It is part of an educational requirement in a complicated society where devious interdependence hides many of the functions of organized, specialized activities.

GOAL-SETTING AND STRATEGY

We have suggested that it is improbable that an organization can continue indefinitely, if its goals are formulated arbitrarily, without cognizance of its relations to the environment. One of the requirements for survival appears to be ability to learn about the environment accurately enough and quickly enough to permit organizational adjustments in time to avoid extinction. In a more positive vein, it becomes important for an organization to judge the amount and sources of support that can be mobilized for a goal, and to arrive at a strategy for their mobilization.

Competition, bargaining, co-optation, and coalition constitute procedures for gaining support from the organizational environment; the selection of one or more of these is a strategic problem. It is here that the element of rationality appears to become exceedingly important, for in the order treated above, these relational processes represent increasingly "costly" methods of gaining support in terms of decision-making power. The organization that adopts a strategy of competition when co-optation is called for may lose all opportunity to realize its goals, or may finally turn to co-optation or coalition at a higher "cost" than would have been necessary originally. On the other hand, an organization may lose part of its integrity, and therefore some of its potentiality, if it unnecessarily shares power in exchange for support. Hence the establishment *in the appropriate form* of interaction with the many relevant parts of its environment can be a major organizational consideration in a complex society.

This means, in effect, that the organization must be able to estimate the position of other relevant organizations and their willingness to enter into or alter relationships. Often, too, these matters must be determined or estimated without revealing one's own weaknesses, or even one's ultimate strength. It is necessary or advantageous, in other words, to have the consent or acquiescence of the other party, if a new relationship is to be established or an existing relationship altered. For this purpose organizational administrators often engage in what might be termed a *sounding out process*.

The sounding out process can be illustrated by the problem of the boss with amorous designs on his secretary in an organization that taboos such relations. He must find some means of determining her willingness to alter the relationship, but he must do so without risking rebuff, for a showdown might come at the cost of his dignity or his office reputation, at the cost of losing her secretarial services, or in the extreme case at the cost of losing his own position. The "sophisticated" procedure is to create an ambiguous situation in which the secretary is forced to respond in one of two ways: (1) to ignore or tactfully counter, thereby clearly channeling the relationship back into an already existing pattern, or (2) to respond in a similarly ambiguous vein (if not in a positive one) indicating a receptiveness to further advances. It is important in the sounding out process that the situation be ambiguous for two reasons: (1) the secretary must not be able to "pin down" the boss with evidence if she rejects the idea, and

(2) the situation must be far enough removed from normal to be noticeable to the secretary. The ambiguity of sounding out has the further advantage to the participants that neither party alone is clearly responsible for initiating the change.

The situation described above illustrates a process that seems to explain many organizational as well as personal interaction situations. In moving from one relationship to another between two or more organizations it is often necessary to leave a well defined situation and proceed through a period of deliberate ambiguity, to arrive at a new clear-cut relationship. In interaction over goal-setting problems, sounding out sometimes is done through a form of double-talk, wherein the parties refer to "hypothetical" enterprises and "hypothetical" situations, or in "diplomatic" language, which often serves the same purpose. In other cases, and perhaps more frequently, sounding out is done through the good offices of a third party. This occurs, apparently, where there has been no relationship in the past, or at the stage of negotiations where the parties have indicated intentions but are not willing to state their positions frankly. Here it becomes useful at times to find a discreet go-between who can be trusted with full information and who will seek an arrangement suitable to both parties.

CONCLUSION

In the complex modern society, desired goals often require complex organizations. At the same time the desirability of goals and the appropriate division of labor among large organizations is less self-evident than in simpler, more homogeneous society. Purpose becomes a question to be decided rather than an obvious matter.

To the extent that behavior of organization members is oriented to questions of goals or purposes, a science of organization must attempt to understand and explain that behavior. We have suggested one classification scheme, based on decision-making, as potentially useful in analyzing organizational-environmental interaction with respect to goal-setting and we have attempted to illustrate some aspects of its utility. It is hoped that the suggested scheme encompasses questions of rationality or irrationality without presuming either.

Argument by example, however, is at best only a starting point for scientific understanding and for the collection of evidence. Two factors make organizational goal-setting in a complex society a "big" research topic: the multiplicity of large organizations of diverse types and the necessity of studying them in diachronic perspective. We hope that our discussion will encourage critical thinking and the sharing of observations about the subject.

C. THE DECISION-MAKER'S ROLE

Keeping in mind the limits upon organizational behavior outlined above, this section now turns to some of the more specific factors that seem to affect complex decision-making processes. It might be expected that a book based on the social-psychological sciences would include here a series of papers dealing with personality variables; there has certainly been plenty of speculation on the degree to which these distinguishing characteristics of very diverse humans not only make generalization about human affairs futile, but produce highly disparate foreign policies. Thus, Kremlinologists of the post-World War II era enjoyed comparing Molotov, Vyshinsky, Shepilov, and Gromyko while assigning policy shifts to their personality differences; the same pastime has amused scores of American and other pundits as they "psychoanalyzed" Marshall, Acheson, Dulles, and Rusk.

The effect of top policy-makers' personalities (especially in the more centralized governments) should not be dismissed, but at the same time one must recognize how little variance in diplomatic outcomes can be accounted for by these variables in the bureaucratized decision-making of the mid-twentieth century. Thus, some fascinating data and theory on such personality phenomena as authoritarianism, ambiguity thresholds, manifest anxiety, or the need to achieve are quite consciously omitted here. Where they enter into national character and find fairly uniform expression throughout a society and, hence, affect *public* opinion or the outlooks of *almost all elites,* it is, of course, another story. To put it another way, the assumption here is that those structural and cultural aspects of the decision-making organization found in most of the industrialized, and many of the transitional, societies will exercise an

153

effect which should partly negate *intra*national as well as *cross*national personality discrepancies.[1]

Thus, this section will not be particularly concerned either with who the decision-makers are or with how they are selected,[2] but rather with the sorts of psychological pressures under which they operate, once they are in the foreign policy organization. In other words, are there some factors at work in a decision-making agency or bureau which are likely to produce behavior peculiar to that particular type of structural setting?

1. The Impact of Role

First of all, there is the well-known effect of role (or role change) itself, which suggests that the same individual will perform in appreciably different ways, depending on the role he occupies at any one moment.

When one is a teacher or researcher, for example, he has little direct and immediate responsibility for a nation's security, and there are few internal or external pressures standing in the way of genuine candidness. But when the professor becomes a consultant, his role requirements undergo considerable modification. And if he actually becomes a full-time legislator or foreign ministry official, these requirements can be expected to change even more radically. The same may be said of a lawyer who becomes an official, a businessman or soldier who becomes a legislator, or a legislator who becomes an under-secretary. As Lieberman indicates in the study which follows, the pressure to conform to the expectations of a new peer group is only one of the factors at work; every role change can be expected to produce attitudinal and behavioral change, and, in the same vein, the most diverse personalities will tend to converge if they are put into the same policy-making role.

---

[1]Some compelling evidence in support of this assumption is in James N. Rosenau, "The Socialization of Foreign Policy Officials: An Assessment of the Relative Potency of Individual and Role Variables," in J. David Singer (ed.), *Quantitative Research in International Politics* (New York: The Free Press of Glencoe, in press).

[2]Some important research on this question has been done by Donald R. Matthews, *Social Background of Political Decision-Makers* (New York: Random House, 1954), and *U.S. Senators and Their World* (Chapel Hill: University of North Carolina Press, 1960). See also: Dean E. Mann, *Federal Political Executives* (Washington: Brookings Institution, 1964); and W. Lloyd Warner, *et al., The American Federal Executive: A Study of the Social and Personal Character of Civilian and Military Leaders of the U.S. Federal Government* (New Haven, Conn.: Yale University Press, 1963).

THE EFFECTS OF CHANGES IN ROLES ON THE ATTITUDES OF ROLE OCCUPANTS

SEYMOUR LIEBERMAN

PROBLEM

One of the fundamental postulates of role theory, as expounded by Newcomb, Parsons, and other role theorists, is that a person's attitudes will be influenced by the role that he occupies in a social system. Although this proposition appears to be a plausible one, surprisingly little evidence is available that bears directly on it. One source of evidence is found in common folklore. "Johnny is a changed boy since he was made a monitor in school." "She is a different woman since she got married." "You would never recognize him since he became foreman." As much as these expressions smack of the truth, they offer little in the way of systematic or scientific support for the proposition that a person's attitudes are influenced by his role.

Somewhat more scientific, but still not definitive, is the common finding, in many social-psychological studies, that relationships exist between attitudes and roles. In other words, different attitudes are held by people who occupy different roles. For example, Stouffer *et al.* found that commissioned officers are more favorable toward the Army than are enlisted men. The problem here is that the mere existence of a relationship between attitudes and roles does not reveal the cause and effect nature of the relationship found. One interpretation of Stouffer's finding might be that being made a commissioned officer tends to result in a person's becoming pro-Army—i.e. the role a person occupies influences his attitudes. But an equally plausible interpretation might be that being pro-Army tends to result in a person's being made a commissioned officer—i.e. a person's attitudes influence the likelihood of his being selected for a given role. In the absence of longitudinal data, the relationship offers no clear evidence that roles were the "cause" and attitudes the "effect."

The present study was designed to examine the effects of roles on attitudes in a particular field situation. The study is based on longitudinal data obtained in a role-differentiated, hierarchical organization. By taking advantage of natural role changes among personnel in the organization, it was possible to examine people's attitudes both before and after they underwent changes in roles. Therefore, the extent to which changes in roles were followed by changes in attitudes could be determined, and the cause and effect nature of any relationships found would be clear.

From Seymour Lieberman, "The Effects of Changes in Roles on the Attitudes of Role Occupants," *Human Relations,* IX (1956), 385-402 (the footnotes and the bibliography and references have been omitted). Reprinted by permission of the author and *Human Relations.*

METHOD: PHASE 1

The study was part of a larger project carried out in a medium-sized Midwestern company engaged in the production of home appliance equipment. Let us call the company the Rockwell Corporation. At the time that the study was done, Rockwell employed about 4,000 people. This total included about 2,500 factory workers and about 150 first-level foremen. The company was unionized and most of the factory workers belonged to the union local, which was an affiliate of the U.A.W., C.I.O. About 150 factory workers served as stewards in the union, or roughly one steward for every foreman.

The study consisted of a "natural field experiment." The experimental variable was a change in roles, and the experimental period was the period of exposure to the experimental variable. The experimental groups were those employees who underwent changes in roles during this period; the control groups were those employees who did not change roles during this period. The design may be described in terms of a three-step process: "before measurement," "experimental period," and "after measurement."

Before Measurement

In September and October 1951, attitude questionnaires were filled out by virtually all factory personnel at Rockwell — 2,354 workers, 145 stewards, and 151 foremen. The questions dealt for the most part with employees' attitudes and perceptions about the company, the union, and various aspects of the job situation. The respondents were told that the questionnaire was part of an overall survey to determine how employees felt about working conditions at Rockwell.

Experimental Period

Between October 1951 and July 1952, twenty-three workers were made foremen and thirty-five workers became stewards. Most of the workers who became stewards during that period were elected during the annual steward elections held in May 1952. They replaced stewards who did not choose to run again or who were not re-elected by their constituents. In addition, a few workers replaced stewards who left the steward role for one reason or another throughout the year.

The workers who became foremen were not made foreman at any particular time. Promotions occurred as openings arose in supervisory positions. Some workers replaced foremen who retired or who left the company for other reasons; some replaced foremen who were shifted to other supervisory positions; and some filled newly created supervisory positions.

After Measurement

In December 1952, the same forms that had been filled out by the rank-and-file workers in 1951 were readministered to:
1. The workers who became foremen during the experimental period (N = 23).
2. A control group of workers who did not become foremen during the experimental period (N = 46).
3. The workers who became stewards during the experimental period (N = 35).
4. A control group of workers who did not become stewards during the experimental period (N = 35).

Each control group was matched with its parallel experimental group on a number of demographic, attitudinal, and motivational variables. Therefore, any changes in attitudes that occurred in the experimental groups but did not occur in the control groups could not be attributed to initial differences between them.

The employees in these groups were told that the purpose of the follow-up questionnaire was to get up-to-date measures of their attitudes in 1952 and to compare how employees felt that year with the way that they felt the previous year. The groups were told that, instead of studying the entire universe of employees as was the case in 1951, only a sample was being studied this time. They were informed that the sample was chosen in such a way as to represent all kinds of employees at Rockwell—men and women, young and old, etc. The groups gave no indication that they understood the real bases on which they were chosen for the "after" measurement or that the effects of changes in roles were the critical factors being examined.

*　　*　　*　　*　　*

RESULTS: PHASE 1

The major hypothesis tested in this study was that people who are placed in a role will tend to take on or develop attitudes that are congruent with the expectations associated with that role. Since the foreman role entails being a representative of management, it might be expected that workers who are chosen as foremen will tend to become more favorable toward management. Similarly, since the steward role entails being a representative of the union, it might be expected that workers who are elected as stewards will tend to become more favorable toward the union. Moreover, in so far as the values of management and of the union are in conflict with each other, it might also be expected that workers who are made foremen will become less favorable toward the union and workers who are made stewards will become less favorable toward management.

Four attitudinal areas were examined: 1. attitudes toward management and officials of management; 2. attitudes toward the union and officials of the union; 3. attitudes toward the management-sponsored incentive system; and 4. attitudes toward the union-sponsored seniority system. The incentive system (whereby workers are paid according to the number of pieces they turn out) and the seniority system (whereby workers are promoted according to the seniority principle) are two areas in which conflicts between management and the union at Rockwell have been particularly intense. Furthermore, first-level foremen and stewards both play a part in the administration of these systems, and relevant groups hold expectations about foreman and steward behaviors with respect to these systems. Therefore, we examined the experimental and control groups' attitudes toward these two systems as well as their overall attitudes toward management and the union.

The data tend to support the hypothesis that being placed in the foreman and steward roles will have an impact on the attitudes of the role occupants. As shown in *Tables 1* through *4*, both experimental groups undergo systematic changes in attitudes, in the predicted directions, from the "before" situation to the "after" situation. In the control groups, either no attitude changes occur, or less marked changes occur, from the "before" situation to the "after" situation.

Although a number of the differences are not statistically significant, those which are significant are all in the expected directions, and most of the non-significant differences are also in the expected directions. New foremen, among other things, come to see Rockwell as a better place to work compared with other companies, develop more positive perceptions of top management officers, and become more favorably disposed toward the principle and operation of the incentive system. New stewards come to look upon labor unions in general in a more favorable light, develop more positive perceptions of the top union officers at Rockwell, and come to prefer seniority to ability as a criterion of what should count in moving workers to better jobs. In general, the attitudes of workers who become foremen tend to gravitate in a pro-management direction and the attitudes of workers who become stewards tend to move in a pro-union direction.

A second kind of finding has to do with the relative *amount* of attitude change that takes place among new foremen in contrast to the amount that takes place among new stewards. On the whole, more pronounced and more widespread attitude changes occur among those who are made foremen than among those who are made stewards. Using a *P*-level of .10 as a criterion for statistical significance, the workers who are made foremen undergo significant attitude changes, relative to the workers who are not made foremen, on ten of the sixteen attitudinal items presented in *Tables 1* through *4*. By contrast, the workers who are made stewards undergo significant attitude changes, relative to the workers who are not made stewards, on only three of the sixteen items. However, for the steward role as well as for the foreman role, most of the differences found between the experimental and control groups still tend to be in the expected directions.

The more pronounced and more widespread attitude changes that occur among new foremen than among new stewards can probably be accounted for in large measure by the kinds of differences that exist between the foreman and steward roles. For one thing, the foreman role represents a relatively permanent position, while many stewards take the steward role as a "one-shot" job and even if they want to run again their constituents may not re-elect them. Secondly, the foreman role is a full-time job, while most stewards spend just a few hours a week in the performance of their steward functions and spend the rest of the time carrying out their regular rank-and-file jobs. Thirdly, a worker who is made a foreman must give up his membership in the union and become a surrogate of management, while a worker who is made a steward retains the union as a reference group and simply takes on new functions and responsibilities as a representative of it. All of these differences suggest that the change from worker to foreman is a more fundamental change in roles than the change from worker to steward. This, in turn, might account to a large extent for the finding that, although attitude changes accompany both changes in roles, they occur more sharply among new foremen than among new stewards.

A third finding has to do with the *kinds* of attitude changes which occur among workers who change roles. As expected, new foremen become more pro-management and new stewards become more pro-union. Somewhat less ex- pected is the finding that new foremen become more anti-union but new stewards do not become more anti-management. Among workers who are made foremen, statistically significant shifts in an anti-union direction occur on four of the eight items dealing with the union and the union-sponsored seniority system. Among workers who are made stewards, there are no statistically significant shifts in either direction on any of the eight items having to do with management and the management-sponsored incentive system.

The finding that new foremen become anti-union but that new stewards do not become anti-management may be related to the fact that workers who become foremen must relinquish their membership of the union, while workers who become stewards retain their status as employees of management. New foremen, subject to one main set of loyalties and called on to carry out a markedly new set of functions, tend to develop negative attitudes toward the union as well as positive attitudes toward management. New stewards, subject to overlapping group membership and still dependent on management for their livelihoods, tend to become more favorable toward the union but they do not turn against management, at least not within the relatively limited time period covered by the present research project. Over time, stewards might come to develop somewhat hostile attitudes toward management, but, under the condi- tions prevailing at Rockwell, there is apparently no tendency for such attitudes to be developed as soon as workers enter the steward role.

METHOD: PHASE 2

One of the questions that may be raised about the results that have been presented up to this point concerns the extent to which the changed attitudes

TABLE 1

Effects of Foreman and Steward Roles on Attitudes toward Management

| | Kind of Change | | | | | |
	More favorable to manage- ment	No change	More critical of manage- ment	Total	N	p
	%	%	%	%		
1. How is Rockwell as a place to work?						
New foremen	70	26	4	100	23	N.S.
Control group*	47	33	20	100	46	
New stewards	46	31	23	100	35	N.S.
Control group**	46	43	11	100	35	
2. How does Rockwell compare with others?						
New foremen	52	48	0	100	23	.01-.05
Control group	24	59	17	100	46	
New stewards	55	34	11	100	35	N.S.
Control group	43	46	11	100	35	
3. If things went bad for Rockwell, should the workers try to help out?						
New foremen	17	66	17	100	23	N.S.
Control group	17	66	17	100	46	
New stewards	26	74	0	100	35	N.S.
Control group	14	69	17	100	35	
4. How much do management officers care about the workers at Rockwell?						
New foremen	48	52	0	100	23	<.01
Control group	15	76	9	100	46	
New stewards	29	62	9	100	35	N.S.
Control group	20	80	0	100	35	

*Workers who did not change roles, matched with future foremen on demographic and attitudinal variables in the "before" situation.

**Workers who did not change roles, matched with future stewards on demographic and attitudinal variables in the "before" situation.

TABLE 2

Effects of Foreman and Steward Roles on Attitudes toward the Union

| | Kind of Change | | | | | |
	More favorable to the union	No change	More critical to the union	Total	N	p
	%	%	%	%		
5. How do you feel about labor unions in general?						
New foremen	30	48	22	100	23	N.S.
Control group*	37	48	15	100	46	
New stewards	54	37	9	100	35	.01-.05
Control group**	29	65	6	100	35	
6. How much say should the union have in setting standards?						
New foremen	0	26	74	100	23	<.01
Control group	22	54	24	100	46	
New stewards	31	66	3	100	35	N.S.
Control group	20	60	20	100	35	
7. How would things be if there were no union at Rockwell?						
New foremen	9	39	52	100	23	.01-.05
Control group	20	58	22	100	46	
New stewards	14	86	0	100	35	N.S.
Control group	11	72	17	100	35	
8. How much do union officers care about the workers at Rockwell?						
New foremen	22	69	9	100	23	N.S.
Control group	15	78	7	100	46	
New stewards	57	37	6	100	35	.01-.05
Control group	26	68	6	100	35	

*Workers who did not change roles, matched with future foremen on demographic and attitudinal variables in the "before" situation.

**Workers who did not change roles, matched with future stewards on demographic and attitudinal variables in the "before" situation.

TABLE 3

Effects of Foreman and Steward Roles on Attitudes toward the Incentive System

| | Kind of Change | | | | | |
	More favorable to incentive system	No change	More critical of incentive system	Total	N	p
	%	%	%	%		
9. HOW DO YOU FEEL ABOUT THE PRINCIPLE OF AN INCENTIVE SYSTEM?						
New foremen	57	26	17	100	23	.01
Control group*	15	52	33	100	46	
New stewards	17	54	29	100	35	N.S.
Control group**	31	40	29	100	35	
10. HOW DO YOU FEEL THE INCENTIVE SYSTEM WORKS OUT AT ROCKWELL?						
New foremen	65	22	13	100	23	0.5-.10
Control group	37	41	22	100	46	
New stewards	43	34	23	100	35	N.S.
Control group	40	34	26	100	35	
11. SHOULD THE INCENTIVE SYSTEM BE CHANGED?						
New foremen	39	48	13	100	23	.01
Control group	11	69	20	100	46	
New stewards	14	63	23	100	35	N.S.
Control group	20	60	20	100	35	
12. IS A LABOR STANDARD EVER CHANGED JUST BECAUSE A WORKER IS A HIGH PRODUCER?						
New foremen	48	43	9	100	23	.01
Control group	11	74	15	100	46	
New stewards	29	57	14	100	35	N.S.
Control group	26	65	9	100	35	

*Workers who did not change roles, matched with future foremen on demographic and attitudinal variables in the "before" situation.

**Workers who did not change roles, matched with future stewards on demographic and attitudinal variables in the "before" situation.

TABLE 4
Effects of Foreman and Steward Roles on Attitudes toward the Seniority System

| | Kind of Change | | | | | |
	More favorable to seniority system	*No change*	*More critical of seniority system*	*Total*	*N*	*p*
	%	%	%	%		
13. HOW DO YOU FEEL ABOUT THE WAY THE SENIORITY SYSTEM WORKS OUT HERE?						
New foremen	0	65	35	100	23	.01-.05
Control group*	20	63	17	100	46	
New stewards	23	48	29	100	35	N.S.
Control group**	9	71	20	100	35	
14. HOW MUCH SHOULD SENIORITY COUNT DURING LAY-OFFS?						
New foremen	9	52	39	100	23	.05-.10
Control group	24	59	17	100	46	
New stewards	29	48	23	100	35	N.S.
Control group	29	40	31	100	35	
15. HOW MUCH SHOULD SENIORITY COUNT IN MOVING TO BETTER JOBS?						
New foremen	17	44	39	100	23	N.S.
Control group	20	54	26	100	46	
New stewards	34	46	20	100	35	.01-.05
Control group	17	34	49	100	35	
16. HOW MUCH SHOULD SENIORITY COUNT IN PROMOTION TO FOREMAN?						
New foremen	17	70	13	100	23	N.S.
Control group	15	52	33	100	46	
New stewards	31	35	34	100	35	N.S.
Control group	17	43	40	100	35	

*Workers who did not change roles, matched with future foremen on demographic and attitudinal variables in the "before" situation.

**Workers who did not change roles, matched with future stewards on demographic and attitudinal variables in the "before" situation.

displayed by new foremen and new stewards are internalized by the role occupants. Are the changed attitudes expressed by new foremen and new stewards relatively stable, or are they ephemeral phenomena to be held only as long as they occupy the foreman and steward roles? An unusual set of circumstances at Rockwell enabled the researchers to glean some data on this question.

A short time after the 1952 re-survey, the nation suffered an economic recession. In order to meet the lessening demand for its products, Rockwell, like many other firms, had to cut its work force. This resulted in many rank-and-file workers being laid off and a number of the foremen being returned to non-supervisory jobs. By June 1954, eight of the twenty-three workers who had been promoted to foreman had returned to the worker role and only twelve were still foremen. (The remaining three respondents had voluntarily left Rockwell by this time.)

Over the same period, a number of role changes had also been experienced by the thirty-five workers who had become stewards. Fourteen had returned to the worker role, either because they had not sought re-election by their work groups or because they had failed to win re-election, and only six were still stewards. (The other fifteen respondents, who composed almost half of this group, had either voluntarily left Rockwell or had been laid off as part of the general reduction in force.)

Once again, in June 1954, the researchers returned to Rockwell to readminister the questionnaires that the workers had filled out in 1951 and 1952. The instructions to the respondents were substantially the same as those given in 1952 — i.e. a sample of employees had been chosen to get up-to-date measures of employees' attitudes toward working conditions at Rockwell and the same groups were selected this time as had been selected last time in order to lend greater stability to the results.

In this phase of the study, the numbers of cases with which we were dealing in the various groups were so small that the data could only be viewed as suggestive, and systematic statistical analysis of the data did not seem to be too meaningful. However, the unusual opportunity to throw some light on an important question suggests that a reporting of these results may be worthwhile.

RESULTS: PHASE 2

The principal question examined here was: on those items where a change in roles resulted in a change in attitudes between 1951 and 1952, how are these attitudes influenced by a reverse change in roles between 1952 and 1954?

The most consistent and widespread attitude changes noted between 1951 and 1952 were those that resulted when workers moved into the foreman role. What are the effects of moving out of the foreman role between 1952 and 1954? The data indicate that, in general, most of the "gains" that were observed when workers became foremen are "lost" when they become workers again. The results on six of the items, showing the proportions who take pro-management positions at various points in time, are presented in *Table 5* [omitted]. On almost all of the items, the foremen who remain foremen either retain their favorable attitudes toward management or become even more favorable toward management between 1952 and 1954, while the demoted foremen show fairly consistent drops in the direction of re-adopting the attitudes they held when they had been in the worker role. On the whole, the attitudes held by demoted foremen in 1954, after they had left the foreman role, fall roughly to the same levels as they had been in 1951, before they had ever moved into the foreman role.

The results on the effects of moving out of the steward role are less clear-cut. As shown in *Table 6* [omitted], there is no marked tendency for ex-stewards to revert to earlier-held attitudes when they go from the steward role to the worker role. At the same time, it should be recalled that there had not been particularly marked changes in their attitudes when they initially changed from the worker role to the steward role. These findings, then, are consistent with the interpretation offered earlier that the change in roles between worker and steward is less significant than the change in roles between worker and foreman.

DISCUSSION

A role may be defined as a set of behaviors that are expected of people who occupy a certain position in a social system. These expectations consist of shared attitudes or beliefs, held by relevant populations, about what role occupants should and should not do. The theoretical basis for hypothesizing that a role will have effects on role occupants lies in the nature of these expectations. If a role occupant meets these expectations, the "rights" or "rewards" associated with the role will be accorded to him. If he fails to meet these expectations, the "rights" or "rewards" will be withheld from him and "punishments" may be meted out.

A distinction should be made between the effects of roles on people's attitudes and the effects of roles on their actions. How roles affect actions can probably be explained in a fairly direct fashion. Actions are overt and readily enforceable. If a person fails to behave in ways appropriate to his role, this can immediately be seen, and steps may be taken to bring the deviant or non-conformist into line. Role deviants may be evicted from their roles, placed in less rewarding roles, isolated from other members of the group, or banished entirely from the social system.

But attitudes are not as overt as actions. A person may behave in such a way as to reveal his attitudes, but he can — and often does — do much to cover them up. Why, then, should a change in roles lead to a change in attitudes? A number of explanatory factors might be suggested here. The present discussion will be confined to two factors that are probably generic to a wide variety of situations. One pertains to the influence of reference groups; the other is based on an assumption about people's need to have attitudes internally consistent with their actions.

A change in roles almost invariably involves a change in reference groups. Old reference groups may continue to influence the role occupant, but new ones also come into play. The change in reference groups may involve moving into a completely new group (as when a person gives up membership in one organization and joins another one) or it may simply involve taking on new functions in the same group (as when a person is promoted to a higher position in a hierarchical organization). In both situations, new reference groups will tend to bring about new frames of reference, new self-percepts, and new vested interests, and these in turn will tend to produce new attitudinal orientations.

In addition to a change in reference groups, a change in roles also involves a change in functions and a change in the kinds of behaviors and actions that the role occupant must display if he is to fulfil these functions. A change in actions, let us assume, comes about because these actions are immediately required, clearly visible, and hence socially enforceable. If we further assume a need for people to have attitudes that are internally consistent with their actions, then at least one aspect of the functional significance of a change in attitudes becomes clear. A change in attitudes enables a new role occupant to justify, to make rational, or perhaps simply to rationalize his change in actions. Having attitudes that are consistent with actions helps the role occupant to be "at one" with himself and facilitates his effective performance of the functions he is expected to carry out.

The reference-group principle and the self-consistency principle postulate somewhat different chains of events in accounting for the effects of roles on attitudes and actions. In abbreviated versions, the different chains may be spelled out in the following ways:

1. Reference-group principle: A change in roles involves a change in reference groups ... which leads to a change in attitudes ... which leads to a change in actions.

2. Self-consistency principle: A change in roles involves a change in functions ... which leads to a change in actions ... which leads to a change in attitudes.

In the former chain, a person's attitudes influence his actions; in the latter chain, a person's actions influence his attitudes. Both chains might plausibly account for the results obtained, but whether either chain, both chains, or other chains is or are valid cannot be determined from the data available. A more direct investigation of the underlying mechanisms responsible for the impact of roles on attitudes would appear to be a fruitful area for further research.

But apart from the question of underlying mechanisms, the results lend support to the proposition that a person's attitudes will be influenced by his role. Relatively consistent changes in attitudes were found both among workers who were made foremen and among workers who were made stewards, although these changes were more clear-cut for foremen than for stewards. The more interesting set of results—as far as role theory in general is concerned—would

166

seem to be the data on the effects of entering and leaving the foreman role. It was pointed out earlier that the foreman role, unlike the steward role, is a full-time, relatively permanent position, and moving into this position entails taking on a very new and different set of functions. When workers are made foremen, their attitudes change in a more pro-management and anti-union direction. When they are demoted and move back into the worker role, their attitudes change once again, this time in a more pro-union and anti-management direction. In both instances, the respondents' attitudes seem to be molded by the roles which they occupy at a given time.

The readiness with which the respondents in this study shed one set of attitudes and took on another set of attitudes might suggest either that 1. the attitudes studied do not tap very basic or deep-rooted facets of the respondents' psyches, or 2. the character structures of the respondents are such as not to include very deeply ingrained sets of value orientations. Riesman deals with this problem in his discussion of "other-directedness" vs. "inner-directedness." How much the rapid shifts in attitudes observed here reflect the particular kinds of respondents who underwent changes in roles in the present situation, and how much these shifts reflect the national character of the American population, can only be speculated on at the present time.

SUMMARY

This study was designed to test the proposition that a person's attitudes will be influenced by the role he occupies in a social system. This is a commonly accepted postulate in role theory but there appears to be little in the way of definitive empirical evidence to support it. Earlier studies have generally made inferences about the effects of roles on attitudes on the basis of correlational data gathered at a single point in time. The present study attempted to measure the effects of roles on attitudes through data gathered at three different points in time.

In September and October 1951, 2,354 rank-and-file workers in a factory situation were asked to fill out attitude questionnaires dealing with management and the union. During the next twelve months, twenty-three of these workers were promoted to foreman and thirty-five were elected by their work groups as union stewards. In December 1952, the questionnaires were re-administered to the two groups of workers who had changed roles and to two matched control groups of workers who had not changed roles. By comparing the attitude changes that occurred in the experimental groups with the attitude changes that occurred in their respective control groups, the effects of moving into the foreman and steward roles could be determined.

The results on this phase of the study showed that the experimental groups underwent systematic changes in attitudes after they were placed in their new roles, while the control groups underwent no changes or less marked changes from the "before" situation to the "after" situation. The workers who were made foremen tended to become more favorable toward management, and the workers who were made stewards tended to become more favorable toward the union. The changes were more marked among new foremen than among new stewards, which can be probably accounted for by the fact that the change from worker to foreman seems to be a more significant and more meaningful change in roles than the change from worker to steward.

In the months following the second administration of the questionnaire, a number of the workers who had become foremen and stewards reverted to the rank-and-file worker role. Some of the foremen were cut back to non-supervisory positions during a period of economic recession, and some of the stewards either did not run again or failed to be re-elected during the annual steward elections. In June 1954, the questionnaires were once again administered to the same groups of respondents. By comparing the attitude changes that occurred among foremen and stewards who left these roles with the attitude changes that occurred among foremen and stewards who remained in these roles, the effects of moving out of these roles could be assessed.

The results of this phase of the study showed that foremen who were demoted tended to revert to the attitudes they had previously held while they were in the worker role, while foremen who remained in the foreman role either maintained the attitudes they had developed when they first became foremen or moved even further in that direction. The results among stewards who left the steward role were less consistent and less clear-cut, which parallels the smaller and less clear-cut attitude changes that took place when they first became stewards.

The findings support the proposition that a person's role will have an impact on his attitudes, but they still leave unanswered the question of what underlying mechanisms are operating here. A more direct investigation of these underlying mechanisms might comprise a fruitful area for further research.

2. The Pressures toward Internal Consensus

That the role has a distinct impact on the person who occupies it should now be clear, but a comprehensive explanation of why this should be so is still lacking. Every individual is under frequent, if not continuous, pressure to modify his beliefs and behavior in response to certain nonrational forces. Even a high-ranking official in a foreign ministry or a very senior legislator must, in order to be effective — or at least to "get along" — adhere more to group norms and expectations than his professional judgment might dictate. The implications for policy-making are, of course, ominous, and the inevitable consequence is that decisions move somewhat in the direction of the "conventional wisdom." In the selection which follows, Hollander, building upon some of the experimental literature, proposes a very useful model by which the policy-maker's dilemma might be more fully understood.

CONFORMITY, STATUS, AND IDIOSYNCRASY CREDIT

E. P. HOLLANDER

Something of a paradox exists in the prevailing treatments of conformity and status. Students of social psychology are likely to be left with the pat impression that *the freely chosen leader conforms to,* and perhaps tenaciously upholds, *the norms of his group* [emphasis added]. Yet this kind of leadership is also presented as *a status sufficient to provide latitude* for directing and altering group norms [emphasis added]. From their recent experimental work in this area, Dittes and Kelley have voiced a doubt that the relationship between conformity and status is ever a simple one. The evidence favors their assertion.

Although these phenomena may be treated as discrete entities, they both arise from interaction between an individual and a set of relevant other individuals constituting a group. To say that an individual conforms, or that he has status, is not to say that these are independently determined states nor that they are terminal; they have some common origin in a phenomenal relationship which persists over time. Conformity and status may be thought of therefore as mutually dependent, and transitionally effective upon subsequent interactions. With this as a framework, several general conceptions will be expressed here regarding mechanisms which produce these phenomena and govern their relationship to one another.

In a gross way, three classes of variables, or elements, are necessary to this conceptual scheme: characteristics of the individual himself; characteristics of the group with which he interacts; and outcomes of interaction representing a past history which may alter the relationship of the former elements.

Of particular importance as a mediating process is the changing perception brought about in the individual and the group by their interaction; the third element is, in effect, this process. A distinction is required, therefore, between the phenomenal and perceptual features of behavior. An individual's behavior is not only phenomenally present in interaction but is also subject to view and appraisal by the other members of the group. If there are to be consequences involving these others, it is essential that there be a perceptual intake on their part. And so too must the individual perceive a group norm; the fact that it is manifestly *there* is not enough [emphasis added].

It is worth emphasizing that the focus here is upon how the individual fares in the group rather than upon more global consequences to the group. Two kinds of interlocking mechanisms are of concern: those giving rise to behavior in conformity with group demands, and those giving rise to status. The issues at stake may be put simply as follows: What *produces* conformity [emphasis added]? And what *allows for non*conformity [emphasis added]?

From E. P. Hollander, "Conformity, Status, and Idiosyncrasy Credit," *Psychological Review,* LXV (1958), 117-27 (the footnotes and the bibliography and references have been omitted). Reprinted by permission of the author and the American Psychological Association.

Some Questions on Conformity

Fundamental to these issues is the matter of determining *when* an individual may be said to be conforming. One may note that a twofold assumption underpins the usual view of conformity, i.e., that the individual is aware of the existence of a given group norm, and that his behavior in accordance with this norm is evidence of conformity. It is doubtful that both features of this assumption necessarily hold simultaneously. This being so, difficulties of interpretation will arise. If the individual were to be insensitive to the norm he could hardly be said to be conforming to it, whatever his behavior seemed to betray; correspondingly, a kind of "conformity" might prevail in terms of adherence to an incorrectly perceived norm; and thus, an evident failure to conform might or might not be "nonconformity" depending upon the accuracy of the individual's perception of the norm in the first place.

A related question concerns the individual's motivation. Is there a motive for nonconformity identifiable? Insofar as they are distinguishable, is it necessarily so, after all, that a conflict obtains between the individual's dispositions and the group's demands? Since behavior is taken to be more than a random event, the motivation for instances of conformity or nonconformity should be accountable, once the presence of an adequate recognition of the norm is established.

There remains too the question of who perceives a given behavior to be conforming, i.e., an external observer, a group member, or the actor himself. Employing a fixed-norm baseline for observation, as is often done, serves to obscure differential expectations which render conforming behavior for one individual nonconforming for another—with regard, that is, to others' perceptions *in situ*. Thus, the degree of familiarity with the unique properties of the group context is critical in verifying and understanding conformity.

Norms, Roles, and Group Expectancies

The usual conception of conformity examined here requires some group referent and a standard of behavior abstracted therefrom and defined as a norm. Probably because many studies of groups have involved highly manifest behaviors, norms are conceived to be quite literally evident. On the other hand, in the related concept of role a recognition exists that the behavioral standard may not be manifest, but rather may be an *expectancy*.

Though persisting, the distinction between norms and roles is neither essential nor easy to maintain. Roles are normative in that they involve some implicit shared expectancy among group members; and norms themselves, lacking visibility, may nonetheless dwell in expectancies. It is these expectancies, then, which may be normative, in the sense of typicality. Norms and roles are only distinguishable insofar as norms usually imply expectancies applicable to many persons, while roles are expectancies restrictive to one or a very few individuals in a group.

170

Objective observers might delimit common expectancies appropriate to group members in general from differential expectancies having reference to particular individuals as such. For the individual in the setting, however, manifest conformity probably comes about without regard to a separate awareness of norms as distinct from roles, but more likely in terms of behaviors which he perceives to be expected of him by relevant others, i.e., "doing the *right* thing."

In the world of daily interaction, the perception an individual holds of what relevant others expect of him is a singularly important determinant of his social behavior; and the degree to which an individual perceives the group to be rewarding serves to enhance or elaborate the effect produced by his motivation to belong. An alternative sequence may be seen to occur as well: motivation having reference to some fulfillment through the group serves to heighten the individual's perception of its expectancies.

⁎ ⁎ ⁎ ⁎ ⁎

STATUS EMERGENCE

The foregoing points have concentrated on individual characteristics that absorb and deal with features of the social context. Ultimately, these have consequences in *behavior,* which in its turn has an impact upon the group [emphasis added]. It is appropriate now to consider the implications of this process to the emergence of status.

At bottom, status may be taken to be an outcome of the group's differentiated perception of the individual, leading to a set of particularized expectancies regarding his behavior. This occurs as a function of certain of the behaviors or characteristics evidenced by the individual in interaction, which then yield a reconstruction of the group's perception of him. Cast in these terms, status has special value as a kind of middle ground in relating the individual to the group. It exists in the first place as a feature in someone's perceptual field, for without reference to a perceiver status has no intrinsic value or meaning in itself. And, similarly, role cannot be divorced from its perceptual locus; behavior is only appropriate to status insofar as someone perceives it to be so. Perceptual differentiation by the group has consequences, then, in terms of the behaviors it expects the individual to display.

Though not necessarily the case, it is desirable to conceive of status within this framework as having hierarchical properties on some sort of group-acceptance continuum. This is by no means critical as a feature, but is of heuristic value. Still further, it is convenient to represent status as permitting greater latitude in the manifestation of behaviors which would be seen to be nonconformist for the other members of the group; we refer here to common expectancies, a term introduced earlier. The implications of this aspect of status are of especial relevance to what follows.

Idiosyncrasy Credit

Status will hereafter be considered to be an outcome of interaction referred to as "idiosyncrasy credit" (C). This represents an accumulation of positively-disposed impressions residing in the perceptions of relevant others; it is defined operationally in terms of the degree to which an individual may deviate from the common expectancies of the group. In this view, each individual within a group — disregarding size and function, for the moment — may be thought of as having a degree of group-awarded credits such as to permit idiosyncratic behavior in certain dimensions *before* group sanctions are applied. By definition, affiliation with the group — as perceived by the group — ceases when the individual's credit balance reaches zero.

It is noteworthy that this concept is applicable to the limited, artificially produced laboratory group as well as to the total society. And, since the individual may have simultaneous membership in many groups, he may be considered to have a distinct credit balance in all groups with which he is in some sense involved; in each case he has achieved some level of status. Affixed to this concept of "credit" is the further consideration that "debits" of varying magnitudes may be charged against the credit balance, depending upon the gravity and frequency of the idiosyncrasy manifested, and the credit level which the individual holds.

Taking our society today as an illustration, one's credit balance very likely will be rapidly exhausted by publicly espousing Communist doctrine. In a different sphere, a fraternity man may experience comparable rejection by his peers for growing a beard, though other factors would come into play, so that for some individuals the consequences — in terms of group sanctions — would be disastrous and for others hardly disturbing. This requires some consideration of factors which determine the awarding of credit.

Among other determinants, the credit balance that a group member achieves depends upon the group, its function, and other properties to be considered below. It is useful for our purposes here to conceive of an "open system," i.e., an autonomous group providing focal activities, as well as free face-to-face interaction yielding expectancies; this would permit the simultaneous observation of an individual's behavior by all group members and the generation of impressions representing credit.

There are three general variables which can be delineated as determinants of these impressions. The first of these is alpha value (V_α), referring to the individual's task competence or performance in regard to focal group activities; the second is beta value (V_β), referring to characteristics of the individual not specific to these activities, e.g., status in a broader group, *bonhomie,* and the like; the third is immediate past idiosyncratic behavior (B), constituting a drain on credits. It is not contended that credit is necessarily related linearly to these variables, nor is their very likely interrelationship ignored. They are doubtless intercorrelated, though of varying degrees of significance in generating or dissipating credits. As a generalization, value (V) tends to increase credit while idiosyncratic behavior (B) acts to decrease credit—though the potential for negative value exists, e.g., in the case of prejudice.

*   *   *   *   *

SUMMARY OF VARIABLES

For convenience, the variables described may now be set forth definitionally.

B—*Idiosyncratic behavior*, i.e., any group member's behavior which may be perceived by the group to deviate from a given group expectancy.

C—*Idiosyncrasy credit*, i.e., the extent to which a given group member's idiosyncratic behavior (B) is allowable, in terms of gravity and frequency, before group sanctions are applied.

V_α—*Alpha value*, i.e., the weight assigned the current performance of a given individual, which may be perceived by the group as bearing upon its focal activities, e.g., task competence.

V_β—*Beta value*, i.e., the weight assigned the characteristics of a given individual which may be perceived by the group, but are not specific to its current focal activities, e.g., status external to the group.

P_a—The *perceptual ability* of a given individual, in the sense of a capacity to perceive events and relationships in the social field.

P_e—The *perceptual error* of a given individual in perceiving events or relationships in a particular social field, e.g., group expectancies.

M_a—The *motivation* of a given individual to affiliate with a given group, in terms of a gaining or sustaining *social approval*.

M_g—The *motivation* of a given individual to affiliate with a group, in terms of interest in focal *group activity*.

M—*Individual motivation to gain or sustain membership*, i.e., some composite of a given individual's motivation of both the M_a and M_g variety.

A—In general, *attraction of the group to its members*, i.e., some aggregate of all group members' M.

Y—The *communicality of a given group expectancy*, in terms of the degree to which a given expectancy is evident.

SCHEMATIC REPRESENTATION

In Fig. 1 our symbolic notation has been employed to represent relationships schematically. Since a sequential pattern is of particular importance, a time dimension is involved throughout; thus, subscripts are introduced to indicate the time interval to which reference is made; e.g., t_1 is read as the first time interval; or, P_{e2} as perceptual error in the second time interval.

The system originates at the top with group attraction as a motivational context, and three individual variables, perceptual ability, motivation to gain or sustain social approval, and motivation with reference to the group's activity. At the next level, group attraction has given rise to the communicality of certain expectancies which are then perceived by the individual, thus yielding a perceptual error; and motivation to belong has been aggregated at this level, as well. Beta value is also introduced to signify the group's [modal] perception of the individual's characteristics, e.g., pleasant appearance.

Moving down in time, the individual's idiosyncratic behavior during the period just elapsed has been generated by his error in perceiving expectancies together with his motivation—within the constraints imposed by the level of group attraction. The group's perception of the individual's contribution to its focal activities, alpha value, is influenced by the immediately prior perception of his characteristics, beta value.

In the next stage, status is generated—in the form of group-awarded credits—

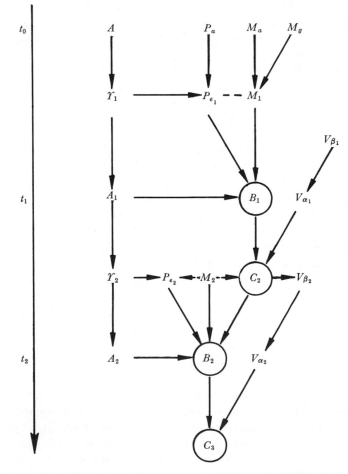

Figure 1. Schematic representation of mechanisms demonstrating relationships over time

by the effects of behavior relative to expectancies and the sequence of beta value to alpha value to credits. At this point the full set of interactions are in play, with credits affecting beta value; the latter serving as a repository of group perceptions of the individual's characteristics; perceptual error and motivation are reintroduced for this new phase, with the former affected by communicality of expectancies. Idiosyncratic behavior is subsequently determined by available credits, as this is checked by motivation, in particular, and perceptual error.

DISCUSSION AND IMPLICATIONS

Early in interaction, conformity to group expectancies serves to maintain or increase status, particularly as it is seen to be combined with manifest contributions to the group; at a later phase, however, the status thus generated permits greater latitude for idiosyncratic behavior. Thus, if an individual conforms to expectancies early in his exposure to the group and if he shows characteristics of competence, he accrues credits. For evident deviations from expectancies, or poor performance, he loses credits. If he exhausts his credit balance completely, pressures are applied to remove him from the group, or, at the very least, he is no longer perceived to be a member. At the other pole, if he continues to amass credits he attains a threshold permitting deviations from common expectancies, but with constraints imposed by newly differentiated expectancies.

The apparent paradox — that leaders both conform to group norms and yet may act to alter them by an exercise of influence — may be explained by reference to this sequential process. In this regard, it should not be supposed that an abundance of credits must lead perforce to influence. While an individual thus endowed has the potential to display more idiosyncratic behavior than others, he might not do so, nor would he of necessity become a leader thereby. Some further points of clarification are in order.

It is easy enough for the individual to continue to do habitually that which is rewarded by relevant others, so long as expectancies remain relatively stable. Consider the state of affairs which holds, however, in the case of the person who has marked [upward] status mobility in the group. He cannot simply continue to redisplay behaviors which were appropriate to the group's earlier expectancies, because the expectancies applicable to him are now altered in keeping with his rising status.

*　　*　　*　　*　　*

Certain of the assumptions made here — e.g., that an individual will have a level of credit reposing unitarily in others' perceptions of him, and that he may know and make use of the credits at his disposal — are only approximations of reality. Their literal tenability is not crucial to the mechanisms postulated, however. One could argue that the individual operates *as if* these assumptions were in fact true: the "they" commonly invoked to denote the upholders of some social pattern are never quite as homogeneous as the term suggests; but, to the individual, the use of "they" to represent a supposed uniformity is a necessary convenience as a basis for behavior. Furthermore, in accordance with this position, the individual apparently does react differentially to what he believes to be the view of him held by the "they," as Dittes and Kelley have demonstrated by manipulating the level of group "acceptance" which an individual is permitted to sense. In general, then, it appears that the individual seeks to know where he stands and does the best he can with the information available to him. These conceptions therefore do no violence to the reality with which the individual deals, but rather describe this reality in terms congruent with his concern.

Summary

Beginning with the consideration that social behavior depends upon attributes of the individual, conditions of the situation, and inputs to a dynamic system arising from their interaction, a theoretical conception relating conformity and status is presented.

The major mediating construct introduced is "idiosyncrasy credit," taken to be an index of status, in the operational sense of permitting deviations from common "expectancies" of the group.

Credits are postulated to increase or decrease as a function of the group's perception of the individual's task performance and generalized characteristics, and of his "idiosyncratic behavior," i.e., deviations from its expectancies. Though increases in credit are seen to permit greater latitude for idiosyncratic behavior, motivational and perceptual states of the individual, and group-level phenomena, are also considered.

Given the structural pressures at work on the member of a decision-making organization and the incentives he has for responding to many of these pressures, a fairly predictable drift toward consensus in such organizations can be expected. Now it might be argued that there are, in this world, a great many individuals who are not likely to acquiesce in such a fashion. True; but it can be asserted that this sort of "rugged individualist" is generally screened out from the beginning; there is very little room for someone who is not a "team man" in bureaucracies. Moreover, those few who do enter government ministries (and, to some extent, legislatures) seldom remain long enough to acquire much influence and usually depart by mutual consent. In the selection which follows, Breed describes the informal processes at work in a newspaper office; this article is of interest to us not only because the news organization is quite similar to a policy organization, but because the press is, itself, a major factor in foreign policy-making. The implications of the latter aspect of this study will be dealt with again in Section E of this part.

SOCIAL CONTROL IN THE NEWSROOM: A FUNCTIONAL ANALYSIS

Warren Breed

Top leaders in formal organizations are makers of policy, but they must also secure and maintain conformity to that policy at lower levels. The situation of the newspaper publisher is a case in point. As owner or representative of ownership, he has the nominal right to set the paper's policy and see that staff activities are coordinated so that the policy is enforced. In actuality the problem of control is less simple, as the literature of "human relations" and informal group studies and of the professions suggests.

Ideally, there would be no problem of either "control" or "policy" on the newspaper in a full democracy. The only controls would be the nature of the event and the reporter's effective ability to describe it. In practice, we find the publisher does set news policy, and this policy is usually followed by members of his staff. Conformity is *not* automatic, however, for three reasons: (1) the existence of ethical journalistic norms; (2) the fact that staff subordinates (reporters, etc.) tend to have more "liberal" attitudes (and therefore perceptions) than the publisher and could invoke the norms to justify anti-policy writing; and (3) the ethical taboo preventing the publisher from commanding subordinates to follow policy. How policy comes to be maintained, and where it is bypassed, is the subject of this paper.

Several definitions are required at this point. As to personnel, "newsmen" can be divided into "staffers" and executives. Executives include the publisher and his editors. "Staffers" are reporters, rewrite men, copy readers, etc. In between there may be occasional city editors or wire editors who occupy an interstitial status. "Policy" may be defined as the more or less consistent orientation shown by a paper, not only in its editorial but in its news columns and headlines as well, concerning selected issues and events. "Slanting" almost never means prevarication. Rather, it involves omission, differential selection and preferential placement, such as "featuring" a pro-policy item, "burying" an anti-policy story in an inside page, etc. "Professional norms" are of two types: technical norms deal with the operations of efficient news gathering, writing, and editing; ethical norms embrace the newsman's obligation to his readers and to his craft and include such ideals as responsibility, impartiality, accuracy, fair play, and objectivity.

From Warren Breed, "Social Control in the Newsroom: A Functional Analysis," *Social Forces*, XXXIII (1955), 326-35 (all footnotes, except note 7, have been omitted). Reprinted by permission of the author and The University of North Carolina Press.

Every newspaper has a policy, admitted or not. One paper's policy may be pro-Republican, cool to labor, antagonistic to the school board, etc. The principal areas of policy are politics, business, and labor; much of it stems from considerations of class. Policy is manifested in "slanting." Just what determines any publisher's policy is a large question and will not be discussed here. Certainly, however, the publisher has much say (often in veto form) in both long-term and immediate policy decisions (which party to support, whether to feature or bury a story of imminent labor trouble, how much freespace to give "news" of advertisers' doings, etc.). Finally, policy is covert, due to the existence of ethical norms of journalism; policy often contravenes these norms. No executive is willing to risk embarrassment by being accused of open commands to slant a news story.

While policy is set by the executives, it is clear that they cannot personally gather and write the news by themselves. They must delegate these tasks to staffers, and at this point the attitudes or interests of staffers may—and often do—conflict with those of the executives. Of 72 staffers interviewed, 42 showed that they held more liberal views than those contained in their publisher's policy; 27 held similar views, and only 3 were more conservative. Similarly, only 17 of 61 staffers said they were Republicans. The discrepancy is more acute when age (and therefore years of newspaper experience) is held constant. Of the 46 staffers under 35 years of age, 34 showed more liberal orientations; older men had apparently "mellowed." It should be noted that data as to intensity of attitudes are lacking. Some staffers may disagree with policy so mildly that they conform and feel no strain. The present essay is pertinent only insofar as dissident newsmen are forced to make decisions from time to time about their relationship to policy.

We will now examine more closely the workings of the newspaper staff. The central question will be: How is policy maintained, despite the fact that it often contravenes journalistic norms, that staffers often personally disagree with it, and that executives cannot legitimately command that it be followed? The frame of reference will be that of functional analysis, as embodied in Merton's paradigm.[7]

The present data come from the writer's newspaper experience and from intensive interviews with some 120 newsmen, mostly in the northeastern quarter of the country. The sample was not random and no claim is made for representativeness, but on the other hand no paper was selected or omitted purposely and in no case did a newsman refuse the request that he be interviewed. The newspapers were chosen to fit a "middle-sized" group, defined as those with 10,000 to 100,000 daily circulation. Interviews averaged well over an hour in duration.

There is an "action" element inherent in the present subject—the practical democratic need for "a free and responsible press" to inform citizens about

---

[7]Robert K. Merton, *Social Theory and Social Structure* (Glencoe: Free Press, 1949), esp. pp. 49-61. Merton's elements will not be explicitly referred to but his principal requirements are discussed at various points.

current issues. Much of the criticism of the press stems from the slanting induced by the bias of the publisher's policy. This criticism is often directed at flagrant cases such as the Hearst Press, the *Chicago Tribune* and the New York tabloids, but also applies, in lesser degree, to the more conventional press. The description of mechanisms of policy maintenance may suggest why this criticism is often fruitless, at least in the short-run sense.

How the Staffer Learns Policy

The first mechanism promoting conformity is the "socialization" of the staffer with regard to the norms of his job. When the new reporter starts work he is not told what policy is. Nor is he ever told. This may appear strange, but interview after interview confirmed the condition. The standard remark was "Never, in my ——— years on this paper, have I ever been told how to slant a story." No paper in the survey had a "training" program for its new men; some issue a "style" book, but this deals with literary style, not policy. Further, newsmen are busy and have little time for recruit training. Yet all but the newest staffers know what policy is. On being asked, they say they learn it "by osmosis." Sociologically, this means they become socialized and "learn the ropes" like a neophyte in any subculture. Basically, the learning of policy is a process by which the recruit discovers and internalizes the rights and obligations of his status and its norms and values. He learns to anticipate what is expected of him so as to win rewards and avoid punishments. Policy is an important element of the newsroom norms, and he learns it in much the following way.

The staffer reads his own paper every day; some papers *require* this. It is simple to diagnose the paper's characteristics. Unless the staffer is naive or unusually independent, he tends to fashion his own stories after others he sees in the paper. This is particularly true of the newcomer. The news columns and editorials are a guide to the local norms. Thus a southern reporter notes that Republicans are treated in a "different" way in his paper's news columns than Democrats. The news about whites and Negroes is also of a distinct sort. Should he then write about one of these groups, his story will tend to reflect what he has come to define as standard procedure.

Certain editorial actions taken by editors and older staffers also serve as controlling guides. "If things are blue-pencilled consistently," one reporter said, "you learn he [the editor] has a prejudice in that regard." Similarly an executive may occasionally reprimand a staffer for policy violation. From our evidence, the reprimand is frequently oblique, due to the covert nature of policy, but learning occurs nevertheless. One staffer learned much through a series of incidents:

> I heard [a union] was going out on strike, so I kept on it; then the boss said something about it, and well—I took the hint and we had less coverage of the strike forming. It was easier that way. We lost the story, but what can you do?
> We used a yarn on a firm that was coming to town, and I got dragged out of bed for that. The boss is interested in this industrial stuff—we have to clear it

all through him. He's an official in the Chamber. So . . . after a few times, it's irritating, so I get fed up. I try to figure out what will work best. I learn to try and guess what the boss will want.

In fairness it should be noted that this particular publisher was one of the most dictatorial encountered in the study. The pattern of control through reprimand, however, was found consistently. Another staffer wrote, on his own initiative, a series about discrimination against Jews at hotel resorts.

It was the old "Gentlemen's Agreement" stuff, documented locally. The boss called me in . . . didn't like the stuff . . . the series never appeared. You start to get the idea. . . .

Note that the boss does not "command"; the direction is more subtle. Also, it seems that most policy indications from executives are negative. They veto by a nod of the head, as if to say, "Please don't rock the boat." Exceptions occur in the "campaign" story, which will be discussed later. It is also to be noted that punishment is implied if policy is not followed.

Staffers also obtain guidance from their knowledge of the characteristics, interests, and affiliations of their executives. This knowledge can be gained in several ways. One is gossip. A reporter said:

Do we gossip about the editors? Several of us used to meet — somewhere off the beaten path — over a beer — and talk for an hour. We'd rake 'em over the coals.

Another point of contact with executives is the news conference (which on middle-sized papers is seldom *called* a news conference), wherein the staffer outlines his findings and executives discuss how to shape the story. The typical conference consists of two persons, the reporter and the city editor, and can amount to no more than a few words. (Reporter: "One hurt in auto accident uptown." City editor: "Okay, keep it short.") If policy is at stake, the conference may involve several executives and require hours of consideration. From such meetings, the staffer can gain insight through what is said and what is not said by executives. It is important to say here that policy is not stated explicitly in the news conference nor elsewhere, with few exceptions. The news conference actually deals mostly with journalistic matters, such as reliability of information, newsworthiness, possible "angles," and other news tactics.

Three other channels for learning about executives are house organs (printed for the staff by syndicates and larger papers), observing the executive as he meets various leaders and hearing him voice an opinion. One staffer could not help but gain an enduring impression of his publisher's attitudes in this incident:

I can remember [him] saying on election night [1948], when it looked like we had a Democratic majority in both houses, "My God, this means we'll have a labor government." (Q: How did he say it?) He had a real note of alarm in his voice; you couldn't miss the point that he'd prefer the Republicans.

It will be noted that in speaking "how" the staffer learns policy, there are indications also as to "why" he follows it.

REASONS FOR CONFORMING TO POLICY

There is no one factor which creates conformity-mindedness, unless we resort to a summary term such as "institutionalized statuses" or "structural roles." Particular factors must be sought in particular cases. The staffer must be seen in terms of his status and aspirations, the structure of the newsroom organization and of the larger society. He also must be viewed with reference to the operations he performs through his workday, and their consequences for him. The following six reasons appear to stay the potentially intransigent staffer from acts of deviance — often, if not always.

1. Institutional Authority and Sanctions

The publisher ordinarily owns the paper and from a purely business standpoint has the right to expect obedience of his employees. He has the power to fire or demote for transgressions. This power, however, is diminished markedly in actuality by three facts. First, the newspaper is not conceived as a purely business enterprise, due to the protection of the First Amendment and a tradition of professional public service. Secondly, firing is a rare phenomenon on newspapers. For example, one editor said he had fired two men in 12 years; another could recall four firings in his 15 years on that paper. Thirdly, there are severance pay clauses in contracts with the American Newspaper Guild (CIO). The only effective causes for firing are excessive drunkenness, sexual dalliance, etc. Most newspaper unemployment apparently comes from occasional economy drives on large papers and from total suspensions of publication. Likewise, only one case of demotion was found in the survey. It is true, however, that staffers still fear punishment; the myth has the errant star reporter taken off murders and put on obituaries — "the Chinese torture chamber" of the newsroom. Fear of sanctions, rather than their invocation, is a reason for conformity, but not as potent a one as would seem at first glance.

Editors, for their part, can simply ignore stories which might create deviant actions, and when this is impossible, can assign the story to a "safe" staffer. In the infrequent case that an anti-policy story reaches the city desk, the story is changed; extraneous reasons, such as the pressure of time and space, are given for the change. Finally the editor may contribute to the durability of policy by insulating the publisher from policy discussions. He may reason that the publisher would be embarrassed to hear of conflict over policy and the resulting bias, and spare him the resulting uneasiness; thus the policy remains not only covert but undiscussed and therefore unchanged.

2. Feelings of Obligation and Esteem for Superiors

The staffer may feel obligated to his paper for having hired him. Respect, admiration and gratitude may be felt for certain editors who have perhaps schooled him, "stood up for him," or supplied favors of a more paternalistic sort. Older staffers who have served as models for newcomers or who have otherwise given aid and comfort are due return courtesies. Such obligations and warm personal sentiments toward superiors play a strategic role in the pull to conformity.

3. Mobility Aspirations

In response to a question about ambition, all the younger staffers showed wishes for status achievement. There was agreement that bucking policy constituted a serious bar to this goal. In practice, several respondents noted that a good tactic toward advancement was to get "big" stories on Page One; this automatically means no tampering with policy. Further, some staffers see newspapering as a "stepping stone" job to more lucrative work: public relations, advertising, free-lancing, etc. The reputation for troublemaking would inhibit such climbing.

A word is in order here about chances for upward mobility. Of 51 newsmen aged 35 or more, 32 were executives. Of 50 younger men 6 had reached executive posts and others were on their way up with such jobs as wire editors, political reporters, etc. All but five of these young men were college graduates, as against just half of their elders. Thus there is no evidence of a "break in the skill hierarchy" among newsmen.

4. Absence of Conflicting Group Allegiance

The largest formal organization of staffers is the American Newspaper Guild. The Guild, much as it might wish to, has not interfered with internal matters such as policy. It has stressed business unionism and political interests external to the newsroom. As for informal groups, there is no evidence available that a group of staffers has ever "ganged up" on policy.

5. The Pleasant Nature of the Activity

A. In-Groupness in the Newsroom

The staffer has a low formal status vis-à-vis executives, but he is not treated as a "worker." Rather, he is a co-worker with executives; the entire staff cooperates congenially on a job they all like and respect: getting the news. The newsroom is a friendly, first-namish place. Staffers discuss stories with editors on a give-and-take basis. Top executives with their own offices sometimes come out and sit in on newsroom discussions.

B. Required Operations Are Interesting

Newsmen like their work. Few voiced complaints when given the opportunity to gripe during interviews. The operations required — witnessing, interviewing, briefly mulling the meanings of events, checking facts, writing — are not onerous.

C. Non-Financial Perquisites

These are numerous: the variety of experience, eye-witnessing significant and interesting events, being the first to know, getting "the inside dope" denied laymen, meeting and sometimes befriending notables and celebrities (who are well-advised to treat newsmen with deference). Newsmen are close to big decisions without having to make them; they touch power without being responsible for its use. From talking with newsmen and reading their books, one gets the impression that they are proud of being newsmen. There are tendencies to exclusiveness within news ranks, and intimations that such near out-groups as radio newsmen are entertainers, not real newsmen. Finally, there is the satisfaction of being a member of a live-wire organization dealing with important matters. The newspaper is an "institution" in the community. People talk about it and quote it; its big trucks whiz through town; its columns carry the tidings from big and faraway places, with pictures.

Thus, despite his relatively low pay, the staffer feels, for all these reasons, an integral part of a going concern. His job morale is high. Many newsmen could qualify for jobs paying more money in advertising and public relations, but they remain with the newspaper.

6. News Becomes a Value

Newsmen define their job as producing a certain quantity of what is called "news" every 24 hours. This is to be produced *even though nothing much has happened.* News is a continuous challenge, and meeting this challenge is the newsman's job. He is rewarded for fulfilling this, his manifest function. A consequence of this focus on news as a central value is the shelving of a strong interest in objectivity at the point of policy conflict. Instead of mobilizing their efforts to establish objectivity over policy as the criterion for performance, their energies are channeled into getting more news. The demands of competition (in cities where there are two or more papers) and speed enhance this focus. Newsmen do talk about ethics, objectivity, and the relative worth of various papers, but not when there is news to get. News comes first, and there is always news to get. They are not rewarded for analyzing the social structure, but for getting news. It would seem that this instrumental orientation diminishes their moral potential. A further consequence of this pattern is that the harmony between staffers and executives is cemented by their common interest in news. Any potential conflict between the two groups, such as slowdowns, occurring among informal work groups in industry, would be dissipated to the extent that news is a positive value. The newsroom solidarity is thus reinforced.

The six factors promote policy conformity. To state more exactly how policy is maintained would be difficult in view of the many variables contained in the system. The process may be somewhat better understood, however, with the introduction of one further concept—the reference group. The staffer, especially the new staffer, identifies himself through the existence of these six factors with the executives and veteran staffers. Although not yet one of them, he shares their norms, and thus his performance comes to resemble theirs. He conforms to the norms of policy rather than to whatever personal beliefs he brought to the job, or to ethical ideals. All six of these factors function to encourage reference group formation. Where the allegiance is directed toward legitimate authority, that authority has only to maintain the equilibrium within limits by the prudent distribution of rewards and punishments. The reference group itself, which has as its "magnet" element the elite of executives and old staffers, is unable to change policy to a marked degree because first, it is the group charged with carrying out policy, and second, because the policy maker, the publisher, is often insulated on the delicate issue of policy.

In its own way, each of the six factors contributes to the formation of reference group behavior. There is almost no firing, hence a steady expectation of continued employment. Subordinates tend to esteem their bosses, so a convenient model group is present. Mobility aspirations (when held within limits) are an obvious promoter of inter-status bonds as is the absence of conflicting group loyalties with their potential harvest of cross pressures. The newsroom atmosphere is charged with the related factors of ingroupness and pleasing nature of the work. Finally, the agreement among newsmen that their job is to fasten upon the news, seeing it as a value in itself, forges a bond across the status lines.

As to the six factors, five appear to be relatively constant, occurring on all papers studied. The varying factor is the second: obligation and esteem held by staffers for executive and older staffers. On some papers, this obligation-esteem entity was found to be larger than on others. Where it was large, the paper appeared to have two characteristics pertinent to this discussion. First, it did a good conventional job of news-getting and newspublishing, and second, it had little difficulty over policy. With staffers drawn toward both the membership and the reference groups, organization was efficient. Most papers are like this. On the few smaller papers where executives and older staffers are not respected, morale is spotty; staffers withhold enthusiasm from their stories, they cover their beats perfunctorily, they wish for a job on a better paper, and they are apathetic and sometimes hostile to policy. Thus the obligation-esteem factor seems to be the active variable in determining not only policy conformity, but morale and good news performance as well.

SITUATIONS PERMITTING DEVIATION

Thus far it would seem that the staffer enjoys little "freedom of the press." To show that this is an oversimplification, and more important, to suggest a kind of test for our hypothesis about the strength of policy, let us ask: "What happens when a staffer *does* submit an anti-policy story?" We know that this happens infrequently, but what follows in these cases?

The process of learning policy crystalizes into a process of social control, in which deviations are punished (usually gently) by reprimand, cutting one's story, the withholding of friendly comment by an executive, etc. For example, it is punishment for a staffer when the city editor waves a piece of his copy at him and says, "Joe, don't *do* that when you're writing about the mayor." In an actual case, a staffer acting as wire editor was demoted when he neglected to feature a story about a "sacred cow" politician on his paper. What can be concluded is that when an executive sees a clearly anti-policy item, he blue-pencils it, and this constitutes a lesson for the staffer. Rarely does the staffer persist in violating policy; no such case appeared in all the interviews. Indeed, the best-known cases of firing for policy reasons — Ted O. Thackrey and Leo Huberman — occurred on liberal New York City dailies, and Thackrey was an editor, not a staffer.

Now and then cases arise in which a staffer finds his anti-policy stories printed. There seems to be no consistent explanation for this, except to introduce two more specific subjects dealing first, with the staffer's career line, and second, with particular empirical conditions associated with the career line. We can distinguish three stages through which the staffer progresses. First, there is the cub stage, the first few months or years in which the new man learns techniques and policy. He writes short, non-policy stories, such as minor accidents, meeting activity, the weather, etc. The second, or "wiring-in" stage, sees the staffer continuing to assimilate the newsroom values and to cement informal relationships. Finally there is the "star" or "veteran" stage, in which the staffer typically defines himself as a full, responsible member of the group, sees its goals as his, and can be counted on to handle policy sympathetically.

To further specify the conformity-deviation problem, it must be understood that newspapering is a relatively complex activity. The newsman is responsible for a range of skills and judgments which are matched only in the professional and entrepreneurial fields. Oversimplifications about policy rigidity can be avoided if we ask, "*Under what conditions* can the staffer defy or by-pass policy?" We have already seen that staffers are free to argue news decisions with executives in brief "news conferences," but the arguments generally revolve around points of "newsiness," rather than policy as such. Five factors appear significant in the area of the reporter's power to by-pass policy.

1. The norms of policy are not always entirely clear, just as many norms are vague and unstructured. Policy is covert by nature and has large scope. The paper may be Republican, but standing only lukewarm for Republican Candidate A who may be too "liberal" or no friend of the publisher. Policy, if worked out explicitly, would have to include motivations, reasons, alternatives, historical developments, and other complicating material. Thus a twilight zone permitting a range of deviation appears.

2. Executives may be ignorant of particular facts, and staffers who do the leg

(and telephone) work to gather news can use their superior knowledge to subvert policy. On grounds of both personal belief and professional codes, the staffer has the option of selection at many points. He can decide whom to interview and whom to ignore, what questions to ask, which quotations to note, and on writing the story which items to feature (with an eye toward the headline), which to bury, and in general what tone to give the several possible elements of the story.

3. In addition to the "squeeze" tactic exploiting executives' ignorance of minute facts, the "plant" may be employed. Although a paper's policy may prescribe a certain issue from becoming featured, a staffer, on getting a good story about that issue may "plant" it in another paper or wire service through a friendly staffer and submit it to his own editor, pleading the story is now too big to ignore.

4. It is possible to classify news into four types on the basis of source of origination. These are: the policy or campaign story, the assigned story, the beat story, and the story initiated by the staffer. The staffer's autonomy is larger with the latter than the former types. With the campaign story (build new hospital, throw rascals out, etc.), the staffer is working directly under executives and has little leeway. An assigned story is handed out by the city editor and thus will rarely hit policy head on, although the staffer has some leverage of selection. When we come to the beat story, however, it is clear that the function of the reporter changes. No editor comes between him and his beat (police department, city hall, etc.), thus the reporter gains the "editor" function. It is he who, to a marked degree, can select which stories to pursue, which to ignore. Several cases developed in interviews of beat men who smothered stories they knew would provide fuel for policy—policy they personally disliked or thought injurious to the professional code. The cooperation of would-be competing reporters is essential, of course. The fourth type of story is simply one which the staffer originates, independent of assignment or beat. All respondents, executives and staffers, averred that any employee was free to initiate stories. But equally regularly, they acknowledged that the opportunity was not often assumed. Staffers were already overloaded with beats, assignments, and routine coverage, and besides, rewards for initiated stories were meager or non-existent unless the initiated story confirmed policy. Yet this area promises much, should staffers pursue their advantage. The outstanding case in the present study concerned a well-educated, enthusiastic reporter on a conventional daily just north of the Mason-Dixon line. Entirely on his own, he consistently initiated stories about Negroes and Negro-white relations, "making" policy where only void had existed. He worked overtime to document and polish the stories; his boss said he didn't agree with the idea but insisted on the reporter's right to publish them.

5. Staffers with "star" status can transgress policy more easily than cubs. This differential privilege of status was encountered on several papers. An example would be Walter Winchell during the Roosevelt administration, who regularly praised the president while the policy of his boss, Mr. Hearst, was strongly critical of the regime. A *New York Times* staffer said he doubted that any copy reader on

the paper would dare change a word of the copy of Meyer Berger, the star feature writer.

These five factors indicate that given certain conditions, the controls making for policy conformity can be bypassed. These conditions exist not only within the newsroom and the news situation but within the staffer as well; they will be exploited only if the staffer's attitudes permit. There are some limitations, then, on the strength of the publisher's policy.

*   *   *   *   *

SUMMARY

The problem, which was suggested by the age-old charges of bias against the press, focussed around the manner in which the publisher's policy came to be followed, despite three empirical conditions: (1) policy sometimes contravenes journalistic norms; (2) staffers often personally disagree with it; and (3) executives cannot legitimately command that policy be followed. Interview and other data were used to explain policy maintenance. It is important to recall that the discussion is based primarily on study of papers of "middle" circulation range, and does not consider either non-policy stories or the original policy decision made by the publishers.

The mechanisms for learning policy on the part of the new staffer were given, together with suggestions as to the nature of social controls. Six factors, apparently the major variables producing policy maintenance, were described. The most significant of these variables, obligation and esteem for superiors, was deemed not only the most important, but the most fluctuating variable from paper to paper. Its existence and its importance for conformity led to the sub-hypothesis that reference group behavior was playing a part in the pattern. To show, however, that policy is not ironclad, five conditions were suggested in which staffers may by-pass policy.

Thus we conclude that the publisher's policy, when established in a given subject area, is usually followed, and that a description of the dynamic socio-cultural situation of the newsroom will suggest explanations for this conformity. The newsman's source of rewards is located not among the readers, who are manifestly his clients, but among his colleagues and superiors. Instead of adhering to societal and professional ideals, he re-defines his values to the more pragmatic level of the newsroom group. He thereby gains not only status rewards, but also acceptance in a solidary group engaged in interesting, varied, and sometimes important work. Thus the cultural patterns of the newsroom produce results insufficient for wider democratic needs. Any important change toward a more "free and responsible press" must stem from various possible pressures on the publisher, who epitomises the policy-making and coordinating role.

3. Reconciling the Conflicting Role Pressures

The two preceding papers have given some idea of (a) the sorts of variables which predispose the incumbent of a decision-making role to conform to the norms of his group, and (b) the rather informal way in which those norms act upon that individual. In the following paper, Miller and Shull present their theory of the way in which decision-makers will handle that type of role conflict which stems from conflicting pressures, and then test the theory against the experiences of a sample of these decision-makers. It should be borne in mind that such conflicting pressures need not necessarily come from two or more well-identified subunits or individuals in the organization, but might just as easily come from a temporary and informal faction in the organization or from the individual's own sense of duty or ambition.

THE PREDICTION OF ADMINISTRATIVE ROLE CONFLICT RESOLUTIONS

DELBERT C. MILLER AND FREMONT A. SHULL, JR.

The purpose of this study was to secure further knowledge about role conflict and to attempt to predict role conflict resolutions by business and labor leaders. Neal Gross and his associates presented a theory of role conflict resolution which they employed to predict the behavior of Massachusetts school superintendents. A modification of their theory served as a basis for this study.

Role conflict refers to role behavior which is experienced by a person who perceives that he is exposed to incompatible expectations. The person studied here is an incumbent in a formal position who must decide on a specific course of action.

THEORETICAL BASIS OF PROBLEMS

Briefly, the theory developed by Gross, Mason, and McEachern states that the incumbent of a position chooses one of four different actions when confronted with two conflicting role expectations. These are conformity to expectation *A*, conformity to expectation *B*, compromise, or avoidance. Thus, in a role conflict dealing with salary recommendations, a school superintendent may make a strong recommendation in accord with higher salary expectations of the teach-

From Delbert C. Miller and Fremont A. Shull, Jr., "The Prediction of Administrative Role Conflict Resolutions," *Administrative Science Quarterly*, VII (1962), 143-60 (the footnotes have been omitted). Reprinted by permission of the authors and *Administrative Science Quarterly*.

ers; he may recommend no increase to follow the wishes of the taxpayers' association; he may compromise by recommending a slight increase; or he may avoid a decision by delaying or even refusing to make a recommendation.

It was hypothesized that *three factors account for the incumbent's choice:* legitimacy, sanctions, and personal orientation [emphasis added]. Legitimacy refers to whether the incumbent believed that the individual or group making the claim had a right to expect him to conform to the expectations. Sanctions refer to penalties perceived as a consequence of following either of the conflicting role expectations. The respondent was asked to indicate how those who expected him to conform to expectation *A* and to expectation *B* would react if he did not do what each expected of him.

Some persons react differently to the moral aspects of a situation as well as to the varying pressures that either promise to reward or threaten to penalize them. Thus, the third factor in the theory was the personal orientation of the incumbent as he brought his own values to bear upon a decision. Personal orientation refers to three possible evaluations of legitimacy and sanctions which the incumbent might make. The morally oriented person places more weight on legitimacy than upon sanctions. The expediently oriented person places more weight on sanctions than upon legitimacy. The moral-expedient person weighs both dimensions relatively equally. On the basis of these three factors, role resolutions were predicted and then compared with actions taken by school superintendents.

Modification of Theory of Gross, Mason, and McEachern

Gross and his associates assumed that personal orientation could be treated as a stable personality trait and measured this dimension with an attitude scale especially constructed to identify the moral, moral-expedient, and expedient types of personality.

The present study is based on a theoretical assumption that reliable predictions of role conflict resolution can be made by ascertaining *only the two* variables, legitimacy and sanctions [emphasis added]. First, judgments about the legitimacy of the opposing expectations must be secured from the respondent. Secondly, the negative sanctions he perceives from failure to follow either of the contesting claimants must be recorded. The concept of personal orientation as a stable personality trait is rejected and is replaced with a concept of variable choice. It is held that the same individual may make different choices in role conflict situations according to the nature of the situation; i.e., he is moral, moral-expedient, or expedient in his choice, depending on personal and organizational goals, group support, values at stake, and so on. A set of rules was constructed to predict the act of resolution solely through the subjective weighing of legitimacy and sanctions that the person might make in each role conflict situation. The research hypothesis may be simply put; the hypothesis to be tested states: *The decisions of a position incumbent when confronted with role conflicts can be predicted with a high degree of accuracy if the incumbent's perceptions of legitimacy and sanctions are given.*

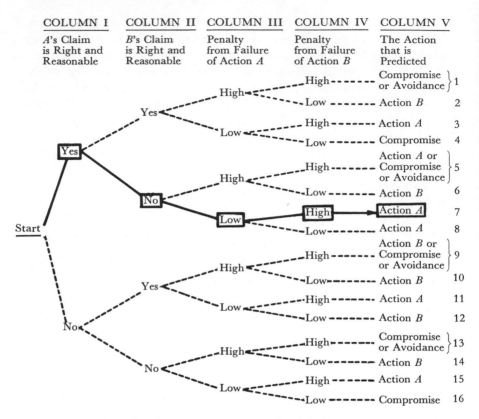

COLUMN I	COLUMN II	COLUMN III	COLUMN IV	COLUMN V
A's Claim is Right and Reasonable	B's Claim is Right and Reasonable	Penalty from Failure of Action A	Penalty from Failure of Action B	The Action that is Predicted

Figure 1. Schematic diagram of predicted decision process
Source: Supplied by the authors for inclusion in this reprinting of their paper, and originally reproduced in Delbert C. Miller and William H. Form, *Industrial Sociology* (New York: Harper & Row, 1964), pp. 737-41. Reprinted by permission of the authors and the publisher.

RESEARCH DESIGN

Populations Studied

Four populations were selected: two groups of business managers, one group of training directors, and one group of labor leaders. The business managers were from many different companies in the United States. These business leaders, a first- and second-year participant group, were assembled for a three-week executive development institute at Indiana University in June, 1960. The training directors were members of the Indiana chapter of the American Society of Training Directors and held positions in various Indiana firms. The labor leaders were international, state, and local labor leaders holding posts in and around Indianapolis, Indiana. In each case the respondents met criteria which stamped them as representative of wider populations, although no generalizations are made beyond the specific populations studied.

Method of Securing Data

Role conflicts encountered by business and labor leaders were secured by questionnaire and by individual and group interviews. The training directors were sent a specially designed questionnaire. The questionnaire was completed after considerable interviewing had been carried out to define typical role conflicts. The first part of the questionnaire presented a structured situation to evoke answers and to instruct the respondent in the legitimacy and sanction dimensions and in the choice of an appropriate action pattern from the list provided. The second part asked the respondent (1) to describe an actual conflict situation in which he had participated, (2) to judge the legitimacy and sanctions he perceived, and to describe his action. The final section of the questionnaire included data on the organizational aspects of his position and a brief description of his career. Thirty-three per cent of the questionnaires mailed to training directors were returned. Considerable protective behavior was encountered. One company insisted that its public relations office had to clear this kind of questionnaire; this office did not release it. Many said that, while we promised anonymity and did not ask for a signature, the personal data requested destroyed such anonymity.

*   *   *   *   *

Design of the Questionnaire

Gross and his associates recorded answers to legitimacy of expectations as yes or no, and answers to negative sanctions expected as weak or strong. Upon completion of their research they suggested that some measures of the degree of legitimacy and sanction perceived would bring greater precision. Accordingly, in this study negative sanctions were put on a five-point scale (see Assessment of Negative Sanctions in the summary of the questionnaire which follows). We also tried to add more weight to the perception of sanction by asking the respondent to perceive the consequences of failure if he conformed to either of the designated expectations. The respondent was asked to combine the thwart pressures which might be imposed by the persons denied as well as his perception of consequences of failure of his decision choice. The question was put: "What did you anticipate would happen to you if you followed this expectation and then failed?" In this way, the respondent was asked to calculate the full consequence of negative sanctions.

Legitimacy was left in a dichotomous form, but a change was made to give the concept a broader meaning. The question put was: "Did you think it was right and reasonable for X to expect you to act as he asked?" The phrase "right and reasonable" was believed to encompass ideas of moral right as well as notions of reasonable practicality. To be reasonable in organizational life is to ask what is feasible in terms of resources, time and energy, as well as legitimate authority.

191

To ask more is to make an illegitimate request of a decision maker. (See Legitimacy Assessments in the summary of the questionnaire which follows.)

These changes may be observed in the following summary of one structured role conflict presented in questionnaire form to the business managers and training directors.

Summary of Part I of Questionnaire

ROLE EXPECTATIONS

Expectation A: A supervisory training director was asked by the president of his company to prepare a supervisory training program for all plant supervisors and to administer it according to the best known practices. (The training director believes that these instructions call for a compulsory program *on* company time [emphasis added].)

Expectation B: The general plant superintendent now operating under a heavy production schedule insists that the training program be voluntary and *off* company time [emphasis added]. (The president has said that he will order the plant superintendent to comply with the conditions specified by the training director if this is needed.)

LEGITIMACY ASSESSMENTS

[Note that this dimension is treated as a dichotomous variable.]

1. Assuming that you are the training director, do you think it was right and reasonable for the president to expect you to present a successful program under the conditions described above? ____ Yes ____ No
2. Still assuming that you are the training director, do you think it was right and reasonable for the plant superintendent to expect you to present a successful program voluntary in nature and off company time? ____ Yes ____ No

ASSESSMENTS OF NEGATIVE SANCTIONS

[Note that this dimension is treated as a 5-point scale.]

3. What do you anticipate will happen to you, the training director, if you do not follow the wishes of the plant superintendent and go ahead with compulsory meetings on company time, invoking the authority of the president and then fail to produce good results? (Use scale below for your answer.)
4. What do you anticipate will happen to you, the training director, if you fail to produce a successful program under the conditions that you go ahead with voluntary meetings, off company time? (Use scale below.)

   0   No disapproval
   1   Mild disapproval
   2   Strong disapproval but no formal action taken
   3   Lose possibility of salary increases or promotion
   4   Placed in a lower-status position or discharged

192

CHOICE OF ACTION

5. What would you do in the situation described above? (Encircle your answer.)
   a. Request presidential order to plant superintendent and set up compulsory program on company time. [*Maximize A*]
   b. Conduct program according to plant superintendent's wishes. [*Maximize B*]
   c. Conduct program off company time but insist that it be compulsory. [*Compromise*]
   d. Conduct program on company time but agree that it be voluntary. [*Compromise*]
   e. Postpone program. [*Avoidance*]

PREDICTION MODELS

It must be remembered that each respondent in the study answered a *hypothetical* structured role conflict incident and then gave similar information about an *actual* conflict situation in which he had become involved on his job [emphasis added]. The research task then posed the problem of constructing a model that would predict the act of conflict resolution. According to the hypothesis, this model should forecast the outcome of each act, providing the legitimacy and sanction perceptions could be assessed. Legitimacy and sanctions were given by the questionnaire or interview schedule which reported the subjective perceptions of the respondent. A set of operating rules [was] formulated to interpret these perceptions and to construct three prediction models for moral, moral-expedient, and expedient choices. The operating rules were constructed to give varying weights to the legitimacy and sanction perceptions paralleling the logic and values we estimated the incumbent would use in coming to a decision.

TABLE 1
Subjective Evaluations of Incumbents

Incumbent's Evaluation of:	Expectation	
	A	B
Legitimacy	Yes[1]	No[2]
Negative sanctions	Strong[3]	Weak[4]

To illustrate in oversimplified fashion, assume, as in Table 1, the following subjective evaluations made by the incumbent: legitimate expectations associated with A (1) and a strong penalty for failure to conform to A (3); illegitimate expectations associated with B (2) but a weak penalty for failure to conform to B (4).

If the incumbent acts in terms of a moral orientation, i.e., weighs legitimacy exclusively or more heavily, it is apparent that he would choose to follow expectation A; on the other hand, if the incumbent acts expediently, he would

193

choose to follow expectation *B;* if a moral-expedient choice is made he would weigh a positive legitimacy against a strong opposing penalty and would choose to compromise or to avoid a decision.

TABLE 2
Prediction Model as Defined by Choice (Mechanism)

Choice	Both Expectations Legitimate*					Expectation A Legitimate, B Illegitimate					Expectation A Illegitimate, B Legitimate					Both Expectations Illegitimate				
	0	1	2	3	4	0	1	2	3	4	0	1	2	3	4	0	1	2	3	4
Moral-Expedient^x																				
0	c	a	a	a	a	a	a	a	a	a	b	c	a	a	a	c	c	c	a	a
1	b	c	a	a	a	c	a	a	a	a	b	b	c	a	a	c	c	c	d	a
2	b	b	c	a	a	b	c	a	a	a	b	b	b	c	a	c	c	d	c	c
3	b	b	b	c	a	b	b	c	a	a	b	b	b	b	c	b	d	c	c	c
4	b	b	b	b	c	b	b	b	c	a	b	b	b	b	b	b	b	c	c	c
Moral^y																				
0	*	c	*	*	*	*	*	*	*	*	*	b	c	*	*	*	*	*	*	*
1	c	*	c	*	*	a	*	*	*	*	*	*	b	c	*	*	*	*	c	*
2	*	c	*	c	*	c	a	*	*	*	*	*	*	b	c	*	*	c	d	d
3	*	*	c	*	c	*	c	a	*	*	*	*	*	*	c	*	c	d	d	d
4	*	*	*	c	*	*	*	c	a	*	*	*	*	*	*	*	*	d	d	d
Expedient^z																				
0	*	*	*	*	*	*	*	*	*	*	*	*	*	*	*	*	*	*	*	*
1	*	*	*	*	*	*	*	*	*	*	*	*	*	*	*	*	*	d	*	*
2	*	*	*	d	*	*	*	dc	dc	*	*	*	dc	d	*	*	d	*	*	*
3	*	*	d	d	d	*	*	d	dc	dc	*	*	dc	dc	d	*	*	*	*	*
4	*	*	*	d	d	*	*	*	d	dc	*	*	*	dc	dc	*	*	*	*	*

The horizontal scale indicates negative sanctions associated with expectation *B;* the vertical scale, negative sanctions associated with expectation *A.*

Sanction scale

0 = no disapproval

1 = mild disapproval

2 = strong disapproval but no formal action taken

3 = lose possibility of salary increase or promotion

4 = placed in a lower status position or discharged

Acts of conflict resolution

a = maximize expectation *A*

b = maximize expectation *B*

c = compromise

d = avoidance

*An asterisk in the table denotes the same as the action predicted by the moral-expedient mechanism.

^{x}This program predicts for the person who weighs both legitimacy and sanctions relatively equally when placed in the midst of a role conflict. This is the modal model.

^{y}This program predicts for the person who weighs legitimacy of the opposing claims more heavily than the sanction penalties that may be suffered.

^{z}This program predicts for the person who weighs negative sanctions more heavily than the legitimacy of the opposing claim.

194

Table 2 shows the prediction models which result when negative sanctions are placed on a five-point scale and each combination of legitimate and illegitimate expectations are assessed. These prediction models may be likened to a computer program in which real acts are to be examined against a set of programmed predictions.

Two general principles guided all predictions made for each "choice" model. The first principle was that as the difference between the opposing penalties grows smaller, the legitimacy assessments become more important as the basis for choice. A second principle was that heavy penalties, shown by higher penalties expected from opposing claimants, would predict avoidance or compromise, since the person seeks to escape the "failure" penalty which he perceives will be evoked, regardless of the legitimacy of the expectation.

Each predicted decision is based on the rule sets which were, in turn, the assumed assessments the incumbent might make of sanctions and legitimacy at the 100 different choice points. Applying the rules to the moral-expedient model gives predicted actions for each of the 100 choice points; when the rules are applied to the moral choice model, 33 predicted acts result, and when applied to the expedient choice model, 32 predicted acts emerge. Across the entire range of these choices we have provided 165 predictions within the matrix of 400 possible actions (there are four possible actions a, b, c, and d at each of the 100 choice points).

The challenge to prediction then resided in the capacity of the program to forecast the actions of the incumbents as it was *assumed* they behaved under different assessments of legitimacy and sanctions [emphasis added]. Actual choice in seven sample sets of conflict situations by the business and labor leaders were examined and compared with predicted actions. First, the results of the correct predictions for the moral-expedient choice model will be presented. Finally the over-all success of the prediction table will be shown combining the moral-expedient results with those of the moral and expedient models.

RESULTS

Table 3 makes a comparison of the proportions of correct predictions obtained for each of the situation samples as programmed into the moral-expedient model. This model was considered the modal type, i.e., it was assumed that most decision makers would weigh legitimacy and sanction relatively equally. We observe correct predictions of 59, 60, 70, 60, 43, 52, and 35 per cent for the various samples. The over-all predictive accuracy for the moral-expedient choice is 52 per cent. It can be noted that an average of 62 per cent correct predictions were secured for the open-end role conflict cases and 43 per cent correct predictions for the structured type of role conflict situation. This suggests that the data given by respondents out of their own experience may enable the researcher to predict more accurately.

Not shown in Table 3 are the results obtained for the extreme *moral* and *expedient* choice models [emphasis added]. The moral choice model which holds 33 alternate predictions (see Table 2) showed that an additional 10 per cent of the cases (12 out of 115) were predicted correctly. The expedient choice model with its 32 alternate predictions provided correct prediction of another 9 per cent (10 out of 115). Thus, the moral and expedient models provided accurate predictions for an additional 19 per cent of the cases (22 out of 115).

TABLE 3

Analysis of the Predicted Accuracy of the *Moral-Expedient* Choice Model by Type of Role Conflict Situation and Sample Population [Emphasis Added]

Test Population	Structured Situation		Open-End Situation	
		%		%
Business managers 1			10/17[a]	59
Business managers 2	9/21	43	9/15	60
Training directors	7/20	35	9/13	70
Labor leaders	10/19	52	6/10	60
Total[b]	26/60	43	34/55	62

[a]The numerator gives the number of correct predictions; the denominator indicates the total number of responses.

[b]For both structured and open-end situations, the ratio of correct predictions to total number of responses was 60/115 or 52 per cent.

The percentage of correct predictions secured from the summation of all cases based on the 165 predicted actions in the 400-cell probability matrix is shown in Table 4. This table shows the difference between the proportions expected in each situation according to chance expectancy and the proportion actually obtained on the basis of all three choice mechanisms. The differences are shown

TABLE 4

Comparison of Correct Predictions for Seven Situation Samples of Test Population for All Three Choice Models

Test Population	Number of Cases	Correct Predictions	Percentage of Correct Predictions	t
Business managers 1	———	———	———	———
	17	13	76	4.0
Business managers 2	21	14	67	3.3
	15	11	73	3.4
Training directors	20	14	70	3.5
	13	11	85	5.0
Labor leaders	19	13	68	3.3
	10	6	60	1.8
Total	115	82	71	6.9

196

to be at the .01 level of significance, except for one sample. The over-all predictive accuracy is shown to be 71 per cent. It may be concluded that the hypothesis can be accepted: there is evidence that role conflict resolutions of business and labor leaders in the population studied can be predicted with a high degree of accuracy. Seven situations sampled provided high proportions of successful predictions. These predictions fall below the 91 per cent accuracy which Gross and his associates obtained for their total population. However, Ehrlich, Rinehart, and Howell report predictions in the 50 to 60 per cent range for a number of studies of police patrolmen confronted by typical on-the-job conflicts.

Improvement of Predictive Accuracy

It is not unreasonable to strive for higher predictability. The theory of role conflict resolution has yielded 71 per cent correct predictions. The possibility of increasing validity is challenging. We know that various errors were introduced and certain variables escaped measurement. Four modifications are suggested for improved predictability: (1) inclusion of a more exhaustive set of factors relevant to the decision-making process; (2) improvements in research and statistical methodologies; (3) refinement and quantification of the factors in the Gross theory of role conflict resolution; and (4) search for more parsimony in predictive factors.

Inclusion of More Variables

A decision-making model has been suggested by Irwin Bross in which the decision-making process involves a rational and intelligent calculation of: (*a*) a set of alternative actions, (*b*) an array of outcomes for each action, (*c*) probabilities associated with the outcomes, and (*d*) values resulting from each outcome.

Bross suggests that, when these data are available, a course of action is selected through the application of a decision criterion or choice mechanism. This refers to a generalized action principle utilized by the decision maker who sorts out a particular mode of action from his own hierarchy of values to fit the expected outcomes in order to make a specific choice. For example, in our study the decision criterion is: The decision maker minimizes some composite of negative sanctions and illegitimate expectations following a moral-expedient, a moral, or an expedient choice.

The key elements in decision making are possible actions, outcomes, probabilities, values, and a decision criterion. The theory of role conflict resolution as employed here follows closely these key elements but with variations and some omissions. Respondents were asked to focus on four possible actions and to weigh outcomes based on legitimacy of expectations and on negative sanctions associated with thwart and failure pressures. Value definitions were secured by gathering the managers' subjective evaluation of legitimacy and sanctions.

197

Certain omissions, if included in the theory and future research, might improve predictive efficiency:

Loss of Probability Estimates of Success or Failure

Bross has said that decision making involves both a value system and a prediction system. The prediction system includes estimates of probability of success or failure of alternate courses of action. We asked the respondent to consider the (negative) *values* associated with each of the expectations but *not* the *probabilities* [parentheses and emphasis added]. Sometimes, for example, respondents said that the question of failure was not appropriate — that they did not expect to fail or that failure was almost impossible in the situation.

Loss of Positive Sanction as an Influencing Factor

The sanction factors were restricted to negative sanctions, but positive rewards do impel some actions even when an expectation is considered illegitimate and strong negative sanctions are expected. Therefore, positive sanctions should be included if some types of actions are to be understood. The *net* desirability of an outcome may be its most important feature.

Loss of Measures of Super Sanctions, Job Preservation

Respondents often found themselves forced to act against the direction of specific legitimacy and sanction because they were forced to act according to their interpretation of the requirements of their jobs. Avoidance and even compromise were sometimes impossible choices if they wished to retain their positions.

Loss of a Predominantly Moral or Predominantly Expedient Response

In our study, we assumed that the respondent weighed both legitimacy and sanctions. We lost a certain number of predictions because some respondents acted on wholly legitimate evaluations or for wholly expedient reasons.

Improvements in Methodologies

Research experiences have made us aware of certain errors that may have reduced the accuracy of prediction.

Coding Error

There were coding errors because there was no initial agreement on the coding of a number of types of action when independent judgments of the respondents' answers to the open-end cases were made. Agreement was obtained, however, when we thoroughly discussed the evidence offered, but there was undoubtedly some unreliability in the coding. Two major problems were encountered here: (*a*) the degree of deviation from conforming behavior which constituted compromise, and (*b*) the distinction between compromise and avoidance.

Irrationality or Failure of Comprehension

Some errors were introduced because the respondent did not weigh his action in the light of the problem as given. On some occasions when respondents were interviewed it was found that they simply did not understand what was wanted. This may have reflected their insensitivities to the social environment as well as deficiencies on the researchers' part. For example, the questionnaire failed to communicate to some respondents how they were to draw an example of role conflict from their experiences.

Quantification of the Variables

For improvement, Gross and his associates stress primarily the refinement and quantification of the factors in their model. This was done in this study by placing the sanction variable on a five-point scale. But the study could be improved in at least two ways.

Loss of Quantitative Measures of Legitimacy

Legitimacy was treated as a dichotomous attribute. This meant that a very strong feeling about legitimacy was treated in the same way as a very weak reaction. This lack of precision caused errors. In numerous cases respondents said both parties presenting conflicting expectations were perceived as making legitimate requests. These requests often involved a super legitimacy factor — a legitimacy not only of a position or department responsibility but also of responsibility to the company policy or higher-ranking personnel. This is similar to the problem of suboptimization discussed in current management literature.

Classification and Measures of Personal Orientation

The personal orientation of the decision maker is a crucial issue in conflict situations. It was a major assumption of this study that the personal orientation of an individual changes over time and with the specific features of the conflict situation. It may be that the Gross model of conflict resolution which assumes that moral, moral-expedient, and expedient orientations are stable personality types may be a more useful model. This would imply that there should be a refinement of the measurement of individuals with respect to personal orientation. Gross is currently constructing a Guttman-type scale. There is an important assumption at stake here as to the validity of situational or trait psychology when dealing with this variable. Only research tests of these conflicting theories can throw light on this problem.

In summary, the researcher who would improve prediction must decide which of these possible errors should be remedied and how [he] should isolate and measure influencing variables that are not now included in the theory of conflict resolution. It appears that the refinement of the measures of legitimacy and sanctions should get priority in future research. Both measures could be converted into cardinal scales and the sanction dimension enlarged to provide for a measure of both positive and negative sanctions. The future researcher should be warned, however, that two five-point scales — one each for legitimacy and sanction — will create 625 choice points. The use of a single five-point scale (for sanctions) increased the choice points to be considered from Gross's original 16 to 100.

Summary and Suggested Future Research

An over-all predictive accuracy of 71 per cent was discovered for the type of action taken by training directors, labor leaders, and two populations of business managers when confronted by certain role conflicts. Our hypothesis stated that the decisions of an executive confronted with role conflicts can be predicted with a high degree of accuracy if his perceptions of legitimacy and sanctions are given. However, a decision criterion cannot be ignored. The decision maker sorts out a particular mode of action from his own hierarchy of values to fit the expected outcomes in order to make a specific choice. It is postulated that the decision maker minimizes some composite of negative sanctions and illegitimate expectations following a moral-expedient, a moral, or an expedient choice. It was a major assumption of this study that the personal orientation of an individual changes over time and with the specific features of the conflict situation. Choice models were constructed to provide alternate predictions for decisions arrived at by the incumbent's perceptions of legitimacy and sanctions. Gross reports that school superintendents — and this research also confirms — that most decision makers follow a moral-expedient orientation, weighing both factors relatively equally in their final decision.

Many fruitful research challenges are opened by the search for more understanding of role conflict. Further increases in predictive accuracy seem possible. Refinements in methodology have been suggested in this paper to specify the means by which this might be accomplished.

Three other goals seem especially compelling. First, the prospect of preparing social psychological job descriptions is wide open to exploration. We have barely entered the field of role stress in hierarchical structures. Social psychological job descriptions would specify the aspects of the job which, besides simple duties, make socioemotional demands on the person. The theory of role conflict resolution could provide more meaningful definitions of position stresses and strains facing a business or labor leader. Role conflicts of course have all sorts of costs to the organization, from turnover and absenteeism to ulcers and coronary pathology in executives. Social psychological job descriptions could capture the persistent conflict elements in the job and could constitute a useful tool in job placement and training.

Secondly, a new executive training method might be developed as a social scientist applied the theory of role conflict resolution in a consultative role. The social scientist would assist the administrator to work through role conflict situations as they were encountered in his actual work role. This would involve assistance in directing the assessment of alternate actions and in the rehearsal of consequences for each of these actions as the legitimacy and sanctions of opposing claimants were weighed.

Finally, the impact of the work group upon the administrator could be examined. What is the effect upon a decision maker when he is surrounded by expediently oriented superiors? What difference does it make if the group to which the administrator reports is viewed as morally oriented? What happens over time to a man who makes a series of decisions within a particular milieu? How soon can a moral orientation be replaced in a person or a group by an expedient orientation and with what consequences? In such a search a number of reality-testing techniques should be developed. How sensitive, for example, is the respondent to his position in a role conflict situation? How clearly and accurately does he perceive expectation? How rational is his weighing of sanctions? What is his tolerance for stressful situations? These are among the major questions now awaiting an answer.

D. EXTERNAL STRESSES

In addition to those forces—characteristic of almost all large, formal organizations—which propel the individual decision-makers toward the easiest consensus, there are those dysfunctional stresses which arise not so much out of the internal structure as out of the external stimuli. Three of these seem particularly striking in terms of their relevance for foreign policy-making: (1) information overload, (2) shortage of time, and (3) externally induced crisis.

1. Information Overload

Every human organization, from the individual to the national state, has some limit beyond which it cannot possibly process all the information inputs from the environment as they arrive. The following paper summarizes the experimentation in this field and indicates the types of response which the organization can make to this particular form of stress.

THE INDIVIDUAL AS AN INFORMATION PROCESSING SYSTEM

James G. Miller

Considering human beings as information processing systems has in the last decade proved useful in both experiment and theory. Some of the hoary old problems of behavior and learning theory have received a new form or have

From pages 301-28, James G. Miller, "The Individual as an Information Processing System," in Fields, William S., and Abbott, Walter (eds.), *Information Storage and Neural Control,* 1963. Courtesy of Charles C Thomas, Publisher, Springfield, Illinois, and the author. (The bibliography and references have been omitted.)

been bypassed, and some fruitful approaches to human individual, group, and social behavior have arisen.

It has been estimated that in fifty years of waking life an individual may process 10^{16} (ten thousand trillion) bits of information. A person may be looked upon as a component in an interpersonal system in which messages are sent from one node to another along channels and through nets. As an individual, he may be studied as a "black box" whose input-output relationships can be determined, or as a system of interrelated components whose performance and capacities are increasingly available to experimental investigation.

At the Mental Health Research Institute of The University of Michigan some of us work within the general systems orientation, which regards all life as a part of the physical space-time continuum. We consider this continuum to be organized into a hierarchy of levels of systems, all of which have subsystems and are themselves subsystems of larger organizations or supersystems.

* * * * *

Deciding

Deciding, as we have said, goes on in each subsystem, as well as at the system level. Much of psychology concerns choices and judgments of various sorts—psychophysical judgments, sociometric choices, economic and social decisions, and so forth. Recent work in game theory, utility theory, statistical decision theory, and group effects on judgments of their members is clarifying the processes of complex decisions. In complex reaction-time experiments it is possible to calculate accurately the amount of time which is added to the response time when a choice of behaviors is involved. This time falls to zero as the task is better practiced and the choice becomes automatic.

We have been interested in one aspect of channel capacity which can be studied at five levels of living systems. What happens at each level when a channel is overloaded?

INFORMATION INPUT OVERLOAD

From a review of the literature we were able to draw a curve which appeared to apply at each level. The general shape of this performance curve shows the output (in bits per second) rising as a more or less linear function of input until channel capacity is reached, then leveling off and finally decreasing in the confusional state. This cross-level generality appeared fairly convincingly in the empirical work of others, even though it was not recognized as such by them. At the same time, we also found suggestions as to hierarchical differences among the levels. The overall impression of the findings is that channel capacity decreases from cells to organs, to individuals, to groups, to social organizations. Processes of adjustment appear to be comparable at different levels.

We have hypothesized that there are limited numbers of such adjustment processes which behaving systems can enlist as stresses on them increase. The following adjustment processes, or mechanisms of defense, seem to be used by living systems against the stresses of information input overload. Not all living systems have all these mechanisms. The smaller systems, like neurons, appear to have fewer than the larger systems, like societies, which not only have all of them but also have complicated variations of them. These appear to be the fundamental mechanisms, but this may not be an exhaustive list:

1) *Omission,* which is simply not processing information whenever there is an extreme of overload;

2) *Error,* which is processing incorrectly, then not making the necessary adjustment;

3) *Queuing,* which is delaying responses during peak load periods and then catching up during lulls;

4) *Filtering,* which is systematic omission of certain categories of information, according to some priority scheme;

5) *Approximation,* which is an output mechanism whereby a less precise or less accurate response is given because there is no time to be precise;

6) *Multiple channels,* which parallel transmission subsystems that can do comparable tasks at the same time and consequently together can handle more information than a single channel can transmit alone;

6a) *Decentralization,* which is a special case of this; and, finally there is

7) *Escape,* which is leaving a situation entirely or taking any other steps that effectively cut off the flow of information.

Thus we have searched for quantitative similarities and differences among living systems at all levels in the way they react to information input overload, and have given special attention to (a) performance characteristics of a system as an information processing channel; and (b) associated adjustment processes used to relieve stress on the information processing subsystem and maintain performance.

*   *   *   *   *

Individual Research

For this study we designed and built an IOTA (Information Overload Testing Aid) apparatus [Figure 3 omitted].

This is a piece of equipment by which stimuli are presented to a subject on a transparent ground-glass screen, about 3 x 4 feet in size. The apparatus is placed on a table in front of the subject, who responds by pushing appropriate buttons arrayed before him. Stimuli are thrown on the back of the screen by a Perceptoscope, which is a projector capable of showing movie film at rates of from one to twenty-four frames per second. The film contains a program which presents black arrows on a white background, which can appear in from one to eight of the eight two-inch wide vertical slots which run down the screen. Arrows can assume any one of eight angular positions, like clock hands. Before the subject is a set of eight buttons for each of the slots being used. Since he can see stimuli in a maximum of four slots at once, altogether he has thirty-two buttons, four sets of eight buttons each. If an arrow in Position *B* appears in Slot 3, the correct response is to push Button *B* of the set for Slot 3. Any other response is an error. If the subject pushes none, that is an omission.

Queuing is also possible. The subject has a foot pedal with which he can lower or raise opaque strips behind each of the slots. At the beginning of each test, only the top square in each of the slots being used is open so that light can come through. If the subject pushes the pedal, he can move the opaque strips to open as many as eleven more squares, a maximum of twelve; or by pushing the pedal in the other direction he can close these up again, as he wishes. The moving picture film is made so that if an arrow appears in Position *B* in Slot 3 in Frame 1 of the film, it goes to the next lower position in that slot in Frame 2, and to the next lower position in Frame 3, until having gone through all twelve positions, it finally disappears from the screen. In the meantime other stimuli may be appearing higher in the same slot, or in other slots. Therefore, when the subject pushes his queuing pedal he gives himself more time to respond to the stimulus before it disappears. He can filter by paying attention only to the arrows pointing up, or to those pointing to the left, rather than to those pointing to all eight positions. He can approximate by pushing all four left buttons in Slot 3, if he is not certain in which of the four left directions the arrow pointed, but knows it pointed toward the left; or by pushing all eight buttons for Slot 3 if he simply saw an arrow but has no idea of its direction. On occasion, he can use multiple channels by working with both hands at the same time. Finally, escape is possible, if he gives up and refuses to continue the task. So all the mechanisms of adjustment that we have mentioned are possible on the IOTA.

This apparatus can increase the amount of information per second in several ways: (1) by increasing the ensemble, or the number of alternate positions for the arrows from two (1 bit) to eight (3 bits); (2) by speeding the movie; (3) by increasing the range, or raising the number of slots used simultaneously; or (4) by altering the degree of regularity or randomness of the presentations.

Two male college students were used as subjects in this study. Before being tested, they were thoroughly trained in the procedure, including the use of all the adjustment processes.

The button-pushing performance of each subject was recorded on a kymograph and was compared with the program of stimuli presented. These raw data were fed into a computer programmed to calculate the input (stimulus presentation) and output (subject's response) rates in bits of information per second, using the Shannon information statistic.

Data obtained with this equipment (Figure 4) produce a curve of the same general shape as do data at the level of cell and organ when input in bits per second is plotted against output in bits per second. Within the range tested, there is some question as to whether the output falls below channel capacity at high input rates, or whether some cut-off mechanism prevents this from happening.

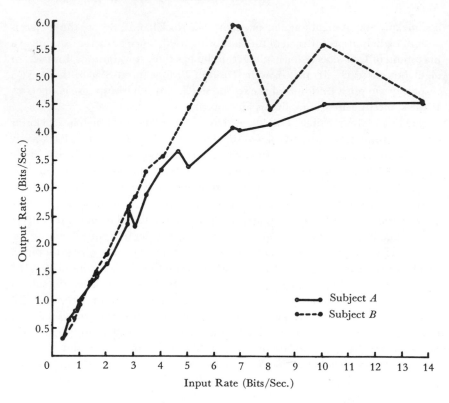

Figure 4. Performance curves for Subjects A and B

It is probable, however, that ultimately, at very high input rates, output does fall. The maximum channel capacity for an individual operating the IOTA was determined to be about six bits per second. Other experimenters have found maximum channel capacities for random material up to about thirty bits per second. With the IOTA, however, output rate is limited by partial incompatibility between the nature of the stimulus and the organization of the response mechanism, by the difficulty of making the response, and by many other factors.

Our subjects were trained regarding the possible mechanisms of adjustment available to them, and were free to select them as they saw fit. They used few or none of the mechanisms at slow rates of transmission. They tended to attempt them all at medium rates. At higher rates, under our experimental conditions, the subjects showed preference for filtering and, particularly, for omission [Figure 5 omitted]. Whether this preference is genetically determined or learned, we do not know.

Group Research

We also used the IOTA apparatus with two four-man groups. The procedure was as follows: Three members of the group, A, B, and D, face the screen. A calls out the number of the slot in which an arrow appears, and *B* calls out a letter representing the position. *C,* who is facing the buttons, but whose back is turned to the screen, then pushes the button indicated by the information he got from *A* and *B*. When *C* pushes a button a small red light appears over one of the slots, indicating which button he pushed. If his push is correct, *D* says nothing. If the push is incorrect, *D* corrects *C* and *C* tries to push the right button. The performance curves from our pretest runs with two groups have the same general appearance as the performance curves of the individual subjects, though at lower channel capacities — about 3 bits per second (Figure 6).

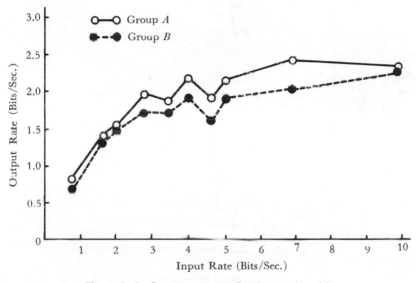

Figure 6. Performance curves for Groups A and B

This is, of course, a very specialized sort of small group in which roles are strictly differentiated. Only some members can receive sensory inputs, while others make responses or perform other tasks. There are structural similarities to certain role-differentiated groups in military life, like tank crews, bomber crews, or submarine crews. We recognize this as only one type of group, just as we used only one type of individual in our individual-level study.

The use of adjustment processes by groups was comparable to their use by individuals, although queuing was not employed. The reason for this is not clear. Figure 7 presents these findings.

Social Institution Research

My colleagues and I have conducted two investigations on informational overload of social organizations. In one project, much of which was carried out by Jay and McCornick, we studied a simulator of the air raid warning system of

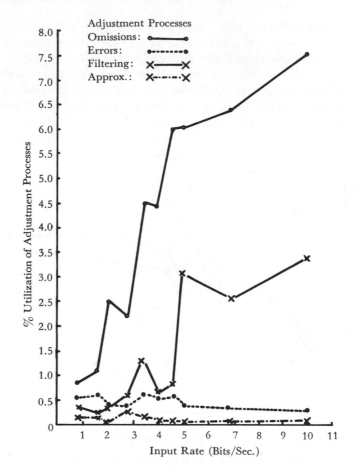

Figure 7. Average utilization of adjustment processes by both groups at various input rates

the United States and Canada. The simulator, at System Development Corporation in California, which cooperated in the study, consisted of three groups of three men, each in three separate rooms. Because of these three echelons, and because all members were not face to face, we called this an institution rather than a group, though it was a very small unit. The first room simulated a radar station in the air raid warning network; the second room simulated the room at headquarters in which the message from the local station was received; and the third room simulated a plotting board on which the location of planes was indicated at headquarters. Dots, presumably representing airplanes in geographical sectors, appeared randomly on a 21 x 21 matrix [Figure 8 omitted]. These dots, each with an associated message number, were thrown on a board by a movie projector. Each of three readers in the first room was responsible for one-third of the total board. When a dot and its number appeared in his sector, the appropriate reader wrote down on a card the coordinates of the cell in which the dot appeared and also the number of the dot. He then presented the card to his corresponding teller in the next room by passing it through a slot. The teller in turn read the card by telephone to the corresponding plotter in the third room, who wrote the message number in the proper cell on the plotting board. This board was photographed automatically at 6-second intervals, so that a continuous record of the appearance of numbers on the plotting board could be obtained. Thus, there were three entirely separate channels in this system, since Reader *A* always gave his information only to Teller *A,* who passed the message only to Plotter *A,* and so on for Team 2 and Team 3. The performance curves for these teams had shapes similar to those curves obtained at the individual and group levels when input in bits per second was plotted against output in bits per second. Maximum channel capacity was about four bits per second, approximately in the range of the group, probably because information passed through about as many components as in the group, rather than through more, as would have been the case in a larger social institution (Figure 9). These subjects also had much more practice than those in our group research and had greatly improved their transmission rates since their earlier trials.

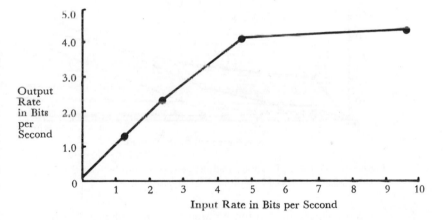

Figure 9. Average performance curves for teams in Social Institution Experiment

Four adjustment processes were used by the teams in these studies — omission, error, queuing, and filtering. The experimental instructions prevented use of approximation and multiple channels. Utilization of all adjustment processes was measured in percentages, except for queuing, which was measured in average number of seconds of delay (Figure 10).

An associated study directed by Meier dealt with the effects of overloads of demands upon the Undergraduate Library of The University of Michigan at periods of peak use. The inflow of students and faculty into this library, each person with special needs, is not an overload of energy or matter, for the library is never actually physically unable to hold them. The demands upon members of the library staff for service, however, can constitute what is essentially an information overload.

Participant observation and other operations research procedures were employed to find how much the library was used at top load periods and what changes occurred in library functions at such times. Since no significant difference in average time of getting a book was found between periods of light and of heavy use, the library may not have been under real performance overload at any time. Rough efforts were made to calculate the number of bits of information flowing through the library. It was determined that the average book title in the card catalog contains about 135 bits of information, and that the average reader processes between 50,000 and 90,000 bits per hour of reading.

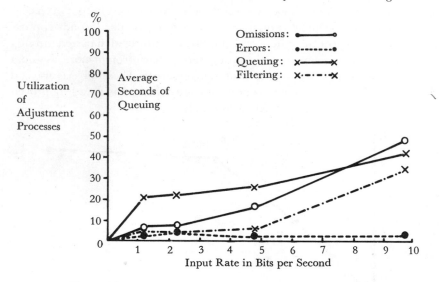

Figure 10. Average utilization of adjustment processes by teams in Social Institution Experiment

Perhaps the most significant finding by Meier and his colleagues was that a series of adjustment processes occurred, or could occur, in the library to cope with the overload. He recognizes the similarity of his list to the one presented earlier in this chapter. However, he found more complex forms of these adjustment processes, or "policies" as he calls them, in this complicated social institution with its many subsystems carrying out numerous activities. His list follows: Queuing; priorities in queues and backlogs; destruction of low priority inputs (filtering); omission; reduction of processing standards (approximation); decentralization (a special case of use of multiple channels); formation of independent organizations near the periphery (multiple channels); mobile reserve (multiple channels); rethinking procedures; redefinition of boundaries of the system; escape; retreat to formal, ritualistic behavior; and dissolution of the system with salvage of its assets. Whether there are new adjustment processes here, or simply special cases of those we have listed is a question for debate; but that such adjustment policies are used, there can be no question.

Summary of Our Research

For five levels of organization, or systems, viewed as information processing channels, the following propositions appear to have support:

A. When information input in bits per second is increased, the output at first follows the input more or less as a linear function, then levels off at a channel capacity, and finally falls off toward zero. We have yet to determine whether the larger systems have a cut-off mechanism which prevents the final fall in output. Though such a mechanism may delay this fall, the weight of evidence suggests that it must finally occur.

This decrease of information output rate in living systems is not the result of destruction of the system by an overload of the energy which conveys the information because (1) the process is reversible—decrease of input rate immediately raising output rate back to channel capacity, and (2) final irreversible change of such systems by energy input undoubtedly occurs when the energy is orders of magnitude greater than that involved in informational overload.

B. There is a hierarchical, cross-level difference in maximum channel capacity. Assuming pulse-interval coding, we found this to be of the order of 4,000 bits per second for neurons in the frog sciatic nerve, and about fifty bits per second for a single channel in the visual nervous system of the rat. It was six bits per second for the individual, three bits per second for a single-channel group, and three to four bits per second per channel in a small social institution with about the same number of components in each channel as there were in the group.

Apparently the more components there are in an information processing system, the lower is its channel capacity. There are several reasons for this. Two of the most obvious are that recoding of information is necessary at the border between each component and the next, and that such recoding always results in loss of a certain amount of information. Moreover, if there are n components in any system, one must have a lower channel capacity than the others, and the statistical probability of there being such a slow component is always greater as n increases. This sluggish component constitutes a bottleneck, since no channel is faster than its slowest component.

C. Several of the adjustment processes are used by all of these systems, the use increasing as input rate rises.

D. Fewer adjustment processes seem to be available to the systems at the lower levels. Those employed at the higher levels appear to be more complex as well as more numerous, although their fundamental similarity to the lower level processes is clear.

Of course the findings for other types of systems at each of the levels might be different in significant ways from our findings in the particular systems we chose to study. The goal of these projects was to determine whether a cross-level formal identity could be confirmed for any examples of systems at different levels.

It is apparent that interesting insights arise when not only individuals, but all living organisms and organizations are viewed as information processing systems.

2. The Compression of Time

Closely related to the problem of *too much information* is that of *too little time,* a condition which is so normal a part of the decision-maker's life. Whereas Miller focussed on the response of the organism *qua* organism to its stress, Lanzetta focusses here on some of the internal details and concerns himself with those effects which can, in turn, hamper the problem-solving effectiveness of the group. His introduction of nagging and badgering as additional stress is appropriate since they are quite often the normal concomitants of time shortage.

GROUP BEHAVIOR UNDER STRESS

JOHN T. LANZETTA

The primary aim of this study was to investigate the effects of situational stress on the behavior of individuals interacting in small groups. Motivation, as an independent variable, was also introduced because it was felt its interaction with stress was not thoroughly understood and because, on a priori grounds, it seemed that the effects of stress on problem-solving behavior would be a function of the motivation of the group.

Rosenzweig, in his attempt to conceptualize reactions to frustration, called specific attention to the necessity for including a consideration of the defense reactions of social groups for an adequate account of these adjustive mechanisms. Since that time the effects of stress on social groups have assumed increasing practical importance as a result of work done by social scientists during World War II. The data collected by the Research Branch, Information and Educational Division of the Army, as reported in the *American Soldier* series, indicated the importance of stress as a determiner of attitudes, morale, and group efficiency, while the work of Grinker and Speigel documented the effects of stress on combat performance and motivation. This work, as well as much

From John T. Lanzetta, "Group Behavior under Stress," *Human Relations,* VIII (1955), 29-52 (the footnotes and the bibliography and references have been omitted). Reprinted by permission of the author and *Human Relations.*

unsystematized observation, implies that one of the possible variables affecting a person's reaction to stress is the presence of other individuals with whom he must interact in the performance of some common task. If this is so, the effects of stress on individuals in groups will differ from the effect of stress on individuals in an "alone" situation.

Despite the apparent importance of this variable, an examination of the literature indicates that previous studies have centered attention on the behavior of individuals working alone or co-acting. These studies of the effects of stress on emotional, cognitive, and performance aspects of behavior are a possible source of valuable tentative hypotheses in the investigation of group behavior. However, hypotheses deduced from this work can only be held tenuously, since it is fairly well established that the behavior of one member of a group is to some degree a function of the behavior of other group members.

To the author's knowledge there is only one experimental study of the behavior of interacting individuals under what could be called "stress" conditions. This excellent experiment by French is an exploratory study of the dynamics of group behavior in strongly emotional situations. It differs from the present investigation primarily in that it does not concern itself with changes in dynamics within the same group under "stress" and control conditions.

The present study can thus contribute to the growing body of empirical knowledge about the functioning of small groups, as well as shed light on the experimentally neglected area of stress and interpersonal relations.

PROBLEM

Primary interest was focused on studying the effects of situational stress on the behavior of individuals interacting in small groups under two levels of motivation. The concern was with the effects stress might have on the interaction of group members as they attempt to work cooperatively on a group task—effects not only on interactions of members with each other, but of members with the task materials. The emphasis was on both social-emotional and problem-solving behavior. In addition we attempted to investigate particular group properties (e.g., morale, cohesiveness) as they were affected by stress; properties which are probably the synthesis of certain interaction patterns but which we find difficult to describe in terms of interactions alone.

It seemed necessary because of the lack of pertinent data to consider the present study an exploratory one, and as such it demanded a rather comprehensive experimental technique. The methodology utilized was patterned directly after that used by Carter *et al.*, and can be considered as yielding data at three descriptive levels:

(a) group properties (e.g., cohesiveness)
(b) interaction patterns (e.g., agreeing, disagreeing behaviors)
(c) individual characteristics (e.g., striving for group recognition, leadership)

These levels are essentially those Cattell advances. He argues that groups can be described at three levels: (a) syntality, or the behavior of the group *per se* (group properties), (b) internal structural arrangements or relationships of parts (patterning of interactions), and (c) characteristics of the average member of the population (averaged individual characteristics).

Method

The basic method used was that employed by Carter *et al.* in their studies of small groups, as reported in a series of papers. Groups composed of four subjects worked on two types of tasks in a laboratory setting. The subjects were observed by two separated observers who immediately classified their ongoing behavior in terms of a large number of categories, and after each task rated each subject on a number of traits. After completion of the two tasks, both the observers and the subjects rated the group on a series of group characteristics.

The two tasks used, a Reasoning, and a Mechanical Assembly task, are described in detail elsewhere. They represent the task which had high loadings in a factor analysis of leadership ratings on a series of six tasks, as reported by Carter. His results indicate: "... that each individual has certain abilities which, related to a particular task, are unique and enable him to fulfil leadership functions as the group attempts to accomplish the task. While each person may have some amount of 'general leadership ability' it is clear that his leadership ability is to a large extent relative to the task."

Since leadership is a variable with which we were concerned, it was thought best to use the two representative tasks.

The Experimental Situations

The two independent variables in this investigation were imposed stress and motivation. Three stress and two motivating conditions were used, i.e., an attempt was made to create three experimental stress atmospheres and two experimental motivating atmospheres for the purpose of inducing in the subjects a perception of varying degrees of stress and motivation. Checks on the adequacy of the experimental atmospheres were afforded by the recording of criteria behaviors (tension indicators and signs of frustration) and by a rating on the motivation of the group by the observers and the subjects. A description of the experimental atmospheres follows:

Stress

An attempt was made to create a non-stressful atmosphere, a mildly stressful atmosphere, and a fairly high stress atmosphere.

The non-stress (NS) situation was comparable to the situations used in previous studies by Carter *et al.* The subjects were brought into the situation and shown the materials for the tasks. They were informed that we were interested in observing how groups interact while performing certain types of task, and then told to proceed. No mention was made of how long we expected the tasks to take or how well they were expected to perform them. The only stresses that would appear to exist in such a situation are those which are inherent in any experimental situation that is unfamiliar and requires face to face contact with comparative strangers.

The mildly stressful (MS) situation was essentially the same as the above with the addition of a time limit for performance of the tasks. To make the time barrier more prominent the time remaining for completion of the task was called off to the subjects every five minutes, until only five minutes remained. In the last five minutes time remaining was told to the subjects at one minute intervals. Time limitations have served as stressful conditions in assessment work done during World War II, and by Lindsley and McKinney in experiments. All found that it served effectively to produce frustrating reactions.

The high stress (HS) situation consisted of the above procedure, time limitations, plus the addition of other barriers. For the reasoning task the additional stress was imposed by:

(a) informing the subjects when a conclusion reached was in error. The informing was done over a loudspeaker, the experimenter being in a separate room. This tended to make the time barrier more prominent since subjects were not allowed to rush through the task, coming to many false conclusions.

(b) the experimenter continually offered comments over the loudspeaker to the effect that the group was rather stupid, that the items were extremely easy and they should be doing much better on them, that "X" minutes had passed and they were not accomplishing much, and that the experimenter was surprised that they were having difficulty since he felt these items to be extremely simple.

For the mechanical assembly task additional stress consisted of the same badgering as in (b) above. In addition:

(a) a barrier was imposed which thwarted completion of the task. The task was assembly of a bridge out of pre-cut and pre-drilled lumber. The subjects were asked to "use your imagination on this task since you are to visualize yourselves as a combat engineering team whose job is to build a bridge across this river (the river was two strips of tape on the floor). The side of the river you are on was orginally completely mined but a small area (this area was defined by two lights) has been cleared and you have only that space to work in." When subjects crossed into the mined area two photo tubes and accessory circuits tripped a relay causing a bell to sound rather loudly and they were told harshly by the experimenter, "You are in the mined area, move out of it immediately." Initially, the subjects were informed that "...on the basis of present information from intelligence headquarters the enemy is sufficient distance away to allow you about 20 minutes to build the bridge across the river." After 10 minutes had elapsed, however, they were told that new information showed the enemy to be much closer than was thought, and they would have only 5 more minutes in which to work. The work space to which they were confined was extremely small, being barely larger than the largest pieces of lumber for the task, and manipulating materials and constructing were extremely difficult inside the barriers. Every time a barrier was violated they were harshly reprimanded and made to move back into the work area. In addition, as was mentioned above, they were continually reminded of the remaining time and badgered as to their stupidity, slowness, and lack of ability.

The addition of time barriers conformed to Rosenzweig's definition of a passive external stress, in that no threat to the organism was produced. The badgering technique, the implications of inadequacy, seems to conform to Rosenzweig's definition of an active external stress in that it *is* threatening to the group. A further justification for assuming the badgering to be stressful is that the technique was used effectively by Bruner and Postman in creating stress.

*　　*　　*　　*　　*

DISCUSSION

Stress

Attention will be directed to two main questions concerned with interpersonal relations and problem-solving behavior respectively, as they are affected by stress. No attempt will be made to discuss all the nuances of the data. It is felt that the methodology utilized is not sufficiently refined to allow conclusions to be drawn from any isolated correlation or test of significance. Therefore, only data which are supported by results obtained with other instruments, or data which integrate well into the total picture, will be discussed.

Interpersonal Relations under Stress

Analysis of the interaction indices indicates that the behavior changes under stress could be considered to fall into three classes: (a) changes in behavior which would tend to cause tension, friction, or disequilibrium in the group, (b) changes in behavior which would tend to cause a decrease in tension, and increased integration of the group, and (c) changes in problem-solving behavior. The first two certainly reflect a change in interpersonal relations. It was found that as stress increased there was a decrease in behaviors associated with internal friction in the group; a decrease in the number of disagreements, arguments, aggressions, deflations and other negative social-emotional behaviors, as well as a decrease in self-oriented behaviors. Concomitant with this decrease was an increase in behaviors which would tend to result in decreased friction and better

216

integration of the group; an increase in collaborating, mediating, cooperating behaviors. Apparently, as stress increases, individuals attempt to keep interpersonal tensions at a low level, substituting positive, group-oriented behaviors for negative, individually-oriented behaviors.

These changes in behavior should result in changes in characteristics of the group as perceived by both observers and subjects. The analysis of the ratings of group characteristics indicates that both observers and participants saw the groups as less competitive, more cooperative, and more friendly under increased stress. These changes are almost certainly a reflection of the changes in behavior noted above, and they indicate decreasing friction and tension within the group, and increasing internal harmony.

The data from still another source, the ratings of individual characteristics, lend more support to this finding. Individuals were rated as being more cooperative, less aggressive, less oriented toward individual solution, and less confident under high stress than under non-stress. The first three changes can be interpreted as leading to a decrease in friction and an increase in harmony within the group, while the fourth gives a clue as to why such changes might have occurred.

It can be said then, that under increased stress members of a group show more behavior which tends to reduce interpersonal tension and friction and less behavior which might lead to increased disharmony. They will become less argumentative and aggressive, and more cooperative and friendly. It is conceivable that in the face of the external stress and increasing anxiety the group members perceive the group to be a source of security and thus attempt to maintain their position in it and prevent rejection by more cooperative and friendly behavior. That the group members do become less confident, and probably more anxious, is supported by the decrease in the self-confidence ratings made by observers.

The majority of the studies on stress have been concerned with the performance of individuals in non-group situations, and in general they find that stress leads to the typical reactions of: (a) aggression, (b) withdrawal or escape behavior, (c) regression, (d) neurotic symptoms, etc. They also find that the strength or degree of the above reactions is positively related to the degree of stress. Therefore, these rather negative emotional behaviors should increase as stress increases. We find the opposite occurring.

Some incidental observations made on the groups may shed some light on this apparent discrepancy. It will be recalled that the order of exposure of a group to high stress was varied systematically, some groups receiving high stress on the first session. It was noted that groups receiving stress at their first session were much more recalcitrant about returning for further sessions than the groups which had worked under non-stress. On the average about 30 per cent more cancellations were received from "high stress on first session" groups. It was also apparent that individuals in these groups were more often late for the next session, and when they arrived were often sullen and irritable with the experimenter. Finally, it may be said that no aggression against the experimenter was recorded for the non-stress sessions, whereas some aggression against the experimenter occurred under the stress conditions, although the frequency was so low that no analysis could be attempted.

All the above can be interpreted as manifestations of aggression, withdrawal, or escape behavior with regard to the experimental situation. This would be in agreement with the literature since in almost all the reported studies the behavior noted, in fact the only behavior possible, was a reflection of the interaction between the subject and the experimental conditions, or the experimenter, *both probably being associated with the imposed stress.*

Wright, in a study of the influence of frustration upon the social relations of young children, found essentially similar results. He reports that, "There was a significant increase in the cohesiveness of the groups under the influence of frustration. The amount of time spent in cooperative behavior significantly increased, and time spent in conflict behavior decreased." This change in inter-child social emotional behavior was accompanied by a marked change in attitude toward the experimenter. The predominantly friendly attitude in the free play situation changed to one of considerable hostility in the frustrating situation.

Both Wright's and the present study seem to indicate that where the stimuli are perceived to be associated with the imposed stress the subjects react in a fashion predictable from previous experiments on individuals, but where the stimuli (other individuals) are not associated with the imposed stress and are in fact probably perceived as supports in facing this threat, the behavior is the opposite of what would be predicted.

This increase in integrative behavior is by no means a unique observation. It coincides, more or less, with the layman's observation that disaster sometimes leads to decreased bickering and increased integration of group members in families, athletic teams, cities, or nations.

Problem-Solving Behavior under Stress

We include in our discussion of problem-solving not only behaviors which are considered to be directly related to solution of the problems, but also those characteristics of the group which are probably interrelated with or resultant from such behaviors.

From the interaction categories it was noted that under increased stress there was a decrease in initiating behaviors, mainly in terms of "diagnoses situation, makes interpretation" kinds of behavior, and an increase in a more "general discussion of the task" kind of behavior. In the light of the recorded increase in equalitarian, group-oriented behaviors, these changes probably reflect a more democratic, less individually-oriented approach to solution rather than a more disorganized, less efficient approach. This would also be supported by the observers' ratings of group and individual characteristics. They rated productivity, efficiency, and morale as being highest under mild stress and about the same under non-stress and high stress conditions, while talkativeness was rated lowest under mild stress. These results would indicate that the problem-solving performance of the groups was best under mild stress and about equal under non-stress and high stress.

The subjects did not perceive the situation in this way. They rated productivity as similar under non-stress and mild stress, and lower under high stress although their other ratings are inconsistent with this. Activity, interest in job completion, motivation, and morale are all perceived to be highest under mild stress and about the same under the other two stress conditions. These characteristics would presumably be highly related to the productivity of the group, and would lead one to believe that perceived productivity would also be highest under mild stress. It is possible that this apparent discrepancy is simply a reflection of a change in ego-involvement and level of aspiration of the group members. If one assumes that level of aspiration increases monotonically as stress increases, then one would expect the above co-variations to occur. Under non-stress, although the group does not see itself as especially active, motivated, interested in job completion, or with very high morale, its low level of aspiration would still lead it to perceive productivity as adequate. Under mild stress even though activity, motivation, etc., are felt to be high, the increased level of aspiration would result in no increase in perceived productivity, *even if productivity were actually higher*. Then under high stress, with activity, motivation, etc., perceived to be at about the non-stress level, the high aspiration level would result in a much lower rating of productivity. That such a change in ego-involvement and level of aspiration is probably occurring is supported by the participants' ratings of "pride in group" and attitude towards the situation. It would be expected that with increased level of aspiration and concomitant decreased productivity, the "failure" experienced would become more acute, and satisfaction with the situation would decrease. The ratings indicate that the subjects felt less pride in their groups and also had an increasingly less favorable attitude toward the situation as stress increased.

3. Crisis

A third possible external stress is that of a crisis — an event which tends to combine a number of more specific stresses. Most crises subject decisional groups not only to the need for handling too much information in too little time, but to such additional ones as frustration, intolerable ambiguity, depletion of resources, and so on. Part of the folklore in political science is that totalitarian (and even other) leaders will often try to precipitate a diplomatic crisis in order to unify dissident forces at home; if the generalization is correct, the following article may shed some light on why the ploy is not always successful.

GROUP INTEGRATION DURING A CRISIS

Robert L. Hamblin

The purpose herein is to report a laboratory study designed to test further a hypothesis which was evidently first suggested by Emile Durkheim, namely, group integration increases during a crisis.

THEORY

A Crisis

All groups, whether they be large or small, powerful or weak, have the possibility of experiencing a crisis. Nations face a crisis in every sudden economic depression or inflation and in every attack by another nation. A not uncommon crisis experienced by family groups is reduction in or loss of income through unemployment, sickness, or death. When the environment changes, religious groups often face a crisis because their traditional beliefs and practices no longer suffice for solving their members' moral problems. Otherwise, religious groups may face crises of persecution of one type or another. Political parties and groups usually experience a crisis in every election or, if there is lack of electoral machinery, in every revolution. A crisis, an urgent situation in which all members of a group face a common threat, is a generic social experience.

Group Integration

Durkheim seems to have used the term integration to refer to the degree to which the behavior of group members is group-oriented rather than self-oriented. Recently, however, Lanzetta re-defined integration as the tendency to build harmony and reduce conflict among group members. Both definitions have been used in previous research and both definitions will be used in this study.

Previous Research

The first empirical study of group integration during crises is found in Durkheim's classic, *Suicide*. Early in his study, Durkheim established that egoistic suicide rates vary inversely with social integration. Then he observed that national suicide rates decrease during certain crises—political revolutions,

---

From Robert L. Hamblin, "Group Integration During a Crisis," *Human Relations,* XI (1958), 67-76 (the footnotes and the bibliography and references have been omitted). Reprinted by permission of the author and *Human Relations*.

elections, and popular wars. After examining and rejecting several different explanations of these phenomena, he suggested that the reason for the decreases in suicide rates was that group integration had increased during the crises. At another point, he (perhaps unknowingly) applied the same principle to account for a decrease in suicide rates of religious groups experiencing crises of persecution.

During the last few years, a half-century after Durkheim's monumental work, a number of studies have been reported which give evidence in support of Durkheim's hypothesis. Stouffer *et al.* report an increase in behavior indicative of integration among American troops during the crisis of battle. Lanzetta, Schachter *et al.*, Sherif, and Swanson, using very different designs, have reported an increase in behavior indicative of integration in urgent situations involving a common threat which were produced experimentally. Hence, Durkheim's hypothesis has received considerable support.

The Reason for this Study

This study resulted from asking two simple questions. The first was, Why should group integration increase during a crisis? The answer does not seem obvious until the above-mentioned studies are examined rather closely. Present in every crisis situation studied is *a likely solution* to the crisis problem — a solution that requires the cooperation of all or most of the members of the groups involved [emphasis added]. When such a solution is present, it seems very reasonable for group members to give their all to cooperation, as cooperation is the most obvious way to avoid the common threat. Also, it seems very reasonable for group members to avoid self-oriented behavior, to suppress aggressive impulses, and to act on positive impulses. This is the way to avoid alienating those whose help is very important in avoiding the threat. Although this explanation seemed to satisfy the initial question, it raised the second question: Will integration increase if a likely solution to the crisis problem is *unavailable* during the crisis [emphasis added]? A laboratory experiment, described in detail below, was designed in an attempt to find a reliable answer to this question.

METHOD

The Experimental Populations

Twenty-four populations of three were used in the experiment. The participants were either personal acquaintances of the experimental staff or residents of a housing development for married students. Ages ranged between 25 and 30 years. Half of the participants were men; the other half, women. To reduce barriers to cooperation, participants composing any given experimental population were of the same sex and were approximately the same age.

221

The Experimental Situation

An experimental situation was developed to allow the experimenter to create a "crisis" for half of the experimental populations. The situation was produced as follows:

After ushering a population into the testing-room (see *Figure 1*), the experimenter gave each participant a copy of instructions and asked them to follow as he read aloud:

Tonight you three people are going to work together as a team to play a game. You will use the equipment you see here to get a high score. We can tell you only a few things about the way to get a high score. . . .

1. Points are gained by shooting these golf balls either against the barriers down there or through the slot between the barriers.

2. When shooting a golf ball you must use a pusher and a disc or the shot will not count.

3. When you are shooting you must stand back of this line or your shot will not count.

There are other rules that you will need to know in order to get a high score.

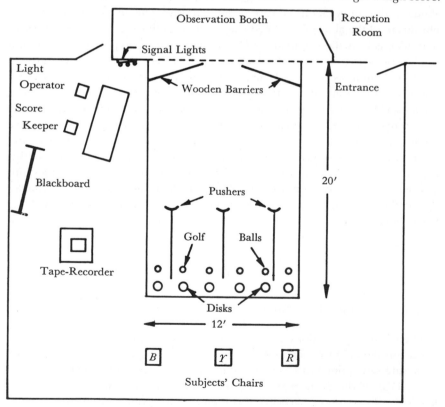

Figure 1. Diagram of experimental room

Penalties will be given each time you break these rules. You may figure out these other rules by watching the light board. The red bulb will flash every time you do something that is giving you a penalty. By figuring out what you did to get the red light, you can determine what these other rules are. The green light will flash on every time you do something that is gaining points for you.

The plan is that you will have a total of $28\frac{1}{2}$ minutes to learn these other rules and gain points. You will play for $3\frac{1}{2}$ minutes, take a $1\frac{1}{2}$-minute intermission, and so on. During the intermissions you will return to your present seat.

After each $3\frac{1}{2}$-minute playing period, your group's performance score will be recorded on the blackboard over there. These performance scores are total group scores. . . . The points you gain are cumulative. . . . The scores are the remainder left over from subtracting the penalties you receive from the points you gain. . . . The different ways of getting points and penalties have different weights. . . .

Please speak up so the observers behind the screen can hear you. The success of the experiment depends upon their being able to hear you.

Once we get underway, we cannot answer any questions. When the test period starts, you will get your instructions from this recording machine. It will tell you what to do and how much time you have remaining.

Notice the colors on your armbands correspond to the colors on the light board over there and to the colors of the golf balls.

You may consult these instructions at any time.

At this point the experimenter asked the participants for points that needed clarification. If they asked questions which could not be answered from material in the instructions, they in turn were asked to determine the answer themselves by watching the light board. The experimenter then continued:

Notice on the blackboard that there are some high-school scores. These are average scores of 12 groups of high-school students who participated in a pretest of this experiment in Michigan four years ago. We put these scores on the board to give you an idea of how well you are doing as the game progresses.

I might say that the ability to analyse a rather complex situation is the important skill in this game. I have seen many groups work very hard to make many successful shots only to lose most of the points gained through penalties because they failed to learn these other rules. For this reason we expect mature college graduates to do better than high-school students. If you do get more points, however, you will have to work hard. These high-school students did.

With this the tape recorder was started and the experimental session began. During the first three playing periods, the light operator flashed a green light whenever a participant, by driving a disc with a pusher, shot a golf ball of the color of his armband against a barrier or into the space between the barriers. She flashed a red light when a participant shot from any position other than from behind the baseline, touched the golf balls lying within the playing area with

223

anything but discs propelled by pushers, shot golf balls other than those colored like his armband, or allowed any golf ball to roll outside the playing area. In addition, a red light was flashed every time one of the three rules given in the instructions was violated.

Sixteen experimental sessions were conducted while these procedures were changed and tested. With the procedures described above, the usual group acted as though they were in a tournament. They rushed, ran, and not infrequently shouted. It was a rowdy experiment, but we feel confident that motivation was high and emotions were very real.

The Crisis

Since red and green lights were used in teaching the participants the rules of the game, the lights could be used to change the rules at the beginning of the fourth period and, hence, create a crisis.

At the beginning of each experimental session, the light operator flipped a coin. If the coin landed tails, a "crisis" was produced at the beginning of the fourth playing period by changing the rule that discs had to be used when shooting golf balls. A red light flashed every time a participant shot his ball using a disc. Green lights would flash if pushers alone were used. If, through experimentation, the participants found out the new rule, another rule was changed to continue the crisis throughout the last three playing periods. Consistent with the rule change, these "crisis" groups were not given an increment in points during the last three periods.

If the coin landed heads, the procedure described for the first three playing periods was followed during the last three periods. These "control" groups were given standard scores which slightly increased their lead over the high-school scores as the game progressed. (The scoring procedure was so ambiguous that the participants seldom questioned the validity of these scores.) These standard scores eliminated "crises" that would have occurred if true scores were given, because some of the control groups did not do as well as the "high-school students," and, thus, would have been threatened.

Measurement of Integration

1. Of all of the behavior in the experimental situation, helping seemed to be the most indicative of how much the participants were giving their all for a *common* cause. A participant could pick up and carry several balls or shove back several pucks with little extra effort. This helping saved fellow participants time and effort which could be used in finding out about the rules of the game or in gaining points to beat the high-school students. Refusal to help seemed to indicate a lack of concern for the group, and to indicate that participants were behaving as isolated individuals.

An observer was trained to put down a mark on an observation form whenever a participant retrieved another's ball or puck, handed another a pusher, or helped in any other way. Since helping in this situation was limited somewhat to the amount of shooting a group did, the final helping scores were corrected. This was done by recording the number of shots each group took and dividing that number into the number of times participants helped one another.

2. Foriezos, Hutt, and Guetzkow have developed a set of categories to facilitate the coding of behavior designed to satisfy self-oriented needs. Swanson used these categories to obtain scores which he considered a negative measure of integration. Certainly, self-oriented behavior that is designed to satisfy individual emotional needs rather than to help the group achieve its goal is the opposite of the social integration that Durkheim talked about.

An observer put down a pre-coded symbol each time a participant acted overly dominant, overly dependent, sought status in the eyes of the group, or released tension (nervous laughter, hostility, or self-disgust). According to Swanson, self-oriented behavior is, in part, a function of the volume of communication. Therefore it is desirable to subtract out the effect of communication. This was done by training an observer to record each clause spoken during the various periods and then dividing the raw, self-oriented behavior scores by the number of clauses spoken.

3. Counts of the number of positive and negative sanctions were also made. Preliminary observation indicated that the participants restricted themselves to the use of verbal sanctions. Hence, an observer was trained to put down a mark each time a participant (a) was considerate enough to praise another for action well done or (b) was upset enough to show antagonism toward either another participant or the "crazy" experiment.

Reliability

Observers were trained by having them code the behavior of training groups who read scripts aloud. Written to simulate the communication that typically occurred in the experimental situation, the scripts made possible an accurate check of the observers' coding. Immediately after a script was coded, the experimenters and the observers cooperated in recoding the script. Since this coding was done cooperatively and at leisure, it was used as a standard in computing observer error. An error was counted for every relevant unit of behavior an observer scored in the wrong category, for every relevant unit of behavior that was not scored, and for every score for which there was no relevant unit of behavior. Training continued until observer error within each category levelled off at at least ten per cent.

An exception to the above procedure was made for the helping dimension. It was decided to code this dimension just before the first sessions of the final experiment began. Since this category is rather uncomplicated, it was just explained to an observer who had previously achieved high competence on other categories. She was, however, unaware of the hypothesis to be tested.

RESULTS

The data for each index were used as follows: (a) Scores were computed for the last 13½ minutes — the "crisis" period for the crisis groups and the comparable period for the control groups. (This last 13½ minutes will be called "Period II.") (b) For each group scores were computed for the first 13½ minutes (Period I). (c) For each group the Period I score was subtracted from the Period II score. (d) These differences were averaged for the crisis groups and for the control groups. For the control groups this average of the differences shows the normal change that is expected to occur in this experimental situation. For the crisis groups this average of the differences shows both the normal change that is expected to occur in this experimental situation and the change due to the crisis. (e) The average change observed for the control group was subtracted from the average change in the crisis groups. The resulting difference should be due to the crisis but it could be due to the chance variations involved in randomization (the flipping of the coin). (f) The t-test statistic was used to calculate the probability that the difference is due to randomization. The results of this analysis for each of the indices are presented in *Table 1*.

TABLE 1
Summary of Results

| Indices of Integration | Changes for | | Difference (1)-(2) | p[a] |
	Crisis Groups	Control Groups		
Helping	−1.3	20.9	−22.2	.05
Self-oriented behavior	18.2	9.0	9.2	.10
Frequency of positive sanctions	−1.7	0.9	−2.6	.02
Frequency of negative sanctions	4.9	0.0	4.9	.0002

[a]These probabilities are for a two-tailed t-test.

The helping scores and the frequencies of positive sanctions are *positive* indices of integration. Since the differences in *Table 1*, Column 3, are *negative* in sign, the inference is that integration *decreased* during the crisis.

The self-oriented behavior scores and the frequencies of negative sanctions are negative indices of integration. Since the differences in *Table 1*, Column 3, are positive in sign, again the inference is that integration *decreased* during the crisis.

The question that directly initiated the inquiry was, Will integration increase if a likely solution to the crisis problem is unavailable during the crisis? The several indices of integration used in this experiment imply an identical answer. No, integration does not *increase* during a crisis in the absence of a likely solution; rather, it *decreases*.

226

DISCUSSION

The Validity of the Test

The experiment was obviously frustrating to the crisis groups. As a rule the members of the crisis groups were very upset during the post-experimental period. The experimenter had to exercise considerable skill and effort to reduce the tension during the half hour available. The threat was real; there is little doubt that the crisis groups experienced a real crisis. Of course, the crisis groups did not have a likely solution to the crisis problem available during Period II. Hence, the context seems to have been validly produced. Although no single index of integration used is completely valid (for example, including "antagonism against the experiment" in the frequencies of negative sanctions seems to be an obvious error), each index produced a reliable difference which leads to an identical inference. This consistency of the results argues for the overall validity of the indices. Yet the results, as evidence, seem obviously limited because *ad hoc* groups were used in a game situation in a laboratory.

Previous Research

Because of the above-mentioned limitations and because the results were not particularly anticipated, the experimental literature was searched again for evidence which might either lend support to or bring into question the findings of this study. Relevant evidence was found in Durkheim's *Suicide*, and in studies by Hovland and Sears and Moore.

As mentioned above, when the environment changes, sometimes religious groups experience obsolescence crises because their traditional beliefs and practices no longer suffice for solving their members' moral problems. Durkheim evidently assumed that certain groups in the Catholic Church had experienced such obsolescence crises and, because of it, had become Protestants. He pointed out, however, that they had up until his time failed to find new beliefs and practices that were satisfactory enough to become generally accepted in these groups and, hence, solve their crisis problem. He argued that these crises had decreased the integration of these groups as evidenced by the fact that they still had higher suicide rates than other religious groups who had evidently not experienced obsolescence crises and, hence, had remained Catholics.

Hovland and Sears's data indicate that the frequency of lynchings (intra-group aggression from the point of view of the total community) increases during economic depressions. Moore's data, in a cross-cultural community study, support the hypothesis that inter-class conflict (again intra-group aggression from the point of view of the total community) increases during periods of economic deprivation. Of course, periods of economic deprivation (including depressions) have generally been identified as crises. And until recently, at least, likely techniques for manipulating the economic system to avoid general economic deprivation have been absent. Thus, these data as well as the Durkheim data seem to agree with the results of this study—that is, they seem to show also that group integration decreases during a crisis if a likely solution to the crisis problem is absent.

Although no evidence was found in the search of the literature that negates the inferences made thus far, evidence from two studies does supplement these inferences. This evidence shows that group integration may decrease during crises for reasons other than the absence of a likely solution to the crisis problem.

Mintz has experimented with a novel crisis situation analogous to the situation in which people find themselves in a theater fire. Merton has cited bank suspension rates before and after the establishment of the Federal Deposit Insurance Corporation. Their data show that groups completely disintegrate when two rather special competitive conditions are operative during crises, namely, *the possibility of avoiding the threat by withdrawing from the crisis situation coupled with the probability that those who withdraw last will not avoid the threat.* Notice that a likely solution to the crisis problem is present in these conditions. But the likely solution, individual withdrawal, is essentially a competitive solution. Group members compete with one another to withdraw in time to avoid the common threat. It will be remembered that in the crisis situations where integration was observed to increase, a likely solution to the crisis problem was present too. But this likely solution implied cooperation rather than competition.

Theoretical Considerations

The evidence from this and previous research has led to generalizations about group integration in three different crisis situations. The theoretical basis for the first generalization has been considered already. It was observed that an increase in integrative behavior is a plausible reaction for group members in a crisis situation if a likely, cooperative solution to the crisis problem is present. Are the other two generalizations equally plausible?

Why do groups disintegrate during a crisis when a likely, but competitive, solution to the crisis problem is present? In the Mintz and Merton examples, one type of self-oriented behavior seemed to involve quick withdrawal from the crisis situation. This quick withdrawal was, of course, the only way to escape the threat. On the other hand, group-oriented behavior, that is, refusing to withdraw from the crisis situation lest others be hurt, only increases the chance of experiencing the threatened deprivation. Thus, on the basis of a simple rational model, a type of self-oriented behavior is expected to be evoked, and group-oriented behavior is expected to be avoided. In addition, the quick-acting members may be perceived by the slower acting members as frustrating agents and, thus, become targets for direct and displaced aggression. The situation offers few, if any, reasons for responding positively and suppressing negative (or aggressive) impulses.

Why does integration decrease during a crisis when a likely solution to the crisis problem is not available? A search for a possible solution is, of course, expected in this situation. But in this search there is probably little to be gained either in cooperating or going it alone. This absence of a good reason for cooperating may be enough to explain the decrease in mutual aid (or helping) that was observed during the crisis in this experiment. However, other factors may have contributed to this decrease. Undoubtedly, as one possible solution after another fails, frustration mounts. Using the principle of displacement, this mounting frustration would probably cause the group members to over-react to the things that they normally do to irritate one another. Of course this over-reaction could take the form of antagonism, as it was observed to take in this experiment. But very much antagonism is unlikely both because of the normal inhibitions against showing antagonism and because antagonism might alienate those whose help may be important if an effective solution is found. The withdrawal of help and the withdrawal of positive reactions are, of course, more subtle (and less risky) forms of aggression which this over-reaction could take. But then, aggression is not the only way to handle mounting frustration or tension. Foriezos, Hutt, and Guetzkow have pointed out that the type of self-oriented behavior measured in this experiment is an alternative way for individuals to reduce tensions in a group situation.

Future Research

The generalizations (or principles) and the explanations presented were fabricated from evidence from a number of very dissimilar studies. Although this dissimilarity increases confidence in the generality of the principles and, perhaps, the explanations, it also increases the possibility of error. Hence, it seems appropriate for these conclusions to be checked in an appropriate experiment. The experiment should involve three crisis variations and a control variation. In one crisis variation, a likely, cooperative solution to the crisis problem should be available, and in the other, a solution to the crisis problem should not be available. Of course, the intensity of the threat ought to be comparable in each crisis situation. Also, apart from the crisis experiences indicated, the treatment in the crisis and control variations should be alike. There are a number of untested hypotheses implied in the above discussion that could be tested in such an experiment. For example, it was implied that group integration ought to decrease more during a crisis when a likely, competitive solution is present than when a solution is not available.

SUMMARY AND CONCLUSIONS

A number of crisis situations were examined when an increase in integration has been observed, and it was discovered that a likely, cooperative solution to the crisis problem was present in all the situations. This discovery led to the question, Will group integration increase in the absence of a likely solution to the crisis problem? An experiment was designed to answer this question. Twenty-four *ad hoc* groups were brought into a laboratory situation. Half of these groups experienced an appropriate and seemingly genuine crisis. Four indices of integration based on observational data showed reliable differences in the behavior of the crisis and the control groups. These indices all indicated that integration decreased rather than increased as a result of the crisis. These unexpected results led to the consideration of other previous research. The evidence from all the previous research and the evidence from this experiment seem to support the following conclusions: Group integration decreases during a crisis if a likely solution to the crisis problem is unavailable. Group integration increases during a crisis if a likely cooperative solution to the crisis problem is present. Groups disintegrate during a crisis if a likely, competitive solution to the crisis problem is present.

E. PUBLIC OPINION AS A DECISIONAL INPUT

Up to this juncture Part Two has treated the foreign policy decision-making process as one in which the major inputs are those which originate within the decisional unit itself (Section C), or in its very immediate environment in the form of stressful stimuli (Section D). Such a treatment omits three very crucial classes of inputs, one of which is, of course, the broad environment within which the nation as a whole must operate—the international system and its technological, cultural, and structural characteristics, as discussed in Part One. The second is the behavior of those other nations with which the nation under consideration is interacting, these factors will be treated in Part Three. The third class of decisional inputs includes those phenomena alluded to in Section B of this part—the national character, which is the range of values, preferences, beliefs, attitudes and opinions which are held with varying intensity by the population as a whole or by relevant subgroups within the population. As was suggested there, this complex of outlooks finds expression not only in the nature of the goals which the nation pursues (or eschews) but in the diplomatic and strategic style which it displays as a goal-seeking actor.

The problem, of course, is to ascertain the way in which these vague, ill-defined, and often incompatible psychological predispositions (a) are created, modified, strengthened and weakened, and (b) find their way into the decision-making process. It is perhaps in this area that the behavioral social sciences are already making their major contribution to the study of international politics. Social psychologists have made impressive progress in their understanding of the origins and manifestations of individual human attitudes, particularly those germane to public social issues, but neither they nor the sociologists seem to have gone beyond the political scientists when it comes to the processes by which such attitudes affect political decision-making; this latter aspect of the public opinion problem requires much more careful and imaginative research, probably of a collaborative nature, among all the relevant disciplines.

Given the nature of present knowledge, however, it is certainly possible to go ahead with a preliminary examination of the role of public opinion in foreign policy decision-making with some expectation of success. Thus, this section will offer several papers which present some important data and some equally important concepts regarding the formation, change, and diffusion of *individual* opinions. It is crucial, however, to note that all of the research reported here is based on American data and is, hence, relatively culture-bound; some of the generalizations may not, therefore, be applicable to other societies.

1. A Typology of Opinion Formation and Change

One of the reasons that the student of international politics may have trouble understanding attitudinal variables is the plethora of models and approaches he encounters. One model that I have found exceptionally clear and relevant is that developed by Kelman on the basis of several of his own experiments and many which preceded them. In this paper he brings together data and concepts which shed considerable light on the antecedents and consequences of three different types of attitude or opinion change.

COMPLIANCE, IDENTIFICATION, AND INTERNALIZATION: THREE PROCESSES OF ATTITUDE CHANGE

HERBERT C. KELMAN

A crucial issue in communication research relates to the *nature* of changes (if any) that are brought about by a particular communication or type of communication. It is not enough to know that there has been some measurable change in

From Herbert C. Kelman, "Compliance, Identification, and Internalization: Three Processes of Attitude Change," *The Journal of Conflict Resolution,* II (1958), 51-60 (the footnotes and the bibliography and references have been omitted). Reprinted by permission of the author and *The Journal of Conflict Resolution.*

attitude; usually we would also want to know what kind of change it is. Is it a superficial change, on a verbal level, which disappears after a short lapse of time? Or is it a more lasting change in attitude and belief, which manifests itself in a wide range of situations and which is integrated into the person's value system? Or, to put it in other terms, did the communication produce public conformity *without* private acceptance, or did it produce public conformity coupled with private acceptance? Only if we know something about the nature and depth of changes can we make meaningful predictions about the way in which attitude changes will be reflected in subsequent actions and reactions to events.

⚹   ⚹   ⚹   ⚹   ⚹

I. Theoretical Framework

The experiment reported here grows out of a broader theoretical framework concerned with the analysis of different processes of attitude change resulting from social influence. It is impossible to present this framework in detail in the present paper, but I should like to outline its main features.

The starting point of the theoretical analysis is the observation discussed in the preceding paragraphs, i.e., that changes in attitudes and actions produced by social influence may occur at different "levels." It is proposed that these differences in the nature or level of changes that take place correspond to differences in the *process* whereby the individual accepts influence (or "conforms"). In other words, the underlying processes in which an individual engages when he adopts induced behavior may be different, even though the resulting overt behavior may appear the same.

Three different processes of influence can be distinguished: compliance, identification, and internalization.

Compliance can be said to occur when an individual accepts influence because he hopes to achieve a favorable reaction from another person or group. He adopts the induced behavior not because he believes in its content but because he expects to gain specific rewards or approval and avoid specific punishments or disapproval by conforming. Thus the satisfaction derived from compliance is due to the *social effect* of accepting influence.

Identification can be said to occur when an individual accepts influence because he wants to establish or maintain a satisfying self-defining relationship to another person or a group. This relationship may take the form of classical identification, in which the individual takes over the role of the other, or it may take the form of a reciprocal role relationship. The individual actually believes in the responses which he adopts through identification, but their specific content is more or less irrelevant. He adopts the induced behavior because it is associated with the desired relationship. Thus the satisfaction derived from identification is due to the *act* of conforming as such.

Internalization can be said to occur when an individual accepts influence because the content of the induced behavior—the ideas and actions of which it is composed—is intrinsically rewarding. He adopts the induced behavior because it is congruent with his value system. He may consider it useful for the solution of a problem or find it congenial to his needs. Behavior adopted in this fashion tends to be integrated with the individual's existing values. Thus the satisfaction derived from internalization is due to the *content* of the new behavior.

The three processes represent three qualitatively different ways of accepting influence. A systematic treatment of the processes might, therefore, begin with an analysis of the determinants of influence in general. These determinants can be summarized by the following proposition: The probability of accepting influence is a combined function of (a) the relative importance of the anticipated effect, (b) the relative power of the influencing agent, and (c) the prepotency of the induced response. A variety of experimental findings can be cited in support of this proposition.

Compliance, identification, and internalization can each be represented as a function of these three determinants. For each process, however, these determinants take a qualitatively different form. Thus the determinants of the three processes can be distinguished from one another in terms of the *nature* of the anticipated effect, the *source* of the influencing agent's power, and the *manner* in which the induced response has become prepotent.

In other words, each process is characterized by a distinctive set of *antecedent* conditions, involving a particular qualitative variation of a more general set of determinants. Given the proper set of antecedents, then, influence will take the form of compliance, identification, or internalization, respectively. Each of these corresponds to a characteristic pattern of internal responses (thoughts and feelings) in which the individual engages while adopting the induced behavior.

Similarly, each process is characterized by a distinctive set of *consequent* conditions, involving a particular qualitative variation in the subsequent history of the induced response. Responses adopted through different processes will be performed under different conditions, will be changed and extinguished under different conditions, and will have different properties.

Since each of the three processes mediates between a distinct set of antecedents and a distinct set of consequents, the proposed distinctions between the three processes can be tested by experiments which attempt to relate the antecedents postulated for a given process to the consequents postulated for that process. The present experiment was designed to vary one of the antecedents— the source of the influencing agent's power—and to observe the effects of this variation on one of the consequents—the conditions of performance of the induced response.

Power is defined as the extent to which the influencing agent is perceived as instrumental to the achievement of the subject's goals. The sources of the agent's power may vary. The following hypotheses are offered regarding the variations in *source* of power [emphasis added]:

1. To the extent to which the power of the influencing agent is based on means-control, conformity will tend to take the form of compliance.

2. To the extent to which the power of the influencing agent is based on attractiveness, conformity will tend to take the form of identification.

3. To the extent to which the power of the influencing agent is based on credibility, conformity will tend to take the form of internalization.

Now let us look at the *consequent* side [emphasis added]. One of the ways in which behaviors adopted through different processes can be distinguished is in terms of the conditions under which the behavior is performed. The following hypotheses are offered regarding the conditions of performance:

1. When an individual adopts an induced response through compliance, he tends to perform it only under conditions of surveillance by the influencing agent.

2. When an individual adopts an induced response through identification, he tends to perform it only under conditions of salience of his relationship to the agent.

3. When an individual adopts an induced response through internalization, he tends to perform it under conditions of relevance of the issue, regardless of surveillance or salience.

II. PROCEDURE

The subjects in this experiment were Negro college Freshmen in a border state. The experiment was conducted in the spring of 1954, just prior to the announcement of the Supreme Court decision on desegregation in the public schools. The social influence situation to which the students were exposed consisted of a fixed communication designed to change their attitudes on an issue related to the impending Court decision. Specifically, each of the communications employed in the study presented essentially the following message: If the Supreme Court rules that segregation is unconstitutional, it would still be desirable to maintain some of the *private* Negro colleges as all-Negro institutions, in order to preserve Negro culture, history, and tradition. Preliminary testing indicated that a large majority of the subjects would initially oppose the message presented in the communication.

The communications were tape-recorded interviews between a moderator and a guest (the communicator). They were presented to the subjects as recordings of radio programs which we were interested in evaluating. By varying the nature of these communications, it was possible *to manipulate* experimentally *the source and degree of the communicator's power*, while keeping *the message* of the communication *constant* [emphasis added]. Four different communications were used, as can be seen from Table 1, which outlines the basic design of the experiment (see left-hand column).

In one communication the attempt was made to present the communicator in such a way that he would be perceived as possessing *high means-control* [emphasis added]. He was introduced as the president of the National Foundation for Negro Colleges. In the course of the interview it became evident that his foundation had been supporting the college in which the study was being conducted; that he had almost complete control over the funds expended by the foundation; and that he was the kind of person who would not hesitate to use his control in order to achieve conformity. He made it clear that he would withdraw foundation grants from any college in which the students took a position on the issue in question which was at variance with his own position.

TABLE 1[a]

Design of the Experiment and Predictions

Experimental Groups: Variations in Communicator Power	Questionnaires: Variations in Conditions of Performance		
	Questionnaire I	Questionnaire II	Questionnaire III
	Surveillance Salience Issue-Relevance	Non-Surveillance Salience Issue-Relevance	Non-Surveillance Non-Salience Issue-Relevance
High power, based on means-control	H	L	L
High power, based on attractiveness	H	H	L
High power, based on credibility	H	H	H
Low power	L	L	L

[a]H = high probability that attitude will be expressed; L = low probability that attitude will be expressed.

In the second communication the communicator was presented in such a way that he would be perceived as possessing *high attractiveness* [emphasis added]. He was introduced as a Senior and president of the student council in a leading Negro university. He was also chairman of his university's chapter of an organization called Student Poll, which recently did a study on the attitudes of Negro college Seniors on issues relating to the Supreme Court decision. He presented the same message as the first communicator, but he made it clear that he was presenting not simply his own opinions but the overwhelming consensus of opinion of the college students represented in the polls. He was portrayed as a representative of one of the subjects' reference groups and as a person who was in a position to supply valid information on the group norms.

In the third communication the communicator was presented in such a way that he would be perceived as possessing *high credibility* [emphasis added]. He was introduced as a professor of history in one of the country's leading universities. In the course of the interview, it became evident that he was one of the top experts on the history and problems of minority groups; that he was highly respected both by his colleagues and by members of minority groups; and that he had a profound concern for the welfare of the American Negro community. He presented the same position as the other speakers, but he made it clear that this position was based on his research and on the evidence of history.

For purposes of comparison, a fourth communication was used in which the communicator was presented in such a way that he would be perceived as possessing *low power* [emphasis added], that is, as being low in means-control, attractiveness, *and* credibility. He was introduced as an "ordinary citizen," who had no control over the subjects and no special knowledge about the topic. His attractiveness and credibility were further undermined by the fact that he was portrayed as a white man with a southern accent, who had recently come from Mississippi and who did not clearly dissociate himself from a pro-segregation point of view.

Each of the four communications was presented to a different experimental group. There was also a control group, which was not exposed to any communication at all. This group provided a base line for post-communication attitudes, since we did not obtain before-scores from the experimental subjects.

After exposure to the communication, the subjects in each experimental group filled out attitude questionnaires, designed to measure the extent of their agreement with the communicator. The questionnaire consisted of eighteen statements which were directly or indirectly related to the central message of the communication. Subjects were asked to respond to each item on a six-point scale. Scores for each item ranged from 1 for extreme disagreement with the communicator's position to 7 for extreme agreement (the score of 4 was not used, since the scale did not contain a neutral position). A total score for each subject was computed by adding up the individual scores on the 18 items. Thus the range of possible total scores was from 18 (complete disagreement) to 126 (complete agreement).

To vary the conditions of performance, we presented these eighteen statements to each subject on three separate questionnaires. As can be seen from Table 1, it is assumed that issue-relevance was present on all three questionnaires, since the attitude items dealt with the issues involved in the communication. The questionnaires differed, however, with respect to surveillance and salience.

Questionnaire I was completed under conditions of *salience and surveillance* [emphasis added]. In order to maximize the salience of the communicator and the communication, the questionnaire was administered immediately after the communication. In order to maximize surveillance by the communicator, it was made clear — both by the appearance of the questionnaire and by the instructions — that this questionnaire was being administered at the communicator's request and that he would see each subject's answers. Moreover, the subjects were asked to sign their names and to give other identifying information.

237

Questionnaire II was completed under conditions of *salience and non-surveillance* [emphasis added]. In order to maximize salience, the questionnaire was administered immediately after Questionnaire I, so that the relationship between the questionnaire and the communication was still clearly apparent. In order to minimize surveillance, Questionnaire II was anonymous, and it was made clear to the subjects that their responses would not be seen by the communicator or by anyone other than the research staff.

Questionnaire III was completed under conditions of *non-salience and non-surveillance* [emphasis added]. In order to minimize the salience of the communicator and the communication, the questionnaire was administered from one to two weeks after the communication session, in a different place, under different auspices, and by a different experimenter. The questions were imbedded in a large number of other attitudinal items; and no mention of the communication was made. In order to minimize surveillance, Questionnaire III was anonymous and was in no way tied in to the communication.

III. HYPOTHESES

The specific hypotheses that were tested were as follows:

1. Attitudes adopted from a communicator whose power is based on means-control will tend to be expressed only under conditions of surveillance by the communicator. The mediating process postulated here is compliance.

The specific prediction can be noted in Table 1. In the means-control group there will be a greater amount of acceptance of the communicator's position on Questionnaire I than on Questionnaires II and III, since Questionnaire I is the only one completed under conditions of surveillance. There should be no significant difference between Questionnaires II and III.

2. Attitudes adopted from a communicator whose power is based on attractiveness will tend to be expressed only under conditions of salience of the subject's relationship to the communicator. The mediating process postulated here is identification.

Specifically, it is predicted that in the attractiveness group there will be a smaller amount of acceptance of the communicator's position on Questionnaire III than on Questionnaires I and II, since Questionnaire III is the only one completed under conditions of non-salience. There should be no significant difference between Questionnaires I and II.

3. Attitudes adopted from a communicator whose power is based on credibility will tend to be expressed under conditions of relevance of the issue, regardless of surveillance or salience. The mediating process postulated here is internalization.

The specific prediction for the credibility group is that there will be no significant differences between the three questionnaires, since they were all completed under conditions of issue-relevance.

IV. RESULTS

Before proceeding to examine the data which bear directly on the hypotheses, it was necessary to check on the success of the experimental variations. Did the subjects really perceive each of the variations in communicator power in the way in which we intended it? To provide an answer to this question, Questionnaire II included a series of statements about the speaker and the communication to which the subjects were asked to react. An analysis of these data indicated that, by and large, the experimental manipulations succeeded in producing the conditions they were intended to produce, thus making possible an adequate test of the hypotheses.

The findings which are directly relevant to the hypotheses are summarized in Tables 2 and 3. Table 2 presents the mean attitude scores for the four experimental groups on each of the three questionnaires. All subjects who had completed the three questionnaires were used in this analysis.

It can be seen from the summary of the significance tests that all the experimental predictions were confirmed. In the means-control group, the mean score on Questionnaire I is significantly higher than the mean scores on Question-

TABLE 2

Effects of Variations in Communicator Power on Acceptance of
Induced Attitudes under Three Conditions of Measurement

Groups	N	Mean Attitude Scores		
		Quest. I	*Quest. II*	*Quest. III*
Means-control (compliance)	55	63.98	60.65	58.04
Attractiveness (identification)	48	56.81	55.94	49.67
Credibility (internalization)	51	59.51	56.39	56.10
Low power	43	49.33	50.58	53.35

Summary of Significance Tests

Groups	Sources of Variation	F	p
Means-control	(1) Between questionnaires	3.6	<0.05
	(2) I versus II and III	5.8	<0.05
	(3) II versus III	1.4	n.s.
Attractiveness	(1) Between questionnaires	7.2	<0.01
	(2) I and II versus III	14.2	<0.01
	(3) I versus II	0.2	n.s.
Credibility	Between questionnaires	2.3	n.s.
Low power	Between questionnaires	2.0	n.s.

naires II and III; and there is no significant difference between the scores on Questionnaires II and III. In the attractiveness group, the mean score on Questionnaire III is significantly lower than the mean scores on Questionnaires I and II; and there is no significant difference between the scores on Questionnaires I and II. In the credibility group, there are no significant differences between the three questionnaires.

While these results are all in line with the hypotheses, examination of the means in Table 2 reveals that the findings are not so clear-cut as they might be. Specifically, we should expect a relatively large drop in mean score for the means-control group from Questionnaire I to Questionnaire II. In actual fact, however, the drop is only slightly higher than that for the credibility group. This might be due to the fact that the analysis is based on *all* subjects, including those who were not influenced by the communication at all. The hypotheses, however, refer only to changes from questionnaire to questionnaire for those people who *were* initially influenced.

It was not possible to identify the subjects who were initially influenced, since there were no before-scores available for the experimental groups. It was possible, however, to approximate these conditions by using only those subjects who had a score of 60 or above on Questionnaire I. If we make certain limited assumptions (which I cannot spell out in this brief report), it can be shown that

TABLE 3

Effects of Variations in Communicator Power on Acceptance of
Induced Attitudes under Three Conditions of Measurement[a]

Groups	N	Mean Attitude Scores		
		Quest. I	Quest. II	Quest. III
Means-control (compliance)	30	78.20	70.76	67.56
Attractiveness (identification)	23	71.30	69.57	59.70
Credibility (internalization)	26	73.35	71.04	69.27

Summary of Significance Tests

Groups	Sources of Variation	F	p
Means-control	(1) Between questionnaires	5.2	<0.01
	(2) I versus II and III	9.4	<0.01
	(3) II versus III	0.9	n.s.
Attractiveness	(1) Between questionnaires	14.5	<0.01
	(2) I and II versus III	28.4	<0.01
	(3) I versus II	0.6	n.s.
Credibility	Between questionnaires	1.1	n.s.

[a]Data based on a selected sample, containing a higher proportion of influenced subjects. Criterion for selection was a score of 60 or above on Questionnaire I.

the use of a cutoff point of 60 "purifies" the experimental groups to some degree. That is, the subsamples selected by this criterion should have a higher ratio of influenced to uninfluenced subjects than the total groups from which they were selected. It was anticipated that an analysis based on these subsamples would provide a better test of the hypotheses and would yield more clear-cut results. This did, in fact, happen, as can be seen from Table 3.

Table 3 presents the mean attitude scores for the three high-power groups, using only those subjects who had scores of 60 or above on Questionnaire I. Examination of the means reveals a pattern completely consistent with the hypotheses. In the means-control group, agreement with the communicator is relatively high on Questionnaire I and declines on Questionnaires II and III. In the attractiveness group, agreement is high on Questionnaires I and II and declines on Questionnaire III. In the credibility group, changes from questionnaire to questionnaire are minimal. Analyses of variance clearly confirmed all the experimental predictions.

V. Conclusions

It would be premature to accept the hypotheses tested in this experiment as general principles that have been proved. The experiment does, however, lend considerable support to them. To the extent to which the hypotheses were substantiated, the experiment also gives support to the theoretical framework from which these hypotheses were derived. The mediating concepts of compliance, identification, and internalization seem to provide a unified and meaningful way of organizing the present experimental findings and of relating them to a more general conceptual framework.

The framework presented here can be applied directly to the analysis of the effects of various communications and other forms of social influence on attitudes and actions in the international sphere. In the study of public opinion, for example, it should help us identify some of the conditions which are likely to produce one or another of these processes and predict the subsequent histories and action implications of attitudes adopted under these sets of conditions. This framework may also be helpful in the study of the social influences which affect decision-making processes and negotiations on the part of various elites.

Some of the concepts presented here might be useful not only for the study of change but also for the analysis of existing attitudes and their motivational bases. Let us take, for example, people's attitudes toward their own country's system of government. Even if we look only at those individuals who have favorable attitudes, various distinctions suggest themselves. For some individuals, acceptance of their system of government may be based largely on compliance: they may go along with the accepted norms in order to avoid social ostracism or perhaps even persecution. For others, attitudes toward their government may be largely identification-based: their relationship to their own nation and its major institutions may represent an essential aspect of their identity, and acceptance of certain political attitudes and beliefs may serve to maintain this relationship and their self-definition which is anchored in it. For a third group of individuals, belief in the country's system of govenment may be internalized: they may see this political form as fully congruent and integrated with their value systems and likely to lead to a maximization of their own values. Our evaluation of the meaning of "favorable attitudes" on the part of a particular individual or group or subpopulation and our prediction of the consequences of these attitudes would certainly vary with the motivational processes that underlie them. The conditions under which these attitudes are likely to be changed, the kinds of actions to which they are likely to lead, and the ways in which they are likely to affect reactions to particular events will be different, depending on whether these attitudes are based on compliance, identification, or internalization.

2. Predisposition toward Foreign Policy Opinions

With Kelman's typology of the opinion change process as background, it is now possible to look at the "raw material" upon which the forces for opinion change must operate: the values and attitudes which people hold prior to any specific effort or event that might produce a change in direction or intensity of the individual's views. That is, no citizen is a "tabula rasa"; he is being socialized and politicized almost from birth, and at any moment he is the possessor of a cluster or syndrome of views which have (if he is relatively sane) a measure of coherence and con- sistency, at least as far as the holder himself is concerned.

Perhaps the most well-known of these syndromes is the "authoritatian personality," a concept and set of operational measures designed by Adorno and others at the University of California. I am not, however, presenting any excerpts from that specific body of research because (a) it is probably familiar to the reader, and (b) it has come in for some severe criticism on methodological grounds.[1] Rather, I am including one rather novel application of that approach. In the selection below, Fensterwald presents an experiment which illustrates the degree to which personality type predicts the foreign policy attitudes of the subject, and then goes on to demonstrate a striking relationship between isolationist and interna- tionalist views, depending upon the foreign region in question.

---

[1]See T. W. Adorno, Else Frenkel-Brunswik, Daniel Levinson, and R. Nevitt Sanford, *The Authoritarian Personality* (New York: Harper, 1950); the major critique is in Richard Christie and Marie Jahoda, *Studies in the Scope and Method of "The Authoritarian Personality"* (Glencoe, Ill.: The Free Press, 1954). A provocative set of case studies dealing with the relationship between personality structure and political outlook is found in M. Brewster Smith, Jerome S. Bruner, and Robert W. White, *Opinions and Personality* (New York: Wiley, 1956).

AMERICAN "ISOLATIONISM" AND EXPANSIONISM

BERNARD FENSTERWALD, JR.

IV. QUESTIONNAIRE

*   *   *   *   *

The conclusions to be tested were: (1) that attitudes on foreign relations are intimately connected (in a psychological sense) with attitudes on a number of wholly unconnected subjects and, further, that nationalistic attitudes favoring "isolationism" and "imperialism" are part of an authoritarian ideology and (2) that attitudes favoring "isolationism" toward Europe and expansionism toward other areas of the world are entirely compatible from a psychological standpoint.

After all, dislike and distrust of "foreigners" is ethnocentrism's most outward concentric circle, and the nation-state is the ingroup par excellence. It has been demonstrated before that attitudes of exaggerated love for this ingroup (i.e., superpatriotism) correlate very high with other ethnocentric attitudes. Whereas patriotism forms one side of the coin of nationalism, dislike and distrust of national outgroups forms the other. Attitudes on foreign relations which reflect such dislike and distrust (i.e., anti-internationalism) should also correlate very high with ethnocentrism and, further, with authoritarianism. This has long been recognized popularly, at least in part, in the concept that "isolationists" are usually "conservatives."

Construction of the Questionnaire

It was determined that the optimum number of items for the questionnaire would be sixty, divided equally between items covering international and domestic matters. Since nationalism and authoritarianism (rather than their opposites) were the primary objects of scrutiny, it was believed that the items would be more discriminating if they were so phrased that a nationalist (i.e., "isolationist," "imperialist," and "anti-internationalist") and authoritarian (i.e., "ethnocentrist," "patriot," and "economic conservative") would tend to *disagree* with them. However, to obviate the danger that subjects filling out the questionnaire might fall into a "set" tendency to agree or disagree with all items, nine were "turned around," so that a nationalist-conservative would *agree* with them. (For the sake of convenience, these are given in italics in this article.) The questionnaire was pretested, and a number of items were deleted or changed to make them more discriminating.

From Bernard Fensterwald, Jr., "American 'Isolationism' and Expansionism," *The Journal of Conflict Resolution,* II (1958), 280-307 (the footnotes and the bibliography and references have been omitted). Reprinted by permission of the author and *The Journal of Conflict Resolution.*

The subjects were given a wide choice of responses, from strong agreement through moderate agreement, slight agreement, slight disagreement, moderate disagreement, to strong disagreement. They were asked to circle one of the following numbers to register their response: +3, +2, +1, −1, −2, −3, with +3 indicating strong agreement, +2 indicating moderate agreement, etc. These responses were converted into scores as follows: $+3 = 7, +2 = 6, +1 = 5, -1 = 3, -2 = 2, -3 = 1$; unmarked items were given the intermediate score of 4. Needless to say, "turned-around" items were scored in reverse, with $+3 = 1$, etc.

As each questionnaire was graded, it was transferred to an IBM card which reflected the score on each item, as well as certain factual information relating to the person completing the questionnaire. The purpose of this was to make possible the use of IBM machines to determine the "correlation coefficients" between the various groups of items in the questionnaire.

A "correlation coefficient," or simply a "correlation," as it is generally spoken of by psychologists, is the mathematical expression of the degree of co-variation that exists for any two variable items. For example, we know that people who are above average height *tend to be slightly* smarter than people who are below average height. Or we know that a person's right arm is *usually about* the same length as his left. However, such expressions as "tend to be slightly" and "usually about" are entirely subjective in meaning, and they are unsatisfactory for any kind of scientific experimentation. So that everyone will be talking about the same thing and accuracy will be given to the degree of alignment or disalignment between two variables, psychologists have agreed on a single mathematical equation to record the relationship. For our purposes, it is not necessary to be familiar with the exact nature of the formula. It is only necessary to know that when there is no similarity between the variables, the correlation is zero; when there is perfect similarity, the correlation is +1; and when there is perfect *dis*similarity, the correlation is −1. As for the examples that we chose, the correlation between arm lengths is +.96. In other words, if we know the length of one of a person's arms, we can predict the length of the other with 96 per cent accuracy.

Furthermore, if there is a high degree of correlation between two variables, X and Y, there is a strong implication that there is a causal link between the two variables.

The two primary groups or scales of items to be correlated were the "international scale" ("INT") and the "domestic scale" ("DOM"), each of which contained thirty items.

The INT Scale

The INT Scale consisted of the following thirty items dealing with international matters:

1. We should get out of the United Nations if they hire any more Americans who have not been cleared by the F.B.I.
5. If the free world is to win its battle against international communism, the

U.S. will have to forget about being "leader" and assume the role of "boss."

6. After defeating Spain in the war of 1898, it was our duty to take over the Philippines and help them along the road to civilization.

8. Our sovereignty is an indivisible whole which should never be surrendered to any international organization.

11. It was the "manifest destiny" of the original 13 American colonies that they should expand and take over the continent from coast to coast.

13. The U.S. got into World War I not because of any real interest, but because of British propaganda, the munitions makers, and Wilsonian idealism.

14. Instead of just annexing Texas, we should have annexed all of Mexico in the 19th Century when we had the chance.

15. Unless the French Government agrees to cooperate wholeheartedly in Western defense, we should withdraw our forces from the continent of Europe.

17. Our failure to join the League of Nations had little or nothing to do with its failure.

18. Since the American Indians made little or no use of the vast resources of North America and stood in the way of progress and civilization, we were justified in putting them on reservations.

19. The Marshall Plan may have helped the Europeans, but it hasn't done much for us.

22. *The Chinese Nationalists lost their war against the Communists in large measure because of their own internal corruption.*

25. American industries which cannot compete with cheap foreign labor should be protected by tariffs.

27. *The United States should stay in the United Nations if and when Red China is seated.*

28. Our position in the Far East would be stronger today if we had not given up voluntarily our military administration and occupation of Japan.

29. *Just as the original 13 colonies in North America formed a unified government, the sovereign states of the world, including the U.S., shall have to organize some sort of world government.*

31. We made a mistake in letting the United Nations settle in New York, since all sorts of dangerous people are invited to its meetings.

34. In the Korean War, General MacArthur should have been allowed to bomb across the Yalu River even though there was a chance that this might have gotten us into war with Red China.

36. We should tell European countries to clean up their political messes or expect no aid from us.

40. If George Washington were alive today, he would still believe in as few entangling alliances as possible.

45. We should never have ratified the North Atlantic Treaty Organization (NATO) Agreement, since it is the worst sort of entangling alliance.

46. Looked at from a purely realistic and cold-blooded standpoint, most of our Allies aren't worth bothering about.

47. The Philippine demand for independence from the United States was an act of ingratitude.

245

48. If the Europeans form a common army, the U.S. should keep its armed forces completely outside such an organization.
49. We could have avoided war with the Nazis if we had not aided England by supplying her with destroyers, Lend-Lease, etc.
53. We should stop giving economic aid to India until Nehru quits running around behind the Iron Curtain.
56. Since the United Nations has 60 Member States, the United States should refuse to pay one-third of all its expenses.
57. It is no concern of ours whether or not the countries of Europe are able to get together and form some sort of federal system of government for their part of the world.
59. Chiang Kai-shek is one of the few remaining symbols of liberty and freedom in Asia today.
60. There is a great deal of good sense in General MacArthur's well-known advice to "go it alone" if our Allies don't agree with us on general strategy.

With the exception of three "turned-around" items (22, 27, and 29), all the above were so stated that persons with nationalist, as opposed to internationalist, attitudes would be expected to agree with them. Most items were purposely worded to bring out slight or moderate, rather than strong, agreement or disagreement. Inevitably, in regard to many of them, a rational, though often strained, argument can be made to show how an internationalist might agree with them. The only way to avoid this difficulty would be to phrase all questions blatantly, but this would cause more serious difficulties than it would eliminate.

The items in the INT Scale cover a sufficient number of areas of international concern to test thoroughly a person's general attitudes toward the conduct of foreign relations. A high-scorer on all thirty items would have a collection of highly nationalistic attitudes. He would favor aloofness from Europe (13, 15, 49); he would oppose alliances (40, 45, 46, 48, 60); he would justify American expansionism (6, 11, 14, 18); he would favor a policy of "new imperialism" for America (5, 36, 53, 27, 28); he would favor interventionism in the "weaker" areas of the world (22, 34); he would be unenthusiastic concerning United States participation in international co-operation (1, 8, 17, 29, 31, 56); and he would be an economic nationalist (19, 25). An internationalist might get a high score *on a few* of these items, but a consistent high-scorer must certainly be a person who is nationalistically inclined [emphasis added].

The DOM Scale

The DOM Scale consisted of thirty items dealing with matters of domestic concern. This scale was subdivided into five subscales, each designed to test one aspect of authoritarianism. These subscales were as follows:

(P) *Patriotism Subscale*

4. One of the best slogans that we have ever had is: "My country, right or wrong."

10. It was wrong to make our boys in Korea fight under the United Nations flag.
21. The American system of government may not be perfect, but it is far and away the best system of government anywhere in the world today.
33. All conscientious objectors should be made to serve jail sentences.
42. Patriotism is the most important requirement of a good citizen.

(ETH) *Ethnocentrism Subscale*

7. In view of the present world crisis, it is highly important to limit responsible government jobs to native-born citizens.
26. The U.S. Supreme Court overstepped its bounds when it ordered schools to stop segregating Negro and white children.
39. The main internal threat to basic American institutions during this century has come from the infiltration of foreign ideas, doctrines, and agitators.
43. *There was little or no justification for placing Japanese-American citizens in detention camps after Pearl Harbor.*
55. Sincere Catholics can't be really 100% Americans because of the influence of the Pope.

(PEC) *Political and Economic Conservatism Subscale*

2. The best political candidate to vote for is the one whose greatest interest is in fighting vice and graft.
9. Public power projects, such as TVA, are basically unfair because they benefit one small area of the country at the expense of the rest of the citizens.
16. *It should be one of the functions of the Federal Government to help make sure that everyone has a good standard of living.*
23. What this country needs most is a strong leader who can restore our faith in a system of free enterprise.
30. Our government is better off when most of the important jobs in Washington are in the hands of businessmen rather than college professors.
37. *The best way to provide adequate medical care for the entire population is through some federal health program.*
41. Some of the power of the Federal Government should be given back to the 48 States.
44. *The Social Security program should be expanded to cover all workers who might want to be covered.*
51. *Congress should appropriate money to help the States finance their public schools.*
58. *The Federal Government should do more in trying to deal with the problems of unemployment.*

(CCE) *Child Care and Education Subscale*

20. The old saying about "sparing the rod and spoiling the child" still makes good sense today.
32. The most important things that a child should be taught are the value of the dollar and the vast importance of ambition, efficiency, and determination.

38. The value of modern child psychology is vastly over-rated.
50. Obedience and respect for authority are the most important virtues children can learn.
54. American schools waste a great deal of time and effort on so-called progressive education.

(AP) *Authoritarian Personality Subscale*

3. Every decent person should have a feeling of love, gratitude, and respect for his parents.
12. America is spending too much money on the education of mentally defective people who won't amount to anything no matter how much is done for them.
24. The true American way of life is disappearing so fast that force may be necessary to preserve it.
35. Homosexuals are degenerates who ought to be severly punished.
52. Most people who don't get ahead simply don't have enough will power.

Since most of these domestic items are fairly standardized in tests of this type, they do not require any extended discussion. Items on anti-Semitism were deleted from the Ethnocentric (ETH) Subscale partly to shorten the questionnaire and partly because the anatomy of anti-Semitism has been exhaustively covered elsewhere. Although several items on child-raising and education are frequently included in scales for the measurement of social attitudes, childhood was considered so important to the formation of ethocentric and nationalistic attitudes that a separate subscale (CCE) on this subject was included in the questionnaire. The items in the Authoritarian Personality (AP) Subscale were taken almost verbatim from the F Scale of the California group.

The questionnaires were printed in booklet form, with the sixty items on two inside sheets, and with instructions and questions about the subjects' background on the cover sheet. Each subject was requested to indicate his age, sex, religion, occupation, political affiliation, citizenship, place of birth, national origin, home state, size of community, and economic or social class.

The questionnaire was completed by a total of 882 persons in all sections of the country. It was administered to large groups of college students, at the University of Miami, Vanderbilt University, San Diego State College, and Fisk University; to 106 student nurses at Bellevue Hospital; to 26 employees of a Republican newspaper in New York City; to 37 women who belonged to a southern chapter of the League of Women Voters. Unfortunately, it was not possible to have the questionnaire administered to any sizable groups of individuals in the lowest-income or education brackets.

Correlation of Attitudes on International and Domestic Questions

Each subject's score on the International Scale (INT) and Domestic Scale (DOM) was totaled, as well as his score on the subscales of the DOM Scale, i.e.,

Patriotism (P), Ethnocentrism (ETH), Political and Economic Conservatism (PEC), Child Care and Education (CCE), and Authoritarian Personality (AP). The International Scale (INT) was correlated with the Domestic Scale (DOM) and all its subscales. Correlations were found not only for the whole group of 882 subjects but also for four relatively homogeneous subgroups: 379 white undergraduates, 58 Negro undergraduates, 106 student nurses, and 37 members of the League of Women Voters. These correlations are tabulated in Table 1.

TABLE 1
The International Scale Correlated with Domestic Scale and Its Subscales

Group	DOM	INT Correlated with				
		P	ETH	PEC	CCE	AP
Total (882)	.76	.65	.61	.44	.53	.64
White undergraduates (379)	.76	.57	.58	.31	.49	.57
Negro undergraduates (58)	.70	.52	.42	.20	.64	.71
Student nurses (106)	.60	.43	.42	.28	.36	.44
Women voters (37)	.78	.74	.61	.61	.62	.48

The primary correlations of INT with DOM, ranging from .60 to .78, are of considerable significance. The two scales contain items relating to such diverse areas of social living that the high degree of correlation strongly suggests that well-knit personality patterns must play a large role in determining the subject's attitudes toward the different types of issues. Naturally, care must be taken not to draw too broad conclusions from these figures. However, it would seem fair to say that, although nationalism and authoritarianism are imperfectly related, nationalistic attitudes toward foreign relations definitely fit into the authoritarian ideology.

Social Background and Attitudes

Although no attempt was made to obtain either a representative or a random sampling of the American public, it was believed that the backgrounds of the subjects to whom the questionnaire was administered would indicate the trends that should be expected from a more perfect sampling. Table 2 contains an analysis of the average scores on the scales and subscales, arranged according to various groupings determined from the factual information submitted by the subjects on the front page of the questionnaire. In each division (by age, by sex, etc.) the grouping is arranged in descending order, with the group with the highest average score on all scales at the top of the division.

Although scores can range from 1.0 to 7.0, the vast majority of average scale scores fall under 4.0, the "neutral" score. However, this is not believed to be a drawback, since the items were phrased to be discriminatory and provide meaningful correlations, not to measure the level of authoritarianism and nationalism (or anti-authoritarianism and internationalism) in the country.

249

TABLE 2

Analysis of Scores Arranged by Sociological Groupings
of Subjects Filling in Questionnaires

Groupings	N in Group	Per Cent of Total Group	All Scales	Average Score Per Item						
				INT	DOM	P	ETH	PEC	CCE	AP
All groups (for comparison)	882	100.0	3.11	2.97	3.24	3.58	2.86	3.19	3.63	3.02
By age (years):										
70-79	6	0.7	4.14	3.90	4.37	4.03	4.57	4.20	4.67	4.57
60-69	29	3.3	3.71	3.41	3.99	4.10	3.40	4.08	4.70	3.63
16-19	187	21.2	3.26	3.19	3.33	3.74	2.94	3.11	3.70	3.37
50-59	56	6.3	3.18	2.88	3.46	3.66	3.17	3.49	3.95	3.05
20-29	419	47.5	3.06	2.94	3.17	3.53	2.77	3.13	3.53	2.95
30-39	82	9.3	3.00	2.87	3.12	3.49	2.82	3.17	3.40	2.70
40-49	93	10.5	2.82	2.63	3.00	3.24	2.66	3.10	3.46	2.54
By sex:										
Males	424	48.1	3.14	2.97	3.30	3.61	2.92	3.20	3.72	3.17
Females	455	51.6	3.08	2.97	3.19	3.55	2.81	3.17	3.55	2.88
By religion:										
Catholic	179	20.3	3.31	3.22	3.38	3.90	2.76	3.27	4.03	3.08
Protestant	477	54.1	3.18	3.03	3.33	3.58	3.07	3.26	3.70	3.19
Jewish	162	18.4	2.89	2.74	3.03	3.53	2.53	3.01	3.26	2.85
None	59	6.7	2.49	2.31	2.66	2.71	2.35	2.81	2.83	2.48
By political party:										
Republican	205	23.2	3.43	3.23	3.62	3.90	3.13	3.75	4.04	3.17

Independent	344	39.0	3.01	2.89	3.1?	3.41	2.68	3.14	3.37	2.95
Democrat	298	33.8	2.97	2.84	3.10	3.51	2.84	2.85	3.62	2.94
By section of country:[a]										
Plains & Mts.	88	10.0	3.37	3.13	3.60	3.80	3.21	3.66	4.10	3.25
South	275	31.2	3.16	3.02	3.29	3.63	2.96	3.22	3.57	3.16
Great Lakes	92	10.4	3.06	2.93	3.18	3.41	2.75	3.21	3.52	3.07
New England & N. Atlantic	329	37.3	3.05	2.93	3.17	3.56	2.73	3.07	3.76	2.84
Pacific & S.W.	81	9.2	2.97	2.86	3.07	3.40	2.84	3.06	3.09	2.96
By size of community: Less than 5,000	99	11.2	3.59	3.42	3.76	3.93	3.48	3.71	4.27	3.51
Rural	40	4.5	3.36	3.17	3.57	4.11	3.38	3.50	4.20	3.16
5,000-50,000	225	25.2	3.22	3.12	3.32	3.75	2.94	3.24	3.62	3.13
More than 50,000	508	57.6	2.95	2.80	3.03	3.42	2.68	3.03	3.46	2.87

[a]"New England and N. Atlantic" consists of Connecticut, Delaware, Maine, Maryland, Massachusetts, New Hampshire, New Jersey, New York, Pennsylvania, Rhode Island. Vermont, D.C.; "South" consists of Alabama, Arkansas, Florida, Georgia, Kentucky, Louisiana, Mississippi, North Carolina, South Carolina. Tennessee, Virginia; "Pacific Coast and S.W." consists of Arizona, California, New Mexico, Oregon, Texas, Washington; "Great Lakes" consists of Illinois, Indiana, Michigan, Minnesota, Ohio, West Virginia, Wisconsin; "Plains and Mts." consists of Colorado, Idaho, Iowa, Kansas, Missouri. Montana, Nebraska, Nevada, North Dakota, Oklahoma, South Dakota, Utah, and Wyoming.

Furthermore, the results obtained from certain factual questions were so in-conclusive that they were omitted from Table 2. For example, the subjects' occupations were so diverse as to give no intelligible basis for analysis.

The division by age groups shows that the oldsters and the youngsters are the high-scorers. The low-scoring twenty- to forty-nine-year-olds are joined by the fifty- to fifty-nine-year-olds in low scores on the INT Scale.

The division according to sex shows that there is no significant difference in the scores of males and females.

Religion appears to be significantly related to the attitudes being tested. Catholics scored highest on INT, DOM, P, PEC, and CCE. Protestants were generally close to the neutral point, but on top on ETH and AP ("white Protestant Americans"). Jews were lower than average but, significantly, not so low as those who professed to belong to no organized religion.

As to political parties, the cleavage is between high-scoring Republicans and low-scoring Democrats and Independents. The differences are smaller than might be expected. As with religion, those with no professed party allegiance (i.e., no ingroup tie) take a more tolerant view of ingroup-outgroup relations in general than do persons with a more partisan approach.

The significant thing to note regarding sectionalism is the relatively low score of the Great Lakes area and the relatively high score of the southern area. As many commentators have pointed out, "Midwest isolationism" is no longer centered in the Mississippi Valley but has moved westward. Our results would also indicate that much of the South's alleged internationalism may have been only skin-deep—limited to questions of tariffs, motivated by party loyalty, or, possibly, in large measure non-existent. And to the extent that one kind of prejudice (i.e., "white supremacy") fosters others, the general level of ethnocen-trism in the South may add a slight authoritarian aroma to the life of the area, which would run counter to internationalism. It is not a long jump from "I hate all niggers" to "I hate all foreigners."

A person's attitudes toward group relations seems to be more affected by the size of his community than by the geographical section of the country in which he lives. The small towns and rural areas vie for top honors as the favorite habitat of high-scorers.

The Two Sides of Nationalism

Throughout our history those persons who have most strongly favored "no entangling alliances" with European countries have been those who most fa-vored militant nationalist expansion. In fact, one of the, if not *the,* primary objectives of aloofness toward Europe in the nineteenth century was to permit expansion in other directions. Those who wanted the United States to expand across the continent, then to dominate the whole Western Hemisphere, and then to become a power in the Far East quite naturally turned their backs on Europe and consistently faced in the opposite direction.

*　　*　　*　　*　　*

In short, during the nineteenth century there were two nationalistic policies, both of which were highly successful: one was a policy of aloofness toward Europe, the other of continental expansion westward and later of intervention in Latin America and the Pacific. Political events have conspired to link these policies together, to nurture them together, and to place both of them in opposition to internationalism. Simultaneously, political events have conspired to fuse together attitudes opposed to expansionism and in favor of international co-operation.

Part of the explanation for the apparent inconsistency of attitudes favoring intervention in Asia and aloofness from Europe lies in the basic nature of ethnocentrism. An American ethnocentrist in the nineteenth century might have disliked and distrusted all national outgroups, but he must have feared some more than others. He must have felt that, though we were morally "superior" to Europeans, they were powerful, and we might get a bloody nose or a broken neck if we messed with them. He also felt superior to the American Indians, Mexicans, Cubans, Hawaiians, etc., and believed that we could attain our "manifest destiny" at their expense and without running any serious risks.

This same feeling has persisted down through the twentieth century. It is well illustrated by our isolationism from Europe and our propensity for dabbling in the affairs of Latin America and Asia in the 1920's and 1930's. Furthermore, in 1950, there were still many people who believed, on the one hand, that General MacArthur should be allowed to bomb beyond the Yalu (admittedly at the risk of war with China) and who also believed that we should not "risk" stationing more than a handful of troops on the Continent of Europe. That the possibility of war in Europe seemed so much more dangerous to them than the probability of war in Asia is mute testimony of the influence of tradition upon their thinking. They were willing to risk all in order to "teach the Chinese Communists a lesson" but were willing to risk very little to try to bolster western Europe against the threat of Russian Communist expansion.

Active and Passive Nationalism

The tendency to look westward might be called the *active* part of nationalism. It is the expansionist, imperialist, militant part. It is strenuous and aggressive. Continental expansion was always westward. Imperialism was always southward and westward, and the militant aspects of nationalism are focused on the continent of Asia today. Conversely, the reluctance to face eastward might be called the *passive* part of nationalism. It is characterized by caution and withdrawal. It is "isolationist" and anti-internationalist. It is against European "entanglements." It is against too deep involvement in international organizations, which are pictured as dominated by Europeans.

If nationalism consists of these two active and passive segments, one would expect most nationalistically inclined individuals to hold both sets of attitudes toward our foreign relations—a retiring one toward Europe and an aggressive one toward Asia. It was to test the correctness of this hypothesis that the INT Scale was divided into two halves. One half contains items which would be agreed to by a person favoring aloofness toward Europe; the other half contined items which would be agreed to by a person favoring expansionism and interventionism toward Asia. A high correlation between scores on these two subscales would lend credence to the correctness of the basic hypothesis concerning the structure of American nationalism.

For lack of better names, the aggressive-expansionist subscale was designated as "W" (westward-looking), and the passive subscale named "E" (eastward-looking).

Construction of the "W" Subscale

The W, or westward-looking, Subscale contains three different types of questions, all aimed at different aspects of the aggressive side of American nationalism. The following five items relate directly to expansionism and imperialism:

6. After defeating Spain in the war of 1898, it was our duty to take over the Philippines and help them along the road to civilization.
11. It was the "manifest destiny" of the original 13 American colonies that they should expand and take over the continent from coast to coast.
14. Instead of just annexing Texas, we should have annexed all of Mexico in the 19th Century when we had the chance.
18. Since the American Indians made little or no use of the vast resources of North America and stood in the way of progress and civilization, we were justified in putting them on reservations.
47. The Philippine demand for independence from the United States was an act of ingratitude.

Although four of these five items pertain to nineteenth-century situations, they all strike responsive chords in most Americans today. All are stated in such a way as to appeal to the tough-minded nationalistic personality. For example, "manifest destiny" (Item 11) was used by generations of expansionists to rationalize and gloss over the ruthlessness with which the United States took over the continent. Item 18 is a standard rationalization for the particularly shabby way in which we treated the Indians in our continental expansion. Items 6 ("White man's burden") and 47 ("grateful Filipinos") deal with extra-continental expansion.

The following five items were included in the W Scale to cover what might best be described as the "new imperialism":

5. If the free world is to win its battle against international communism, the United States will have to forget about being "leader" and assume the role of "boss."
36. We should tell European countries to clean up their political messes or expect no aid from us.
46. Looked at from a purely realistic and cold-blooded standpoint, most of our Allies aren't worth bothering about.

254

53. We should stop giving economic aid to India until Nehru quits running around behind the Iron Curtain.
60. There is a great deal of good sense in General MacArthur's well-known advice to "go it alone" if our Allies don't agree with us on general strategy.

Imperialism has changed; it no longer means territorial expansion. Today it consists of telling "inferior" countries what to do and how to do it. Realizing that we cannot remain aloof from the world, many former isolationists are now in the front ranks of the new imperialists. All five of the above items express the same idea of running the free world rather than leading it.

Five current items, dealing with our relations with Far Eastern countries (and particularly China), were included in the W Subscale:

22. *The Chinese Nationalists lost their war against the Communists in large measure because of their own internal corruption.*
27. *The United States should stay in the United Nations if and when Red China is seated.*
28. Our position in the Far East would be stronger today if we had not given up voluntarily our military administration and occupation of Japan.
34. In the Korean War, General MacArthur should have been allowed to bomb across the Yalu River even though there was a chance that this might have gotten us into war with Red China.
59. Chiang Kai-shek is one of the few remaining symbols of liberty and freedom in Asia today.

Items 22 and 27 are "reversed," and it was expected that Asia-firsters would *disagree* with them. Conversely, it was expected that they would agree with Item 59. All three of these items are based on the premise that there are large groups of Americans who believe that China was "lost" because America did not intervene sufficiently and, further, that China might eventually be "saved" by Chiang and the Nationalists if they are given sufficient help. Items 28 and 34 reflect attitudes of continued intervention in Japan and new intervention in China.

Construction of the "E" Subscale

The E (eastward-looking) Subscale was designed to cover several different aspects of passive nationalism. Five "isolationist" items were included:

13. The U.S. got into World War I not because of any real interest, but because of British propaganda, the munitions makers and Wilsonian idealism.
17. Our failure to join the League of Nations had little or nothing to do with its failure.
25. American industries which cannot compete with cheap foreign labor should be protected by tariffs.
40. If George Washington were alive today, he would still believe in as few entangling alliances as possible.

49. We would have avoided war with the Nazis if we had not aided England by supplying her with destroyers, Lend-Lease, etc.

At least two of these (13 and 49) deal specifically with Europe and are tailored for the unreconstructed isolationist of 1917-18 and 1939-41. The League of Nations (Item 17) has been thought of as a "European project." It was thought that Item 17 would bring out anti-League sentiment better than an item specifically directed to whether we should have joined the League. As to Items 25 and 40, historically the doctrines of "protective tariffs" and "no entangling alliances" have been addressed almost entirely to our economic and political relations with Europe. They are both timeless nationalist shibboleths, representing the withdrawal aspects of American nationalism.

Five items were included on international co-operation:

1. We should get out of the United Nations if they hire any more Americans who have not been cleared by the F.B.I.
8. Our sovereignty is an indivisible whole which should never be surrendered to any international organization.
29. *Just as the original 13 colonies in North America formed a unified government, the sovereign states of the world, including the U.S., shall have to organize some sort of world government.*
31. We made a mistake in letting the United Nations settle in New York since all sorts of dangerous people are invited to its meetings.
56. Since the United Nations has 60 Member States, the United States should refuse to pay one-third of all its expenses.

Three of the items (1, 31, 56) deal with carping and peripheral attacks on the United Nations, which greatly appeal to those who basically dislike and distrust that organization but who believe it has a certain popularity which makes direct attacks unprofitable. Items 8 and 29 on "indivisible sovereignty" and "world government" are purposely vague and are designed to elicit emotional responses.

Another five items were included to cover the survival into the post-World War II era of attitudes favoring "aloofness from Europe" and "no entangling alliances":

15. Unless the French Government agrees to cooperate wholeheartedly in Western defense, we should withdraw our forces from the continent of Europe.
19. The Marshall Plan may have helped the Europeans, but it hasn't done much for us.
45. We should never have ratified the North Atlantic Treaty Organization (NATO) Agreement, since it is the worst sort of entangling alliance.
48. If the Europeans form a common army, the United States should keep its armed forces completely outside such an organization.
57. It is no concern of ours whether or not the countries of Europe are able to get together and form some sort of federal system of government for their part of the world.

These are all straightforward items, and their inclusion in the E Subscale requires no explanation or commentary.

Correlations of W and E

The correlations of expansionist-western-looking (W) and isolationist-eastern-looking (E) Subscales are shown in Table 3.

The W-E correlations of .48-.80 are of considerable significance. Despite the fact that the W and E Subscales contain only half as many items as the INT and DOM Scales, they correlate almost as high; as Table 3 shows, the correlations for the whole group, the white undergraduates, and the student nurses declined somewhat, but those for the Negro undergraduates and the women voters increased slightly.

The general high level of correlations of W and E leads to the conclusion that it is a common phenomenon today among young American nationalists to have strong attitudes of aloofness toward Europe and, at the same time, equally strong attitudes of intervention toward other areas of the world. As to the commonness of this phenomenon, the correlations speak for themselves.

V. CONCLUSIONS

Attitudes on questions of the international relations of the country (i.e., the national ingroup) are closely allied with attitudes on other ingroup-outgroup relations. Nationalistic attitudes on such questions, like patriotic attitudes, correlate very well with other ethnocentric attitudes, and they would seem to form an integral part of an authoritarian ideology. Logic alone would never lead one to conclude that there was any great connection between attitudes toward child-raising or the punishment of sex offenders and attitudes toward the conduct of foreign relations. However, the correlations between the International (INT) Scale and the Domestic (DOM) Scale point to just such a conclusion. If a person has an authoritarian personality, he will have authoritarian views on how he will treat his children and how he thinks we (as Americans) should treat the Russians or the British—or, for that matter, how Jews, Negroes, Martians, etc., should be treated. Although it is not absolutely safe to predict that if a person favors aloofness toward Europe and international organizations he will also favor interventionism in Asia, the chances are very much in favor of it.

In the preceding article, the emphasis was largely upon "personality type" as a predictor of certain attitudinal predispositions. In the one which follows, Pettigrew reports on a diverse body of data revealing the extent to which attitudes (in this case, racial attitudes) are a function of the social and political environment within which the holders live. It should also be mentioned in passing that this study makes a dual contribution: it not only brings out the role of nonpersonality variables in the development of social attitudes, but it also presents data on a factor which is still understressed by students of international politics. That is, one normally thinks of racial prejudice as primarily affecting domestic politics, and of its foreign policy effects as indirect at most. Yet the colonial policies of nineteenth-century Europe, and today's vestiges thereof, have rested heavily upon assumptions of racial superiority. It might also be argued that British errors vis-à-vis Turkey, before and during World War I, stemmed largely from a belief in the relative insignificance of the nation, with ethnic prejudice a key ingredient. Racism was likewise a major variable in the diplomatic strategy of Nazi Germany, as it was in French brutality vis-à-vis Algeria. In other words, racial or ethnic differentiation (and its normal concomitant, attributed inferiority) permits and produces policies of a negative sort which are somewhat less likely to be directed against nations or groups whose racial characteristics are similar to one's own.

PERSONALITY AND SOCIOCULTURAL FACTORS IN INTERGROUP ATTITUDES: A CROSS-NATIONAL COMPARISON

THOMAS F. PETTIGREW

I. INTRODUCTION

Along the continuum of prejudice theories, two extreme positions have been popular. One strongly emphasizes the personality of the bigot and neglects his cultural milieu; the other views intolerance as a mere reflection of cultural norms and neglects individual differences. Recent evidence lends *little support to either pole* [emphasis added]. As further data are gathered with more refined research tools, it becomes increasingly apparent that the psychological and sociological correlates of prejudice are elaborately intertwined and that both are essential to provide an adequate theoretical framework for this complex phenomenon.

Carrying this viewpoint further, Smith, Bruner, and White have delineated three functions that attitudes may serve for an individual. First, there is the *object-*

From Thomas F. Pettigrew, "Personality and Sociocultural Factors in Intergroup Attitudes: A Cross-National Comparison," *The Journal of Conflict Resolution,* II (1958), 29-42 (the footnotes and the bibliography and references have been omitted). Reprinted by permission of the author and *The Journal of Conflict Resolution.*

appraisal function; attitudes aid in the process of understanding "reality" as it is defined by the culture. Second, attitudes can play a *social-adjustment* role by contributing to the individual's identification with, or differentiation from, various reference groups. It should be noted that both these functions — object appraisal and social adjustment — are important reflections on the personality level of sociocultural conditions. But the most studied function of attitudes, *externalization,* is somewhat unique. "Externalization occurs when an individual, often responding unconsciously, senses an analogy between a perceived environmental event and some unresolved inner problem . . . [and] adopts an attitude . . . which is a transformed version of his way of dealing with his inner difficulty." Such a process may serve to reduce anxiety. The principal psychological theories of prejudice — frustration-aggression, psychoanalytic, and authoritarianism — all deal chiefly with this third process.

External expression of inner conflict is relatively more independent of sociocultural factors than are the other functions of attitudes. Indeed, a heuristic distinction between externalized personality variables and sociological variables contributes to our understanding of much that is known about intergroup conflict.

Minard's observations of race relations in the coal-mining county of McDowell, West Virginia, serve as a direct illustration of the point. The general pattern in this region consists of white and Negro miners being integrated below the ground and almost completely segregated above the ground. Minard estimates that roughly 60 per cent of the white miners manage to reverse roles almost completely; they can accept Negroes as equals in the mines but cannot accept them as equals elsewhere. Furthermore, he feels that, at one extreme, about 20 per cent accept the black miners as equals in both situations, while, at the other extreme, about 20 per cent never accept them in either situation. In our terms, the behavior of the *majority* of these whites studied by Minard can be predicted largely by sociocultural expectations, and the behavior of the *consistent minorities* can be accounted for largely by externalized personality variables [emphasis added].

The research literature abounds with further examples in which a separation of psychological and sociological factors is helpful. The many papers on interracial contact in housing, at work, and in the army show the marked effects that can be brought about by certain changes in the social situation between races. But personality factors are still operating. Usually these studies report that some individuals hold favorable attitudes toward minorities even before the contact and that other individuals still hold unfavorable attitudes after the contact. Many of these studies also find that the changes brought about by the contact are quite specific and delimited in nature. That is, the intergroup changes occur only under a narrow range of conditions, since the basic personality orientations of the participants have not changed fundamentally. Thus white department-store employees become more accepting of Negroes in the work situation after equal status contact but not in other situations. And the attitudes of white army personnel toward the Negro as a fighting man improve after equal status contact in combat, but their attitudes toward the Negro as a social companion do not change.

Desegregation findings furnish further illustrations where the distinction is useful. Social demands for racial desegregation and the irresistible trend of the times are counteracting personality predispositions in many communities. Thus a 1954 public opinion survey in Oklahoma found an overwhelming majority of the residents sternly against desegregation, and yet today mixed schools have become accepted throughout most of the state without incident. And in Wilmington, Delaware, two years after successful school integration without apparent public opposition, a poll indicated that only a minority approved of the school desegregation decision of the Supreme Court. Indeed, this discrepancy between opinions and demands is a general phenomenon throughout the border states. Hyman and Sheatsley report that only 31 per cent of the white population in those border areas that have already integrated their school systems indorse desegregation.

This conflict between *authority-supported cultural changes* and *personal preferences* is underscored by another finding that public opinion polls have uncovered in the South [emphasis added]. Several investigators have independently shown that respondents themselves make a distinction between what they individually favor and what they expect to happen in their community. Thus the huge majority of southern whites favor racial segregation, but most of them also feel that desegregation is inevitable.

Finally, the work originally done by La Piere in 1934 and more recently replicated in different contexts by Saenger and Gilbert and by Kutner, Wilkins, and Yarrow furnishes further justification for a theoretical separation of social and externalization aspects of intergroup conflict. These investigations illustrate the results of conflicting personality predispositions and actual social situations with minority-group members; frequently the face-to-face conditions override previous practices.

Such work has led several authorities in the field to make the sociocultural and personality differentiation. Psychologist G. W. Allport discusses the two classes of factors separately in his definitive volume, *The Nature of Prejudice,* and sociologist Arnold Rose makes a similar distinction in a recent theoretical article on intergroup relations.

The present paper is a summary report on research conducted chiefly to gain cross-national perspective on these two sets of prejudice factors. The studies were made in two parts of the world where racial conflict today is highlighted and cultural sanctions of intolerance are intense and explicit: the Union of South Africa and the southern United States. First, a more detailed report of previously unpublished data will be presented on the South African study. Following this, a comparison will be made with the southern United States based on a summary of data presented in detail elsewhere.

II. Racial Prejudice in the Union of South Africa

The limited evidence available supports the general belief that white South Africans are unusually prejudiced against Africans. This raises the intriguing question as to whether this increased hostility represents (*a*) more externalizing personality potential for prejudice among South Africans, (*b*) the effects of different cultural norms and pressures, or (*c*) both of these.

To provide a tentative answer, a questionnaire study was undertaken of the racial attitudes of students at the English-speaking University of Natal in the Union of South Africa. A non-random sample of 627 undergraduates — approximately one-third of the entire university — completed an anonymous instrument containing three scales and a number of background items. The three scales are a thirteen-item measure of authoritarianism (F scale) whose statements are shown in Table 2, a sixteen-item measure of social conformity (C scale) whose statements are shown in Table 3, and an eighteen-item measure of anti-African attitudes (A scale) whose statements are shown in Table 8. Background information includes place of birth, political party preference, father's occupation, and ethnic-group membership.

Taken as a group, these students evidence considerable hostility toward Africans, accepting in large degree the white-supremacy ideology so adamantly propounded by the present government of their country. Thus 72 per cent of the sample agree that "there is something inherently primitive and uncivilized in the native, as shown in his music and extreme aggressiveness"; and 69 per cent agree that "manual labor seems to fit the native mentality better than more skilled and responsible work." And yet their F-scale responses are roughly comparable to those of American student populations. Thus these South Africans are sharply prejudiced against blacks without possessing any greater externalizing personality potential for intolerance than peoples in more tolerant areas.

In addition, authoritarianism correlates with anti-African attitudes at a level comparable to relationships between authoritarianism and prejudice in other parts of the world. Table 1 [omitted] shows that the A and F scales correlate +0.56 among the Afrikaans-speaking members of the sample and +0.46 among the English-speaking members. Similar scales typically correlate in the fifties in American college samples. The C-scale measure of social conformity — employed for the first time in this investigation — relates to the A-scale scores significantly, too, in both ethnic groups.

More detailed analyses of the F and C scales' relationships with anti-African attitudes are provided in Tables 2 and 3. Each of the thirteen authoritarian statements separates the less and more prejudiced halves of the sample in the predicted direction, seven of the differences proving to be significant at better than the 0.001 level of confidence. The sixteen C-scale items predict almost as well; the more anti-African students in every case agree more often than the less

TABLE 2
Anti-African Prejudice and F-Scale Items

F-Scale Item	Percentage Agreement[a]		$2\times2\chi^2$	p
	Less prejudiced half	More prejudiced half		
a) Nowadays when so many different kinds of people move around and mix together so much, a person has to be especially careful not to catch an infection or disease from them	13.6	33.2	33.5	0.001
b) There is hardly anything lower than a person who does not feel a great love and respect for his parents	52.6	70.5	21.2	.001
c) People can be put into two distinct classes: the weak and the strong	23.5	37.8	15.1	.001
d) Most of our social problems would be solved if we could somehow get rid of the immoral, crooked, and feebleminded people	45.4	60.6	14.8	.001
e) The most important thing a child should learn is obedience to his parents	79.8	90.2	13.2	.001
f) Every person should have faith in some supernatural power whose decisions he obeys without question	46.7	60.9	13.0	.001
g) When a person has a problem or worry, it is best for him not to think about it, but to keep busy with more cheerful things	39.4	53.2	11.8	.001
h) Nowadays more and more people are prying into matters that should remain private and personal	63.5	74.5	8.6	.01
i) If people would talk less and work more, everybody would be better off	67.8	78.2	8.3	.01
j) An insult to our honor should always be punished	31.8	40.3	4.7	.05
k) No sane, normal person would ever think of hurting a close friend or relative	67.9	76.6	4.3	.05
l) Science has its place, but there are many important things that can never possibly be understood by the human mind	80.7	85.8	2.9	0.10
m) Some day it will probably be shown that astrology can explain a lot of things	44.4	48.0	0.9	n.s.

[a]The respondent was given four categories: agree strongly, agree, disagree, and disagree strongly. Percentage agreement is calculated by combining the first two of these replies.

TABLE 3

Anti-African Prejudice and C-Scale Items

C-Scale Item	Percentage Agreement[a]		$2 \times 2 \chi^2$	p
	Less prejudiced half	More prejudiced half		
a) It's better to go along with the crowd than to be a martyr	34.8	53.2	21.8	0.001
b) When almost everyone agrees on something, there is little reason to oppose it	16.6	31.1	18.5	.001
c) Adherence to convention produces the best kind of citizen	31.8	46.8	14.9	.001
d) To be successful, a group's members must act and think alike	45.7	60.0	12.5	.001
e) It is important for friends to have similar opinions	28.5	42.2	12.1	.001
f) It is more important to be loyal and conform to our own group than to try to co-operate with other groups	25.6	38.5	11.7	.001
g) We should alter our needs to fit society's demands rather than change society to fit our needs	42.4	55.1	11.4	.001
h) A good group member should agree with the other members	21.2	33.2	11.1	.001
i) It is best not to express your views when in the company of friends who disagree with you	23.8	32.9	6.1	.02
j) Before a person does something, he should try to consider how his friends will react to it	54.6	63.1	4.4	.05
k) To become a success these days, a person has to act in the way that others expect him to act	33.2	41.5	4.2	.05
l) A group cannot expect to maintain its identity unless its members all think and feel in very much the same way	59.3	66.8	3.9	.05
m) It is one's duty to conform to the passing demands of the world and to suppress those personal desires that do not fit these demands	43.7	51.1	3.4	.10
n) A person should adapt his ideas and his behavior to the group that happens to be with him at the time	45.7	52.6	3.1	.10
o) It is extremely uncomfortable to go accidentally to a formal party in street clothes	78.5	83.1	2.0	.20
p) To get along well in a group, you have to follow the lead of others	27.2	31.1	1.1	0.30

[a]Percentage agreement calculated as in Table 2.

prejudiced. Perhaps the conforming attitude of the bigots is capsuled in the first item of Table 3. While only a third of the tolerant members of the group agree with the statement, over half the prejudiced students feel that "it's better to go along with the crowd than to be a martyr."

These personality relationships suggest (*a*) that personality factors are as important correlates of prejudice in this sample as they are in other, non-South African samples; (*b*) that social conformity (as measured by the C scale) is a particularly crucial personality variable in this sample's attitudes toward Africans; and (*c*) that personality components do not in themselves account for the heightened intolerance of this sample.

We must turn to sociocultural factors to explain the extreme prejudice of these respondents, and the unusual importance of these variables is made clear by the data. For instance, the 560 students who were born on the African continent are significantly more intolerant of Africans than the remaining 65, but they are *not* more authoritarian. Table 4 shows that those *not* born in Africa are much less likely to fall into the most prejudiced third of the distribution than other sample members [emphasis added]. And yet the two groups do not differ significantly in their F-scale scores. More thoroughly influenced throughout their lives by the culture's definition of the white man's situation in Africa, students born on the Dark Continent are more anti-African without the usual personality concomitants of ethnocentrism.

TABLE 4
Place of Birth and Anti-African Prejudice[a]

| Anti-African Attitudes[b] | N | Place of Birth | |
		On African Continent	Not on African Continent
		560	65
Least prejudiced	176	28%	29%
Medium prejudiced	246	38	54
Most prejudiced	203	34	17

[a]2 × 3 chi-square = 9.33; $p < 0.01$.
[b]The least prejudiced are the students who rated A-scale scores from 0 through 4 by disagreeing with a heavy majority of the items; the medium prejudiced received scores of either 5 or 6 by agreeing with roughly half of the 18 A-scale items; and the most prejudiced obtained scores of 7 through 10 by agreeing with a majority of the statements.

Another such relationship involves students who support the Nationalist party —the pro-*Apartheid* political faction that is presently in power. Table 5 indicates that these respondents score significantly higher on the A scale than their fellow undergraduates, but these two groups do not differ on the F scale. Again a prejudice difference is not accompanied by a personality potential difference. These relationships with political party preference and prejudice hold for each of the major ethnic groups—Afrikaners and English—considered separately.

Two other comparisons yield statistically significant differences in both author-

TABLE 5
Political Party Preference and Anti-African Prejudice[a]

Anti-African Attitudes	N	Political Party Preference[b]	
		Nationalist Party	Other Parties
		72	483
Least prejudiced	157	8%	35%
Medium prejudiced	210	26	36
Most prejudiced	188	66	29

[a]2×3 chi-square $= 38.60$; $p < 0.001$.
[b]Seventy-two of the 627 students did not indicate any political preference.

itarianism and anti-African prejudice. Table 6 indicates that those sample members whose fathers are manually employed are significantly more intolerant of the African than those whose fathers are non-manually employed. The two groups differ in the same manner in their F-scale scores. But when authoritarianism is controlled for, the groups still differ significantly in their attitudes toward blacks. In other words, the children of manual fathers are more prejudiced and more authoritarian than other students, and they remain more prejudiced even after the difference in authoritarianism is partialed out of the relationship. These upwardly mobile students must be carefully in step with the mores to establish firmly their rise in the social structure, and the mores of South Africa lead to intolerance.

TABLE 6
Father's Occupational Status and Anti-African Prejudice[a]

Anti-African Attitudes	N	Father's Occupational Status[b]	
		Manual	Non-manual
		146	417
Less prejudiced half	280	34%	55%
More prejudiced half	283	66	45

[a]2×2 chi-square $= 18.90$; $p < 0.001$.
[b]Sixty-four of the 627 students did not indicate their fathers' occupations.

Table 7 shows the sharp difference between the Afrikaner and English subjects in the sample. Afrikaners are both more anti-African and more authoritarian, and, when the F-scale differences are corrected for, they remain significantly more hostile to the African. These 50 students are directly subject to the national ethos and have no conflicting national reference, as many English-speaking South Africans have in Great Britian. Like the upwardly mobile, they are in roles that demand unusual conformity.

Table 8 clarifies further the ethnic differences in attitudes toward the African.

265

Sixteen of the A scale's eighteen statements significantly separate the Afrikaners from the English, the former scoring higher in all cases. And, moreover, there is a definite trend in these differences. The five items which discriminate poorest between the ethnic groups (items *n* through *r*) are all stereotyped-belief statements; they refer to the standard traits frequently associated with Africans — lazy, primitive, happy-go-lucky, and bad-smelling. Conversely, five of the six best discriminators (items *b* through *f*) are all exclusion-discrimination statements;

TABLE 7
Ethnic Group and Anti-African Prejudice[a]

Anti-African Attitudes	N	Ethnic Group[b]	
		Afrikaners	English
		50	513
Less prejudiced half	264	14%	50%
More prejudiced half	299	86%	50%

[a]2×2 chi-square $= 23.7$; $p < 0.001$.
[b]Ethnic group is determined by both the student's own ethnic identification and the principal language spoken in his home. Sixty-four of the students identified with other groups (e.g., Jewish, French, German) and are not included in this analysis.

they deny equal rights to Africans in employment, housing, and voting. Afrikaans-speaking and English-speaking students, then, do not differ sharply in the degree to which they harbor the traditional *stereotype* of the African, but they do possess markedly divergent views on *discrimination* against the African [emphasis added]. A key to these differences may be provided in the lone exception to this trend, item *a*. Seven out of every ten Afrikaners, as compared with only a third of the English, believe that the "natives will always have a greater tendency toward crimes of violence than Europeans." Strong projection may be operating for those agreeing with this statement, but, in any event, it suggests that physical fear of the black man is especially prevalent among our Afrikaans-speaking respondents and that this may be the fundamental motivation for their emphasis on excluding and discriminating against the African.

All these findings point to the crucial role of the cultural milieu in shaping the attitudes of the white South African toward the blacks in his midst. While externalizing personality factors do not account for the students' unusually prejudiced attitudes concerning Africans, variables which reflect the dominant norms of the white society prove to be important. Students who are especially responsive to these norms — those who were born in Africa, those who identify with the Nationalist party, those who are upwardly mobile, and those who have been molded by the conservative traditions of the Afrikaans-speaking people — tend to be intolerant of Africans to some degree, regardless of their basic personality structure.

III. RACIAL PREJUDICE IN THE SOUTHERN UNITED STATES

Similar considerations led to an earlier comparative study of anti-Negro prejudice in the southern and northern United States. While considerable evidence indicates that white southerners are typically more intolerant of the Negro than white northerners, little work has been focused on the factors underlying this difference. But, like the South African data, the scant data available suggest that sociocultural and not externalization [i.e., personality] factors may be the crucial determinants of the contrasting regional attitudes toward the Negro.

Thus, if the South did have more externalizing personality potential for prejudice than other American areas, it should also be more anti-Semitic. But Roper has twice found in his national polls that the South is one of the most tolerant regions toward Jews, and Prothro has noted that 40 per cent of his adult white Louisiana sample is at the same time favorable in its attitudes toward Jews and highly anti-Negro. Furthermore, there is no evidence that the stern family pattern associated with "prejudiced personalities" is more prevalent in the South than in the North. And, finally, the few white southern populations that have been given the F scale have obtained means that fall easily within the range of means reported for non-southern populations.

Rose categorically concludes: "There is no evidence that 'authoritarian personality' or frustration-aggression or scapegoating, or any known source of 'prejudice' in the psychological sense, is any more prevalent in the South than in the North." And Prothro adds: "Situational, historical and cultural factors appear to be of considerable, perhaps major, import in addition to personality dynamics" in determining anti-Negro attitudes in the South.

In testing these ideas in the two regions, different methods were employed than those used in South Africa. Public opinion polling techniques were utilized with 366 randomly selected white adults in eight roughly matched communities in the North and South. The four small southern towns, located in Georgia and North Carolina, were chosen to have Negro population percentages ranging from 10 to 45 per cent, while the small northern towns, all located in New England, have less than 1 per cent Negroes each.

The interview schedule contained a ten-item measure of authoritarianism (F scale), an eight-item measure of anti-Semitism (A-S scale), and a twelve-item measure of anti-Negro prejudice (N scale), together with numerous background questions. The poll purported to be concerned with the effects of the mass media upon public opinion, and it seems largely due to this guise that the blatantly phrased prejudice statements caused no interview breakoffs.

Of greatest immediate interest is the striking similarity in these results with those of the South African investigation. First, the southern sample is considerably more anti-Negro than the northern sample but is *not* more authoritarian. Similar to the Afrikaner-English differences (Table 8), the southerners respond in the more prejudiced direction on each of the N-scale statements but are most

TABLE 8

Ethnic-Group Differences on A-Scale Items

| A-Scale Items | Percentage Agreement[a] | | $2 \times 2 \chi^2$ | p |
	Afrikaners	English		
a) Because of their primitive background, natives will always have a greater tendency toward crimes of violence than Europeans	70.0	34.9	33.6	0.001
b) Native musicians are sometimes as good as Europeans at swing music and jazz, but it is a mistake to have mixed native-European bands	86.0	54.2	18.8	.001
c) Most of the natives would become officious, overbearing, and disagreeable if not kept in their place	80.0	48.3	18.2	.001
d) Laws which would force equal employment opportunities for both the natives and Europeans would not be fair to European employers	74.0	44.2	16.2	.001
e) The natives have their rights, but it is best to keep them in their own districts and schools and to prevent too much contact with Europeans	86.0	63.7	9.9	.01
f) The natives do not deserve the right to vote	64.0	41.3	9.5	.01
g) The natives will never have the intelligence and organizing ability to run a modern industrial society	42.0	23.2	8.7	.01
h) As the native will never properly absorb our civilization, the only solution is to let him develop along his own lines	68.0	46.3	8.6	.01

i) Manual labor seems to fit the native mentality better than more skilled and responsible work	88.0	68.9	8.0	.01
j) Seldom, if ever, is a native superior to most Europeans intellectually	72.0	52.2	7.1	.01
k) The natives tend to be overly emotional	66.0	46.5	7.1	.01
l) Because of his immaturity, the South African native is likely to be led into all sorts of mischief and should therefore be strictly controlled in his own best interests	92.0	75.6	6.9	.01
m) The granting of wide educational opportunities to natives is a dangerous thing	36.0	19.9	6.9	.01
n) Most natives are lazy and lack ambition	60.0	44.1	4.6	.05
o) There is something inherently primitive and uncivilized in the native, as shown in his music and extreme aggressiveness	86.0	72.1	4.4	.05
p) Due to the differences in innate endowment, the Bantu race will always be inferior to the white race	54.0	39.6	4.0	.05
q) Most of the natives are happy-go-lucky and irresponsible	70.0	60.0	1.9	0.20
r) In spite of what some claim, the natives do have a different and more pronounced body odor than Europeans	84.0	81.5	0.2	n.s.

[a]Percentage agreement calculated as in Table 2.

unique in their extreme attitudes concerning excluding and discriminating against the Negro. That is, southerners and northerners in the samples both share in large degree the lazy, primitive, happy-go-lucky, and bad-smelling stereotype of the Negro, but southerners far more than northerners wish to deny equal rights to the Negro in employment, housing, and voting. And yet there is no difference in the externalization potential for intolerance; the F-scale means of the two samples are almost identical.

Further similarities to the South African data support the contention that personality dynamics, such as authoritarianism, are not responsible for the sharp North-South divergence in attitudes toward the Negro. When age and education are partialed out, the N and F scales correlate to a comparable degree in the two populations. Moreover, with age and education partialed out again, the N and A-S scales relate at equivalent levels in the two regional samples. In other words, the externalizing prejudiced personality as tapped by the F and A-S scales does not account for any more of the anti-Negro variance in the southern sample than it does in the northern sample. This finding, combined with the previously mentioned fact that the two groups do not differ in their F-scale responses, indicates that externalization factors do not explain the heightened bigotry of the southerners. As with the South African results, we must turn to social variables in an effort to account for the regional discrepancy in attitudes toward the Negro.

All six of the sociocultural dimensions tested yield meaningful relationships with Negro prejudice in the southern sample: sex, church attendance, social mobility, political party identification, armed service, and education. These variables reflect southern culture in a manner similar to the social variables tested in the South African study. And as in South Africa, those southerners, who by their roles in the social structure can be anticipated to be conforming to the dictates of the culture, prove to be more prejudiced against Negroes than their counterparts. For example, females, the "carriers of culture," are significantly more anti-Negro than men in the southern sample but *not* in the northern sample.

Two other groups of southerners who manifest conforming behavior in other areas are also more intolerant of Negroes. Respondents who have been to church within the week are significantly more anti-Negro than those who have not been within the month, and there is a tendency (though not statistically significant) for the upwardly mobile to be more anti-Negro than others in the non-manual occupational class. The latter result recalls the finding in the South African study that students whose fathers are manual workers tend to be more anti-African (Table 6). In the northern sample, no such trends appear. Protestant church-goers in the North tend to be more tolerant of the Negro than Protestant non-attenders, and no relationship between upward mobility and attitudes toward Negroes is discernible. Conformity to northern norms—unlike conformity to southern or South African norms—is not associated with hostility for the black man.

In contrast to the conformers, southerners who evidence deviance from the mores in some area of social life tend to be *less* anti-Negro. Non-attenders of church furnish one example. Another example are respondents who explicitly identify themselves as political independents, which also represents a degree of deviance: they tend to be considerably more tolerant of the Negro than are southerners who consider themselves either Democrats or Republicans. Again, no such discrepancy occurs in the northern population.

Downward mobility has been noted by other investigators to be positively related to intolerance in the North, and this finding is replicated in the present northern data. But in the southern data a striking reversal occurs. The downwardly mobile in the South are much less anti-Negro than other manually employed respondents, though the two groups do not differ in authoritarianism. Perhaps in a culture that emphasizes status and family background, that makes a sharp distinction between "poor whites" and "respectable whites," and that cherishes its aristocratic traditions, the downwardly mobile southerner learns to reject much of his culture. And rejecting the culture's stress on tradition and status makes it easier to reject also the culture's dicta concerning the Negro.

Two groups of southerners—armed service veterans and the highly educated—are potential deviants from southern culture simply because their special experience and study have brought them into contact with other ways of life. And, as we might expect, we find that both veterans and college-educated southerners are considerably more tolerant of the Negro than non-veterans and the poorly educated. Veterans in both regions prove to be more authoritarian than non-veterans, and, consistent with this, northern veterans are less tolerant of Negroes than northerners who had not served. Education is negatively related to N-scale scores in the northern sample, too, but significantly less than in the southern sample. Exposure to non-southern culture leads to deviance from the strict southern norms concerning the Negro; little wonder that southerners who have been out of the region for any considerable length of time are generally viewed as suspect by their neighbors upon return.

These consistent relationships with social factors in the southern data have been interpreted in terms of conformity and deviance from the narrowly prescribed mores of small-town southern life. Evidence for such an analysis comes from a final intra-southern difference. Southern communities with high Negro population ratios (38 and 45 per cent) have significantly higher N-scale means than the other communities sampled in the South with low Negro ratios (10 and 18 per cent), though they are *not* different in authoritarianism or anti-Semitism. In southern areas with the most intensely anti-Negro norms, prejudice against the black southerner is greater, even though there is not a greater amount of externalizing personality potential for prejudice.

Though limited by the restricted samples employed, this evidence indicates that sociocultural factors—as in the South African sample—are indeed the key to the regional difference in attitudes toward the Negro. In spite of the marked contrast in samples and method between the two investigations, both the South

African and the southern results underline the unique importance of social variables in prejudice that is sanctioned by the cultural norms.

IV. SUMMARY AND CONCLUSIONS

Finely interwoven personality and sociocultural variables together form the foundation upon which a broad and satisfactory theory of racial prejudice must be built. Neither set of factors can be neglected, but a heuristic separation between the relatively culture-free externalization factors and social factors aids analysis. The present paper uses this distinction to interpret prejudice data from two parts of the world with tense racial conflict — the Union of South Africa and the southern United States.

Externalization factors such as authoritarianism are associated with prejudice in both the South African and the southern samples at levels roughly comparable with other areas. Data from the South African students hint, however, that susceptibility to conform may be an unusually important psychological component of prejudice in regions where the cultural norms positively sanction intolerance. In addition, there is no indication in either of these samples that there is any more externalizing personality potential for prejudice in these areas than in more tolerant parts of the globe.

The extensive racial prejudice of the South African and southern groups seems directly linked with the antiblack dictates of the two cultures. Sociocultural factors which reflect the mores consistently relate to prejudice — place of birth, political party preference, upward mobility, and ethnic-group membership in the South African data and sex, church attendance, social mobility, political party identification, armed service, and education in the southern data. The pattern is clear: conformity to South African or southern mores is associated with racial intolerance, while deviance from these mores is associated with racial tolerance.

Taken together with other published work, these limited results suggest a broad, cross-national hypothesis:

In areas with historically imbedded traditions of racial intolerance, externalizing personality factors underlying prejudice remain important, but sociocultural factors are unusually crucial and account for the heightened racial hostility.

Should future, more extensive, research support such a hypothesis, its implications for prejudice theory would be considerable. Regions or peoples with heightened prejudice against a particular outgroup would not necessarily be thought of as harboring more authoritarianism; the special conflict may reflect the operation of particular historical, cultural, and social factors. Such a prospect may be encouraging to many action programs — efforts which typically are more successful at changing a person's relation to his culture than they are at changing basic personality structure. Desegregation is a case in point. The success of the movement in the South does not depend — this hypothesis would contend — on changing the deeply ingrained orientations of prejudice-prone personalities;

rather, it rests on the effectiveness with which racial integration now going on in the South can restructure the mores to which so many culturally intolerant southerners conform.

A second implication of the hypothesis is that personality factors such as authoritarianism and susceptibility to conform cannot be overlooked in understanding bigotry even in parts of the world like the Union of South Africa and the southern United States. Most psychological approaches to prejudice, it has been noted, are concerned chiefly with the externalization function of attitudes. Perhaps, as the object-appraisal and social-adjustment functions of attitudes are studied in more detail, the direct personality concomitants of cultural pressures will be isolated and better understood.

3. The Malleability of Citizen Opinion

The two previous selections indicated the types of personality and environmental factors that account for many attitudinal predispositions; in a sense they attempted to summarize the cumulative effects of socialization upon the individual up to some given point in time. But all the while that attitudes, and predispositions to such attitudes, are being slowly shaped by the interaction of personality and environment, important events occur to slow or hasten the pace, or to change its direction. In other words, the individual's attitudes and opinions are not only shaped to an impressive degree by the gradual processes of maturation in his given sociopolitical milieu, but by people and/or phenomena which impinge much more dramatically upon him under conditions of relevance and salience. This effect is particularly pronounced when the subject is confronted with the views of those whom he regards as popular, respected, or knowledgeable—"reference figures."

The two American psychologists who have focussed on this manipulability to the greatest extent are probably Muzafer Sherif and Solomon Asch, but their experiments have been so widely reported as to make their inclusion here superfluous. Rather, since the reader's general awareness of these data and interpretations has been assumed, the paper selected goes beyond the *frequency* with which manipulation (in the form of distorted judgment) can be generated, to focus upon the *magnitude* of such possible opinion change. In this study, Livant found it a remarkably simple task to induce—over a sequence of thirty estimates and "confirmations"—distortions of up to 300 per cent. In other words, a judgment which could not possibly be generated by a one-shot propaganda volley may readily be generated by a series of continuing, incremental exaggerations.

CUMULATIVE DISTORTION OF JUDGMENT

WILLIAM PAUL LIVANT

Distortion-producing influences on judgment have been extensively studied, particularly those due to social influence of an authority or a group of peers. In the classical group-pressure studies, some attention has been directed to the time course of induced judgmental distortion over successive occasions. Asch found no time trend in the proportion of Ss who yield in their judgments, and noted also the high degree of consistency for individual Ss. However, as Cohen *et al.* point out, we cannot conclude that no temporal process is operating; the experimental run may be too short. More important, the pressure experiment may be regarded as a conflict extended in time. It is possible to build a model of temporal conflict such that a change in parameter values can predict constant or altering proportions of judgmental distortion over time.

Cohen has formalized this temporal conflict in a Markovian model. He has found that group pressure on judgment extended over time tends to divide a population into those who regularly yield to the group in their judgments and those who do not. All persons who switch back and forth will eventually settle into one of these two states. This conception agrees with a general observation on the effects of continued stress on a population: continued stress tends to magnify small initial differences in the ability to deal with it.

Cohen's treatment of conflict over time does not attempt to examine the manner in which successive judgments build upon their predecessors. Once an initial direction of distortion is established, each successive judgment of the same phenomenon becomes a distortion of a distortion of a distortion. The importance of this temporal process in natural life has been discussed by Bettelheim among others. If the distorting influence on judgments operates on the level of judgment established by past distortion, persons find themselves eventually making judgments or performing actions they would consider outrageous initially. Willingness to undertake such actions under hypnosis appears also as a matter of progressive degrees. Extreme behavior in general may result from the operation of bias on the results of previously biased actions.

This study is a demonstration of a method to produce such striking effects in the classical laboratory situation.

We consider a situation in which a party judges each of a succession of

From William P. Livant, "Cumulative Distortion of Judgment," *Perceptual and Motor Skills,* XVI (1963), 741-45 (the bibliography and references have been omitted). Reprinted by permission of the author and *Perceptual and Motor Skills.*

recurring events (e.g., ABCBCACAB . . .). Correction is given after each judgment. But this "correction" is biased. It contains a bias applied onto the party's *own previous judgment of that event.* The present demonstration illustrates the cumulative effects of a systematic bias. Since the judgments investigated are magnitudes, line lengths, each "correction" of a given length, A, was 20% greater than S's last judgment of A. Successive judgments, therefore, reveal the degree to which S adopts the bias of the "correcting" authority in advance in judging future events. And since the recurring sets of stimulus events are identical, the limits to which judgments can be distorted may be investigated.

The present method was tried and discarded in the context of a larger study with a different purpose; but the two cases run and reported suggest the nature of the phenomena which may appear.

METHOD

Setting

Two Ss were brought into a darkened room and seated across a table; each was 15 ft. from a movie screen on the front wall of the room. At the rear center E operated the projector.

Materials

On 45 5- × 8-in. white cards, were ruled straight lines, one to a card; the slope and direction of line was randomized across cards. There were 15 line lengths varying, when projected on the screen, from 6 in. to 48 in. in steps of 3 in.; thus, each line length was represented three times in a complete run of the deck. The order of projection was randomized.

Procedure

After the two Ss were seated, E instructed them as follows: "This is an experiment to study how people agree about making judgments on the lengths of lines. I will flash a line on the front screen. You two must arrive within a minute at a common guess: — how many inches long is it? You may talk it over freely; in fact, I encourage you to. You *must* arrive at a common guess. You will report your common guess, then I will tell you how long *I* think it is. Then we will go on to the next line."

The schedule of experimental correction was as follows. On two trials out of every three, the test trials, E reported a length approximately *20% more than the group's previous guess.* This was true for each line length. On the first trial for each length, correction was 20% more than the groups' present guess. On one guess

275

of every three *E* reported *approximately 20% more than the true line length;* this report was intended to provide some "realistic" effect.

*S*s were two groups with two college men in each group.

RESULTS

Figs. 1 and 2 show the cumulative course of judgment distortion for both groups on the test trials. The data were averaged over all line lengths. It appears that both groups' data can be fitted with a linear function. No careful record was kept of group discussion or terminal interview, but both groups were becoming suspicious of being influenced. Group A in the interview definitely verbalized that "you keep pulling us up, and it has something to do with our guesses," although they could not say what. If the experiment had been prolonged, it is possible that the data would not be linear.

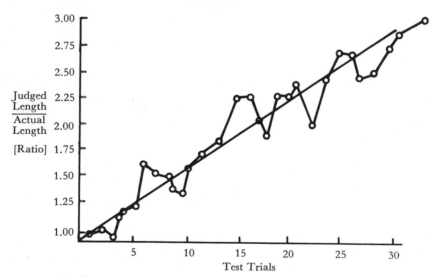

Figure 1. Successive judgments of line length: Group 1

Obviously, for these two groups, cumulative distortion was very large; lines which were initially judged as long as a man's arm were judged at the end as long as a man's whole height. Although it is not demonstrated here, it is very doubtful that *S*s would be prepared initially to accept such a monstrous correction.

The present demonstration points especially to the fact that judgments, in serving as the basis for further judgments, have consequences. In judgmental conflict over time, not only is the judge modified by influence, but also the judgment he is called upon to make. The *kind* of judgment has been shown to be an important prediction of induced distortion. But, to date, kinds of judgments have been studied independently of each other. Very likely there are sequential schedules of interdependent judgments which produce striking differences in distortion.

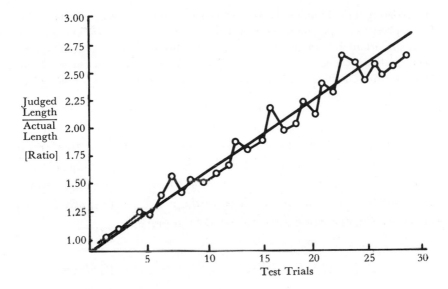

Figure 2. Successive judgments of line length: Group 2

The present method is a way of investigating the development of progressive distortion. With slight alteration it may serve to distinguish different components of judgments as well. The process of weighing influences upon judgment is structured in depth. Kelman, for example, has created experimental conditions where increasingly powerful effects of authority upon judgment are revealed. He calls these (a) compliance, (b) identification and (c) internalization. Each successive condition demands less actual supervisory presence of coercive authority to induce an effect of authority upon judgment.

The present method may be modified slightly to distinguish these effects in the same single experiment. A party (1) makes a judgment and, (2) after each judgment he observes the judgment of another, and then (3) he reconsiders, and makes a second judgment of the same event. If the judgment of the other is a systematic distortion of the party's first judgment, the effects of cumulative distortion in judgments (1) and (3) can be observed over time. The change in (3) affords a measure of the *tendency to yield to the judgment of another.* The judgment (1) affords a measure of the *tendency to internalize the bias of another* before the other's judgment is rendered.

It may be possible to examine Kelman's third process, internalization, with a further modification. Let the party continue judging without any "correction" at all. Continued progressive distortion may be taken to indicate that S not only projects the authority's bias on his own past judgments in making future ones, but he also regards his cumulative bias as "correct" without explicit correction. Thus, the same situation may be made to yield differing, perhaps scalable, measures of judgmental alteration.

Finally, these effects can likely be magnified in situations where the stimuli are not recurring, but changing. If the successive stimuli *themselves* were based on a bias applied to S's past judgment, distortion might progress indefinitely. This case is important in bargaining behavior, where two parties offer stimuli for each other's judgment, e.g., make "offers." These offers may interact to reach some stable norm, or they may grow progressively distorted leading to an eventual breakdown of bargaining.

On the other hand, there is some evidence to suggest that certain limits to such malleability nevertheless exist. In the following selection, Jacobs and Campbell indicate the extent to which serious misperceptions and distortions may be reduced or perhaps even extinguished as the sources of the distortion are weakened or removed.

THE PERPETUATION OF AN ARBITRARY TRADITION THROUGH SEVERAL GENERATIONS OF A LABORATORY MICROCULTURE

ROBERT C. JACOBS AND DONALD T. CAMPBELL

According to Sumner "the mores can make anything right," and he went on to illustrate with a chapter on sacral harlotry and child sacrifice. According to Tarde "imitation is the key to the social mystery," "society is imitation," "social man is a veritable somnambulist." Such quotations indicate the late 19th century awareness of the power of culture to perpetuate arbitrary beliefs. Less drastically expressed, some such perspective permeates present day social science, although tempered somewhat by functionalism in anthropology and sociology. In social psychology, for example, cultural tradition tends to be invoked primarily as an "explanation" for social evils, prejudice, resistance to ameliorative social change, and the like. The current emphasis upon conformity reinforces this view, in spite of Asch's demurrer. Yet there are, no doubt, restraints upon a complete arbitrariness to culture, particularly with regard to beliefs that lie within people's direct range of observation. Thus arbitrary and erroneous superstitions about the shape of fishhooks probably would not long survive the systematic drift pressures resulting from continual minor variations some of which are in the direction of noticeably more effective form. Here lies the problem in the theory of culture for which a laboratory analogue was sought.

From Robert C. Jacobs and Donald T. Campbell, "The Perpetuation of an Arbitrary Tradition through Several Generations of a Laboratory Microculture," *Journal of Abnormal and Social Psychology*, LXII (1961), 649-58 (the bibliography and references have been omitted). Reprinted by permission of the authors and the American Psychological Association.

Since Sherif's classic studies on the formation of "social norms" in laboratory groups, there have been sporadic efforts to bring the process of cultural transmission into the laboratory. While much small group research might be so interpreted, the present study was in particular inspired by Sherif's studies, by Rose and Felton's "experimental histories of culture," and by the preliminary report of experiments on the evolution of "microcultures" by Gerard, Kluckhohn, and Rapoport. In the latter two studies and in the present one, there is an effort to demonstrate a perpetuation of "cultural" characteristics that transcends the replacement of individual persons. In the present study confederates have been employed to establish an extreme cultural norm, the inculcation and survival of which is then studied as the confederates are one by one taken out of the group, naive new members gradually introduced, who then unwittingly become the further transmitters of the belief to still newer entrants.

The specific culture trait and the ecology of the group relative to such traits should obviously affect the success in the indoctrination of each new generation, and the rate of erosion of the tradition by innovation. In the Rose and Felton study, group interpretations of Rorschach cards were employed, a material offering considerable latitude for cultural arbitrariness and idiosyncrasy. In the Gerard, Kluckhohn, and Rapoport study, the groups were continually faced with new instances of a very difficult puzzle series, and were continually confronted with evidences of the lack of perfection of their traditional solutions, a situation encouraging the evolution of more adaptive norms, and unfavorable to the perpetuation of pure superstition. For the present study, a task was sought which would allow as much latitude for cultural arbitrariness as the Rose and Felton situation, and which would, in addition, make possible the ready quantification of effects. The original Sherif autokinetic movement situation was judged to provide this: if a person views a pinpoint of light in an otherwise totally blacked-out room, the light soon appears to move. The illusion is a strong one for most persons, and is apparent even to those who know the light to be stationary. As Sherif has shown, naive respondents are very suggestible as to the degree of movement seen, and laboratory group norms on the amount of movement are rapidly established without the respondents being aware of the fictitiousness of their judgments.

So labile is the autokinetic experience or at least the translation of it into judgments of linear extent, that one reading the reports of studies employing it might expect that an arbitrary group norm once established would be passed on indefinitely without diminution; that once well indoctrinated, the naive group members would become as rigid and reliable spokesmen for the norm as were the confederates who preceded them; that each new generation would unwittingly become a part of a self-perpetuating cultural conspiracy propagating superstition and falsehood.

But the autokinetic experience is not completely labile. The very fact that sophisticated observers under strong "suggestion" to see the light remain fixed still perceive movement, shows this. Haggard and Rose, in attempting to condi-

279

tion perceived movement on a right-left dimension, found for most respondents a strong rightward bias. In preliminaries to the present experiment, we learned that for our setting, respondents reporting alone produced mean individual judgments over 30 trials of from .64 to 6.67 inches, and with individual judgments rarely if ever approaching the arbitrary cultural norm of 15 to 16 inches which the confederates in our study provide. It is the presence of this potential natural norm that makes our inculcated cultural norm truly "arbitrary," and provides a counterpressure to the cultural tradition in its transmission across the experimental generations.

METHOD

Respondents

The 175 respondents who took part in this experiment were students, enrolled in introductory social sciences courses. They were unsophisticated concerning the autokinetic phenomenon and were unadvised as to the nature of the experiment previous to the time of serving in it. The respondents were assigned randomly to the six conditions involved. The number of respondents participating per group is shown in Table 1.

Materials, Apparatus, and Common Procedure

The experiment took place in a completely darkened, windowless, fan-ventilated room. The respondents were seated in a row 8 feet from a box designed to emit a small pinpoint of light. A 1 rpm induction motor was attached in series with the lamp, and a single switch controlled both. The motor was used solely as an auditory effect supporting the illusion of movement.

All respondents were blindfolded when brought into the experimental situation and were asked to put their blindfolds on whenever the door was opened to allow old respondents to leave and new ones to enter. This gave the respondents little if any knowledge of the size and arrangement of the experimental room. The individual respondents received the following instructions:

> This is a movement experiment. It is designed to test the students' visual perception with respect to space. In the next room is an apparatus that will project a small light. A few seconds after we begin, the light will move. It may move in a wavy motion or pattern or it may follow a recognizable course. However, your specific task will pertain merely to judging the distance that the light moves from the time that it appears until it is turned off. All judgments should be made in inches along a straignt line connecting the starting point and the ending point on each trial.

Respondents going into group conditions received these additional instructions:

> You are going to join a student (or number of students) who are already serving in this experiment. . . . You will be seated in the seat on the far left. To

simplify recording prodecure I will ask you to report your judgments beginning with the person on the far right and ending with you on the far left. When I stop you the person on the far right will leave, each of you inside will move right one seat, and a new person will be brought in.

Each trial was 5 seconds in length and after each block of 30 trials a ventilation fan was turned on by the experimenter. During this time in the group conditions, the "oldest" member of the group was taken out, other members moved to the right one seat, and a new member introduced. In the solitary conditions, respondents were told that ventilation took place as a health requirement. The ventilation period was timed to take approximately the same amount of time that was necessary to give instructions to a new respondent and bring him in in the other conditions.

Experimental Conditions

Table 1 shows the main feature of the six treatment conditions. (These have been given designations summarizing the group's constuction. C and X stand for control and experimental. The first digit indicates the size of the group, while the second digit indicates the number of confederates present in the first generation.) There are two control conditions. In C-1-0 each respondent judged the movement of the light in solitude for four periods (called generations for the group conditions) or 30 judgments each. In C-3-0 respondents were run in groups of three, replacing one each generation (or 30 trials), for a total of nine generations.

A major dimension of experimental variation was the number of "culture-bearing" confederates with which the first naive respondent found himself

TABLE 1
Experimental Paradigm

Condition	Size of Group	Number of Confederates	Trials per Generation	Number of Generations	Generations per Respondent	Number of Replications	Number of Naive Respondents
C-1-0	1	0	30	—	4	24	24
C-3-0	3	0	30	10	3	3	30
X-2-1	2	1	30	9	2	3	27
X-3-2	3	2	30	10	3	3	30
X-4-3	4	3	30	11	4	3	33
X-3-1	3	1	30	9	3	3	29

placed. In experimental groups X-2-1, X-3-2, and X-4-3, the initial generation consisted of a solitary naive respondent sitting to the left of one, two, or three confederates who gave their judgments before he did, and who had been instructed to give judgments between 15 and 16 inches. The experimental variation in number of confederates was expected to produce cultural traditions of increasing strength. Confederates were recruited from the same subject pool as were the naive respondents. All were pledged to secrecy, with apparent success.

Another mode of manipulating cultural strength was explored by adding X-3-1, a group of two naive respondents led by one confederate. Thus C-3-0, X-3-1, and X-3-2 provide a set of three-person groups of 0, 1, and 2 confederates in the first generation.

The confederates who were present in the starting condition were removed one at a time, after each round of 30 judgments. Thus the groups with more confederates present in the first generation likewise had some stooging present for more generations. The shifting of members one chair to the right each generation, plus the rule of responding in turn from right to left, insured that on each trial a confederate or the eldest member of the group spoke first.

Each of the groups was replicated three times, while 24 respondents were run in the solitary control condition. The conditions were given in a counterbalanced order insuring that the differences in respondent selection from one part of the term to the other were kept independent of treatments.

RESULTS

Control Treatments

Figure 1 [not shown] shows the results for the two control conditions. It will be noted that for C-1-0 the mean of the 24 respondents starts at 3.80 and decreases steadily generation by generation to a value of 2.90. This decrease is highly significant statistically, being found in the individual records of 21 of the 24 respondents, for which, by a two-tailed sign test, $p < .0002$.

The three-person group control, C-3-0, shows very comparable mean levels, and likewise a general decline. The effect is not so clearly significant and is beclouded by the mutual influence that the group situation introduces. In the three replications, two groups declined, while one started abnormally low and increased. Comparing Generation 1 with the last generation with three persons present, Number 8, average judgment changes were 3.93-2.90, 6.72-2.03, and 1.72-2.49. Notice that in spite of the idiosyncratic norms of Generation 1, the three replications became more similar as the process of successive replacement went on. Of the 27 respondents present in more than one generation, 16 showed declines between their first and last generations.

In graphing C-3-0, the data have been averaged in a different fashion from the foregoing. To show the successive replacement and overlapping generational character, the careers of each successive replacement have been plotted separately. The plotted points represent the average of the three replications; that is, each plotted point represents the average judgment of three individual respondents, each taking the corresponding role in the three separate groups replicating this control treatment.

The two types of control established such similar reference standards that they cannot both be used conveniently as visual base lines in the graphing of the results of the experimental treatments. For this reason, in Figures 2, 3, and 4, only C-1-0 has been plotted. This plotting has been done in such a manner as to provide a parallel for each new starting generation in the experimental group. Thus in Figure 2, where each respondent stays only two generations, the first two generations of data from C-1-0 have been repeatedly plotted. In Figure 4, all four generations of C-1-0 are needed as a comparison base.

Transmission of Arbitrary Norms over Total Replacement of Indoctrinator

Figures 2, 3, 4, and 5 [only Figure 4 is shown] present the transmission results from X-2-1, X-3-2, X-4-3, and X-3-1. The first question that we ask of the data is whether or not the naive respondents, once indoctrinated by the confederates, have themselves transmitted any vestiges of the arbitrary cultural norm once the original indoctrinators have passed on. To test this, one can examine the

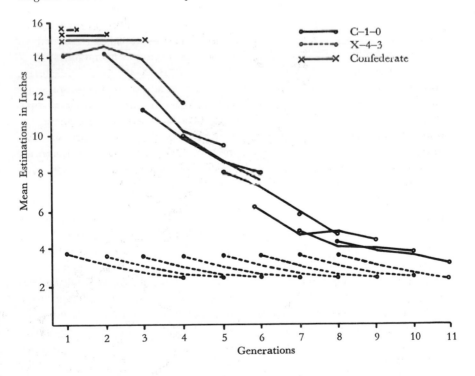

Figure 4. Transmission of arbitrary norm in four-person groups

judgments of the first generation of respondents to judge without any confederates present. For X-2-1, X-3-2, and X-4-3 these values are 12.07, 9.79, and 9.82. Each of these differs significantly ($p < .01$) from the C-1-0 control group by t test, when the mean of the 3 experimental respondents is compared with the mean of the 24 control respondents. For X-3-1, the mean is 5.34, not significantly different from the C-1-0 value of 3.80.

By pooling groups X-2-1, X-3-2, and X-4-3, we can compare to the 24 C-1-0 respondents 9 experimental respondents newly introduced at each of several generations beyond the final confederate. For the first such generation, $M = 10.57$, $t = 7.25$, $p < .0001$; for the second, $M = 7.80$, $t = 3.74$, $p < .0001$; for the third, $M = 6.06$, $t = 4.02$, $p < .0001$; for the fourth, $M = 5.08$, $t = 2.04$, $p < .03$; for the fifth, $M = 4.37$, $t = 1.31$, $p < .10$. Thus the arbitrary norm is transmitted in some degree up through the fourth and perhaps the fifth generation beyond the last confederate. By the sixth it has entirely disappeared, the mean of 3.60 being slightly below the control value of 3.80.

*   *   *   *   *

Judgments as a Compromise between Own and Other's Observations

The deterioration of the cultural norm occurs, in part, because each naive respondent makes judgments somewhat lower, somewhat closer to the natural norm, than do the confederates or elder citizens serving as his mentors. Of 36 naive respondents serving for the first time in X-2-1, X-3-2, and X-4-3 during the first four generations (where some significant strength to the cultural norm was still present) 34 made mean judgments lower than the average of their mentors (for which, $p < .0000001$). This clear-cut fact we take as supporting the interpretation that each judgment represents a pooling of the person's own observations (the value for which we infer from the control group) with the reported observations of others. In the resulting compromise the person's own observations are not given much weight, but they are given some.

In the first generation of the experimental groups, the conditions are simple enough so that we can make some estimates of this relative weighting of own observations and other's reports. For the first naive respondent in X-2-1, the other's (confederate's) report averages 15.52. The own observation is inferred from C-1 to be 3.80. If the naive respondent weighted his own observation equally with the report of the confederate, his judgment would fall halfway between these values, at 9.66. Instead, the judgment is 12.23, much closer to the confederate's. Rather than regarding the confederate as an equally good observer as himself, the respondent has weighted the confederate's opinion 2.6 times as heavily as his own. The formula for the weighting ratio is $(12.23 - 3.80)/(15.52 - 12.23)$. Assuming each confederate to be equally weighted, and solving for the weight given a single confederate's opinion, we get values of 4.6 for X-3-2 and 2.5 for X-4-3. Since these ratios are based upon the performances of but three naive respondents each, they are quite unstable, and are provided here primarily for illustrative purposes. Similar computations for the later generations have been omitted because of the difficulty of taking into account the reciprocal effect of new respondents upon the older naive respondents acting as indoctrinators. The first generation situation is computable just because the confederates were unresponsive to the judgments of their fellows.

Whatever the weighting ratio, as long as some weight is given own observations, and as long as own observations deviate in a consistent direction from the cultural norm, the arbitrary culture is doomed to deterioration eventually, at least in the limited sanction system of this laboratory. While the question has not been stated in this form, the relative respect for own observations over the reports of others is much higher in less ambiguous situations, as Asch has shown. It is easy to understand how the ambiguities of the autokinetic situation lead to lack of confidence in own opinion, but it is perhaps an indication of human trust that this same ambiguity does not lead to a proportional lack of confidence in the reports of others.

Forgetting and Reciprocal Influence

If the previous factor of compromise weighting were all that was involved, the deterioration in culture as graphed in Figures 2, 3, and 4 might have been of a stair-step fashion, with each new inductee starting lower than his indoctrinator, but once started, holding to his initial level through the several generations of his life in the group. As can be seen from the graphs, this is not the case. Instead, the respondent is less loyal to the old culture the longer he stays in the group. Of the 36 naive respondents introduced in the first four generations of X-2-1, X-3-2, and X-4-3, 31 made lower mean judgments on their last session than on their first (for which, $p < .00001$).

In the present design, three factors are confounded in generating this effect. While we have not extricated them, it seems well to mention them. The first factor is the autonomous decline noted previously in the control groups. In terms of absolute magnitude, this would seem to account for little of the total effect.

A second factor is forgetting. Were a respondent to judge with the leadership of a culture-bearing confederate, and then to judge in isolation for several sessions, he would in these later sessions be pooling his immediate visual impression of the stimulus with the remembered reports of the other in a previous session. As these memories dimmed, their weighting could be expected to diminish, and the relative weighting of own observation could be expected to increase. No doubt in the present situation forgetting of indoctrination provides some of the decline within the judgment series of a single respondent.

A third possible source of this within-respondents decline in loyalty to the arbitrary culture is the effect of the new group member upon his elders. Since judging was always from eldest to youngest on any given stimulus presentation, this would have to involve an influence carrying over from one turn to the next. We feel sure that some such influence was present, but its demonstration would require a separate experiment placing confederates in the final answering position.

DISCUSSION

In presenting these materials to our colleagues, we have found them most fascinated by the fact of the cultural transmission surviving total replacement of specific individuals, and by the fact of naive respondents becoming unwitting conspirators in perpetuating a cultural fraud. This demonstration was of course our main intent, and this outcome was inevitable if the conformity research upon which we built had any transfer validity. But while these results are highly significant statistically, they fall short of our expectations. The inculcated arbitrary norms turn out to be eroded by innovation at a much more rapid rate than we had expected. We have hardly provided a laboratory paradigm for the examples of tenacious adherence to incredible superstition with which anthropologists and students of comparative religion provide us.

Of course, a relative weakness in strength is to be expected in a laboratory example. Mature individuals are undergoing transient indoctrination by unknown age-mates, as opposed to the natural setting of the teaching of the very young by tribal adults over a period of years. Fewer confederates are involved than in the tribal situation, although the effect of number upon degree of conformity is unclear in the laboratory. More important, there are no sanctions rewarding conformity nor punishing innovation. Furthermore, it is even possible that the subject of judgment in our experiment is less ambiguous than the subject material of religious belief, for example. There is, after all, a fairly clear consensus among our naive solitary observers. In our situation, the spontaneous deviations from orthodoxy were all in the same direction, whereas for many arbitrary items of culture the deviations may lack such concerted direction.

Nonetheless, the outcome may well warn us against the assumption that a purely arbitrary cultural norm could be perpetuated indefinitely without other sources of support. Even if people weigh the opinions of their elders many times that of their own direct observations, the collective effect of their own observations probably soon erodes a *functionless* arbitrary belief. Where we observed tenacious bizarre cultural belief we must look to more than mere tradition, suggestibility, or conformity, to explain its retention. Latent functions (e.g., Merton) at the personal or societal level must be present to counteract the pressures from continuous spontaneous innovation in a more natural direction. For example, Moore and Aubert have recently suggested such latent functions to superstitious magical lotteries used in the selection of hunting and fishing sites. As our understanding of the requisites of individual and social life further increases, we may expect to discover such latent functions for many if not all of those "meaningless" superstitions which stubbornly persist.

SUMMARY

In an autokinetic judgment situation in which solitary judgments of movement averaged 3.8 inches, confederates were used to establish arbitrary "cultural norms" of 15.5 inches. The transmission of this norm was studied as one at a time confederates and old members were removed from the group while new members were added. Significant remnants of the culture persisted for four or five generations beyond the last confederate. Gradually in each of the 12 experimental groups the arbitrary norm decayed and the group judgments drifted away from it back to the natural norm found in the control groups. The size of group had no clear effect upon the endurance of the norm established, although a group beginning with one confederate and two naive respondents was markedly weaker than the others and transmitted no culture beyond one generation.

Major effects are interpreted in terms of a judgment process in which each respondent weighs the reports of others and his own observations, achieving a compromise between them. Even with the respondents giving the reports of others from 2.5 to 4 times the weight of their own observations, slight "innovations" result which rapidly cumulate to erode the original arbitrary cultural norm. Details of the process and analogues to the cultural transmission of bizarre beliefs are discussed.

Public opinion tends to be responsive not only to the views of reference figures, but to more tangible phenomena as well. One of these influences on the individual is the behavior of his society—or more particularly, those who act authoritatively for it—in preparing for future, but uncertain, events. In the foreign-policy field, uncertainty about the future is an inherent part of the perceptions of both the public and the policy-makers, yet allocation of attention and resources must continuously be made. In the experiment reported here, Yaryan and Festinger shed light on two very important generalizations concerning preparation for an uncertain future contingency. First, the higher the subjective probability that a given event will occur, the less likely are the decision-makers or the public to take any action to forestall that event, regardless of the disutility which they attach to it: "you don't fight the inevitable." Second, the greater the investment made in preparing for that contingency, the greater the actor's certainty that it will occur. If one bears in mind the similarities among preparing for a painful test, a stressful contest, or war, the following study, which deals specifically with the second of these generalizations, should seem relevant.

PREPARATORY ACTION AND BELIEF IN THE PROBABLE OCCURRENCE OF FUTURE EVENTS

Ruby B. Yaryan and Leon Festinger

People are frequently faced with the possibility that a future event that would have important consequences for them may actually occur. Usually, in such a situation, it is possible to take some action in preparation for the possible future event so that, if it should occur, its impact on the person would be more favorable than would otherwise have been the case. Such preparatory action, however, may involve considerable inconvenience and, if the possible future event should not occur, the preparatory action will have been useless.

Obviously, the more a person in such a situation believes that the possible future event will really occur, the more willing he should be to take action in preparation for it. This statement is almost self-evident and, of course, is *not* our concern here. The problem we wish to deal with is, indeed, the reverse of this. That is, if a person has somehow been induced to take preparatory action of a rather inconvenient or effortful kind, will this, in and of itself, lead him to believe that the future event is even more likely to occur?

The theory of dissonance (Festinger) would lead one to give an affirmative answer to this question. Consider the cognitions of a person who has expended considerable effort preparing for some possible future event and who also knows many things that indicate to him that the event will not actually occur. These two sets of cognitions are dissonant with one another. Considering only those facts the person knows which indicate that the event will *not* occur, it would follow psychologically that the person would not expend effort in preparation for it [emphasis added]. Hence, the information that he did expend effort in preparation is dissonant with information he has that indicates the event will not occur.

Given this dissonance, then, let us examine how it may be reduced. There are three major ways in which such dissonance can be reduced:

1. The person may somehow be able to persuade himself that the preparation was really effortless and not at all inconvenient.

2. The person may find for himself some other objectives, in addition to the possible future event, which "justify" the actions he has taken.

3. The person may persuade himself that the possible future event is, indeed, very likely to occur.

To the extent that this last means of reducing dissonance is employed by people, we emerge with the prediction that, after a person engages in effortful

---

From Ruby B. Yaryan and Leon Festinger, "Preparatory Action and Belief in the Probable Occurence of Future Events," *Journal of Abnormal and Social Psychology,* LXIII (1961), 603-6 (the footnotes and the bibliography and references have been omitted). Reprinted by permission of Professor Festinger and the American Psychological Association.

preparation for a future event, he should believe the event is even more likely to occur than he had previously believed. The present experiment was designed to test this derivation under controlled laboratory conditions.

METHOD

The basic design of the experiment was simple. All subjects were given a standard set of instructions concerning the exact probability of occurrence of a future event (that they might have to take an examination). One group of subjects, selected at random, was then induced to engage in effortful preparation while another group was induced to engage in relatively effortless preparation. The major dependent variable in which we were interested was how likely the subject thought it was that the event would actually occur (that she herself would have to take the examination). The details of the procedure follow.

Subjects and Volunteering Procedure

The subjects were 60 female high school students, ranging from 14 to 18 years of age, who had volunteered to participate in an experiment on "Techniques of Studying."

In asking for volunteers the experimenter said:

We are doing research on the techniques of studying; specifically, we are looking into the guessing process that seems to be involved when students study for tests.

Now, here is what we are asking you to do. We are requesting that everyone volunteer for two hours. The experiment takes one hour for 50% of the subjects and two hours for the other 50%. I can't tell you now in which group, the one hour or the two hour group, you will be placed, for this is part of the experiment itself. That is why we are asking everyone to volunteer for two hours, although half of you will be finished at the end of one hour.

Thus, before the experiment each subject knew that, even though each appointment was for 2 hours, 50% of the subjects would be finished at the end of 1 hour.

Course of the Experiment

When each subject arrived for the experiment she was told the following:

We are studying the techniques that students use to study for exams. We know that in the process of studying, students form hypotheses, hunches, or guesses about an exam (for example, if there will be essays on the exam, what the essays will be about, the type of material to be asked, and so on), and then they orient their behavior according to their guesses. As yet we don't know the hows or the whys or the types of conclusions that students reach and their relative accuracy. These are the questions we hope to answer in this experiment.

As I told you before, this experiment takes one hour for half of the subjects and two hours for the others. We won't tell you which group you are in until we finish the first part of the experiment. We have the experiment designed this way so that we can get at the answers we want. What we have done is to divide the people that have volunteered for the experiment into two experimental conditions; we have done this on the basis of certain criteria (we have access to high school records and other things). Now I can't tell you what these criteria are at this point, for we want you to guess about them later. In short, however, you have already been put in one of the two conditions, so no matter what you do now this will not change.

In one condition the people will take a new, highly reliable aptitude test, one developed specifically for people above the ages of 14. If you happen to be in this condition, the time you will be here will be two hours. The other half of the people will not take any aptitude test at all; these people will be finished in one hour. We had everyone volunteer for two hours, so that people wouldn't know which condition they were in.

So that you will be familiar with the total situation, even though you may or may not have to take the test, we tell everyone generally about it.

As I mentioned before, this test that half the people that signed up will be taking is a new type of aptitude or IQ test, "The Revised Standardized Aptitude Test 1958." It has been specifically developed for people above the ages of 14 and has proved to be very successful in accurately indicating IQ. The test goes on the assumption that the reason past IQ tests have been unreliable with people above these ages is that through studying specific areas, these students have a specialized knowledge of the factual information in the area of their concentration and relatively little extensive knowledge of the information in other areas. This, you can see, leads to noncomparable groups of people and, as a consequence, leads to noncomparable measures of the aptitudes. In order to get around this problem and to standardize the conditions for all students, this test requires that the people taking it be given some specific information beforehand, which will give them all the necessary tools to work with the questions on the test; this way everyone approaches the test with the same information. What the test measures is not this information, but rather the way that they work with the information that they have been given.

In order to establish the "high preparatory effort condition," the experimenter said:

Now in a few minutes I shall give you the "Information Sheet." As you will see, it is crucial for taking the test. If you happen to be one of those selected to take it, which you may not be, it is of utmost importance that you memorize these definitions, for the test is not valid if the people do not learn them. We are requiring everyone to commit these definitions to memory, no matter which condition they are in.

Thus far, it has taken people around 25-30 minutes to memorize these. You may take as much time as you need to learn this material thoroughly, for you will not be able to have this sheet later, if you happen to be one of those previously designated to take the test.

After you have memorized these definitions, we will give you a short questionnaire and interview; then we will tell you in which group you have been placed. If you have not been selected to take the test, you can leave then; if you are one of the people that have been selected, you will then take the test.

The "low preparatory effort condition" was established by the following instructions:

Now in a few minutes I shall give you the "Information Sheet." As you will see, it is crucial for taking the test, if you happen to be one of those selected to take it, which you may not be. In any case, we want everyone to briefly look over it.

You will have a minute or so to look over the information, just to get an idea of what it is all about. You need not attempt to commit it to memory or study it, for you will be able to have the "Information Sheet" with you, if you should be one of the people previously designated to take the test.

After you have looked over these definitions, we will give you a short questionnaire and interview; then we will tell you in which group you have been placed. If you have not been selected to take the test, you can leave then; if you are one of the people that have been selected, you will then take the test.

Each subject was then handed an "Information Sheet" containing 25 symbols with arbitrary abstract definitions of each symbol. After each subject had finished either memorizing the list (high effort condition) or briefly familiarizing herself with it (low effort condition), she was asked a number of questions which we will describe exactly when we discuss the results of the experiment. When the questionnaire had been completed, the true nature of the experiment was explained to each subject in detail. Of course, no aptitude test was administered.

Although each subject was asked not to talk about the experiment with others in the school, some talking about the details of the experiment did occur. Seven subjects, four from the "high effort" and three from the "low effort" condition, had to be discarded because they had heard what the experiment was all about. Such subjects, of course, realized beforehand that there was no aptitude test to take. Two other subjects were discarded (one form each condition) because of misunderstanding of instructions and directions. Valid data remained for 51 subjects, 26 in the high preparatory effort condition and 25 in the low preparatory effort condition.

RESULTS

Effectiveness of the Manipulation

In order to determine whether or not we had effectively created a high preparatory effort and a low preparatory effort condition, we asked all subjects the following question:

Do you think that the work you had to do in preparation was . . .

(−3)	(−2)	(−1)	(+1)	(+2)	(+3)
very	somewhat	slightly	slightly	somewhat	very
easy	easy	easy	difficult	difficult	difficult

The mean rating for subjects in the high preparatory effort condition was +.7. The comparable figure for those in the low preparatory effort condition was −.9. The difference between the two conditions is significant beyond the .05 level. In other words, our experimental manipulation was successful. Those in the high effort condition felt they had worked harder in preparation for the test than did those in the low effort condition.

Expectation of Taking the Test

Let us recall the hypothesis this experiment was designed to test. We would expect, from considering the theory of dissonance, that, if a person is induced to engage in effortful activity in preparation for a possible future event, the person will subsequently believe that the event is more likely to occur. If this hypothesis is correct, we would expect the subjects in the high preparatory effort condition to believe that they would actually have to take the test more than would subjects in the low preparatory effort condition. To obtain the data necessary to test this hypothesis, we asked the subjects the following question:

Do you believe that you are one of the people that have been selected to take the test?

(+3)	(+2)	(+1)	(−1)	(−2)	(−3)
certain	probably	slightly	slightly	probably	definitely
		likely	unlikely	not	not

The mean rating on this scale for subjects in the high effort condition was +1.1; for those in the low effort condition the mean rating was only +.2. The difference is significant at the .01 level ($t = 2.70$). Another way of looking at these data is in terms of the number of subjects who checked the plus side of the scale, indicating that they thought they would probably have to take the test. In the high effort condition 24 of the 26 subjects (92%) checked the plus side of the scale while in the low effort condition only 15 out of 25 (60%) checked this side of the scale. In other words, as a group, the subjects in the low effort condition reflect fairly well what they have been told, namely, that 50% of them would have to take the test. The low effort condition subjects divided themselves 60% to 40%, which is not very different from an "expected" 50%. In the high effort condition, however, there is clearly a stronger belief that they would have to take the test. Since subjects were allocated to experimental conditions at random, it seems clear that this stronger belief in having to take the test is a consequence of the amount of effort expended in preparation. We may confidently conclude that the data support the hypotheses.

4. Large-Scale Opinion Change

The previous section focussed on studies which clarify the processes by which individual opinions are formed and modified. But it will not suffice to treat collective or large-scale opinion formation either as that of individuals written large or as the sum total of individual opinion formation. Though several of the above experiments recognized the importance of the views of the *entire* group under study, this was not their primary concern. Thus, the next two selections are intended to explore the process by which opinion (and behavior) change spreads throughout a society by dint of two intimately connected phenomena: mass communication and interpersonal communication.

THE TWO-STEP FLOW OF COMMUNICATION: AN UP-TO-DATE REPORT ON AN HYPOTHESIS

Elihu Katz

Analysis of the process of decision-making during the course of an election campaign led the authors of *The People's Choice* to suggest that the flow of mass communications may be less direct than was commonly supposed. It may be, they proposed, that influences stemming from the mass media first reach "opinion leaders" who, in turn, pass on what they read and hear to those of their everyday associates for whom they are influential. This hypothesis was called "the two-step flow of communication."[1]

The hypothesis aroused considerable interest. The authors themselves were intrigued by its implications for democratic society. It was a healthy sign, they felt, that people were still most successfully persuaded by give-and-take with other people and that the influence of the mass media was less automatic and less potent than had been assumed. For social theory, and for the design of communications research, the hypothesis suggested that the image of modern urban society needed revision. The image of the audience as *a mass of disconnected individuals hooked up to the media but not to each other* could not be reconciled with the idea of a two-step flow of communication implying, as it did, networks of

From Elihu Katz, "The Two-Step Flow of Communications: An Up-to-Date Report on an Hypothesis," *Public Opinion Quarterly,* XXI (1957), 61-78 (all footnotes, except note 1, have been omitted). Reprinted by permission of the author and *Public Opinion Quarterly.*
[1]Paul F. Lazarsfeld, Bernard Berelson and Hazel Gaudet, *The People's Choice,* New York: Columbia University Press, 1948 (2nd edition), p. 151.

interconnected individuals through which mass communications are channeled [emphasis added].

Of all the ideas in *The People's Choice,* however, the two-step flow hypothesis is probably the one that was least well documented by empirical data. And the reason for this is clear: the design of the study did not anticipate the importance which interpersonal relations would assume in the analysis of the data. Given the image of the atomized audience which characterized so much of mass media research, the surprising thing is that interpersonal influence attracted the attention of the researchers at all.

In the almost seventeen years since the voting study was undertaken, several studies at the Bureau of Applied Social Research of Columbia University have attempted to examine the hypothesis and to build upon it. Four such studies will be singled out for review. These are Merton's study of interpersonal influence and communications behavior in Rovere; the Decatur study of decision-making in marketing, fashions, movie-going and public affairs, reported by Katz and Lazarsfeld; the Elmira study of the 1948 election campaign reported by Berelson, Lazarsfeld and McPhee; and, finally, a very recent study by Coleman, Katz and Menzel on the diffusion of a new drug among doctors.

These studies will serve as a framework within which an attempt will be made to report on the present state of the two-step flow hypothesis, to examine the extent to which it has found confirmation and the ways in which it has been extended, contracted and reformulated. More than that, the studies will be drawn upon to highlight the successive strategies which have been developed in attempting to take systematic account of interpersonal relations in the design of communications research, aiming ultimately at a sort of "survey sociometry." Finally, these studies, plus others which will be referred to in passing, will provide an unusual opportunity to reflect upon problems in the continuity of social research.

FINDINGS OF *The People's Choice*

The starting point for this review must be an examination of the evidence in the 1940 voting study which led to the original formulation of the hypothesis. Essentially, three distinct sets of findings seem to have been involved. The first had to do with *the impact of personal influence.* It is reported that people who made up their minds *late* in the campaign, and those who changed their minds during the course of the campaign, were more likely than other people to mention personal influence as having figured in their decisions [emphasis added]. The political pressure brought to bear by everyday groups such as family and friends is illustrated by reference to the political homogeneity which characterizes such groups. What's more, on an average day, a greater number of people reported participating in discussion of the election than hearing a campaign speech or reading a newspaper editorial. From all of this, the authors conclude that *personal contacts appear to have been both more frequent and more effective than the mass media in influencing voting decisions* [emphasis added].

The second ingredient that went into the formulation of the hypothesis concerned *the flow of personal influence.* Given the apparent importance of inter-personal influence, the obvious next step was to ask whether some people were more important than others in the transmission of influence. The study sought to single out the "opinion leaders" by two questions: "Have you recently tried to convince anyone of your political ideas?" and "Has anyone recently asked you for your advice on a political question?" Comparing the opinion leaders with others, they found the opinion leaders more interested in the election. And from the almost even distribution of opinion leaders throughout every class and occupa-tion, as well as the frequent mention by decision-makers of the influence of friends, co-workers and relatives, it was concluded that *opinion leaders are to be found on every level of society and presumably, therefore, are very much like the people whom they influence* [emphasis added].

A further comparison of leaders and others with respect to mass media habits provides the third ingredient: *the opinion leaders and the mass media.* Compared with the rest of the population, *opinion leaders were found to be considerably more exposed to the radio, to the newspapers and to magazines,* that is, to the formal media of communication [emphasis added].

Now the argument is clear: If word-of-mouth is so important, and if word-of-mouth specialists are widely dispersed, and if these specialists are more exposed to the media than the people whom they influence, then perhaps "ideas often flow from radio and print to opinion leaders and from these to the less active sections of the population."

DESIGN OF THE VOTING STUDY

For studying the flow of influence as it impinges on the making of decisions, the study design of *The People's Choice* had several advantages. Most important was the panel method [interviewing the *same* respondents on two or more occasions] which made it possible to locate changes almost as soon as they occurred and then to correlate change with the influences reaching the decision-maker. Secondly, the unit of effect, the decision, was a tangible indicator of change which could readily be recorded. But for studying that part of the flow of influence which had to do with contacts among people, the study design fell short, since it called for a random sample of individuals abstracted from their social environments. It is this traditional element in the design of survey research which explains the leap that had to be made from the available data to the hypothesis of the two-step flow of communication.

Because every man in a random sample can speak only for himself, opinion leaders in the 1940 voting study had to be located by self-designation, that is, on the basis of their own answers to the two advice-giving questions cited above. In effect, respondents were simply asked to report whether or not they were opinion leaders. Much more important than the obvious problem of validity posed by this technique is the fact that it does not permit a comparison of leaders with their respective followers, but only of leaders and non-leaders in general. The data, in other words, consist only of two statistical groupings: people who said they *were* advice-givers and those who did *not* [emphasis added]. Therefore, the fact that leaders were more interested in the election than non-leaders cannot be taken to mean that influence flows from more interested persons to less interested ones. To state the problem drastically, it may even be that the leaders influence only each other, while the uninterested non-leaders stand outside the influence market altogether. Nevertheless, the temptation to assume that the non-leaders are the followers of the leaders is very great, and while *The People's Choice* is quite careful about this, it cannot help but succumb. Thus, from the fact that the opinion leaders were more exposed to the mass media than the non-leaders came the suggestion of the two-step flow of communication; yet, manifestly, it can be true only if the *non-leaders,* are, in fact, *followers* of the leaders [emphasis added].

The authors themselves point out that a far better method would have been based on "asking people to whom they turn for advice on the issue at hand and then investigating the interaction between advisers and advisees. But that procedure would be extremely difficult, if not impossible, since few of the related 'leaders' and 'followers' would happen to be included in the sample." As will be shown immediately, this is perhaps the most important problem which succeeding studies have attempted to solve.

[The author here describes, in some detail, three research studies subsequent to *The People's Choice* which deal with interpersonal influence: 1. *the Rovere study,* 2. *the Decatur study,* and 3. *the drug study.* Since the problem of *designing* such research is not directly relevant to the purposes of this book, this rather lengthy section has been omitted, and the reader is given only the results of these studies. — ED.]

*   *   *   *   *

THE FINDINGS OF STUDIES SUBSEQUENT TO
The People's Choice

Having examined the *designs* of these studies, the next step is to explore their *findings* insofar as these are relevant to the hypothesis about the two-step flow of communication. It will be useful to return to the three categories already singled out in discussing *The People's Choice:* (1) the impact of personal influence; (2) the flow of personal influence; and (3) opinion leaders and the mass media. Evidence from the three studies just reported, as well as from the 1948 Elmira study and from others, will be brought together here; but in every case the characteristics of each study's design must be borne in mind in evaluating the evidence presented.

A. THE IMPACT OF PERSONAL INFLUENCE

1. Personal and the Mass Media Influence

The 1940 study indicated that personal influence affected voting decisions more than the mass media did, particularly in the case of those who changed their minds during the course of the campaign. The Decatur study went on to explore the relative impact of personal influences and the mass media in three other realms: marketing, fashions and movie-going. Basing its conclusions on the testimony of the decision-makers themselves, and using an instrument for evaluating the relative effectiveness of the various media which entered into the decisions, the Decatur study again found that personal influence figured both more frequently and more effectively than any of the mass media.

In the analysis to date, the drug study has not approached the problem of the relative effectiveness of the various media from the point of view of the doctor's own reconstruction of what went into the making of his decision. Comparing mere frequency of mention of different media, it is clear that colleagues are by no means the most frequently mentioned source. Nevertheless, exploration of the factors related to whether the doctor's decision to adopt the drug came early or late indicates that the factor most strongly associated with the time of adoption of the new drug is the extent of the doctor's integration in the medical community. That is, the more frequently a doctor is named by his colleagues as a friend or a discussion partner, the more likely he is to be an innovator with respect to the new drug. Extent of integration proves to be a more important factor than any background factor (such as age, medical school, or income of patients), or any other source of influence (such as readership of medical journals) that was examined.

Investigation of why integration is related to innovation suggests two central factors: (1) interpersonal communication—doctors who are integrated are more in touch and more up-to-date; and (2) social support—doctors who are integrated feel more secure when facing the risks of innovation in medicine. Thus the drug study, too, provides evidence of the strong impact of personal relations—even in the making of scientific decisions.

2. Homogeneity of Opinion in Primary Groups

The effectiveness of interpersonal influence, as it is revealed in the studies under review, is reflected in the homogeneity of opinions and actions in primary groups. The medium of primary group communication is, by definition, person-to-person. Both of the voting studies indicate the high degree of homogeneity of political opinion among members of the same families, and among co-workers and friends. The effectiveness of such primary groups in pulling potential deviates back into line is demonstrated by the fact that those who changed their vote intentions were largely people who, early in the campaign, had reported that they intended to vote differently from their family or friends.

The drug study, too, was able to examine the extent of homogeneity in the behavior of sociometrically related doctors, and was able to demonstrate that there were situations where similar behavior could be deserved. For example, it was found that, when called upon to treat the more puzzling diseases, doctors were likely to prescribe the same drug as their sociometric colleagues. The study also showed that, very early in the history of a new drug, innovating doctors who were sociometrically connected tended to adopt the new drug at virtually the same time. This phenomenon of homogeneity of opinion or behavior among interacting individuals confronting an unclear or uncertain situation which calls for action has often been studied by sociologists and social psychologists.

3. The Various Roles of the Media

The 1940 voting study explored some of the reasons why personal influence might be expected to be more influential in changing opinions than the mass media: It is often non-purposive; it is flexible; it is trustworthy. It was suggested that the mass media more often play a reinforcing role in the strengthening of predispositions and of decisions already taken. Nevertheless, it was assumed that the various media and personal influence are essentially competitive, in the sense that a given decision is influenced by one *or* the other. The Decatur study tended toward this assumption too, but at one point the study does attempt to show that different media play different parts in the decision-making process and take patterned positions in a sequence of several influences. The drug study elaborates on the roles of the media even further, distinguishing between media that "inform" and media that "legitimate" decisions. Thus in doctors' decisions, professional media (including colleagues) seem to play a *legitimating* role, while commercial media play an *informing* role [emphasis added].

B. THE FLOW OF PERSONAL INFLUENCE

The 1940 voting study found that opinion leaders were not concentrated in the upper brackets of the population but were located in almost equal proportions in every social group and stratum. This finding led to efforts in subsequent studies to establish the extent to which this was true in areas other than election campaigns and also to ascertain what it is that *does* distinguish opinion leaders from those whom they influence.

The first thing that is clear from the series of studies under review is that the subject matter concerning which influence is transmitted has a lot to do with determining who will lead and who follow. Thus, the Rovere study suggests that within the broad sphere of public affairs one set of influentials is occupied with "local" affairs and another with "cosmopolitan" affairs. The Decatur study suggests that in marketing, for example, there is a concentration of opinion leadership among older women with larger families, while in fashions and movie-going it is the young, unmarried girl who has a disproportionate chance of being turned to for advice. There is *very little overlap of leadership:* a leader in one sphere is not likely to be influential in another unrelated sphere as well [emphasis added].

Yet, even when leadership in one or another sphere is heavily concentrated among the members of a particular group—as was the case with marketing leadership in Decatur—the evidence suggests that people still talk, most of all, to others like themselves. Thus, while the marketing leaders among the older "large-family wives" also influenced other kinds of women, most of their influence was directed to women of their own age with equally large families. In marketing, fashions, and movie-going, furthermore, there was no appreciable concentration of influentials in any of the three socio-economic levels. Only in public affairs was there a concentration of leadership in the highest status, and there was some slight evidence that influence flows from this group to individuals of lower status. The Elmira study also found opinion-leaders in similar proportions on every socio-economic and occupational level and found that conversations concerning the campaign went on, typically, between people of similar age, occupation, and political opinion.

What makes for the concentration of certain kinds of opinion leadership within certain groups? And when influential and influencee are outwardly alike—as they so often seem to be—what, if anything, distinguishes one from the other? Broadly, it appears that influence is related (1) to the *personification of certain values* (who one is); (2) to *competence* (what one knows); and (3) to *strategic social location* (whom one knows). Social location, in turn, divides into whom one knows within a group: and "outside."

Influence is often successfully transmitted because the influencee wants to be as much like the influential as possible. That the young, unmarried girls are fashion leaders can be understood easily in a culture where youth and youthfulness are supreme values. This is an example where "who one is" counts very heavily.

But "what one knows" is no less important. The fact is that older women, by virtue of their greater experience, are looked to as marketing advisers and that specialists in internal medicine—the most "scientific" of the practicing physicians —are the most frequently mentioned opinion leaders among the doctors. The influence of young people in the realm of movie-going can also be understood best in terms of their familiarity with the motion picture world. The Elmira study found slightly greater concentrations of opinion leadership among the more educated people on each socio-economic level, again implying the importance of competence. Finally, the influence of the "cosmopolitans" in Rovere rested on the presumption that they had large amounts of information.

It is, however, not enough to be a person whom others want to emulate, or to be competent. One must also be accessible. Thus, the Decatur study finds gregariousness—"whom one knows"—related to every kind of leadership. The Rovere study reports that the leadership of the "local" influentials is based on their central location in the web of interpersonal contacts. Similarly, studies of rumor transmission have singled out those who are "socially active" as agents of rumor.

Of course, the importance of whom one knows is not simply a matter of the number of people with whom an opinion leader is in contact. It is also a question of whether the people with whom he is in touch happen to be interested in the area in which his leadership is likely to be sought. For this reason, it is quite clear that the greater interest of opinion leaders in the subjects over which they exert influence is not a sufficient explanation of their influence. While the voting studies as well as the Decatur study show leaders to be more interested, the Decatur study goes on to show that interest alone is not the determining factor. In fashion, for example, a young unmarried girl is considerably more likely to be influential than a matron with an equally great interest in clothes. The reason, it is suggested, is that a girl who is interested in fashion is much more likely than a matron with an equally high interest to know other people who share her preoccupation, and thus is more likely than the matron to have followers who are interested enough to ask for her advice. In other words, it takes two to be a leader—a leader and a follower.

Finally, there is the second aspect of "whom one knows." An individual may be influential not only because people within his group look to him for advice but also because of whom he knows outside his group. Both the Elmira and Decatur studies found that men are more likely than women to be opinion leaders in the realm of public affairs and this, it is suggested, is because they have more of a chance to get outside the home to meet people and talk politics. Similarly, the Elmira study indicated that opinion leaders belonged to more organizations, more often knew workers for the political parties, and so on, than did others. The drug study found that influential doctors could be characterized in terms of such things as their more frequent attendance at out-of-town meetings and the diversity of places with which they maintained contact, particularly far-away places. It is interesting that a study of the farmer-innovators responsible for the diffusion of hybrid seedcorn in Iowa concluded that these leaders also could be characterized in terms of the relative frequency of their trips out of town.

C. THE OPINION LEADERS AND THE MASS MEDIA

The third aspect of the hypothesis of the two-step flow of communication states that opinion leaders are more exposed to the mass media than are those whom they influence. In *The People's Choice* this is supported by reference to the media behavior of leaders and non-leaders.

The Decatur study corroborated this finding, and went on to explore two additional aspects of the same idea. First of all, it was shown that leaders in a given sphere (fashions, public affairs, etc.) were particularly likely to be exposed to the media appropriate to that sphere. This is essentially a corroboration of the Rovere finding that those who proved influential with regard to "cosmopolitan" matters were more likely to be readers of national news magazines, but that this was not at all the case for those influential with regard to "local" matters. Secondly, the Decatur study shows that at least in the realm of fashions, the leaders are not only more exposed to the mass media, but are also more affected by them in their own decisions. This did not appear to be the case in other realms, where opinion leaders, though more exposed to the media than non-leaders, nevertheless reported personal influence as the major factor in their decisions. This suggests that in some spheres considerably longer chains of person-to-person influence than the dyad may have to be traced back before one encounters any decisive influence by the mass media, even though their contributory influence may be perceived at many points. This was suggested by the Elmira study too. It found that the leaders, though more exposed to the media, also more often reported that they sought information and advice from other persons.

Similarly, the drug study showed that the influential doctors were more likely to be readers of a large number of professional journals and valued them more highly than did doctors of lesser influence. But at the same time, they were as likely as other doctors to say that local colleagues were an important source of information and advice in their reaching particular decisions.

Finally, the drug study demonstrated that the more influential doctors could be characterized by their greater attention not only to medical journals, but to out-of-town meetings and contacts as well. This finding has already been discussed in the previous section treating the *strategic location* of the opinion leader with respect to "the world outside" his group. Considering it again under the present heading suggests that the greater exposure of the opinion leader to the mass media may only be a special case of the more general proposition that opinion leaders serve to relate their groups to relevant parts of the environment through whatever media happen to be appropriate. This more general statement makes clear the similar functions of big city newspapers for the Decatur fashion leader; of national news magazines for the "cosmopolitan" influentials of Rovere; of out-of-town medical meetings for the influential doctor; and of contact with the city for the farmer-innovator in Iowa as well as for the newly-risen, young opinion leaders in underdeveloped areas throughout the world.

CONCLUSIONS

Despite the diversity of subject matter with which they are concerned, the studies reviewed here constitute an example of continuity and cumulation both in research design and theoretical commitment. Piecing together the findings of the latter-day studies in the light of the original statement of the two-step flow hypothesis suggest the following picture.

Opinion leaders and the people whom they influence are very much alike and typically belong to the same primary groups of family, friends and co-workers. While the opinion leader may be more interested in the particular sphere in which he is influential, it is highly unlikely that the persons influenced will be very far behind the leader in their level of interest. Influentials and influencees may exchange roles in different spheres of influence. Most spheres focus the group's attention on some related part of the world outside the group, and it is the opinion leader's function to bring the group into touch with this relevant part of its environment through whatever media are appropriate. In every case, influentials have been found to be more exposed to these points of contact with the outside world. Nevertheless, it is also true that, despite their greater exposure to the media, most opinion leaders are primarily affected not by the communication media but by still other people.

The main emphasis of the two-step flow hypothesis appears to be on only one aspect of interpersonal relations – interpersonal relations as channels of communication. But from the several studies reviewed, it is clear that these very same interpersonal relations influence the making of decisions in at least two additional ways. In addition to serving as networks of communication, interpersonal relations are also sources of pressure to conform to the group's way of thinking and acting, as well as sources of social support. The workings of group pressure are clearly evident in the homogeneity of opinion and action observed among voters and among doctors in situations of unclarity or uncertainty. The social support that comes from being integrated in the medical community may give a doctor the confidence required to carry out a resolution to adopt a new drug. Thus, interpersonal relations are (1) channels of information, (2) sources of social pressure, and (3) sources of social support, and each relates interpersonal relations to decision-making in a somewhat different way.

The central methodological problem in each of the studies reviewed has been how to take account of interpersonal relations and still preserve the economy and representativeness which the random, cross-sectional sample affords. Answers to this problem range from asking individuals in the sample to describe the others with whom they interacted (Elmira), to conducting "snowball" interviews with influential-influencee dyads (Decatur), to interviewing an entire community (drug study). Future studies will probably find themselves somewhere in between. For most studies, however, the guiding principle would seem to be to build larger or smaller social molecules around each individual atom in the sample.

Lest the impression be conveyed that all mass communication generates opinion *change*, however, it is profitable to look now at the other side of the coin. In an effort to summarize the results of what he calls the

302

"cascade" of recent research,[1] Klapper reminds us that communications from the mass media represent only *one* of the factors affecting public opinion, and that, more often than not, it tends to reinforce, rather than modify, prevailing views.

WHAT WE KNOW ABOUT THE EFFECTS OF MASS COMMUNICATION: THE BRINK OF HOPE

JOSEPH T. KLAPPER

* * * * *

... As early as 1948, Berelson, cogitating on what was then known, came to the accurate if perhaps moody conclusion that "some kinds of *communication* on some kinds of *issues*, brought to the attention of some kinds of *people* under some kinds of *conditions* have some kinds of *effects*." It is surely no wonder that today, after eight more years at the inexhaustible fount of variables, some researchers should feel that the formulation of any systematic description of what effects are how effected, and the predictive application of such principles, is a goal which becomes the more distant as it is the more vigorously pursued.

This paper, however, takes no such pessimistic view. It rather proposes that we already know a good deal more about communications than we thought we did, and that we are on the verge of being able to proceed toward even more abundant and more fruitful knowledge.

THE BASES OF HOPE

This optimism is based on two phenomena. The first of these is a new orientation toward the study of communication effects which has recently become conspicuous in the literature. And the second phenomenon is the emergence, from this new approach, of a few generalizations. It is proposed that these generalizations can be tied together, and tentatively developed a little further, and that when this is done the resulting set of generalizations can be extremely helpful. More specifically, they seem capable of organizing and relating a good deal of existing knowledge about the processes of communication effect, the factors involved in the process, and the direction which effects typically take. They thus provide some hope that the vast and ill-ordered array of communications research findings may be eventually molded, by these or other generalizations, into a body of organized knowledge.

---

[1] A useful review of several relevant books in this field is Morris Janowitz, "Mass Persuasion and International Relations," *Public Opinion Quarterly*, XXIV (1961), 560-71.

From Joseph T. Klapper, "What We Know about the Effects of Mass Communication: The Brink of Hope," *Public Opinion Quarterly*, XXI (1957-1958), 453-73 (the footnotes have been omitted). Reprinted by permission of the author and *Public Opinion Quarterly*.

This paper undertakes to cite the new orientation, to state what seem to be the emerging generalizations, and to at least suggest the extent of findings which they seem capable of ordering. In all of this, the author submits rather than asserts. He hopes to be extremely suggestive, but he cannot yet be conclusive. And if the paper bespeaks optimism, it also bespeaks the tentativeness of exploratory rather than exhaustive thought. Explicit note will in fact be taken of wide areas to which the generalizations do not seem to apply, and warnings will be sounded against the pitfalls of regarding them as all-inclusive or axiomatic.

The Phenomenistic Approach

The new orientation, which has of course been hitherto and variously formulated, can perhaps be described, in a confessedly oversimplified way, as a shift away from the concept of "hypodermic effect" toward an approach which might be called "situational," "phenomenistic," or "functional." It is a shift away from the tendency to regard mass communication as a necessary and sufficient cause of audience effects, toward a view of the media as influences, *working amid other influences,* in a total situation [emphasis added]. The old quest of specific effects stemming directly from the communication has given way to the observation of existing conditions or changes — followed by an inquiry into the factors, including mass communication, which produced those conditions and changes, and the roles which these factors played relative to each other. In short, attempts to assess a stimulus which was presumed to work alone have given way to an assessment of the role of that stimulus in a total observed phenomen.

*   *   *   *   *

Emerging Generalizations

The entire set of generalizations will first be presented in their bare bones, and without intervening comment. The remainder of this paper will be devoted to justifying their existence and indicating the range of data which they seem able to organize. Without further ado, then, it is proposed that we are as of now justified in making the following tentative generalizations:

1. Mass communication ordinarily does not serve as a necessary and sufficient cause of audience effects, but rather functions among and through a nexus of mediating factors and influences.

2. These mediating factors are such that they typically render mass communication a contributory agent, but not the sole cause, in a process of reinforcing the existing conditions. (Regardless of the condition in question — be it the level of public taste, the tendency of audience members toward or away from delinquent behavior, or their vote intention — and regardless of whether the effect in question be social or individual, the media are more likely to reinforce than to change.)

3. On such occasions as mass communication does function in the service of change, one of two conditions is likely to obtain. Either:
   a. the mediating factors will be found to be inoperative, and the effect of the media direct; or
   b. the mediating factors, which normally favor reinforcement, will be found to be themselves impelling toward change.

4. There are certain residual situations in which mass communication seems to wreak direct effects, or to directly and of itself serve certain psychophysical functions.

5. The efficacy of mass communication, either as contributory agents or as agents of direct effect, is affected by various aspects of the media themselves or of the communication situation (including, for example, aspects of contextual organization, the availability of channels for overt action, etc.).

Therewith the generalizations, and herewith the application. The schemata will be applied first to the field of persuasive communication, and then, much more briefly, to the data dealing with the effects of mass communication on the levels of audience taste. The hope, in each case, is to show that the data support the generalizations, and that the generalizations in turn organize the data and suggest new avenues of logically relevant research.

THE GENERALIZATIONS APPLIED: PERSUASION

Persuasive communication here refers to those communications which are intended to evoke what Katz and Lazarsfeld have called "campaign" effects, i.e., to produce such short term opinion and attitude effects as are typically the goals of campaigns—political, civic, or institutional. Long-range phenomena, such as the building of religious values, are not here a focus of attention, nor are the marketing goals of most advertising.

Reinforcement

It is by now axiomatic that persuasive communication of the sort we are discussing is far more often associated with attitude reinforcement than with conversion. The now classic *People's Choice* found reinforcement, or constancy of opinion, approximately ten times as common as conversion among Erie County respondents exposed to the presidential campaign of 1940, and a nine to one ratio was found in the more elaborate study of Elmira voters in 1948. Various other studies have attested that, in general, when the media offer fare in support of both sides of given issues, the dominant affect is stasis, or reinforcement, and the least common effect is conversion.

But we are not here proposing merely that the media are more likely to reinforce than to convert. We are also proposing, as some others have proposed before us, and as we have stated in generalization number 1, that the media typically do not wreak direct effects upon their audiences, but rather function among and through other factors or forces. And we are going slightly farther by proposing, in generalization number 2, that it is these very intervening variables themselves which tend to make mass communication a contributing agent of reinforcement as opposed to change. We shall here note only a few such variables, deliberately affecting both from among the long familiar and the newly identified, in order to suggest the extent of findings for which this generalization seems able to account, and which, seen in this light, become logically related manifestations of the same general phenomenon.

Audience predispositions, for example, have been recognized since the very beginnings of communications research as a controlling influence upon the effects of persuasive mass communication. A plethora of studies, some conducted in the laboratory and some in the social world, have demonstrated that such predispositions and their progeny — selective exposure, selective retention, and selective perception — intervene between the supply of available mass communication stimuli and the minds of the audience members. They wrap the audience member in a kind of protective net, which so sifts or deflects or remolds the stimuli as to make reinforcement a far more likely effect than conversion.

Let us turn from these very old friends to newer acquaintances. Communications research has recently "rediscovered" *the group.* Katz and Lazarsfeld, drawing on the literature of small group research, have proposed, with considerable supporting evidence, that primary-type groups to which the audience member belongs may themselves function as reinforcing agents and may influence mass communication to do likewise. People tend, for example, to belong to groups whose characteristic opinions are congenial with their own; the opinions themselves seem to be intensified, or at least made more manifest, by intra-group interaction; and the benefits, both psychological and social, of continued membership in good standing act as a deterrent against opinion change. Group-anchored norms thus serve, on a conscious or unconscious level, to mediate the effects of communications. The proposition has been empirically demonstrated by Kelley and Volkart, who found that, in general, persuasive communications were more likely to be rejected if they were not in accord with the norms of groups to which the audience member belonged; there were indications, furthermore, that the tendency was intensified in regard to issues more salient to the group, and among persons who particularly valued their membership. Groups are further likely to supplement the reinforcing effect by providing areas for oral dissemination. Various studies have shown that communications spread most widely among persons of homogeneous opinion, and especially among those who agree with the communication to begin with. The "rediscovered group," in short, intervenes between the media stimuli and the people who are affected, and it does so, other conditions being equal, in favor of reinforcement.

Consider another phenomenon which is now in the limelight of communication research: *opinion leadership,* or, as it is sometimes called, "the two-step flow of communication." The operation of such leadership is by definition interventive. And opinion leaders, it turns out, are usually super-normative members of the same groups to which their followers belong—i.e., persons especially familiar with and loyal to group standards and values. Their influence therefore appears more likely to be exercised in the service of continuity than of change, and it seems therefore a reasonable conjecture—although it has not, to the author's knowledge, been specifically documented—that their role in the process of communication effect is more likely to encourage reinforcement than conversion.

All the intervening phenomena which has thus far been cited pertain, in one way or another, to the audience members—to the element of *whom* in the old Lasswell formula. But the range of mediating influences is not so restricted. *The nature of mass communication* in a free enterprise society, for example, falls under this same rubric. It is surely not necessary to here rehearse in detail the old adage of how the need for holding a massive audience leads the media, particularly in their entertainment fare, to hew to the accepted, and thus to tend to resanctify the sanctified. But it should here be noted that this is to say that the demands of the socio-economic system mediate the possible effects of mass communication in the direction of social reinforcement.

Such phenomena as these lend some credence to the proposition that the media typically work among and through other forces, and that these intervening forces tend to make the media contributing agents of reinforcement. And the generalization, to which these factors lend credence, in turn serves to organize and relate the factors. Diverse though they may be, they are seen to play essentially similar roles. One is tempted to wonder if they do not constitute a definable class of forces—whether, if the process of communicational effect were reduced to symbolic formulation, they might not be severally represented as, say, Q_1, Q_2, and so forth to Q_n. The author does not propose anything so drastic. He merely notes that the generalization suggests it. It suggests, simultaneously, relevant topics for further research. *Do* opinion leaders actually function, as the generalization suggests, to render mass communication a more likely agent of reinforcement than of change? And what of all those Q's between Q_3 or Q_8 and Q_n? What other phenomena function in a similar manner and toward the same end?

We may note also that this generalization, simple though it is, not only accounts for such factors as provide its life blood. It provides as well a sort of covering shed for various bits and pieces of knowledge which have hitherto stood in discrete isolation.

Consider, for example, the phenomenon of *"monopoly propaganda"*—i.e., propaganda which is vigorously and widely pursued and nowhere opposed. Monopoly propaganda has been long recognized as widely effective, and monopoly position has been cited as a condition which virtually guarantees persuasive success. But monopoly propaganda can exist only in favor of views which already enjoy such wide sanction that no opposition of any significance exists. Viewed in the light of the generalization, monopoly position is seen not as an isolated condition of propaganda success, but as a specific combination of known factors.

It is a name for the situation in which both the media and virtually all the factors which intervene between the media and the audience, or which operate co-existently with the media, approach a homogeneity of directional influence. Monopoly position is, as it were, a particular setting of the machine, and its outcome is logically predictable.

Change, with Mediators Inoperative

Generalization number 3 recognizes that although the media typically function as contributory agents of reinforcement, they also function as agents of attitude change. In reference to this simple point, there is surely no need for lengthy documentation: the same studies that find reinforcement the predominant effect of campaigns typically reveal as well some small incidence of conversion, and a plethora of controlled experiments attest that media, or laboratory approximations of media, can and often do shift attitudes in the direction intended by the communicator. But the generalization further proposes — and in this it is more daring than its predecessors — that such attitude changes occur when either of two conditions obtain: when the forces which normally make for stasis or reinforcement are inoperative, or when these very same forces themselves make for change.

Let us consider first the proposition that change is likely to occur if the forces for stasis are inoperative. A set of experiments which has already been mentioned above is extremely indicative in reference to this proposition. Kelley and Volkart, it will be recalled, found that, in general, communications opposed to group norms were likely to be rejected if the issue was particularly salient to the group, and that they were more likely to be rejected by persons who particularly valued their group membership. But there is another side to the Kelley-Volkart coin, viz., the findings that the communication opposed to group norms was more likely to be *accepted when the issue was not particularly salient* to the group, and that it was more likely to be accepted *by persons who did not particularly value their membership* in the group. Put another way, *changes were more likely to occur in those situations in which the mediating effect of the group was reduced.*

A whole slew of other findings and bits of knowledge, both old and new, and previously existing as more or less discrete axioms, seem susceptible of being viewed as essentially similar manifestations of this same set of conditions. It has long been known, for example, that although the media are relatively ineffectual in conversion, they are quite effective in forming opinions and attitudes in regard to *new issues,* particularly as these issues are the more unrelated to "existing attitude clusters." But it is precisely in reference to such issues that predispositions, selective exposure, and selective perception are least likely to exist, that group norms are least likely to pertain, that opinion leaders are least ready to lead — that the mediating forces of stasis, in short, are least likely to mediate. The intervening forces, in short, are likely to be inoperative, and the media are more likely to directly influence their audience.

Much the same explanation can be offered for the observed ability of the media to influence their audience on peripheral issues while simultaneously failing in the major mission of the moment, and the same situation probably obtains in regard to media's ability to *communicate facts or even change opinions on objective matters without producing the attitude changes* that such facts and opinions are intended to engender. It may well be that the facts and opinions are not related to the desired attitude change sufficiently strongly to call the protective mediating forces into play: the communication content is probably not recognized as necessarily relevant to the attitude, as not salient, and mediation does not occur. This interpretation, by the way, could very easily be tested.

The inverse correlation between the capability of the media to wreak attitude change and the degree to which the attitude in question is ego-involved may well be another case in point. But this paper cannot analyze and rehearse, nor has the author wholly explored, the entire range of phenomena which might be explained on the basis of the forces for stasis being inoperative. If the generalization is at all valid, it will gather such phenomena unto itself. Let it be the role of this paper to present it, to germinate as it will.

Changes through Mediators

Let us turn now to the second part of the proposition about the conditions under which media may serve as agents of opinion change. It has been suggested that such an effect is likely when either of two conditions obtain: when the forces for stasis are inoperative — as in the cases which have just been discussed — and, secondly, when the intervening forces themselves favor change.

Let us look again, for example, at the influence of group membership and of group norms. These typically mediate the influences of mass communication in favor of reinforcement, but under certain conditions they may abet communicational influences for change.

In an ingeniously designed experiment by McKeachie, for example, communications regarding attitudes toward Negroes, and the discussion which these communications engendered, made some group members aware that they had misperceived the pertinent group norms. The great majority of such individuals showed opinion changes in the direction of the norm, which was also the direction intended by the communication. The *newly perceived norms* impelled the audience toward the communicationally recommended change.

A *switch in group loyalties or in reference groups* may likewise predispose an individual toward consonant opinion changes suggested by mass communication. Studies of satellite defectors, for example, suggest that persons who have lived for years as respected members of Communist society, and then fall from grace, develop a new susceptibility to Western propaganda. As their lot deteriorates, they turn their eyes and minds to the west, and their radio dials to VOA and RFE. By the time they defect they have developed a set of extremely anti-Communist and pro-Western attitudes, quite out of keeping with their previous lives, but in accord with what they regard as normative to their new refugee primary group.

Group norms, or predispositions otherwise engendered, may furthermore become dysfunctional; in learning theory terminology, the response they dictate may cease to be rewarding, or may even lead to punishment. In such situations the individual is impelled to find a new response which does provide reward, and communications recommending such a changed response are more likely to be accepted. Some such phenomenon seems to have occurred, for example, in the case of Nazi and North Korean soldiers who remained immune to American propaganda appeals while their military primary group survived, but became susceptible when the group disintegrated and adherence to its normative attitudes and conduct ceased to have survival value. The accustomed group norms in such instances had not merely become inoperative; they had become positively dysfunctional and had sensitized and predisposed their adherents to changes suggested by the media.

Personality pattern appears to be another variable which may mediate the influence of communications, and particular syndromes seem to abet change. Janis, for example, found in a laboratory study that those of his subjects "who manifested social inadequacy, inhibition of aggression, and depressive tendencies, showed the greatest opinion change" in response to persuasive communication. They appeared, as Hovland puts it, to be "predisposed to be highly influenced."

In sum, it appears that the generalization is supported by empirical data — that intervening variables which mediate the influence of mass communication, and which typically promote reinforcement, may also work for change. And again, the generalization, in turn, accounts for and orders the data on which it is based. Group membership, dysfunctional norms, and particular personality patterns can be viewed as filling similar roles in the process of communicationally stimulated opinion change. Other similarly operative variables will doubtless be identified by a continued phenomenistic approach, i.e., by the analysis of accomplished opinion changes.

The generalization furthermore serves, as did the others, to relate and explain various discrete findings and isolated bits of knowledge. It would appear to cover, for example, such hitherto unrelated phenomena as the susceptibility to persuasive appeals of persons whose primary group memberships place them under cross-pressures, and the effects of what Hovland has called "role playing."

The first case — *the susceptibility to persuasive communications of persons whose primary group membership places them under cross-pressure* — is fairly obvious. In terms of the generalization, such people can be said to be at the mercy of mediating factors which admit and assist communicational stimuli favoring both sides of the same issue. We may also observe that any attitude shift which such a person may make toward one side of the issue does not necessarily entail any reduction of the forceful mediation toward the other direction. On the basis of the generalization, we would therefore predict not only change, but inconstancy, which has in fact been found to be the case.

The effects of role playing seem another, if less obvious, example of opinion change occurring as a result of a mediating, or, in this case, a superimposed factor which in turn rendered a communication effective. Hovland reported that if persons opposed to a communication are forced to defend it, i.e., to act in a public situation as though they had accepted the recommended opinion, they become more likely actually to adopt it. The crucial element of role playing is, of course, artificially superimposed. But in any case, the entire phenomenon might be viewed as something very akin to what occurs when an old norm, or an old predisposition, ceases to lead to reward. Successful role playing in fact invests the opposing response with reward. The communication is thus given an assist by the imposition of new factors which favor change. The potentialities of this technique, incidentally, are of course appalling. The Communists have already developed and refined it and we have christened the process "brain-washing."

* * * * *

THE GENERALIZATIONS APPLIED: EFFECTS ON TASTE

Reinforcement

It has been long known that the media do not seem to determine tastes, but rather to be used in accordance with tastes otherwise determined. The typical audience member selects from the media's varied fare those commodities which are in accord with his existing likes, and typically eschews exposure to other kinds of material. His existing likes, in turn, seem largely to derive from his primary, secondary, and reference groups, although they are not uncommonly affected by his special personality needs. Whatever their origin, they intervene between the audience member and the vast array of media fare, and between the specific content and his interpretation of it. The media stimuli are thoroughly sifted and molded, and they serve, typically, as grist for the existing mill. Put in a now familiar way, the effects of mass communication are mediated, and the media serve as contributing agents of reinforcement.

Changes

But the media are also associated with changes in taste. Oddly enough, little attention has been paid to the one change which occurs continually—the changing tastes of growing children. Wolf and Fiske seem to be the only researchers who explicitly noted that the pattern of development in children's comic book preferences precisely parallels the changing needs of their developing personalities, as expressed, for example, in games. And no one, to the author's knowledge, has ever pointed out that the pattern of development in comic book and TV preferences also parallels the previously characteristic patterns of development in regular reading preferences. In short, the development and its integral changes in taste are culturally wholly catholic. In terms of our present set of generalizations, this is to say that such mediating variables as personality, cultural norms, and peer group interests impel the media to function as contributory agents of taste change.

The media have also been observed, although rarely, to play a role in elevating the tastes of adults. Suchman, for example, investigated the previous habits of some 700 persons who regularly listened to classical music broadcasts, and found that in the case of 53 per cent the radio had either "initiated" their interest in music or had "nursed" a mild but previously little exercised interest. But—and here is the essential point—the radio had functioned in almost all of these cases not as a necessary and sufficient cause, but as an "energizing agent" or implementer of tendencies otherwise engendered. The so-called initiates had been urged to listen by friends, or in some cases fiancés, whose tastes they respected and whose good opinion they sought, or by their own belief that a taste for classical music would increase their social prestige. The mediating factors, in short, were at it again.

The literature on taste effects is relatively sparse, and seems to offer no illustration of changes which could be ascribed to the forces of stasis being inoperative. It might be conjectured that such effects occur among extreme isolates, but the possibility seems never to have been investigated.

In any case, our two generalizations which regard both reinforcement and change as essentially products of mediating factors account for virtually all of the hard data on the effect of mass communication on public taste. The generalizations furthermore suggest that the data are neither contradictory nor anomalous, but logically related. Stasis, reinforcement, developmental patterns, and individual change appear as different but understandable and predictable products of the same machines.

5. Elite Response to Public Opinion

The articles above discussed certain aspects of the public opinion problem on the assumption that these variables will have some effect on the sorts of goals which the nation might pursue, as well as on the strategy employed in that pursuit. But a serious question still remains: to what extent do national leaders share or respond to the views of the larger society? Are political leaders attitudinal deviants, or do they largely reflect their nation's outlook? And if they do not personally hold the same general views as their constituents, are they at least able to judge accurately and thus respond to such opinions? In the following experiment the authors present results that suggest a high correlation between the individual's ability to assess his group's views and his likelihood of being selected as a leader.

THE RELATIVE ABILITIES OF LEADERS AND NON-LEADERS TO ESTIMATE OPINIONS OF THEIR OWN GROUPS

KAMLA CHOWDHRY AND THEODORE M. NEWCOMB

According to modern social psychological theory, individuals are not selected for positions of leadership merely because they possess personal qualities which fit them for leadership in general. We must, on the other hand, assume that individual characteristics *in a particular group situation* have something to do with the selection of leaders. Every group is characterized by a set of interests shared by its members, and with regard to these common interests every group has a set of standards which are important determiners of their members' attitudes. Attitudes toward other things, not closely related to the common interests of a particular group, may be expected to be less homogeneous than attitudes toward objects of common interest. It is likely, however, that in every group there is some diversity of attitudes, even with regard to matters of most focal interest in the group.

Other things equal, those members of a group will be most effective leaders who are most familiar with its standards, and most familiar with the degree to which those standards are shared by the group's members. It seems likely, too, that such familiarity with the group is considered desirable by members as they choose their leaders. If so, then chosen leaders should be more accurate than non-leaders in their estimates of the attitudes of other members toward issues relevant to the group's interest. There is no reason, however, to conclude that leaders should judge more accurately than non-leaders the attitudes of members on issues *irrelevant* to their own groups [emphasis added]. On the contrary, if we assume that the characteristics of leaders are more or less specific to particular group situations, we shall expect chosen leaders to be better than average judges of other members' attitudes on relevant, but not on irrelevant issues. It might, of course, turn out that chosen leaders are superior judges of members' attitudes toward irrelevant as well as toward relevant issues; in that event we should have

---

From Kamla Chowdhry and Theodore M. Newcomb, "The Relative Abilities of Leaders and Non-Leaders to Estimate Opinions of Their Own Groups," *Journal of Abnormal and Social Psychology,* XLVII (1952), 51-57 (the footnotes and the bibliography and references have been omitted). Reprinted by permission of the authors and the American Psychological Association.

to conclude that leadership is a function of a *general* capacity to judge the attitudes of associates, but not a function of the particular standards of particular groups.

This study therefore attempts to test the hypothesis that chosen leaders of a group are superior to non-leaders in estimating group opinion on issues of high relevance to that group, but not superior to them on issues of little relevance. This hypothesis makes no assumptions as to the components of interest, social skill, or personality dynamics which go to make up ability to judge group opinion. Nothing is hypothesized beyond the covariance of two variables: *frequency of being chosen for positions of leadership, and ability to judge group opinion on issues of varying relevance to the group* [emphasis added]. The confirmation of the hypothesis, however, would tend to support a theory of leadership which presupposes interaction among group members who share interests and standards. The rejection of the hypothesis would tend to support a theory of leadership based primarily upon individual differences in skills and capacities.

The hypothesis is one that can be tested either by creating groups in the laboratory, or by obtaining the appropriate information from "natural," existing groups; only the latter procedure was employed in this study. Four groups were selected upon the basis of the following criteria:

1. That they be organized around definite interest patterns, like religion or politics.

2. That each group provide a basis for face-to-face interaction, so that the phenomena of leadership and isolation could emerge.

3. That the members be sufficiently familiar with each other and the opinions of the group to be able to evaluate group opinion.

4. That each group be an example of a common interest group in our society.

A religious group, a political group, a medical fraternity, and a medical sorority were chosen for the investigation. Each of these four groups satisfied the above criteria, though in varying degrees. The medical fraternity and sorority were somewhat different from the religious and political groups, in having a wider range of common interests and experience. They had in common social as well as medical interests, whereas the political and religious groups, according to available information, were more nearly limited to a single interest.

METHOD

Each group was administered a different attitude questionnaire which was subdivided into three parts. These three parts were designed to get at three different levels of relevance to the group's common interests. The first part of the questionnaire dealt with issues with which the group was familiar, and which were presumed to be relevant to the group's goals. The third part consisted of issues which were not only little discussed in the group, but which did not seem to be connected with the basic interest pattern of the group. The second part was intermediate in familiarity and relevance.

314

For the religious group, the first part consisted of items dealing with historic Christian doctrines and practices. The second part included items dealing with the church as a social institution, and the attitudes of Christians toward war. The third part included items dealing with general economic and political issues. Almost all the items in this questionnaire were taken from a previously published "Inventory of Religious Concepts."

For the political group, the first part of the questionnaire consisted of items which the Wallace Progressive group was interested in at that time (1948), and which they were discussing in their meetings. It included such issues as civil liberties, the Palestine question, the Czechoslovakian *coup,* Wallace as a presidential candidate, and nationalization of natural resources. The second part dealt with general economic and political issues, and the third part consisted of items dealing with the church as a social institution, and the attitudes of Christians toward war. The second and third parts of the questionnaire were the same as those used for the religious group.

For the medical fraternity and the medical sorority the items in the first part of the questionnaire were selected (with the help of men and women medical students from other groups) to be representative of those usually discussed in the "bull sessions" of medical students, both men and women. The items dealt with the role of professional women at home, the desirability of medical women as wives, the problems of abortion and euthanasia, of equal opportunity of admission for women and Jews to medical schools, etc. These items were taken from a number of sources, the major one being Kirkpatrick's scale on Feminism and Symonds' Social Attitude questionnaire. The second part consisted of general economic and political items, and the third part consisted of religious items dealing with the church as a social institution, and the attitudes of Christians towards war. The second and third parts had also been used in both the religious and political groups.

Sociometric data were also collected in each group according to four criteria of leadership. The questions asked were:

1. Who are the three persons who, in your opinion, are most capable of acting as president of your group?

2. Who are the three persons who, in your opinion, most influence the opinions of the group?

3. Who are the three persons who, in your opinion, are most worthy of acting as representatives of this group to a convention? (The convention was specified according to the nature of the group.)

4. Who are the three persons in this group with whom you would most like to be friends?

Personal information, including name, age, sex, educational status, length of group membership, and positions in previous groups, was also collected.

Each member of the group was requested to make two replies to every item in the questionnaire. The first was a response indicating *his own reaction* to the statement by encircling "A" if he definitely agreed, encircling "D" if he definitely

315

disagreed, encircling "a" if he had a tendency to agree rather than disagree, and encircling "d" if he had a tendency to disagree rather than agree, with the statement [emphasis added]. Secondly, each member was requested to give the percentage of the group which *he believed agreed* with the statement [emphasis added]. The latter procedure has been used by Newcomb and Travers in their investigations.

From the sociometric data the group status of each individual was determined. Those individuals were arbitrarily designated leaders who received the highest fifth of the total choices on the four criteria. The rest were called non-leaders, and among the non-leaders those who did not receive a single vote on any of the four criteria were termed isolates. The use of total choices for differentiating group status was justified by the high correlation of choices received, according to each of the four criteria. Table 1 [omitted] gives the correlations between the total and each of the four significant sociometric criteria, in each of the four groups. All the correlations are significant at high levels of confidence.

Measurement of sensitivity

To determine the individual's ability to judge group opinion, or his sensitivity to group opinion, a mean error score for each individual was computed, as follows. First, actual group opinion was calculated for each item of the questionnaire by taking the percentage of people who actually agreed to each item. ("Definite agreement" was combined with "tendency to agree.") Secondly, the average error score was calculated for each individual by subtracting his estimate from the actual group opinion concerning each item, and averaging the divergences. The algebraic signs were not taken into consideration because we were not interested in the direction of the error, but only in the magnitude of error.

RESULTS

Comparison of Estimates

In Table 2 [omitted] the leaders of each of the four groups are compared to non-leaders and isolates with respect to their ability to evaluate group opinion at the three levels of relevance. The mean error score of the leader group is compared to that of the non-leader and isolate groups, and the significance of difference between the groups is tested.

In the *religious group* on part A (items assumed to be most relevant) the leaders are superior to non-leaders and isolates. The difference between leaders and non-leaders is significant at the .05 level, and between leaders and isolates at the .01 level. On part B (items assumed to be of intermediate relevance) the leaders again have a tendency to be better evaluators than non-leaders and isolates. The difference between leaders and non-leaders is not significant, but the difference between leaders and isolates is significant at the .05 level. On part C (items assumed to be of least relevance) there is hardly any difference in the error scores of leaders, non-leaders, and isolates.

In the *political group* on part A the mean error score of leaders is again the least. The difference between leaders and non-leaders is significant at the .07 level, and between leaders and isolates at the .02 level. On parts B and C there are no significant differences in the mean error scores of leaders, non-leaders, and isolates.

In the *fraternity* on part A the mean error of leaders in evaluating group opinion is less than that of non-leaders or of isolates. The differences in mean error of leaders and non-leaders, and of leaders and isolates, are both significant at the .01 level. On part B the difference between the mean errors of non-leaders is not significant; the difference between leaders and isolates is significant at the .05 level. On part C the difference in mean errors is too small to be significant.

In the *medical sorority* on part A the leaders make a smaller average error than non-leaders and isolates, but the differences are not significant. On part B, however, the differences in error scores of leaders and non-leaders, and of leaders and isolates are both significant at the .01 level. On part C the differences in the mean errors of leaders, non-leaders, and isolates are small enough to be accounted for by chance variations.

In the medical sorority we used the same questionnaire as we did for the medical fraternity. The leaders in the fraternity are superior to non-leaders and isolates in their knowledge of group opinion on part A, but this superiority on the same issues is not shown by the sorority leaders. The latter finding is opposite to the hypothetical prediction. On the other hand, the sorority leaders are significantly superior to non-leaders and isolates in their ability to evaluate group opinion on part B. This superiority on part B is not shared by the fraternity leaders. On part C, however, neither the fraternity nor the sorority leaders are better in evaluating group opinion than non-leaders and isolates. There seem to be two possible explanations of this difference of results on parts A and B in the fraternity and the sorority. First, our assumption that the same type of things are familiar and relevant to the fraternity and sorority members may be wrong. It is possible that items on part A were more discussed and more relevant to the members of the fraternity, and the items on part B were more discussed and more relevant to the members of the sorority. Secondly, the fraternity was a much more homogeneous group than the sorority; the sorority included Chinese, Filipinos, Negroes, and South Americans. The fraternity included only white North Americans. It is possible that evaluating group opinion of a homogeneous group is easier than evaluating group opinion of a comparatively heterogeneous one.

In summarizing the results of the four groups in sensitivity to group opinion we may say that, on issues designed to be familiar and relevant to the group (A), the leaders are superior to non-leaders and isolates in their ability to evaluate group opinion, the differences between leaders and isolates usually being greater than between leaders and non-leaders. On issues designed to be relatively nonfamiliar and nonrelevant (C), there are no differences in leaders, non-leaders, and isolates in their ability to evaluate group opinion. On issues intermediate in nature to the above two, there are no consistent results.

Supplementary Data from Other Groups

Data from two quite different groups (Bennington College students and a C.I.O. local) were obtained concerning relevant issues only. In the former group, the mean error score of leaders was smaller than that of both non-leaders and isolates, at the .01 level of confidence. Similar differences were obtained in the C.I.O. group at the .03 level.

Chronological Age

The average age of religious leaders (twenty-six) is about three years greater than that of non-leaders and isolates in the same group, while political leaders are on the average two years younger (thirty) than other members of the same group. Neither of these differences is statistically significant. In the fraternity and in the sorority the average age of leaders (twenty-five) is only a few months greater than that of all other members of the same groups. Chronological age is thus not related to leadership and isolation in these data, and evidently has no relation to ability to evaluate group opinion.

Length of Membership in Group

The longer a person has been a member of a group the more likely it is, other things equal, that he will be able to evaluate group opinion accurately. Is it possible that leaders in these groups were those individuals whose memberships were of relatively long duration, and who, therefore, knew more members and their opinions?

Table 3 [omitted] shows that leaders in the religious group have a shorter period of membership, while leaders in the fraternity and sorority groups have a little longer period of membership in their groups than non-leaders and isolates. In the political group the leaders' length of membership is intermediate between that of non-leaders and of isolates.

Length of membership, in these groups, is not consistently related to leadership and isolation, nor to an individual's ability to evaluate group opinion. Travers' data confirm this finding.

Academic Status

Since all or most members of all groups were college students, it is possible to note whether academic status of a person is connected with his status in the group. The chi-square test of significance was used to test whether graduates and seniors were more often in the leader group than in the non-leader and isolate groups. None of the relationships found was significant, indicating that there is no association between leadership and the academic status of an individual, in these groups.

Relations of Elected Positions in Other Groups and Present Status

The chi-square test was again used to see whether there was any significant association between past and present status. Only in the fraternity and sorority groups did we find that leaders have occupied elected positions in other groups significantly more often than non-leaders and isolates ($p < .02$). The other leadership positions held by fraternity and sorority leaders were (according to own statements) predominantly in social and recreational organizations. Such findings suggest that leadership may be "transferable" among similar kinds of groups.

INTERPRETATION

It was found that leaders of a group are significantly superior to non-leaders and isolates in their ability to judge group opinion on familiar and relevant issues, the difference between leaders and isolates being usually greater than the difference between leaders and non-leaders. This differential ability on the part of leaders, non-leaders, and isolates to judge group opinion is, however, *not* evident in *unfamiliar* or less familiar or *less relevant* issues [emphasis added].

It is possible that leaders are accorded the leader status because of this superior ability in evaluating group opinion, and that isolates sink into psychological isolation because of this lack of understanding of the group. An alternative explanation might be that leaders have a superior knowledge of the group because of the greater opportunities afforded to them in their official position, since they come into greater contact with the members and can therefore evaluate their opinions better. That familiarity alone is not a sufficient explanation for the greater understanding of leaders is evidenced by a number of facts gathered from other studies, as well as from some of the preceding data.

In the community studied by Jennings some individuals, because of the work situations they had chosen, had greater opportunities of social contact than others. These individuals who had a greater opportunity to know and be known by others were not more often chosen than ones who lacked similar opportunities; 35 per cent (13/37) of the overchosen subjects were individuals of the high opportunity group, whereas 65 per cent (24/37) attained a similar status without having the same kind of exceptional opportunities.

Further relevant evidence is to be found in the Bennington College data, which show that individuals who later acquire prestige and leadership status are those who possess more than the average amount of sensitivity to group opinion. "Entering freshmen who later acquire leader status have less conservative attitudes than those who are later to achieve little or no prestige. This is significant primarily by way of showing that the histories and the personal characteristics of entering freshmen are such that they are impelled to varying degrees of leadership and prestige, and that *within a few weeks of entering college they have already sized up the dominant community trends,* toward which they adapt themselves in proportion to their habits of seeking leadership and prestige." Those freshmen who had ability enough to "size up" the situation were the individuals who later acquired the leader status.

Group understanding or knowledge, then, seems to be an important factor in the status that an individual may acquire in the group. Understanding or knowledge presupposes communication between individuals, and it seems that some individuals have a better ability to keep these channels of communication open than others. Jennings says, "Each [leader] appears able to establish rapport quickly and effectively with a wide range of other personalities. . . . By contrast, the isolates and near-isolates appear relatively 'self-bound,' unable to bridge the gap between their own personalities and those of other persons."

Also the leaders seem to possess attitudes and personality characteristics which make it possible for them to be in fuller communication with the members of the group. According to Jennings, "The overchosen individuals are personalities who are not concerned with personal problems, but direct their energies to group problems. The underchosen individual is self-centered and is not outgoing in emotional expansiveness."

This suggests that certain personality traits of the overchosen make it possible for them to be in fuller communication with the members than can be said of the underchosen. The leaders' thinking is in terms of the group, and this attitude makes it necessary for them to keep the channels of communication open. The isolates, on the other hand, are "self-centered" and "relatively self-bound." Their channels of communication do not operate in both directions, and are often blocked entirely. They are relatively incapable of going out of themselves to understand the groups' problems. There is a lack of group understanding on their part because they fail to establish a two-way communication.

The ability to function as an effective group member would also seem to be related to the ability to perceive the opinions and attitudes of the group. The more awareness an individual has of an environment, the more satisfactorily he can adjust to it, other things equal. Each individual adjusts to the situation according to the way he perceives it, and not as it "really" is. Since the leaders' perceptions of the prevailing attitude trends existing in a group tend to be more realistic than those of non-leaders and isolates, the chances of their adequate adjustment are greater than those of the non-leaders and isolates.

Our evidence, thus interpreted, suggests that group status, understanding, communication, and adjustment are interdependent variables; it seems likely that better understanding, ready communication, adequate adjustment, and high status are apt to be associated, whereas relative lack of understanding and adjustment, blocked communication, and low status are similarly apt to be found together.

It seems reasonable to conclude, therefore, that leaders of groups like these are chosen, in part at least, because of recognized qualities of "sensitivity" to other members of the group. If so, such qualities may or may not be *potentially* of a general nature. That is, the same ability which enables an individual to be a good judge of others' religious attitudes in a religious group might also enable him to be a good judge of political attitudes in a political group. The fact is, however, that leaders excel primarily in judging attitudes of special reference to their own groups. They are not just good judges of others' attitudes in general; if they have the ability to become such all-around good judges, they are not motivated to develop it equally in all directions.

And so we conclude that in groups like these the ability to be a good judge of others' attitudes is a necessary but not a sufficient condition of being chosen for leadership. A further necessary condition is that the ability be demonstrated within the confines of a specific membership character. Leadership *potentiality* may be adaptable to a wide range of membership characters. But leaders of particular groups seem to be chosen because their potentialities have been developed in particular directions, as called for by the differentiated interests of group members.

One aspect of the public opinion factor which we have not yet discussed is the degree to which *it* is influenced by those very individuals who claim to *be influenced by it*. Political elites, in autocratic as well as democratic societies, never tire of describing their responsiveness to public opinion. Foreign policy-makers are constantly using public opinion as a justification and as a bargaining lever in both the domestic and diplomatic settings. But they are, in the twentieth century, extremely bashful about recognizing the degree to which they themselves are the "opinion-makers." In the following experiment this process is clarified, albeit on a much more modest scale.

THE ASSESSMENT OF GROUP OPINION BY LEADERS, AND THEIR INFLUENCE ON ITS FORMATION

George A. Talland

In a recent study Chowdhry and Newcomb tested the relative abilities of leaders in estimating group opinion and found strong evidence to confirm their hypo-

From George A. Talland, "The Assessment of Group Opinion by Leaders, and Their Influence on Its Formation," *Journal of Abnormal and Social Psychology*, XLIX (1954), 431-34 (the footnotes, the bibliography and references, and the tables have been omitted). Reprinted by permission of the author and the American Psychological Association.

thesis that "leaders should be more accurate than non-leaders in their estimates of the attitudes of other members toward issues relevant to the group's interest." The authors advanced two complementary explanations to account for their findings. Leaders may be accorded their status because of their superior ability in assessing group opinion, and their more accurate evaluation may be due to their position which furnishes them with better opportunities for assessing the attitudes of their followers. The latter was not considered as sufficient explanation in itself.

While Chowdhry and Newcomb did not indicate that only these two circumstances could account for their results, they certainly omitted considering a third which, in their experimental setting, appears equally probable. Leaders may know best the opinions of their groups because they, more than any other member, were influential in formulating these opinions. This line of reasoning would also apply to leaders more generally. Everyday experience in industry, in the services, in political and social organizations, as well as history, demonstrates the fact that leaders are not invariably in close touch with the opinions of their followers. Action leaders in a battle or mob situation, for instance, are likely to assume that role exactly through their insensitivity to the attitudes of those they impel with their commands. The purpose of the present report is to support the argument that leaders know best the opinions of their groups because by their prestige, authority, or other influence they bring their followers in line with their own views.

METHOD

The experiment formed part of a series of psychometric studies of therapeutic groups at the Maudsley Hospital, London. Data collected for the purposes of other researches were utilized, and only a minor modification of the testing procedure was introduced in order to create experimental conditions for the present research.

The applicability of Chowdhry and Newcomb's findings to this type of group was first tested on ten psychotherapeutic groups, totaling 64 members. These had been in treatment for varying periods of from 2 to 18 months, and each consisted of five to eight members, some being all male, others all female, and others of both sexes.

As in the sociometric procedure, leadership status was based on one's fellow group members' assessments. The information, however, was not that of choices and rejections on specified criteria but complete rankings of all other group members. Group scales were derived from the summation of individual ranking scales. This procedure was designed by F. K. Taylor, two of whose status scales were employed in the present study, *public popularity* and *dominance*. The individual rankings from which the popularity scale is derived are given in answer to a question: ". . . estimate the general popularity of each member in the group

... you should not allow your own feelings towards a particular member to influence your judgment." The criterion of dominance rankings was the degree of a member's domination of, and influence upon, group discussion, irrespective of the helpful or harmful effect of this influence. To these was added a new scale, *leadership role*, derived from rankings of the members according to the leadership they had displayed in the group.

*   *   *   *   *

Group opinion was probed in one of the few areas which could be safely assumed to be of common interest to all members within a group: the therapeutic usefulness of various topics of discussion to the group. A list of 15 topics was submitted to the subjects (*S*s), each of whom was asked to rank these individually with a view to their usefulness to the group as a whole. Concordances of rankings within each group were significantly higher than chance at the 1 per cent level of confidence as measured by Taylor's modification of Kendall's *W* coefficient. In view of this, a measure of group opinion could be obtained by summating the individual rank scales. This summated scale was ranked, and accuracy of evaluating group opinion was measured by the rank correlation coefficient between each member's individual rank scale and the ranked summated scale. The coefficient used was rho. The applicability of Chowdhry and Newcomb's conclusions to the therapeutic groups was tested by examining the positions of the most and least accurate assessors of group opinion on the composite scale of leadership and the dominance scale of each group.

Up to this point ten groups provided data for the research. The final experiment, however, could be applied to seven groups only, with a total membership of 44. The topics were ranked by each member on the basis of (*a*) personal helpfulness, and (*b*) helpfulness to the group. These were submitted, and the groups were then asked to furnish a collective rank scale which would express the opinion of the group as a whole. In order to provide this information, the groups were told to discuss the matter, and the experimenter (*E*) left them to proceed with the task. Three of the ten groups were not available for this experiment, and in one of the remaining five groups two members could not attend the discussion. Neither of these occupied extreme positions on either the composite leadership or the dominance scale.

RESULTS

Nine leaders and nine "isolates" emerged from the ten composite scales. In one group the lowest score was above 90, in another the highest was below 210. None of these nine leaders had the highest assessment coefficient in his group, nor did these leaders tend to score in the clusters of best assessors, which are an artifact of the method by which group opinion was obtained. Two leaders made the least accurate evaluation of group opinion in their groups, and one of these leaders tied for top score on the composite scale. Two isolates gave the least accurate, but two others gave the most accurate, evaluation in their group. None of the most dominant members surpassed all his group colleagues in accuracy of assessment. Two gave the least accurate evaluation in their group, as did two of the least dominant members. Two bottom scorers on dominance made the best assessment of group opinion.

*　　*　　*　　*　　*

Replacing the summated scales of group opinion by the collective rankings we find that the association between leadership and accuracy of assessment becomes clearly marked. Five of the six leaders surpass their fellow group members in evaluating the collective opinion. Only two of the five isolates gave the least accurate assessment. Six of the seven top scorers on dominance gave the best assessment of collective opinion, only one bottom scorer the worst.

DISCUSSION

The results confirm the hypothesis that leaders influence the formation of group opinion when this emerges in the course of discussion, and that this influence is likely to account to some extent for the finding that leaders make the most accurate evaluations of group opinion. Before the matter at issue was publicly discussed, not one of the nine leaders in the ten groups had assessed the group opinion more accurately than had other members. One group was leaderless according to the criterion adopted.

After the question had been publicly discussed, i.e., the psychotherapeutic groups had become discussion groups in the commonly accepted sense of the term, all but one of the six leaders or seven top scorers on dominance were found to have assessed the group's collective opinion more accurately than any of their colleagues. The one exception to this rule may be accounted for as a chance occurrence, though it can be explained by the unusually high agreement among the individual opinions of the four members who followed the leader on the composite scale. With correlation coefficients ranging from .80 to .93 they established a group norm which hardly changed in the course of discussion, and from which the leader had markedly deviated. The results throw little light on the isolate, except that in this situation he does not tend to assess group opinion less accurately than other members. The change in the accuracy of the leader's assessment of group opinion is highly significant. It would be difficult to account for it otherwise than by his direct influence on the shaping of group opinion, whether this influence is exerted by deliberate pressure or by prestige, because of more forceful advocacy or more clearly formulated views on the question at issue.

The departing point of the present experiment was Chowdhry and New-comb's research. The groups examined satisfied three of their four criteria. They were organized around a definite interest pattern, they provided a basis for face-to-face interaction and for phenomena of leadership to emerge, and their members were sufficiently familiar with each other to be able to evaluate group opinion. Leadership, too, was defined on criteria similar to those adopted by Chowdhry and Newcomb. Admittedly, the presence of the therapist did not allow for a formal recognition of leadership, but this role did emerge in a functional sense. The principles of the therapeutic technique employed pre-scribed the minimum of interference by the therapist, and, in fact, it was found that the latter's personal judgment had little influence on the shaping of his patients' opinions as far as the usefulness of the topics of discussion is concerned. While psychotherapeutic groups are not meant to be representative of groups in general, nor rankings of discussion topics for their usefulness a typical example of collective opinion, there is no reason to doubt that what has been found in these groups would also occur in others. If the influence of leaders in shaping group opinion is so marked when their status, far from being officially recog-nized, is established under the shadow of an appointed authoritative conductor, it is likely that official leaders who discharge their functions as a matter of duty would exert at least as great an influence. Also, if this influence is so effective, after each member had first to form his opinion independently on the same issue and has therefore some motivation to resist prestige suggestion, it may be expected that the leader's influence would be at least as effective when opinions in a group are initially formed by means of public discussion.

The conclusions drawn from this study are intended to complement those of Chowdhry and Newcomb and the discordant findings of Hites and Campbell. The results suggest that the leader's more accurate evaluation of group opinion need not be attributed primarily to his more sensitive perception of attitudes and atmosphere in the group, nor to this factor combined with his greater opportu-nities of communication. They also suggest that publicity rather than familiarity is the operative attribute of opinions in this context. In order to discover the circumstances by which leaders arrive at more accurate evaluations of group opinion than do followers, investigations carried out after such opinions had been formulated by public discussion fail to assess the leader's influence on the outcome of these discussions. Concerning Chowdhry and Newcomb's second hypothesis, i.e., that the leaders' more accurate assessment of group opinion may be due to their better opportunities for communication, though this factor would not in itself account for the finding, the present experiment gives support to the qualifying clause. Theoretically all members of a therapeutic group have the same opportunities of communication. In fact, leaders communicate more frequently and more explicitly to others and receive more communications from their fellow group members. It would therefore have been expected that their views should be most influential on judging group opinion before its explicit formulation. The results did not confirm this expectation.

SUMMARY

Leadership status was defined and established for each member of ten psychotherapeutic groups on a combined criterion of *dominance, popularity,* and *leadership role.*

By asking the members of these groups to rank 15 topics of discussion in the order of their usefulness in therapy, group opinions and individual evaluations of these group opinions were obtained on a matter of common interest.

It was found that leaders were not more accurate in assessing group opinion than were other members, before a public discussion in the course of which group opinion was formulated.

When groups were asked to discuss the relative usefulness of these topics publicly and to present a collective ranking, it was found that the collective opinion was, in six cases out of seven, closer to the leader's individual opinion than to those of other members.

The results confirm the hypothesis that leaders influence the formation of group opinion, bringing this in line with their personal views. It is suggested that this influence should be considered in accounting for the finding that leaders evaluate group opinion more accurately than other members.

F. THE DECISION-MAKING PROCESS

Up to this point the variety of factors which impinge upon the foreign policy decision-makers has been considered, but no particular attention has been paid to the process *itself*.[1] If one realizes that most bona-fide decisions (i.e., authoritative allocation of resources to a given policy) are made in small or middle-sized groups, it becomes apparent that an impressive amount of behavioral science research may be considered relevant. That is, group dynamics or small group experiments constitute a very large share of the work in sociology and social psychology. But the application of these findings to foreign policy-making concerns could constitute a project of some magnitude, in and of itself, and, therefore, only a small sample of the literature is presented here.[2]

1. The Size of Decisional Groups

One particular question to which small group experiments have given considerable attention is that of group size, especially as this variable affects the speed and quality of problem-solving performance. These data are relevant not only to the matter of effective organization for the formulation and execution of foreign policy, but also to the issue of whether autocratic or democratic societies enjoy any specific advantage in the diplomatic game as a result of the size of their decisional units. In the study excerpted below, Lorge and his colleagues present a survey of

---

[1]An excellent interdisciplinary source is Paul Wasserman and Fred S. Silander, *Decision-Making: An Annotated Bibliography* (Ithaca, N.Y.: Cornell School of Business and Public Administration, 1958). More specific is Richard C. Snyder, H. W. Bruck, and Burton Sapin, *Foreign Policy Decision-Making* (New York: The Free Press of Glencoe, 1962).
[2]An excellent examination of the application of some of the small group research to political science is Sidney Verba, *Small Groups and Political Behavior* (Princeton, N.J.: Princeton University Press, 1961).

the findings which emerge from their own and others' experiments comparing groups and individuals.

A SURVEY OF STUDIES CONTRASTING THE QUALITY OF GROUP PERFORMANCE AND INDIVIDUAL PERFORMANCE, 1920-1957

IRVING LORGE, DAVID FOX, JOEL DAVITZ, AND MARLIN BRENNER

This is an analysis of studies done in the years 1920-1957 which contrast the quality of performance by individuals and by groups in diverse situations. A number of studies are included which add to our understanding of this aspect of human behavior. However, an unpublished review by Lorge et al. prepared in 1953 served as an important source for this presentation. In fact, some of the organization of that report is carried into this study. The existence of this report is due to a literature search made in connection with research into group performance and group process in problem solving.

* * * * *

PROBLEM SOLVING IN MORE REALISTIC SETTINGS

Studies using genuine and significant situations are less numerous than those involving judging, learning, etc., partly because concern with the more genuine human relations problems has emerged quite recently and partly because of the practical difficulties in working experimentally with problems involving decisions. These decisions require the individual or the group to weight alternatives for relative adequacy, followed by the selection of one or some combination of several as the most feasible solution rather than determination of the correct answer. Thus, the criterion for appraising decisions in these experimental studies should differ from agreement with the *one true order or the one correct answer;* rather, the evaluation of decision, ultimately, should be based on some system of credits for coverage and adequacy.

Timmons used as criterion the experts' rank-order of five possible options to the genuine problem, "What type of parole system should Ohio adopt?" His research was oriented primarily to estimate the effect of [group] discussion on the individual's ranking of the five options. The Ss were high school students in Ohio. Classes were divided so that some Ss worked as individuals throughout the

From Irving Lorge, David Fox, Joel Davitz, and Marlin Brenner, "A Survey of Studies Contrasting the Quality of Group Performance and Individual Performance, 1920-1957," *Psychological Bulletin,* LV (1958), 337-72 (the footnotes and the bibliography and references have been omitted). Reprinted by permission of Professor Davitz and the American Psychological Association.

experiment and others worked in specially constituted groups during part of the experiment. The controls (as individuals throughout) 1: on Day 1, ranked the five different options and took an attitude scale toward parole; 2: on Day 2, read a pamphlet containing authoritative information about parole, then again took the attitude scale and ranked the options; 3: on Day 3, reread the information pamphlet under motivation of competing with groups discussing the problem, and then again took the attitude scale and ranked the options; and 4: after an interval of a month, were measured for attitude and for ranking of options.

The experimental section was treated identically for Steps 1, 2, and 4. The essential difference was in Step 3 in which six different kinds of groups were formed, based on the performance on the first day. Each group was supplied with a copy of the informational pamphlet, discussed the problem in leaderless groups and formulated a ranking of the options as a group. When that had been completed, each member of each group took the attitude scale and ranked the options as individuals.

Timmons' measure was the *individual's* ranking of options, so much so that Timmons considered ranking by groups only incidentally and tangentially [emphasis added]. In terms of the individual's agreement with expert ranking, the informational pamphlet produced a tremendous shift toward experts' rank (Day 2 minus Day 1). Individual study and group discussion resulted in further movement toward expert ranking (Day 3 minus Day 2). The individuals who participated in *group* discussion were closer to the experts than the individuals who restudied the pamphlet [alone] [emphasis added]. These changes were maintained, in general, a month later. For attitudes, gains only followed the reading of the pamphlet on Day 2 and at no other time, and showed no difference at any time between those who *discussed* and those who *restudied* the pamphlet [emphasis added].

In this major aspect, Timmons demonstrated a significant transfer from group discussion to subsequent individual rankings. Unfortunately, Timmons considered the group's ranking a very minor aspect of his research. He reported that after discussion the groups' average agreement score was 2.93, which was not significantly different from the immediately subsequent individual (from those groups) average agreement score of 3.31. The 3.31, however, was significantly better than the 6.70 of the individuals who had restudied the pamphlet.

Although Timmons formed six different kinds of groups based on the amount of their agreement with experts' ranks initially, he failed to report the ranking of the various groups. Methodologically, the six groups were made up as: I. 4 Ss with good scores; II. 4 Ss with intermediate scores; III. 4 Ss with poor scores; IV. 2 Ss with good scores, 2 Ss with poor scores; V. 2 Ss with good scores, 2 Ss with intermediate scores; and VI. 2 Ss with intermediate scores, 2 Ss with poor scores.

He reported, however, in terms of individual change that the gains were largest for the poor, smaller for the intermediate, and least for the good, student. The *good* made greater gains after discussing with other *good* than after discussing with the *poor* or the *intermediate*. The *good* did not get worse after discussing with the so-called *poor*. The *poor* gained as much from discussion with the *good* as from the *intermediate,* but always significantly more than from discussion with the *poor*. From the viewpoint of learning by individuals, all individuals seem to benefit from discussion even when the discussants were relatively less adequate.

In 1941, Robinson investigated the effects of group discussion upon attitudes toward two social problems: capital punishment, and American policy to keep out of war. He contrasted college sophomores in 43 *ad hoc* groups of from 8 to 20 members as experimental samples, and 225 college sophomores as individuals. The experimental sample (*a*) studied group discussion theory for one month and had weekly practice discussions, (*b*) studied material on the problems, then, (*c*) took Thurstone Attitude Scales relevant to both problems, (*d*) had a two-hour discussion on each of the questions, and finally, (*e*) took the attitude scales a second time. The control sample had *no* group discussion, but were given successively the two forms of the Thurstone Scales on each problem [emphasis added]. In one variation, an information test was added before and after discussion; in other variations, discussion theory and the study of the informational material were omitted.

Although significant changes in mean scores were made only in attitudes about how to keep out of war, Robinson noted that a consideration of the magnitude of the attitude shifts by individuals revealed significant changes on both problems in all groups. When the informational test was used, the individuals showed gains after discussion. However, without comparable data for the control, this gain cannot be referenced to individual versus group superiority. In a third experiment, Robinson, comparing change in attitude after reading informational material with that after 30-minute group discussion found that the magnitude of the shifts by individuals after reading not only exceeded those after 30-minute discussion, but also those after the two-hour discussions in the earlier experiments. This lack of shift after discussion, contrary to Timmons' findings, may be attributable to the inadequacy of experimental designs, or to a genuine difference between the sequelae of reading or of discussion.

Robert Thorndike hypothesized that much of the superiority of groups over individuals was attributable to the elimination of (*a*) individual chance errors and (*b*) those errors differing from individual to individual and from time to time. The second hypothesis had been confirmed partly in the Gordon experiments. Thorndike attempted to isolate that part of group superiority that was due to averaging or summing individual contributions, from that part due to the elimination of each individual's chance errors. He used 1,200 college students formed into 220 *ad hoc* groups of from four to six members. They worked on 30 problems, e.g., selecting the better of two poems, the more socially significant of two headlines, etc. The design required choice by an individual together with a measure of confidence; then, after discussion, a group choice. Both the individual and the subsequent group choice were completed for each problem before the *S*s proceeded to the next problem. There were significant differences between the mean scores for all individuals before discussion, for "concocted" groups before discussion, and for *ad hoc* groups after discussion.

The analysis of the group product revealed that part, but not all, of the difference between group and individual results can be explained as a consequence of the pooling of the individual products. As Gurnee found in group judgments, the group product was more than an expression of the majority of the members comprising the group, and Thorndike found this "more" attributable to the discussion among the group's members.

The data also were analyzed for the consequences of grouping, i.e., the effects when the majority were correct before discussing in the group, as opposed to when the majority were incorrect. When at least 70% of the individuals were correct before discussion, there was a gain after group discussion of 11%. When less than 50% of the individuals were correct before discussion there was a loss after group discussion of 7%. This result indicated the necessity of qualifying Jenness' earlier hypothesis that disagreement among members is more conducive for group improvement than is agreement. His hypothesis may be correct with judgments, where awareness that others do differ results in restudy, but may not apply in problem solving or decision making when disagreement involves a majority with an erroneous view. Indeed, Farnsworth and Williams made the same point in their demonstration that when all group members were likely to be in error, there was no reason to expect the group product to be *better* than that of individuals.

Timmons concluded that after allowance for the averaging of individual contributions is made, a significant superiority for all groups still remains; similarly, after allowing for the effect of majority influence, an insignificant amount of superiority is reported. When allowances both for averaging effects and for majority influence are made, there is "a large, but not significant" difference favoring the group. Timmons suggested that considering the rigor of his methods, "it seems probable that the differences are even more significant than they seem to be." He suggested four factors possibly inherent in discussion that may account for unexplained differences: the group (*a*) has more suggestions leading toward the solution (cf. Shaw), (*b*) has a wider range of interpretations of the facts of the problems, (*c*) has a wider range of criticism and suggestion (cf. Shaw), and finally (*d*) has more information (cf. Lorge and Solomon).

In 1955 Lorge et al. experimented with the difference in the quality of solution to a practical problem which was presented in four settings differing in degree of remoteness from reality. The problem was presented either as a verbal description, a photographic representation, a miniature scale model, but not allowing manipulation of parts and materials; or a miniature scale model allowing manipulation of parts and materials. The problem consisted of finding a way to get a squad of soldiers across a specified segment of mined road as quickly and secretly as possible using a limited number of available props. The problem was adaptable to many solutions of varying quality, and had the characteristics of a genuine field situation. Ten *teams* of five AFROTC students and 10 *individuals* worked on the problem [emphasis added]. Any individual or group had the right to ask as many questions of the experimenter as he so desired, and the experimenter made an effort to answer all questions as long as they did not directly divulge a method of solution. The results indicated no significant differences among the solutions at the four levels of remoteness from reality. However, at all levels the solutions of the groups were markedly superior to the solutions of the individuals. It was concluded that the differences may be due in large part to the amount and kind of information the Ss had at their command. It was noted that the number of questions asked of the examiner increased with the remoteness of the model from reality. This worked toward equalization of the information available to all groups. Groups asked more questions than the individuals at all levels of remoteness, which meant that the groups had more information to work with than did the individuals, and may account, in part, for their superiority.

Lorge et al. completed a study in 1953 comparing the quality of group and individual solutions of human relations problems before and after class instruction in staff procedures. At the beginning of the course, one half of the Ss spent one period in problem solving as individuals, while the other half worked as groups. In the very next period, those who had worked as individuals were formed into groups, while the earlier groups were dissolved and their members worked individually. The design was replicated six months later, at the termination of the course. The results indicated that as a result of this particular form of instruction, the quality of decisions prepared by *ad hoc* staffs after training is significantly superior to that of those prepared by *ad hoc* staffs in the opening week of class. By contrast, and of interest, the decisions written by *individuals* after instruction are not significantly different from those they had prepared as individuals in the opening days of the course [emphasis added]. This indicated the possibility of individuals being able to improve in their performance of a given task *as members of a group,* without showing improvement in their performance of the same task *as individuals* [emphasis added].

These results emphasize the fact that the group is not necessarily superior to the individual in human relations decisions. The quality of individual decisions *before* instruction is significantly superior to that of groups [emphasis added]. This difference in favor of individuals may indicate merely the relative ineffectiveness of *ad hoc* groups to solve the problem in the given time. In some of the appraisals it was found that groups, before instruction, lost upwards of 80% of the ideas that their constituent members as individuals had for the solution of the problems. Many of these lost ideas were important. At the beginning of instruction, more than 75% of the individual decisions were superior in quality to the best of group decisions. Since the decisions of the individuals at the end of instruction do not differ in quality from those at the beginning, the presumption was that there was a gain in group interaction but not in problem-solving skills whether among individuals or in groups.

The data also indicated that the probability that any individual's idea will be expressed in the group decision is a function of the *commonality* of the idea, i.e., of the number of individuals who had the same idea *prior* to the group meeting. Of all the ideas that were held in common by two or more group members prior to the group meeting, half appeared in the group decision. Only 10% of the unique ideas, those possessed by only one person prior to the group meeting, ultimately appeared in the group decision. Similarly, only one third of the ideas evolved in group decisions were original, i.e., ideas which none of the group members had mentioned in their earlier individual decisions, whereas two thirds of the ideas had already been so expressed. These data suggested that group process does not generate original ideas but relies heavily upon ideas formulated prior to the group meeting.

2. Friction and Friendliness in Decisional Groups

One of the corollaries which emerged from the papers in Section C is that decision-makers are under considerable pressure to modify their views prematurely in the direction of the emerging consensus, merely in order to maintain friendly interpersonal relations with their colleagues. But it is by no means certain that the absence of friction is conducive to optimal performance in such groups. In the selection which follows, Guetzkow and Gyr present an experiment which suggests that certain types of intragroup conflict may well be functional. It is also worth noting that they were confronted with some qualititive phenomena which tend to elude easy observation and classification; their handling of this methodological problem is quite germane to the study of international relations.

AN ANALYSIS OF CONFLICT
IN DECISION-MAKING GROUPS

HAROLD GUETZKOW AND JOHN GYR

Conflict is an important ingredient of our day-by-day social relations. It often results in frustration and disappointment. Yet many speculate as to its creative potential. This study explores some aspects of its operation in the small, face-to-face, decision-making group. The analysis is intended to clarify, to a degree, the conditions under which the participants in a conference terminate their deliberations in consensus or disagreement.

From Harold Guetzkow and John Gyr, "An Analysis of Conflict in Decision-Making Groups," *Human Relations,* VII (1954), 367-82 (the footnotes have been omitted). Reprinted by permission of the authors and *Human Relations.*

I. Nature of the Empirical Data

The basic data used for this analysis of conflict within conferences were gathered by the Conference Research project during 1949 by observing business and governmental decision-making conferences in operation. This analysis is based on group meetings involving in all about 700 persons. Each conference group had been operating within its parent organization for some time before it was observed. The groups usually consisted of five to twenty persons, representing a number of departments or bureaux within the organization, called together to make policy and staff decisions. The research team studied one meeting of each group. Before the meeting, background information was obtained about the group by interviewing its chairman. The Conference Research team of three specialists then actually observed the conference during a bona fide meeting. One observer kept a running record of each participation, who gave it and to whom it was directed. This observer also classified the contribution according to the function it performed in the "problem-solving" process of the conference. He decided whether the remark "gave information," "proposed a solution," "developed another participant's contribution," or fell into any other of the eleven classes of "problem-solving behaviors." A second specialist observed the extent to which the behaviour of each participant was instigated by the personal, self-oriented needs of the individual—needs to be dominant in social situations, to express aggression against others, etc. He noted the incidence of behavior based on "self-oriented needs" as contrasted with behavior arising from problem-centered or task-oriented motives. The third specialist made more global observations and kept a running record of the agenda being handled in the meeting. Immediately after the conference, reactions to the meeting were obtained from each participant by questionnaire. A day or so later, in the privacy of each participant's office, a personal interview was used to supplement the observational and questionnaire material. The interviewer encouraged free and full responses to questions concerning "behind-the-scenes" information about the conference in which the respondent had participated. A holistic view of the entire meeting is obtained when these data are assembled into a single picture. In all, approximately 100 measures were employed to characterize the meeting. Further information about the observational techniques, the questionnaires, and the interview procedures are available on microfilms which have been prepared for those who desire technical details.

II. Definition of Concepts

The basic question of the analysis is the following: are there conditions under which tension or conflict within a conference terminates in agreement or consensus among the participants, as contrasted with other conditions under which conflict ends in disagreement? This question demands definition of two basic concepts—*conflict* and *consensus*. It further requires comparison of groups in *conflict* which eventuate in *high* [emphasis added] amounts of *consensus* with those conferences in which *conflict* results in *low* [emphasis added] amounts of *consensus*, so that the conditions under which each occurs may be contrasted.

A. Definition of Conflict

After making its observation of the conferences, the research team estimated the extent to which the interactions of each meeting were characterized by important differences of opinion among the group members, intellectual or personal in origin. This estimate by each of the three observers was made in answer to the question, "How much overt conflict was there within the group?" The inter-observer reliability of the rating was +.88.

Let us make a conceptual distinction between at least two types of conflict — conflict rooted in the *substance of the task* which the group is undertaking, and conflict deriving from the emotional, affective aspects of the group's *interpersonal relations* [emphasis added]. On the surface, both kinds of conflict would be similar in their overt manifestations — for example, both would delay the meeting. However, one could predict that the two types of conflict would arise and dissipate under different conditions. For example, one might expect much substantive conflict when the members in the group are *task*-oriented, striving to achieve their group goals [emphasis added]. On the other hand, one might expect affective conflict when the members are using the group to satisfy their *self*-oriented needs, their needs for dominance or status [emphasis added]. One might expect substantive conflict to be dissipated by willingness to evaluate another member's suggestions — criticizing some and accepting others. Contrariwise, one might expect affective conflict to be alleviated by reducing the intensity of the self-oriented needs or through conduct within the group which insulates the members from disruptive effects of interpersonal aggression and hostility. . . .

Two of the measures made on the meetings seem useful in appraising the extent to which each of the groups was permeated by substantive and affective conflict, as defined immediately above.

1. The measure of substantive conflict was based on a tally by the problem-solving observer. This tally contrasted the "opposing" and "supporting" comments made during the course of the meeting. This observer counted each time a participant's verbal behavior could be classified into one of the two classes:

Opposing: These contributions are characterized by an opposition, resistance to, or disagreement with a suggestion, solution, interpretation, etc. Responses which point out obstacles, difficulties or objections are included here. A special reliability study made by Heyns and Fouriezos indicates an inter-observer reliability of .76 for contributions coded as "opposing" in nature.

Supporting: These contributions serve the function of indicating agreement or approval of a suggestion or solution proposal. The special study referred to above yielded an inter-observer reliability of .95 for "supporting" contributions.

An index of *substantive* conflict was constructed by determining the ratio of "opposing" contributions to the total of [both] "opposing" and "supporting" comments, made in the course of the meeting [emphasis added]. . . . The scores actually used for characterizing the groups were the average of the three observers' ratings.

2. The index of affective conflict was an estimate made by the three conference observers on a more holistic basis in response to the question, "To what extent did the group seem to be frustrated?" The inter-observer reliability for this rating was .66, not as high as would be desirable.

At first it seemed this measure would hardly be suitable for use as an indicator of affective conflict, for frustration may arise from many sources besides person-to-person conflict. However, this frustration measure was unrelated to non-personal frustration-inducing factors. For instance, there was no relation between frustration and insufficient information about agenda problems being considered, nor was there any relation between frustration and the group's having decision authority incommensurate with the problems being discussed. Contrariwise, the group frustration measure was highly related to other indices of the affective atmosphere of the groups. For instance, group frustration correlated with the observer's estimate of how critical and punishing the group was to its members ($r = .81$). The frustration measure was inversely related to a global measure of the pleasantness of the group's emotional atmosphere ($r = .76$). Thus, it seems justified to utilize the frustration measure as an index of affective conflict.

*   *   *   *   *

Meetings on conflict are characterized by delays and blockages. Those meetings in which there was above average conflict tended to last about half as long again as those conferences in which there was less than average of either or both types of conflict. Thus, both measures delineate groups in which observers gained an over-all impression of the existence of conflict and which lasted for a significantly longer time.

Conflict, then, as defined in this study, is not a single, unified thing. It has at least two relatively independent components. Our basic question now needs to be reformulated as two questions: 1. Under what conditions is substantive conflict resolved in consensus? and 2. under what conditions is affective conflict resolved in consensus? It may also be that certain conditions will influence the conference's process identically, whether the conflict is substantive or affective.

B. Definition of Consensus

Usually the minimal requirement of a decision-making conference is agreement upon some decisions, even though these decisions may be of varying quality. In the post-conference interview the participants were asked, "How much difference was there between your final opinion(s) on the questions discussed and the decision(s) which the group reached?" What is implied in answers to this question? Groups of participants who *agree* with the decision may or may not be *satisfied* with the decision [emphasis added]. When the decision is the best of a number of very unsatisfactory alternatives, the group may agree with it but be dissatisfied with it. However, there tended to be a substantial association between consensus on the decisions and satisfaction with the decisions among the groups studied (r = .46). In interpreting these results the assumption must not be made that agreement among participants implies agreement with the decision by all for the same reason. One participant may agree because the decision means more finances for his department, while another may agree because the same decision means less work for his unit.

III. DESIGN OF THE ANALYSIS

The aim of this study is to find out the differences, if any, between groups which terminated their conflict in consensus and groups which did not. Thus, the analysis design requires that we be able to compare groups in which conflict ended in consensus with groups in which conflict was never resolved. Since conflict was broken down into two types we need to make these comparisons for groups which were characterized [primarily] by *substantive* conflict as well as for groups in which *affective* conflict was predominant [emphasis added]. A further breakdown will be made for those groups which ranked high on either type of conflict and for those which ranked low on [either type of] conflict. Table 2 presents the break-downs which were made and the number of conference groups in each breakdown category.

The analysis would be adequate were we to concern ourselves only with the four high conflict classes specified in the upper part of Table 2. Yet it is interest-

TABLE 2
Number of Conference Groups within Each Class[a]

	Group in Substantive Conflict		Group in Affective Conflict	
	High Consensus	*Low Consensus*	*High Consensus*	*Low Consensus*
High conflict	13	16	9	14
Low conflict	19	9	20	7

[a]The mean of the population distribution on any particular dimension was used to make the separations into "High" and "Low" Conflict.

ing to check whether the same conditions that are conducive to high or low consensus in groups in *high* conflict also operate in groups having *little* conflict—those classes enumerated in the lower part of Table 2 [emphasis added]. Data obtained in analysis of this complementary set of classes with low conflict were helpful in guiding interpretation of the results obtained in the classes with high conflict.

Our analysis aimed to determine which conditions were associated with high or low consensus in the various classes of groups. It was necessary first to choose which of over 100 measures available might be of interest and should be subjected to analysis. Approximately half of them seemed relevant, in the sense that some relatively sound social, psychological hypotheses might be given in their support as being factors or conditions which might "make a difference" in determining whether the conflict ended in consensus or disagreement. Given a particular measure, a t-test was made to check whether a difference on the measure between high and low consensus groups in high or low conflict, substantive or affective, was statistically significant.

*   *   *   *   *

V. Summary

This is an exploratory study of the conditions under which tension or conflict in a conference may be either harmful or helpful. A large number of decision-making meetings in government and business were observed, so that groups in conflict that terminated in consensus might be contrasted with groups in conflict that did not so terminate.

Study of the conflict itself revealed it not as a single characteristic, but rather consisting of two relatively unrelated traits. "Substantive conflict" is associated with intellectual opposition among participants, deriving from the content of the agenda. "Affective conflict" is tension generated by emotional clashes aroused during the interpersonal struggle involved in solving the group's agenda problems.

Certain conditions existing within the conference in either type of conflict are associated with the conference ending in high consensus.

A. Conditions associated with High Consensus in Groups in *either Substantive or Affective* Conflict [emphasis added].
  (i) When there is little expression of personal, self-oriented needs.
  (ii) When whatever self-needs are expressed tend to be satisfied during the course of the meeting.
  (iii) When there is a generally pleasant atmosphere and the participants recognize the need for unified action.

(iv) When the group's problem-solving activity is understandable, orderly, and focused on one issue at a time.

B. Conditions associated with High Consensus in Groups in *Substantive* Conflict [emphasis added]. (These conditions do not hold for groups in affective conflict.)

(i) When facts are available and used.

(ii) When chairman, through much solution-proposing, aids the group in penetrating its agenda-problems.

(iii) When the participants feel warm and friendly toward each other in a personal way.

C. Conditions associated with High Consensus in Groups in *Affective* Conflict [emphasis added]. (These conditions do not hold for groups in substantive conflict.)

(i) When the group withdraws from its problem-solving activities by tackling only discrete, simpler agenda items and postpones consideration of others.

(ii) When the participants withdraw from the problem-situation and have little interest in what is being discussed.

(iii) When the participants withdraw from interpersonal contact with each other.

The conditions related to consensus may be regarded as of two kinds—those positive factors that promote consensus, and certain negative conditions that prevent consensus from occurring. In addition, there are those forces which serve to promote consensus indirectly by restraining the effects of the negative factors. Substantive conflict ending in agreement is largely associated with factors that promote consensus. Conversely, affective conflict terminating in consensus is associated with factors restricting the operation of forces that hinder consensus.

3. Aspiration Levels in Decisional Groups

Earlier in this part it was suggested that organizations must not only match their aspirations and goals to their capabilities but also maintain a modicum of internal harmony. These considerations raise the question of whether national or other decisional organizations attempt to (a) maximize their preferences, (b) optimize them, or (c) settle for something less. Most of the texts and journals in the field of international relations indicate the degree to which nations are thought of as highly efficient organizations, pursuing rationally calculated objectives in an aggressive and alert manner. As the above selections may have hinted, I find very little evidence for this type of model. On the contrary, the many "case studies" of foreign policy decision-making point in a rather different direction.[1]

Just as the industrial organization must sacrifice a total preoccupation with profit in order to meet other demands such as employee morale, a reputation for honesty, minimizing inventories, internal distribution of power, and so on, so must the nation. As a political system with a multitude of incompatible internal and external demands made upon it, the national government and its decision-making units cannot afford to subordinate all other considerations to the maximixation of power or any other foreign policy imperative. In the selection which follows, March and Simon articulate a conclusion which sharply challenges some of the traditional models of economic, political, or other administrative behavior. The key element here is that of aspiration level, which the word "satisfice" represents.

THE CONCEPT OF RATIONALITY

James G. March and Herbert A. Simon

How does the rationality of "administrative man" compare with that of classical "economic man" or with the rational man of modern statistical decision theory? The rational man of economics and statistical decision theory makes "optimal" choices in a highly specified and clearly defined environment:

1. When we first encounter him in the decision-making situation, he already has laid out before him the whole set of alternatives from which he will choose his action. This set of alternatives is simply "given"; the theory does not tell how it is obtained.

2. To each alternative is attached a set of consequences—the events that will ensue if that particular alternative is chosen. Here the existing theories fall into three categories: (a) *Certainty*: theories that assume the decision maker has complete and accurate knowledge of the consequences that will follow on each alternative. (b) *Risk*: theories that assume accurate knowledge of a probability distribution of the consequences of each alternative. (c) *Uncertainty*: theories that

---

[1]Two useful volumes in this regard are Bernhard C. Cohen, *The Political Process and Foreign Policy: The Making of the Japanese Peace Settlement* (Princeton, N.J.: Princeton University Press, 1957); and Warner Schilling, Paul Hammond, and Glenn Snyder, *Strategy, Politics, and Defense Budgets* (New York: Columbia University Press, 1962).

From James G. March and Herbert A. Simon, *Organizations* (New York: Wiley, 1958), Ch. 6, pp. 137-41 (the bibliography and references have been omitted). Reprinted by permission of the authors and John Wiley & Sons, Inc.

assume that the consequences of each alternative belong to some subset of all possible consequences, but that the decision maker cannot assign definite probabilities to the occurrence of particular consequences.

3. At the outset, the decision maker has a "utility function" or a "preference-ordering" that ranks all sets of consequences from the most preferred to the least preferred.

4. The decision maker selects the alternative leading to the preferred set of consequences. In the case of *certainty,* the choice is unambiguous. In the case of *risk,* rationality is usually defined as the choice of that alternative for which the expected utility is greatest. Expected utility is defined here as the average, weighted by the probabilities of occurrence, of the utilities attached to all possible consequences. In the case of *uncertainty,* the definition of rationality becomes problematic. One proposal that has had wide currency is the rule of "minimax risk": consider the worst set of consequences that may follow from each alternative, then select the alternative whose "worst set of consequences" is preferred to the worst sets attached to other alternatives. There are other proposals (e.g., the rule of "minimax regret"), but we shall not discuss them here.

SOME DIFFICULTIES IN THE CLASSICAL THEORY

There are difficulties with this model of rational man. In the first place, only in the case of certainty does it agree well with common-sense notions of rationality. In the case of uncertainty, especially, there is little agreement, even among exponents of statistical decision theory, as to the "correct" definition, or whether, indeed, the term "correct" has any meaning here.

A second difficulty with existing models of rational man is that it makes three exceedingly important demands upon the choice-making mechanism. It assumes (1) that all the alternatives of choice are "given"; (2) that all the consequences attached to each alternative are known (in one of the three senses corresponding to certainty, risk, and uncertainty respectively); (3) that the rational man has a complete utility-ordering (or cardinal function) for all possible sets of consequences.

One can hardly take exception to these requirements in a normative model—a model that tells people how they *ought* to choose. For if the rational man lacked information, he might have chosen differently "if only he had known." At best, he is "subjectively" rational, not "objectively" rational. But the notion of objective rationality assumes there is some objective reality in which the "real" alternatives, the "real" consequences, and the "real" utilities exist. If this is so, it is not even clear why the cases of choice under risk and under uncertainty are admitted as rational. If it is not so, it is not clear why only limitations upon knowledge of consequences are considered, and why limitations upon knowledge of alternatives and utilities are ignored in the model of rationality.

From a phenomenological viewpoint we can only speak of rationality relative to a frame of reference; and this frame of reference will be determined by the limitations on the rational man's knowledge. We can, of course, introduce the notion of a person observing the choices of a subject, and can speak of the rationality of the subject relative to the frame of reference of the observer. If the subject is a rat and the observer is a man (especially if he is the man who designed the experimental situation), we may regard the man's perception of the situation as objective and the rat's as subjective. (We leave out of account the specific difficulty that the rat presumably knows his own utility function better than the man does.) If, however, both subject and observer are men—and particularly if the situation is a natural one not constructed for experimental purposes by the observer—then it becomes difficult to specify the objective situation. It will be safest, in such situations, to speak of rationality only relative to some specified frame of reference.

The classical organization theory, like classical economic theory, failed to make explicit this subjective and relative character of rationality, and in so doing, failed to examine some of its own crucial premises. The organizational and social environment in which the decision maker finds himself determines what consequences he will anticipate, what ones he will not; what alternatives he will consider, what ones he will ignore. In a theory of organization these variables cannot be treated as unexplained independent factors, but must themselves be determined and predicted by the theory.

ROUTINIZED AND PROBLEM-SOLVING RESPONSES

The theory of rational choice put forth here incorporates two fundamental characteristics: (1) Choice is always exercised with respect to a limited, approximate, simplified "model" of the real situation. We call the chooser's model his "definition of the situation." (2) The elements of the definition of the situation are not "given"—that is, we do not take these as data of our theory—but are themselves the outcome of psychological and sociological processes, including the chooser's own activities and the activities of others in his environment.

Activity (individual or organizational) can usually be traced back to an environmental stimulus of some sort, e.g., a customer order or a fire gong. The responses to stimuli are of various kinds. At one extreme, a stimulus evokes a response—sometimes very elaborate—that has been developed and learned at some previous time as an appropriate response for a stimulus of this class. This is the "routinized" end of the continuum, where a stimulus calls forth a performance program almost instantaneously.

At the other extreme, a stimulus evokes a larger or smaller amount of problem-solving activity directed toward finding performance activities with which to complete the response. Such activity is distinguished by the fact that it can be dispensed with once the performance program has been learned. Problem-solving activities can generally be identified by the extent to which they involve *search:* search aimed at discovering alternatives of action or consequences of action. "Discovering" alternatives may involve inventing and elaborating whole performance programs where these are not already available in the problem solver's repertory.

When a stimulus is of a kind that has been experienced repeatedly in the past, the response will ordinarily be highly routinized. The stimulus will evoke, with a minimum of problem-solving or other computational activity, a well-structured definition of the situation that will include a repertory of response programs, and programs for selecting an appropriate specific response from the repertory. When a stimulus is relatively novel, it will evoke problem-solving activity aimed initially at constructing a definition of the situation and then at developing one or more appropriate performance programs.

Psychologists (e.g., Wertheimer, Duncker, de Groot, Maier) and observant laymen (e.g., Poincaré, Hadamard) who have studied creative thinking and problem-solving have been unanimous in ascribing a large role in these phenomena to search processes. Search is partly *random*, but in effective problem-solving it is not *blind* [emphasis added]. The design of the search process is itself often an object of rational decision. Thus, we may distinguish substantive planning—developing new performance programs—from procedural planning—developing programs for the problem-solving process itself. The response to a particular stimulus may involve more than performance—the stimulus may evoke a spate of problem-solving activity—but the problem-solving activity may itself be routinized to a greater or lesser degree. For example, search processes may be systematized by the use of check lists.

Satisfactory Versus Optimal Standards

What kinds of search and other problem-solving activity are needed to discover an adequate range of alternatives and consequences for choice depends on the criterion applied to the choice. In particular, finding the *optimal* alternative is a radically different problem from finding a *satisfactory* alternative [emphasis added]. An alternative is *optimal* if: (1) there exists a set of criteria that permits all alternatives to be compared, and (2) the alternative in question is preferred, by these criteria, to all other alternatives. An alternative is *satisfactory* if: (1) there exists a set of criteria that describes minimally satisfactory alternatives, and (2) the alternative in question meets or exceeds all these criteria.

Most human decision-making, whether individual or organizational, is concerned with the discovery and selection of satisfactory alternatives; only in exceptional cases is it concerned with the discovery and selection of optimal alternatives. To optimize requires processes several orders of magnitude more complex than those required to *satisfice* [emphasis added]. An example is the difference between searching a haystack to find the *sharpest* needle in it and searching the haystack to find a needle sharp enough to sew with.

PART THREE

POLITICS
AS
INTERACTION

Part One examined the idea of a complex social system serving as an environment within which smaller social systems or groups behave and interact with one another. The international system provides the organizational-institutional, the attitudinal-cultural, and the technological-physical settings within which the drama of world politics is acted out. Then Part Two focussed upon the subsystems which are the major actors in the larger, total system: in world politics, the nations. Although the legitimacy of considering so large and complex a social organization an actor was upheld, it was emphasized that no anthropomorphizing was intended; the nation, despite its many discrete and divergent component parts, is both a conceptual convenience of considerable magnitude to the scholar, and a powerful psychic reality to the overwhelming proportion of twentieth-century mankind.

The difference between Part Two and Part Three, then, lies in the "level of analysis";[1] the focus shifts away from the actor (or comparative foreign policy) level and back again to the systemic level, but this time with concentration on the interactions which occur in the system. That is, Part One looked at the total system in terms of its essentially stable and *continuing* characteristics, whereas here the emphasis is upon its more rapid-changing *dynamics*, even though the line of demarcation between the two is far from clear and unambiguous. Perhaps the distinction is best expressed by referring to the former attributes of the system as its *structural* characteristics and to the latter as its *behavioral* ones; if the two are in harmony, we may speak of a condition of "moving equilibrium," to paraphrase Jean Bodin, the sixteenth-century political philosopher.

A semantic note is also in order here. If Part Two is thought of as an indirect inquiry into comparative foreign policy, this part might well be conceived of as an indirect inquiry into inter-nation relations. But, as I have hinted earlier, the word "relations" is more passive in its implications than is appropriate to this field of study. Thus I have used the more dynamic "international politics," even though some object to its being too

---

[1]See J. David Singer, "The Level of Analysis Problem in International Relations," *World Politics*, XIV (1961), 77-92.

narrow a concept, emphasizing, as it does, interaction among governments at the expense of nongovernmental interaction across national boundaries. In this book, however, the usage is satisfactory, since there is a quite intentional exclusion of almost everything but national governments as they act and interact on behalf of, and in the context of, their respective national societies or nations.

A. THE OBSERVATION AND MEASUREMENT OF INTERACTION

It is often asserted that international politics constitute such a complicated and invisible web of behaviors that no systematic observation is possible; as a consequence, it is argued, the field can never become a scientific discipline. As might be expected, similar prognostications have been made in the past regarding physics, astronomy, biology, sociology, and psychology, to mention a few. Yet in each of these cases, a combination of ingenuity and diligence has produced steady improvement in the scholar's ability to classify and describe the complex and elusive phenomena of his particular discipline.

Highly suggestive for the student of international relations is the methodological innovation devised by Bales for the observation and measurement of interpersonal relations in the admittedly more manageable setting of small group experimentation.

A SET OF CATEGORIES FOR THE ANALYSIS OF SMALL GROUP INTERACTION

Robert F. Bales

In a recent review of the state of research in the field of small groups, Edward Shils makes some remarks which aptly point up the problem to which this paper is addressed:

From Robert F. Bales, "A Set of Categories for the Analysis of Small Group Interaction," *American Sociological Review*, XV (1950), 257-63 (the footnotes have been omitted). Reprinted by permission of the author and The American Sociological Association.

Because problems are dimly "felt," because they are neither related to a general theory of behavior on the one side, nor rigorously connected with the categories and indices to be chosen for observation on the other, the results of the research can very seldom become part of the cumulative movement of truth which constitutes the growth of scientific knowledge. When concrete indices (and classifications) are not clearly related to the variables of a general theory of human behavior in society, they tend to be *ad hoc*. Under these conditions they are only with difficulty applicable, i.e., translatable into another concrete situation by an investigator who seeks to confirm, revise, or disconfirm the previously "established" proposition.

Probably most of us have some difficulty in thinking of a session between a psychiatrist and patient, a corner boy's gang in a political huddle, and a staff conference of business executives as comparable within a single frame of reference. It is probably more difficult, for example, than thinking of the social systems of China, of Bali, and the United States as legitimate objects for comparative analysis. At least the latter three constitute full scale, and in some sense, complete social systems.

What do the former three groups have in common? They are small face-to-face groups. If we call them social systems, we shall have to say that they are partial, as well as microscopic social systems. To place a slightly different emphasis, it can be said that they are systems of human interaction. At this degree of abstraction there is no necessary incongruity in comparing them with each other, or with full-scale social systems. Both small groups and complete societies can be viewed as types of interaction systems, even though one is tremendously more inclusive than the other. If this point of view turns out to be excessively formal or abstract, we may have to retreat to less generalized frames of reference.

To take the more hopeful view, it may very well be that one of the main contributions of the study of small groups will be an expanding of the range of available empirical data in such a way as to force our theory of social systems to a more general and powerful level of abstraction. If the theory of social systems has been generalized and strengthened by the necessity of making it applicable to a range of full-scale social systems, non-literate as well as literate, Eastern as well as Western, then there is at least the possibility that it will be further strengthened by the necessity of making it applicable up and down the scale from large to small.

However this may be, the present set of categories was developed with this hope, and took its initial point of departure from a body of theory about the structure and dynamics of full-scale social systems. This will not be immediately apparent in viewing the set of categories, nor can it be spelled out to any satisfactory degree in this article. A manual dealing with both the theoretical and practical aspects of the method for those who may wish to apply it in their own research has recently been published. The present paper will give only a simplified introductory description of the method and some of its possible uses.

DESCRIPTION OF THE METHOD

The method is called interaction process analysis. It is a type of content analysis in the basic sense, but the type of content which it attempts to abstract from the raw material of observation is the type of problem-solving relevance of each act for the total on-going process. Hence it has seemed less confusing to refer to what we are doing as "process analysis" rather than as "content analysis."

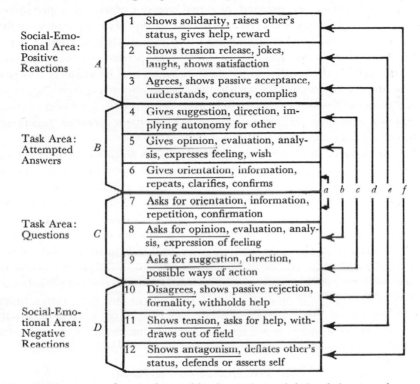

Chart I. The system of categories used in observation and their relation to major frames of reference

Key:

a. Problems of orientation   c. Problems of control   e. Problems of tension-management

b. Problems of evaluation   d. Problems of decision   f. Problems of integration

The heart of the method is a way of classifying behavior act by act, as it occurs in small face-to-face groups, and a series of ways of analyzing the data to obtain indices descriptive of group process, and derivatively, of factors influencing that process. The set of categories as it actually appears on the observation form is shown under the twelve numbers in Chart I. The outer brackets and labels do not appear on the observation form, but constitute a part of the mental set of the observer. The twelve observation categories are numbered from the top down, but are arranged in a series of complementary pairs proceeding from the center pair, 6 and 7, outward. The phrases and terms within the numbered categories are only catch-phrases designed to be concretely descriptive of the implied theoretical content of the categories in their usual forms. Actually there are extended definitions of each of the categories, and the central meaning of each is given by its position in the frames of reference to which they are all related as indicated by the labeled brackets on the Chart.

The set of twelve categories (and the actual behavior which is classified under them) are brought into working relation to other bodies of theory in terms of the frame of reference. The key assumption which provides this articulation is the notion that all organized and at least partially cooperative systems of human interaction, from the smallest to the most inclusive, and of whatever concrete variety, may be approached for scientific analysis by abstracting from the events which go on within them in such a way as to relate the consequences of these events to a set of concepts formulating what are hypothetically called "functional problems of interaction systems."

For purposes of the present set of categories we postulate six interlocking functional problems which are logically applicable to any concrete type of interaction system. As indicated in Chart 1, these are in one-word terms: problems of orientation, evaluation, control, decision, tension-management, and integration. These terms are all related to a hypothetical conception of an over-arching problem-solving sequence of interaction between two or more persons. As a concrete first approximation we may find it helpful to think of the functional problems as related in an order of "stages" or "steps" in a problem-solving sequence, as their order suggests. Actually this is an over-simplified view. However, in order to illustrate the notion of stages as they may appear under certain conditions, let us take a short description of a fictional group meeting. The same example will serve to illustrate the method of scoring with the categories.

How the Scoring is Done

Let us imagine we are observing a group of five persons who are meeting together to come to a decision about a point of policy in a project they are doing together. Three or four of the members have arrived, and while they wait they are laughing and joking together, exchanging pleasantries and "small talk" before getting down to business. The missing members arrive, and after a little more scattered conversation the chairman calls the meeting to order. Usually, though not necessarily, this is where the observer begins his scoring.

Stage 1. Emphasis on problems of orientation: (deciding what the situation is like). The chairman brings the meeting up to date with a few informal remarks. He says, "At the end of our last meeting we decided that we would have to consider our budget before laying out plans in greater detail." The observer, sitting with the observation form in front of him, looks over the list of twelve categories and decides that this remark is most relevant to the problem of orientation, and specifically that it takes the form of an "attempted answer" to this problem, and so he classifies it in Category 6, "Gives orientation, information, repeats, clarifies, confirms." The observer has already decided that he will designate the chairman by the number 1, and each person around the table in turn by the numbers 2, 3, 4, and 5. The group as a whole will be designated by the symbol 0. This remark was made by the chairman and was apparently addressed to the group as a whole, so the observer writes down the symbols 1-0 in one of the spaces following Category 6 on the observation form.

In this one operation, the observer has thus isolated a unit of speech or process which he considers a proper unit for classification, has classified it, identified the member who performed the act, and the person or persons to whom it was directed. If he were writing on a moving tape instead of a paper form, as we do for some purposes, he would also have identified the exact position of the act in sequence with all others. In practice we find that we obtain from 10 to 20 scores per minute in keeping up with most interaction, and that this speed is not excessive for a trained observer.

As the chairman finishes his remark, Member 2 asks the chairman, "Has anybody gone over our expenditures to date?" The observer decides that this is a "question" indicating that a problem of orientation exists, and so should be classified in Category 7, "Asks for orientation, information, repetition, confirmation." He so records it by placing the symbols 2-1 in a box following this category. The chairman replies, "I have here a report prepared by Miss Smith on the expenditures to date." The observer marks down the symbols 1-2 under Category 6, as an "attempted answer" to the indicated problem of orientation. As the chairman goes over the report the observer continues to score, getting a good many scores in Categories 6 and 7, but also occasional scores in other categories.

Stage 2. Emphasis on problems of evaluation: (deciding what attitudes should be taken toward the situation). As the chairman finishes reviewing the items on the report he may ask, "Have we been within bounds on our expenditures so far?" The observer puts down a score under Category 8, "Asks for opinion, evaluation, analysis, expression of feeling." Member 3 says, "It seems to me that we have gone in pretty heavily for secretarial help." The observer puts down a score in Category 5, "Gives opinion, evaluation, analysis, expresses feeling." Member 4 comes in with the remark, "Well I don't know. It seems to me. . ." The observer puts down the symbols 4-3 in Category 10, "Disagrees, shows passive rejection, formality, withholds help," and continues with scores in Category 5 as Member 4 makes his argument. The discussion continues to revolve around the analysis of expenditures, with a good many scores falling in Category 5, but also in others, particularly Categories 10 and 3, and interspersed with a number in Categories 6 and 7 as opinions are explained and supported.

Stage 3. Emphasis on problems of control: (deciding what to do about it). Finally the chairman says, "Well a little more than half our time is gone." The observer scores 1-0 in Category 6. "Do you want to go ahead and decide whether we should buy that piece of equipment or. . ." The observer scores 1-0 in Category 9, "Asks for suggestion, direction, possible ways of action." Member 2 says, "I think we should get it." The observer scores 2-0 in Category 4, "Gives suggestion, direction, implying autonomy for other." As Member 2 begins to support his suggestion, Member 3 breaks in with a counter argument, and the discussion begins to grow more heated.

The observer begins to have trouble in keeping up as the members are talking more rapidly and some remarks are left unfinished. He does not forget to keep scanning the group, however, and presently he notices that Member 5, who has said little up to this point, sighs heavily and begins to examine his fingernails. The observer puts down a score under Category 11, "Shows tension, asks for help, withdraws out of field." He enters this score as 5-y, since he has decided ahead of time to use the symbol y to stand for "self," and to use it when activity is directed toward the self, or is expressive and non-focal, that is, not directed toward other members.

Meantime, Member 3, the chronic objector, comes through with a remark directed at Member 2, "Well, I never did agree about hiring that deadhead secretary. All she's got is looks, but I guess that's enough for Joe." The others laugh at this. The observer scores the first and second remarks under Category 12, "Shows antagonism, deflates other's status, defends or asserts self." The laugh which follows is scored in Category 2, "Shows tension release, jokes, laughs, shows satisfaction." In this case the score is written 0-3, all to Member 3.

At this point Member 5 comes in quietly to sum up the argument, and by the time he finishes several heads are nodding. The observer scores both the nods and the audible agreements in Category 3, "Agrees, shows passive acceptance, understands, concurs, complies." The chairman says, "Then it looks like we are in agreement." The observer scores in Category 6, and scores the answering nods in Category 3. Member 3, the chronic objector, who is also the chronic joker, comes in with a joke at this point, and the joking and laughing continue for a minute or two, each member extending the joke a little. The observer continues to score in Category 2 as long as this activity continues. As the members pick up their things one of them says, "Well, I think we got through that in good shape. Old Bill certainly puts in the right word at the right time, doesn't he." The observer marks down two scores under Category 1, "Shows solidarity, raises other's status, gives help, reward," and after a few more similar remarks the meeting breaks up.

The Possibility of Empirical Norms

The foregoing is a fictional example, designed to illustrate the nature of the scoring operation, as well as a kind of hypothetical sequence of stages which may occur under certain conditions. To summarize, we might say that during the course of this meeting there were a series of "phases" portrayed, during which one or more of the functional problems included in our conceptual framework received more than its usual share of attention. The temporal order of these phases in this fictional example follows in a rough way the logical order in which we arrange the categories on the observation form in pairs from the center line outward, that is, as dealing with problems of orientation, evaluation, control, and then in rapid order, a special emphasis on final decision, tension reduction, and reintegration. Each of the major functional problems has been made into an implicit "agenda topic."

The categories of activity as classified by the present system are assumed to bear a functional relation to each other similar to the relation of the phases in the meeting just portrayed. The example has been constructed so that in its phases the relations of the categories to each other are "written large," to borrow an idea from Plato. Hence it is relevant to ask what degree the notion of phases on the larger scale is actually to be taken as an empirical description rather than as a logical model. It is important to emphasize in answer to this question that we do not assume nor believe that all group meetings actually proceed in just this way. One of the thorniest problems in the history of thinking about the process of small groups is whether or not, or in what sense there may be a series of "steps" or "stages" in group problem solving. Data will later be published which indicate that under *certain conditions,* which must be carefully specified, a group problem-solving process essentially like that sketched above, does it tend to appear. The data indicate that the sequence described is a kind of average sequence for problem-solving groups, that is, an empirical norm. It further appears that departures from the average picture can be used as diagnostic indicators of the nature of the conditions under which interaction takes place.

Similarly, it appears that there are empirical uniformities in the way activities are distributed between persons. We have some data which indicate that, on the average, if we rank order participants according to the total number of acts they originate, they will then also stand in rank order as to (1) the number of acts they originate to the group as a whole (to 0), (2) the number of acts they originate to specific other members of the group, and (3) the number of acts they receive from all other members of the group. In addition, (4) each person in the rank order series addresses a slightly larger amount of activity to the person just above him in the series than the person above addresses to him, with the top person addressing the group as a whole to a disproportionate degree. It seems likely that these uniformities can be tied together in a more comprehensive theory, and that departures from this average picture can be used as a diagnostic indicator of the nature of the conditions under which interaction takes place. Data on this problem will be published later.

Similarly, ignoring time sequence and the specific persons who initiate or receive acts, empirical uniformities appear in the gross frequency with which each category of activity tends to occur. Preliminary data on these uniformities are given below.

FREQUENCY OF OCCURRENCE OF EACH TYPE OF ACTIVITY

We have available for this tabulation some 23,000 scores in terms of the present twelve categories, from observations of groups of different sizes and kinds, ranging through nursery school children, high school and college students, married couples, college faculty discussions, etc., on tasks of widely different kinds. We do not know how badly biased this collection of scores may be as a sample of something larger. They are simply all of the raw scores we have to date on all of the groups and tasks we happen to have observed for a variety of reasons. The scorings were made by the present author. The general problems of reliability are treated in the manual mentioned above. Very briefly it may be said that satisfactory reliability has been obtained between observers, but requires intensive training which should be regarded as an integral part of the method.

Table 1 shows the raw scores and their percentage distribution (or rates) in the twelve categories. In order to have certain conventional limits for inspection of the variability of particular profiles we have employed an external criterion rather than utilize the variance of our samples, which are known to be quite

TABLE 1

Raw Scores Obtained on All Interaction Observed to Date,
Percentage Rates, and Suggested Limits, by Categories

Category	Raw Scores	Percentage	Suggested Limits for Inspection of Profiles[a]	
			Lower	Upper
1	246	1.0	0.0	5.0
2	1675	7.3	3.0	14.0
3	2798	12.2	6.0	20.0
4	1187	5.2	2.0	11.0
5	6897	30.0	21.0	40.0
6	4881	21.2	14.0	30.0
7	1229	5.4	2.0	11.0
8	809	3.5	1.0	9.0
9	172	.8	0.0	5.0
10	1509	6.6	3.0	13.0
11	1009	4.4	1.0	10.0
12	558	2.4	0.0	7.0
	22970	100.0		

[a]Suggested limits shown have been established for each category by use of binomial confidence limits given in Snedecor, *Statistical Methods,* 1946, p. 4, with p equal "Percentage of total" and n equal 100. This provides relatively wider ranges for the smaller values and although such conventions do not properly reflect the multinomial character of the variation, they provide a first approximation for present purposes.

heterogeneous. Our experience indicates that when the rate for a given category on a particular profile is outside the range suggested in Table 1, we are usually able to connect the deviation with some more or less obvious source of variation in the conditions under which the interaction took place. For example, we find that a profile of nursery school children at free play is over the suggested limits on showing solidarity and showing antagonism, on giving direct suggestions and on disagreement, and is under the limits on asking for opinion, giving orientation, and giving opinion. A group of high school boys in group discussion is over the limits on laughing and joking, and under the limits on giving orientation. A group of faculty members planning a thesis problem with a graduate student is within the limits on all categories. Pending the development of a satisfactory typology of groups, tasks, and other sources of variation, and the accumulation of more experience, this arbitrary procedure for detecting "significant variations" may serve a useful purpose.

APPLICABILITY OF THE METHOD

Verbal interaction accounts for the largest part of the scores, but the categories apply to non-verbal interaction as well. Groups of manageable size for the method fall in the range between two and perhaps twenty, but there is no definitely established top limit—the top manageable size depends upon the character of the interaction. The method is most easily applied in groups where the attention of the members tends to focus in turn on single speakers or members, as in most discussion groups. Hence it might be said to apply to groups small enough so that each member potentially takes into account the reactions of each of the others.

In concrete terms, the groups which one might be able to study with the method are very diverse. They would include a series of groups concerned primarily with substantive problems external to their own process, such as discussion groups, planning groups, policy forming and executive committees, boards and panels, diagnostic councils in clinical work, seminars and classroom groups, teams and work groups, certain kinds of problem-solving groups in experimental social psychology and sociology, etc. In addition, there are certain groups with a primary focus on their own procedure in an impersonal way, for training purposes, such as those formed for training in basic human relations skills, now an important branch of small group research. In a less impersonal way, there are large numbers of small groups which have the interaction or interpersonal relations of the members as a primary focus, whatever their concern with substantive external problems. These would include family and household groups, children's play groups, adolescent gangs, adult cliques, social and recreational clubs, and small associations of a great many kinds. Finally there are groups which might be said to have a primary focus on problems of personal content or experience of members, such as therapy or confessional groups of various kinds, and groups of two, such as therapist and patient, counselor and client, interviewer and interviewee, and a number of others in the general class of professional specialist and client.

Some of these types of groups have been studied with the present method or others similar to it. Some of them are unexplored as yet. Taken together, however, the total range of possible types of groups constitutes a challenging array. If interaction in groups of the diverse sorts mentioned can be brought within the range of a single frame of reference, and can be made to yield data by the same method of analysis, we should be some distance along toward meeting the difficulties which Shils indicates in the comments at the beginning of this paper.

B. INCOMPATIBLE GOALS AS A SOURCE OF INTERACTION

Part Two explored at some length the nature of the goals which nations tend to pursue, as well as the variables which produce these goal orientations. In those selections, it should have been evident that many of these national goals are incompatible—in more ways than one. Not only do the various future states of affairs which a given set of national decision makers might prefer conflict with one another, but they also conflict with those preferred by the corresponding members of decision-making groups in other nations. The processes by which the various groupings *within* the nation reconcile their conflicting preferences, predictions, and goals have already been investigated—and, hopefully, illuminated. There remain, however, the less structured, and, hence, more conflicting, processes by which those national goals which are incompatible with the goals *of other nations* are more or less reconciled.

Before examining those processes, however, this section will first look at the source and nature of these incompatibilities. Are they "real" and objective, or merely the result of erroneous perceptions, faulty communications, or misunderstandings? A useful introduction to the problem is Bernard's vigorous presentation of the "sociological" as distinguished from the "psychological" approach to intergroup conflict.

THE CONCEPTUALIZATION OF INTERGROUP RELATIONS WITH SPECIAL REFERENCE TO CONFLICT

Jessie Bernard

INTRODUCTION: THE SEVERAL TYPES OR LEVELS OF INTERGROUP CONCEPTUALIZATION

Intergroup relations have traditionally been a preoccupation of social scientists. More recently psychologists have likewise attacked problems of intergroup relations, with so much vigor, indeed, that they now almost dominate the field so far as theory and conceptual formulations are concerned. A large proportion of presumably intergroup research at the present time is prosecuted by psychologists, it is based on psychological concepts, and is oriented within a psychological framework. This psychological approach is characterized by an emphasis on subjective factors, for the psychologist, because of the nature of his science, sees primarily what goes on in the human mind. The psychological *Tendez* is of necessity, therefore, in the direction of an "it's all in the mind" orientation. Thus in conceptualizing intergroup relations the tendency is to minimize objective conditions and to concentrate on such phenomena as stereotypes, prejudice, hostility, aggression, threat orientation, and to lay great emphasis on the allegedly non-rational nature of these subjective phenomena.

At the present time, therefore, the conceptualization of intergroup relations may be thought of in terms of a continuum so far as emphasis on subjective factors is concerned. At one extreme we have the ecologist's theoretical system with its concepts of symbiosis, commensalism, predation, parisitism, etc., in which there is little if any room for recognition of subjective factors, or, indeed, of individuals at all. Next comes the economist's system, which in its analyses of the division of labor, especially in the international market, verges closely on the ecological point of view, but makes room for some emphasis on subjective factors in its considerations of value. (The Marxist conceptualization of intergroup relations, of course, makes room for a good deal of subjective emphasis.) Next on the continuum would probably come the political scientist's system which, with its emphases on nations and nationalism, has a large component of subjective material. Then comes the sociologist's formulations which place considerable stress on objective relations, but also deal with subjective factors in his emphases on cultural factors. Finally we have the psychologist's conceptual system which is wholly in terms of subjective elements.

From Jessie Bernard, "The Conceptualization of Intergroup Relations with Special Reference to Conflict," *Social Forces*, XXIX (1951), 243-51 (the footnotes have been omitted). Reprinted by permission of the author and The University of North Carolina Press.

Because of the inherent interest and appeal of the data secured by this psychological approach it has seduced many workers who have, as a result, neglected the—in many ways—less appealing because less personal sociological approach. Thus sociological research in intergroup relations has lagged behind psychological research. In the field of conflict, for example, we know more about the personality mechanisms underlying hostility, prejudice, aggression, and group stereotypes than we do about the techniques for determining whether or not a conflict exists and of measuring the extent of incompatibility of group goals, if it does.

The psychological or subjective approach has a great deal of value, and nothing said here is intended to disparage it in any sense. It does, however, raise a number of theoretical questions. Are intergroup relations to be conceived as existing independently of, or at least separately from, the inner reactions or the interpersonal relations of members, as the social sciences have tended to conceptualize them; or are they to be conceived subjectively, either as the sum total of individual interpersonal relations among members of the groups, or as the subjective reactions of the members of the groups, as the psychologists tend to conceive them? Can one always tell what the intergroup relations are from a scrutiny, however careful, of interpersonal relations? Does the fact that Group A has no prejudice, hostility, or wrong stereotypes of Group B mean in fact that there is no conflict between them?

The present article, written by a sociologist with, presumably, a sociological bias, will deal primarily with the contrast between the sociological and the psychological conceptualizations of conflict in intergroup relations, omitting reference to the ecological, economic, and political.

SOCIOLOGICAL AND PSYCHOLOGICAL CONCEPTUALIZATIONS OF CONFLICT

Sociologically speaking, conflict exists between groups when there is a fundamental incompatibility in their values, goals, interests, etc., so that if one group gets what it wants, the other group cannot get what it wants. Conflict so conceived can exist independently of the subjective reactions of members of the groups. The members of the groups in conflict may and, indeed, often do need and bear affection toward one another, as in the case of the conflict between the sexes or age groups. Nor is hostility a necessary concomitant of conflict, viewed sociologically. Conflict in this sociological sense should be distinguished from misunderstanding; in a misunderstanding, groups *may* feel that a conflict exists when in fact none does [emphasis added]. Nor should conflict be confused with aggression. Aggression may occur where there is no conflict; and conflict may occur without aggression. It is not, in fact, always possible to determine whether a *conflict actually exists*, that is, whether the goals, values, interests, etc., of two groups are actually *incompatible* [emphasis added].

In contrast to this concept is that of the psychologist according to which conflict appears to exist in the minds of group members. There is, for example, much written on "threat orientation" but little on actual threat. In a recent text in social psychology, the author is at great pains to emphasize that groups may conceive of one another as threats, but he lays little stress on the fact that maybe this threat-consciousness is well based in fact. Sociologically speaking, one group may actually constitute a threat to another and the threat-consciousness of the threatened group is not nonrational but well founded in fact, as we shall indicate below.

Intergroup Relations Conceived as the Sum-Total of Interpersonal Relations among Group Members

One way to conceptualize intergroup relations psychologically is to view them as the sum-total of interpersonal relatons among members of the groups. Although this point of view is not usually precisely formulated, it often lies back of practical programs for improving intergroup relations. The assumption is made that improving interpersonal relations will *ipso facto* improve the relationship between the groups. It is basic to the principle that "getting people together," or "getting people to work on a common project" will improve intergroup relations. The Sub-Commission on Prevention of Discrimination and Protection of Minorities of the United Nations has erected this into a basic educational measure. Perhaps such interpersonal relations will improve intergroup relations under certain specified circumstances. But in and of themselves there is no reason to believe they will. The following analysis of a community set-up which appears to conform almost ideally to the prescription by the United Nations Sub-Commission, illustrates a situation in which warm, even intimate, interpersonal relations grew up among members of two groups under factory conditions without in any way changing the fundamental patterns of intergroup relations in the community at large.

Ohsylvania is located in the fruit region of Pennsylvania, near the Ohio border. The entire community recognizes its common dependence on the successful harvesting and preservation of the fruit crop. When the harvest fails, everyone suffers; when it is successful, everyone profits. The entire organization of the community is aimed at achieving this common goal . . . For instance, the custom has developed that every woman regardless of status, pitches in to work in the canneries at the peak of the season. Hence from June to October the banker's daughter and the day laborer's daughter may work side by side. In the cannery, status is a matter of efficiency on the job. Outside the cannery, and from October to June, an altogether different status structure prevails, one in which Italians are relegated to a position not too dissimilar to that of Negroes in a southern community. In the cannery, intimacy may develop; outside, social distance, even discrimination exists. The fact that all share the community enterprise of saving the harvest does not mitigate the status discrimination outside the common experience. . . .

B. Incompatible Goals as a Source of Interaction

Within the plant it is quite usual to have females representing all four classes working on the same belt. Of two girls working over the first pitter, one may be from a prominent local family, the other of Italian descent. The position over the pitter is noisy, hot, and undesirable; but the girls are proud that they have been chosen for a position which demands concentration and reliability. They must not only sort the fruit, as all the women on the belt do, but they must also be responsible for the functioning of the pitter as well. If a mechanical defect is noted, they must quickly report it. If the flow of the fruit is too great, they must strive to keep the pitter unclogged. They must be able to estimate its capacity, and above all they must remain calm in emergencies. Realizing this, they begin to function as a team, with no thought of background — class or ethnic — differences. Within a short time, each develops the greatest respect for the other as a worker and eventually even as a person. Each is proud of the accomplishments of the team rather than of herself. To relieve the grueling monotony, they converse as equals with complete freedom. The upper class girl discusses her date of the night before — a college man, a new car, a corsage — and the Italian girl is sincerely happy for her partner. The Italian girl tells of her new nephew, that he cried all night, that he is the eleventh child in the home, that he has just been baptized in the Roman Catholic faith; and the upper class girl is well aware of the unspoken love for the child. One feels ill; the other silently does more than her share. One is injured; the other sympathetically aids. This continues for weeks, and soon the two girls fully understand each other — thoughts and hopes and beliefs, spoken and unspoken. Then the season is over. A month later, the girls pass on the street, seeing each other for the first time since their common experience of the summer. There is no evidence of the former relationship, and they merely utter a brief "Hi." Their common interest of processing the fruit gone, they have nothing further to say. The bond of understanding has been broken.

In brief, a thousand friendships between members of two groups — German and American scientists, for example, or a thousand love affairs between soldiers and forbidden enemy women — will not add up to friendly group relations. Nor conversely, will a thousand quarrels between American tourists and French taxi-drivers add up to Franco-American conflict.

For the laws which govern interpersonal relations are not necessarily the same as those which regulate intergroup relations. We recognize this fact in intersexual relations. Men and women have found themselves attracted to one another in spite of the widest and deepest group barriers. Negro and white, Mongolian and Caucasian, Oriental and Occidental, Jew and gentile, Greek and barbarian, conqueror and vanquished have leaped group barriers from time immemorial. Even among men, personal attractions have often subverted intergroup patterns. In static trench warfare, as in World War I, fraternization between enemies can be a constant danger to intergroup hostility. It is reported that in both World Wars American soldiers often found their enemies, the Germans, personally more congenial than their allies, the French. We are told that even in Nazi Germany many high officials had their "pet" Jews of whom they were fond and whom they wished to protect.

363

Nothing here said should be interpreted as opposing any effort to bring the members of conflicting groups into warm, friendly relations. The argument is, simply, that such relations will not necessarily bring about equally friendly group relations. This interpersonal approach might be labelled the "cosmetic" approach; it glosses over the surface but does not always come to grips with the fundamental bases for group conflict.

INTERGROUP RELATIONS CONCEIVED AS SUBJECTIVE REACTIONS OF GROUP MEMBERS

More often explicitly stated is the psychological conceptualization of group relations in terms of the subjective reactions of groups members. The tendency of psychologists to conceptualize group conflict in terms of stereotypes, prejudice, hostilities, and aggressions is illustrated in a number of recent works. Otto Klineberg, in his outstanding and valuable memorandum on *Tensions Affecting International Understanding,* deals with such topics as personality in relation to nationality, national stereotypes, attitudes and their modification, and influences making for aggression. He recognizes the existence of demographic and technological factors in intergroup relations but—justifiably—begs to be excused from discussing them, as outside the competence of a psychologist. Newcomb, who as professor of both psychology and sociology, could be expected to represent a sociological orientation (and does, more than most psychologists), in a chapter in his recent text on group conflict discusses prejudices, hostilities, stereotypes, barriers to communication (especially segregation), lynching, and the reduction of hostility (by reducing personal susceptibility to threat orientation, reducing barriers to communication, changing norms through joint participation). These two important works illustrate the typical or characteristic conceptualizations of intergroup conflict by the psychologist today—the current psychological "line" in intergroup relations.

The question may perhaps legitimately be raised as to whether such a frame of reference even deals with intergroup relations at all. It certainly deals with human beings and tells us a good deal about them. Does it, however, tell us anything about group relations?

An important embodiment of the psychological conceptualization of intergroup relations is the basic psychological premise on which the UNESCO constitution rests, namely that "wars begin in the minds of men." This type of statement has a specious kind of authenticity about it which sounds well until one tries to interpret it. It is either a truism, meaning that war is a kind of human behavior, which is conceived and executed through the human mind. Or else it is, unless considerably modified and qualified, something of a fallacy. For what, exactly, does it mean? No one save perhaps the orthodox Freudian psychoanalysts would argue today that war is the result of an instinct (of pugnacity or aggression, or what-have-you) that periodically requires mass expression. Modern warfare is a highly complex technological enterprise for which nothing in man's instinctive equipment prepares him. Indeed, modern warfare is so contrary to our instincts that a considerable amount of training, indoctrination, and outside motivation is necessary to convert men into fighters. Modern psychologists do not, therefore, invoke instincts (excepting again the psychoanalysts who posit a death instinct) to explain wars. But they have created a number of concepts to substitute for the concept of instinct. They are, as we have seen, such concepts as stereotypes, prejudice, hostility, aggression, and threat orientation.

Stereotypes

The current doctrine with respect to stereotypes tends to challenge the older "kernel of truth" theory and to emphasize the wholly nonrational element in them. It is argued, although not demonstrated, that stereotypes among nations are more important than the facts about the nations themselves. "More important than the truth about America is what Europe thinks about America—if we view the matter from the standpoint of relationships; for Europe will be more influenced by its own picture of America than by America itself." Klineberg agrees with Den Hollander that stereotypes become "a psychological reality of tremendous importance, which operates in both directions in determining group relations and group behavior."

In support of the argument that stereotypes are independent of actual experience, psychologists offer data to show that whether one has had little or much contact with minority groups, one tends to hold similar stereotypes. The person who has had no contact with Negroes reacts much like one who has had a great deal. How then could his picture of Negroes be based on fact? It is, obviously, true that the origin of stereotypes within the individual does not require first hand experience with the stereotyped group. But vicarious experience can be, and in fact is, just as effective. Teachers and propagandists depend on it as a matter of course. Thousand of students in the social sciences during the past 15 years have acquired stereotypes of the Zuni, Kwakiutl, and Dobuans; of the Arapesh, the Tchambouli, and the Mundugumor. Perhaps less than one in a thousand have had any direct contact with these peoples. Yet their stereotypes are the same as those of Benedict and Mead, who have. Most people must of necessity acquire their stereotypes of other peoples of the world through this kind of vicarious rather than through direct contacts. But this tells us little about the accuracy of the stereotype itself; it may be favorable or unfavorable, accurate or inaccurate whether it is acquired directly or vicariously. But none of this informs us about the origin or the validity of the stereotypes as collective representations in the first place. We can explain why John Smith, who has had little contact with Negroes, has a stereotype of the Negro as superstitious and lazy, or of the Arapesh as cherishing and gentle. But this explanation does not account for the origin of the stereotype in John Smith's world. Are stereotypes wholly arbitrary? If so, can we invent arbitrary stereotypes about any group and make them stick? Why are certain adjectives chosen as part of the stereotypes of particular groups? If there is little in the "kernel of truth" theory, it should be possible to create any kind of stereotype about any people—ferocious Arapesh and gentle Mundugumor.

Whether or not stereotypes do or do not have a "kernel of truth" as their base, no evidence has been presented to show that they cause or prevent intergroup conflict. The stereotypes of German children with respect to America resemble those of French children more than they do those of British children; all are fairly friendly and favorable. Yet twice in this century Germany and the United States have fought wars. Most Americans hold unfavorable stereotypes about, let us say, the Turks. These stereotypes are not likely to lead us to war with the Turks; nor do they even imply the existence of conflict.

Hostile stereotypes are more likely to be the *result* of conflict than its *cause* [emphasis added]. When a conflict exists, each side attempts to create hostile stereotypes of the enemy in order to whip up fighting drive. It is, in fact, one of the functions of propagandists to create such stereotypes—of the ruthless Hun, of the aggressive communist, of the sneaking Jap, etc. Stereotypes, in brief, may be used as weapons in intergroup conflict; they have not been shown to be causes of such conflict.

Prejudice

Prejudice is undoubtedly an important sociological as well as psychological fact. Yet its relationship to intergroup conflict is no more clear and unequivocal than that of the stereotype. As in the case of the stereotype, prejudice appears to be one of the results rather than a cause of intergroup conflict. Can we, for example, say that the slave trader was prejudiced against the Africans he captured and sold? There certainly was a conflict here; was it a consequence of prejudice? Was prejudice responsible for the conflict between the American Indian and the white colonist? Or was it a consequence? Thousands if not millions of Americans during the thirties were, if anything, prejudiced in favor of the Russians. Many found it difficult to accept the existence of conflict between the Soviet Union and the United States in the postwar forties; some do not still. There has been little if any prejudice against the Germans in this country. Nevertheless conflict has existed.

In brief, the existence of a causal relationship between prejudice and group conflict objectively considered has yet to be demonstrated. In order to prove such a relationship we would have to show that prejudice existed between the parties of all intergroup conflict and that no such prejudice existed where no conflict existed. Prejudice, like the hostile stereotype, is a weapon in intergroup conflict; it is used in conflict; it does not cause conflict. Until a causal relationship can be established between prejudice and intergroup conflict, the conceptualization of intergroup conflict in terms of prejudice has limited significance.

Hostility

Conflict objectively considered can exist between groups without hatred or hostility on the part of the members. Conversely, hostility can exist without conflict. Hostility, like adverse stereotypes and prejudice, results from, rather than causes, conflict.

Aggression

A convenient substitute for instinct is the recently evolved concept of "free floating aggression." The blows and buffets of the world create in us — more in some than in others — those agressive impulses which seek an outlet in war. As a matter of fact, it is highly questionable whether individual aggression has any more to do with modern warfare than do instincts. Americans are, so far as individual personality is concerned, generally considered — "stereotyped" — as aggressive; yet the United States has been traditionally pacifistic. Russians, conversely, who are, as individuals, almost archetypes of the amenable, belong to the most aggressive nation of the world today. There is little demonstrable relationship between the aggressiveness of individuals, the kind psychologists deal with, and group conflict as such.

Threat Orientation

The subjective or psychological concept which seems to have the most direct bearing on intergroup conflict is that dealing with the consciousness of threat on the part of group members. The chief limitation to this concept lies in the fact that the psychologist as psychologist can tell us only what the members of a group conceive as threats; he cannot tell us whether or not an actual threat exists. He can say only that the members of one group perceive the members of another group as threats: he cannot say that one group actually is a threat to another. Even psychologists do, however, occasionally look up from their preoccupation with the internal attitudes of people to gaze at the world about them. Thus Newcomb, discussing group conflict, finally concedes that perhaps there is an objective basis for threat orientation:

> ... segregated groups almost invariably differ in regard to power, privilege, and prestige. The more complete the segregation, the more certainly this is true. Segregation tends to "freeze" such differences, because it usually enables the group with the greater power and privilege to maintain its advantage. The result of these facts is that members of the more privileged group have something to gain, and the less privileged group have something to lose, by segregation. Hence most members of the more privileged group will view as threatening any lowering of the barriers to association, whereas to the less privileged group the barriers themselves are threatening. Thus segregation gives rise to threat-oriented attitudes out of which prejudice springs.

367

In brief, prejudice results from the objective conflict of group interests. There is a good, that is, rational basis for "prejudice" if such "prejudice" will preserve one's privileges or help one fight for privileges. Such "prejudices" may not be gentlemanly or Christian or "American" in the ideal sense, but they are certainly not non-rational in a threat-situation. They represent an empirically reasonable technique in conflict. Carey McWilliams has called anti-Semitism "a mask for privilege." Perhaps all kinds of discriminatory prejudices have something of this character. A threat to privilege may produce them.

It is the sociologist who should be able to tell us something of the "real" or "objective" relations between groups, regardless of how they may appear subjectively within the minds of the members; he should be able to tell us whether or not a threat exists. To be sure, no group is likely to think of itself as a threat to any other group; on the contrary, members of one group are likely to conceive of other groups as threats to themselves. The sociologist should, however, be able to tell whether the threat actually exists and in which direction. The psychologist, training his microscope on the subjective reactions of his subjects, is not in a position to tell us about the outside world, however much he may know of threat orientation. Was the white man a threat to the American Indian? Was the American Indian a threat to the white man? The psychologist cannot answer such questions because his theoretical conceptualization of inter-group relations makes no room for such problems. He can tell us what the white man felt and thought about the Indian, but not whether or not a true conflict existed. Is the capitalistic United States a threat to Soviet Russia? Russian children are taught to believe so. The idea seems to us wholly false. Is Soviet Rissia a threat to capitalistic United States? We think so; Russians deny the charge. Psychologists can tell us how Russians and Americans look to one another in terms of threat; as psychologists they can not tell us whether the two peoples do actually threaten one another.

The concept of threat-orientation comes nearer than the others so far discussed to the heart of intergroup conflict; it is the logical subjective counterpart to objective conflict, for in true conflict one group actually is a threat to the other. The difficulty is, however, that threat-orientation may exist even where true conflict does not.

THE AUTHORITARIAN PERSONALITY

The logical embodiment of the above theories of stereotypes, prejudice, hostility, aggression, and threat, is found in the recently elaborated theory of the prejudice-prone personality. The theory is that if one exposes a number of people to the same experiences with, or the same information or data about, minority groups, a certain proportion will give intolerant reactions, whereas others, on the basis of the same stimuli, will give tolerant reactions. This is, in a way, the epitome of the "it's all in the mind" point of view. Earlier work by Angus Campbell, *Fortune* magazine, and Gardner Murphy and Rensis Likert, had shown that hostility toward one minority group tended to be extended to others also. The most elaborate formulation of the theory that prejudice and intolerance represent a reaction-system of a definite personality type and are relatively independent of objective fact as a basis, and that people who harbor such intolerant attitudes constitute a definite type is that expressed in *the Authoritarian Personality* by Adorno, Sanford, Levinson, and Frenkel-Brunswik (New York: Harper, 1950). These authors believe the differences between tolerant and intolerant personalities can be accounted for by early mothering experience.

This prodigious study of the authoritarian personality seems to establish the fact — a matter of common observation — that some people look out upon a hostile world, whereas others live in a world they conceive of as friendly. Some are essentially sour, suspicious; they interpret everything as threatening. Others are sanguine, everything is for the best. The distinction is an old one and real enough. The use to which it is now being put is new. We used to think of such differences as temperamental (whatever that might mean), or glandular or hereditary or based on physique or constitutional type. The current theory is that they result from differences in mothering experience in infancy. And one special set of attitudes is singled out for emphasis — attitudes toward Jews. It is not difficult to accept the fact that a suspicious person who feels the world is his enemy will hate minority groups, nor the fact that a person who views the world as friendly will feel tolerant toward them. The thing that puts the solution in a unique focus is the emphasis on this one facet of personality and labeling a type long distinguished in the literature, as "authoritarian" or "fascistic" or "anti-Semitic."

There is no doubt that these analyses give us a good deal of information about and insight into certain personality configurations. But they tell us little about intergroup relations. The fact that one type of person is tolerant and another intolerant, for whatever reasons, does not tell us whether from his point of view the tolerance or intolerance is justified by the facts. We have long since learned that we cannot discount behavior because of its motivations, it has to be judged on its own merits. A work of art is no less great because it is the product of a personality motivated by parental frustrations; the revolutionary is no more and no less justified because he is reacting against authority on the basis of an infantile pattern. The fact that some people are tolerant and others intolerant tells us only that some are secure, others insecure. As in the case of threat-orientation, we are looking in, not out. During the thirties the secure or sanguine type of person interpreted almost everything Russia did in a favorable way, just as others were as convincedly hostile to Russia. Both were presented with the same set of facts; one interpreted them favorably the other unfavorably. One type was "tolerant," or appeasing, of communism; the other, "intolerant." This fact, however, does not describe, any more than threat-orientation, the true relations between Russia and the United States. The fact that some people were sympathetic toward Russia proves nothing about Russia, though it might reveal a good deal about the sympathetic people. Nor does the fact that so many people were hostile to Russia prove anything about Russia. Only an objective, sociological analysis could tell us whether or not a conflict existed between Russia and the United States. Scrutinizing the attitudes of people, however scientifically, cannot tell us. In other words, the approach to intergroup relations by means of psychological or psychiatric data, as in *the Authoritarian Personality,* is interesting so long as it does not pretend to be more than it is—an analysis of individual people—and recognizes that it is not a contribution to intergroup relations.

To test the hypothesis basic to *The Authoritarian Personality* even as a strictly psychological concept we ought to have companion studies of Jews who are hostile to non-Jews. If the hypothesis on which this book is based is correct, the anti-gentile Jew—or anti-white Negro—should have a psychological personality structure like that of the authoritarian or anti-Semitic or fascistic or anti-democratic personality, a similar mothering history. Jewish stereotypes of the hating, persecuting gentile have, perhaps, no more kernel of truth than the non-Jewish stereotypes of the wily, shrewd Jew. Probably not one American Jew in a thousand has suffered personally in a pogrom or liquidation program. Perhaps after all anti-Semitism is all in his mind.

Unless we conceive the world in terms of an essential harmony, there *will* be times when the "authoritarian" or "fascistic" or "anti-Semitic" personality will be right in his hostile reactions [emphasis added]. Similarly, the tolerant personality will be wrong in terms of the survival of his group when he fails to give a hostile reaction to a group that constitutes a *real* threat to his own [emphasis added].

VALUES AS CLEWS TO INTERGROUP CONFLICT

The above discussion does not imply that subjective factors in intergroup relations are to be discounted. There is a sense in which it may be said that wars and other conflicts begin in the minds of men. Men have certain hierarchies of values in their minds. War is, for most people, low on their list. But there are, again for most people, certain things that are worse than war. Most Americans, for example, consider war extremely bad; but most of them consider domination by communism even worse than war. Few people actually want war. But there are other things they want even less. Historically the cultures and peoples that have been willing to pay any price at all to avoid war have probably been destroyed as separate cultures and peoples by other groups that were not willing to pay the price of cultural self-destruction in order to maintain peace. It is in the values in men's minds, not in their stereotypes, prejudices, hostilities, and aggressions, that one must, perhaps, look for the subjective "causes" of conflict. When these values are incompatible, so that one set can survive only at the expense of the other, we have intergroup conflict, no matter how the individual members may feel toward one another personally.

The UNESCO tensions project would probably learn a good deal about the beginnings of war in the minds of men if it addressed itself to the question of group hierarchies of values. In communities throughout the world let people be

370

asked to list their values (by the method, let us say, of paired comparisons). Using such an instrument it would be possible to determine the "war threshold" of different peoples, that is, how much or how little they were willing to pay in terms of their values to avoid war. Attempts to minimize war by changing subjective attitudes would have to concentrate on these value hierarchies, although it would seem presumptuous for outsiders to come in to tell people what they should value more or less than war. It might, presumably, be possible for a powerful propaganda agency to change our attitude toward communism so that we would not mind Russian aggression, or so that we would prefer appeasement to war. It is interesting that when we talk of changing attitudes it is always the other person's attitudes we conceive of as needing change.

C. POWER AND INFLUENCE AT WORK

The essence of inter-nation politics is, of course, the application of—and resistance to—influence attempts; some social scientists would even argue that influence is the essence of all social relations, and I would tend to agree. Yet it is a phenomenon which is seldom examined systematically, and about which there is little data and no adequate theory; as Cartwright put it recently, twentieth-century social scientists have been "soft on power."[1]

1. Two Models of Power

In the following two selections there are some signs of progress, however halting. That is, I would rate these as two of the most important efforts in the study of social influence, yet, even though they are separated by almost five years, there has been very little gain in empirical evidence. Because Dahl and Harsanyi are talking in very much the same terms (as well as in the same journal) there will be no need to comment separately upon the latter's paper.

THE CONCEPT OF POWER

Robert A. Dahl

That some people have more power than others is one of the most palpable facts of human existence. Because of this, the concept of power is as ancient and

---

[1]Dorwin Cartwright (ed.), *Studies in Social Power* (Ann Arbor: University of Michigan, Institute for Social Research, 1959), p. 2; he is specifically challenging social psychologists, but the charge would seem applicable to all of us. My own effort at least to conceptualize and interrelate the key variables is J. David Singer, "Inter-Nation Influence: A Formal Model," *American Political Science Review*, LVII (1963), 420-30.

From Robert A. Dahl, "The Concept of Power," *Behavioral Science*, II (1957), 201-15 (the footnotes and the bibliography and references have been omitted). Reprinted by permission of the author and the Mental Health Research Institute.

ubiquitous as any that social theory can boast. If these assertions needed any documentation, one could set up an endless parade of great names from Plato and Aristotle through Machiavelli and Hobbes to Pareto and Weber to demonstrate that a large number of seminal social theorists have devoted a good deal of attention to power and the phenomena associated with it. Doubtless it would be easy to show, too, how the word and its synonyms are everwhere embedded in the language of civilized peoples, often in subtly different ways: power, influence, control, pouvoir, puissance, Macht, Herrschaft, Gewalt, imperium, potestas, auctoritas, potentia, etc.

I shall spare the reader the fruits and myself the labor of such a demonstration. Reflecting on the appeal to authority that might be made does, however, arouse two suspicions: First (following the axiom that where there is smoke there is fire), if so many people at so many different times have felt the need to attach the label power, or something like it, to some Thing they believe they have observed, one is tempted to suppose that the Thing must exist; and not only exist, but exist in a form capable of being studied more or less systematically. The second and more cynical suspicion is that a Thing to which people attach many labels with subtly or grossly different meanings in many different cultures and times is probably not a Thing at all but many Things; there are students of the subject, although I do not recall any who have had the temerity to say so in print, who think that because of this the whole study of "power" is a bottomless swamp.

Paradoxical as it may sound, it is probably too early to know whether these critics are right. For, curiously enough, the systematic study of power is very recent, precisely because it is only lately that serious attempts have been made to formulate the concept rigorously enough for systematic study. If we take as our criterion for the efficiency of a scientific concept its usability in a theoretical system that possesses a high degree of systematic and empirical import, then we simply cannot say whether rigorous definitions of the concept of power are likely to be useful in theoretical systems with a relatively large pay-off in the hard coin of scientific understanding. The evidence is not yet in.

I think it can be shown, however, that to define the concept "power" in a way that seems to catch the central intuitively understood meaning of the word must inevitably result in a formal definition that is not easy to apply in concrete research problems; and therefore, operational equivalents of the formal definition, designed to meet the needs of a particular research problem, are likely to diverge from one another in important ways. Thus we are not likely to produce —certainly not for some considerable time to come—anything like a single, consistent, coherent "Theory of Power." We are much more likely to produce a variety of theories of limited scope, each of which employs some definition of power that is useful in the context of the particular piece of research or theory but different in important respects from the definitions of other studies. Thus we may never get through the swamp. But it looks as if we might someday get around it.

With this in mind, I propose first to essay a formal definition of power that will, I hope, catch something of one's intuitive notions as to what the Thing is. By "formal" I mean that the definition will presuppose the existence of observations of a kind that may not always or even frequently be possible. Second, I should like to indicate how operational definitions have been or might be modelled on the formal one for some specific purposes, and the actual or possible results of these operational definitions.

I should like to be permitted one liberty. There is a long and honorable history attached to such words as power, influence, control, and authority. For a great many purposes, it is highly important that a distinction should be made among them; thus to Max Weber, *"Herrschaft ist ... ein Sonderfall von Macht,"* Authority is a special case of the first, and Legitimate Authority a subtype of cardinal significance. In this essay I am seeking to explicate the primitive notion that seems to lie behind *all* of these concepts. Some of my readers would doubtless prefer the term "influence," while others may insist that I am talking about control. I should like to be permitted to use these terms interchangeably when it is convenient to do so, without denying or seeming to deny that for many other purposes distinctions are necessary and useful. Unfortunately, in the English language power is an awkward word, for unlike "influence" and "control" it has no convenient verb form, nor can the subject and object of the relation be supplied with noun forms without resort to barbaric neologisms.

POWER AS A RELATION AMONG PEOPLE

What is the intuitive idea we are trying to capture? Suppose I stand on a street corner and say to myself, "I command all automobile drivers on this street to drive on the right side of the road"; suppose further that all the drivers actually do as I "command" them to do; still, most people will regard me as mentally ill if I insist that I have enough power over automobile drivers to compel them to use the right side of the road. On the other hand, suppose a policeman is standing in the middle of an intersection at which most traffic ordinarily moves ahead; he orders all traffic to turn right or left; the traffic moves as he orders it to do. Then it accords with what I conceive to be the bedrock idea of power to say that the policeman acting in this particular role evidently has the power to make automobile drivers turn right or left rather than go ahead. My intuitive idea of power, then, is something like this: A has power over B to the extent that he can get B to do something that B would not otherwise do.

If Hume and his intellectual successors had never existed, the distinction between the two events above might be firmer than it is. But anyone who sees in the two cases the need to distinguish mere "association" from "cause" will realize that the attempt to define power could push us into some messy epistemological problems that do not seem to have any generally accepted solutions at the moment. I shall therefore quite deliberately steer clear of the possible identity of "power" with "cause," and the host of problems this identity might give rise to.

Let us proceed in a different way. First, let us agree that power is a relation, and that it is a relation among people. Although in common speech the term encompasses relations among people and other animate or inanimate objects, we shall have our hands full if we confine the relationship to human beings. All of the social theory I mentioned earlier is interesting only when it deals with this limited kind of relationship. Let us call the objects in the relationship of power, actors. Actors may be individuals, groups, roles, offices, governments, nation-states, or other human aggregates.

To specify the actors in a power relation—A has power over B—is not very interesting, informative, or even accurate. Although the statement that the President has (some) power over Congress is not empty, neither is it very useful. A much more complete statement would include references to (*a*) the source, domain, or *base* of the President's power over Congress; (*b*) the *means* or instruments used by the President to exert power over Congress; (*c*) the *amount* or extent of his power over Congress; and (*d*) the range or *scope* of his power over Congress. The base of an actor's power consists of all the resources— opportunities, acts, objects, etc.—that he can exploit in order to effect the behavior of another. Much of the best writing on power—Bertrand Russell is a good example—consists of an examination of the possible bases of power. A study of the war potential of nations is also a study of the bases of power. Some of the possible bases of a President's power over a Senator are his patronage, his constitutional veto, the possibility of calling White House conferences, his influence with the national electorate, his charisma, his charm, and the like.

In a sense, the base is inert, passive. It must be exploited in some fashion if the behavior of others is to be altered. The *means* or instruments of such exploitation are numerous; often they involve threats or promises to employ the base in some way and they may involve actual use of the base. In the case of the President, the means would include the *promise* of patronage, the *threat* of veto, the *holding* of a conference, the *threat* of appeal to the electorate, the *exercise* of charm and charisma, etc.

Thus the means is a mediating activity by A between A's base and B's response. The *scope* consists of B's responses. The scope of the President's power might therefore include such Congressional actions as passing or killing a bill, failing to override a veto, holding hearings, etc.

The *amount* of an actor's power can be represented by a probability statement: e.g., "the chances are 9 out of 10 that if the President promises a judgeship to five key Senators, the Senate will not override his veto," etc. Clearly the amount can only be specified in conjunction with the means and scope.

Suppose now we should wish to make a relatively complete and concise statement about the power of individual A over individual a (whom I shall call the respondent) with respect to some given scope of responses. In order to introduce the basic ideas involved, let us restrict ourselves to the 2 by 2 case, where the actor A does or does not perform some act and the respondent a does or does not "respond." Let us employ the following symbols:

$(A, w) = A$ does w. For example, the President makes a nation-wide television appeal for tax increases.

$(A, \overline{w}) = A$ does not do w.

(a, x) = a, the respondent, does x. For example, the Senate votes to increase
    taxes.

$(a, \bar{x})$ = a does not do x.

$P(u|v)$ = Probability that u happens when v happens.

Then a relatively complete and concise statement would be symbolized:

$$P(a, x|A, w) = p_1$$
$$P(a, x|A, \bar{w}) = p_2$$

Suppose now, that $p_1 = 0.4$ and $p_2 = 0.1$. Then one interpretation might be: "The probability that the Senate will vote to increase taxes if the President makes a nationwide television appeal for a tax increase is 0.4. The probability that the Senate will vote to increase taxes if the President does not make such an appeal is 0.1."

PROPERTIES OF THE POWER RELATION

Now let us specify some properties of the power relation.

1. A necessary condition for the power relation is that there exists a time lag, however small, from the actions of the actor who is said to exert power to the responses of the respondent. This requirement merely accords with one's intuitive belief that A can hardly be said to have power over a unless A's power attempts *precede* a's responses [emphasis added]. The condition, obvious as it is, is critically important in the actual study of power relations. Who runs the XYZ Corporation? Whenever the president announces a new policy, he immediately secures the compliance of the top officials. But upon investigation it turns out that every new policy he announces has first been put to him by the head of the sales department. Or again, suppose we had a full record of the times at which each one of the top Soviet leaders revealed his positions on various issues; we could then deduce a great deal about who is running the show and who is not. A good bit of the mystery surrounding the role of White House figures like Sherman Adams and Harry Hopkins would also be clarified by a record of this kind.

2. A second necessary condition is, like the first, obvious and nonetheless important in research: there is no "action at a distance." Unless there is some "connection" between A and a, then no power relation can be said to exist. I shall leave the concept of "connection" undefined, for I wish only to call attention to the practical significance of this second condition. In looking for a flow of influence, control, or power from A to a, one must always find out whether there is a connection, or an opportunity for a connection, and if there is not, then one need proceed no further. The condition, obvious as it is, thus has considerable practical importance for it enables one to screen out many possible relations quite early in an inquiry.

3. In examining the intuitive view of the power relation, I suggested that it seemed to involve a successful attempt by A to get a to do something he would not otherwise do. This hints at a way of stating a third necessary condition for the

power relation. Suppose the chances are about one out of a hundred that one of my students, Jones, will read *The Great Transformation* during the holidays even if I do not mention the book to him. Suppose that if I mention the book to him and ask him to read it, the chances that he will do so are still only one out of a hundred. Then it accords with my intuitive notions of power to say that evidently I have no power over Jones with respect to his reading *The Great Transformation* during the holidays—at least not if I restrict the basis of my action to mentioning the book and asking him (politely) to read it. Guessing this to be the case, I tell Jones that if he does not read the book over the holidays I shall fail him in my course. Suppose now that the chances he will read the book are about 99 out of 100. Assume further that nothing else in Jones's environment has changed, at least nothing relevant to his reading or not reading the book. Then it fully accords with my intuitive notions of power to say that I have some power over Jones's holiday reading habits. The basis of my power is the right to fail him in his course with me, and the means I employ is to invoke this threat.

Let me now set down symbolically what I have just said. Let

(D, w) = my threat to fail Jones if he does not read *The Great Transformation* during the holidays.

$(D, \overline{w})$ = no action on my part.

(J, x) = Jones reads *The Great Transformation* during the holidays.

Further, let

$p_1 = P(J, x|D, w)$ the probability that Jones will read *The Great Transformation* if I threaten to fail him.

$p_2 = P(J, x|D, \overline{w})$ the probability that Jones will read the book if I do not threaten to fail him.

Now let us define the *amount of power*. To avoid the confusion that might arise from the letter p, let us use the symbol M (from *Macht*) to designate the amount of power. Then, in accordance with the ideas set out in the illustration above, we define A's power over a, with respect to the response x, by means of w, as M, or, more fully:

$$M\left(\frac{A}{a} : w, x\right) = P(a, x|A, w) - P(a, x|A, \overline{w}) = p_1 - p_2$$

Thus in the case of myself and Jones, M (my power over Jones, with respect to reading a book during the holidays) is 0.98.

We can now specify some additional properties of the power relation in terms of M:

a. $p_1 = p_2$, then $M = 0$ and no power relation exists. The absence of power is thus equivalent to statistical independence.

b. M is at a maximum when $p_1 = 1$ and $p_2 = 0$. This is roughly equivalent to saying that A unfailingly gets B to do something B would never do otherwise.

c. M is at a minimum when $p_1 = 0$ and $p_2 = 1$. If negative values of M are to be included in the power relation at all—and some readers might object to the idea—then we shall have a concept of "negative power." This is not as foolish as it may seem, although one must admit that negative control of this kind is not ordinarily conceived of as power. If, whenever I ask my son to stay home on Saturday morning to mow the lawn, my request has the inevitable effect of inducing him to go swimming, when he would otherwise have stayed home, I do have a curious kind of negative power over him. The Legion of Decency sometimes seems to have this kind of power over movie-goers. Stalin was often said to wield negative power over the actions on appropriations for foreign aid by the American Congress. A study of the Senate that will be discussed later suggested that at least one Senator had this kind of effect on the Senate on some kinds of issues.

Note that the concept of negative power, and M as a measure, are both independent of the *intent* of A. The measure does, to be sure, require one to assign a positive and negative *direction* to the responses of the respondent; what one chooses as a criterion of direction will depend upon his research purposes and doubtless these will often include some idea as to the intent of the actors in a power relation. To take a specific case, p_1 *could* mean "the probability that Congress will defeat a bill if it is contained in the President's legislative program," and p_2 could mean "the probability that Congress will defeat such a bill if it is not contained in the President's legislative program." By assigning direction in this way, positive values of M would be associated with what ordinarily would be interpreted as meaning a "negative" influence of the President over Congress. The point of the example is to show that while the measure does require that direction be specified, the intent of A is not the only criterion for assigning direction.

MEASUREMENT OF SOCIAL POWER, OPPORTUNITY COSTS, AND THE THEORY OF TWO-PERSON BARGAINING GAMES

John C. Harsanyi

INTRODUCTION

Recent papers by Simon, by March, and by Dahl have suggested measuring person A's power over person B in terms of its actual or potential *effects*, that is, in terms of the changes that A causes or can cause in B's behavior. As Dahl puts it, A has power over B to the extent to which "he can get B to do something that B would not otherwise do."

From John C. Harsanyi, "Measurement of Social Power, Opportunity Costs, and the Theory of Two-Person Bargaining Games," *Behavioral Science*, VII (1962), 67-80 (the footnotes and the bibliography and references have been omitted). Reprinted by permission of the author and the Mental Health Research Institute.

As Simon and March have obtained very similar results, I shall restrict myself largely to summarizing Dahl's main conclusions. Dahl distinguishes the following constituents of the power relation:

(a) the *base* of power, i.e., the resources (economic assets, constitutional prerogatives, military forces, popular prestige, etc.) that *A* can use to influence *B*'s behavior;

(b) the *means* of power, i.e., the specific actions (promises, threats, public appeals, etc.) by which *A* can make actual use of these resources to influence *B*'s behavior;

(c) the *scope* of power, i.e., the set of specific actions that *A*, by using his means of power, can get *B* to perform; and finally

(d) the *amount* of power, i.e., the net increase in the probability of *B*'s actually performing some specific action *X*, due to *A*'s using his means of power against *B*.

If *A* has power over several individuals, Dahl adds a fifth constituent:

(e) the set of individuals over whom *A* has power—this we shall call the *extension* of *A*'s power.

Dahl points out that the power of two individuals can be compared in any of these five dimensions. Other things being equal, an individual's power is greater: (a) the greater his power base, (b) the more means of power available to him, and the greater (c) the scope, (d) the amount, and (e) the extension of his power. But Dahl proposes to use only the last three variables for the formal defintion and measurement of social power. He argues that what we primarily mean by great social power is an ability to influence many people (extension) in many respects (scope) and with a high probability (amount of power). In contrast, a large power base or numerous means of power are not direct measures of the extent of the influence or power that one person can exert over other persons; they are only instruments by which great power can be achieved and maintained, and are indicators from which we can normally *infer* the likely possession of great power by an individual.

Among the three variables of scope, amount, and extension, amount of power is the crucial one, in terms of which the other two can be defined. For the scope of *A*'s power over *B* is simply the set of specific actions *X* with respect to which *A* has a nonzero amount of power over *B*, i.e., the set of those actions *X* for which *A* can achieve a nonzero increase in the probability of these actions actually being performed by *B*. Similarly, the extension of *A*'s power is the set of specific individuals over whom *A* has power of nonzero scope and amount.

While the amount of power is a difference of two probabilities, and therefore is directly given as a *real number,* all other dimensions of power are directly given as lists of specific objects (e.g., a list of specific resources, a list of specific actions by *A* or by *B*, or a list of specific individuals over whom *A* has power). But Dahl and March suggest that at least in certain situations it will be worthwhile to develop

379

straight numerical measures for them by appropriate aggregating procedures – essentially by counting the number of comparable items in a given list, and possibly by assigning different weights to items of unequal importance (e.g., we may give more "marks" for power over an important individual than for power over a less important one). In other cases we may divide up a given list into several sublists and may assign a separate numerical measure to each of them, without necessarily aggregating all these numbers into a single figure. That is, we may characterize a give dimension of power not by a single number, but rather by a set of several numbers, i.e., a vector. (For instance, we may describe the extension of President de Gaulle's power by listing the numbers [or percentages] of deputies, of army officers of various ranks, of electors, etc., who support him, without trying to combine all these figures into one index number.)

Two Additional Dimensions of Social Power

A quantitative characterization of a power relation, however, in my view must include two more variables not mentioned in Dahl's list:

(f) the opportunity costs to A of attempting to influence B's behavior, i.e., the opportunity costs of using his power over B (and of acquiring this power over B in the first place if A does not yet possess the required power), which we shall call the *costs* of A's power over B; and

(g) the opportunity costs to B of refusing to do what A wants him to do, i.e., of refusing to yield to A's attempt to influence his behavior. As these opportunity costs measure the strength of B's incentives for yielding to A's influence, we shall call them the *strength* of A's power over B.

More precisely, the *costs* of A's power over B will be defined as the *expected value* (actuarial value) of the costs of his attempt to influence B. It will be a weighted average of the net total costs that A would incur if his attempt were successful (e.g., the costs of rewarding B), and of the net total costs that A would incur if his attempt were unsuccessful (e.g., the costs of punishing B).

Other things being equal, A's power over B is greater the smaller the costs of A's power and the greater the strength of A's power.

Both of these two cost variables may be expressed either in physical units (e.g., it may cost A so many bottles of beer or so many working hours to get B to adopt a given policy X; and again it may cost B so many bottles of beer or so many years' imprisonment if he does not adopt policy X), in monetary units (e.g., A's or B's relevant costs may amount to so many actual dollars, or at least may be equivalent to a loss of so many dollars for him), or in utility units. (In view of the theoretical problems connected with interpersonal comparisons of utility, and of the difficulties associated with utility measurement even for one individual, in practice the costs and the strength of power will usually be expressed in physical or in monetary units. But for the purposes of theoretical analysis the use of utility costs sometimes has important advantages, as we shall see.)

Unlike the power base and the means of power, which need not be included in the definition of the power relation, both the costs of power and the strength of power are essential ingredients of the definition of power. *A*'s power over *B* should be defined not merely as an ability by *A* to get *B* to do *X* with a certain probability *p*, but rather as an ability by *A* to achieve this at a certain total cost *u* to himself, by convincing *B* that *B* would have to bear the total cost *v* if he did not do *X*.

THE COSTS OF POWER

One of the main purposes for which social scientists use the concept of *A*'s power over *B* is for the description of the policy possibilities open to *A*. If we want to know the situation (or environment) which *A* faces as a decision-maker, we must know whether he can or cannot get *B* to perform a certain action *X*, and more specifically how sure he can be (in a probability sense) that *B* will actually perform this action. But a realistic description of *A*'s policy possibilities must include not only *A*'s ability or inability to get *B* to perform a certain action *X*, but also the *costs* that *A* has to bear in order to achieve this result. If two individuals are in a position to exert the same influence over other individuals, but if one can achieve this influence only at the cost of great efforts and/or financial or other sacrifices, while the other can achieve it free of any such costs, we cannot say in any useful sense that their power is equally great. Any meaningful comparison must be in terms of the influence that two individuals can achieve at comparable costs, or in terms of the costs they have to bear in order to achieve comparable degrees of influence.

For instance, it is misleading to say that two political candidates have the same power over two comparable constituencies if one needs much more electioneering effort and expenditure to achieve a given majority, even if in the end both achieve the same majorities; or that two businessmen have the same power over the city government if one can achieve favorable treatment by city officials only at the price of large donations to party funds, while the other can get the same favorable treatment just for the asking.

Of course, a power concept which disregards the costs of power is most inaccurate when the costs of using a given power become very high or even prohibitive. For instance, suppose that an army commander becomes a prisoner of enemy troops, who try to force him at gun point to give a radio order to his army units to withdraw from a certain area. He may very well have the power to give a contrary order, both in the sense of having the physical ability to do so and in the sense of there being a very good chance of his order being actually obeyed by his army units—but he can use this power only at the cost of his life. Though the scope, the amount, and the extension of his power over his soldiers would still be very great, it would clearly be very misleading in this situation to call him a powerful individual in the same sense as before his capture.

More generally, measurement of power merely in terms of its scope, amount, and extension tends to give counterintuitive results when the possessor of power has little or no real *opportunity* to actually use his power [emphasis added]. For example, take the case of a secretary who has to compile various reports for her employer, according to very specific instructions which leave her little actual choice as to how to prepare them. Suppose that her employer then uses these reports as a basis for very important decisions. Physically she could exert considerable influence on her employer's policies by omitting certain pieces of information from her reports, or including misleading information. In this sense, the scope and the amount of her power over her employer is considerable. But normally she will have little opportunity for using this power, and social scientists would hardly wish to describe her as a powerful individual, as they would have to do if they used Dahl's power concept without modification.

In terms of our own power concept, however, the secretary in question has little real power if all dimensions of her power are taken into account. Though she does have power of great scope and great amount over her employer, this fact is normally more than offset by the very high costs of using her power. If she intentionally submits misleading reports she probably will be found out very soon and will be dismissed and/or punished in other ways. Moreover, if she is a loyal employee such flagrant violation of her instructions would in itself involve very high disutility costs to her.

To conclude, a realistic quantitative description of A's power over B must include, as an essential dimension of this power relation, the costs to A of attempting to influence B's behavior.

THE STRENGTH OF POWER

While the costs of power must be included in the definition of our power concept in order to ensure its descriptive validity, the variable of *strength* of power must be included to ensure the usefulness of our power concept for explanatory purposes.

As March has pointed out about the concept of influence, one of the main analytical tasks of such concepts as influence or power (which essentially is an ability to exert influence) is to serve as *intervening variables* in the analysis of individual or social decision-making. Therefore we need a power or influence concept which enables us in the relevant cases to explain a decision by a given private individual or by an official of a social organization, in terms of the power or influence that another individual or some social group has over him. But fundamentally, the analysis of any human decision must be in terms of the variables on the basis of which the decision-maker concerned actually makes his decision — that is, in terms of the advantages and disadvantages he associates with alternative policies available to him. In order to explain why B adopts a certain policy X in accordance with A's wishes, we must know what *difference it makes* for B whether A is his friend or his enemy — or more generally, we must know the *opportunity costs* to B of not adopting policy X. Hence, if our power concept is to serve us as an explanatory intervening variable in the analysis of *B*'s decision to comply with *A*'s wishes, our power concept must include as one of its essential dimensions the opportunity costs to *B* of noncompliance, which measure the strength of *B*'s incentives to compliance and which we have called the strength of *A*'s power over *B*.

For instance, if we want to explain the decision of Senator Knowland to support a certain bill of the Eisenhower administration we must find out, among other things, which particular individuals or social groups influenced his decision, and to what extent. Now suppose that we have strong reasons to assume that it was President Eisenhower's personal intervention which made Senator Knowland change his mind and decide to support the bill in question. Then we still have to explain *how* the variables governing the Senator's decision were actually affected by the President's intervention. Did the President make a promise to him, i.e., did he attach new *advantages,* from the Senator's point of view, to the policy of supporting the bill? Or did the President make a threat, i.e., did he attach new *disadvantages* to the policy of opposing the bill? Or did the President supply new information, pointing out certain already *existing* advantages and/or disadvantages associated with these two policies, which the Senator had been insufficiently aware of before? In any case we must explain how the President's intervention increased the opportunity costs that Senator Knowland came to associate with opposing the bill.

If we cannot supply this information, then the mere existence of an influence or power relationship between President Eisenhower and Senator Knowland will not *explain* the latter's decision to support the bill. It will only pose a *problem* concerning this decision. (Why on earth did he comply with the President's request to support the bill, when it is known that he had many reasons to oppose it, and did actually oppose it for a while?)

There seem to be four main ways by which a given actor *A* can manipulate the incentives or opportunity costs of another actor *B*:

1. *A* may provide certain *new* advantages or disadvantages for *B*, subject to *no condition.* For instance, he may provide certain facilities for *B* which make it easier or less expensive for *B* to follow certain particular policy objectives desirable to *A*. (For example, country *A* may be able to induce country *B* to attack some third country *C*, simply by supplying arms to *B*, even if *A* supplies these arms "without any strings attached"—and in particular without making it a condition of her arms deliveries that *B* will actually attack *C*.) Or *A* may withdraw from *B* certain facilities that could help *B* in attaining policy objectives undesirable to *A*. More generally, *A* may provide for *B* goods or services complementary to some particular policy goal *X*, or competitive to policy goals alternative to *X*, so as to increase for *B* the net utility of *X*, or to decrease the net utility of its alternatives; or *A* may achieve similar results by depriving *B* of goods or services either competitive to *X* or complementary to its alternatives.

2. *A* may set up *rewards* and *punishments*, i.e. *new* advantages and disadvantages subject to certain *conditions* as to *B*'s future behavior.

3. *A* may supply *information* (or misinformation) on (allegedly) already *existing* advantages and/or disadvantages connected with various alternative policies open to *B*.

4. *A* may rely on his legitimate *authority* over *B* or on *B*'s personal *affection* for *A*, which make *B* attach *direct disutility* to the very act of disobeying *A*.

Of course, in a situation where *A* has certain power over *B*, either party can be mistaken about the true opportunity costs to him of various alternatives. Therefore both in discussing the costs of *A*'s power over *B*, and in discussing the strength of his power, we must distinguish between *objective* costs and *perceived* costs—between what these costs actually are and what the individual bearing these costs thinks them to be. For the purpose of a formal definition of the power relation, the *costs* of *A*'s power over *B* have to be stated as the *objective* costs that an attempt to influence *B* would actually entail upon *A,* while the *strength* of *A*'s power over *B* has to be stated in terms of the costs of noncompliance as *perceived* by *B* himself. The reason is that the costs of *A*'s power serve to describe the objective policy possibilities open to *A,* whereas the strength of *A*'s power serves to explain *B*'s subjective motivation for compliant behavior. (Of course, a full description of a given power situation would require listing both objective and perceived costs for both participants.)

2. Relative Power and Its Effects

Though power remains, even in the contemporary phase of the international system, the central and dominant phenomenon, it is of interest here only insofar as it permits an examination of the types of relationships which are generated by the exercise of power. In the next paper, Dubin, a sociologist, presents a fairly general theory of industrial conflict, with power as his central organizing variable. Even though he presents no operational (as distinguished from anecdotal) data, he suggests an insight which may be highly relevant to the student of international relations: that the relative power of the two protagonists is not the only power ratio of importance. Equally crucial to the outcome of conflict in any system is the power ratio between the larger system and the conflicting component actors: what is referred to as the "autonomy" of the *sub*systems vis-à-vis the larger system.

Worth bearing in mind here is the degree to which political scientists are willing to assume the heuristic value of analogizing from labor-management relations, while expressing greater skepticism when the model is one of interpersonal or other intergroup relations. Why this should be so is not altogether clear, unless it is because the size discrepancy between a nation and an industrial union is smaller than that between a nation and, for example, an experimental small group. Though size may be a good predictor of behavioral difference, there are enough *other* variables to justify a relatively uniform skepticism of all analogy.

Be that as it may, this selection should suggest a number of fascinating hypotheses in which power is the independent variable and conflict is the variable to which we are predicting. When Dubin speaks of "state," "society," or "industrial institution," it is necessary to think in terms of the international system; and when he speaks of "labor" or "management," to posit any two nations or blocs of nations.

A THEORY OF CONFLICT AND POWER IN UNION-MANAGEMENT RELATIONS

Robert Dubin

Two concepts are almost universally used by analysts of union-management relations. The first is that of *conflict;* the second is *power*. In this article we examine these twin concepts and present models of their relationships.

The Analysis of Industrial Conflict

Conflict may be defined as the actual or threatened use of force in any continuing social relationship. Force is the attempt to override opposition by an act designed to produce injury to the other party. Specifically, in collective bargaining the typical manifestations of force are: the threat or carrying out of a strike and lockout; the threat or carrying out of cessation of face-to-face negotiations; the threat or carrying out of slowdowns, sabotage, physical seizure of property (as in the sitdown strike); and the implied or actual use of verbal abuse, in its many forms, toward negotiators of the other side.

In our society, conflict has been a characteristic social process in all realms of life. We still tend to have attitudes of dismay and distaste for it, even though experience makes it abundantly clear that the ubiquity of conflict has *not* torn the society apart and made it incapable of functioning.

The data of industrial life reveal many kinds of characteristic conflicts.

From Robert Dubin, "A Theory of Conflict and Power in Union-Management Relations," *Industrial and Labor Relations Review,* XIII (1960), 501-18 (the footnotes have been omitted). Reprinted by permission of the author and *Industrial and Labor Relations Review.*

Although the most obvious is that between company and union, there are other kinds of industrial conflict as well: between functionally specialized departments within a company; between cliques fighting for controlling positions within business firms; among factions within the ranks of labor unions; among ethnic and racial groups within the employed population; between work groups in the daily round of working life; and the more disguised form of conflict among business competitors in a product market. This listing does not exhaust the range of conflicts observable and already studied by students of working life. The list does make clear, however, that conflict is a continuous kind of social interaction in and around productive organizations.

Students have tried to make analytical sense out of industrial conflict in two general ways. (1) A number of students have analyzed conflict by relating it to other modes of interaction between management and unions. (2) Where attention has centered on reducing conflict, the analytical framework used at arriving at the "cure" is derived from a model of the causes of conflict. Let us briefly examine these two approaches to understanding industrial conflict.

In contrasting conflict with other modes of group interaction, students of labor relations have generally pointed to cooperation, collusion, competition, accommodation, and assimilation as characterizing the essential types of interaction between company and union. Where conflict occurs, it tends to be viewed as the breakdown of other modes of union-management relations. Conflict is thus given the standing of a residual form of interaction, a second level of relationship used as a last resort.

An alternative formulation, still viewing conflict as a secondary level of interaction, sees the inception of collective bargaining characterized by conflict. In this alternative formulation, the subsequent evolution of collective bargaining is considered to represent a transmutation of conflict into other, more primary, modes of union-management interaction.

Where attention has been focused on reducing conflict, two principal analytical approaches have been used. The first has been to proclaim that all those engaged in a productive enterprise really can share values and, once perceiving these shared values, will behave in ways to eliminate the conflict which destroys the values or prevents their fulfillment. The second approach has been to view conflict as a psychological phenomenon, whose elimination is attempted by removing the stimuli which call forth conflict behavior.

The appeal to common values takes the general form of asserting that the production of goods and services is the reason for the existence of work organizations. All those who engage in the enterprise are willy-nilly "partners in production," however diverse may be their individual contributions and their respective payoffs. It follows that if everyone believes that this sense of partnership must be shared by all participants in the work organization, then the process of sharing should serve to eliminate constant frictions and conflicts which inhibit the achievement of this goal.

The main difficulty with this approach is that it implies a questionable social dynamic. The fundamental assumption of this position, that social values or goals actually guide behavior, becomes doubtful when viewed against the history of general social values. Democracy and equality are shared values in our society, whose meaning in daily life leads to quite different behaviors for today's southern white citizen and his Negro neighbor. Individualism has been celebrated in Western thought for several centuries and is still a strongly held value, even among contemporary "organization men." Success has frequently been considered a dominant American value, but its consequences for behavior have been repeatedly shown to be highly variable among different institutions of American society.

In short, the burden of proof still remains with those who conclude that values guide action. The alternative formulation, that action results from imperative conditions imposed by the situation in which behavior takes place, is still a viable, if not a preferred, theory.

Without more elaborate analysis of the functions of values in human life, we can simply conclude that the belief that conflict may be eliminated through the sharing of common values results from an inadequate theory of the relations between values and action.

The second commonly used approach to the psychological analysis of conflict sees it as the product of individual orientation in circumstances of frustration. The individual caught up in a social situation in which "normal" behavior is ineffective becomes aggressive, hostile, and turns the social relationship into a conflict situation. What has *not* been established, and this is crucial, is that conflict between groups is caused by the same psychological mechanisms and takes the same course as conflict among individuals.

CONFLICT BETWEEN GROUPS

When we turn to an examination of conflict between groups the psychological approach has limited usefulness. Unless we work with a kind of old fashioned "group mind" construct, which becomes the locus of feelings of frustration and corresponding aggression, it is difficult, if not impossible, to find a useful way of conceptualizing psychological mechanisms in group conflict. Aggressive behavior is used, of course, to carry out industrial conflict. Aggressive behavior, however, does not arise out of the collective conscience of a group of industrial workers frustrated by the conditions of their employment. We can characterize the difference by saying that workers do not demand more wages solely because of their perceived dissatisfactions with work. On the other hand, the demand for more pay may make use of very aggressive actions to achieve it.

We have to move to an entirely different level of analysis when we examine conflicts between groups. The starting point is to ask: "What is the conflict about?" Here the answer seems to center on gaining a policy to guide future behavior. The union contract is a statement of policy for the future; so is a personnel program. Unions and management are vitally interested in the control of policies governing the conditions of employment in the private sectors of the economy, achieved through collective bargaining or personnel policy. They are equally concerned with public policies affecting the same realm through legislation and administration of laws. Once we perceive group conflict as centering on the content of public or private policies affecting group members, we then place conflict within the social structure rather than the psyches of the actors.

The history of union-management relations makes abundantly clear that *the control of policy in the public and private sectors of the economy is the stuff over which the parties are fighting* [emphasis added]. Viewed in the context of the social structure, we can conclude that conflict is one process by which public and private policy is determined. It is, of course, not the only method, being coordinate with bargaining, arbitration, compulsion, and other methods for reaching consensus on policy.

Put in its broadest terms one of the important functions of conflict in industrial relations is *to affect the direction and amount of social* [systemic] *change* [emphasis added]. New policies established through industrial conflict may determine the direction in which the future of industrial life evolves; or this conflict may affect the rate at which changes in a given direction take place. Conflict in process may be costly. The results of industrial conflict are changes in the direction toward which society is moving.

If this kind of formulation of conflict makes sense, then we come full round by concluding that conflict, however distasteful it may be in process, has a consequence that is useful for the society, namely, to determine the next steps it will take. An older tradition in sociology made conflict a social process *coordinate* with competition, accommodation, assimilation, and cooperation. We may have to go back at least as far as this tradition to find a theoretical conceptualization useful in understanding and making sense out of industrial conflict.

*   *   *   *   *

POWER AND CONFLICT

The relations between power and conflict in union-management relations will now be examined from two standpoints. Attention will first be directed at the amount of industrial conflict produced by the *joint* power of companies and unions in relation to state power over the industrial institution [emphasis added]. We will then consider variations in the amount of industrial conflict in individual bargaining situations as a consequence of the balance of power between the parties.

Conflict in the Social System

The state exercises some control over all its constituent institutions. Participants in an institution also have some control of, or power over, institutional functions. The balance between state power and the power of institutional participants over the functioning institution is our first focus of attention.

For the industrial institution we predict that the amount of *conflict between its participants,* management and unions, will *increase* as the amount of *their joint power over the institution increases* in relation to the power of the state [emphasis added]. That is, where there are things of importance to control, then the contest over their control will generate conflict. On the other hand, where control of important areas of industrial behavior is beyond the reach of the parties, as for example, when it is in the hands of the state, then there is nothing to fight about, and the amount of conflict between the parties will be correspondingly reduced.

In Figure 1 we have suggested the idealized relationship between the amount of industrial conflict in the society and the ratio of power of companies plus unions to state power over the industrial institution. The curve suggests a positive relationship between the sum of power of unions and companies over institutional functioning, and the amount of conflict between them. It is further indicated that the curve is of the general logistic form. The upper limit is viewed as reaching some asymptote [curve approaches but does not meet axis] on the general grounds that the society as a whole never abdicates completely its control over any constituent institution. Thus, the amount of power of the institutional participants can never be absolute in their institutional setting. The asymptote for the lower section of the curve is suggested by the general conclusion that the

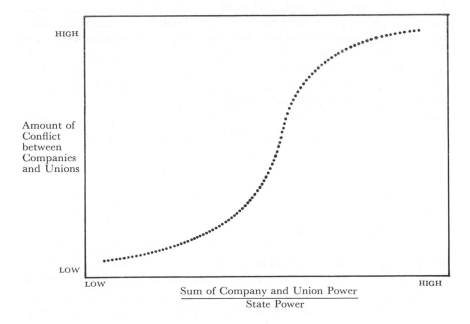

Figure 1. Conflict between companies and unions in relation to the ratio of their joint power to state control over the industrial institution

participants in an institution are never completely powerless; they do control some functions of the institution, however minor they may be.

*   *   *   *   *

Conflict in Collective Bargaining

We now shift attention to bargaining in the individual firm. We are here concerned with the amount of conflict as it relates to the disparity between company and union in their control of (power over) industrial functions. In this analysis it is immaterial whether the company or union has the greater amount of power.

Two broad categories of collective bargaining issues are defined for analytical purposes. *Fundamental* issues are those not yet incorporated in collective bargaining. Control over the functions defining such issues may be in the hands of either party exclusively, or located at some other point in the social system. *Conventional* issues are defined as those which have been included in collective bargaining through past negotiation between the parties and incorporated in union contracts. Differences between the parties may arise as to future solutions of those issues which have previously been settled, and therefore, conflict may be employed in achieving new solutions.

In Figure 2, the curve representing the amount of conflict as a function of disparity in power of company and union on *fundamental* issues expresses an inverse relationship. That is, where there is *great disparity* between the individual *power* of the company and the union over the productive institution, the amount of *conflict* between them will be relatively *low* [emphasis added]. Conversely, where there is *little discrepancy* between company and union in control over the institutional functions, the amount of *conflict* over fundamental issues is predicted as relatively *high* [emphasis added].

Given great disparity in power between the parties, the weaker would not be inclined to introduce fundamental issues because of the high probability of losing. The more powerful party, on the other hand, would certainly not introduce fundamental issues that might broaden the scope of functions over which control would be shared with the weaker party. Thus, there is a mutual reluctance to introduce fundamental issues where a great deal of power disparity is recognized by both parties. Hence, the prediction that little conflict would result over fundamental issues with great power disparity.

At the other end of the spectrum of power disparity, these calculations of outcome of open conflict on fundamental issues are materially modified by the relative parity in power of the parties. Either side would calculate that the probable outcome of conflict over a fundamental issue is uncertain, due to the relative equality in power of each side. Consequently, both sides would be more likely to risk open conflict in introducing or resisting the inclusion of fundamental issues in the bargaining situation. This provides the rationale for the negatively inclined slope to the curve relating power of the parties and amount of conflict between them over fundamental issues.

Consider now the relation between Figure 1 and Figure 2. From Figure 1 we conclude that the *joint* power of companies and unions over the industrial institution, if high in relation to the power of the state, will result in considerable conflict. From Figure 2 we conclude that if the disparity between a company and union in power over the industrial institution is great, there will be relatively little conflict over fundamental issues in collective bargaining. Thus, an apparent anomaly is posed. Suppose, as in pre-New Deal United States, the sum of union and company power is high in relation to state power, but that this sum is made up of much company power and little union power. From the analysis of Figure 1 alone, we would conclude that there might be considerable industrial conflict.

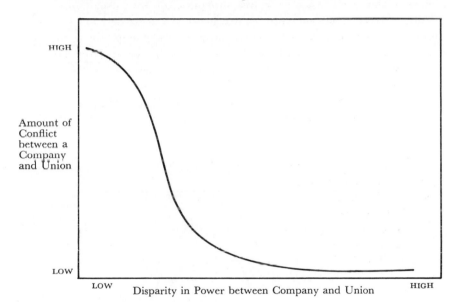

Figure 2. Amount of conflict on *fundamental* issues between a company and union in relation to the disparity of power between them

But from the analysis of Figure 2 (assuming almost all companies had much power and almost all unions had little power) we would conclude that there would be little conflict on *fundamental* issues. The predictions do not necessarily cancel each other. The relative weakness of unions in pre-New Deal days meant that they were making little progress in winning fundamental issues in collective bargaining. The conflict that did occur in this early era was largely over conventional issues. We conclude, then, that the imbalance between company and union power has a dampening effect on industrial conflict over fundamental issues in an era where the sum of their joint power over the industrial institution is great.

When we turn to a consideration of the relationship between power and conflict on *conventional* issues, the accompanying Figure 3 displays the predicted linkage. It will be recalled that conventional issues are those already within the scope of collective bargaining and are issues on which balance points between the demands of the parties need to be found. Our prediction is this: As the disparity increases between the total power held by each party, up to about the mid-point of power disparity, the amount of conflict on conventional issues will also increase to a maximum, and then rapidly fall off.

Disputes over conventional issues represent disagreements on means for accomplishing already agreed-upon ends. The collective bargaining problem is to find some acceptable balance point between the stated and visible disparate demands of the parties. On conventional issues the parties are already half way down the road to agreement because they have both defined the issue as requiring joint acceptance of a compromise on means for its solution.

Under circumstances of power parity between the parties, the weapon of conflict is largely neutralized as the parties focus attention on the substance of the issue between them. With power parity, conflict methods employed on conventional issues have the face appearance of irrational behavior by the parties, since the range of determinant solutions is already visible, falling within the limits of maximum demands of both sides. This leads to the prediction that conflict will be minimum on conventional issues where power of the parties is balanced.

In the mid-range of power disparity, Figure 3 suggests that conflict between the parties will be maximum. We assume that each side is aware of the distribu-

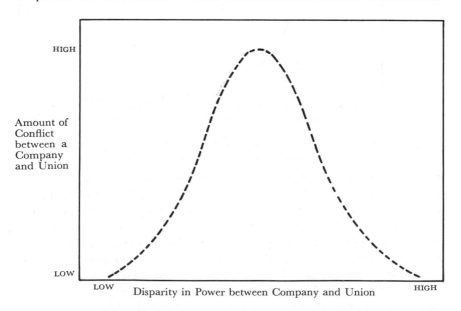

Figure 3. Amount of conflict on *conventional* issues between a company and union in relation to the disparity of power between them

tion of power between them and the general amount of the disparity. Then, for a conventional issue, the party having less power can anticipate the out-come of negotiations as favorable (for example, securing gains beyond those already attained, or beyond the best offer of the other side) only if extraordinary means are used to accomplish this. That is, *the perception of inequality* of power in the situation leads the weaker bargainer to consider pressure techniques of sufficient threat to make it seem desirable for the stronger party to eschew some of its power and make concessions [emphasis added]. For the more powerful bargainer, the knowledge of power advantage will be a deterrent to making concessions until the conflict methods employed to achieve them begin to hurt. Consequently, the more powerful party will accept the challenge of conflict as the means for resolving the issue, with some confidence of triumphing.

Beyond the mid-point on the power disparity scale, it is indicated that the amount of conflict rapidly falls off. Within this range of much power disparity the weaker bargainer would tend to view conflict methods as an improbable means for securing gains on conventional issues. There is no reason to predict that the stronger bargainer will make any new concessions under the impact of conflict methods employed by the weaker party. There is similarly no reason for the stronger party to fear open conflict and to bargain away some of its power in order to avoid the effects of conflict. Consequently, conflict as a mode of interaction in solving problems of conventional issues appears improbable under circumstances of much power disparity.

POWER DISPARITY AND TOTAL CONFLICT

If we now put fundamental and conventional issues on the same scale of power disparity, and the same scale of amount of conflict, the pattern depicted in Figure 4 emerges. The curve showing total conflict between the parties over fundamental *and* conventional issues is made up of the sum of conflict for both kinds of issues.

Figure 4 shows three critical features. (1) Total conflict drops sharply beyond the mid-range of power disparity. (2) There is a dip in total conflict at the point of moderate disparity in power. (3) At any given point in time there may be very sudden shifts in the amount of conflict, depending on whether fundamental or conventional issues are the focus of attention of the parties. Let us examine each of these points in turn.

The sharp drop in the amount of total conflict beyond the mid-point of power disparity can be articulated with the myth of the general strike and revolutionary activity in general. Where labor leaders perceived the balance of power as overwhelmingly favoring management across the board in the industrial institu-tion (that is, in all companies) then only heroic measures, like revolution, are viewed as the solution to the problems of power distribution, and adopted as the strategy of the weaker party. This should presumably be equally true of manage-ment use of the state and capture of political power through a totalitarian

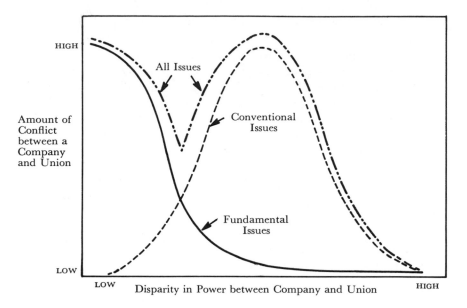

Figure 4. Amount of total conflict between a company and union as the sum of conflict on fundamental and conventional issues

regime, where management collectively perceives itself as the weaker in total power over the industrial institution.

The dip in the curve of total conflict at the lower quartile of power disparity suggests interesting analytical problems. The curve predicts that the total amount of conflict will be minimized over the lower half of the range of power disparity when one side or the other has some power advantage. Thus, if social policy demands minimum conflict between antagonists in the industrial institution, the predicted point at which this occurs is *not* the point of absolute power parity between them. The Wagner Act, for example, had as its stated policy balancing the power of companies and their organized employees *and* promoting industrial peace. If our analysis, as represented in Figure 4, is correct, then the optimum condition of industrial peace (when both management and unions are strong) is reached when there remains some mild power disparity between the parties.

What is the consequence of this result? The result seems to make sense when we note that the major contribution to industrial conflict in the lower quartile of power disparity is from disputes on fundamental issues. Fundamental issues have already been defined as those changing the scope of collective bargaining. They are additions to the previously accepted issues in bargaining. As such they are the vehicles of major social change in the bargaining relationship. Change is always disruptive of institutional arrangements, however desirable the goals of the change may be. A moderate brake is imposed on the rate of such change by some degree of power disparity between the bargainers. Thus, we would

394

conclude that mild power disparity between the parties to collective bargaining is functional in maintaining stability of the industrial institution because it serves to reduce the amount of total conflict between them.

The formulation of Figure 4 also proves useful when we examine the volatile character of collective bargaining. At any given time in the bargaining situation there may be very dramatic shifts from open conflict to serious negotiation designed to resolve the issues before the parties. If we examine the left-hand portion of Figure 4, it will be noted that the amount of conflict may be dramatically reduced in a bargaining situation, if the issue in dispute is shifted from a fundamental one to a conventional one. Thus, granting that there is little disparity in the power of the bargainers (and this is what the left portion of the x-scale tells us) their shift from one kind of an issue to the other would significantly reduce the amount of conflict between them at that point in time.

The same type of situation obtains if the middle portion of Figure 4 is examined. Here, however, a sudden shift in attention of the bargainers from conventional issues to fundamental issues may markedly reduce the amount of conflict in the negotiation sessions.

It is also predicted that the volatile shift in the amount of conflict at a given point in collective bargaining would occur in the opposite direction if the change in kinds of issues were reversed from those just examined. That is, with low disparity in power between the parties, a shift from conventional issues to fundamental issues could suddenly increase the amount of conflict. If there is a medium disparity in power between the parties, a change from fundamental issues to conventional issues might materially increase the amount of conflict.

In general, we conclude that the magnitude of conflict is not solely related to the amount of disparity in power between the parties. It is also a product, at any given point in time, of the focus of attention of the bargainers on either conventional issues or fundamental issues. If their attention can shift rapidly from fundamental issues to conventional issues, and back again, this can have dramatic consequences for the amount of conflict in the relationship when the shift occurs.

This now suggests that the formulation represented in Figure 4 is one way of visualizing two quite disparate aspects of collective bargaining. If we consider the total curve of conflict as it relates to the disparity in power, we secure a generalized picture which may be useful in characterizing a continuous and prolonged relationship. If, on the other hand, attention focuses on much smaller units of time in the bargaining relationship, then the left-hand half of Figure 4, and the x-like intersecting curves portrayed there, suggest a model for analyzing the volatile character of conflict in hour-by-hour or day-by-day bargaining.

ALTERNATIVES TO CONFLICT

There are factors in addition to the disparity of power between bargainers that enter into the amount of conflict in a particular union-management relationship.

We have already examined the consequences of the bargainers' shift of attention from fundamental to conventional issues as this affects the amount of conflict between them. Alternative modes of interaction, as these are related to the shape of the conflict-power curves, must also be considered.

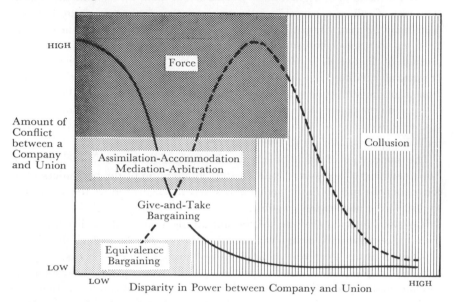

Figure 5. The relation of substitute forms of interaction to the curves of industrial conflict between a company and union

In Figure 5 the essential features of Figure 4 are duplicated, eliminating only the curve for total conflict. Superimposed on the two curves of Figure 5 there is a set of boxes, each labelled as an area of particular kinds of collective bargaining interaction. The topmost box represents the area in which force is most likely to be used in bargaining, in accordance with the preceding arguments. The middle area box is labelled the area of assimilation, accommodation, mediation, and arbitration. In terms of the power disparity scale, this area is approximately one-quarter of the way from the lower end. This indicates low, moderate disparity in power between the parties.

The proposition that this level of power disparity is a condition of mutual assimilation and accommodation between the parties, or their willingness to turn to third parties for mediation and arbitration, calls on the following arguments.

Mutual Assimilation and Accommodation

The bargaining strategy in mutual assimilation and accommodation differs for the weaker and the stronger power holders. For the weaker power holder, the posture of being assimilated or accommodated by the stronger party can be rationalized as a way of translating fundamental issues into future conventional

396

issues. That is, the weaker party is willing to accept the definition of the issue by the stronger, simply to get it into the realm of the union contract, and thus making it a conventional issue. With possible future favorable shifts in power towards the weaker party, better bargains on the issue can be anticipated. On conventional issues the weaker party may accept assimilation and accommodation as a means for deferring direct bargaining on the issue in the hope that a future shift in power in its favor will improve the outcome of such direct bargaining.

From the standpoint of the stronger bargainer the granting of an accommodation to the weaker, or the assimilation of the weaker to its position may represent a subjective working out of a social psychological posture of *noblesse oblige*. It is anticipated that this display of *noblesse oblique* will perhaps contribute to "understanding" and "reasonableness" on the part of the weaker bargainer in future relations.

Where third parties are brought into the bargaining situation, as in mediation and arbitration, the motivations of the stronger and weaker group also differ. For the weaker bargainer, the acceptance of arbitration or mediation is based on the belief that nothing more can be lost than the last offer of the stronger party, and conceivably something more may be gained through the mediator's recommendations or the arbitration award. For the party holding the greater power in the situation, the acceptance of mediation and arbitration may be the result of a desire to get the issues settled, and a willingness to risk some of its power position should the mediator's recommendations or the arbitration award favor the weaker bargainer.

Assimilation and accommodation are forms of interaction which the parties substitute for conflict. Similarly, bringing in a third party to help resolve differences, as in mediation and arbitration, replaces conflict as a form of interaction. The very possibility of substituting other forms of interaction for conflict makes clear the continuity among all forms of bargaining interaction.

Give-and-Take Bargaining

The next box in Figure 5 is labelled give-and-take bargaining. Give-and-take bargaining occurs where two noncomparable issues are considered simultaneously. In this type of bargaining, solutions to the noncomparable issues are traded off against each other. One party may accept its maximum, or near-maximum, demands on one issue, at the same time making similar concessions to the other party on the coupled issue. This typically occurs where so-called "package deals" constitute the basis for reaching collective bargaining agreements.

Package deals usually have two parts. The manifest part (incorporated in the agreement) is what each side gains on its favored issues. The latent part is what has been originally demanded at an early stage of the bargaining, and then traded off by each side for gains on noncomparable issues. The latent part of package deals becomes visible only by examining the history of a particular bargaining agreement. It is often the strategy of bargainers on both sides to "pad" initial demands with issues that can become trading pawns in give-and-take bargaining.

On conventional issues, give-and-take bargaining takes the form of "you take one, we'll take another" negotiation. For example, the employer's wage offer might be accepted in return for strengthening the union security clause, or health and welfare benefits may be improved if the union will make concessions on work rules. On fundamental issues, negotiations follow the same characteristic pattern in which new areas may be incorporated in an agreement by matching "pet" demands of each side.

The social roots of motivation that enter into give-and-take bargaining relate to the relative power equality of the parties. Where power is balanced, there is an *ethic of symmetry* characterizing the bargaining situation. This ethic declares that the gains of each side to the bargain should roughly balance, or be symmetrical over the entire contract. The number and importance of issues won by each party should roughly balance out, as should the number of issues each loses. We use the term "should" advisedly. It is a "should" from the perceptive stance of the bargainers, not from that of the outside observer. Hence, it is not the observer's value judgment being denoted, but that of the participants. The ethic of symmetry in give-and-take bargaining is generated by the conditions of the bargaining situation, and particularly the relative power equality of the parties.

Equivalence Bargaining

The box in the lower left hand portion of Figure 5 designates the lower portion of the curve of conventional issues as the area of "equivalence" bargaining. In "equivalence" bargaining, the single issue remains constantly in the attention of the negotiators, and they are constrained to compromise between the two stated positions of each side in reaching their solution. This is called "equivalence" bargaining because the solution is determined for a single issue, and falls between previously established upper and lower limits, stated in the initial demands of each party.

A good deal of collective bargaining on conventional issues is of precisely this sort, where "splitting the difference" can be the commonest balance point of compromise. This kind of bargaining, of course, minimizes the use of force and is therefore low on the scale of conflict. It is also characteristic of a situation in which there is minimal disparity in the power of the bargainers.

The ethic of symmetry would also seem to be a characteristic of equivalence bargaining. In this instance, however, the ethic is a constraint toward splitting differences, making the middle range between the extreme demands of the parties the most probable area of compromise.

398

Collusive Bargaining

The area of collusion is illustrated in Figure 5 as pertaining to fundamental and conventional issues under circumstances of wide disparity in power. Collusion is a situation in which two parties make an agreement directed against a third or "sucker" party. In collective bargaining the third party may be the work force for whom the agreement is negotiated, or business competitors.

Where collusive or "sweetheart" agreements are made between a company and a union organizer it is usually under circumstances of little labor power and much management power. The intent of the power holder in making such an agreement flows from the assumption that the body of workers, presumably its beneficiary, will be suckered into a tractable stance beneficial to company operations. Management is willing to risk some control over business functions in the hope that by sharing them with collusively-inclined union organizers, labor peace and worker complacency may be the payoff.

Where the union is clearly the stronger power holder in a situation, collusive agreements may be forced on an employer either on grounds that he can thereby equalize competition in the industry through total unionization (because of union force and sanctions against noncooperating employers—as in local service industries), or because the union threat of force against noncooperation will worsen the individual company's competitive position vis à vis the firms which have entered into the collusive agreements with the union.

SUMMARY

This analysis provides models for the full range of the two principal curves depicting the relationship between disparities in power and the amount of conflict in industrial relations. In particular, we have considered the strategies involved under varying circumstances of power balance as this alone would affect conflict between the parties. We then examined in more detail the possibilities of substituting other interaction processes for conflict in the resolution of collective bargaining issues. These two analyses together seem to give plausibility to the particular models here offered for the relationship between power and conflict in union-management relations. The amount of conflict not only changes with shifts in the disparity in power between union and management, but it is also modified by the possibility of substituting other kinds of interactions between the parties. The models suggest that the direct relationship between power and conflict, on the one hand, and the points at which substitution of nonconflict methods enters into the bargaining on the other, supplement each other. Together they constitute a theoretical model of conflict and power in union-management relationships.

D. TWO STYLES OF CONFLICT BEHAVIOR

When two or more actors with some incompatible interests come into contact, the interaction is, by definition, competitive. When both parties become aware of (a) the existence of the other, and (b) the presence of incompatible interests, and if they then allocate any resources to defeating or besting the other, conflict results. Thus, it is relatively safe to say that conflict is inherent in almost all social systems and that almost all social relationships will have some element of conflict. The problem, of course, is not the elimination of conflict, but the *management* of it, so that the interaction does not become destructive of the very interests it is meant to protect. In the sections following this, two interesting approaches to the management of conflict will be looked at, but first there are presented two papers that illustrate the range of behaviors and strategies that the actors are likely to use in inter-nation as well as other social conflicts.

1. Tactical Sophistication in a One-Shot Conflict

One of the really difficult problems for parties in conflict is the choice between emphasizing long-run or short-run considerations. Leaving ethics aside for the moment, the calculating actor must decide whether it is either possible or desirable to eliminate his adversary. If both conditions seem to obtain, then one is free to use all ploys, gambits, and means which seem likely to succeed. There is no need to ask questions regarding future relations with the adversary, because the future is almost irrelevant: victory is what counts.

400

TAXICAB RATE WAR:
COUNTERPART OF INTERNATIONAL CONFLICT

RALPH CASSADY, JR.

Business rivalry has been likened unto war even in its ordinary aspects. This similarity is accentuated when firms become engaged in price warfare. It is interesting that price wars possess many of the elements of armed conflict — "enemy" moves in the form of price reductions which may be interpreted as unfriendly by a competitor; ultimata followed perhaps by countermoves by firms which are adversely affected: the use of strategems to mislead the "enemy"; additional hostile activity in the form of further reductions or threatened reductions; the dissemination of propaganda to influence public opinion; the "signing" of peace treaties; and, finally, postwar problems. A taxicab rate war waged in Hawthorne, California, in 1949 included most of these elements, as well as others seldom found in price wars. It therefore makes an interesting case study for students of conflict.

Price wars involving taxicab service appear to be rare, partly perhaps because in most communities rates are regulated by city ordinance and operators are not free to price as they please. However, a very interesting price battle occurred among cab companies in Hawthorne, California, in the fall of 1949. Three taxicab firms were serving the community at the time — City Cab Company, Yellow Cab Company, and Veteran Cab Company. The cab fare charged by all three companies before the "war" was 30¢ per flag drop and 30¢ per mile.

INCEPTION OF THE "WAR"

The price dispute started, according to reports, when one company offered a $10 ride book for $9 (although one of the participants stated that this initial offer was a $6 book for $5). The owners of the rival companies tried to persuade the price-cutter to rescind the bargain offer. When this course failed, one of the rivals countered by reducing his rate to a flat 25¢ per ride anywhere in town. The latter also let it be known that, if his price were met, he would drastically undercut this rate (to 10¢). After some weeks, the competing cab concerns (the original cutter and one of the two operators who attempted to persuade him to rescind the reduction) retaliated with a flat fee of 10¢ per ride. The initiator of the 25¢ rate continued to maintain his price at that level, although he continually threatened to reduce rates below those charged by competitors.

From Ralph Cassady, Jr., "Taxicab Rate War: Counterpart of International Conflict," *The Journal of Conflict Resolution*, I (1957), 364-68 (the footnotes and the bibliography and references have been omitted). Reprinted by permission of the author and *The Journal of Conflict Resolution*.

STRATEGY OF OPPONENTS AND TACTICAL MOVES

It is perfectly clear from factual information available concerning this taxi "war" that the over-all plans of battle (strategy) of the opposing forces differed greatly. The battle plan of the "coalition" appears to have been simple—merely to undercut the rival's prices and render him *hors de combat* as quickly as possible. The plan of the opposing operator was much more complex—to avoid deep cutting but pretend to be about to undercut rivals at any moment—and was conditioned to some extent at least by limited resources, combined with a determination to avoid unprofitable operation if at all possible. It follows from this that the maneuvering of forces (tactics) would, of necessity, be substantially different.

Ordinarily, one would expect that the same rates would be charged by taxi companies operating in a market. Otherwise, there would be a strong tendency for concentration of customers with the competitor offering the lower-priced service, which, in turn, would force competitors to meet the low quotations. It is an interesting fact that at no time after the first reduction in the Hawthorne taxicab rate war until the final settlement of the dispute were the rates charged for taxi service by the competing factions identical or even close to identical.

There is no doubt that the shape of this encounter was determined to a large extent by one competitor's extreme reluctance to reduce his rates "below costs," combined with the use of unusually skilful (and to some extent unethical) tactics in maneuvering the "enemy" into a disadvantageous position. There were several aspects of this which should be of interest to students of warfare.

1. It is an interesting fact that this competitor had an aversion, if not an actual fear, of dropping his rate below a profitable level. In fact, he reported to the author that if his opponents had met him at 25¢ he would have been ruined because he would have had to make the threatened move to 10¢ and, obviously, could not have operated profitably on this basis. When the author suggested to him that this might have brought the conflict to a head more promptly, he said, in effect, "But suppose it had not."

This fear evidently conditioned his tactical behavior. After his opponents dropped their rate to 10¢ flat, this operator first began ostensibly to consider a reduction from 25¢ to 5¢ and even perhaps to 1¢. He saw to it that his purported intention gained currency. He even had 5¢ signs made and indeed had been leaning them against the building near his taxi stand, although he informed the author later that he had had no intention of dropping his price at that time and that this diversionary tactic was designed only to confound the opposition.

2. This operator actually attempted to influence public opinion in the community by word-of-mouth propaganda toward the point of view that the opposition was attempting to put him out of business. He utilized as an example the Yellow Cab—Veteran Cab Company struggle in the city of Los Angeles a year or two earlier, which had resulted in the withdrawal of the latter company from that

market. Consequently, many people in Hawthorne were loyal to his company despite the substantially higher rate which he charged for taxicab service.

3. With the rate still posted at 25¢ (which reportedly was profitable), the owner of this taxicab company made another competitively advantageous tactical move. This one was designed to force the "enemy" to waste his resources. Observing the "10 cents to any point in Hawthorne" signs on opposition cabs, he enlisted the aid of a score or more of high-school students in his battle with opposing companies. This cab operator provided the youngsters with dimes and instructed each of them to take a cab of one of the two competitors to destinations at the far end of town. A refusal by a rival to accept a fare at rates publicly offered would have resulted in a complaint against the cut-rate cab company and a possible revocation of license. Thus this operator's competitors were kept busy providing cab service at below-cost rates while he continued to serve his patrons at the relatively profitable 25¢ rate.

4. From the point of view of his "enemies," even if this operator was forced to reduce his rates, time appeared to be on his side. The owner of the company with the 25¢ price enjoyed a tactical advantage from the general impression held by people in the community, including his opponents, that he possessed strong resources and could hold out indefinitely, even in an all-out campaign. This impression was gained by the fact that this man had had an interest in a large superservice station before going into the taxicab business and had presumably sold out at a huge profit (which incidentally was not true but was not denied by the operator).

The foregoing clearly demonstrates a triumph of tactical superiority over material resources. The fact that success depended upon the use of deceit and the dissemination of falsehoods is not a pertinent element in this evaluation. War is like that.

TERMINATION OF WAR

The 10¢ rate under which the two competing companies operated was reportedly very unprofitable, especially on long hauls. After about three weeks of conducting business on this basis, these cab companies reverted to the rate which had prevailed before the outbreak of the price war (30¢ per flag drop and 30¢ per mile). Ordinarily, one would expect all rates to revert to pre-"war" levels. It is interesting that the operator charging the 25¢ fare retained this price for several months after others raised their rates. During this stage he enjoyed a genuine competitive advantage.

Interestingly enough, termination of this price war did not result from one of the participants seeking out the other and suggesting that they "lay down their arms." Indeed, one of the competitors reported that this would have been impracticable because it might have indicated weakness and therefore might have encouraged the opponent to continue the war. Actually, subtle arrangements were made for an outside person to negotiate a settlement among the parties. Mediation is, of course, not unknown in international conflict.

Subsequently, a city ordinance was enacted providing for the regulation of taxicab operations and rates within the city of Hawthorne. Under this ordinance, licenses are issued only on a basis of certificates of public convenience and necessity, and rates must be approved by the city council. Such rates must be posted in the cabs, and no variations may be made above or below these rates. Moreover, no changes in the schedule are permitted without application in writing and the city council's approval. Thus taxicab rate wars were effectively prevented by legislative means.

Just as in the case of real war, price wars are eventually terminated, and they may be won by one side or the other or result in a stalemate. It is an interesting fact that this one evidently was won not by those firms which outdid their competitor in rate-cutting but by the firm which maneuvered its opponents into a losing operation and then devised ways of preventing them from deriving any gains from the rate advantage they enjoyed. Because of the low rates charged and the tactical superiority of their opponent, the deep-cutting operators appear to have emerged from the encounter with heavy casualties (financial losses) and no new territorial gains (new customers).

Like real war, the conditions which obtain following a price war depend on which of the opposing factions prevails in the encounter and the philosophy of the victors. The cost of price warfare may go way beyond the losses experienced by participants during the engagement (offset perhaps by consumer gains derived from the lower rates). An evaluation of price wars should include any changes which have occurred in the intensity of rivalry in the market in question by virtue of a shift in competitive alignment. It appears that competition might have been adversely affected by the Hawthorne taxicab rate war in 1949 by the defeat of the liberal forces and the strengthening of the hand of a would-be monopolist. If so, this rate war can be judged as socially disadvantageous.

2. Strategic Sophistication in Recurrent Conflict

Suppose now that an equally amoral actor concludes that short-run victories are desirable, but that "unconditional surrender" is most unlikely and that a fairly enduring "competitive coexistence" is in the cards. In that case, it behooves him (as well as the opposing actor) to consider the need for rules under which the conflict will be conducted. If he is rational, he will sacrifice some possibilities of short-run gain in order to protect himself from equally vicious measures, should the tables be turned in subsequent rounds.

BARGAINING STRATEGY AND UNION-MANAGEMENT RELATIONSHIPS

PAUL DIESING

By a union-management relationship I mean the set of understandings and attitudes that have developed in joint dealings. Attitudes include such things as trust, suspicion, hostility, respect, determination to get even. Understandings include the beliefs each side has about the purposes, character, and methods of the other, and also beliefs about the proper procedures, standards, and objectives of joint dealings. Some understandings are shared and some are not. However, if no understandings are shared, not even on proper procedures, one can hardly say that a relationship exists. When misunderstandings are extreme, attempts at communication and negotiation must miscarry, and even open hostilities can hardly lead to a clear result if their meaning is interpreted differently by the two sides. Thus Dubin argues that the successful settlement of strikes is made possible by the fact that both union and management share certain beliefs about them. Without these shared beliefs, strikes would be vague, meaningless, aimless affairs.

All union-management dealings are shaped by the relationships within which they occur. The kinds of proposals that are made and the reception they get, the manner of moving away from initial positions and the ranges of possible agreement are all determined by the beliefs and attitudes of the two sides. When relationships are good, genuine agreements become possible, and the feeling that the agreements are fair or at least not too unfair prevents motives of revenge from poisoning future dealings. When relations are poor, chances of agreement are missed through misunderstanding, energies are absorbed in useless belligerency, and dealings are distorted by attempts to retaliate for imagined past injustices and insults.

No one kind of relationship is best for all the varied circumstances of industrial life. However, all good relationships have some common characteristics: they all include some minimum of trust and respect, some shared understandings, and some possibilities of communication. Without some understanding and some communication channels, no joint discussion can occur, and without some trust no paper agreement can succeed in practice. Beyond these minima the ingredients may vary considerably, ranging from strong hostility and suspicion to firm respect and cooperation. In this article I shall deal in general terms with ways of

From Paul Diesing, "Bargaining Strategy and Union-Management Relationships," *The Journal of Conflict Resolution,* V (1961), 369-78 (the footnotes and the bibliography and references have been omitted). Reprinted by permission of the author and *The Journal of Conflict Resolution.*

achieving and maintaining any kind of good relationship. After that I shall deal briefly with some of the circumstances that make different kinds of relations appropriate or possible.

I am adopting Harbison and Coleman's classification of union-management relationships in this article purely for reasons of convenience and simplicity. The three relationships they single out for attention — armed truce or power bargaining, working harmony, and cooperation — represent a good cross-sectional sample of the varieties of relationship actually found. Consequently principles which are illustrated by reference to them can easily be applied to other kinds of relationships by making the appropriate changes. Other well-known classifications introduce complexities which are irrelevant for present purposes.

Union-management relations are affected by every contact between representatives of the two, and also by transactions with third parties such as newspapers. However, in this article I shall concentrate on contract negotiations, since the problems involved are typical of those facing any union and management representatives who meet regularly. There are four principles which are basic to the establishment of good working relations among negotiators.

I. Avoid Extreme Weakness

Good relations are not necessary when one side has an overwhelming and permanent superiority of power. In such cases the strong power takes what it wants and the weak one must be satisfied with what it can get. Indeed, one can hardly say that a relationship exists when one side makes decisions unilaterally. But when each side is powerful enough to inflict considerable damage on the other, unilateral dictation is no longer possible and bargaining becomes necessary. Consequently the first step in establishing a relationship is to organize enough power to prevent dictation by one's opponent.

The chief danger here is that an increase of power may be seen as a threat by one's opponent, to be answered by the development of deterrent power. If this happens the energies of the two sides are likely to be absorbed in a spiraling power race, and the resulting hostility and suspicion will make the development of relations more and more difficult.

To avoid this result power must be built up in such a way as to minimize threat to one's opponent. Although there is no sure formula for doing this, threat can usually be reduced by putting recognizable limits on one's own power. Thus a slow, short-term buildup with definite objectives and definite moral limits is less threatening than a fast, general, unscrupulous, and apparently unlimited buildup. The reduction of misunderstanding and suspicion and the building up of mutual confidence also decreases the threatening effect of one's power. Since the three following principles deal with the problem of developing confidence and understanding, their application will help reduce the danger of threat and retaliation.

II. RESPECT THE CENTRAL POWER POSITION
OF THE OTHER SIDE

It is to be expected that each side, in working to increase its relative power and so improve its negotiating position, will try to weaken the power of the other side; but this attempt should always have limits. Neither side should try to penetrate and destroy the basic power resources of the other side, and should clearly signal its intention not to do so. Any such attempt will threaten the extermination of the other side, and will consequently provoke a desperate struggle for survival. Conversely, a demonstrated respect for the vital power resources of the other side signals acceptance of it as a permanent partner, and thus creates the security that enables both sides to begin working together.

Acceptance of this principle has been urged as the necessary first step in setting up good union-management relations. Ordinarily it is the union which faces the greater immediate danger of extinction, so the principle is expressed as a restraint on management. Management is advised to signal its acceptance of the union by refraining from attacking its central power, the loyalty of the union members and the jobs of the union leaders. Once this acceptance has been clearly expressed, and perhaps formalized as maintenance-of-membership clauses and the like, the union can shift from a militant struggle for existence to the less militant task of coexistence.

Note that this development requires a voluntary self-restraint on both sides; it cannot be forced or induced by one side only. The union may force management to accept all sorts of union security clauses, but if management clearly indicates that its acceptance is involuntary and that it will evade or overthrow these clauses on first opportunity, working relations cannot be established. Nor can management automatically induce a union to abandon militancy by offering security clauses and other signs of acceptance, since the union leaders' suspicions and beliefs may be too strong to be immediately overcome. This is especially true if the suspicion has deep ideological roots. But without strong evidence of voluntary management acceptance, union suspicions can never be overcome.

When unions are powerful enough to be a threat to management, union self-restraint is necessary. The central power position of management is its profit balance, since this affects its credit rating, the price of stocks, and stockholders' attitudes. If a union demonstrates that it has no respect for at least minimum profits, even well-established relations can be quickly destroyed.

III. FIND PRINCIPLES AND GOALS
WHICH CAN BE SHARED

Principles and goals are the main bulk of the shared understandings which are basic to any relationship, even hostile ones. Procedural principles and goals give meaning to actions by specifying the range of responses that are expected and appropriate. Substantive principles are basic to negotiation, in that they provide the arguments by which proposals can be validly defended and criticized. Shared goals provide additional criteria of appropriateness for joint activities, enabling them to proceed without too much confusion and misunderstanding. For example, in a strike procedural principles clarify the meaning of such activities as picketing, banking the fires, admitting supervisory personnel. These activities become normal routines demanding normal responses, with no mysterious overtones and no power to produce anxiety or unnecessary hostility. The shared goal of settling the strike soon so the strikers can return to their former jobs provides the general outline of the activities to be expected from each side. Procedural principles specify the detailed steps to be taken by each side in reaching a settlement—calling a conciliator, etc. Substantive principles, such as the principle that the prevailing wage for the area (or the industry, or the union, or the wage leader) should be paid, set the terms and limits within which negotiations proceed.

Some principles and goals, such as those associated with picketing, collective bargaining in general, and the union shop, are very generally shared and form part of the national system of industrial relations. But many other more specific principles must be worked out locally to fit local circumstances and history, and in some cases even nationally accepted principles may be rejected by one side or may be inappropriate or misunderstood. Consequently, one of the main tasks in the development of a local relationship is the working out of the detailed shared understandings that give form to a relationship.

Ordinarily each side tries to carry out this task by urging its own ideology on the other side. Each side supposes that its own principles are entirely sound and adequate for all purposes, and that the only obstacle to cooperation is the failure of the other side to recognize this obvious truth. (The same supposition is constantly made in international affairs.) As a result, negotiation sessions turn into persuasion contests, and disappointment at the obstinacy of one's opponent soon turns into suspicion of his intentions.

This approach is mistaken. The beliefs of either side are, as a rule, not suitable for sharing because they are too closely bound up with the partisan interests of that side. Acceptance by the other side would normally involve a heavy sacrifice of its claims and interests and thus would be a defeat.

For example, management frequently argues for the acceptance of a "management responsibility" theory during negotiations. This theory states that management has the legal responsibility, the ability, the experience, and the information necessary for making all major financial and administrative decisions. These decisions are not arbitrary; they are made according to well-established administrative principles and procedures, which normally, though not inevitably, insure that the results are beneficial to all. The proper task of the union is to check on management's application of these principles and procedures, call attention to errors, misinformation, arbitrary action, and thus insure the correctness of decisions. Another check is provided by competition, which penalizes mistakes and corrects inequitable distribution of resources, such as over-low wages, by creating shortages which force an equitable distribution.

The application of this theory to collective bargaining produces the conclusion that wage levels as determined by management are adequate unless the union can show that management's facts or predictions of business trends are mistaken. Any increase of wages above their proper level will damage the competitive position of the firm, and this will cause hardship for everyone, including the workers most of all.

The truth or falsity of this theory is not in question here. What is relevant is that its acceptance would nullify most union wage claims. In addition a parallel application of the theory would nullify most claims to job security based on seniority, as well as many claims for improved working conditions with regard to job scheduling and assignment. Any union that accepted this theory without qualification would be imposing a heavy, continuous, and unilateral sacrifice on itself.

A similar result would follow from management acceptance of the union "living wage" theory. This theory states that, in the richest country on earth, workers are entitled to a decent standard of living. The exact definition of "decent" varies, sometimes even in a single negotiation session. Sometimes Bureau of Labor Statistics figures on adequate living standards are cited, sometimes rises in living costs or abnormally high local prices are referred to, or more frequently, a comparison is made with some other group of people who are better off. Management acceptance of this theory would entail rapid and continuous wage rises, particularly when the criterion of decency is vague enough to shift occasionally. Similar results follow from labor's "antidepression purchasing power" theory, management's goal of efficiency, and management's "welfare of the consumer" theory.

The adoption of the beliefs of one side would usually also have the effect of minimizing the participation of the other side in decision-making. For example, the "management responsibility" theory assigns the entire positive decision-making process to management, with the union limited to criticism and appeal. The "decent living standard" theory, because of the multiple criteria of decency, assigns unions almost the entire burden of deciding which criterion is relevant and what level of wages is decent. The efficiency goal and the consumer welfare principle are usually interpreted to mean that management has primary responsibility for decision-making.

Because of this, when one side argues the validity of its principles and goals, it is in effect trying to get a larger place for itself in the joint scheme of things, both in the distribution of rewards and in decision-making authority. The other side is naturally well-advised to be suspicious of such arguments, and to look behind lofty ideological pronouncements for the one-sided advantages they imply. But when this happens, discussion between the two sides ceases entirely, and they are actually addressing the bystanders, government, and the public, trying to win supporters for a power struggle.

What sort of principles and goals are suitable for sharing? Only those which imply a clear and definite limitation on the interests of both sides, *especially* on the side proposing the principle. Suspicions of ulterior motive can be overcome and a principle accepted only when its proponent is clearly limiting himself and sacrificing a short-run advantage.

For example, the "decent living standard" theory becomes shareable when decency is defined by a single unambiguous criterion, such as cost-of-living index, and when this index goes *down* as well as up. Tying the theory down to a single neutral criterion removes the union's unilateral ability to decide the adequacy of wage standards as it pleases, and acceptance of an index that goes down as well as up shows that the union is really holding to an objective criterion, and is not merely rationalizing a limitless desire for more. Even here, if the "downs" of the index are rare and the "ups" are frequent, the index is likely to generate suspicion that it is a cleverly disguised trick. Management's goal of efficiency becomes shareable if *most* of the rewards of increased efficiency go to union members in a clear, unambiguous way, and if decisions on how to increase efficiency are jointly made.

Bargaining relations require three kinds of shared values, and the principle that both sides must be plainly limited by a shared value applies to all three.

1. Procedural rules are necessary for any kind of joint discussion, even power bargaining. They include understandings as to when is the proper time to make an offer, whose turn it is to make an offer, when clarifications of offers are in order, when is the time to make concessions, whose turn it is to make a concession, and what to do when there is a deadlock. A satisfactory procedural rule is one in which gives both sides relatively equal participation in discussion, that is, opportunities to state a position, to respond, and to be responded to. An unsatisfactory rule is one which gives one side the whole responsibility for determining the content of a decision, and leaves the other side only the alternatives of accepting or rejecting it. For instance, a frequent rule in wage negotiations is that each side should make an initial demand which is moderately in excess of its maximum hopes, and then make several concessions in return for counter-concessions. This rule is shareable because it gives each side an equal opportunity to plan strategy, to deceive or outmaneuver the other side, to conceal its own position, and to change targets or strategy when necessary. In contrast, sometimes the understanding is that management's initial wage offer is also its final one, and no deception or concealment is allowable. This rule is satisfactory only if wages are of minor importance and there is room for discussion and maneuver on major clauses of the contract. A rule which states that management or union should work out unilaterally a complete package and then devote the bargaining sessions to its explanation and justification is always unsatisfactory and unshareable.

410

2. In "working harmony" a large variety of criteria or standards is necessary as a basis for criticizing and modifying suggestions and moving toward agreement. These include such things as criteria for what constitutes a genuine offer or demand, what constitutes a genuine concession, what kind of justifying arguments or objections are valid, and what topics are open to negotiation. The requirement for a shareable standard is that it be clear enough to be applicable by both sides without too much disagreement, that it provide a clear basis for limiting as well as justifying proposals, and that the limits are set relatively close to existing practices. For example, both sides may agree that a satisfactory wage level is one that is either perceptibly better than all others in the industry, or equal to the highest in the industry or the area, or equal to the average in the industry or the area, or not too far below the average. Any one of these standards is shareable if it implies only a small departure from present practice, because they are all clear and capable of limiting both sides. However, the first criterion is acceptable only if suggested initially by management, while the last must be suggested by the union, because in this way the initiating side will bear the major short-run sacrifice. The opposite course, in which the initiating side gets a considerable advantage, tends to turn the rule into an expedient rationalization for private interest. A rule that wages ought to be equal to what other workers are getting is unshareable because its vagueness allows the union unlimited discretion in its choice of reference group. A rule that wages ought to approximate the level that would be set by supply and demand is unshareable because it does not adequately limit managerial discretion in estimating hypothetical supply and demand levels.

3. Shared goals are necessary as a basis for coordination when there is considerable positive cooperation, or indeed for any joint activity. A goal is shareable if it provides a place for most of the current activities of both sides or offers substitutes for the omitted activities (this avoids the unilateral sacrifice of stopping customary activities); and if both burdens and rewards are distributed about equally, or if the burdens initially fall mainly on the proposing side and the rewards mainly to the other side. For example, management's productivity and reputation-for-quality goals become shareable if most of the short-run gains clearly go to the workers. This means they should be distributed as a separate bonus, not merely as an improvement in the firm's position which "benefits everybody." Labor's goals of job security, advancement opportunities, and challenging work become shareable when most of the initial burdens are clearly assigned to labor. Otherwise the recognition of these goals represents a sacrifice by management which must be compensated for by a union sacrifice elsewhere.

It is possible to achieve a real sharing of principles even if the proposing side gains most of the short-run benefits, but these cases represent a gift and an act of trust by the accepting side, which must be reciprocated if the sharing is to continue. If the proposing side, like Jack Horner, views them as a personal triumph resulting from shrewd strategy, the trust will disappear and relations deteriorate.

IV. BE HONEST TO THE PROPER DEGREE

Honesty is sometimes called "good faith" in contract negotiations, although this term by now has acquired other meanings as well. Another version of the principle is *respect your lines of communication.* Honesty is a prerequisite of communication, and without some communication no negotiations are possible. The penalty for dishonesty is immediate and automatic: a breakdown of communication channels in the immediate area involved. As soon as one's words are discovered to be deceitful, all future words on that subject begin to lose their trustworthiness, and one's power to communicate is narrowed. Dishonesty is useful when one wishes to break up established communication channels, as when children wish to overthrow the constant supervision of their elders. But the task in contract negotiations is the opposite one of establishing and maintaining communication channels, so here honesty is quite essential.

Since honesty is prerequisite to communication, the exact degree of honesty required depends on the kinds of communication channels found to be necessary for negotiation. I will offer three examples to illustrate this point.

In *power bargaining* the problem of each side is to extract as many concessions as possible without having to carry out one's threat of using force, and to concede as little as possible without inducing the other side to use force [emphasis added]. The problem of negotiations is to find a bargain that is thought by each side to be more advantageous than the use of force. One resorts to force when the loss resulting from an agreement would be greater than the anticipated eventual loss from battle, or when the gain from agreement would be less than the anticipated gain from battle. During negotiations each side tries to obtain an objective estimate of the other side's power and readiness to act, and to exaggerate its own power position. The stronger one's position is thought to be, the more one can gain from negotiations, so it is advantageous to try to induce one's opponent to make as high an estimate as possible. Consequently, deception rather than honest communication is advantageous, and each side tries to bluff the other. Elaborate rules for bluffing tactics are followed, and the experienced negotiator learns to avoid detection by continually varying his bluffing pattern.

The regular use of bluffing leads each side to discount the statements of the other, so that it becomes increasingly difficult to exaggerate one's power position. Eventually, discounting proceeds so far that one's power or readiness to act is even underestimated. However, there is no advantage in having one's position underestimated, so low estimates must be corrected by a statement of one's true position. This is where honesty is essential. There must always be some way to communicate one's true position without deception and without misunderstanding. For instance, bargaining parties may reserve some special form of words for honest statements: "We really mean it this time," "We're not bluffing," "I'm warning you"; or they may reserve some special intermediary for urgent honest statements. If all channels of communication have been destroyed by constant deception so that honesty is impossible, power bargaining is in serious danger of

412

breaking down into unnecessary hostilities. Occasionally hostilities may be necessary, for instance because of internal union or management politics, but when they are unnecessary a good relationship should be able to prevent them.

In power bargaining the agreement is supported by its conformity to the estimated power positions of the two sides. Negotiators justify the agreement by saying "It's the best we could do under the circumstances." In *working harmony* the agreement is supported by a mutual feeling that it is fair [emphasis added]. "Fairness" here means that some clauses have been justified according to shared standards, such as the "prevailing wages for the area" standard, and that other clauses represent approximately equivalent concessions by each side. Bargaining proceeds by means of alternating concessions, and expert negotiators learn to work out compromises and equivalences.

The crucial kind of honesty required is in promises to make a concession in return for a counter-concession, and in claims that a real concession has been made. For instance, if a negotiator says "I don't think we'll have much trouble with this point if we can get that other one settled right," he is signaling an intention to make a concession on the first point if he gets an adequate concession on the other point. If there is disagreement on whether a real concession has been promised or made, discussion breaks down or turns into power bargaining. In other words, dishonesty and a failure of communication here is fatal to the maintenance of working harmony.

It is not necessary to be honest about just how extensive a concession has been promised or made, so long as the concession itself is genuine. The two sides expect to try to deceive each other about the extent of their concessions, in hopes of getting by with a minimum sacrifice. This kind of mutual deception does not disrupt the movement of negotiations, so it is not wrong.

Cooperative union-management relations are characterized by some mutual goodwill, based on numerous shared standards and some shared goals [emphasis added]. Force and haggling move into the background and there is an attempt to achieve benefits for both sides rather than just oneself. The ideal bargain is one in which each clause of the contract provides maximum benefit to one side at minimum cost to the other, and the two sets of benefits are vaguely balanced. The attempt at mutual benefit is based on an expectation that any benefits freely given to the other side will sooner or later be reciprocated, and partly on an identification of interest that results from sharing activity and goals. But when discussion is aimed at mutual benefit, it is necessary for both sides to be acquainted with each other's real aims, frustrations, and real resources. Otherwise, it is impossible to determine what action will most benefit one's partner at smallest cost to oneself, and vice versa. Therefore, in this kind of relationship it is necessary to be honest about the real reasons for one's requests or refusals, and about one's ultimate aims and discontents. When communication in this area breaks down, the aim at mutual benefit becomes impossible, and each side is forced to look out for itself.

For example, Whyte mentions an instance in which management proposed a five-minute cut in rest periods. Its reason was frustration over the abuse of the rest period by certain employees who overstayed their leave. Once the union representatives discovered the real reason behind the proposal, they could propose an alternative, union policing of the delinquent employees, which was more efficient and of greater benefit to both sides. In this case had management concentrated on its formal five-minute demand, and talked about management prerogatives, the need for efficiency, and the like, they would have been dishonest and would have weakened the relationship—even though their arguments may have been entirely valid.

In the above three examples I do not mean to imply that a particular union-management relationship falls clearly into any one of the three categories described. A relation may involve power bargaining on some issues, working harmony on others, and cooperation on still others; or it may shift from one to the other with circumstances, personalities, and shifts of mutual trust. The abstract distinctions are made only to illustrate the various degrees of honesty that are necessary in maintaining various discussion relations.

So far I have dealt with principles common to all good relations. I have used three kinds of relationships to illustrate my principles: (1) power bargaining, in which each side tries to extract as much as possible and concede as little as possible without using or inducing the use of force; (2) working harmony, where the aim of fairness is achieved through removal of inequities and through approximately equivalent concessions by each side; (3) cooperation, where the aim is to provide maximum advantage to each side at minimum cost to the other, and the sacrifices are vaguely balanced out over an indefinite period rather than in each separate contract. I shall now touch briefly on the question of what relations are best in what circumstances.

In terms of contract benefits, it is plain that cooperation is the best of the three relationships mentioned. In cooperation both sides work for the maximization of the real aims of each, and the mutual problem-solving approach to maximization turns up alternatives that could not have been conceived by either side working alone. When cooperation is impossible each side must work for its own welfare against the minimizing efforts of the other side. Of the other two relationships, armed truce is advantageous to a side which has a considerable superiority of power, because it does not have to be fair. But when both sides are more nearly equal, working harmony is more advantageous because it reduces the necessity of constant vigilance against petty harassment, power buildups, and cold war tactics.

Certain internal political circumstances favor the maintenance of armed truce. When an organization is characterized by weak loyalty, vague goals, and general apathy, its inner cohesiveness can be increased by a fight against a vicious enemy. Hard-won victories mean more in terms of loyalty than generous concessions, and even defeat and punishment can be the basis for a militant unity leading to eventual triumph. This is particularly true for a new union. When recognition is too easily achieved and the employer is too reasonable, the union is likely to remain a paper organization with low levels of loyalty and participation.

Factionalism is another circumstance favoring armed truce. The existence of an opposition union or management faction ready to take advantage of errors reduces the maneuvering space of the negotiators and forces them to emphasize immediate, tangible results rather than more speculative long-run advantages. A move toward cooperation is particularly risky and difficult to take, because this involves the setting of limits on one's own power, making concessions in hopes of vague future returns, accepting alien ideological principles, and consorting with the enemy. Negotiators need considerable internal political security to take these risks. And even if they have the security, too rapid a movement toward cooperation at the top may create factional deviation among more militant foremen, stewards, or rank and file workers.

Some special risks inherent in cooperation make working harmony a safer type of relationship. If cooperation is too enthusiastic there is a danger of one side losing sight of real and permanent differences of interest and sacrificing too much. Thus a union may be too ready to forego a wage demand when it should rather pressure management to increase efficiency elsewhere, or management may be too ready to soften piecework rates at the cost of weakening its competitive position. In general, cooperation requires an emphasis on joint problem-solving, and simple concessions are more appropriate for working harmony.

Other considerations of a similar nature have been cited in the literature as relevant to the evaluation of a specific relationship. My primary concern in this article has not been to list all these considerations, but to discuss principles which are basic to any good, effective relationship. Even armed truce, when it is appropriate, is not a chaotic outpouring of hostilities but a structured relationship based on definite rules and principles.

E. MODES OF CONFLICT MANAGEMENT

As was suggested in the previous section, the conflict strategy to be adopted by the actors involves a complex range of considerations. *Every* conflict is costly to the participants, whether or not those costs are exceeded by the gains that are made, or by the other losses that are, hopefully, prevented. That is, there is almost always *some* incentive to reduce the intensity or duration of the conflict by means of various techniques for managing or resolving it.

Normally, however, sheer self-interest (no matter how enlightened) is insufficient to bring the conflict within tolerable bounds; some external, environmental stimulus must be at work. That stimulus may be found in any of the three dimensions discussed in Part One: the physical-technological, the cultural-attitudinal, or the structural-institutional. In the contemporary international system, the first dimension certainly offers many incentives and inducements for conflict management, but it also offers serious temptations for conflict exacerbation.[1] The same may be said for both of the other dimensions, except that the *structure* is probably more conducive to heightened aggressiveness while the *culture* seems to exert a slightly stronger pull in the direction of resolution. The two papers that follow should be highly suggestive in this regard, with the first stressing primarily the cultural dimension and the second the structural one.

1. Changing the Actors

Regardless of whether the extra impetus necessary for conflict management comes from the cultural or the structural aspects of the system,

---

[1] This dual effect is spelled out in J. David Singer, "Weapons Technology and International Stability," *Centennial Review,* V (1961), 415-35.

416

an impressive range of ideas on the subject is found in the literature of the behavioral sciences. These ideas appear to range from the totally irrelevant to the highly promising, but there is almost no systematic and operationally gathered evidence on the matter as far as inter-nation conflict is concerned. All that is available so far is a number of hunches and opinions, buttressed for the most part by historical anecdote or — as is the case here — intuitively plausible argument. In the analogy suggested below, there is emphasis upon the degree to which the culture prescribes and permits the extension of the conflict to third parties, who, once involved, may play a catalytic role in its resolution.

EXTENSION OF CONFLICT
AS A METHOD OF CONFLICT RESOLUTION
AMONG THE SUKU OF THE CONGO

Igor Kopytoff

This paper describes particular methods of resolving conflict found among the Suku of southwestern Congo (formerly the Belgian Congo). The emphasis is on resolution and not on the sources of the conflict itself. That is, we shall treat Suku culture and social structure as given conditions under which conflicts occur. The immediate, and perhaps "superficial," sources of conflict are seen to reside in the universal phenomenon that culturally approved norms (from the point of view of someone in the society, at least) are sometimes broken and that this calls up some patterned reaction from the party which is defined as "offended" and which, depending on the cultural contexts, may be an individual, a group, the state, or even that somewhat amorphous entity usually called "society as a whole." The more fundamental question as to why norms are broken, and with what frequency, lies beyond the concern of this paper. Assumptions that some cultures and social structures tend to generate more conflict, or less, or, viewing the same facts from the other side, to resolve conflict less or more successfully, are entirely avoided, each being the converse of the other and empirically inseparable from it insofar as real data are concerned.

We shall begin by giving briefly the general background of Suku society, its culturally defined social units, the way conflicts between them are conceptualized, and the formally approved or "normal" methods of their settlement. Next, we shall turn to the methods resorted to when the "normal" ones fail or are

From Igor Kopytoff, "Extension of Conflict as a Method of Conflict Resolution among the Suku of the Congo," *The Journal of Conflict Resolution,* V (1961), 61-69 (the footnotes and the bibliography and references have been omitted). Reprinted by permission of the author and *The Journal of Conflict Resolution.*

deliberately discarded. Finally, we shall examine the consequences of these methods for the social structure as a whole.

Suku Society

The Suku, numbering some 80,000 persons, are located in the Kwango District of southwestern Congo. They occupy an area of rolling savanna of about fifty by one hundred miles. The region is sparsely populated. Traditional villages vary in size between fifteen and seventy-five inhabitants; the distance between neighboring villages is seldom less than two miles. Suku economy is based on the cultivation of manioc, practiced exclusively by the women, and on hunting and fishing, activities pursued primarily by the men. While intermittent contacts with individual European traders date to the beginning of this century, more or less effective Belgian administration was established in the middle of the 1920's. In the following description, although the present tense is used, the political relations discussed are those which prevailed before European occupation [and withdrawal].

The functional unit of Suku society is the corporate matrilineage. Several such matrilineages, known to be related through a common but forgotten ancestor in the maternal line, are further grouped into a major lineage, or clan. The main function of the latter lies in the residual rights of a related lineage to the property and political positions of an extinct lineage; also, small lineages of the same clan may reintegrate into a single lineage.

The corporate matrilineage usually has a depth of five or six generations. It possesses a recognized and ritually sanctioned head who is the oldest male in the lineage and who takes up residence in the lineage center, which is the village originally built by the founder of the lineage in the process of lineage segmentation. The corporate matrilineage carries a name (assumed by its current head), holds the ultimate rights in all the property of its members, often possesses hunting rights in certain lands, and is sometimes vested with a position in the formal political organization. The matrilineage is responsible as a unit for the infractions of any of its members *vis-à-vis* another lineage; the lineage head always represents the lineage in negotiations and in the chiefs' tribunals. In cases of self-help, it is culturally accepted that revenge may be taken indiscriminately against any member of the offending lineage.

While Suku descent is matrilineal, residence at marriage is virilocal; that is, the wife leaves her previous residence to live with her husband. Ideally, male children are expected to remain in their father's village, and as a rule do so at least until their father's death and often thereafter. These patterns obviously tend to disperse the lineage territorially. This tendency toward dispersion is, however, countered by a variety of mechanisms whose description is beyond the scope of this paper, and these result in maintaining the lineage center as a point of what may be called "psychological," if not necessarily physical, residence for its members.

418

Thus, every village which is a lineage center has a core of residents belonging to the founding lineage, and it also has additional residents who are usually the sons of the lineage members and, as such, participate actively in its affairs. Other lineage members ordinarily reside in villages not far removed from this center. The dispersal of a lineage is thus over a relatively small area, so that face-to-face contacts between its members and back-and-forth visiting are possible. While this cross-cutting of lineage membership, patrilineal ties, and residential affiliation prevents the rigid coincidence of residential units with the strongly corporate lineages and results in a complex integrative network of social and political relations, lineage loyalty remains paramount in situations of conflict.

Superimposed upon this "horizontal" structure of essentially dyadic relationships between individuals or groups is the structure of formal political authority whose model is pyramidal, with the king standing at the apex and with chains of delegated power descending from him to regional chiefs and subchiefs. Every position of chief and subchief is vested in particular lineages whose current heads automatically occupy them. In the same way, the king himself is simultaneously the head of the royal lineage.

It may be noted that the varying units of this "vertical" political organization do not coincide with the units of the social organization previously described. Related lineages and even portions of the same lineage may reside in different chieftainships. Some lineages even possess branches outside of the Suku region and are thus divided between two different "tribes" and two different supreme political authorities.

SUKU CONCEPTUALIZATION OF INTERLINEAGE CONFLICT

The consequence of the strongly corporate nature of Suku lineages is that the important conflicts which occur in the society are those *between* different lineages, while conflicts *within* any one lineage tend, by comparison, to be minimal [emphasis added].

The settlement of *intra*lineage conflicts, including capital offenses, is entirely an internal matter, and it is achieved through the consensus of lineage elders whose authority is "mystically" sanctioned [emphasis added]. Suffice it to say for our present purposes that as far as internal matters are concerned, the lineage is a completely independent political unit, with no outside authority impinging upon it.

The corporateness of lineages results, at the same time, in automatically pitting one lineage against another whenever conflicts occur between members of different lineages. Here, the principle of total reciprocity prevails. A homicide must be compensated with the payment of two slaves, regardless of whether it was accidental or premeditated. A theft may be cancelled only by the return of an object of equivalent value. The dissolution of a marriage, through divorce or death, must be accompanied by the return of the bridewealth, appropriate readjustments being made for the number of children to whom the husband had acquired paternal rights; if he relinquishes these rights, the original sum is returned *in toto*. Reciprocity is also maintained by balancing an action with a similar counteraction. A theft is wiped out by an anwering theft, an insult returned effaces an insult given, a murder is compensated by a reciprocal murder; in these cases, no further settlement is necessary.

The sources of *inter*lineage conflict lie in a real or imagined imbalance in the system of reciprocity, and the initiative toward the restoration of the balance belongs to the offended lineage and to no one else [emphasis added]. A further consequence of the conception of reciprocity is that since it defines clearly the claims of every side in every given situation and the exact compensations involved, a conflict between lineages develops from a disagreement over the events held to be responsible for the imbalance, and it will be so phrased. Agreement on these events is ideologically equivalent to the resolution of the conflict. There is no place, in this system, for arguments over the amount of compensation, for that is clearly defined, nor over such matters as premeditation or accident, for these are legally irrelevant and compromise cannot take place in these terms. Thus, a solution of the conflict must be a redefinition of the reciprocal imbalance, which is mutually acceptable and from which settlement automatically results.

The "Normal" Methods of Conflict Resolution

We have described the two networks of socio-political relations — the "horizontal" system of dyadic relations, and the formal "vertical" political organization. Both of these possess socially approved mechanisms for the solution of interlineage conflicts, and, to a large extent, the choice between them lies with the lineage.

Formally, the king is the supreme executive and the supreme judge, and, in every region, the same powers are vested in his representatives, the local political chiefs. These are responsible for maintaining the peace in their regions; should violent conflict erupt, it is their duty to intervene and mediate the dispute with the advice of elders selected for the occasion. If their authority is defied, they can call upon the help of neighboring chiefs and of the king himself.

So much for the theoretical structure. In practice, the traditional political system lays primary emphasis on the periodic collection of tribute which flows, in principle if not always in fact, along the chains of delegated authority to the king. The sheer physical distances involved, the relatively meager technological resources, the limited means of communication in a sparsely populated region, the lack of any standing force of warriors under the immediate orders of the chiefs, suspicions of favoritism — all these contribute to the inefficiency of the system. It may also be noted that while the territorial dispersion of the lineages makes, in some measure, for the "horizontal" integration of the society, it militates at the same time against the kind of integration demanded by the pyramidal political structure. The channels to be followed in the latter are based on regional affiliation and thus cross-cut the direct lines of lineage loyalty.

In view of the above, it is not surprising that methods of conflict resolution, congruent with the "horizontal" socio-political structure of dyadic relationships, are extremely important. Such socially approved methods rest on negotiation between the two parties, and in cases where the facts are known to all, agreement is easily achieved. Thus, theft in which the culprit is caught red-handed, or an accidental murder during a communal hunt, or a debt known to all would not be ordinarily disputed. If direct negotiation fails, the case may be taken to a judge whose position is validated only by his reputation and on whom both parties must agree; his decision is reinforced by divination and the method of enforcement consists in the preliminary deposition with him by each party of a sum of money or objects equivalent to the compensation under dispute. Conflicts involving "mystical" causes, such as deaths blamed on adultery, are usually resolved by the diviner who determines the "facts" of the case and thus, in a *quasi* judicial capacity, decides on the merits of the dispute. However, there is no mechanism for enforcing a diviner's decision.

ALTERNATIVE METHODS OF RESOLVING CONFLICT

It cannot be emphasized too strongly that the methods so far described are not only culturally approved but are also successful in most cases. If we have dwelt on some of their negative aspects, it was to make it clear that occasionally they do fail, and the stress on the possibilities of failure is necessary to understand why the alternative methods to be presently described exist at all. This must be kept in mind if proper perspective on the total Suku political organization is to be preserved. However, the subsidiary nature of these alternative methods does not detract from their theoretical significance.

When any of the socially approved methods cannot be agreed upon, or even when a lineage considers that its claim is likely to be rejected outright with no further negotiations possible, direct self-help is resorted to, sometimes immediately. Thus, a stolen pig is compensated for at once by appropriating a pig from the thief's lineage and if the case is clear-cut, no more is said of it, the balance of reciprocity being regarded as restored. Sometimes, a hostage from the offending lineage may be captured to insure greater speed of settlement.

True conflict appears when the two parties disagree fundamentally on the premises of the case. An accusation of theft is denied, the exact sum of an unpaid debt is contested, the responsibility for a death rejected out of hand. Self-help is then seen by the other party as an unprovoked attack demanding reciprocal retaliation. It is clear that this system, if restricted to the two lineages, would result in an impasse or a spiraling series of counter-retaliations. In such an impasse, continued self-help is often increasingly difficult since both sides are prepared for it and take the necessary precautions; animals are kept under surveillance and people take special care not to wander off singly and unarmed. The situation may be defined as one of total external conflict, in which the claims are mutually exclusive since satisfaction on one side generates counter-claims on

421

the other. At the same time, the abandonment of its claims by a lineage results in an internal conflict, for this militates directly against the strongly held principle of reciprocal balance *vis-à-vis* other lineages.

Resolution of this impasse by force suggests itself as a feasible way out, and it may in fact be used. "War" is declared by one of the parties. Each lineage invites neighboring villages to participate on its side, with the unstated understanding that any deaths or wounds will be compensated by it according to the usual scale. These alliances are ephemeral, the new participants regard the "war" as a kind of dangerous but exciting game, and people joining one lineage in one "war" may be opposed to it in another. The "wars" seldom result in many deaths, and their function is primarily to bring pressure upon the opponent to settle before the costs become too high and also, more indirectly, to involve the regional chief in the settlement of the quarrel since, once violence has occurred, he is duty-bound to investigate the original cause. The disadvantage of "wars" is that they may turn out to be too costly for both parties who are legally bound to pay for the damages done by participants. The latter, knowing this, can afford to be irresponsible. Thus, the costs of this solution may be judged sometimes to outweigh its advantages.

The other solution, which we shall now examine in detail, consists of a deliberate enlargement of the conflict, creating a new situation in which other socio-political units are forcibly involved. An example should make this pattern clear. If lineage A steals a goat from lineage B, the latter may resort to self-help with regard to a third party, lineage C, which has nothing to do with the original quarrel. In such cases, lineage B is said to act "because of," that is, in the name of, lineage A to which it transfers the blame for its action. Thus, lineage B will simply capture a goat from the unsuspecting lineage C, informing it that any claims about this theft should be taken directly to lineage A, that of the original thief. This transfer of blame is accepted by C which always presents its complaints as suggested and demands that A settle its obligations, threatening retaliation if this is not done. The Suku say that the third party is angry at both lineages for involving it in the quarrel, but more so at the lineage of the first thief which is responsible for the affair in the first place. The next step is for the three lineages to get together, the third party acting as an informal mediator. If the affair is not settled, the third party will pressure the recalcitrant lineage to agree upon a judge to examine the case.

While the involvement of a third party in the conflict does not automatically lead to its solution, it is achieved more easily in this manner. From a simple dyadic relationship between two autonomous units whose quarrel was legally confined to them alone, the structure of the conflict now involves a third party, neutral yet highly interested in finding a solution. Such mediation may, in fact, be preferred to taking the case to a tribunal. The original conflict being irreconcilable in its opposing interpretation of previous events, its presentation in these terms to a judge or a chief means that, given Suku legal conceptions, each party stands to win all or lose all; hence, the presentation tends to lead to extreme rather than reconcilable claims. With a third party whose judgment carries no finality, a mutual readjustment of opposing versions is more easily achieved, no concession being binding.

It is tempting to view this forcible enlistment of a mediator as an example of an extension of conflict leading to its solution, a corollary of the "peace in the feud" proposition recently advanced by Gluckman, among others. But no matter how appealing the paradoxical turn of the phrase may be, certain qualifications, or conditions, must be explicitly stated. In the case of the Suku, the mechanism of extension works only as long as the third party accepts the role of mediator, and this it does because it accepts the cultural premise that the wronged lineage is justified in compensating itself in the name of the wrongdoer. This cultural premise is indispensable, and the success of the pattern derives from it and not from the bare structural fact that the conflict has been expanded.

It is also important to stress here that mediation by a third party is not the goal of the lineage resorting to this pattern but rather a consequence of an autistic view that its balance in the system of reciprocity need not be strictly a balance between it and every lineage taken singly, but between it and the surrounding social universe as a whole. The lineage seeks first of all compensation; once that is obtained, it considers its claims satisfied. Its eventual participation in the final settlement is never automatic nor spontaneous, and it participates mainly because of fear of retaliation or war. If it considers itself safe from retaliation, as when great distances are involved, it may fail to participate at all in the settlement. Hence, the situation must be clearly understood in terms of individual motivation and action before it is analyzed at the level of social structure which is the consequence of action.

THE EXTENSION OF CONFLICT IN CASES OF HOMICIDE

That extension of conflict does not necessarily result in successful settlement is seen in those cases where the same method, still used to reestablish reciprocal balance, is applied to cases of homicide. Here, the socio-structual consequences appear to be far from integrative in any immediate sense.

When lineage A is held by lineage B to be responsible for the death of one of its members (be the killing deliberate, accidental, or, in some cases "mystical"), extension of the conflict may take place through the murder of a member of some third lineage. This pattern stresses the way in which the system of reciprocity is conceptualized. The equation of reciprocity may be maintained either by a return of a subtracted unit or by equal subtraction from both sides. The loss of a man is compensated either by its legal equivalent—two persons—or by the infliction of a similar loss on the other side. The other side, in an impasse, becomes the whole society. In both cases, equilibrium is achieved, but the consequences for futher action differ. In the previously described example of theft, negotiation is facilitated by the fact that the object under dispute, for example a goat, may be returned; whatever equilibrium exists is flexible and may be changed without entailing additional losses for any side. Theft, in effect, is reversible; death is not.

Thus, in the case of homicide, lineage B, by subtracting a person from lineage C, has achieved irrevocable equilibrium but has not replaced its loss in the process. It is usually unwilling to participate in any further negotiations because any readjustment that these may necessitate can either demand two people as compensation, or simply confirm that it has already "collected" through the second killing. No gain existed in the first place, nor is any gain forthcoming. Finally, compromise in terms of a reconciliation of different versions of events is impossible because with an object, it may be agreed, even if it is not believed, that the "theft" was a "mistake"; with death, when no mitigating circumstances are allowed, the conflict cannot be settled except through the total surrender by one of the parties of all its claims. These considerations make the first lineage equally uncooperative in negotiation.

These difficulties in reaching a settlement are known to the third lineage which has been forcibly involved in the conflict. It may appeal to the regional chief; the difficulties of which have already been commented on and what interests us at present is the situation which results when normal channels fail. The other alternative for the third lineage, desperate as it is to solve the external conflict, is to settle at least its own internal conflict—between inaction and the principle of reciprocity—by killing a member of yet some other lineage. This triggers off a chain of further killings, the whole process being known as *kembi.*

When news of a *kembi* spreads in a region, no lineage may regard itself as safe. Even the chiefs' lineages are not immune; because murder is always committed in the name of the previous killers, a lineage, angry at having been caught in a situation of whose very origin it may be ignorant, will deliberately kill an important person in order to make the eventual settlement as costly as possible for the original offender. The chances for settlement appear when the lineage that has been last victimized refuses to continue the *kembi* and calls upon the political chief to settle the issue. This demands an obviously laborious and lengthy process of retracing each step in the *kembi,* which may have crossed several regional political boundaries, sometimes even into neighboring non-Suku groups. In principle, the lineage judged to have committed the first unjustifiable murder compensates the last lineage to have lost a member. The intermediate links in the chain receive no compensation, since they have already achieved their balance in the system of reciprocity. Some *kembi* are known to have never been settled, as far as the Suku are concerned; they literally "disappeared over the horizon" into neighboring groups.

The socio-structural consequences of *kembi* may now be considered. We do not venture to say whether *kembi* "integrates" the society and whether it prevents in any way a potentially greater disruption of the social order. We shall simply present a shortened description of a region at the time of *kembi* given by an informant, and let the reader judge for himself this particular aspect of the problem.

424

When people heard there was a *kembi,* women did not go to the fields by themselves, but several armed men accompanied them; once the work was accomplished, they would quickly return to the village. At night, people did not sit around the fires outside the houses, so that no arrow would be shot at them from the dark. The chiefs of lineages and of the land did not sleep in their own houses, but in some small hut, for fear of an arrow shot through the (grass) wall. My own lineage chief was killed in a *kembi* this way: he heard a voice outside the door, asking for fire. When he opened the door, the man shot him in the chest and ran away into the dark, shouting, "We are of such-and-such, and we killed for such-and-such, because of *kembi.*"

We may now examine certain less immediate consequences of *kembi* in relation to the social structure. If the extension of conflict over a theft is seen to result in a kind of forcible induction of a mediator, the utilization of the same principle in murder results in a continuous displacement of localized conflict. It may be viewed as a variant of the deliberately localized war in international relations, the localization, however, shifting between different units of the socio-political organization. Conflict between any two parties in the chain is effectively and often quickly settled, and it has no chance to increase through mutual aggressive stimulation. While the displaced conflict may "never" be resolved, resolution, in the sense of elimination of logically irreconcilable claims, is achieved locally and between specific units.

Considering the occasional failures of "normal" Suku methods of conflict settlement, the absence of this pattern of displacement of conflict would, theoretically, result in its permanent localization and in its increasing intensity, one of the possible outcomes being a full-fledged blood-feud. It is, of course, difficult to say what "preserves" or "maintains" the social structure better, a localized blood-feud or one spread wide and thin.

SOME GENERAL OBSERVATIONS

We have examined two quite different structural consequences of a single cultural pattern in which the principle of reciprocity, often illustrated in anthropological literature, takes on a modified guise in Suku culture under conditions of unresolved conflict. The initial consequence of the pattern is, in every case, to extend a conflict between any two social units to a third one. The further consequence, however, depends on the characteristics of the new structural situation thus created and on the view of it by the parties involved. In one case, the extension of conflict facilitates its settlement. In another, it leads to a chain-like introduction of conflict to ever new and unaffected units while automatically resolving the conflict between all the preceeding units in the chain.

On the level of anthropological theory and method, the situation we have dealt with has some relevance to the relation between culture, or "custom," and social structure. One prevalent view of culture assigns it no dynamic role in explanatory schemes and seeks its generalizations or principles exclusively on the level of

425

social structure, while seeing culture simply as symbolizing existing social relations, or, at least, granting the concept of culture the role of an alternative view of human behavior, unnecessary to and functionally unintegrated with the structural view.

The logical consequence of this approach should be that the cultural conceptions of a society are unnecessary to the formulation of structual "explanations" and that every structual situation should reflect, and perhaps even explain, any customs associated with it. Thus, in the above example, it would be tempting to explain the pattern of conflict displacement as a function of some kind of imperative of a social structure to provide mechanisms for conflict resolution in the case of minor conflicts where such resolution is in fact facilitated. Yet, the same cultural conception is directly associated with situations of major and proliferating conflict. The direction of the explanatory chain in which one custom is derived from two dissimilar structual situations appears to be, at best, uneconomical.

We have preferred, therefore, to deal with the conception underlying the pattern as a cultural given (whatever its historic sources may have been), and we see nothing illogical in finding that quite dissimilar structural situations may be the consequences of a single cultural idea applied to behavior in combination with other factors which are themselves also significant variables.

On a more general level, the ethnographic example above underscores the necessity of viewing any conflict not simply as a dyadic relationship possessing internal characteristics but also in terms of the cultural context in which it occurs. A clear-cut logical incompatibility of goals can be seen to exist and to be so perceived, fully and consciously, by the parties to the conflict. Such situations of impasse have usually been analyzed in terms of the possibilities of reducing the conflict or at least of preventing the conflict from breaking out into violence. Thus, recently Deutsch called attention to the need for determining a "point of no return," in which one or both parties achieve a "loss of freedom of decision" and thus forcible solution threatens to become inevitable. Similarly, Schelling points out that "the problem is to develop a *modus vivendi* when one or both parties either cannot or will not negotiate explicitly. . . ." It is understandable that, given the present framework of international relations, both authors should concentrate heavily on the genesis of conflict in terms of communication and restrict the view largely to the two parties involved. The attempt is to prevent conflict from becoming total and irreconcilable.

In our example, the "point of no return" clearly could not be defined exclusively in terms of the internal characteristics of the conflict and of the parties to it; reference to different social and cultural contexts in which otherwise structually similar conflicts may occur becomes necessary. It is clear, for example, that in labor-management disputes, the "point of no return," when only mediation exists, ceases to be that when compulsory arbitration is introduced. Thus, resolution may lie in a modification of the social structure itself, as well as in the introduction into a given social structure of new forces which would counteract the development of irreconcilability in conflicts.

The Suku example, however, shows that this still does not exhaust the possibilities. When the formal Suku political structure fails, the situation superficially reverts to one of independent units, locked in total conflict and with the resolution resting entirely on them. The only possibilities may be thought to be total surrender by one of the parties of all its goals, or, finally, resort to war. Yet, *kembi* illustrates another possible method of resolution which is of theoretical interest. It lies neither in the creation of a new, more inclusive, social structure nor in the prevention of the development of total conflict. It is, to be sure, obvious that the method can only work when the social field that it "plays" embraces a great number of quasi-autonomous units. Nevertheless, it represents another "logical" outcome of a conflict which has reached a "point of no return."

2. Changing the Objectives

Instead of changing (by addition) the *parties* to the conflict, the utility of a change in the *objectives* which the actors pursue might be considered, and again it is modification by addition. In the well-known experiments excerpted below, Sherif presents some persuasive evidence for this particular mode. Yet the important disparities between his conflict problem and conflicts in the area of international politics cannot be overlooked. First of all, his protagonists had almost no enduring contact with one another prior to the introduction of his experimental manipulation, and, therefore, no well-established norms to overcome. Second, and most relevant here, the modification of their goals was largely imposed by the investigator; the initiative, at least, did not come from the protagonists.

INTERGROUP CONFLICT AND COOPERATION: THE ROBBERS' CAVE EXPERIMENT

MUZAFER SHERIF, ET AL.

MAIN CONCLUSIONS

Individual Characteristics and Intergroup Behavior

In this experiment, the rigorous criteria and painstaking procedures for selecting subjects ruled out explanations of hostile or friendly intergroup attitudes in terms of differences in socio-economic, ethnic, religious, or family backgrounds.

From Muzafer Sherif, *et al., Intergroup Conflict and Cooperation: The Robbers' Cave Experiment* (Norman: University of Oklahoma, Institute of Group Relations, 1961), pp. 205-12. Reprinted by permission of Professor Sherif.

Similarly, the criteria for subject selection insured against explanations on the basis of unusual individual frustrations, failures, maladjustment or instability.

The subjects came from families who were established residents of the same city. They were stable families composed of natural parents and siblings. No subjects came from broken homes. Their religious affiliations were similar. They were from the middle socio-economic class. They were of the same chronological and educational level. They had all made satisfactory progress academically; none had failed in school. In school and neighborhood, their social adjustment was above average. None was a behavior problem in home, neighborhood or school. In short, they were normal, healthy, socially well-adjusted boys who came from families with the same or closely similar socio-economic, ethnic, and religious backgrounds.

Since none of the individuals was personally acquainted with others prior to the experiment, pre-existing positive or negative interpersonal relations did not enter into the rise of intergroup attitudes.

The conclusion that explanations of the intergroup trends and attitudes on the basis of individual characteristics are ruled out in this experiment should not be construed to mean that the relative contributions of individuals within their own groups and in intergroup relationships are unimportant. Individuals do contribute differentially both in shaping and carrying on the trend of group relationships. This experiment does indicate, however, that intergroup attitudes are not merely products of severe individual frustrations or background differences brought to the situation.

Formation of Group Organization and Norms

When the individuals interacted in a series of situations toward goals with common appeal value which required interdependent activity for their attainment, definite group structures arose. These groups developed stable, but by no means immutable *status hierarchies* and *group norms* regulating experience and behavior of individual members.

More concretely, a pattern of leader-follower relations evolved within each group as members faced compelling problem situations and attained goals through coordinated action. As group structure was stabilized, it was unmistakably delineated as an "in-group." Certain places and objects important in group activities were incorporated as "ours." Ways of doing things, of meeting problems, of behaving under certain conditions were standardized, permitting variation only within limits. Beyond the limits of the group norms, behavior was subject to group sanctions, which ranged from ridicule, through ignoring the offender and his behavior, to threats, and occasionally to physical chastisement.

In-Group Cooperativeness Is Not Directly Transferable

When two groups met in competitive and reciprocally frustrating engagements, in-group solidarity and cooperativeness increased. Toward the end of intergroup friction (Stage 2), in-group solidarity became so strong that when the groups were taken to a public beach crowded with outsiders and affording various distractions, our groups stuck almost exclusively to activities within their respective in-groups. Psychologically, other people did not count as far as they were concerned. In the presence of so many people and distractions, this intensive concentration of interests and activities within the group atmosphere would have been impossible had the groups gone there before attaining such a high degree of solidarity.

This heightened in-group solidarity and cooperativeness were observed at the very time when intergroup hostility was at its peak, during the period when the groups asserted emphatically that they would not have anything more to do with each other. This can only mean that the nature of intergroup relations cannot be extrapolated from the nature of in-group relations. In-group solidarity, in-group cooperativeness and democratic procedures need not necessarily be transferred to the out-group and its members. Intergroup relations cannot be improved simply by developing cooperative and friendly attitudes and habits within groups.

Consequential Intergroup Relations Affect In-Group Relations

Special note should be made of a related finding, namely that consequential intergroup relations have an impact on the in-group organization.

When it became evident that certain members of one group, including the leader, were not living up to the responsibilities expected of them by other members during the eventful course of intergroup competition, leadership changed hands. Those individuals who distinguished themselves by giving a good account for their group rose in the status hierarchy. Internal shifts in status were observed again during the cooperative intergroup activities of Stage 3. Functional relations between groups which are of consequence tend to bring about changes in the pattern of in-group relations.

Limiting Conditions for Intergroup Attitude and Behavior

We have seen that the individuals studied in this experiment were selected in ways which rule out explanations for the direction of intergroup behavior on the basis of differences in their backgrounds or on the basis of their individual frustrations, instabilities and the like. In the preceding sections, we have seen evidence that in-group properties were affected by consequential intergroup relations. Thus the intergroup hostility and its reduction cannot be explained merely by the nature of relationships within the groups.

Our findings indicate that the limiting condition determining friendly or hostile attitudes between groups is the nature of functional relations between them, as defined by analysis of their goals. When the groups competed for goals which could be attained by only one group, to the dismay and disappointment of the

429

other, hostile deeds and unflattering labels developed in relation to one another. In time, derogatory stereotypes and negative attitudes toward the out-group were crystallized. These conclusions are based on observations made independently by observers of both groups and other staff members. Sociometric indices pointed to the overwhelming preponderance of friendship choices for in-group members. Experimental assessment of intergroup attitudes showed unmistakable attribution of derogatory stereotypes to the villainous out-group and of favorable qualities to the in-group. Laboratory-type judgments of performance showed the tendency to overestimate the performance attributed to fellow group members and to minimize the performance of members of the out-group.

What Kind of Contact between Groups Is Effective?

The novel step in this experiment was Stage 3, in which intergroup friction was reduced. We have already stated why we discarded certain procedures in this stage, such as introducing a "common enemy" or disseminating information. In order to clarify the term "contact," we tried the method of bringing the groups into close proximity in a series of activities. Most of these contact situations involved activities which were satisfying in themselves, such as eating good food in the same room, attending a movie together, or engaging in an exciting activity like shooting fireworks. But none of them created a state of interdependence between the groups. Such contact situations did not prove effective in reducing friction. Instead contact situations not conducive to interdependence were used by our groups for overt acts of hostility and further exchanges of unflattering invectives.

The ineffectiveness of contacts during which hostile groups engaged, while in close physical contiguity, in activities which were themselves satisfying to each individual has obvious implications for psychological theorizing.

The Introduction of Superordinate Goals

During the final period of the experiment, the prevailing friction between groups was reduced. Reduction of the conflict and hostility was observed in reciprocally cooperative and helpful intergroup actions, in friendly exchanges of tools, in developing standard procedures for alternating responsibilities and in meeting problems. The change in behavior and patterns of interaction between the groups was striking to all observers. The reliability of these observations is established by sociometric indices which showed increases of friendship choices for the erstwhile antagonists and also in the sharp decrease of unfavorable stereotypes toward the out-group. Favorable conceptions of the out-group developed, so that ratings of the in-group and out-group were no longer a set of contrasted polarities.

The end result was obtained through introduction of a series of superordinate goals which had compelling appeal value for both groups but which could not be achieved by the efforts and resources of one group alone. When a state of interdependence between groups was produced for the attainment of superordinate goals, the groups realistically faced common problems. They took them up as common problems, jointly moving toward their solution, proceeding to plan and to execute the plans which they had jointly envisaged.

In this experiment, the setting and circumstances for the introduction of superordinate goals were elaborately prepared by the experimenters. But beyond setting the scene, the methods followed, the discussion necessary for the solution, the plans to be made and executed were left to the groups themselves. Faced with superordinate goals, the groups carried on discussion when necessary, listened to the advice and suggestions of members of both groups who were resourceful, made decisions, and even combined discussion, decision and deeds simultaneously when the goal was attained more effectively this way.

Cumulative Effects of Superordinate Goals

If the hostile attitudes generated during intergroup friction had any stability, it could not be expected that one or two situations embodying superordinate goals could wipe them out. Indeed intergroup antagonisms did not disappear in one stroke. At first, cooperative interaction involving both groups developed in specific situations in response to common problems and goals, only to be followed by a renewal of sharply drawn group lines and intergroup friction after the challenge had been met. Patterns and procedures for intergroup cooperation were laid down at first on a small scale in specific activities. Only during interaction in *a series of situations involving superordinate goals* did intergroup friction begin to disappear and the procedures for intergroup reciprocity developed in specific situations extend spontaneously to widening areas of activity [emphasis added].

In the sequential events of Stage 3, . . . it was abundantly evident that the series of activities conducive to superordinate goals provided opportunities for members of the two groups to work out and develop procedures for cooperation in various spheres of action. Once a cooperative pattern was effective in a specific activity, it was extended by members of both groups to related actions. In the face of successful functioning of such procedures, the occasional dissident member who preferred the old days of intergroup strife or self-imposed separation found it more difficult to make his voice count in his own group.

Some procedures successful in intergroup interaction had previously been used by the groups in meeting problems *within* their own groups [emphasis added]. But their transfer to intergroup interaction involved a significant step: the tacit recognition that the procedures now involved *groups* of individuals and not merely so many individual members within a group [emphasis added]. Each individual within his group had been expected and encouraged by others to contribute to group efforts to the best of his abilities. Now, each group expected the other to contribute its share to meeting intergroup problems. While previously solutions were experienced as equitable or not relative to the individual's expectations and contributions within his group, now justice was also evaluated relative to equitable participation and opportunity for the groups as well.

The Same Tools May Serve Intergroup Conflict or Cooperation

In planning and working towards superordinate goals, there were times when the groups used jointly the tools and techniques which had been used by one or both groups separately in the service of fights during the intergroup conflict. Tools and techniques can be put to the service of harmony and integration as well as of deadly competition and conflict. Tools, in themselves, are not opposed to cooperation among individuals using them. It is the individuals as group members who put the tool to use in their opposition to other groups.

Even the proprietary pride that a place, a technique, a tool is "ours" takes on a different significance when the trend in intergroup relations is cooperation toward superordinate goals. Use of the technique or the tool in intergroup activities now implies a contribution toward a goal common to both groups — a contribution by the group in which members may take personal pride and which can be reciprocated by the other group equally enjoying its benefits through its own contributions at that or future occasions.

Superordinate Goals Alter the Significance of Other Influences

Contacts between groups in the course of actions towards superordinate goals are effective [emphasis added]. They are used for developing plans, making decisions, and for pleasant personal exchanges. *Information* about the out-group becomes a matter of interest to group members and is actually sought in the course of interactions between members of the two groups [emphasis added]. *Leaders* find that the trend toward intergroup cooperation in activities involving superordinate goals widens the spheres in which they may take positive steps toward working out procedures for joint endeavors and planning future contacts [emphasis added]. Mingling with members of the other group and sharing in activities with them is no longer perceived by in-group members as "betrayal" or "treason." Similarly, the out-group member who engages in activities with the in-group is no longer seen by them as a strange and threatening figure in "our midst." On the contrary, intermingling of persons from different groups becomes a joint opportunity to work towards goals shared by both groups.

These are products of interaction toward goals superordinate to all groups, which are genuinely appealing to all, whose attainment requires equitable participation and contributions from all groups in interdependent activities.

F. ATTRIBUTED RATIONALITY AND CONFLICT MANAGEMENT

As several of the previous papers in this part have indicated, one of the major variables contributing to the continuation, if not the exacerbation, of conflict is mutual suspicion. Social organizations in conflict with one another develop mutual suspicions of two distinct but related sorts. One is the perfectly normal and expected suspicion regarding one another's motives and intents; superimposed upon the objective incompatibilities are those which flow from the conflict process itself and which lead to exaggeration of the original clashes of interest. This effect by itself inhibits the management of conflict, but almost inexorably it is joined by another, and perhaps even more destructive, type of suspicion: the suspicion of irrationality. Here, the actors (or more accurately, their decision-makers) begin to doubt whether the adversary is even capable of *recognizing and pursuing his own self-interest*. It is this combination of incompatible interests and great distrust of both motives and rationality that produces the situation known in game-theory parlance as "the prisoners' dilemma."[1]

Briefly stated, two prisoners (*A, B*) are in a dilemma because the district attorney has enough evidence to convict both of them on a charge of *petty* larceny but strongly suspects that they have together

---

[1]Game theory, essentially a branch of formal mathematics, most often attributed to John von Neumann, a mathematician, and Oskar Morgenstern, an economist, was first fully articulated in their *Theory of Games and Economic Behavior* (Princeton, N.J.: Princeton University Press, 1944). Among the more useful introductory treatments of this heuristically powerful conceptual approach to social bargaining and conflict are Karl W. Deutsch, "Game Theory and Politics," *Canadian Journal of Economics and Political Science*, XX (1954), 76-83; and Martin Shubik (ed.), *Readings in Game Theory and Political Theory* (New York: Doubleday, 1954). Important applications are often found in *The Journal of Conflict Resolution* (which now has a special game-theory section in each issue) and in *Behavioral Science*.

committed *grand* larceny. But he needs a confession from *either one* in order to get a conviction of both on the more serious charge, and he tries to get that confession by offering each of them, separately, his freedom in exchange for the confession. If *neither* prisoner confesses, each will receive only a two-year sentence, and if *only one* confesses, that one goes free while the other goes to jail for ten years. But if *both* confess, then both receive the heavier, ten-year penalty. In graphic terms, their so-called "payoff matrix" looks like this, with *A*'s payoffs for each of the four possible outcomes listed first and *B*'s payoffs second:

		B's CHOICES	
		Confession	No Confession
A's CHOICES	Confession	$-10, -10$	$0, -10$
	No Confession	$-10, \quad 0$	$-2, \quad -2$

The best outcome from *A*'s point of view (assuming that there is no "honor among thieves") is the upper-right corner one, in which *he* confesses and goes free; conversely *B*'s preferred outcome is that in the lower-left, where he goes free and *A* takes the "full rap." But what happens if *each* acts in order to get the best outcome for himself? Obviously, they both confess; their choices lead to the outcome in the upper-left corner, and each spends ten years in jail. If each had, in the absence of effective communication, only been able and willing to assume that the other was rational (in the psychological rather than the mathematical sense), each could have expected the other to remain quiet and thus both would have received the lighter penalty.

The relevance of this situation to inter-nation bargaining and conflict should be quite evident. To the extent that both protagonists assume that the other is both malevolent *and* irrational, arms races go on, conflicts spiral, and both parties suffer. Neither trusts that the other is able or willing to recognize its own self-interest. Of course, there is generally some mixture of trust and suspicion in diplomatic relations, and the problem is one of establishing the highest possible trust-to-suspicion ratio. But this requires more than good will: it requires the presence of certain properties within the system and within the relationship, so that each actor is more likely to (a) behave rationally himself, and (b) attribute a similar rationality to the other.

1. The Effect of Communication on Trust

In the first of two experimental studies excerpted here, Morton Deutsch (a social psychologist and no relation to Karl Deutsch, the political scientist) explores the effects of differing induced motivations (cooperative, competitive, and individualistic) and of differing communication possibilities. The results of the first part are quite predictable, while those in the second part should be more interesting to the student of international politics.

TRUST AND SUSPICION

Morton Deutsch

Taken together, the results clearly support the hypotheses concerning the effects of motivational orientation. Somewhat oversimplifying the results, one can say that a co-operative orientation will produce trusting (and trustworthy) behavior even when the situational facilities do not encourage it—e.g., when no communication is permitted and when one has to choose without knowledge of the other person's choice. On the other hand, even when situational facilities are encouraging, a competitive orientation will result in suspicious and/or untrustworthy behavior rather than trust and trustworthiness. In contrast to both the co-operative and the competitive orientations, the behavior resulting from an individualistic orientation is very much influenced by situational determinants. The implication of this last statement is important and is worth emphasizing because of the common assumption that mutual trust is possible only when people are oriented to each other's welfare. Our results indicate that trust in co-operative behavior from another can reside *in the situational determinants* of his behavior *rather than in his character* [emphasis added].

The purpose of some of our later experiments was to investigate some of the social or situational conditions under which mutual trust could arise in subjects with an individualistic orientation. These studies focused upon (*a*) the influence of communication; (*b*) the influence of power; and (*c*) the influence of third parties.

The Influence of Communication

Our initial study of the influence of communication indicated that subjects with an individualistic orientation were more likely to trust each other if they

From Morton Deutsch, "Trust and Suspicion," *The Journal of Conflict Resolution*, II (1958), 265-79 (the footnotes, the bibliography and references, and the tables and figures have been omitted). Reprinted by permission of the author and *The Journal of Conflict Resolution*.

could communicate freely before they made their choices [Table 1 and Table 2 omitted]. However, it was evident that a sizable percentage of these subjects did not utilize the communication opportunity effectively. It was also apparent that the notes of the subjects who established mutual trust were different in a number of respects from the notes of the subjects who did not succeed in this. These results suggested the general question: "How can communication opportunities be used to raise the individual's confidence that his trust will be fulfilled and also used to elicit trustworthy or responsible behavior?"

An approach to answering this question is by rephrasing it and asking what the minimum ingredients of a co-operative interchange are. In essence, they are a complementarity of *intention* and *expectation*. That is, Person I expects Person II to perform certain activities which are necessary to I's gratifications and, in turn, intends to perform certain activities which are necessary to II's gratifications; a complementary situation exists for II vis-à-vis his intentions and expectations. However, for the co-operative interchange to be a stable ongoing system, each person must have *a way of reacting to violation of his expectation* which is known to the other and which can serve as an inhibitor of violation, since the frequent occurrence of violations will break down the system of interchange. However, the nature of any ongoing system is such that violation is likely to occur, if only by chance. Hence, for the system to endure, there must be some way of avoiding the following self-perpetuating cycle: violation on the part of Person I, leading to a reaction to I's violation on the part of Person II, leading to expectation of distrust from II and hence, to repeated violation by I, leading to a reaction to I's violation on the part of II, etc. That is, the system must have some means of restoring complementarity, once it has been violated. It must have, in effect, a *method of absolution* and of recognizing when a return to complementarity has occurred. In sum, the following elements appear to be involved in a stable co-operative system: (1) expectation, (2) intention, (3) retaliation, and (4) absolution.

An experiment was designed in which prepared notes were constructed using one or more of these four elements. There were five different notes in all. The simplest note (which stated the note writer's expectation) said, in effect, "I would like you to co-operate so that I can win." The most complete note included all four elements. It stated, "I will co-operate and I would like you to co-operate. That way we can both win. If you don't co-operate, then I will choose so that you can't win. If you decide to co-operate and make a co-operative choice after first not doing so, then I will co-operate." The intermediate notes contained one, two, or three of these elements. Some of the subjects received notes and others sent notes; but there was never any two-way communication. As a control, one group of subjects played the game without any opportunity to communicate.

The experiment proceeded as follows. The game was explained. It was indicated that there would be five trials during the game. Then the subjects were tested to see whether they understood the implications of the various combinations of choices. The subjects were all given the individualistic orientation. Next, the subjects either sent or received a note. It may be noted that the subjects were induced to send a note of a given type by instructions and by the message form on which they were asked to write. After the note writing and reading was completed, the game was begun. The subject and the other person, without knowledge of what each other's choice would be on that trial, made their choices. After the choices were made on each trial, they were announced.

We expected that trust and co-operation would increase as a function of the completeness of the communication. Results on the first trial [Table 3 omitted], where the subjects had not yet experienced how the other person would play, indicated that 11 per cent of the control subjects, 31 per cent of the subjects who received the simple communication treatment, and 80 per cent of the subjects who received the full communication treatment trusted the other person and made co-operative choices (i.e., they were "trustworthy" as well as "trusting"). The results at the intermediate levels were consistent with this trend.

Although there were about the same number of note senders and note receivers who were both trusting and trustworthy on the first trial, the subject's communication position did have differential effects. The note receivers more frequently tended to expect the other person to be trusting and trustworthy than did the note senders. On the other hand, the note receiver was more likely than the note sender to violate the trust he perceived the other person to have, even when he expected the other person to be trustworthy as well as trusting. In other words, there was a clear tendency for the note receiver to expect more trustworthiness and to be less trustworthy, despite this expectation, than the note sender. In considering these results, one should keep in mind that the notes which were sent or received were always co-operatively oriented.

A possible explanation for the differences due to the communication position of the subject is in terms of "commitment." The note sender had, by sending the note, "committed" himself to co-operation and hence was more likely to choose co-operatively. The note receiver, as a result of the note and its implicit commitment, had a better basis for expecting the other person to be trusting and trustworthy, but, since he had not written a note, he had not committed himself to choose co-operatively.

What are the conditions under which a person will be "committed" to what he communicates? This study throws no light upon this question. However, our earlier studies of two-way communication suggest that, when subjects are competitively oriented, there is little commitment to what one communicates and hence little basis for trust as a result of the communication one receives. It would seem that the situation has to be ambiguous as to whether the individuals will interrelate themselves co-operatively or competitively, rather than clearly competitive, before an individual will assume that communications are informative rather than misleading. The greater trustworthiness of communications in an individualistic as compared with a competitive situation possibly reflects the greater social restraints against deception in the individualistic situation: more customarily, "anything goes" under intense competition.

To sum up our research on the influence of communication, it is evident that mutual trust can be established in people with an individualistic orientation through communication. Communication is likely to be effective in so doing to the extent that the basic features of a co-operative interrelationship are made explicit in what is communicated. These basic features are (1) expression of one's intention; (2) expression of one's expectation; (3) expression of one's planned reaction to violations of one's expectation; and (4) expression of a means of restoring co-operation after a violation of one's expectation has occurred.

2. The Effect of Relative Power on Trust

Another factor which is likely to have some impact on the degree to which the actors are able to attribute rationality, if not good will, to the adversary is that of relative power. In addition to summarizing the results of other experiments in the area of trust and suspicion, Solomon presents below his hypotheses and findings on the impact of the relative power of the two actors. Note the degree to which they coincide with, or differ from, the less empirical papers by French and Raven, Dahl, Harsanyi, and Dubin.

THE INFLUENCE OF SOME TYPES OF POWER RELATIONSHIPS AND GAME STRATEGIES UPON THE DEVELOPMENT OF INTERPERSONAL TRUST

LEONARD SOLOMON

*   *   *   *   *

A bargaining relationship is one in which the participants have a conflict of interests, yet are dependent upon each other in order to avoid a mutually detrimental outcome [emphasis added]. One rather striking finding to emerge from Deutsch's study was the fact that under conditions of noncommunication the individualistically

From Leonard Solomon, "The Influence of Some Types of Power Relationships and Game Strategies upon the Development of Interpersonal Trust," *Journal of Abnormal and Social Psychology,* LXI (1960), 223-30 (the footnotes and the bibliography and references have been omitted). Reprinted by permission of the author and the American Psychological Association.

oriented dyads did not differ from the competitive ones with respect to the number of trusting choices made in a ten-trial game. Contrary to what would have been predicted on a common sense basis, the individualistic subjects (Ss) were unable to act rationally in the absence of mutual trust. Each player was unable to subordinate immediate self-interest for long range group gain and the relationship tended to deteriorate into a self-defeating competition. These findings stimulated several follow-up studies that attempted to determine the minimal social or situational conditions under which mutual trust could arise in dyads with an individualistic orientation. Thus, Loomis examined the effects of variations in the opportunity to communicate while Farr dealt with the influence of a mutually disliked third person upon the development of mutual trust.

The present study sought to determine how a player in different positions of relative power could exercise this power in the form of various game playing strategies so as to induce an individualistic S to adopt a cooperative orientation. Deutsch's formulations concerning the situational conditions necessary for the realization of mutual trust, along with Heider's principle of cognitive balance provided a theoretical basis for the derivation of several hypotheses.

Trust and Suspicion

For the purposes of economy and clarity of exposition, the symbol S is used to refer to the perceiver (also the subject) and his experiences or cognitions; O refers to another person whose action affects S. In the terms of the dyadic game employed in this study, S refers to Player 1 and O refers to Player 2.

Deutsch has proposed the following conceptualizations of interpersonal trust and suspicion:

A person (S) may be said to have trust in the occurrence of an event, if S expects its occurrence and his expectation leads to behavior that he perceives to have positive motivational consequences if the expectation is confirmed and negative motivational consequences if it is not. S may be said to be suspicious of the occurrence of an event if the disconfirmation of the expectation of the event's occurrence is preferred to its confirmation, and if the expectation of its occurrence leads to behavior that is intended to reduce its negative motivational consequences.

Interpersonal trust or suspicion exists when S trusts or suspects that O will do something and he perceives that O is aware that his behavior has relevance for S. Trust refers to expectations of benevolence; whereas suspicion refers to expectations of malevolence. Deutsch exemplifies these notions when he states (paraphrased):

If a mother trusts a baby sitter enough to leave her baby in her care and the sitter does not live up to this trust, the mother suffers an unpleasant consequence — harm to her baby. The trusting mother, when her trust is fulfilled, is in a more advantageous position than if she had not trusted. However, the disadvantages of trusting and having her trust unfulfilled are considerably greater than the advantages of being able to do things she could otherwise not do.

Cognitive Balance

Heider has proposed that the process of social perception is steered by a need to achieve cognitively balanced states. The need for cognitive balance has been defined as a tendency for the person to cognize various aspects of his environment in such a way that the behavioral implications of his cognitions are not in contradiction. If an imbalanced state exists, the person will attempt to reduce or remove the imbalance through either cognitive reorganization or behavior. This principle and several of its derivations have been elaborated and tested by Festinger and Deutsch and Solomon.

Interpersonal Power

Heider has defined social power as the ability to produce intentionally events that have a particular degree of positive or negative motivational consequences for a recipient. In line with this conception the interpersonal power balance has been defined in this paper in the following ratio form: O's ability to produce motivational consequences for S relative to S's ability to produce motivational consequences for O. The nature of the events to be produced will determine what dimensions of ability [are] required (i.e., physical strength or intelligence).

Game Strategies

The two person bargaining games are so contrived that they represent a mixture of mutual and divergent interests. In such relationships the term *game strategy* is used to refer to the pattern of O's choice behavior as it affects the preferences of O and S. As a first approximation, situations which result in both lesser loss as well as greater gain are treated, hereafter, as involving gain; loss is extended to include lesser gain as well as greater loss. The two modal forms of game strategy dealt with in this experiment are the Cooperative Strategy wherein O's choice pattern promotes the maximum mutual gain, and the Noncooperative Strategy wherein O blocks the attainment of maximal mutual gain. The motivational source of such behavior patterns may vary. For example, O's cooperation could stem from fear of retaliation (individualism) or a sincere liking for S (altruism). A guiding conception of this study is that the nature of the power relationship influences the kind of motive S attributes to account for O's game strategy.

In terms of the game, O's power over S is a reflection of his ability to achieve a preferred outcome relatively independent of S's cooperation. Thus, if O had absolute power, he could employ a Noncooperative Strategy to obtain his optimal gain whereas if the players had equal power, O would have to reckon with potential losses derivable from *S*'s use of his retaliatory power. This reasoning suggests a more general proposition; the greater *S*'s power relative to *O* the more likely is *S* to expect cooperative as opposed to noncooperative behavior and to behave with trust rather than suspicion. In addition, the principle of cognitive balance serves to predict that an *S* who receives a Cooperative Strategy should tend to develop a liking for *O*, whereas, the contrary would be true if *S* received a Noncooperative Strategy. The intensity of the like or dislike is expected to be influenced by the particular power relationship that exists between *S* and *O*, or to put it another way, the perceived cost of cooperation or noncooperation to *O* influences *S*'s motive attribution and subsequent feelings toward *O*.

The specific hypotheses associated with this rationale are elaborated in the presentation of the results.

METHOD

A laboratory experiment was designed employing a two-person nonzero-sum game (see Fig. 1) in which the gains or losses incurred by each player were a joint function of the choices made between two alternatives by both players. Two sets of independent variables, namely, four types of power relationships and three types of game strategies, were created experimentally and analyzed as a 4 × 3 factorial design. A total of 256 undergraduate Queens College students served as *S*s. Thirty-six experimental groups each composed of from four to eight *S*s were randomly assigned to one of the four power conditions. Each *S* within a particular group was then exposed (by a random procedure) to one of three game strategies from his partner.

Procedure

Laboratory Setting

Once in the laboratory, the *S*s were placed in cubicles so that they were unable to determine the identity of their game partners. In order to communicate their game choices, the *S*s used an electric signal switch. The two switches on each *S*'s box were wired separately to the *E*'s master control panel, which was hidden from the *S*s. The wiring scheme permitted the *E* to receive information separately from each *S* as well as to send preprogrammed choices to all *S*s simultaneously. At the outset of the experiment, the *S*s were given a standard set of instructions which are outlined below:

> You are going to participate in a study concerned with game playing behavior. You will be playing with another person whom you cannot see or communicate with. One of you will be called Person 1 (*S*), the other of the pair will be Person 2 (*O*). In this game you can either win money or lose money. This money will be *imaginary,* but we want you to feel and act as if it were real money.

441

Creation of Power Conditions

Groups of Ss were randomly assigned to one of four game matrices, each corresponding to a particular power condition (Fig. 1). The power conditions are defined from the point of view of *O*'s position:

O in Absolute Power 1 (AP 1). O (Person 2) has absolute power over *S*. *O* can determine whether *S* wins (Column A) or loses (Column B). *S* however cannot affect *O*'s payoff; *O* wins $30 for any combination of choices. *O* and *S*'s preferences are thus *coordinated*.

O in Absolute Power 2 (AP 2). This condition is the same as AP 1 with one difference; *O* can win more by choosing B ($40) rather than A ($30). If, however, *O* does choose B, *S* must lose. *O* and *S*'s preferences are *divergent*.

O in Partial Power (PP). O can determine whether *S* wins or loses. *S* in this condition can, however, exert some control over *O*'s payoffs. By choosing Row Y rather than Row X, S forces O into a position whereby he can win only $10 or $20, rather than a possible $30 or $40. This condition differs from AP 2 only with respect to the fact that S has retaliatory power in the Partial Power Condition.

O in Equal Power (EP). Both players are equally powerful in terms of the extent to which each player can determine the gains or the losses of the other. Each player can achieve his maximal gain by a choice which is detrimental to the interests of the other. (Row Y for *S* and Column B for *O*.) If a YB combination does occur then both players lose. The EP condition differs from the PP condition for *S* in two important respects: (*a*). *S* can exert a greater control over *O*'s payoffs and; (*b*) *S* has greater incentive to choose Y since he can maximize his gain ($40). Under PP a choice of X would enable *S* to maximize his gain ($30).

O in Absolute Power 1 (AP₁) (Coordinated Preferences)			O in Partial Power (PP)		
	A	*B*		*A*	*B*
X	(+30, +30)	(−30, +30)	*X*	(+30, +30)	(−30, +40)
Y	(+20, +30)	(−10, +30)	*Y*	(+20, +10)	(−10, +20)
O in Absolute Power 2 (AP₂) (Divergent Preferences)			O in Equal Power (EP)		
	A	*B*		*A*	*B*
X	(+30, +30)	(−30, +40)	*X*	(+30, +30)	(−30, +40)
Y	(+20, +30)	(−10, +40)	*Y*	(+40, −30)	(−20, −20)

(*S*) chooses between Rows *X* and *Y*, whereas (0) chooses between columns *A* and *B*. *S*'s payoffs are the first numbers in the parentheses; *O*'s are the second numbers.

The EP game matrix is similar in structure to that used by Deutsch...

Figure 1. The game matrices for four power conditions

Game Playing Instructions

Regardless of the particular matrix utilized, the social implications of any combination of choices were explained to the Ss in the following manner (illustration is based upon the EP condition):

Person 1 chooses first between Row X or Y for each trial. Person 2 knowing Person 1's choice then makes his choice of Column A or B. (Before each of you makes his choice you will answer two questions on your game score form.) If Person 1 were to choose X he could either win $30 or $40 depending upon what Person 2 decides to choose. If Person 2 chooses A, both players win $30 whereas if he chooses B, Person 2 would win $40 while Person 1 loses $30. If Person 1 chose Y he could win $40 or lose $20. Here if Person 2 chose A he would lose $30 (Person 1 wins $40) whereas, if he chose B, both would lose $20.

All groups were given the same instructions regarding their goal in playing the game. They were instructed as follows:

This is the orientation, or the attitude you should have in playing this game. *If you are Person 1 (S), your motivation should be to win as much money as you can for yourself.* You are not interested in what happens to the other person. You are not out to help the other person or to beat him. You are merely out to win as much as you can and lose as little as possible and you should feel it's important for you to do so. *If you are Person 2 (O), you can decide for yourself just how and for what purpose you want to play the game.*

A basic requirement of the experimental situation was that the Ss understand the mechanics of the game playing procedure as well as the interpersonal effects of their game choices. A twelve-item test was administered to the Ss just before the game to check on the adequacy of their game understanding. Any S who made more than one error on this test was dropped from the experimental sample. Only nine Ss (4%) failed by this criterion.

Creation of Three Game Strategies

The E fed back a preprogrammed series of choices to the Ss in his role as Person 2. Before describing the game strategies, it is necessary to list and define the basic types of game choices and their social implications:

Cooperative Choice (coop. choice) refers to a choice of X or A which serves to maximize the mutual gain.

Noncooperative Choice (noncoop. choice) refers to a choice of Y or B which serves to maximize the recipient's loss and minimizes the combined gain of the dyad.

Trusting Behavior refers to a coop. choice based upon expectation of receiving a coop. choice from the other player (O).

Suspicious Behavior refers to a noncoop. choice based upon an expectation of receiving a noncoop. choice from O.

Exploitative Behavior refers to a noncoop. choice based upon an expectation of receiving a coop. choice from O. (EP [Equal Power] condition only)

Risk-Taking Behavior refers to a coop. choice based upon an expectation of receiving a noncoop. choice from O.

Each S received one of three types of game strategies from O:

1. *An Unconditionally Cooperative Strategy: O* makes a coop. choice (A) on every trial regardless of what S chooses.

2. *A Conditionally Cooperative Strategy:* On the first trial O makes a coop. choice. However, for each trial thereafter O's choice is *reciprocal* to that of S. O makes a coop. choice only when he receives one from S.

TABLE 1

Percentage of Ss with Trusting and Suspicious Choices in Each Power Condition
(Trial 1)

	Absolute Power 1	Absolute Power 2	Partial Power	Equal Power
Trust[a]	43.1	22.0	30.9	24.2
Suspicion[b]	27.6	39.0	32.4	45.2
Residual[c]	29.3	39.0	36.7	30.7
	100%	100%	100%	100%
	$N = 58$	$N = 59$	$N = 68$	$N = 62$
		χ^2	df	p (1 tail)
Hypothesis 1	$AP_2 > AP_1$	5.92	2	<.03
Hypothesis 2	$AP_2 > PP$	—	2	n.s.
	PP vs. EP	—	2	n.s.

[a]S expects a coop. choice from O and makes a coop. choice.
[b]S expects a noncoop. choice and makes a noncoop. choice.
[c]Residual category includes both of the following:
 (a) S expects a coop. choice and makes a noncoop. choice (exploitative for the EP condition).
 (b) S expects a noncoop. choice and makes a coop. choice (risk taking).

3. *A Noncooperative Strategy: O* makes a noncoop. choice (B) for every trial regardless of what S chooses.

After the data were analyzed, it was discovered that because some Ss consistently made a cooperative offering in the face of a prescheduled cooperative strategy, they had the experience of mutual cooperation for six trials. These Ss, therefore, satisfied the requirements for assignment to both the Conditional and the Unconditionally Cooperative Strategy. Moreover, they represented a select group in terms of personality predispositions as well as game experience. For these reasons this group was partialled out for separate analysis and labeled the *Residual Cooperative Group.*

Reverse Trial and Postgame Questionnaire

After six trials of the game, Ss were informed that for the seventh trial their roles would be reversed. S would now choose last. E "fed" Ss in all conditions a coop. choice for the Reverse Trial. At the close of the game, Ss were asked to complete a postgame questionnaire that tapped their attitudes toward O and interpretations of his game playing patterns.

Informal interviews with a number of the Ss after they played the game revealed that they became quite involved in the game interaction. Several demanded to know the identity of their partners whom they felt had "exploited" or "double-crossed" them.

RESULTS AND DISCUSSION

Hypothesis 1

The greater the gain O can derive from noncooperative as compared to cooperative behavior, the more likely is S to behave suspiciously.

Hypothesis 2

The greater the power O has relative to S, the more likely is S to behave suspiciously.

In order to capture the effects of differences in power relationships in their purest form, the percentage of Ss who were trusting or suspicious at the outset of the game (Trial 1) were compared for the four power conditions. These data are presented in Table 1.

Hypothesis 1 receives support by virtue of the fact that a significantly greater proportion of Ss act suspiciously when initiating an interaction with an Absolutely Powerful O who stood to gain from a noncoop. choice as compared to one who did not ($AP_2 > AP_1$). This prediction is also supported by the finding that Ss make a significantly greater mean number of suspicious choices during the game (Trials 2-6) in the AP_2 as compared to the AP_1 condition (see Table 2).

TABLE 2

Mean Frequency of Trusting and Suspicious Choices
for the Cooperative Strategies under Three Power Conditions
(Trials 2-6)

	Means			t	
	AP_1	AP_2	PP	AP_1 vs. AP_2	AP_2 vs. PP
Trust	2.80	2.26	2.83	1.33[a]	1.31[a]
Suspicion	0.97	1.50	0.85	1.75[a]	2.20[a]

[a]$p < .05$, one-tailed test.

The test of Hypothesis 2 was based upon a comparison of S's behavior when confronted with an O who has Absolute Power (AP_2) as compared to where O has

Partial Power and S could retaliate. Although Table 1 indicates that the differences in the percentage of suspicious choices for Trial 1 were in the predicted direction, they did not attain statistical significance. Table 2, however, shows that the Ss made a significantly lower mean number of suspicious choices in a relationship where they could retaliate (PP) as compared to one where they could not (AP$_2$). These findings (Trials 2-6) taken together with the first trial data substantiate Hypothesis 2.

Of interest is a comparison of the Equal Power with the Partial Power Condition for Trial 1. The EP conditions differ from the PP condition in two respects: although S can exert greater control over O's outcome this is accompanied by a greater incentive to make a noncoop. choice (see Fig. 1). The absence of a reliable difference between the EP and PP conditions suggests that an increase in S's relative power does not necessarily increase the probability of trusting behavior if the heightened power is accompanied by an inducement to be noncooperative. (See Table 1.)

Hypothesis 3

Under the conditions where S receives a Cooperative as compared with a Noncooperative Strategy: (a) S is more likely to trust O; (b) S tends to develop a greater liking for O.

Hypotheses 3a and 3b were tested by applying an analysis of variance to test the effects of four power conditons and four game strategies upon the development of trust and sentiment. With respect to the mean number of trusting choices made during the game (Trials 2-6) the only significant F ratio was derived from the main effects of game strategies ($p < .01$). Postmortem t tests support Hypothesis 3a in that any type of Cooperative Strategy employed by O induced a significantly greater number of trusting choices than the Noncooperative Strategy. There was no reliable difference between the Conditional and Unconditionally Cooperative Strategy.

The index of sentiment was based upon the mean of S's responses to nine evaluative items of the Osgood Semantic Differential. The scores ranged from 1 (dislike) to 7 (like). An analysis of variance of the mean sentiment score for the 16 experimental groups yielded a significant F ratio for the main effects of game strategies ($F = 43.7$, $p < .001$) as well as significant interaction effect. (Power × strategies, $F = 2.1$, $p < .01$) Postmortem t tests indicated, as predicted by Hypothesis 3b, that any type of Cooperative as compared to Noncooperative Strategy induced a greater liking for O.

An inspection of the 16 cells suggest that the interaction effect was a function of the reversals in the direction of the differences between the two types of Cooperative Strategies. Under the EP condition the Conditional Cooperative group had a higher mean sentiment score than the Unconditionally Cooperative group; however, under the Unequal Power Conditions (AP$_1$, AP$_2$, PP) this difference reversed itself. A t test of the mean difference between these two pairs

446

of means yielded a significant interaction ($t = 2.21$, $df = 41$, $p < .02$). Thus, a Conditionally Cooperative O was evaluated more favorably than an Unconditionally Cooperative O if S had Equal Power; however, the Unconditionally Cooperative O was evaluated more favorably under conditions where S was *dependent* upon O.

A behavioral index of sentiment was available through the fact that on the final *trial (#7)* S and O reversed roles so that O chose first with a programmed coop. choice and S chose last. In this situation the Ss (under conditions AP$_2$, PP, and EP) were provided with an opportunity of gaining an additional $10 at a cost of $30 to O (noncoop. choice) or of accepting a lesser gain (−$10) thereby enabling O to win $30 (coop. choice). In effect, a coop. choice at this point represents an abandonment of a purely individualistic orientation. The results, in terms of the proportion of coop. choices made under each strategy are as follows: Residual Cooperative, 88%; Conditional Cooperative, 52%; Unconditional Cooperative, 39%; and Noncooperative, 21%. In line with Hypothesis 3 each Cooperative Strategy differed significantly from the Noncooperative Strategy ($p < .05$; cells corrected for unequal n). There were no significant differences between the Conditional and the Unconditional Cooperative Strategy.

Hypothesis 4

Under conditions where S and O are in an Equal Power relationship and can achieve their respective maximal gain via noncooperative behavior, the application of a Conditional rather than an Unconditionally Cooperative Strategy is more effective in inducing S to play cooperatively. Hypothesis 4 presumes that S learns that O's cooperation is not contingent upon his own cooperation when playing with an Unconditionally Cooperative O, whereas in playing with a Conditionally Cooperative O he learns that his own cooperation is necessary in order to elicit O's cooperation.

TABLE 3

Mean Number of Cooperative Choices for Three Game Strategies
(Equal Power Condition)

| | Means | | | t test |
| | | | | |
Strategies	*Cooperative Choices*	*Groups Compared*		*p(2 tailed)*
Cond. Coop.	3.47	Cond. vs. Uncond. Coop.		< .01
Uncond. Coop.	1.43	Cond. vs. Noncoop.		< .01
Noncoop.	1.00	Uncond. vs. Noncoop.		n.s.

The data in Table 3 corroborates Hypothesis 4. Ss chose a significantly greater number of coop. choices when playing with a Conditional as compared to an

Unconditionally Cooperative *O*. There was no significant difference, however, between the mean number of coop. choices between the Unconditionally Cooperative and the Noncooperative Strategy. By teasing out those noncoop. choices which were based upon an expectation of cooperation (exploitation) from those based upon an expectation of noncooperation (suspicion) it was possible to make a precise analysis of *S*'s intentions.

TABLE 4
The Radio of Exploitative/Noncooperative
Choices for Three Motivational Strategies
(Equal Power Condition)

Exploitative <hr> *All-Noncooperative*[a]	*Noncooperative*	*Unconditional Cooperative*	*Conditional Cooperative*
Ratio = 0	20	7	15
Ratio > 0	2	7	4
p Value[b]			
Uncond. vs. Cond. Coop.	<.01		
Uncond. vs. Noncoop.	<.01		
Cond. vs. Noncoop.	*n.s.*		

[a]The ratio of exploitative/noncoop. choice is based upon the proportion of
$$\frac{\text{Y choices and A expectation}}{\text{Y choice with A or B expectation}}$$
for each *S*. The distributions were highly skewed, thus a dichotomy at *O* and *>O* was made.
[b]Fisher exact test.

Table 4 presents the proportion of noncoop. choices based upon an exploitative intention for the three types of game strategies. The results indicated that the *S*'s noncoop. choices are more likely to be based upon an exploitative intention when playing with an Unconditionally Cooperative *O* as compared with a Noncooperative or Conditionally Cooperative *O*. Apparently *S* was quick to learn that he could satisfy his individualistic goals most efficiently by exploiting *O*'s rigid pattern of cooperation. In spite of the fact that *Ss* in this condition won more money they did not show as great a liking for the Unconditional as compared to the Conditionally Cooperative *O*. How can this finding, which on the surface contradicts reinforcement theory as well as the notion of cognitive balance be explained?

S is confronted with a pair of inconsistent cognitions; *O* (who is presumed to like himself) consistently rewards *S*'s exploitative behavior. *O*, in effect, acts in a "self-defeating" manner. *S* can resolve the cognitive imbalance in one of three basic ways: by disengaging *O* from any responsibility for his self-defeating behavior; by reinterpreting the meaning of the loss for *O*; or by inverting the tacit assumption that O likes himself to O dislikes himself. The data on motive attribution serves to shed some light on the nature of S's cognitive reorgainzation.

S's Motive Attribution

Data pertaining to the type of motive S attributes to O are derived from S's response to Item 3 of the Postgame Questionnaire which asked: "What do you think O's purpose or goal was in playing the game in this manner?" Ss could select from one of four fixed alternatives or choose to write in their own response. (11% of the Ss chose the open-ended alternative.) All of the Ss' responses were classified into one of the three following categories: (*a*) A *Cooperative Motive* defined as O seeks to maximize the mutual gain, (*b*) an *Individualistic Motive* defined as O seeks to maximize his own gain and/or O seeks to outdo S, and (*c*) an *Out of the Field Motive* defined as O does not wish to win money or O does not understand the game. Table 5 presents the proportion of Ss who attribute each of these three motives for two types of Cooperative Strategies and two types of Power Conditions. It shows that where S has equal power the Unconditionally Cooperative Strategy is more likely to induce the attribution of an Out of the Field Motive, whereas, under conditions where S is dependent upon O, this strategy is more likely to induce S to attribute a Cooperative Motive.

Thus, an S who interacts with an Unconditionally Cooperative O (EP) resolves his incompatible impressions of O by attributing to O a disinterest in the goal or sheer cognitive confusion. In effect, the meaning of the loss for O has been reinterpreted, and/or O is disconnected from responsibility for his behavior. These findings also serve to parallel and complement the results with respect to S's sentiment toward O. On theoretical grounds we would expect S to have a

TABLE 5

The Percentage of Ss Who Attribute Each of Three Motives to O
under Two Power Conditions and Two Game Strategies

O's Motive	Equal Power Condition[a]		Unequal Power Condition[b]	
	Conditional Cooperative ($N = 20$)	Unconditional Cooperative ($N = 14$)	Conditional Cooperative ($N = 43$)	Unconditional Cooperative ($N = 32$)
% Cooperative	75.0	57.1	52.4	100.0
% Individualistic	25.0	7.1	35.7	00.0
% Out of field	00.0	35.8	11.9	00.0
	100.0%	100.0%	100.0%	100.0%

[a]In Equal Power Condition $\chi^2 = 9.01$; $df2$; $p < .02$.
[b]In Unequal Power Condition $\chi^2 = .9$; $df2$; $p < .01$.
[c]Although the requirements of expected cell frequencies of 5 for using χ^2 were not met, the p value obtained suggests that the null hypothesis may be rejected.

greater liking for an O whose coop. choices stem from an intrinsic desire for group gain than for an O whose coop. choices are accidental or only a derivative of a more primary self-centered purpose.

SUMMARY

A two-person nonzero-sum game was devised to test some hypotheses regarding the influence of differences in social power and the strategy with which it is used upon the development of interpersonal trust. One member of the dyad was an S while the other was a programmed experimental confederate (O). O interacted with S in one of three conditions of relative power: O in Absolute Power, Partial Power, and Equal Power. O employed one of three types of game strategies in each power condition: Conditional Cooperation, Unconditional Cooperation, and Noncooperation.

The major findings supported Deutsch's theory of trust. They were the following:

1. S is more likely to engage in trusting behavior the greater the power he has relative to O.

2. Under conditions of Equal Power, S tends to respond to an Unconditionally Cooperative O with *exploitative* game behavior and less liking, whereas he tends to be *cooperative* and have a greater liking for the Conditionally Cooperative O [emphasis added]. This difference reversed itself under the Unequal Power Conditions.

These findings are of particular relevance to the problems inherent in the socialization of a child or a patient and they suggest some of the conditions under which exploitative or altruistic motives may develop. More specifically this experiment demonstrates that a Conditionally Cooperative Strategy is most likely to facilitate the transformation of an individualistic to a cooperative orientation, particularly under conditions where there is a high degree of mutual interdependence.

PART FOUR

SYSTEM
TRANSFORMATION

By now, there should be little doubt that I find the present international system less than adequate as an environment within which nations may interact in pursuit of their separate — and seldom compatible — goals. The major inadequacy is the relative "autonomy" of the *actors* vis-à-vis the larger *system;* but, by this, I do not mean that the nations enjoy a wide range of freedom or a large number of alternative modes of behavior. On the contrary, given the nature of the internal and the external constraints within which national policy-makers must operate, it is sometimes surprising that there is as diverse a repertory of behaviors as there is. What I do mean by "autonomy" here is the degree to which the shape of global institutions and norms is determined by the component subsystems (nations), as contrasted with the influence which the larger system may exert on its own characteristics. In *System and Process in International Politics,* Morton Kaplan refers to this type of international system as "*sub*system dominant," and he sees it as more or less opposite to the "system dominant" one in which "the essential rules . . . act as parametric 'givens' for any single subsystem. . . . The criterion for dominance depends upon the degree of influence."[1]

To drop the general systems metaphor for a moment, it might be said that both the political organization of, and the normative restraints on, the international community are far too weak to provide the nations with the sort of incentives and disincentives which could produce greater cooperation on their part. When the normative and ethical, or the utilitarian, incentives for cooperative behavior are weak, the coercive ones need to be stronger. Or, to put it quite simply, the world needs a great deal more "government" than it now has at the *international* level, and probably quite a bit less government than it now has at the *national* level.

To move in that direction would imply a fair degree of system (and subsystem) transformation. It is not that such transformation is not already taking place; it is, but at too slow a pace. The system has, in the past, gone through a number of transformations, some rapid and dramatic, others slow and barely perceptible. As a matter of fact, one

---

[1](New York: Wiley, 1957), pp. 16-17.

recent author has gone so far as to suggest that we have witnessed nine separate and distinct historical systems since the early eighteenth century.[2] While this seems a rather strong assertion (and the empirical evidence he adduces is essentially intuitive and unoperational), my quarrel with him may be merely a semantic one. In any event, the system has been, and continues to be, changing in many of its characteristics, even though there is hardly discernible any linear progression from subsystem dominance to system dominance.

It is at this juncture, however, that the most useful contribution of this general systems approach becomes evident. That is, the moment one concerns himself with system change or transformation, the conceptual convenience of sharply differentiating between actors and their environment becomes either a liability or an asset, depending on the larger framework utilized. To assume either no interaction, or a one-way interaction, between actor and environment deprives him of any chance of fully understanding system change. The essence of understandable system change is the recognition of the interdependence between and among the subsystem, its own subcomponents, and the larger, total system. And the central notion here is one mentioned by Bertalanffy in the opening selection of this book: feedback.[3]

In the discussion which follows, the tempo shifts, then, from a more or less "cross-sectional" view of international relations to what is often called the "longitudinal" view. Here the focus is on the interaction of a number of dynamically changing variables, at a variety of interdependent levels of human organization. It may be emphasized that no one seems to have come close to a fully-developed model of transformation of the system he happens to be examining, but everyone is preoccupied — implicitly, if not explicitly — with the phenomena of inter-level interdependence and feedback.[4]

The pattern set by the rest of this book would require that I present at

---

[2] Richard N. Rosecrance, *Action and Reaction in World Politics* (Boston: Little, Brown, 1963).
[3] Two political scientists have relied very heavily upon this concept, with considerable success: see David Easton, *The Political System* (New York: Knopf, 1959); and Karl W. Deutsch, *The Nerves of Government* (New York: The Free Press of Glencoe, 1963). Also suggestive for the international-relations student are Kenneth Boulding, *Conflict and Defense* (New York: Harper, 1962); and James G. Miller, *Living Systems* (New York: Wiley, in press).
[4] My own tentative views on the problem are expressed in J. David Singer, "The Political Science of Human Conflict," in Elton McNeil (ed.), *The Nature of Human Conflict* (Englewood Cliffs, N.J.: Prentice-Hall, 1965).

least a few selections which indicate the way in which the behavioral social sciences have attempted to understand such complex, large-scale transformation of social systems. Unfortunately, I did not discover any papers that met these particular needs, but I must confess that my search was less than exhaustive. The volume is already long enough; and, furthermore, I wanted to have the "last word" for some speculations of my own. Thus, let me conclude with two brief remarks.

First—and this perhaps explains why relevant papers were not to be found—most scientific studies of social change reveal an emphasis on *imposed* transformation. That is, with the exception of minor environmental modifications resulting from a change in the actors' behaviors, most radical but legitimate change at any level of social organization seems to be a response to forces emanating either from a parallel organization of equal or greater power, or, more likely, from a superordinate one whose capability normally exceeds that of the component parts. To put it another way, sociology (the discipline most relevant here) has had little opportunity to study peaceful change in *subsystem-dominant* settings; normally, officers exercise more control over enlisted men, and management over employees, than vice versa; a modern *nation's* economy has more influence over the economies of its *regions* than the reverse; and changes in norms are initiated more often by reference figures and opinion-makers than by anonymous citizens.

Moreover, on those isolated occasions when transformation does originate at the subsystem level, the larger system must itself manifest one of two conditions in order to be susceptible to this upward influence. Either it must be so *highly organized* that pressure exerted at one or several points in it will be effectively transmitted throughout the remainder of the system, or it must be so *disorganized* that it is rather easily destroyed and replaced. It seems fairly evident that the present organization of the international system falls somewhere between these two poles of vulnerability.

Finally, whatever probability of subsystemically induced transformation still remains is further reduced by the absence of incentives for those subsystems that might have the power to initiate such change. More specifically, those individuals who act for the nations are caught in a situation (admittedly, largely of their own and their predecessors' making) in which the rewards and punishments which can be meted out by their own societies tend to push them primarily *away* from efforts at

455

system transformation. Under conditions which require some measure of attitudinal and organizational hostility toward one or more other actors, appeals which tap that hostility are more likely to succeed — and be rewarded — than those which deny, or seek to vitiate, that hostility.

These comments lead, in turn, to my second and concluding remark. It is most unlikely that the dilemma facing the nations and those who decide for the nations will be resolved by good will. To express that good will is often costly at home and most difficult to make credible abroad. In the short run, the best that the decision-makers can do is to try to suggest to the decision-makers of other nations that they are "rational," and, even more difficult, to assume the possibility of rationality on the part of those others.

Here, of course, is where the behavioral science approach to international politics becomes most germane. To put it bluntly, decision-makers *do not know* what foreign policy strategies are most likely both to (a) preserve the short-run security of their own nation, and (b) move toward a system change which would enhance the security of all the nations.[5] In order to take serious risks with short-run security, they must be able to predict the responses of the other nations with considerably more confidence than is now possible. It is insufficient — from where they sit — to believe that the adversary *may* reciprocate with a conciliatory gesture, and *may not* exploit a unilateral (or even bilateral) measure which produces a momentary weakness in the military or diplomatic sector. No matter how low the *probability* of such exploitation may seem to the policy-maker, he sees its *disutility* as so enormous that the risk is unlikely to be taken.[6]

In other words, the application of social science methods, concepts,

---

[5]Some readers will object that I largely prejudge the issue by assuming that system transformation in the direction of greater global integration *will* enhance the security of its members. Given the quality of our research to date, this prediction can hardly be stated with much confidence, so I have no choice but to put it in the form of an assumption. Hopefully the empirical basis for — or against — it will not be long in coming. A promising start will be found in the work of Karl W. Deutsch and his colleagues on "security communities," and in the early formulations found in Richard W. Van Wagenen, *Research in the International Organization Field: Some Notes on a Possible Focus* (Princeton, N.J.: Princeton University, Center for Research on World Political Institutions, 1952).

[6]Moreover, there is considerable experimental evidence to indicate that extremely high utilities or disutilities attached to any potential outcome will contaminate the probability dimension as well; thus highly desired and highly feared outcomes often increase the subjective, perceived probability that such outcomes will in fact eventuate. See Ward Edwards, "Utility and Subjective Probability: Their Interaction and Variance Preferences," *The Journal of Conflict Resolution*, VI (1962), 42-51; and Robert M. Thrall, *et al., Decision Processes* (New York: Wiley, 1954).

and data to the study of international politics might well provide the decision-makers with that additional increment of accuracy and confidence in their predictions which could permit slightly less conventional policies, especially on the part of the major powers. The increment might not be large, and it is unlikely to be gained in the immediate future, but with so much at stake, we should find the challenge an important and attractive one.

Equally compelling, of course, is the possibility that, one day, international politics may stand alongside psychology, sociology, and economics as a bona fide social science discipline. For humanitarian and intellectual reasons, then, the enterprise suggested in this volume must command our dedicated attention. In that enterprise, the political scientist and diplomatic historian can get considerable assistance from the behavioral sciences. We have labored too long without utilizing the tools that lie near at hand. The judicious and careful application of the findings, concepts, and techniques of sociology, psychology, and, to a lesser extent, anthropology might well hasten the speed and lengthen the stride of those who see in international politics today, the embryo of what could and should become a coherent, well-integrated, systematic area of intellectual inquiry.

SELECTED BIBLIOGRAPHY

The purpose of this bibliography is to indicate the extent to which progress in establishing a social science of international relations has been made. While the intent of the present volume is to encourage such progress, by presenting sociological and psychological research which *could be* applied to our discipline (even though the authors seldom intended such application), it would be misleading to suggest that no progress toward this end has yet been made. Some indication of what has been done is given by the listing, in two categories, of already completed research: (a) work by scholars in the social-psychological sciences, who are trying to apply their conceptual and methodological skills, as well as their data, to problems in international relations; and (b) work by international relations specialists who are trying to combine their own expertise with the concepts, methods, and data of the social-psychological sciences.

A word or two regarding selection criteria are in order. First, the two listings are by no means exhaustive, although they do seem to bring together the most comprehensive grouping of this sort yet available. Second, work by political scientists which is more relevant to *comparative* politics than to *international* politics is omitted, despite the increasing interdependence of the two fields. Several recent studies are, however, of such empirical importance that they warrant mention here: Gabriel Almond and Sidney Verba, *The Civic Culture: Political Attitudes and Democracy in Five Nations* (Princeton, N. J.: Princeton University Press, 1963); Arthur Banks and Robert Textor, *A Cross-Polity Survey* (Cambridge: M.I.T. Press, 1963); R. L. Merritt and S. Rokkan (eds.), *Comparing Nations: The Use of Quantitative Data in Cross-National Research* (New Haven, Conn.: Yale University Press, 1965); and Bruce Russett, Hayward Alker, Karl Deutsch, and Harold Lasswell, *World Handbook of Political and Social Indicators* (New Haven, Conn.: Yale University Press, 1964). Third, articles whose primary purpose is to discuss the "state of the art" in international relations, especially in its relationships to the behavioral sciences, are omitted. Perhaps the most useful of these are Karl W. Deutsch, "The Place of Behavioral Sciences in Graduate Training in International Relations," *Behavioral Science*, III (1958), 278-84; Harold Guetzkow, "Long Range Research in International Relations," *American Perspective*, IV (Fall 1950), pp. 421-40; Stanley Hoffman, "International Relations: The Long Road to Theory," *World Politics*, XI (1959), 264-74; Harold D.

Lasswell, "The Scientific Study of International Relations," *Yearbook of World Affairs* (London), XII (1958), 303-37; J. David Singer, "The Relevance of the Behavioral Sciences to the Study of International Relations," *Behavioral Science*, VI (1961), 324-35; and Richard C. Snyder, "Some Recent Trends in International Relations Theory and Research," in Austin Ranney (ed.), *Essays on the Behavioral Study of Politics* (Urbana: University of Illinois Press, 1962). For a more critical evaluation, however, see Kenneth Waltz, *Man, the State, and War* (New York: Columbia University Press, 1959). Fourth, I have not listed separately a number of important articles when they are also to be found in any of the books or special journal issues that are cited; many of the most important articles in both categories, for example, are found in James N. Rosenau (ed.), *International Politics and Foreign Policy* (New York: Free Press of Glencoe, 1961). Likewise, several important studies have appeared in a variety of forms, and only the most accessible form of each is listed. Fifth, the material on attitudes and foreign policy is quite sketchy since a more complete listing would run to extraordinary length. For the most comprehensive bibliography available, see Leroy Rieselbach, *Personality and Political Attitudes: Available Questionnaire Measures* (Ann Arbor: University of Michigan, Mental Health Research Institute, 1964).

Several other points are worth noting. First, a few of the anthologies (books or special issues of journals) defy dichotomization and have been classified according to which type of author is dominant in the collection. Second, no evaluation of the materials is intended, so that the works cited are extremely uneven in quality. Third, as the bibliography makes evident, there is one journal which has served as the major vehicle for bringing behavioral science and international relations together: *The Journal of Conflict Resolution,* published by the Center for Research on Conflict Resolution at the University of Michigan. Also valuable in this regard are the new *Journal of Peace Research,* published by the Oslo Peace Research Institute since 1964, and the *Papers of the International Peace Research Society,* published in 1964 and 1965 by the University of Pennsylvania, Department of Regional Science. The official journal of the International Studies Association — *Background* is also tending to move in this direction, while *World Politics* and the *American Political Science Review* have done so to a much more limited extent. Finally, such a cross-breeding of international relations and behavioral science scholars could not have progressed as far as it has without certain environmental catalysts. Most significant of these has been the United States Naval Ordnance Test Station at China Lake, California. As the major "consumer" of policy-oriented interdisciplinary research, Dr. Thomas W. Milburn, Director of Project Michelson, has initiated, encouraged, and helped finance some of the best applied research in the field. Of the approximately forty-four studies contracted by NOTS to date, thirty-eight would appear to qualify as efforts to apply behavioral science concepts, methods, and data to problems of international relations; summaries and titles of these reports are found in Louis Higgs and Robert Weinland, *Project Michelson: Status Report I* (China Lake, Calif.: USNOTS, April 1964).

A. Works by Social-Psychological Scientists

I. BOOKS

Bauer, R. A., Pool, I. de S., and Dexter, L. A. *American Business and Public Policy: The Politics of Foreign Trade.* New York: Atherton Press, 1963.

Bernard, Luther Lee. *War and Its Causes.* New York: Holt, 1944.

Bluemel, C. S. *War, Politics and Insanity.* Denver: World Press, 1948.

Bramson, L., and Goethals, G. W. *War: Studies from Psychology, Sociology, and Anthropology.* New York: Basic Books, 1964.

Buchanan, William, and Cantril, Hadley. *How Nations See Each Other: A Study in Public Opinion.* Urbana: University of Illinois Press, 1952.

Cantril, Hadley (ed.). *Tensions That Cause Wars.* Urbana: University of Illinois Press, 1950.

Christiansen, B. *Attitudes toward Foreign Affairs as a Function of Personality.* Oslo, Norway: Oslo University Press, 1959.

Daugherty, W. E., and Janowitz, Morris (eds.). *A Psychological Warfare Casebook.* Baltimore: Johns Hopkins Press, 1958.

Doob, Leonard W. *Patriotism and Nationalism.* New Haven, Conn.: Yale University Press, 1964.

Durbin, E. F. M., and Bowlby, J. *Personal Aggressiveness and War.* London: Kegan Paul, 1939.

Eisenstadt, Shmuel N. *Political Systems of Empires.* New York: Free Press of Glencoe, 1962.

Fisher, Roger (ed.). *International Conflict and Behavioral Science: The Craigville Papers.* New York: Basic Books, 1964.

Free, Lloyd A. *Six Allies and a Neutral.* Glencoe, Ill.: Free Press, 1959.

George, Alexander L. *Propaganda Analysis.* Evanston, Ill.: Row, Peterson, 1959.

Gillespie, James M., and Allport, Gordon W. *Youth's Outlook on the Future: A Cross-National Study.* New York: Doubleday, 1955.

Glover, Edward. *War, Sadism and Pacifism.* London: Allen & Unwin, 1935.

Janowitz, Morris. *The Professional Soldier.* Glencoe, Ill.: Free Press, 1960.

Kisker, George W. (ed.). *World Tension: The Psychopathology of International Relations.* New York: Prentice-Hall, 1951.

Klineberg, Otto. *The Human Dimension in International Relations.* New York: Holt, Rinehart, & Winston, 1964.

—— *Tensions Affecting International Understanding: A Survey of Research.* New York: Social Science Research Council, 1950.

Lentz, Theodore F. *Towards a Science of Peace: Turning Point in Human Destiny.* London: Halcyon Press, 1955.

McNeil, Elton B. (ed.). *The Nature of Human Conflict.* Englewood Cliffs, N.J.: Prentice-Hall, 1965.

May, Mark. *A Social Psychology of War and Peace.* New Haven, Conn.: Yale University Press, 1943.

Murphy, Gardner (ed.). *Human Nature and Enduring Peace.* Boston: Houghton Mifflin, 1945.

Nef, John U. *War and Human Progress.* Cambridge: Harvard University Press, 1950.

Ogburn, William F. *Technology and International Relations.* Chicago: University of Chicago Press, 1948.

Osgood, Charles E. *An Alternative to War or Surrender.* Urbana: University of Illinois Press, 1962.

Pear, T. H. (ed.). *Psychological Factors of Peace and War.* New York: Philosophical Library, 1950.

Richardson, Lewis F. *Arms and Insecurity.* Chicago: Quadrangle Books, 1960.

Sorokin, P. A. *Social and Cultural Dynamics.* 4 vols. New York: American Book Co., 1937. See especially Vol. III.

Speier, Hans. *Social Order and the Risks of War.* New York: G. W. Stewart, 1952.

Stanton, Alfred H., and Perry, Stewart E. (eds.). *Personality and Political Crisis: New Perspectives from Social Science and Psychiatry for the Study of War and Politics.* Glencoe, Ill.: Free Press, 1951.

Strachey, Alix. *The Unconscious Motives of War.* New York: International Universities Press, 1957.

Tolman, E. C. *Drives Toward War.* New York: Appleton-Century, 1942.

Turney-High, H. H. *Primitive War: Its Practice and Concepts.* Columbia: University of South Carolina Press, 1949.

West, Ranyard. *Psychology and World Order.* London: Penguin Books, 1945.

Withey, Stephen, and Scott, William. *The United States and the United Nations; The Public View.* New York: Manhattan Publishing Co., 1958.

Wright, Quincy, Evan, W. M., and Deutsch, M. (eds.). *Preventing World War III: Some Proposals.* New York: Simon & Schuster, 1962.

II. MONOGRAPHS AND RESEARCH REPORTS

Bernard, Jessie, Pear, T. H., Aron, Raymond, and Angell, Robert C. *The Nature of Conflict: Studies on the Sociological Aspects of International Tensions.* Paris: UNESCO, 1957.

Buchanan, William, Krugman, H. E., and Van Wagenen, Richard W. *An International Police Force and Public Opinion: Polled Opinion in the United States, 1939-1953.* Princeton, N.J.: Princeton University Center for Research on World Political Institutions, 1954.

Guetzkow, Harold. *Multiple Loyalties.* Princeton, N.J.: Princeton University Center for Research on World Political Institutions, 1955.

Hero, Alfred O. *Americans in World Affairs.* Boston: World Peace Foundation, 1959.

—— *Mass Media and World Affairs.* Boston: World Peace Foundation, 1959.

461

———— *Opinion Leaders in American Communities*. Boston: World Peace Foundation, 1959.

———— *Voluntary Organizations in World Affairs Communication*. Boston: World Peace Foundation, 1960.

International Communications Research, Public Opinion Quarterly, XVI, No. 4 (1953).

Paul, John, and Laulicht, Jerome. *In Your Opinion: Leaders' and Voters' Attitudes on Defence and Disarmament*. Clarkson, Ont.: Canadian Peace Research Institute, 1963.

Relevance of Social Research in War Prevention—A Symposium, Journal of Human Relations, III (Spring, 1954).

Research Approaches to the Study of War and Peace, Journal of Social Issues, XI, No. 1 (1955).

The Techniques of International Conference, International Social Science Bulletin, V (1953), 233-391.

III. ARTICLES

Adler, Kenneth P., and Bobrow, Davis. "Interest and Influence in Foreign Affairs," *Public Opinion Quarterly*, XX (1956), 89-101.

Alexander, Franz. "Psychiatric Aspects of War and Peace," *The American Journal of Sociology*, XLVI (1941), 504-20.

Angell, Robert C. "A Study of Social Values: Content Analysis of Elite Media," *Journal of Conflict Resolution*, VIII (1964), 329-85.

Bronfenbrenner, U. "The Mirror Image in Soviet-American Relations: A Social Psychologist's Report," *Journal of Social Issues*, XVII (1961), 45-56.

Cooley, Charles Horton. "Social Control in International Relations," *Publications of the American Sociological Society*, XII (1917).

Cottrell, L. "Cultural Growth of Internationalism," *American Sociological Review*, X (1945), 586-95.

Crow, Wayman J. "A Study of Strategic Doctrines Using the Inter-Nation Simulation," *Journal of Conflict Resolution*, VII (1963), 580-89.

Davison, W. Phillips. "Political Significance of Recognition via Mass Media— An Illustration from the Berlin Blockade," *Public Opinion Quarterly*, XX (1956), 327-33.

Dicks, H. V. "Personality Traits and National Socialist Ideology," *Human Relations*, III (1950), 141-54.

Doob, Leonard W. "South Tyrol: An Introduction to the Psychological Syndrome of Nationalism," *Public Opinion Quarterly*, XXVI (1962), 172-84.

Fried, Morton H. "Warfare, Military Organization, and the Evolution of Society," *Anthropologica*, III (1961).

Galtung, Johan. "Summit Meetings and International Relations," *Journal of Peace Research* (Oslo), I (1964), 36-54.

Ginsburg, Morris. "The Causes of War," *Sociological Review*, XIII (1939).

Guetzkow, Harold. "Isolation and Collaboration: A Partial Theory of Inter-Nation Relations," *Journal of Conflict Resolution*, I (1957), 48-68.

462

Keller, Suzanne. "Diplomacy and Communication," *Public Opinion Quarterly,* XX (1956), 176-82.

Levinson, Daniel J. "Authoritarian Personality and Foreign Policy," *Journal of Conflict Resolution,* I (1957), 37-47.

Lifton, Robert J. "Psychological Effects of the Atomic Bomb in Hiroshima: The Theme of Death," *Daedalus,* XCII (1963), 462-97.

McNeil, Elton B. "Personal Hostility and International Aggression," *Journal of Conflict Resolution,* V (1961), 279-90.

Perry, Stewart E. "Notes on the Role of the National: A Social-Psychological Concept for the Study of International Relations," *Journal of Conflict Resolution,* I (1957), 346-63.

Pruitt, Dean G. "An Analysis of Responsiveness between Nations," *Journal of Conflict Resolution,* VI (1962), 5-18.

Putney, S., and Middleton, R. "Some Factors Associated with Student Acceptance or Rejection of War," *American Sociological Review,* XXVII (1962), 655-67.

Queener, Llewellyn. "The Development of Internationalist Attitudes," *Journal of Social Psychology,* XXIX (May 1949), 221-52.

Schein, Edgar H. "Some Observations on Chinese Methods of Handling Prisoners of War," *Public Opinion Quarterly,* XX (1956), 321-27.

Schneider, Joseph. "On the Beginnings of Warfare," *Social Forces,* XXXI (1952), 68-74.

Smoker, Paul, "Fear in the Arms Race: A Mathematical Study," *Journal of Peace Research* (Oslo), 1 (1964), 55-64.

Stagner, Ross. "Needed Social-Psychological Research on War and Peace," *Social Problems,* II (1954), 88-92.

Stagner, Ross, Brown, J. F., Gundlach, R. H., and White, R. K. "A Survey of Public Opinion on the Prevention of War," *Journal of Social Psychology,* XVI (1942), 109-30.

B. Works by International Relations Scholars

I. BOOKS

Alker, Hayward R., Jr., and Russett, Bruce M. *World Politics in the General Assembly.* New Haven, Conn.: Yale University Press, 1965.

Almond, Gabriel. *The American People and Foreign Policy.* New York: Harcourt, Brace, 1950.

Deutsch, Karl W., *et al. Political Community in the North Atlantic Area.* Princeton, N.J.: Princeton University Press, 1956.

Dunn, Frederick S. *War and the Minds of Men.* New York: Harper, 1950.

Grassmuck, George. *Sectional Biases in Congress on Foreign Policy.* Baltimore: Johns Hopkins Press, 1951.

Guetzkow, Harold, Alger, Chadwick F., Brody, Richard A., Noel, Robert C., and

Snyder, Richard C. *Simulation in International Relations: Developments for Research and Teaching.* Englewood Cliffs, N.J.: Prentice-Hall, 1963.

Haas, Ernst B. *Consensus Formation in the Council of Europe.* Berkeley: University of California Press, 1960.

Hovet, Thomas. *Bloc Politics in the United Nations.* Cambridge: Harvard University Press, 1960.

Jacobson, Harold K. *Imperialism, Colonialism and the United States.* New York: Random House, 1965.

Kaplan, Morton. *System and Process in International Politics.* New York: Wiley, 1957.

— Knorr, Klaus, and Verba, Sidney (eds.). *The International System: Theoretical Essays.* Princeton, N.J.: Princeton University Press, 1961.

Lasswell, Harold D. *World Politics and Personal Insecurity.* New York: McGraw-Hill, 1935.

Lerche, Charles. *The Uncertain South: Its Changing Patterns of Politics in Foreign Policy.* Chicago: Quadrangle Books, 1964.

North, Robert C., Holsti, Ole R., Zaninovich, M. George, and Zinnes, Dina A. *Content Analysis: A Handbook with Applications for the Study of International Crisis.* Evanston, Ill.: Northwestern University Press, 1963.

Rieselbach, Leroy N. *The Roots of Isolationism.* Indianapolis: Bobbs-Merrill, 1965.

Robinson, James A. *Congress and Foreign Policy-Making: A Study in Legislative Influence and Initiative.* Homewood, Ill.: Dorsey Press, 1962.

Rock, Vincent P. *A Strategy of Interdependence: A Program for the Control of Conflict Between the United States and the Soviet Union.* New York: Scribner, 1964.

Rosenau, James N. (ed.). *International Politics and Foreign Policy: A Reader in Research and Theory.* New York: Free Press of Glencoe, 1961.

—— *National Leadership and Foreign Policy: A Case Study in the Mobilization of Public Support.* Princeton, N.J.: Princeton University Press, 1963.

Russett, Bruce M. *Community and Contention: Britain and America in the Twentieth Century.* Cambridge: M.I.T. Press, 1963.

Synder, Richard C., Bruck, H. W., and Sapin, B. (eds.). *Foreign Policy Decision-Making.* New York: Free Press of Glencoe, 1962.

Wright, Quincy. *A Study of War.* 2 vols. Chicago: University of Chicago Press, 1942.

—— *The Study of International Relations.* New York: Appleton-Century-Crofts, 1955.

II. MONOGRAPHS AND RESEARCH REPORTS

Deutsch, Karl W. *Political Community at the International Level: Problems of Definition and Measurement.* Garden City, N.Y.: Doubleday, 1954.

Haas, Michael. *Some Societal Correlates of International Political Behavior.* Ph.D. dissertation, Stanford University, 1964.

Holsti, Ole R. *Perceptions of Time, Perceptions of Alternatives, and Patterns of Communications as Factors in Crisis Decision-Making.* Stanford, Calif.: Stanford University Studies in International Conflict and Integration, 1964.

Holsti, Ole R., Brody, Richard A. and North, Robert C. *Theory and Measurement of Interstate Relations: An Application of Automated Content Analysis.* Stanford, Calif.: Stanford University Studies in International Conflict and Integration, 1964.

Riggs, Robert E. *Politics in the United Nations.* Urbana: University of Illinois Press, 1958.

Snyder, Richard C., and Robinson, James A. *National and International Decision-Making.* New York: Institute for International Order, 1961.

Tanter, Raymond. *Dimensions of Conflict Behavior within and between Nations, 1958-60.* Ph.D. dissertation, Indiana University, 1964.

Van Wagenen, Richard W. *Research in the International Organization Field: Some Notes on a Possible Focus.* Princeton, N.J.: Princeton University Center for Research in World Political Institutions, 1952.

Wright, Quincy, Cottrell, W. Fred, and Boasson, Charles. *Research for Peace.* Amsterdam: North-Holland Publishing Company, 1954.

Zaninovich, M. George. *Sino-Soviet Behavior in International Crisis.* Ph.D. dissertation, Stanford University, 1964.

III. ARTICLES

Alger, Chadwick F. "Non-Resolution Consequences of the United Nations and Their Effect on International Conflict," *Journal of Conflict Resolution,* V (1961), 128-45.

Bloomfield, L., and Padelford, N. "Three Experiments in Political Gaming," *American Political Science Review,* LIII (1959), 1105-15.

Brody, Richard A. "Some Systemic Effects of the Spread of Nuclear Weapons Technology: A Study through Simulation of a Multi-Nuclear Future," *Journal of Conflict Resolution,* VII (1963), 663-753.

Deutsch, Karl W. "Mass Communications and the Loss of Freedom in National Decision-Making," *Journal of Conflict Resolution,* I (1957), 200-211.

—— "Shifts in the Balance of Communication Flows: A Problem of Measurement in International Relations," *Public Opinion Quarterly,* XX (1956), 143-60.

—— "Toward an Inventory of Basic Trends and Patterns in Comparative and International Politics," *American Political Science Review,* LIV (1960), 34-57.

Fagen, Richard. "Some Assessments and Uses of Public Opinion in Diplomacy," *Public Opinion Quarterly,* XXIV (1960), 448-57.

Fuchs, Lawrence H. "Minority Groups and Foreign Policy," *Political Science Quarterly,* LXXIV (1959), 161-75.

Haas, Ernst B. "System and Process in the International Labor Organization: A Statistical Afterthought," *World Politics,* XIV (1962), 322-52.

Holsti, K. J. "The Use of Objective Criteria for the Measurement of International Tension Levels," *Background,* VII (1963), 77-95.

Holsti, Ole R. "The Belief System and National Images: A Case Study," *Journal of Conflict Resolution,* VI (1962), 244-52.

Jensen, Lloyd. "Soviet-American Bargaining Behavior in the Post-War Disarmament Negotiations," *Journal of Conflict Resolution,* VII (1963), 522-41.

Klingberg, Frank L. "Studies in Measurement of the Relations among Sovereign States," *Psychometrics,* VI (1941), 335-52.

McClelland, Charles. "System and History: Some Perspectives for Empirical Research and Theory," *General Systems, Yearbook of the Society for General Systems Research,* III (1958), 221-47.

Masters, Roger D. "World Politics as a Primitive Political System," *World Politics,* XVI (1964), 595-619.

Rieselbach, Leroy N. "The Basis of Isolationist Behavior," *Public Opinion Quarterly,* XXIV (1960), 645-57.

—— "Quantitative Techniques for Studying Voting Behavior in the U.N. General Assembly," *International Organization,* XIV (1960), 291-306.

Rummel, R. "Dimensions of Conflict Behavior Within and Between Nations," *General Systems, Yearbook of the Society for General Systems Research,* VIII (1963), 1-50.

Russett, Bruce M. "Demography, Salience, and Isolationist Behavior," *Public Opinion Quarterly,* XXIV (1960), 658-64.

Singer, J. David. "Cosmopolitan Attitudes and International Relations Courses: Some Tentative Correlations," *Journal of Politics,* XXVII (May, 1965), 318-38.

—— "Inter-Nation Influence: A Formal Model," *American Political Science Review,* LVII (1963), 420-30.

—— "Media Analysis in Inspection for Disarmament," *Journal of Arms Control,* I (1963), 248-60.

—— "Soviet and American Foreign Policy Attitudes: A Content Analysis of Elite Articulations," *Journal of Conflict Resolution,* VIII (1964), 424-85.

—— "Threat-Perception and the Armament-Tension Dilemma," *Journal of Conflict Resolution,* II (1958), 90-105.

Sprout, Harold, and Sprout, Margaret. "Environmental Factors in the Study of International Politics," *Journal of Conflict Resolution,* I (1957), 309-28.

Zinnes, Dina A. "Hostility in International Decision-Making," *Journal of Conflict Resolution,* VI (1962), 236-43.

Zaninovich, M. George. "Pattern Analysis of Variables with the International System: The Sino-Soviet Example," *Journal of Conflict Resolution,* VI (1962), 253-68.

PRINTED IN U.S.A.